From Policy to Practice: Challenges and Ways Forward on the Implementation of the AfCFTA

Denis Nfor Yuni • Boopen Seetanah
Tabitha Kiriti-Nganga
Editors

From Policy to Practice: Challenges and Ways Forward on the Implementation of the AfCFTA

Springer

Editors
Denis Nfor Yuni
University of Namibia
Windhoek, Namibia

Boopen Seetanah
University of Mauritius
Reduit, Mauritius

Tabitha Kiriti-Nganga
University of Nairobi
Nairobi, Kenya

ISBN 978-3-032-14050-0 ISBN 978-3-032-14051-7 (eBook)
https://doi.org/10.1007/978-3-032-14051-7

This Springer imprint is published by the registered company Springer Nature Switzerland AG
The registered company address is: Gewerbestrasse 11, 6330 Cham, Switzerland

Foreword

The African Continental Free Trade Area (AfCFTA) represents one of the most transformative economic initiatives in Africa's modern history. With its ambition to unify 55 nations into a single market, the AfCFTA goes beyond a trade agreement—it is a bold vision for a more integrated, prosperous, and self-reliant Africa. As the largest free trade area in the world by the number of participating countries, encompassing a population of 1.3 billion and a combined GDP of $3.4 trillion, the AfCFTA holds the promise of reshaping the continent's economic landscape.

The significance of the AfCFTA lies in its potential to unlock intra-African trade, which currently stands at a modest 18%, far below the levels seen in Europe and Asia. By reducing tariffs, eliminating non-tariff barriers, and harmonising trade regulations, the AfCFTA aims to catalyse industrialisation, enhance competitiveness, and foster economic diversification. The World Bank projects that, if fully implemented, the AfCFTA could lift 30 million Africans out of extreme poverty and increase the continent's income by $450 billion by 2035, which would be a gain of 7%. These gains are not merely economic—they are deeply human. Women and youth, in particular, stand to benefit from expanded opportunities, higher wages, and greater inclusion in regional value chains.

Yet, the road to realising this vision is fraught with challenges. Despite the initial enthusiasm and political momentum, implementation has been uneven and slower than anticipated. As of recent assessments, only a handful of countries have met the necessary customs and trade infrastructure requirements to trade effectively under AfCFTA terms. Regulatory misalignment, infrastructure deficits, limited administrative capacity, and varying levels of political will have continued to hinder progress. These gaps underscore the urgent need for a more coordinated, data-driven, and context-sensitive approach to implementation.

This book, '*From Policy to Practice: Challenges and Ways Forward on the Implementation of the AfCFTA*', arrives at a critical juncture. It offers a timely and comprehensive examination of AfCFTA implementation through a series of country-specific case studies spanning North, West, East, Central, and Southern Africa. By focusing on national-level experiences, this book provides a granular understanding of the diverse challenges, innovations, and policy responses shaping the

AfCFTA's rollout. This empirical approach not only highlights best practices and lessons learned but also facilitates peer learning and comparative analysis across regions.

What sets this volume apart is the calibre and independence of its contributors. This book brings together leading trade researchers from institutions across the continent, including ten African Chairs from the WTO Chairs Programme. These scholars offer objective, evidence-based insights grounded in rigorous research and deep contextual knowledge. Their collective expertise bridges the gap between policy and practice, offering actionable recommendations for governments, businesses, and development partners.

Critical themes addressed in this volume include legal and institutional frameworks, trade facilitation, border management, and the socio-economic impacts of the AfCFTA. The case studies explore how political leadership, economic structures, and institutional readiness shape the pace and effectiveness of implementation. Importantly, this book also addresses the broader implications of the AfCFTA for Africa's development trajectory, including its potential to drive structural transformation, reduce poverty, and enhance regional cooperation.

This book is more than a scholarly contribution—it is a call to action. Governments must prioritise policy alignment, infrastructure investment, and institutional strengthening to harness the benefits of the AfCFTA fully. The private sector, academia, and civil society also have vital roles to play in supporting research, innovation, and advocacy. The successful implementation of the AfCFTA is a historic opportunity to advance African unity, resilience, and its global standing.

I have no doubt that this book will serve as a vital resource for all stakeholders committed to shaping Africa's trade future. It provides a road map for navigating the complexities of implementation and a vision for a more connected and empowered continent. I commend the editors and contributors for their dedication to this important work and invite readers to engage deeply with the insights it offers.

World Trade Organization
Geneva, Switzerland

Xiangchen Zhang,

Acknowledgements

This edited volume emerged from a simple yet compelling idea: to take stock of the implementation of the African Continental Free Trade Area (AfCFTA). Its value in fostering peer learning and informing policy decisions across the continent cannot be overstated. We extend our heartfelt appreciation to the World Trade Organisation (WTO) Chairs Programme for providing both the platform and financial support that brought together WTO research chairs in Africa and other international trade scholars to contribute to this work.

Special thanks go to the National University of Lesotho World Trade Organisation (NUL-WTO) Research Chair, under the leadership of Prof. M. Kapa and Dr. Tsotang Tsietsi, for conceiving this idea and steering its successful execution. We are also deeply grateful to Prof. Stephen Karingi and Dr. Clemens Boonekamp for approving the project and offering insightful comments during its conceptualisation phase.

We express profound appreciation to all contributors who, despite their demanding schedules, devoted significant time and effort to developing their chapters. We also acknowledge the authors of the published and unpublished works, as well as the data sources, that informed this study.

Finally, we extend our gratitude to you, the reader, for there would be no reason to write a book without someone to read it. We hope that your engagement with this volume enhances your understanding of how to facilitate and optimise international trade in Africa, wherever your sphere of influence may lie.

Contents

Contributors

Boris Awa Kigali Independent University ULK, Kigali, Rwanda

Jonas Barayandema Department of Finance, University of Rwanda, Huye, Rwanda

Nabil Boubrahimi Ibn Tofail University, Kenitra, Morocco

Alouis Chilunjika Department of Political and Administrative Studies, National University of Lesotho, Roma, Lesotho

Ngozi Eunice Egbuna Prof. Ngozi E. Egbuna International Centre for Regional Integration and Trade Research, Nnamdi Azikiwe University, Awka, Nigeria

Sheereen Fauzel Department of Finance and Accounting, University of Mauritius, Reduit, Mauritius

Azzedine Ghoufrane Mohammed V University, Rabat, Morocco

Insaf Guedidi WTO Chairs Programme (WCP), University of Tunis, Tunis, Tunisia

Department of Economics, Universitat Jaume I, Castelló de la Plana, Spain

Agyapomaa Gyeke-Dako University of Ghana, Accra, Ghana

Tabitha Kiriti-Nganga Department of Economics and Development Studies, University of Nairobi, Nairobi, Kenya

Manfred Kouty International Relations Institute of Cameroon (IRIC), Yaoundé, Cameroon

Marie-Luce Kuhn School of Economic Sciences, North-West University, Potchefstroom, South Africa

Rorisang Lesaoana Department of Economics, National University of Lesotho, Maseru, Lesotho

Leseko Makhetha Department of Economics, National University of Lesotho, Roma, Lesotho

Douzounet Mallaye LAEREAG, University of NDjamena, NDjamena, Chad

Aristide Maniriho Department of Economics, University of Rwanda, Kigali, Rwanda

Carol Chi Ngang Department of Public Law, National University of Lesotho; Free State Centre for Human Rights, University of the Free State, Bloemfontein, South Africa

François Niragire Department of Applied Statistics, University of Rwanda, Huye, Rwanda

Adelia Jansen van Rensburg School of Economic Sciences, North-West University, Potchefstroom, South Africa

Sawkut Rojid Ministry of Tertiary Education, Science and Research, Ebene, Mauritius

Tasneem Wafiiqah Rojid United Nation Industrial Development Organization (UNIDO), Vienna, Austria

Boopen Seetanah University of Mauritius, Reduit, Mauritius

University of Mauritius North West University, Reduit, South Africa

University of Mauritius, Moka, Mauritius

Puruweti Siyakiya Department of Economics, National University of Lesotho, Maseru, Lesotho

Verena Tandrayen-Ragoobur Department of Economics and Statistics, University of Mauritius, Reduit, Mauritius

Festus Ebo Turkson University of Ghana, Accra, Ghana

Denis Nfor Yuni Department of Economics, University of Namibia, Windhoek, Namibia

Abbreviations

1D1F	One District, One Factory
ACDD	African Customer Due Diligence
ACHPR	African Commission on Human and Peoples' Rights
AEO	Authorised economic operators
AfCFTA	African Continental Free Trade Area
AfDB	African Development Bank
AGOA	African Growth Opportunity Act
AHS	Applied harmonised system
AMU	Arab Maghreb Union
ASEAN	Association of Southeast Asian Nations
ASYCUDA	Automated system for customs data
ATO	African Trade Observatory
AU	African Union
AUDA	African Union Development Agency
AVE	Ad valorem equivalent
BOS	Bureau of Statistics
C&BC	Customs & Border Control Department
CBAM	Carbon Border Adjustment Mechanism
CBN	Central Bank of Nigeria
CEE	Central and Eastern European
CEMAC	Central African Economic and Monetary Union
CET	Common external tariff
CGE	Computable general equilibrium
CMA	Common Monetary Area
CMDTF	Capital Markets Development Trust Fund
COMECON	Council for Mutual Economic Assistance
COMESA	Common Market for Eastern and Southern Africa
CPI	Corruption perception index
CSO	Civil Society Organization
CU	Customs Union
CUSTA	Canada-U.S. Free Trade Agreement

DAWN	Department Agenda for Western Nigeria
DRC	Democratic Republic of Congo
DSB	Dispute Settlement Body
DTIC	Defense Technical Information Center
DTP	Digital Trade Protocol
DVX	Domestic Value Added
EAC	East African Community
EACJ	East African Court of Justice
EBA	Everything but Arms
EC	European Community
ECA	Economic Commission for Africa
ECCAS	Economic Community of Central African States
ECDPM	European Centre for Development Policy Management
ECOWAS	Economic Community of West African States
EPA	Economic Partnership Agreement
EU	European Union
FAO	Food and Agriculture Organization
FDI	Foreign Direct Investment
FEC	Federal Executive Council
FTA	Free trade agreement
FTA	Free trade area
FTZs	Free trade zones
FXA	Foreign value added
GATS	General Agreement on Trade in Services
GCC	Gulf Cooperation Council
GDP	Gross domestic product
GIPC	Ghana Investment Promotion Centre
GRA	Ghana Revenue Authority
GSP	Generalised System of Preferences
GTI	Guided Trade Initiative
GVC	Global value chains
HDI	Human development index
HHI	Herfindahl-Hirschman index
HS	Harmonised system
IATA	International Air Transport Association
IBM	Integrated border management
ICT	Information and Communication Technology
ICUMS	Integrated Customs Management System
IFC	International Finance Corporation
IMD	International Institute for Management Development
IMF	International Monetary Fund
INEDPS	Integrated National Export Development and Promotion Strategy
IP	Intellectual property
IQR	Interquartile range
ITC	International Trade Centre

ITCEQ	Institute for Competitiveness and Quantitative Studies
KRA	Kenya Revenue Authority
LAC	Latin America and the Caribbean
LAPSSET	Lamu Port, South Sudan-Ethiopia Transport
LCCI	Lesotho Chamber of Commerce and Industry
LLDCs	Landlocked Developing Countries
LNDC	Lesotho National Development Corporation
LPI	Logistics Performance Index
MDA	Municipalities and District Assemblies
MDAs	Ministries, Departments, and Agencies
MENA	Middle East and North Africa
MFN	Most-Favoured Nations
MINECOFIN	Ministry of Finance and Economic Planning
MoTI	Ministry of Trade and Industry
MRA	Mutual recognition agreements
MSMEs	Micro, Small, and Medium Enterprises
NAC	National Action Committee
NACCIMA	Nigerian Association of Chambers of Commerce, Industry, Mines, and Agriculture
NAFTA	North American Free Trade Agreement
NBS	National Bureau of Statistics
NCO	National AfCFTA Coordination Office
NEPAD	New Partnership for Africa's Development
NIC	National Implementation Committee
NPFAP	National AfCFTA Policy Framework and Action Plan
NSW	National Single Window
NTB	Non-Tariff Barriers
NTM	Non-Tariff Measures
OAU	Organisation of African Unity
OECD	Organisation for Economic Co-operation and Development
OHRLLS	Office of the High Representative for the Least Developed Countries, Landlocked Developing Countries and Small Island Developing States
OSBPs	One Stop Border Posts
PAPSS	Pan-African Payment and Settlement System
PIDA	Programme for Infrastructure Development in Africa
PPD	Public-private dialogue
PPP	Public-private partnerships
PTA	Preferential trade agreements
R&D	Research and development
RCA	Revealed comparative advantage
REC	Regional economic communities
RoO	Rules of origin
RRA	Rwanda Revenue Authority
RSL	Revenue Service Lesotho

RTAs	Regional Trade Agreements
RVC	Regional value chain
SACU	Southern African Customs Union
SADC	Southern African Development Community
SDG	Sustainable development goal
SDT	Special and differential treatment
SEZ	Special Economic Zone
SGR	Standard-gauge railway
SIDS	Small island developing states
SMEDAN	Small and Medium Enterprises Development Agency of Nigeria
SMEs	Small and medium enterprises
SPS	Sanitary and phytosanitary measures
SQAM	Standardisation, quality, accreditation, and metrology
SSA	Sub-Saharan Africa
STR	Simplified trade regime
SWS	Single window system
TBT	Technical barriers to trade
TCI	Trade complementarity index
TFA	Trade facilitation agreement
TFTA	Tripartite free trade area
TI	Transparency international
TiVA	Trade in value added
TMEA	Trademark East Africa
TPRM	Trade policy review mechanism
TRALAC	Trade Law Centre
TRIMS	Trade-related investment measures
TRIPS	Trade-Related Aspects of Intellectual Property Rights
UK	United Kingdom
UN	United Nations
UNCTAD	United Nations Conference on Trade and Development
UNDESA	United Nations Department of Economic and Social Affairs
UNDP	United Nations Development Programme
UNECA	United Nations Economic Commission for Africa
UNESCO	United Nations Educational, Scientific and Cultural Organization
UNIDO	United Nations Industrial Development Organization
US	United States
USD	United States Dollars
USMCA	United States-Mexico-Canada Agreement
WACTAF	West African Association for Cross-Border Trade in Agro-Forestry-Pastoral and Fisheries
WCO	World Customs Organization
WDI	World Development Indicators
WEO	World Economic Outlook
WITS	World Integrated Trade Solutions
WTO	World Trade Organization

Part I
Introduction

Chapter 1
The Historical Evolution and Socio-Economic Potential of the AfCFTA

Denis Nfor Yuni, Boopen Seetanah, and Tabitha Kiriti-Nganga

Abstract The African Continental Free Trade Agreement (AfCFTA) ushers in a significant reorientation of trade dynamics in Africa, away from the international trade framework that was established during colonial times and has lingered on to the present. The operational phase of the AfCFTA was formally launched on July 7, 2019, and commenced in January 2021, with 54 of 55 member states signing the agreement. This historic moment marked the largest number of countries to commit to a trade agreement since the World Trade Organisation was founded in 1995. Though concerns exist about dwindling revenue from import duties and uneven growth, as is the case with establishing any regional integration, the potential of the AfCFTA is massive. The World Bank (2020) estimates that the AfCFTA could boost Africa's income by $450 billion by 2035, lift 30 million Africans out of extreme poverty, and boost the incomes of nearly 68 million others living on less than $5.50 a day. Nevertheless, the benefits of the AfCFTA can only be attained if African leaders summon the required political will to manage the political and economic dynamics that necessitate its full and comprehensive implementation.

Keywords Regional integration · African trade history · Economic transformation · Evolution of AfCFTA · Africa

D. N. Yuni (✉)
Department of Economics, University of Namibia, Windhoek, Namibia
e-mail: dyuni@unam.na

B. Seetanah
University of Mauritius, Reduit, Mauritius
e-mail: b.seetanah@uom.ac.mu

T. Kiriti-Nganga
Department of Economics and Development Studies, University of Nairobi, Nairobi, Kenya

D. N. Yuni et al. (eds.), *From Policy to Practice: Challenges and Ways Forward on the Implementation of the AfCFTA*,
https://doi.org/10.1007/978-3-032-14051-7_1

1.1 Introduction

Africa's economic trajectory has been profoundly shaped by historical events that have led to economic fragmentation and trade limitations. From pre-colonial legacies to contemporary challenges, the continent's economic landscape reflects a complex interplay of internal and external factors that have hindered cohesive development and robust intra-continental trade. Africa's pre-colonial economic framework was characterised by diverse production and trade systems well-adapted to local environments and social structures. Far from being economically isolated, many African societies had extensive trade routes that defined their local economies. For example, the Trans-Saharan trade connected West Africa to North Africa and the Mediterranean, exchanging goods like gold, salt, ivory, kola nuts, and later slaves (Chirikure, 2017; Fiveable, 2024). In East Africa, the Swahili Coast developed into a major commercial hub, trading with Arabia, Persia, India, and China via the Indian Ocean between the seventh and tenth century (Horton & Middleton, 2000). Southern Africa had robust internal trade systems among groups like the Shona, with Great Zimbabwe serving as a central node for gold and cattle-based wealth. Archaeological evidence suggests that Great Zimbabwe became a centre for trading, with a trade network linked to Kilwa Kisiwani and extending as far as China, especially between the twelfth and sixteenth centuries (History Guild, n.d.; UNESCO World Heritage Centre, 2025).

The "Scramble for Africa" of the late nineteenth and twentieth centuries led to the partitioning of the continent by the major colonial powers, which included Britain, France, Portugal, Germany, Belgium, Italy, and Spain. The colonial era introduced artificial borders and economic systems designed to serve the interests of colonial powers. These powers carved up Africa with little regard for existing ethnic, cultural, or economic linkages, resulting in over 50 countries with varying degrees of economic viability (Pakenham, 1991). This fragmentation disrupted pre-existing trade networks and established economies that were heavily reliant on exporting raw materials to colonial metropoles, with minimal emphasis on intra-African trade or industrial development. For example, the British and French developed railways and roads that led from the interior to coastal ports, focusing on extractive exports that served their interests while undermining and disrupting pre-colonial trade routes and fragmented markets (Rodney, 1972). Also, each colony was integrated into the global economy as a supplier of raw materials and a consumer of European-manufactured goods which reduced incentives for cross-border trade within Africa. For example, Nigeria was reconfigured to export palm oil, cocoa, and groundnuts to Britain, while Senegal focused on groundnuts for France. In terms of infrastructure, railways and ports were also designed to extract resources from colonies rather than to integrate African regions.

After attaining independence, many African nations adopted economic policies that further entrenched fragmentation. The focus on import substitution industrialisation, while aiming to reduce dependency on former colonial powers, often led to the creation of small, inefficient industries that could not compete globally

(Mkandawire & Soludo, 1999). Additionally, the lack of coordination among African nations resulted in overlapping regional trade agreements with limited effectiveness, such as the Economic Community of West African States (ECOWAS) and the Common Market for Eastern and Southern Africa (COMESA), which often had conflicting regulations and standards (Yang & Gupta, 2005). Infrastructure that could propel intra-African trade was in deficit, given that the existing infrastructure was meant to serve Europe with raw materials and market destinations. Moreover, non-tariff barriers like cumbersome customs procedures and regulatory discrepancies have significantly increased the cost and time of trading within Africa. In 2012, the World Bank reported that "the cost of trading across borders in the sub-Saharan Africa region is the highest globally, over twice as high compared to East Asia and OECD countries" (World Bank, 2012).

The constrained level of intra-African trade has limited the region's economic development despite its comparative advantage globally. Africa is the second-largest continent in the world after Asia, with an area of approximately 30.37 million km^2, representing about 20% of the Earth's total land surface (African History, 2025). Hence, Africa is three times the size of the USA and nearly as large as Europe, the USA, and China combined. Africa is extremely rich in natural resources, retaining about 30% of the world's mineral reserves, 12% of global oil reserves, 8% of the world's natural gas, over 65% of the world's arable land, 40% of the world's gold, and up to 90% of its chromium and platinum (United Nations Environment Programme, 2025). As of 2024, Africa's population was estimated to be 1.52 billion people, which is about 18.83% of the global population and projected to double by 2050, potentially reaching 2.5 billion and accounting for 1 in every four people worldwide (Worldometer, 2025). Africa has the youngest and fastest-growing population globally. The median age in Africa is around 19.3 years, compared to 32.5 in Asia, 42.8 in Europe, 38.5 years in the USA, and 30.6 in the world in 2025 (Worldometer, 2025). On this premise, African leaders perceived that the above-cited resources and several others could best be optimised as a region in the framework of intra-regional trade.

1.2 The Historical Overview of the AfCFTA

The idea of a unified regional force, which has now metamorphosed into the AfCFTA, could be traced to independence pan-African aspirations. In the wake of decolonisation, African leaders championed the idea of continental unity to foster economic self-reliance and political solidarity. Ghana's first President, Kwame Nkrumah, was a prominent advocate for this vision, as evidenced in his famous 1961 speech titled "I Speak of Freedom." Nkrumah stated that:

> Divided we are weak; united, Africa could become one of the greatest forces for good in the world.... Individually, the independent states of Africa, some of them potentially rich, others poor, can do little for their people. Together, by mutual help, they can achieve much. But

> the economic development of the continent must be planned and pursued as a whole. (Nkrumah, 1961)

These sentiments laid the groundwork for the establishment of the then, Organisation of African Unity (OAU) in 1963, aiming to promote unity and cooperation among African states. At the opening ceremony of the OAU in 1963, In his inaugural speech the Emperor of Ethiopia, His Imperial Majesty Haile Selassie I, posited that, "the task, on which we have embarked, the making of Africa, will not wait (Selassie, 1963). He further stated that we must act to shape and mould the future and leave our imprint on events as they slip past into history" (Sandu, 2023). On the same occasion, President Nkrumah again stated that, "We must unite now or perish… We must recognise that our economic independence resides in our African unity" (New African Magazine, 2013). Then Thomas Sankara in 1985, opined that "You cannot carry out fundamental change without a certain amount of madness... It took the madmen of yesterday for us to be able to act with extreme clarity today… We must dare to invent the future" (Sankara, 1987; Murrey & Jackson, 2018).

The 1980 Lagos Plan of Action and the 1991 Abuja Treaty were pivotal in outlining strategies for economic integration. The Abuja Treaty, in particular, proposed the creation of an African Economic Community through consolidating regional economic communities (RECs). This treaty envisioned a phased approach to integration, culminating in a continent-wide free trade area. Recognising the need for a more robust framework, African leaders adopted the Sirte Declaration in 1999, which initiated the process of establishing the African Union (AU) to replace the existing Organisation of African Unity. The African Union was officially launched in July 2002 in Durban, South Africa. Unlike the OAU, which concentrated on decolonising Africa, the AU aimed to accelerate political and socio-economic integration across the continent (African Union, 2025). Central to its vision was establishing a continental free trade area to promote intra-African trade and reduce dependency on external partners. In the 24th AU Summit held in Addis Ababa, a strategic framework for the socio-economic transformation of the African continent over a 50-year period (2013–2063) was initiated and tagged "Agenda 2063." One of the flagship projects of Agenda 2063 of the first 10-year implementation plan is the establishment of the AfCFTA.

At the 18th AU Summit in 2012 in Addis Ababa, African leaders officially endorsed the decision to establish the AfCFTA by 2017 and endorsed an Action Plan for Boosting Intra-Africa Trade (African Union, 2012). The overarching goal of the AfCFTA is to boost intra-African trade by creating a single market for goods and services, fostering economic integration, and promoting sustainable development across the continent (United Nations Development Programme (UNDP), n.d.). More specifically, the Member States are expected to gradually remove custom duties and restrictions that hinder trade, open up service sectors in a phased manner, collaborate on issues related to investment, intellectual property, and competition regulation, work jointly on matters linked to trade and customs, implement measures that streamline trade processes, create a system to resolve conflicts over commitments and entitlements, and set up a governing structure to oversee and manage the functioning of the AfCFTA (Trade Law Centre, 2025). The Action Plan for Boosting Intra-Africa Trade contains seven major clusters, which include: trade policy, trade facilitation, productive capacity, trade-related infrastructure, trade finance, trade information, and factor market integration.

In 2015, the AU launched formal negotiations for the AfCFTA, which were structured in phases. Phase I covered trade in goods and services, and dispute settlement mechanisms, which included negotiations on tariff schedules, rules of origin, and trade remedies; commitments in key sectors like transport, communication, finance, tourism, and business services; and the establishment of procedures for resolving trade disputes among member states. Phase I negotiations were to be completed before the launch of the AfCFTA, while Phase II was to commence after the adoption of the AfCFTA (African Union, 2018a). Phase 2 covers areas of Intellectual Property Rights, Investment, and Competition. And then Phase III negotiations were to be conducted on e-commerce and were scheduled to start after 1 year of deliberation and capacity building (Million, 2020). The first meeting of the African Continental Free Trade Area-Negotiation Forum was held in February 2016, followed by the first meetings of the Senior Trade Officials and African Union Ministers of Trade, both of which were held in May 2016. Between February 2016 and December 2018, over 50 high-level meetings were held by AfCFTA negotiating institutions across Africa (Million, 2020).

On March 21, 2018, 44 of the 55 AU member states signed the agreement establishing the AfCFTA in Kigali, Rwanda, during the official opening ceremony of the tenth Extraordinary Summit of the AU Assembly of Heads of State and Government. In recognition of the journey to this momentous moment and with glaring excitement, the then Chairperson of the AU at the time, H. E. Paul Kagame, reckoned that, "I wish to acknowledge all the leaders, past and present, involved in bringing us to this point. We are reaping the rewards of their foresight" (African Union, 2018b). This historic moment marked the largest number of countries to commit to a trade agreement since the WTO was founded on January 1, 1995. The then head of the AU's administrative body, Mr. Moussa Faki Mahamat then emphasised the "need to summon the required political will for the African Continental Free Trade Area to finally become a reality" (African Union, 2018a). The Kigali signing initiated the ratification process in national parliaments.

By May 30, 2019, the AfCFTA had received 22 ratifications, enabling its entry into force. The operational phase of the AfCFTA was launched on July 7, 2019, during the twelfth extraordinary summit in Niamey, adopting the rules of origin, tariff concession frameworks, online trade observatory, the pan-African payments and settlement system, and the African trade observatory (African Union, 2019). January 1, 2021, marked the official commencement of trading under AfCFTA rules. This event was delayed from the original mid-2020 launch due to the COVID-19 pandemic, which disrupted diplomatic engagements and trade logistics across the continent (United Nations Development Programme (UNDP), 2020).

Worth noting is the fact that, at the 17th Extraordinary Session of the AU Assembly held in Niamey in November 2022, it was agreed that negotiations on the Protocols on Digital Trade and Women and Youth in Trade would be finalised by

July 2023. The negotiations on these Protocols were completed and adopted at the African Union Assembly in February 2024. The protocol provides a legal framework to guide the African countries that are party to the AfCFTA, by creating a favourable trading environment for women. This will build their capacity to trade and, in the process, contribute economically not only to their families but also to their countries' economies and the African continent as a whole. As of May 2025, the African Continental Free Trade Area (AfCFTA) is progressing through its implementation phase, with 54 out of 55 African Union (AU) member states having signed the AfCFTA agreement, and 48 countries have deposited their instruments of ratification, signifying their commitment to the agreement (Africa Visa Openness Index, 2025; Spoor & Fisher, 2025).

1.3 The Socio-Economic Rationale for the AfCFTA

1.3.1 Africa's Pre-AfCFTA Trade Dynamics

The historical overview of trade discussed in Sect. 1.1 above clearly shows that African trade has been predominantly with trade partners outside Africa rather than within. The structural weaknesses of intra-African trade before the AfCFTA were characterised by high transaction costs, non-tariff barriers (NTBs), and consequently low volumes. The high transaction cost is mainly due to the inadequate infrastructure, inefficient logistics and limited digital trade facilitation. In 2014, the AU posited that, over 60% of the existing continental road network was unpaved predominantly consisting of nonengineered gravel, the average port utilisation operated at less than half (50%) its capacity, and African airlines captured less than 2% of the global market share for international flights connecting the continent to the rest of the world (African Union Commission, 2014). Complimentarily, the Africa Transport Policy Program (2020) averred that 40% of the final price of goods in Africa stems from high transport costs, and the cost to import a container in Africa is 56% above the world average. Limited digital trade facilitation, such as the lack of electronic single windows, low adoption of e-customs systems, limited use of e-tracking or freight visibility tools, poor data interoperability, and digital infrastructure gaps, also increased transaction costs.

Non-tariff barriers also contributed significantly to limited intra-African trade. Some include, restrictions based on sanitary and phytosanitary measures, lengthy customs clearance processes, requirement of permits or licences to import/export goods, which can be opaque and slow to obtain, rules of origin complexity, trade restrictions and bans, foreign exchange controls, and preferential treatment of state-owned enterprises or licenced monopolies. Examples of such NTBs abound across Africa. Between 2007 and 2018, Zambia consistently rejected milk imports from Kenya by setting the expected threshold at 200,000 total bacterial count, which was far lower than the 1 million total bacterial count that Kenya adhered to (Andae,

2019). Trademark Africa (2025) further posits that, in 2015, Uganda introduced an export permit requirement for Kenyan-manufactured laundry bar soaps which led to a decline of soap imports from 1.6 million kg (valued at approximately $941,000) to just 86,000 kg (valued at about $100,000), representing an approximate 90% decrease. Trademark Africa further shows that, on August 28, 2019, under NTB Complaint No. NTB-000-910, the Rwanda Revenue Authority denied preferential treatment to silk coat products imported from Tanzania, despite the East African Community trade protocols, which led to a 322 day delay and significant additional cost.

Transaction costs, NTBs, fragmented trade policies, insecurity and political instability, obscure post-colonial agreements with former colonial powers, and several other factors, led to the low volumes of intra-regional trade in Africa. Since the 1970s, Africa's share of global trade has dwindled from about 5% to about 2.6% in 2019 (Brookings Institution, 2023; United Nations Conference on Trade and Development, 2018). Furthermore, a Mo Ibrahim Foundation report opined that, in 2019, the primary export destination for over 90% of African countries was a non-African country, with the most common partners being China (14 countries) and United Arab Emitarate (10 countries) (Chandler, 2021). The report further showed that, intra-continental trade was 14.8% in 2019, one of the lowest regions globally when compared to 67.1% in Europe, 60.5% in Asia, 23.3% in North America, and only equal to Latin America and Caribbean with 14.8%.

This trend signals the level of vulnerability that African trade faces, especially when exposed to global trade dynamics. Global trade shocks such as the Russia-Ukraine war which in 2020 affected at least 15 African countries that imported over 50% of their wheat products (Six imported over 70%) from the Russian Federation or Ukraine (Africa.com, 2023). Hence, the conflict triggered a shortage of about 30 million tons of grains on the continent. Besides demand shocks in terms of the shortage of quantities imported, external dependency of this magnitude, will potentially lead to a surge in inflation, loss in currency value, food insecurity and poverty. Before 2019, other notable global shocks such as the 2008 global financial crisis, the 2011 Eurozone Debt Crisis, and the 2014–2016 Global oil price crash, constrained financial growth in economies outside Africa, but were transmitted to African countries because of the level of African dependence outside Africa. Also, the COVID-19 pandemic had a serious impact on the African continent due to its lack of diversification in the import countries which led to shortages of essential items including health consumables as well as ventilators (Kamara & Essien, 2022)

1.3.2 Projected Economic Gains of the AfCFTA

The economic gains of the AfCFTA is founded in the theoretical literature of market integration and trade creation effects. Classical Theories of Economic Integration such as the customs union theory or the theory of dynamic gains from integration show that economic integration leads to trade creation and diversification that translates to efficiency in resource allocation, lower consumer prices, economies of scale, greater competition and innovation, and ultimately long-term productivity growth (Balassa, 1961; Viner, 1950). In addition, the Neofunctionalism theory, according to Haas (1958), posits that integration is a self-reinforcing process because cooperation in one area (e.g., trade) leads to "spillover" into other areas (Haas, 1958). Also, Mundell (1961) opined that, economic areas with synchronised economies and labour mobility benefit from a common currency, which eliminates exchange rate risks, lowers transaction costs, and enhances price transparency. Moreover, the New Regionalism theory by Hettne and Söderbaum (2000) emphasises open regionalism, where integration is outward-looking and driven by the private sector and civil society, not just states.

It is estimated that the AfCFTA will create a continental market of over 1.3 trillion whose economies of scale over time should significantly reduce impediments to intra-African trade such as the fragmented trade policies, transaction costs and NTBs (United Nations Conference on Trade and Development (UNCTAD), 2019). For example, members are expected to eliminate tariffs on 90% of goods in the initial phase under the AfCFTA tariff modalities, with the long-term objective of granting duty-free access to at least 97% of goods and a wide range of services across the continent (International Trade Centre, 2022). The projected estimates by the World Bank, UNCTAD, the United Nations Economic Commission for Africa (UNECA) and other global development bodies on the potential benefits of the AfCFTA is not just promising, it is mind blowing. The World Bank estimates that the AfCFTA could boost Africa's income by $450 billion by 2035, lift 30 million Africans out of extreme poverty and boost the incomes of nearly 68 million others living on less than $5.50 a day (World Bank, 2020). Also, UNECA (2025) projects that the AfCFTA aims to boost intra-African trade by 45%, with significant benefits expected in agri-business and industrial sectors.

Moreover, the AfCFTA is expected to increase Africa's exports by $560 billion, mostly in manufacturing, thereby promoting industrialisation (World Bank, 2020). And UNCTAD (2024) notes that 61% of Africa's regional exports consist of processed and semi-processed goods, indicating regional supply chain diversification and value addition opportunities. Arbisman et al. (2025) further state that the AfCFTA agreement is anticipated to create employment opportunities across various sectors by fostering industrial growth and enhancing intra-African trade. In addition to the expected effects on economic growth, poverty, trade, income, and value addition, the AfCFTA is also estimated to have potential gender and social equity outcomes. World Bank (2020) also posit that the AfCFTA is projected to boost wages for both skilled and unskilled workers by 9.8% and 10.3%, respectively. Noteworthy is the fact that women are expected to experience larger wage gains (10.5%) compared to men (9.9%), indicating a potential narrowing of the gender income gap on the continent over time. Research by the Maliszewska et al. (2020) and World Trade Organisation (2012) shows that trade in the AfCFTA will create better jobs for women, leading to more benefits, training, job security, and less informal employment. Eliminating import tariffs raises real income for female--headed households more than male-headed ones.

Though global and regional development agencies have highlighted these gains, several quarters have also raised a number of other potential limitations. UNCTAD (2018) posits that the removal of tariffs through the AfCFTA is expected to cause a considerable decline in tariff-related income for many African nations, with short-term annual revenue losses projected at approximately $4.1 billion. World Bank (2020) also shows that the benefits of the AfCFTA are likely to be uneven, with industrialised and export-driven nations gaining more, while smaller, landlocked countries may face initial difficulties in remaining competitive. African Export-Import Bank (2020) cautioned that the successful implementation of the AfCFTA relies heavily on institutional capacity, which is still insufficient in many African nations. These concerns are, however, common with any formation of a regional integration. Interestingly, the evidence shows that most regional integrations have grown economically overtime due to the power of wealth creation and its multiplier effect. For example, Haini and Wei Loon (2023) found that Central and Eastern European (CEE) countries experienced an average total factor productivity (TFP) growth of 5.7%, while Eurozone countries saw 8.5%, and they attributed these gains to increased trade linkages and shared technological advancements within the integrated market.

Other empirical works such as Geda and Yimer (2023) employed trade indices and a gravity model to show that the AfCFTA could raise intra-African exports from the average annual value of US$ 72.7 billion (2015–2017) by about US$ 13.7 billion (by about 19%). Furthermore, International Monetary Fund (2023) used empirical analysis to show that meaningful cuts in tariffs and non-tariff barriers under the AfCFTA, combined with enhancements in the overall trade-supporting environment, such as better infrastructure, stronger financial systems, and improved domestic stability, could significantly increase intra-African trade in both goods and services. Additionally, deeper regional integration may play a critical role in helping African nations address the challenges of fast population growth, climate change, and shifting global geopolitical dynamics.

The AfCFTA represents, arguably, the most significant instrument for economic transformation that Africa has ever pursued, holding immense potential to drive long-term, inclusive, and sustainable development across the continent. Its potential, if well implemented, dwarfs the structural adjustment programme, the Comprehensive Africa Agriculture Development Programme, the Programme for Infrastructure Development in Africa, the Aid for Development Programmes, the debt cancellation initiatives, or several other development programmes that Africa has witnessed post-independence. This is because the AfCFTA is market-based, does not rely on external goodwill and is driven by African countries themselves hence creating a self-reinforcing economic engine that triggers economic transformation from within. The AfCFTA focuses on production and trade, which are more sustainable, which should also promote economic sovereignty, empowers SMEs and the private sector, and ultimately improves long-term resilience against global shocks.

1.4 The Political Economy of AfCFTA Implementation

The role of national interests, political good will, and leadership dynamics in the implementation of the AfCFTA cannot be underestimated. It determines the extent to which the AfCFTA will be implemented and the pre-condition to benefit from the estimated projections as discussed in Sect. 1.3. Divergent national interests often pose challenges to the cohesive implementation of AfCFTA, and may prioritise protecting domestic industries over regional integration, leading to reluctance in fully committing to AfCFTA provisions. National interests, driven by economic priorities and political dynamics, could accelerate or slow down the implementation of the AfCFTA. For example, Niger, Mali, and Burkina Faso recently withdrew from the Economic Community of West African States to preserve their interests as military controlled states. Also, Nigeria initially delayed signing the AfCFTA due to concerns from domestic manufacturing groups fearing unfair competition (The EastAfrican, 2019). Another major concern for most African countries is that a significant portion of their national revenue is derived from import duties, so removing or reducing tariffs under AfCFTA threatens this income stream and creates resistance. Countries facing security threats may resist the free movement of goods and people, from unregulated cross-border flows that raise concerns such as smuggling, terrorism, and health risks.

Elite interests and patronage politics must equally be checked in favour of the smooth implementation of the AfCFTA. Mbeki (2008) opined that, political elites frequently avoid productive economic activities themselves, relying instead on politically connected foreign business elites while stifling local industrialisation, and so this reduces employment and constrains economic diversification. While other studies show that, the elite have the tendency to exert state capture that controls state institutions and contracts (Chilunjika et al., 2022; David-Barrett, 2025). Such predisposition should be expected with the implementation of the AfCFTA. Fierce resistance from protectionist lobbies and domestic industries should be expected and systematically monitored, especially at the earlier stages of implementation.

The influence of existing global trade policies and external economic pressures equally contribute significantly to the political economy of the AfCFTA implementation. Several African countries trade more with the USA and other European countries rather than trading with fellow African countries. In 2012, the then Deputy Director General of the WTO, Rugwabiza stated that, Africa remains the world's most fragmented continent, with its 54 nations and many border crossings, recording just 10% intra-trade in 2011; far below the levels in the EU-27 (70%), Asia (52%), North America (50%), and South America (26%) (World Trade Organisation, 2012). Shah (2025) opines that increased intra-African trade enables businesses to source locally, build regional value chains, and retain economic benefits within the continent instead of losing wealth to distant economies.

The management of the above-mentioned politico-economic intrigues is significantly dependent on the political good will of African leaders. The current trajectory of the implementation of the AfCFTA suggests that African leaders are more committed to sovereignty and bilateralism than multilateral cooperation at the continental level. Besides the political will to commit, the political will to align to national development strategies such as industrial policy, customs reform, and transport infrastructure with AfCFTA goals is also imperative. A higher level of *political good will*, will be to establish the requisite institutional capacity to monitor, enforce, or evaluate AfCFTA commitments. Though the AfCFTA has been officially launched, its implementation has been phased out to include several negotiations and other agreements that should lead to comprehensive political and economic integration.

1.5 Organisation of the Book

The book is made up of 19 chapters and is divided into three main parts: the introductory part, country case studies, and the concluding part. Part 1 is made up of four chapters: Chap. 1 x-rays the historical overview, socio-economic rationale, and the political economy of AfCFTA Implementation. Dr. Awa in Chap. 2 investigates the legal frameworks, foundational legal instruments, the institutional framework governing the AfCFTA, and the key challenges in legal and institutional frameworks experienced by African countries. In Chap. 3, Dr. Makhetha unpacks the premise of global and regional trade agreements with keen interest in their conflicts and overlaps in relation to the AfCFTA implementation. To close this introductory part, Prof. Ngang explores the pursuit of socio-economic self-determination in Africa from a pan-African and right to development perspective, positing that the noble ideals embedded therein are attainable through the AfCFTA Agreement, albeit that its implementation remains constrained for no apparent reason.

Part 2 has 11 chapters that interrogate the AfCFTA implementation processes thus far, challenges and recommendations for two countries in each geopolitical region in Africa. The countries include Tunisia, Morocco, Ghana, Nigeria, Kenya, Rwanda, Lesotho, South Africa, Cameroon, and Chad. The last case study analysis the prospects and limitations of Africa's Small Island Developing States in the Implementation of the AfCFTA. These chapters offer a glimpse into country--specific scenarios that reflect diverse realities influencing trade in Africa, such as island or landlocked geography, population size, climate, topography, and resource endowments.

The last four chapters of the concluding part investigate the trends policy harmonisation across borders, and socio-economic impact of AfCFTA on economic transformation. In Chap. 16, Dr. Siyakiya and Lesaoana synthesises key trends and projections shaping the ongoing implementation of the AfCFTA, highlighting both progress and persistent challenges. Prof Chilunjika then analyses how trade facilitation, border management, and the harmonisation of policies across AfCFTA member states affect the implementation of the AfCFTA. In the penultimate chapter, Prof Fauzel, Seetanah, and Tandrayen-Ragoobur evaluate the social and economic effects of the AfCFTA, taking into consideration the different countries' implementation and institutional capabilities. This concluding chapter critically examines the implementation of the AfCFTA across Africa by analysing the challenges, strengths, lessons learned, indigenous solutions, and policy recommendations from the 11 case studies reviewed in the book.

References

Africa Transport Policy Program. (2020). *Regional integration*. Retrieved May 30, 2025, from https://www.ssatp.org/topics/regional-integration

Africa Visa Openness Index. (2025). *Latest developments on the AfCFTA*. https://www.visaopenness.org/pages-not-in-use/latest-developments-on-the-afcfta/.

Africa.com. (2023). *One year later: The impact of the Russian-Ukrainian conflict on Africa*. https://www.africa.com/one-year-later-the-impact-of-the-russian-ukrainian-conflict-on-africa/

African Export-Import Bank. (2020). *African trade report 2020: Informal cross-border trade in Africa in the context of the AfCFTA*. https://media.afreximbank.com/afrexim/African-Trade--Report-2020.pdf

African History. (2025). *The geography of Africa*. Retrieved May 29, 2025, from https://africanhistory.online/history?id=1735550452

African Union. (2012). *Decision on boosting intra-African trade and the establishment of the CFTA*. https://au.int/en/decisions/18th-ordinary-session

African Union. (2018a). *Agreement establishing the African continental free trade area (AfCFTA)*. https://au.int/sites/default/files/treaties/36437-treaty-consolidated_text_on_cfta_-_en.pdf

African Union. (2018b). *AU member countries create History by massively signing the AfCFTA agreement in Kigali*. https://au.int/en/pressreleases/20180321/au-member-countries-create-history-massively-signing-afcfta-agreement-kigali

African Union. (2019). Operational phase of the African Continental Free Trade Area launched at Niger Summit. https://au.int/en/pressreleases/20190707/operationalphase-african-continental-free-trade-area-launched-niger-summit

African Union. (2025). *African Union*. Retrieved May 29, 2025, from https://www.boost-ae.net/en/7_108/63a6c88e081043769276ac5f/African%20Union.html

African Union Commission. (2014). *Issue paper: Infrastructure and trade. Seventh Conference of African Ministers in Charge of Integration*. https://au.int/sites/default/files/newsevents/workingdocuments/12582-wd-issue_paper_infrastructure_and_trade_en_0.pdf

Andae, G. (2019). *Regional standards woes pose non-tariff barrier in Africa push for free trade area*. Business Daily. https://www.businessdailyafrica.com/bd/news/regional-standards-woes-pose-non-tariff-barrier-in-africa-push-for-free-trade-area-2257576

Arbisman, J., Ahuja, N., & Yong, H. (2025). *Investment in Africa: Free trade area agreement powers continent's energy future*. Reuters. https://www.reuters.com/legal/legalindustry/investment-africa-free-trade-area-agreement-powers-continents-energy-future-2025-01-17/

Balassa, B. (1961). *The theory of economic integration*. Allen & Unwin.

Brookings Institution. (2023). *The future of African trade in the AfCFTA era*. https://www.brookings.edu/articles/the-future-of-african-trade-in-the-afcfta-era/

Chandler, B. (2021). *Weathering the next crisis—The AfCFTA as a tool for resilience*. Mo Ibrahim Foundation. https://mo.ibrahim.foundation/news/2021/weathering-next-crisis-afcfta-a-tool-resilience

Chilunjika, A., Intauno, K., Uwizeyimana, D. E., & Chilunjika, S. R. T. (2022). Dynamics of patronage politics and the tendering process at Zimbabwe's state procurement board. *African Journal of Governance and Development, 11*(1.1), 79–103. https://ajgd.journalofgovernance.com/index.php/ajgd/article/view/151

Chirikure, S. (2017). *Documenting precolonial trade in Africa*. Oxford Research Encyclopedia of African History. Retrieved 29 May 2025, from https://oxfordre.com/africanhistory/view/10.1093/acrefore/9780190277734.001.0001/acrefore-9780190277734-e-68

David-Barrett. (2025). *The economic consequences of state capture: Oligarchs are warping markets and corrupting economies around the world*. Foreign Affairs. https://www.foreignaffairs.com/world/economic-consequences-state-capture?utm

Fiveable. (2024). *4.1 Development of trans-Saharan trade routes—History of Africa—Before 1800*. https://library.fiveable.me/africa-before-1800/unit-4/development-trans-saharan-trade-routes/study-guide/lbuS9YiUsrPU6edn

Geda, A., & Yimer, A. (2023). The trade effects of the African continental free trade area: An empirical analysis. *The World Economy, 46*(2), 328–345.

Haas, E. B. (1958). *The uniting of Europe*. Stanford University Press.

Haini, H., & Wei Loon, P. (2023). Do regional integration and trade linkages promote productivity spillovers? Evidence from the European Union. *Baltic Journal of Economics, 23*(1), 64–90. https://doi.org/10.1080/1406099X.2023.2198284

Hettne, B., & Söderbaum, F. (2000). Theorising the rise of regionness. *New Political Economy, 5*(3), 457–472.

History Guild. (n.d.). *Southern African states*. Retrieved August 13, 2025, from https://historyguild.org/southern-african-states/

Horton, M., & Middleton, J. (2000). The Swahili: The social landscape of a mercantile society. Oxford, UK: Blackwell Publisher.

International Monetary Fund. (2023). *Trade integration in Africa: Unleashing the continent's potential in a changing world (Departmental Paper No. 2023/007)*. https://www.imf.org/en/Publications/Departmental-Papers-Policy-Papers/Issues/2023/05/03/Trade-integration-in--Africa-Unleashing-the-Continent-s-Potential-in-a-Changing-World-529215

International Trade Centre (2022). Frequently asked questions on the African Continental Free Trade Agreement (AfCFTA). ITC, Geneva. https://www.macmap.org/en/learn/afcfta?utm

Kamara, J., & Essien, U. (2022). COVID-19 in Africa: Supply chain disruptions and the role of the Africa Continental Free Trade Agreement. Journal of Global Health, 12, 03085. https://doi.org/10.7189/jogh.12.03085

Maliszewska, M., Ruta, M., Arenas, G., Brenton, P., Calderon, C., Echandi, R., Rodarte, I. O., Mensbrughe, D. V., Pereira, M. F. S., & Vnukova, Y. (2020). *The African continental free trade area: Economic and distributional effects*. World Bank Group. https://doi.org/10.1596/978-1-4648-1559-1

Mbeki, M. (2008). *The private sector, political elites and underdevelopment in sub-Saharan Africa*. South African Institute of International Affairs (SAIIA). https://saiia.org.za/research/the-private-sector-political-elites-and-underdevelopment-in-sub-saharan-africa/

Million, A. (2020). *AfCFTA negotiations and implementation: State of play at WTO accession dialogue, Addis Ababa*. World Trade Organization. https://www.wto.org/english/thewto_e/acc_e/afcfta_negotiations_and_implementation_state_of_play_at_wto_accession_dialogue_addis_ababa_12_1_2020_million.pdf

Mkandawire, T., & Soludo, C. C. (1999). Our continent, our future: African perspectives on structural adjustment. Trenton, NJ: Africa World Press.

Mundell, R. A. (1961). A theory of optimum currency areas. *American Economic Review, 51*(4), 657–665.

Murrey, A., & Jackson, N. A. (2018). *The lives and afterlives of Thomas Sankara*. Pluto Press. https://www.plutobooks.com/blog/lives-afterlives-thomas-sankara

New African Magazine. (2013). *"We must unite now or perish"—President Kwame Nkrumah*. New African Magazine. https://newafricanmagazine.com/3721/

Nkrumah, K. (1961). *I speak of freedom: A statement of African ideology* (pp. xi–xiv). William Heinemann Ltd..

Pakenham, T. (1991). *The scramble for Africa: The white man's conquest of the dark continent from 1876 to 1912*. Random House.

Rodney, W. (1972). *How Europe underdeveloped Africa*. Bogle-L'Ouverture Publications.

Sandu, N. (2023). *A mixed bag as AU turns 60*. https://www.nepad.org/news/mixed-bag-au--turns-60#:~:text=By%20Ndamu%20Sandu%2C%20Member%20of,in%20the%20Africa%20of%20tomorrow

Sankara, T. (1987). *Speech at the OAU summit in Addis Ababa*. Retrieved from the Thomas Sankara Official Archive: https://thomassankara.net

Selassie, H. (1963). *Speech at the founding of the OAU*. Retrieved from the African Union archives: https://au.int/en

Shah D. (2025). *Why should Africa trade more with Africa?* https://www.thehabarinetwork.com/why-should-africa-trade-more-with-africa#:~:text=When%20African%20countries%20trade%20more%20with%20each,stays%20in%20Africa%20rather%20than%20flowing%20outward

Spoor & Fisher. (2025). *African continental free trade area (AfCFTA)*. https://spoor.com/afcfta/

The EastAfrican. (2019). *Nigeria finally buys into Africa free trade*. https://www.theeastafrican.co.ke/tea/business-tech/nigeria-finally-buys-into-africa-free-trade-4965046.

Trade Law Centre (2025). *Continental free trade area (CFTA)*. Retrieved May 29, 2025, from https://www.tralac.org/resources/our-resources/6730-continental-free-trade-area-cfta.html

TradeMark Africa. (2025). *How non-tariff barriers affect trade in the EAC*. https://www.trademarkafrica.com/how-non-tariff-barriers-affect-trade-in-the-eac/

UNCTAD. (2018). *Key statistics and trends in regional trade in Africa*. Retrieved from https://unctad.org/publication/key-statistics-and-trends-regional-trade-africa

UNCTAD. (2024). *Economic development in Africa report 2024*. UNCTAD.

UNECA. (2025). *AfCFTA benefits will be across sectors—Economic Report on Africa 2025*. https://www.uneca.org/stories/afcfta-benefits-will-be-across-sectors-%E2%80%93-economic--report-on-africa-2025?

UNESCO World Heritage Centre. (2025). *Great Zimbabwe national monument*. https://whc.unesco.org/en/list/364/

United Nations Conference on Trade and Development. (2019). World investment report 2019: Special economic zones. United Nations. https://unctad.org/system/files/official-document/wir2019_en.pdf

United Nations Conference on Trade and Development. (2018). *Economic development in Africa report 2018: Migration for structural transformation*. UNCTAD. https://unctad.org/en/PublicationsLibrary/aldcafrica2018_en.pdf

United Nations Development Programme (UNDP). (2020). *The futures report: Making the AfCFTA work for women and youth*. https://www.undp.org/sites/g/files/zskgke326/files/migration/africa/SS_AFCFTAFUTUREREPORT.pdf

United Nations Development Programme (UNDP). (n.d.). *AfCFTA—Supporting the African Continental Free Trade Area*. Retrieved May 29, 2025, from https://www.undp.org/africa/afcfta

United Nations Environment Programme. (2025). *Our work in Africa*. Retrieved May 29, 2025, from https://www.unep.org/regions/africa/our-work-africa

Viner, J. (1950). *The customs union issue*. Carnegie Endowment.

World Bank. (2012). *De-fragmenting Africa: Deepening regional trade integration in goods and services*. https://openknowledge.worldbank.org/server/api/core/bitstreams/dab4b92d-6dbe-5527-abc6-a24be7496366/content

World Bank. (2020). *The African continental free trade area: Economic and distributional effects*. World Bank Publications. https://www.worldbank.org/en/topic/trade/publication/the-african-continental-free-trade-area

World Trade Organisation. (2012). *Africa should trade more with Africa to secure future growth" — DDG Rugwabiza*. https://www.wto.org/english/news_e/news12_e/ddg_12apr12_e.htm#:~:text=Africa%20remains%20the%20most%20fragmented,cent%20for%20South%20American%20countries

Worldometer. (2025). *Africa population*. Retrieved May 29, 2025, from https://www.worldometers.info/world-population/africa-population/

Yang, Y., & Gupta, S. (2005). *Regional trade arrangements in Africa: Past performance and the way forward*. IMF Working Paper, 05/36. Retrieved from https://www.imf.org/en/Publications/WP/Issues/2016/12/31/Regional-Trade-Arrangements-in-Africa-Past-Performance-and-the-Way-Forward-18128

Chapter 2
Legal and Institutional Frameworks Governing the AfCFTA

Boris Awa

Abstract The global success of regional economic communities and the need to promote trade and investment among Africans were at the forefront of the African Continental Free Trade Agreement (AfCFTA). While the seeds of AfCFTA date back to the African independence struggle, the emergence of a formidable institution with a battery of legal texts only dates back to 2019, when the dream finally hits the ground. Globally acclaimed as the largest Free Trade Area by size, AfCFTA is conceived under the aegis of the African Union, as Africa's solution to Africa's problems. This chapter zooms into the legal and institutional framework governing the AfCFTA with a specific interests in its legal framework, underlying rules, dispute resolution mechanism, conflicts of rules among others. Based on doctrinal research method, this chapter argues that the legal and institutional framework of AfCFTA is commendable, but there are some antipodal hurdles, that beset its smooth implementation. Major areas for reforms hover around overlapping rules between RECs and AfCFTA, dispute resolution mechanisms and implementation hurdles. This chapter concludes with recommendations and potential areas for reform.

Keywords AfCFTA agreements · World Trade Organisation · Free trade area · Regional economic communities · African Union · Dispute settlement body

---

B. Awa (✉)
Kigali Independent University ULK, Kigali, Rwanda

D. N. Yuni et al. (eds.), *From Policy to Practice: Challenges and Ways Forward on the Implementation of the AfCFTA*,
https://doi.org/10.1007/978-3-032-14051-7_2

2.1 Introduction

Trade accords are as good as the mechanisms put in place for their enforcement. Should the legal and institutional framework of a trade accord be defective, such accords would likely be reduced to a mere piece of paper. It naturally flows from the foregoing premises that the importance of a robust legal and institutional framework for trade agreements cannot be overemphasised. Guided by this fundamental principle, the AfCFTA (referred to in this chapter both as the Agreement establishing the African Continental Free Trade Area and the African Continental Free Trade Area, as the context so warrants) was built on a corpus of legislation destined to carry out the mission of this agreement.

Before this continental approach, various approaches had been adopted, which were primarily driven by efforts of individual states, such as between the Middle East and Northern Africa (Jamel Zarrouk, Franco Zallio, 2001). We have within the African ranks; the Eastern African Community (EAC) (Emmanuel Ugirashebuja, John Eudes Ruhangisa, Tom Ottervanger, Armin Cuyvers, 2017), the Arab Magreb Union (UMA), the Common Market for Eastern and Southern Africa (COMESA), the Community of Sahel-Saharan States (CEN-SAD), the Economic Community of Central African States (ECCAS), the Economic Community of West African States (ECOWAS), the Intergovernmental Authority on Development (IGAD), and the South African Development Community (SADC), which are all recognised by the African Union as Regional Economic Communities (RECs). Despite this subregional and state effort, there was a need to broaden regional integration so that it covers the African continent. At the same time, RECs' Free Trade Areas remain the building blocs for the AfCFTA (article 5 (b) of AfCFTA).

The AfCFTA is trading system geared at uniting the spaghetti bowl of regional blocs, whose degree of integration is much higher and even older than the umbrella institution itself, the AfCFTA. This is understandable, as the AfCFTA is a deliberate effort to unite these smaller sub-regional blocks into a much larger union at the continental level. Apart from the pan-African vision behind AfCFTA, the economic argument behind its creation has been substantially studied (World Bank, 2020).

In recent years, trade in Africa has been the subject of legal discourse by jurists for decades. Given that Free Trade Agreements (Henceforth FTAs) are sprouting successfull across the worldwide in driving state development, it only became normal that the African Union would use them as a toolkit to drive development in Africa. Away from the global need for continents and regional groupings to forge FTAs, it should be highlighted that in recent times, and with the resurgence of "African consciousness", African renaissance calls have been made for the transfer of sovereignty away from the state to regional and continental institutions (Richard Frimpong Oppong, 2011). The zeal of integrating Africa in all ramifications, to wit, economically and politically, has a long history (Ibid), and the move towards FTAs was one of those inroads towards this broader African dream. Given the global success of FTAs, the AfCFTA is an African initiative aimed at driving development accross the continent. This chapter comprises two parts, and the first explores the legal framework of the AfCFTA, while the second delves into the institutional framework.

2.2 Legal Framework of the AfCFTA

From the preliminary reading of the AfCFTA, it emerges that the general objective of the AfCFTA is to create a single market for goods and services, facilitated by the movement of persons to deepen the economic integration of the African continent and by the Pan-African Vision of "An integration, prosperous and peaceful Africa" enshrined in Agenda 2063 (See article 3(a) of the AfCFA). Subsequent objectives of the AfCFTA are largely hinged on the success of the primary objective. It is this proviso that lays the qualification of the AfCFTA as a free trade agreement from a legal standpoint. On a larger scale, it should be emphasised that pan-Africanism forms part of the toolkit upon which the AfCFTA is built.

The AfCFTA comprises 30 articles, 16 pages, and split into 7 parts. Part I of AfCFTA delves into Definitions, Part II explores the Establishment, Objectives, Principles, and Scope of AfCFTA, Part III on the Administration and Organisation, Part IV zooms into Transparency, Part V on Continental Preferences, Part VI on Dispute Settlement, and finally Part VII on the Final Provisions.

It is worth noting from the reading of article 30 of AfCFTA that the authentic texts of AfCFTA are written in four original texts to wit—Arabic, English, French, and Portuguese languages. Unfortunately, despite the pan-African vision of AfCFTA, no African indigenous language was used to draw up the AfCFTA and can be used to authenticate the same. It is further worrisome that while article 11 of the Protocol on Amendments to the Constitutive Act of the African Union recognises Arabic, English, French, Portuguese, Spanish, Kiswahili and any other African Language as official languages of the AU, the AfCFTA limits itself to four languages only. This flaw would be felt in the long run, especially in rural areas in Africa as there would be limited access to documentation on AfCFTA in some African countries (for example, Rwanda uses Kinyarwanda as a national language while Swahili is used in Tanzania, Kenya among others as a national language). While the transposition of AfCFTA into national norms would automatically lead to a translation of AfCFTA into those local languages, it was expected that the drafters of the AfCFTA would have used pan-African languages in the mother instruments.

2.2.1 Foundational Legal Instruments: Overview of the AfCFTA Agreement

In international law, the legal qualification attributed to the AfCFTA is that of a treaty. The AfCFTA from a strict legal standpoint hinges on a series of rules which emanate primarily from AfCFTA or are a derivative of the same, which are regularly churned by the Assembly (the highest decision-making organ of the African Union). It palpably emerges from the forgoing that the foundational rules of the AfCFTA can be harvested either from the mother instrument, which is the AfCFTA agreement, or from subsidiary legislation, named Protocols. The scope of AfCFTA is succinctly limited to trade in goods, trade in services, investment, intellectual property rights and competition policy. Outside this scope the AfCFTA is completely incompetent.

The AfCFTA is the framework legislation, while the protocols are implementation instruments. Nonetheless, it can be argued that the scope of the AfCFTA legal framework, from a loose perspective, is much larger than jurists may be accustomed to think. This view is tenable from the reading of the preamble and certain provisions of the AfCFTA, especially article 5 (I), which laconically adds neighbouring rules such as best practices governing RECs in the state parties and International Conventions binding the African Union within the corpus of the guiding principles governing the AfCFTA. It is very common to find, especially in the Protocols of the AfCFTA, references to the GATT, and other agreements of the World Trade Organisation (WTO), which either shed light on the AfCFTA or render the WTO legal arsenal fully applicable in the realm of the AfCFTA in those areas duly referenced. Thus, the AfCFTA borrows tremendously from the mother legislative organ that regulates trade at the global level.

The AfCFTA prohibits states from exempting themselves from certain mandatory provisions of the AfCFTA through reservations (article 25 of AfCFTA). This means that upon ratifying the AfCFTA, member states shall *ipso facto* remain compliant and ensure that subsequent laws are in tandem with the AfCFTA, or, if not, ensure withdrawal and waiver as measures of exiting their obligations under the AfCFTA. Though this provision can be acclaimed for protecting the interest of the AfCFTA and promoting homogeneity and maximum harmonisation, the practice elsewhere is that reservations are permitted to the extent provided in the FTA.

The AfCFTA baptises the use of protocols as implementation instruments. At present, pursuant to the AfCFTA, the Protocols on Trade in Goods, Trade in Services, Investment, Intellectual Property Rights, Competition Policy, Rules and Procedures on the settlement of Disputes and their Appendices shall, upon their adoption, form an integral part of the AfCFTA. It should also be underscored that the Protocols on Trade in Goods, Trade in Services, Investment, Intellectual Property Rights, Competition Policy, Rules and Procedures on the Settlement of Disputes, among others and their associated Annexes and Appendices shall form part of the single undertaking, subject to entry into force. The above protocols are of paramount significance as they set the stage for the implementation of the AfCFTA.

It follows that negotiations under the AfCFTA encompass trade in goods, trade in services, investment, intellectual property rights, competition policy, digital trade, Women and Youth in Trade and (section 6 of the AfCFTA).

2.2.2 *Compliance with International Law*

2.2.2.1 Alignment with World Trade Organisation (WTO) Rules and Global Trade Norms

It has been aforesaid that the AfCFTA is not a standalone legal instrument which covers the full breadth of the African Continental Free Trade Area. Flavours of the WTO are imbibed within the corpus of legislation that form part of the building blocks of the AfCFTA. Chief among the rules borrowed from WTO rules are the Most-Favoured Nation Treatment (article 4 of the Protocol on Trade in Goods) which has been copied from General Agreement on Trade in Services (GATS, article II) and article I of GATTS. Most-Favoured Nation Treatment under GATS, GATT and AfCFTA is grounded on the principle of non-discrimination and equality among member states. However, under article 19 of AfCFTA, it is possible to set aside AfCFTA, and by extension, the principle of MFN. This is possible to the extent that members of a particular REC have attained among themselves higher levels of regional integration other than those provided in AfCFTA. The REC members can derogate from its core obligations under AfCFTA and apply the rules of the REC.

Also, National Treatment was further copied from the WTO framework (GATT article III) into AfCFTA (article 5 of Protocol on Trade in Goods). Simply put, national treatment ensures that states give the same legal treatment to local goods with imports from member states. Also, non-tariff barriers (article 12 of the Protocol on Trade in Goods), anti-dumping and countervailing measures (article 17 of Protocol on Trade in Goods), among others (see generally article 5 of AfCFTA, governing the principles of AfCFTA) have been substantially borrowed from the WTO framework. Special and differential treatments is another principle which has been borrowed from the WTO toolkit. In the context of the AfCFTA, special and different treatment is couched as a guiding principle of AfCFTA (article 5(d)) and the Protocol on Trade in Goods (article 6) and article 7 of the Protocol on Trade in Services. Special and differential treatment has been globally acclaimed as a mechanism aimed at improving the position of developing countries by introducing "lighter" disciplines that are applicable to developing countries (Mitsuo Matsushita, Thomas J. Schoenbaum et al., 2015). In the context of AfCFTA, Article 6 of the Protocol on Trade in Goods, stating that "In conformity with the objective of the AfCFTA in ensuring comprehensive and mutually beneficial trade in goods, State Parties shall, provide flexibilities to other State Parties at different levels of economic development or that have individual specificities as recognized by other State Parties. These flexibilities shall include, among others, special consideration and additional transition". It follows from this provision that the yardsticks that qualifies a state to special and differential treatment relates to countries at different "economic development" or in cases of them facing "individual specificities" but subject to the condition that these are "recognized" by other state parties (Lily Sommer and Jamie MacLeod, 2019).

These concepts have not only been copied from the WTO and GATT, but the scope and underlying principles mean the same thing under both rules with a few caveats. This holds true as the WTO and GATT have traditionally been considered as the constitution in the promotion of most free trade norms, hinged on the reduction of tariffs and non-tariff trade barriers (James Thuo Gathii, 2011). The alignment of the AfFCTA to the WTO and GATT rules is hinged on the shared mission of both institutions (FTAs) and the need for the AfFCTA to be in tandem with international and best practices on the subject.

The alignment of AfCFTA with WTO and GATT rules is felt at two levels. Firstly, the foundational rules governing the AfCFTA are rooted in the framework of the WTO and GATT. This is the tenor of article 1 of the Protocol on Trade in Goods where it emerges that some concepts to wit Anti-dumping Agreement, Safeguards Agreement, TBT Agreement are all sourced and referenced from WTO Agreement on the implementation of Article VI of the GATT 1994 and WTO Agreement on Technical Barriers to Trade respectively. *Secundo*, on a lighter note, while the AfCFTA seeks to harmonise trade at the intra-African level, the need to harmonise trade rules at the global level was not completely ignored. The AfFCTA recognises the need for a globalised trading system, and the recognition and usage of global trade norms, is in tandem with linking Africa and other FTAs in the global trade system. This is the tenor of article 3 (f) of AfFCTA which outlines that it seeks, among others to "enhance the competitiveness of the economies of State Parties within the continent and the global market". This competition is best guaranteed in a uniform and homogenous global market rules.

Grosso modo, it can be rightly inferred that the drafters of the WTO and GATT rules, were resurrected in Africa to prepare the AfCFTA. However, the aforementioned statement is not true as the AfCFTA has taken a position on certain issues, that departs from the WTO norm. Specific reference can be made to the adoption of variable geometry (article 5 of AfCFTA) which undercuts the famous non-discrimination principle and MFN under WTO (James Thuo Gathii, 2011).

2.2.2.2 Legal Obligations of Member States Under AfCFTA

The legal obligations of member states under the AfCFTA are multifaceted. Given that the AfCFTA is directed for the enforcement of African states and RECs, the obligation of member states cannot be overemphasised. Legally speaking, a careful reading of AfCFTA reveals that states are legally obliged to;

1. Publication of texts for purposes of transparency (article 16 of AfCFTA)
2. Implement Decisions of the Council of Ministers (11 (5) of AfCFTA)
3. Customs Cooperation, Trade Facilitation and Transit (Part IV of the Protocol on Trade in Goods of AfCFTA)
4. Liberalisation of Trade (article 7 of the Protocol on Trade in Goods of AfCFTA)
5. Cooperation relating to Anti-dumping, Countervailing and Safeguards Investigations (aricle 20 of Protocol on Trade in Goods of AfCFTA)
6. Technical assistance and capacity building in trade and trade-related issues (article 29 of Protocol on Trade in Goods of AfCFTA)
7. Maintain or institute, as soon as practicable, judicial, arbitral or administrative tribunals or procedures (article 9 (2) of Protocol on Trade in Services of AfCFTA)

The above obligations are not exhaustive, as it has been extrapolated from AfCFTA, and the relevant protocols. By extension, the objective of AfCFTA implicitly falls on member states when their collaboration and implementation could defer its application (article 4 of AfCFTA). This translates that the legal obligations of member states under the AfCFTA is not static, but evolves as subsequent legislative instruments of AfCFTA are adopted.

Emphasis should be laid on the fact that member states are expected to transplant and apply the AfCFTA into their local orders, meaning that their legal obligations is express from all legal provisions of AfCFTA which necessitates their mutual recognition and application.

2.2.3 Harmonisation of Laws Within the AfCFTA System

The purpose of FTAs often hinges on their ability to harmonise laws, governing trade among member states. This is a legal presumption often premised on the common understanding that trade barriers often crop up when there is a plethora of conflicting and overlapping rules. In the context of AfCFTA, the term harmonisation has not been defined, but rather described. Given the comprehensive scope of AfCFTA, it can be argued that any effort aimed at integrating the African continent under the umbrella of AfCFTA can be termed harmonisation. While the term harmonisation can be loosely interpreted as uniformity, or a unity of rules from a more legalese sense of the word, it can be argued that the concept of harmonisation in AfCFTA is quite confusing. This arises from the fact that harmonisation can be interpretation under AfCFTA first, as the unificatication of existing RECs (article 3 (h) of AfCFTA) under the AfCFTA and secondly as the unification of African states under the umbrella of AfCFTA (article 3 (a) of AfCFTA). In this sense, harmonisation holds a double meaning, which is not akin to other FTAs.

A key feature in Africa, which has often challenged a broad base adoption and unification of laws at the continental level, often hovers on the fact that most African countries do not share a common legal culture (James Thuo Gathii, 2011). This is palpably evident in the current clusters of RECs, which primarily revolve around countries with shared legal cultures and those belonging to a particular geographic zone.

It can even be argued that when the bond between a group is strenghthened their belonging to a common geographic zone, culture and or legal system, there is a high probability that a RECs can crop up. It is common knowledge that the EAC, SADC, COMESA are predominantly located in the East and Southern Africa, respectively. At the same time, the ECCAS comprises civil law and French-speaking countries. At the same time, ECOWAS has flavours that transcend legal systems (civil and common law) and the UMA, made up primarily of African countries in the northern part of Africa, with shared values on Sharia law.

From a broader perspective, it can be inferred that a broader and in-depth harmonisation of laws at the continental level may prove difficult, given that the practice has always been that states with common interest often cluster among each other.

Despite the above viewpoint, it should be emphasised that one of the pillars of the AfCFTA is to expand intra-African trade through harmonisation, coordination of trade liberalisation and implementation of trade facilitation instruments across

Africa (see preamble of AfCFTA). This largely explains why, within the AfCFTA, the approach has not been to completely outlaw or replace RECs by the AfCFTA. In this sense, the AfCFTA regards these RTAs as building blocks towards the fulfilment of a continent-wide trade bloc—the AfCFTA. This approach has been contested by doctrines such as Bhagwati (1995), who contends that the goal of each of these agreements is to liberalise trade within the group. Bhagwati further argues that these agreements had discriminatory consequences for trade creation (James Thuo Gathii, 2011).

Some arguments behind the inclusion of RECs within the AfCFTA system as building blocks are manifold. It can be questioned why the drafters of the AfCFTA, could not single out the most successful REC in Africa based on global trade norms, and use the underlying rules of to develop the AfCFTA system? Or perhaps, use the best practices of all RECs in Africa to develop the AfCFTA? This way, the AfCFTA would fully harmonise all trade norms at a continental level and prevent the convergence of several microsomes and overlapping trade systems. This argument finds favour in the fact that most of the RECs in Africa, are not fully developed, and have not yet attained the stage of a full REC based on global standards. This way, the AfCFTA could easily swallow these RECs and scale up a continental trade system. These arguments and more indicate that fashioning the AfCFTA around RECs is a hectic process and when it is not well conceptualised, could lead to the spaghetti effect per Bhagwati (ibid). It also indicates how the concept of integration is fluid and capable of several definitions and inclinations (Serge François Sobzé, 2023).

On the contrary, the inclusion of RECs in the AfCFTA finds favour in the fact that the AfCFTA came at a later stage in Africa's development trajectory. As a late comer, it is logical that the AfCFTA would have to build around existing trade structures rather than overhaul it.

The question that begs an answer is how conflicts of laws should be resolved if the provisions of the AfCFTA contradict those found in the RECs and other agreements signed by member states? The drafters of the AfCFTA were conscious of this difficulty which can often lead to a legal enigma, and this justifies why section 19 of the AfCFTA is couched as follows: "In the event of any conflict and inconsistency between this Agreement and any regional agreement, this Agreement shall prevail to the extent of the specific inconsistency, except as otherwise provided in this Agreement. Notwithstanding the provisions of Paragraph 1 of this Article, State Parties that are members of other regional economic communities, regional trading arrangements and customs unions, which have attained among themselves higher levels of regional integration than under this Agreement, shall maintain such higher levels among themselves".

The formula provided in Section 19 is to the effect that the supremacy of the AfCFTA over regional agreements should be based on the level of regional integration between the AfCFTA and the regional agreements. Like an onion, it is expected that the AfCFTA will continue to peel off the obstacles that impede regional integration at the continental level, such that in the end, the AfCFTA could remain the sole FTA within the African continent.

2.3 Challenges of Reconciling Diverse National Legal Systems

The harmonisation of the AfCFTA at the continental level also faces difficulties at the national level in member states. This arises based on two principal reasons to wit; the constitutional principle governing the supremacy of the constitution over treaties in African countries is not unique (monist and dualist), and the fact that states belong to several FTAs and partnership agreements with several countries complicates the legal landscape for the reconciliation of national legal systems under the banner of the AfCFTA. On the first arm, member states that practice the monist system are legally obliged to apply provisions hinging on the AfCFTA, so long as they have ratified, without needing a special legislative enactment to that effect. In contrast, countries practising monism would need to enact specific legislation upon which the treaty obligations would be transposed. Practising monism would require the enactment of specific legislation to translate the treaty obligations into their local legal orders. This transposition process may take time and may vary from one country to another, depending on the sovereign nature of their parliaments.

On the second point, reconciling the AfCFTA with local legislations can be complicated because African countries are trading partners with multiple trading partners both within and outside the African continent (James Thuo Gathii, 2011). This has led to overlapping RTAs in Africa, exemplified by the fact that some African countries decided to go solo by signing Economic and Partnership Agreements (EPAs) with the EU, leaving their RECs behind, further exacerbating the multiplicity of trade and related agreements in Africa (ibid).

2.4 Institutional Framework Governing the AfCFTA

The institutional design that carries the AfCFTA must be formidable enough if the desired outcomes are to be met. In this light, similar to other FTAs, the AfCFTA adopts a governance structure that establishes the rules and ensures their enforcement. Apart from the governance issue, there is the issue of dispute resolution mechanisms under the AfCFTA, the question of monitoring and evaluation of the AfCFTA, as well as the role and contribution of RECs within the AfCFTA institutional framework.

At the heart of the AfCFTA is a governance framework that is pivotal to the implementation of the AfCFTA. These structures are provided in Article 9 of the AfCFTA and include the Assembly, the Council of Ministers, the Committee of Senior Trade Officials and the Secretariat. Apart from these institutions, a plethora of sub-committees and committees has been created by the various protocols, annexes of the agreement (see Babajide Sodipo, 2019) such as the Committee for Trade in Services, Committee for Trade in Goods, Sub-Committee on Trade

Facilitation, Customs Cooperation and Transit 1, Sub-Committee on Rules of Origin, Sub-Committee for Technical Barriers to Trade, Sub-Committee for Non-Tariff Barriers (NTB), Sub-Committee on Trade Remedies, Sub-Committee on SPS Measures and Dispute Settlement Body.

2.5 Role of the African Union Commission (AUC) and AfCFTA Secretariat

The AfCFTA, via its Assembly, sets up a Secretariat which shall be autonomous of the African Union Commission. The primary duty of the Secretariat is to serve as the administrative organ to coordinate the implementation of the AfCFTA, and provide technical assistance and capacity building in trade and trade-related issues for the implementation of the AfCFTA, among others.

2.5.1 Composition and Functions of Key Institutions

The wheels of the AfCFTA are manned and set running by these structures with well-defined missions. The Assembly is considered the highest decision-making organ of the African Union (article 10 of AfCFTA), and in the context of the AfCFTA, it has exclusive authority to adopt interpretations of the AfCFTA on the recommendations of the Council of Ministers. It follows that the Assembly referred herein, is not a novel structure created by AfCFTA, but the scope of the Assembly created by the Constitutive Act of the African Union, has been lengthened under AfCFTA. This is understandable, as the Assembly is the legislative organ of the AU, and would automatically be saddled with the role of adopting and interpreting legislative texts of AfCFTA, given that it is subservient to the AU. This reflects the centrality of the AfCFTA to the African Union's integration agenda, ensuring that the project maintains the political commitment of all member states of the African Union (ibid). It is thus the same hammer striking from Addis Ababa, but the hammer has simply been lengthened.

The Council of Ministers, on its part, is composed of Ministers of Trade in member states and they report to the Assembly. The primary role of the Council of Ministers is to make decisions on the AfCFTA and ensure the implementation of the objectives of the AfCFTA. Similar to the Assembly, the Council of Ministers referred to in article 11 of AfCFTA is not a new institution under AfCFTA, but its scope has been extended to now cover the mandate to which it has been accorded to AfCFTA.

The Committee of Senior Trade Officials is the technical arm of the Council of Ministers, as it implements their decisions; develops programmes for the implementation of the AfCFTA, among others (Article 12 of the AfCFTA). This structure plays the groundwork, and test the implementation of AfCFTA. It also measures how AfCFTA hits the ground, and proposes recommendations to the Council of Ministers. The Committee of Senior Trade Officials reports to the Council of Ministers and shall meet at least twice a year and shall operate in accordance with the rules of procedures as adopted by the Council of Ministers. It is noteworthy that RECs shall be represented in the Committee of Senior Trade Officials, in an advisory capacity.

2.5.2 *Dispute Settlement Mechanism*

Central to FTAs is the issue of dispute resolution mechanisms. Provided that FTAs have their rights and obligations which are peculiar to the AfCFTA, it is normal that the AfCFTA should be adopted with a specific dispute resolution mechanism that is palatable with the rights and obligations that the parties exercise. This justifies why the third protocol of the AfCFTA hinges on the Protocol on Rules and Procedures on the Settlement of Disputes. The scope of application of the AfCFTA is quite large and can be triggered when a dispute arises over the rights and obligations of any member state under the provisions of the AfCFTA.

2.5.3 *Overview of the Dispute Settlement Body (DSB) Under the AfCFTA*

The DSB is a central element in providing security and predictability to the regional trading system. The role of the DSB is to preserve the rights and obligations of state parties as provided in the AfCFTA and in accordance with the customary rules of interpretation of public international law (Article 4 of the AfCFTA). The authority of the DSB per article 5 (3) of the Protocol on Rules and Procedures on the Settlement of Disputes is to;

(a) establish Dispute Settlement Panels and an Appellate Body;
(b) adopt Panel and Appellate Body reports;
(c) maintain surveillance of implementation of rulings and recommendations of the Panels and Appellate Body; and,
(d) authorise the suspension of concessions and other obligations under the Agreement.

The dispute resolution mechanism under the AfCFTA is largely built on the WTO Model of dispute resolution. This model permits that state parties to AfCFTA can sue given that physical and juristic persons of private law are precluded from claiming under the AfCFTA via the DSB. The legal procedures for resolving trade disputes are triggered once the parties have been unable to strike a successful amicable resolution of the dispute. The phase preceding the establishment of a Panel by the DSB to settle the dispute is known as the consultation phase. The primary purpose of consultation, as evinced by section 7 of the AfCFTA, is to encourage parties to strengthen and improve the effectiveness of consultation procedures in the AfCFTA. It is worth noting that consultations are obligatory before a party can directly seize the DSB and consultation procedures cannot exceed 60 days.

This timeline is concise and ensures that consultations are not too lengthy for a party to abuse, thereby avoiding the frustration of the entire dispute resolution process. Chief among the rules applicable at the consultation phase of the AfCFTA dispute resolution process is that it shall be confidential and should unfold without prejudice to the rights of any state party in any further proceedings (Article 7(7)).

Apart from consultations in the dispute resolution process, the Protocol on Rules and Procedures on the Settlement of Disputes also provides for the use of Good Offices, Conciliation, and Mediation. The Protocol on Rules and Procedures on the Settlement of Disputes provides that "Good offices, conciliation or mediation may be requested at any time by any state party to a dispute. They may begin at any time and be terminated at any time by any of the state parties to the dispute. Once procedures for good offices, conciliation or mediation are terminated, a complaining party may then proceed with a request for the establishment of a panel". When good office, conciliation, or mediation is entered into after the 60-day period following the date of receipt of a request for consultations, the complaining party must allow a period of 60 days after the date of receipt of the request for consultations before requesting the establishment of a panel.

Once the amicable settlement phase fails, the complaining party shall, in writing, refer the matter to the DSB and request the establishment of a panel (Article 9 of the Protocol on Rules and Procedures on the Settlement of Disputes). The concerned parties to the dispute shall be promptly informed of the composition of the panel. A meeting of the DSB shall be convened within 15 days of the request to establish a panel, provided that at least 10 days' advance notice of the meeting is given to the DSB. The Panel shall be constituted by individuals whose names appear on a roster prepared by the Secretariat. What catches the eye is the fact that the criteria and mechanism used to select members of the panel is couched in ambiguous terms. Under the current legal framework, member states can nominate two individuals annually to the Secretariat for inclusion on the list of the panel (Ibid, article 10). Should the Secretariat fail to select and establish an indicative list of panellist out of laziness or forgetfulness, it is possible that the indicative list referred in article 10 (2) is crowded with panellist nominated by member states. This raises questions on impartibility, independence and autonomy of panellist of the DSB.

The procedure before the panel has been succinctly outlined in section 6 of the Protocol on Rules and Procedures on the Settlement of Disputes. Panel cases (panel reports) are subject to appeal at the Appellate Body (AB) composed of seven persons, three of whom shall serve on any one case. The rulings of the Appellate Body are binding on the parties to the dispute. However, the Protocol on Rules and Procedures on the Settlement of Disputes has left open the question of how decisions from the DSB will be enforced on defaulting states. This is the tenor of article 24 of the Protocol on Rules and Procedures on the Settlement of Disputes which laconically states that "State Parties shall promptly comply with recommendations and rulings of the DSB". It follows from this legal provision that recommendations and rulings of the DSB are not implemented after its adoption by the panel as State Parties can elect the specific period to implement same (article 24 (3) of the Protocol on Rules and Procedures on the Settlement of Disputes). Further legal provisions of the DSB, indicate that it lacks competence to enforce same, and may likely resort to suspension and suspension of concessions under the AfCFTA only if the aggrieved party refers it to the DSB".

2.6 Monitoring and Evaluation Framework

The monitoring and evaluation framework within the AfCFTA is conceptualised in article 11 of the AfCFTA which outlines a series of obligations on the Council of Ministers to wit; to ensure the effective implementation and enforcement of the AfCFTA, working in collaboration with other organs and institutions of the African Union, supervise the work of all committees and working groups it may establish per the prescripts of the AfCFTA, approve the work programmes of the AfCFTA and its institutions among others. As aforesaid, the Council of Ministers consists of the Ministers responsible for Trade or such other ministers, authorities, or officials duly designated by the State Parties.

The Council of Ministers is thus a key player in the AfCFTA, given that the focal person in the member states of the AfCFTA in charge of trade is duly represented there. It follows from the reading of Article 11(5) that decisions taken by the Council of Ministers while acting within its mandate are binding on state parties. Decisions that have legal, structural, or financial implications shall be binding on state parties upon their adoption by the assembly.

It should be underscored here that apart from the duties of the Council of Ministers as enshrined in article 11 of the AfCFTA, various protocols of the AfCFTA have added more impetus to their ability to monitor and enforce the AfCFTA. This is the tenor of article 26 of the Protocol on Trade in Services which reads thus "The Council of Ministers by Article 11 of the Agreement shall establish the Committee on Trade in Services, which shall carry out such functions as may be assigned to it by the Council of Ministers to facilitate the operation of this Protocol and further its objective. The Committee may establish such subsidiary bodies as it considers appropriate for the effective discharge of its functions". It is noteworthy that the principal mission of the Committee on Trade in Services is to prepare annual reports for state parties to facilitate the process of implementation, monitoring and evaluation of the Protocol on Trade in Services. Similar voices are echoed in other protocols of the AfCFTA, which extends the scope of the Council of Ministers as the central organ for the implementation and evaluation of the AfCFTA.

2.6.1 Mechanisms for Tracking Implementation and Compliance

Given the comprehensive powers attributed to the Council of Ministers, the Committee of Senior Trade Officials was set up, under the supervisory authority of the Council of Ministers, primarily to implement their decisions. In addition to their traditional mission as Senior Trade Officials, they are further tasked with monitoring and conducting regular reviews to ensure the proper functioning and development of the AfCFTA by the relevant provisions governing the AfCFTA. The Committee of Senior State Officials also possesses investigative powers by requesting the Technical Committee to carry out investigations on any particular matter.

To ensure that the activities of the Committee of Senior State Officials runs smoothly, they prepare reports, which are expected to run smoothly, and meet at least twice a year. They shall also submit their reports, which may include recommendations, to the Council of Ministers.

2.6.2 Role of Regional Economic Communities (RECs) in the Institutional Framework of AfCFTA

It need not be stressed that RECs are as old as the African Union itself. It is even based on the success of some of these RECs that have been given a place under the AfCFTA framework, given that a major mission of the AfCFTA is to bring all RECs closer together under the guise of the AfCFTA to closely monitor and bring all RECs together. The recognition of RECs in the AfCFTA regulatory framework is felt at several levels. First, this recognition satisfies the objective of the AfCFTA, as it is built on the initiatives and development of RECs (Article 3(c)). On the second arm, RECs are represented, and the forms form part of the Committee of Senior Trade Officials, serving in an advisory capacity. This formal recognition and inclusion of RECs in the AfCFTA is a conscious effort to harmonise and unite all RECs around the AfCFTA as the latter continues to churn and bring the regulations in all RECs closer together.

2.6.3 Key Challenges in Legal and Institutional Frameworks

A central problem facing the AfCFTA is the fragmentation and overlapping trade agreements. It can be argued that the co-existence of several FTAs in Africa may impede the smooth functioning of the AfCFTA. For example, the same product may receive different tariff treatment depending on its origin, as members of a preferential trade arrangement treat their members more favourably than they would non-members. This is particularly evident in the AfCFTA, where even if a product from a non-member is produced at a lower cost, it may still be subject to higher tariffs

(Bhagwati, 1995). By extension, multiple bilateral and RECs undermine the goal of non-discriminatory practices in international trade (AfCFTA in this case) under the umbrella of the GATT/WTO framework since they create RECs that discriminate across products and countries (Panagariya, 2000).

Secondly, the enforcement of obligations and addressing non-compliance is remains a major issue, and the enforcement of obligations and addressing non-compliance are other areas of concern. This is primarily because the implementation of the AfCFTA is based on the presumed good faith of member states and their commitment to and attachment to pan-African values. Given the youthfulness of the AfCFTA, capacity building remains a major issue, and the enforcement mechanism is still shaky.

In addition to enforcement and non-compliance issues, political will and sovereignty concerns in legal harmonisation still pose a problem. This in turn is due to lack of political and institutional support from the various governments to back what they agree to with action (Benjamin Ofori-Amoah, 2024). It is even questionable whether member states of the AfCFTA, who are non-compliant in the RECs that they have ratified, will become compliant under the AfCFTA. The presumption here is that their non-compliance in their various RECs may slip into the AfCFTA. If these challenges are surmounted, member states to the AfCFTA would be able to unlock all the opportunities that it presents.

2.7 Conclusion

It cannot be gainsaid that FTAs, including the AfCFTA, can only be successful if the legal and institutional frameworks are formidable enough to produce the desired results. The legal framework of the AfCFTA has been succinctly outlined in the first arm of this chapter, such as protocols and appendices. The second arm examines the institutional framework, specifically the machinery responsible for running the AfCFTA.

Moving forward, it is recommended that the institutional machinery be strengthened through capacity building, and that the AfCFTA should expedite the harmonisation of all the RECs under its umbrella to prevent the proliferation of fragmented legislations at the continental level.

References

Babajide Sodipo, "Governance for an effective AfCFTA" in David Luke and Jamie MacLeod (eds), Inclusive Trade in Africa, The African Continental Free Trade Area in Comparative Perspective, Routledge, 2019.

Benjamin, Ofori-Amoah The African Continental Free Trade Area Prospects Problems and Challenges Springer International Publishing Cham

Bhagwati, J. (1995). US trade policy: The infatuation with free trade agreements. In J. Bhagwati & A. O. Krueger (Eds.), *The dangerous drift to preferential trade agreements*. AEI Press.

Emmanuel, Ugirashebuja John Eudes, Ruhangisa Tom, Ottervanger Armin, Cuyvers East African Community Law Institutional Substantive and Comparative EU Aspects Brill | Nijhoff

James Thuo Gathii. (2011). *African regional trade agreements as legal regimes.* Cambridge University Press.

Jamel Zarrouk, Franco Zallio. (2001). Integrating Free Trade Agreements in the Middle East and North Africa. The Journal of World Investment & Trade, 2(2), 404.

Mitsuo, Matsushita Thomas J, Schoenbaum Petros C, Mavroidis Michael, Hahn The World Trade Organization Law Practice and Policy Oxford University Press

Lily Sommer and Jamie MacLeod, "How important is special and differential treatment for an inclusive AfCFTA? in David Luke and Jamie MacLeod (eds), Inclusive Trade in Africa, The African Continental Free Trade Area in Comparative Perspective, Routledge, 2019.

Panagariya. (2000). Preferential trade liberalization: The traditional theory and new developments. *Journal of Economic Literature, 38*(2), 287.

Richard Frimpong Oppong. (2011). *Legal aspects of economic integration in Africa.* Cambridge University Press.

Serge François Sobzé. (2023). *La Zone de Libre-échange continentale africaine à l'épreuve de l'harminisation des processus d'intergration régionale en Afrique subsaharienne, Revue des Douanes et Changes en Afrique Centrale, Numero 001/Janvier-Fevrier-Mars* (pp 79–94).

Word Bank, The African Continental Free Trade Area, Economic and Distributional Effects, International Bank for Reconstruction and Development, 2020.

Chapter 3
Global and Regional Trade Agreements and the Implementation of the AfCFTA

Leseko Makhetha

Abstract The African Continental Free Trade Area (AfCFTA) represents a transformative initiative aimed at creating a single continental market for goods and services, fostering economic integration, and boosting intra-African trade. This paper examines the AfCFTA within the broader context of global and regional trade governance. It explores the historical evolution and impact of multilateral frameworks like the World Trade Organisation (WTO) and the proliferation of Regional Trade Agreements (RTAs). The analysis highlights the significant synergies between these agreements and the AfCFTA, particularly in areas of trade facilitation, standards harmonisation, and capacity building. However, it also identifies critical challenges arising from conflicts and overlaps with existing Regional Economic Communities (RECs), such as divergent rules of origin, tariff schedules, and dispute resolution mechanisms. The paper concludes by proposing strategic policy recommendations for the effective implementation of the AfCFTA. These strategies focus on institutional alignment, infrastructure development, capacity building, and enhanced private sector engagement to overcome structural barriers and realise the agreement's potential as a cornerstone for Africa's economic renaissance.

Keywords AfCFTA · Regional integration · WTO · RTAs · Trade liberalization · Rules of origin · Non-tariff barriers · Intra-African trade · RECs

3.1 Introduction

As argued by Hoekman and Kostecki (2009), trade agreements form the backbone of international commerce, establishing rules that promote predictability and reduce barriers. Historically, multilateral frameworks like the General Agreement on Tariffs

L. Makhetha (✉)
Department of Economics, National University of Lesotho, Roma, Lesotho
e-mail: ls.makhetha@nul.ls

D. N. Yuni et al. (eds.), *From Policy to Practice: Challenges and Ways Forward on the Implementation of the AfCFTA*,
https://doi.org/10.1007/978-3-032-14051-7_3

and Trade (GATT) and the World Trade Organisation (WTO) have played pivotal roles in global economic integration (Baldwin, 2016a). These efforts have been complemented by Regional Trade Agreements (RTAs), such as the European Union (EU) and the United States-Mexico-Canada Agreement (USMCA), which have deepened regional ties and reshaped global value chains.

In Africa, however, trade integration has severely lagged. Intra-African trade accounted for a mere 16.6% of total trade in 2021, compared to 68.1% in Europe and 59.4% in Asia (African Development Bank (AfDB), 2021). This fragmentation, driven by high tariffs and inadequate infrastructure, has limited the continent's ability to harness the benefits of commerce (Hartzenberg, 2011). Launched in January 2021, the African Continental Free Trade Area (AfCFTA) is a direct response to these challenges. According to the (World Bank, 2020), it seeks to create the world's largest free trade area by membership, encompassing 55 AU member states with a combined population of 1.3 billion and a GDP of $3.4 trillion. The significance of the AfCFTA extends beyond borders. It represents a bold step to reconfigure Africa's position in the global economy by reducing external reliance and promoting internal value addition (African Union, 2015). Moreover, it aligns with the African Union's Agenda 2063, which envisions a continent characterised by sustainable growth and deeper global integration.

This section explores the relationship between global/regional trade agreements and the AfCFTA's implementation. It reviews the historical impact of multilateral and regional frameworks before detailing the AfCFTA's objectives and structure. The analysis then examines synergies and conflicts with bodies like the WTO and Regional Economic Communities (RECs) such as the Economic Community of West African States (ECOWAS) and the Southern African Development Community (SADC). Finally, it offers strategic policy recommendations for implementation. By framing the AfCFTA within broader trade governance, this section highlights its potential not just as a trade agreement but as a cornerstone for Africa's economic renaissance (Draper & Ismail, 2021).

3.2 Background on Trade Agreements

3.2.1 Global Trade Agreements

Global trade agreements play a pivotal role in shaping international trade by establishing rules and standards that facilitate cross-border exchanges of goods, services, and capital. According to Bagwell and Staiger (2002), these agreements aim to reduce trade barriers, promote fair competition, and foster worldwide economic growth. The most prominent frameworks include the General Agreement on Tariffs and Trade (GATT) and its successor, the World Trade Organisation (WTO). Established in 1947, the GATT focused primarily on trade in goods and, through eight negotiating rounds, achieved substantial reductions in tariffs and trade barriers that stimulated global commerce. Its core principles encompassed non-discrimination through Most Favoured Nation (MFN) and National Treatment provisions, tariff reduction, and fair-trade practices (Bagwell & Staiger, 2002). The GATT operated until 1995, when the WTO succeeded it.

The WTO expanded its scope to include trade in services through the General Agreement on Trade in Services (GATS), intellectual property rights under Trade-Related Aspects of Intellectual Property Rights (TRIPS), and Trade-Related Investment Measures (TRIMS). Hoekman and Kostecki (2009) explain that the WTO aims to facilitate smooth global trade by ensuring member countries adhere to agreed-upon rules, resolve disputes, and further reduce trade barriers. As of 2020, the WTO serves as the primary institution overseeing global trade regulations among 164 member countries.

These global trade agreements have profoundly influenced international trade patterns by facilitating expanded trade flows. The systematic reduction of tariffs and non-tariff barriers under both GATT and WTO frameworks has significantly contributed to growth in global trade volumes. Baldwin (2016b) documents that the average global tariff declined from over 40% in the 1940s to below 5% by the 2010s. This decline has enabled increased trade liberalisation, expanded networks, and broader market access. The WTO's multilateral system has been particularly instrumental in reducing trade barriers and improving market access. By providing a structured platform for negotiation, dispute resolution, and enforcement, it has fostered greater stability in global trade relations. Mavroidis (2007) emphasises that the WTO's dispute settlement mechanism has effectively prevented trade conflicts from escalating into full-scale trade wars, thereby providing essential predictability for businesses and investors.

Regarding economic development, trade liberalisation under global agreements has accelerated growth, particularly in developing countries. By enhancing access to global markets, developing nations have increased their exports, attracted foreign direct investment (FDI), and integrated into global value chains (GVCs). China's accession to the WTO in 2001, for example, significantly boosted its trade and economic growth, transforming the country into the world's largest exporter (Subramanian & Wei, 2007). Similarly, emerging economies, including India and Vietnam, have benefited from reduced trade barriers and greater global integration (Rodrik, 2011). Furthermore, trade liberalisation has encouraged industrialisation, technology transfer, and poverty reduction. As countries open their markets to international competition, they gain access to advanced technologies, improve productivity, and achieve economic diversification, ultimately leading to increased employment opportunities and reduced poverty rates (Baldwin, 2003).

However, the benefits of global trade agreements have not been distributed evenly across all participants. Some developing countries continue to struggle with full participation due to constraints such as limited infrastructure, low industrial capacity, and economic vulnerabilities. These persistent challenges have generated criticism that the global trade system disproportionately favours developed countries (Stiglitz, 2002). Nevertheless, global trade agreements have established frameworks for addressing these disparities, including special and differential treatment provisions for developing nations in areas such as market access and tariff reductions (Simo, 2020).

3.2.2 Regional Trade Agreements

Regional Trade Agreements (RTAs) are agreements between two or more countries aimed at liberalising trade through reduced tariffs, non-tariff barriers, or other trade restrictions. They are established under Article XXIV of the GATT 1994. While the WTO promotes non-discriminatory trade practices, RTAs permit preferential treatment among member countries as regards the MFN principle. These agreements take various forms (discussed in detail in Sect. 3.2.4), ranging from Free Trade Areas to Customs Unions, Common Markets, Economic Unions, and Political Unions, each reflecting a different level of integration. Following the deadlock of the Doha Development Agenda negotiations in 2015, and the WTO's inability to introduce a new "*single undertaking*," RTAs have become a significant driver of trade liberalisation, particularly in the Global South (Baldwin, 2016a; Wolfe, 2017). Consequently, the RTAs have been on proliferation. On average, each WTO member has trade agreements with over 15 countries (Liu, 2009).

This consistent increase and strengthening of RTAs over the past 30 years within an evolving multilateral trade environment have accelerated noticeably. A key source supporting this observation is the WTO Secretariat, which reported that by March 2002, 250 RTAs had been notified to the GATT/WTO. Notably, from 1948 to 1995, the year the WTO was established, 125 RTAs were notified to the GATT, matching the number notified in just the 7 years following 1995 under the WTO. By December 2024, this figure had risen to 373 RTAs. The WTO Secretariat attributes the acceleration in the early 1990s to uncertainties surrounding the Uruguay Round negotiations and integration efforts within Europe following the collapse of the Council for Mutual Economic Assistance (COMECON) bloc (Godard, 2018; Oesch et al., 2015).

In the late 1990s, reinforced notification requirements under WTO law contributed to the increase; however, they did not entirely explain the trend, indicating that more substantial drivers were at play. This highlights tangible factors behind the surge in RTAs and emphasises their real presence and importance. While periodic fluctuations have occurred, the overall trend indicates a steady growth of regionalism within the multilateral trade system, which has had to adapt and respond to these developments. Table 3.1 presents a summary of recent notifications of regional trade agreements.

Regional integration represents a strategic pathway for countries seeking to enhance economic cooperation, foster political stability, and improve trade flows. It enables nations to reduce barriers to trade and investment, harmonise policies, and enhance the competitiveness of the regional economies on the global stage. This is particularly relevant in Africa, where diverse trade agreements have aimed to unify fragmented markets, address development challenges, and promote sustainable

Table 3.1 Recent RTA notifications

RTA name	Coverage	Date of notification	Date of entry into force
Comprehensive and progressive agreement for trans-Pacific partnership (CPTPP)—accession of the United Kingdom	Goods and services	Dec 10, 2024	Dec 15, 2024
EU—Kenya	Goods	Aug 29, 2024	Jul 1, 2024
EFTA—Moldova, republic of	Goods and Services	Aug 29, 2024	Sep 1, 2024
China—Serbia	Goods	Aug 19, 2024	Jul 1, 2024
China—Ecuador	Goods	Aug 12, 2024	May 1, 2024

Source: WTO OMC Regional Trade Agreements Database; EU (European Union); EFTA (European Free Trade Association)

growth. The World Trade Organization (WTO) framework, which encompasses global trade agreements, recognises the importance of regional integration, allowing for deviations from the principle of Most-Favoured-Nation (MFN) treatment under certain conditions. These conditions facilitate trade without creating unnecessary barriers for non-member countries.

These conditions are governed by specific provisions in key instruments, including Article XXIV of the General Agreement on Tariffs and Trade (GATT), the Enabling Clause, and Article V of the General Agreement on Trade in Services (GATS), which outlines the legal basis for forming Regional Trade Agreements. The GATT, in Article XXIV (1947), governs trade in goods and allows Free Trade Areas (FTAs) and Customs Unions (CUs), while the Enabling Clause (1979) grants developing countries additional flexibility to form preferential trade arrangements, and GATS (Article V (1994)) covers trade in services, ensuring that such agreements meet substantial liberalisation criteria.

3.2.3 Reasons for Countries to Enter into Regional Trade Agreements

This section highlights the diverse factors that influence countries when negotiating regional trade agreements (RTAs). According to Whalley (1998), for some, trade agreements serve as a foundation for strategic alliances and are indirectly linked to security arrangements, as seen in Europe. Smaller nations often view agreements with larger partners as a way to secure stable access to their markets, exemplified by the Canada-U.S. Free Trade Agreement (CUSTA). In certain cases, countries have used RTAs and multilateral agreements as mechanisms to solidify domestic policy reforms, making it more challenging to reverse them later, such as Mexico's approach within the North American Free Trade Agreement (NAFTA).

Additionally, some countries strategically leverage regional agreements to shape future multilateral negotiations, as demonstrated by the role of services in both CUSTA and NAFTA. RTAs around the world are thus different from one another, not at least because countries have different objectives when they negotiate them. As a result, a wide range of differences has to be taken into account in analyzing them. Once the reasons why countries enter into RTAs are understood, the form that the eventual agreement takes becomes more explicable.

What this means is that a primary motivation for a country's involvement in trade negotiations is the expectation of mutual benefits from improved market access achieved through reciprocal reductions in trade barriers. These benefits are anticipated to be shared among all parties to the agreement. Another key reason countries pursue RTAs is the belief that such agreements can support and secure domestic policy reforms. By committing to an international trade treaty, countries make it more difficult to reverse reforms in the future, as they are bound by the terms of the agreement. This objective is not exclusive to regional agreements, as it can apply to both bilateral and multilateral negotiations. However, according to Morrison and Villarreal (2013), it played a central role in Mexico's strategy during the NAFTA negotiations. Mexican negotiators were less focused on exchanging concessions with their counterparts and more focused on making unilateral concessions to larger trading partners with whom they had limited negotiating power. The primary goal was to lock in domestic policy reforms through the agreement.

A further motivation for countries to pursue RTAs is the desire to enhance their bargaining power in negotiations with third parties by establishing common external barriers. This is typically achieved through the creation of a customs union rather than a free trade area. This rationale was a key factor behind the formation of the European Community (EC) in the late 1950s. At that time, it was believed that individual European countries would have limited leverage in negotiations with the United States, particularly on multilateral issues. However, by acting cooperatively and adopting a common external trade policy, European countries could increase their collective negotiating power. One argument often cited is that the establishment of the EC was a driving force behind several rounds of GATT negotiations, including the Dillon Round (1959–1961), the Kennedy Round (1963–1967), and the Tokyo Round (1973–1979). These rounds, initiated by the United States, sought to address access to a unified European market where individual countries had adopted common external trade barriers.

Tuomi (1988) posits that one of the objectives in recent trade negotiations involving large and small countries, particularly starting with the Canada-U.S. agreement, is to use a regional trade agreement to secure more reliable access for the smaller country to the larger country's market. In the case of the Canada-U.S. agreement, Canada's primary goal was to establish a regional trade agreement that would provide Canadians with some exemption from the use of anti-dumping and countervailing duties by U.S. producers. Canada also sought special bilateral arrangements to limit the application of U.S. safeguard measures, offering a form of escape from MFN treatment.

Another objective for countries in negotiating RTAs is the potential to strengthen security arrangements among the participating nations. This was a central concept in the early stages of European integration in the 1950s. The idea was that a regional trade agreement that fostered enhanced trade relations between Germany and France would help prevent the recurrence of war in Europe, particularly considering the historical tensions between the two nations from 1870 to 1945. Consequently, the goal of strategic linkage, promoting peace and preventing further conflict in Europe, became the primary focus of European trade negotiations, overshadowing all other integration goals due to the critical nature of the issue.

A final consideration in a country's decision to pursue RTAs is their potential use as a tactical tool to advance multilateral negotiating objectives. Similarly, multilateral negotiations can shape the direction and outcomes of regional negotiations, as global discussions often create regional opportunities. For instance, during the Uruguay Round, the USA leveraged ongoing regional trade talks to pressure uncooperative multilateral partners into submission. By threatening to prioritise regional agreements or actively engaging with prospective regional partners, the USA aimed to compel multilateral partners to respond more favourably. When progress stalled at the multilateral level, initiating regional negotiations became a strategic alternative.

3.2.4 Forms of Regional Trade Agreements

Regionalism has been a consistent feature since January 1948, when GATT first came into force.[1] The plethora of literature on regionalism tends to assume that RTAs are largely uniform (Baldwin, 2014; Bhagwati, 2008; Schiff & Winters, 2003). This assumption arises in part from the frequent use of symmetric scenarios in analytical studies, where countries are often treated as being of equal size (Krugman, 1991). When distinctions are acknowledged, they are typically limited to categorising agreements as either customs unions [e.g., Southern African Customs Union (SACU)] or free trade areas (e.g., AfCFTA). However, RTAs vary significantly in their characteristics. Some, like the East African Community (EAC), aim for deeper integration, while others have simpler structures or greater complexity, with differences extending far beyond the basic distinction between customs unions and free trade areas (United Nations Economic Commission for Africa (UNECA), 2023).

GATT (Article XXIV) provides a legal framework for RTAs, allowing member countries to form preferential trade agreements while adhering to two core principles. The first core principle is *Internal Trade Liberalisation*, where member countries eliminate tariffs and other restrictive measures on substantially all trade among

[1] As is known, GATT as such never entered into force but found provisional application by the way of the so-called Protocol of Provisional Application (UNTS Vol. 55 No. 814). See J.H Jackson, *The World Trading System*, 1997, 39 et seq.

themselves. The second core principle is the *Neutral Impact on Non-Members,* which posits that RTAs should not raise barriers to trade with non-member countries. In other words, they should facilitate trade among members without restricting trade with non-members. To qualify as a permitted exception under WTO rules, an RTA must meet one of the following two conditions: it must either result in a Free Trade Area or a Customs Union, as defined in Article XXIV:8 of the GATT 1994, or, in the case of interim agreements, it must include a clear plan and schedule for achieving full implementation. While the standard guideline for full implementation is a 10-year period, exceptions may be granted if adequately justified.

Nonetheless, the *Enabling Clause* is a more significant provision for developing countries, offering more flexible rules for RTAs compared to GATT Article XXIV. The key difference between these instruments is in terms of *scope.* The Enabling Clause applies exclusively to agreements among developing countries, while GATT Article XXIV applies universally. The second difference lies in *flexibility.* Developing countries can reduce or eliminate tariffs under the Enabling Clause, whereas GATT Article XXIV requires the elimination of tariffs on substantially all trade. The final difference is in *coverage.* The Enabling Clause includes both tariffs and non-tariff measures, whereas GATT Article XXIV focuses on duties and restrictive regulations of commerce. Resultantly, the African Continental Free Trade Area (AfCFTA) primarily operates under the principles of GATT Article XXIV, while agreements such as the ECOWAS may leverage the flexibility of the Enabling Clause of development-focused integration. Thus, RTAs manifest in several forms, each signifying a different degree of integration. Below is an expanded discussion of the key types:

(a) *Free trade area (FTA):* under the FTA, member countries eliminate tariffs and other barriers to trade among themselves but retain independent trade policies with non-members. For instance, AfCFTA seeks to harmonise intra-African trade by reducing tariffs across member countries, covering a broad range of goods and services.

(b) *Customs union (CU):* CUs are a deeper form of integration in which member countries adopt a common external tariff (CET) for non-member countries while removing internal trade barriers. For instance, the East African Community (EAC) and the Southern African Customs Union (SACU) harmonise external tariffs while promoting free trade with their member states.

(c) *Common market:* The Common Market builds on the Customs Union by enabling the free movement of goods, services, capital and labour. For instance, the Common Market for East and Southern Africa (COMESA) promotes regional economic development through trade liberalisation and mobility of factors of production.

(d) *Economic union:* The Economic Union combines features of a Common Market with coordinated economic, fiscal, and monetary policies, sometimes including a shared currency. For instance, the Common Monetary Area (CMA) in Southern Africa is notable for a shared monetary framework. The CMA includes

Lesotho, Eswatini, Namibia, and South Africa, with the South African Rand serving as the anchor currency.

(e) *Political union:* This is the most advanced form of integration, where member states unify politically under shared governance and policies. While not yet a fully Political Union, the African Union (AU) aspires towards greater political and economic integration, exemplified by initiatives like the AfCFTA.

(f) *Interim agreements:* These are the temporary arrangements aimed at transitioning to an FTA or Customs Union within a defined timeframe. The Tripartite Free Trade Area (TFTA) among COMESA, EAC, and SADC aims to merge these blocs into a single integrated market.

3.2.5 Conflicts and Overlaps Between the AFCFTA and Existing Regional Trade Agreements

The existence of multiple overlapping Regional Economic Communities (RECs) in Africa poses significant challenges to the implementation of the AfCFTA. While these RECs have contributed to regional trade integration, their varied structures, objectives, and rules sometimes conflict with AfCFTA's broader continental vision. These conflicts are rooted in disparities in tariff reduction schedules, rules of origin, trade facilitation practices, and dispute resolution mechanisms.

RECs, such as SADC, ECOWAS, and COMESA, have established tariff liberalisation schedules tailored to their member states' specific needs. These schedules often differ in terms of pace and coverage, creating inconsistencies when member states also commit to AfCFTA's liberalisation timeline. For instance, SADC's Protocol on Trade has a gradual tariff reduction process that allows sensitive products to maintain higher protection for longer periods. South Africa, a dominant player in SADC, benefits from these provisions, particularly in protecting its manufacturing and agricultural sectors. However, under AfCFTA, South Africa is required to negotiate tariff reductions with countries outside SADC, such as Nigeria and Egypt, potentially undermining its existing commitment within the REC framework (Hartzenberg, 2011). This dual obligation creates administrative burdens that sometimes lead to trade distortions as countries prioritise REC commitment over AfCFTA implementation.

Furthermore, rules of origin (RoO) are critical for determining the eligibility of products for preferential treatment under trade agreements. However, African RECs have developed their own RoO frameworks, which are often inconsistent with one another and with AfCFTA's provisions. In East Africa, for instance, Kenya, as a member of both the EAC and COMESA, must adhere to different RoO requirements. A product considered originating under EAC rules might not qualify under COMESA rules, leading to inefficiencies and increased costs for traders (Viljoen, 2020). This issue is particularly pronounced in industries like textile and apparel, where differing thresholds for local content can exclude products from preferential treatment. The automotive sector provides another example. Under SADC's RoO, vehicles assembled in South Africa qualify for preferential treatment if a significant portion of the components are locally sourced. However, if those vehicles are exported to an ECOWAS member state under AfCFTA, they may fail to meet the stricter content requirements of ECOWAS, even if they qualify under SADC. Such discrepancies discourage cross-regional trade and limit the benefits of AfCFTA's integrated market.

In addition, trade facilitation measures such as customs procedures and border controls vary widely among RECs, creating bottlenecks for the seamless movement of goods under AfCFTA. For instance, COMESA has implemented a Regional Customs Transit Guarantee scheme to streamline cross-border trade, while ECOWAS used the Inter-State Road Transit scheme for similar purposes. These systems, however, are not harmonised, leading to delays and additional costs for traders operating across regions. The Northern Corridor, which connects Kenya to landlocked countries like Uganda, Rwanda, and the Democratic Republic of Congo, illustrates the impact of such inconsistencies. While the corridor benefits from COMESA's single customs territory framework, traders face additional inspections and documentation requirements when crossing into EAC territories.

Dispute resolution is another area of conflict between RECs and AfCFTA. Each REC has its own mechanism for resolving trade disputes, which may not align with AfCFTA's Dispute Settlement Protocol (Geda & Seid, 2015). For instance, ECOWAS relies on the ECOWAS Court of Justice, while COMESA uses its Court of Justice. These mechanisms operate independently, leading to potential jurisdictional conflicts when disputes involve parties from different RECs. A notable example is the 2020 trade dispute between Nigeria and Ghana over the closure of Nigeria's land borders. Ghana, citing ECOWAS protocols on the free movement of goods, challenged Nigeria's actions. However, the dispute resolution process within ECOWAS failed to yield a resolution, and the matter remained unsolved. Such cases highlight the limitation of the REC-level mechanism and the need for a robust, continent-wide dispute settlement system under AfCFTA.

Other critical issues are policy divergences and institutional capacities. Differences in policy priorities and institutional capacities among RECs further exacerbate conflict with AfCFTA implementation. For instance, SADC prioritise industrialisation and value addition, while ECOWAS focuses on agricultural development and food security. These differing priorities influence the design of trade policies, leading to misalignment with AfCFTA's objectives. Institutional capacity is another critical factor. Some RECs, such as COMESA, have well-established secretariats capable of coordinating complex trade programmes. In contrast, others like the Arab Maghreb Union (AMU), lack the institutional infrastructure to effectively implement trade agreements (Draper & Ismail, 2021). This disparity in capacities creates uneven progress in aligning REC policies with AfCFTA.

Finally, the commitment of individual member states to both the REC and the AfCFTA agreements often depends on domestic political and economic considerations. Countries with strong regional ties may prioritise REC commitments over AfCFTA to protect established trade relationships. For instance, South Africa's economic dominance within SADC gives it significant leverage, making it less likely to fully embrace AfCFTA provisions that might dilute its influence in the region (Hartzenberg, 2011). Nigeria's initial reluctance to sign the AfCFTA agreement in 2019 further illustrates this point. Despite being a key player in ECOWAS, Nigeria hesitated to join AfCFTA due to concerns about exposing its industries to competition from more industrialised African nations. This tension between national interests and continental integration remains a significant obstacle to the implementation of the AfCFTA.

3.3 The AfCFTA: Institutional Framework and Operational Mechanisms

Building upon its foundational objectives, the AfCFTA's operational strength lies in its sophisticated institutional and legal architecture, which is critical for understanding its interaction with other trade regimes. As outlined in the Agreement (African Union, 2018), the framework is governed by several key protocols. The Protocol on Trade in Goods mandates the elimination of tariffs on 90% of tariff lines, with differentiated phase-out periods of 5–10 years for non-LDCs and LDCs, respectively. It also allows 7% of sensitive[2] products longer protection and permits 3% to be entirely excluded (World Bank, 2022). This complex scheduling directly interfaces with existing REC schedules. Complementing this, the Protocol on Trade in Services targets liberalisation in pivotal sectors like transport and finance, which is essential for enabling cross-border value chains.

A pivotal operational innovation is the Pan African Payment and Settlement System (PAPSS). Designed to facilitate instant cross-border payments in local currencies, PAPSS significantly reduces transaction costs and foreign exchange barriers for traders, especially SMEs (African Export-Import Bank, 2022). Furthermore, a rules-based Dispute Settlement Mechanism provides a continent-wide legal framework for resolving trade conflicts, a critical feature for managing overlaps with REC-specific judicial bodies. The institutional architecture, led by the AfCFTA Secretariat, is tasked with harmonising these protocols. As noted by Draper and Ismail (2021), this operational complexity the specific rules, systems, and institutions, forms the basis for analyzing the AfCFTA's synergies and conflicts with other trade agreements.

[2] Sensitive products (up to 7% of tariff lines) are products that countries consider important to protect in the short to medium term because of their economic, social, or political significance. Therefore, they are subject to delayed tariff liberalisation. Excluded products (up to 3% of tariff lines) are products that countries choose to completely shield from liberalisation to protect strategic domestic industries.

3.4 Synergies Between Regional Trade Agreements, AfCFTA and Global Trade Agreements

A complex web of regional, continental, and global agreements shapes trade integration in Africa. At the continental level, the African Continental Free Trade Area (AfCFTA) emerges as a bold initiative to unify Africa's fragmented trade landscape. It is designed not to replace existing trade agreements but to harmonise and deepen them. The AfCFTA interacts with both Regional Trade Agreements (RTAs), such as those under ECOWAS, SADC, COMESA, and EAC, and with global trade frameworks, particularly those under the World Trade Organisation (WTO). These interactions generate a range of synergies that can accelerate Africa's integration into regional and global value chains, support trade facilitation reforms, and enhance the competitiveness of African economies.

At the global level, the WTO framework provides essential support for AfCFTA implementation. The WTO Trade Facilitation Agreement (TFA), for instance, has guided African countries in reducing trade costs and improving customs efficiency. Countries like Ghana and Rwanda have implemented electronic customs systems and single-window platforms, which not only meet TFA standards but also align directly with AfCFTA objectives of seamless intra-African trade (UNECA, 2021). According to the World Trade Organisation (WTO) (2023), these reforms have led to measurable reductions in border delays, boosting trader confidence and lowering compliance costs.

Global agreements on Technical Barriers to Trade (TBT) and Sanitary and Phytosanitary (SPS) measures further provide a legal foundation for harmonising product standards under the AfCFTA. For example, South Africa's agricultural export regulations have benefited from WTO-aligned SPS rules, which the AfCFTA now seeks to replicate the same rules continent-wide (Viljoen, 2020). The alignment of these standards enhances intra-African agricultural trade, ensuring product safety and promoting consumer confidence across borders.

Moreover, global preferential trade schemes, such as the Generalised System of Preferences (GSP), the African Growth and Opportunity Act (AGOA), and the EU's Everything But Arms (EBA) initiative, offer African exporters duty-free or reduced tariff access to developed markets. These schemes create opportunities for AfCFTA members to develop regional value chains that feed into global exports. For instance, Ethiopia's textile industry sources raw materials from neighbouring countries and exports finished goods to the USA under AGOA (Parshotam, 2018). The AfCFTA, by reducing intra-African trade costs, can further support such integrated export strategies.

In parallel, the AfCFTA seeks to promote the integration of African firms into Global Value Chains (GVCs), where production is fragmented across multiple countries. Global trade agreements play a pivotal role here by providing predictable regulatory frameworks and ensuring market access. For example, South Africa's automotive sector, one of the most integrated into global markets, benefits from

WTO rules and preferential trade agreements with the EU, which it complements with AfCFTA-driven intra-African supply linkages (Rodrik, 2011).

The AfCFTA also draws synergy from capacity-building mechanisms embedded in global trade institutions. Initiatives such as the WTO's Aid for Trade and the Enhanced Integrated Framework (EIF) have funded infrastructure upgrades and customs modernisation across Africa. The development of trade corridors, such as the North–South Corridor connecting South Africa to Tanzania, has been supported by such programmes, directly reinforcing AfCFTA trade routes (UNECA, 2021). These investments support smoother logistics and create enabling environments for private sector participation in continental trade.

Equally significant are the synergies between the AfCFTA and existing Regional Trade Agreements (RTAs). As noted by Hartzenberg (2011), the AfCFTA was built on the foundation laid by eight AU-recognised RECs, including ECOWAS, COMESA, SADC, and the EAC. These RECs already have trade protocols, customs unions, and rules of origin in place. The AfCFTA does not replace these structures; instead, it aims to integrate them into a cohesive continental framework.

Many RECs offer mature and functional trade systems that the AfCFTA can adopt or scale. For example, the EAC's Single Customs Territory and COMESA's Regional Customs Transit Guarantee (RCTG) have significantly reduced border delays and improved the movement of goods across multiple countries. These successful REC-level models can be replicated or extended under AfCFTA to enhance continent-wide trade efficiency (African Export-Import Bank, 2022). In doing so, the AfCFTA leverages tested mechanisms to minimise implementation delays and duplicative systems.

Another critical synergy arises from rules of origin (RoO). Historically, inconsistent RoO frameworks across RECs created barriers to cross-border production and trade. The AfCFTA introduces a unified continental RoO regime, which simplifies compliance and fosters cross-regional value chains. In West Africa, ECOWAS is already working to align its RoO with AfCFTA standards, enabling smoother trade in processed agricultural goods and manufactured products (Viljoen, 2020).

Synergies also exist in industrial policy and regional development strategies. The SADC Industrialisation Strategy and Roadmap, for example, targets sectors like agro-processing, pharmaceuticals, and energy. Under the AfCFTA, these sectoral efforts can be scaled up through continent-wide initiatives that pool investment and technology transfer. According to the African Union (2022), coordinated industrial policy under the AfCFTA will help regional hubs become more competitive globally, while also distributing production more equitably across member states.

Beyond technical and economic synergies, political and institutional alignment is vital. Regional summits, ministerial councils, and technical committees that have existed under RECs offer ready-made channels for advancing AfCFTA negotiations. As Draper and Ismail (2021) argue, building trust through regional cooperation can ease the implementation of continental commitments and reduce interstate trade friction. These platforms allow member states to pilot trade initiatives, share best practices, and develop legal and institutional innovations that the AfCFTA can formalise and scale.

3.5 Strategies for Effective Implementation of AfCFTA

The successful implementation of the African Continental Free Trade Area (AfCFTA) hinges on coordinated strategies that address the complexities of trade integration, harmonise overlapping agreements, and build institutional capacity. These strategies must leverage synergies with global and regional agreements while mitigating conflicts to establish a cohesive framework for continental trade.

A robust institutional framework is crucial for overseeing AfCFTA's implementation and resolving challenges arising from its interplay with regional trade agreements (RTAs) and global frameworks. The AfCFTA Secretariat, located in Ghana, plays a pivotal role in providing oversight, monitoring compliance, and coordinating member states' efforts. To enhance governance, it is imperative to establish clear roles and responsibilities for the Secretariat and align its functions with existing Regional Economic Communities (RECs). For instance, the Secretariat could collaborate with RECs to harmonise rules of origin and streamline trade policies. This approach has already shown success in the East African Community (EAC), where member states aligned tariff reduction schedules with the broader objectives of the AfCFTA (UNECA, 2021). Furthermore, it is essential to leverage digital tools to monitor trade flows, collect data, and track progress. Platforms like the African Trade Observatory, developed under the African Union, offer real-time trade data, enabling policymakers to identify bottlenecks and adjust strategies accordingly. For example, Rwanda has effectively used digital systems for customs clearance, which can serve as a model for broader AfCFTA adoption (Viljoen, 2020).

The "spaghetti bowl" of overlapping trade agreements in Africa presents a significant challenge to the AfCFTA's implementation. Harmonising these agreements is essential to creating a seamless trading environment. A unified approach to rules of origin is particularly critical, as inconsistencies can lead to trade disputes and inefficiencies. A practical strategy involves adopting a Pan-African rule of origin framework under AfCFTA. This would simplify trade procedures and reduce compliance costs for businesses. For instance, under COMESA, harmonised rules of origin for agricultural products have facilitated trade between Zambia and Zimbabwe, an approach that AfCFTA could replicate continent-wide (Parshotam, 2018). Additionally, member states must reconcile tariff schedules under AfCFTA with their commitments in other RTAs. A phased approach, where AfCFTA tariffs are gradually aligned with those of RECs, can minimise disruptions. South Africa's dual membership in SACU and SADC provides an illustrative case where tariff alignment strategies are being explored to avoid conflicting obligations (Hartzenberg, 2011).

The lack of adequate infrastructure remains a critical barrier to intra-African trade. Investments in transport, energy, and digital connectivity are fundamental to reducing the cost of doing business and enabling efficient trade under AfCFTA. One key initiative is the African Union's Programme for Infrastructure Development in Africa (PIDA), which prioritises cross-border projects such as the Trans-African Highway network. This initiative can be leveraged to support AfCFTA's objectives by linking major trade hubs and reducing transport costs. For example, the Northern Corridor, connecting Kenya's Mombasa Port to Uganda, Rwanda, and Burundi, has significantly boosted trade volumes in the region (UNECA, 2021). Digital infrastructure is equally critical. E-commerce platforms and digital payment systems can bridge gaps in trade facilitation, particularly for small and medium-sized enterprises (SMEs). Nigeria's Paystack, acquired by Stripe, illustrates the potential of digital solutions to support cross-border transactions and integrate African markets (Parshotam, 2018).

The effective implementation of AfCFTA requires member states to strengthen their technical and administrative capacities. Many African countries face challenges in aligning national policies with AfCFTA provisions, necessitating targeted capacity-building programmes. The WTO's Aid for Trade initiative offers a blueprint for such efforts. Through this programme, countries like Lesotho have modernised customs procedures and enhanced their capacity to comply with trade agreements (Freund & Rocha, 2011). Expanding such initiatives under AfCFTA can help member states meet their obligations and maximise the benefits of integration. Additionally, training programmes for trade negotiators and policymakers are essential. The African Union could establish a dedicated training institute to build expertise in trade policy, dispute resolution, and economic analysis. For example, the Trade Policy Training Centre in Africa (TRAPCA) has successfully equipped African trade officials with the skills needed to navigate complex trade negotiations, a model that could be scaled up for AfCFTA (Viljoen, 2020).

The private sector is the engine of trade and economic growth, making its involvement critical to AfCFTA's success. Governments and regional bodies must create an enabling environment for businesses to thrive under the new trade framework. Public-private partnerships (PPPs) can be instrumental in addressing infrastructure gaps and fostering innovation. For instance, Ethiopia's Industrial Parks Program, developed in collaboration with private investors, has attracted significant foreign direct investment (FDI) and boosted the country's manufacturing exports (UNECA, 2021). Similar PPP models could be replicated across Africa to support AfCFTA's industrialisation goals. Moreover, engaging SMEs is vital, as they constitute the bulk of Africa's businesses. Simplified trade regimes, access to finance, and capacity-building programmes can empower SMEs to participate in continental trade. The African Export-Import Bank's (Afreximbank), PAPSS is a notable initiative that reduces transaction costs for SMEs and facilitates cross-border payments (Hartzenberg, 2011).

Collaboration with global institutions and external partners is crucial for addressing conflicts and enhancing AfCFTA's implementation. Multilateral organisations like the WTO can provide technical assistance, while bilateral partnerships can offer funding and expertise. For example, the European Union's Economic Partnership Agreements (EPAs) with African countries have included provisions for infrastructure development and capacity building. Aligning these initiatives with AfCFTA's objectives can amplify their impact. Similarly, China's Belt and Road Initiative (BRI) has financed major infrastructure projects in Africa, such as the Addis

Ababa-Djibouti Railway, which could be integrated into AfCFTA's trade networks (Draper & Ismail, 2021).

Non-tariff barriers, including bureaucratic inefficiencies, differing standards, and border delays, significantly impede trade. A strategic approach to eliminating NTBs involves establishing a robust monitoring and reporting mechanism. The AfCFTA Non-Tariff Barriers Reporting, Monitoring, and Elimination Mechanism is a promising tool in this regard. Through this platform, businesses can report NTBs in real time, enabling swift resolution by national authorities. For instance, traders in the EAC have successfully used similar mechanisms to address disputes over agricultural exports, demonstrating the potential of such systems (UNECA, 2021).

3.6 Policy Recommendations

The successful implementation of the AfCFTA requires policy measures that are precisely targeted to address the specific structural, institutional, and operational challenges identified in this analysis. The following recommendations are crafted to directly mitigate the conflicts and leverage the synergies discussed in previous sections.

3.6.1 Harmonise Rules of Origin Through a Pan-African Framework

The analysis revealed that incompatible Rules of Origin (RoO) across RECs are a primary barrier to continental value chains. Therefore, the AfCFTA Secretariat should prioritise the development and mandatory adoption of a simple, product-specific Pan-African RoO. This framework must be designed to supersede REC-specific rules, reducing compliance costs and administrative burdens for businesses operating across multiple regions. This directly addresses the conflict where a product meeting SADC's RoO fails to qualify under ECOWAS rules, thereby facilitating the integrated market that the AfCFTA promises (UNECA, 2021; Viljoen, 2020).

3.6.2 Establish a Supra-REC Dispute Settlement Mechanism

Given the jurisdictional conflicts between the courts of RECs like ECOWAS and COMESA, a robust, continent-wide mechanism is essential. Member states must empower the AfCFTA Dispute Settlement Body as the ultimate arbiter for cross-REC trade conflicts. This requires ratifying the relevant protocol and ensuring its decisions take precedence over those of REC-level mechanisms. This recommendation flows directly from the failure of the ECOWAS Court to resolve the Nigeria-Ghana border closure dispute, highlighting the need for a centralised authority (Geda & Seid, 2015).

3.6.3 Implement a Phased Tariff Alignment Strategy

The conflict between AfCFTA and REC tariff liberalisation schedules creates a dilemma for member states. To avoid this, the AfCFTA Secretariat should guide member states in developing a phased, sequenced approach to tariff alignment. Countries like South Africa, with dual membership in SACU and SADC, could be supported in creating a consolidated tariff schedule that aligns their REC commitments with their broader AfCFTA obligations over a defined transition period, thus preventing trade distortion and administrative overload (Hartzenberg, 2011).

3.6.4 Leverage Digital Tools for Trade Facilitation and NTB Reporting

The paper identified non-tariff barriers (NTBs) and disparate customs procedures as major impediments. Governments should accelerate the implementation of the AfCFTA's Digital Trade Protocol and fully operationalise the online NTB Reporting, Monitoring, and Elimination Mechanism. Learning from the success of Rwanda's digital customs systems and the EAC's NTB reporting platform, this provides a real-time, transparent system for traders to report barriers like border delays, ensuring swift resolution by national authorities and directly reducing trade costs (International Trade Centre (ITC), 2021).

3.6.5 Channel Infrastructure Investment into Specific Corridors

The infrastructure deficit, a recurring theme in the analysis, cannot be solved with a general call for investment. Policymakers should leverage the African Union's Programme for Infrastructure Development in Africa (PIDA) to direct public and private investment towards upgrading specific trade corridors identified as priorities for AfCFTA trade flows, such as the Northern Corridor. This targeted approach, potentially financed through partnerships with initiatives like the EU's EPAs or China's BRI, would directly reduce the transport and logistics costs that currently hinder intra-African trade (Draper & Ismail, 2021; African Development Bank (AfDB), 2022).

3.7 Conclusion

The African Continental Free Trade Area represents a landmark initiative in Africa's economic integration. It aligns with global and regional trade agreements while seeking to overcome barriers that have historically hindered intra-African trade. This section examined trade agreements in global trade and regional dynamics, the role of the AfCFTA in Africa's economic future, and the broader challenges and opportunities it presents. Global trade agreements, such as those under the WTO and GATT, have shaped trade flows and economic growth worldwide. Similarly, RTAs like the EU, EAU and SADC have facilitated regional integration, fostering economic cooperation within distinct geographic areas. The AfCFTA builds upon this tradition, offering Africa an ambitious framework to boost intra-continental trade, reduce tariffs, and address non-tariff barriers. Its key objectives include fostering economic integration, increasing Africa's share in global value chains (GVCs), and advancing industrialisation across the continent.

Despite its potential, the AfCFTA faces significant challenges in implementation. The alignment with existing global trade frameworks, such as WTO rules, and its interaction with regional economic communities like ECOWAS, SADC, and the EAC require careful management to avoid conflicts and fragmentation in trade policy. Overlapping memberships and differing trade rules could create complications, necessitating strategies for harmonisation and reconciliation. Furthermore, political commitment, adequate infrastructure, and overcoming non-tariff barriers are critical for the successful realisation of AfCFTA's goals.

The opportunities within the AfCFTA are vast. The agreement has the potential to unlock significant economic benefits, including the diversification of economies, the creation of new trade flows, poverty reduction, and industrial sector growth. By addressing infrastructure and logistical challenges, fostering political will, and enhancing institutional capacity, the AfCFTA can significantly contribute to Africa's economic transformation. Looking ahead, the AfCFTA's implementation must be accompanied by strong policy measures. Aligning it with global trade frameworks, strengthening governance structures, and ensuring robust trade facilitation are essential for success. With these measures in place, the AfCFTA has the capacity to lead Africa towards a future of greater economic cooperation and prosperity, positioning the continent as a key player in the evolving global trade landscape. Through continued collaboration and strategic investments, Africa can harness the full potential of the AfCFTA to foster a more equitable and sustainable global trade system.

References

African Development Bank (AfDB). (2021). *African economic outlook 2021.*

African Development Bank (AfDB). (2022). *African infrastructure outlook 2022*. AfDB.

African Export-Import Bank. (2022). *Facilitating trade in Africa: The role of digitization.* Afreximbank.

African Union. (2015). *Agenda 2063: The Africa we want.*
African Union. (2018). *Agreement establishing the African continental free trade area (AfCFTA).* African Union.
African Union. (2022). *Program for infrastructure development in Africa (PIDA) progress report.* African Union.
Bagwell, K., & Staiger, R. W. (2002). The WTO and the millennium round: The Doha round of trade negotiations. *The World Economy, 25*(5), 699–717.
Baldwin, R. (2003). *The WTO and the world economy*. The MIT Press.
Baldwin, R. (2016a). *The great convergence: Information technology and the new globalization.* Harvard University Press.
Baldwin, R. (2016b). The World Trade Organization and the future of multilateralism. *Journal of Economic Perspectives, 30*(1), 95–116.
Baldwin, R. E. (2014). *Multilateralising 21st century regionalism.* OECD Global Forum on Trade.
Bhagwati, J. (2008). *Termites in the trading system: How preferential agreements undermine free trade*. Oxford University Press.
Draper, P., & Ismail, F. (2021). *AfCFTA: Challenges and opportunities in the multilateral trading system.* SAIIA Occasional Paper Series.
Freund, C., & Rocha, N. (2011). *What constrains Africa's exports?* World Bank Policy Research Working Paper, No. 5184.
Geda, A., & Seid, E. H. (2015). The potential for internal trade and regional integration in Africa. *Journal of African Trade, 2*(1-2), 19–50.
Godard, S. (2018). The Council for Mutual Economic Assistance and the failed coordination of planning in the socialist bloc in the 1960s. In M. Albrecht & V. Westermann (Eds.), *Planning in cold war Europe: Competition, cooperation, circulations (1950s–1970s)* (pp. 187–210). De Gruyter Oldenbourg.
Hartzenberg, T. (2011). *Regional integration in Africa.* WTO.
Hoekman, B., & Kostecki, M. (2009). *The political economy of the world trading system: The WTO and beyond.* Oxford University Press.
International Trade Centre (ITC). (2021). *The AfCFTA: Unlocking Africa's trade potential.* ITC.
Krugman, P. R. (1991). Is bilateralism bad? In E. Helpman & A. Razin (Eds.), *International trade and trade policy* (pp. 9–23). MIT Press.
Liu, X. (2009). Testing conflicting political economy theories: Full-fledged versus partial-scope regional trade agreements. *Southern Economic Journal, 75*(4), 1209–1233.
Mavroidis, P. C. (2007). *The WTO and the law of the World Trade Organization: Text, cases, and materials*. Thomson Reuters.
Morrison, W. M., & Villarreal, M. A. (2013). *NAFTA at 20: Overview and trade effects (CRS Report R42965).* Congressional Research Service.
Oesch, M., Lachenmann, F., & Wolfrum, R. (2015). Uruguay round. In R. Wolfrum (Ed.), *The max planck encyclopedia of public international law.* Oxford University Press.
Parshotam, A. (2018). *The African continental free trade area: A trillion Dollar opportunity.* Brookings Africa Growth Initiative.
Rodrik, D. (2011). *The globalisation paradox: Democracy and the future of the world economy.* Norton & Company.
Schiff, M., & Winters, L. A. (2003). *Regional integration and development.* The World Bank.
Simo, R. Y. (2020). Developing countries and special treatment. *The World Economy, 43*(5), 1423–1425.
Stiglitz, J. E. (2002). *Globalisation and its discontents.* W.W. Norton & Company.
Subramanian, A., & Wei, S. (2007). The WTO and the developing countries: What does the Doha round mean for the developing world? *The World Economy, 30*(3), 357–373.
Tuomi, A. K. (1988). Canada-U.S. free trade agreement: Implications for the bilateral. *Maryland Journal of International Law, 12*(1), 21–45.
UNECA. (2021). *Assessing regional integration in Africa IX: Next steps for the AfCFTA.* United Nations Economic Commission for Africa.

United Nations Economic Commission for Africa (UNECA). (2023). *Implementing southern Africa FTA acquis and AfCFTA*. UNECA.
Viljoen, W.. (2020). Non-tariff barriers and their impact on regional trade in Africa. Tralac Working Paper.
Whalley, J. (1998). Why do countries seek regional trade agreements? In J. Frankel (Ed.), *The regionalisation of the world economy* (pp. 63–90). University of Chicago Press.
Wolfe, R. (2017). Is World Trade Organisation information good enough? How a systematic reflection by members on transparency could promote institutional learning. *Global Policy, 8*(S1), 39–48.
World Bank. (2020). *The African continental free trade area: Economic and distributional effects*. World Bank.
World Bank. (2022). *The potential of the AfCFTA for Africa's economic development*. World Bank.
World Trade Organisation (WTO). (2023). *Trade policy review report*. WTO.

Chapter 4
Pan-Africanist Right to Development Pursuit of Socio-Economic Self-Determination Under the AfCFTA Agreement

Carol Chi Ngang

Abstract This chapter explores the pursuit of socio-economic self-determination in Africa from a pan-African and right to development points of view, positing that the noble ideals embedded therein are attainable through the African Continental Free Trade Area (AfCFTA) Agreement albeit that its implementation remains constrained for no apparent reasons. Anchoring on the historical ideology of pan-Africanism and the concept of the right to development enshrined in the African Charter on Human and Peoples' Rights, the argument is articulated that there is a legal obligation on African Union member states to cooperate for development, including through intra-African trade. Having establish the common market with the aim of boosting free trade, inclusive economic growth and structural transformation across the continent, member states appear to be reneging on their commitments on the AfCFTA Agreement and its ancillary protocols. This chapter interrogates why states parties are reticent in adhering to the commitments they are enjoined to comply with in good faith. It critically examines the lethargy in implementing the AfCFTA Agreement and the implications of that to the aspirations for pan-Africanism and the legitimate expectations on the right to development. The analysis is predominantly theoretical in nature, hinging on the legal dimensions relating to implementation of the AfCFTA, which has the potential to reshape the development landscape on the continent.

Keywords Pan-Africanism · The right to development · Socio-economic self-determination · AfCFTA · Intra-African trade · Duty to cooperate for development

C. C. Ngang (✉)
Department of Public Law, National University of Lesotho; Free State Centre for Human Rights, University of the Free State, Bloemfontein, South Africa
e-mail: cc.ngang@nul.ls

D. N. Yuni et al. (eds.), *From Policy to Practice: Challenges and Ways Forward on the Implementation of the AfCFTA*,
https://doi.org/10.1007/978-3-032-14051-7_4

4.1 Introduction

This chapter explores the intersection between pan-Africanism and the human right to development under the AfCFTA Agreement (2018) and the extent to which intra-African trade within the AfCFTA could enable the pursuit of socio-economic self-determination. The pursuit of pan-Africanism is explained from a right to development point of view to mean the enthusiasm to advance the aspirations for socio-economic self-determination as a guarantee of better standards of living with dignity for the peoples of Africa in the backdrop of a protracted history of subjugation, fragmentation, dispossession, and impoverishment. Rooted in the liberation struggles against enslavement, colonialism, and racism perpetuated on peoples of African descent, the existentialist pan-African ideology emphasises reconnection to the African ancestry, identity, and a common destiny (Falola & Kwame, 2013; Oloruntoba-Oju, 2012). From its inception in the late nineteenth century, pan-Africanism has witnessed significant milestones. One of these milestones was the establishment of the Organisation of African Unity (OAU) in 1963 with the goal of promoting unity and cooperation among African nations. The OAU eventually transformed into the African Union (AU) in 2002 and has continued to uphold pan-African ideals and development on the continent (AKERC, 2025) and promoting trade relations among its member states.

Central to the discussion in this chapter is the point worth reiterating that the collective aspirations for a common African ancestral identity, political status, economic, social, and cultural development are attainable goals, but not achievable through wishful thinking. Pitted against the odds that persist, comprising a blend of continuous external pressures and a lowering of guard in revolutionary enthusiasm for transformation, I posit that the entitlement to self-determination obligates taking concrete measures and actions in righting the wrongs that have robbed Africa of its inexhaustible potential. Pan-Africanism has, in this regard, consistently reinvented itself as a philosophical creed that permeates scholarly discourses, political inclinations, and populist sentiments about Africa. It has also dominated the framing of development agendas on the continent over the decades following the acquisition of nominal political independence. Agenda 2063 is worth drawing attention to, particularly concerning the AfCFTA project conceived therein, which is envisaged to accelerate trade among member states and hence, contribute to inclusive growth and structural transformation of the development landscape across the continent (African Union, 2021).

Significant about the overarching ideology of pan-Africanism is that it eventually birthed the post-independence claim to the right to development that has evolved into recognition and protection in several instruments of law, notably the African Charter on Human and Peoples' Rights, among others. The concept of development, which is portrayed as a vehicle for achieving the pan-African vision, necessitates its understanding from a legal perspective as a human right, both in an individual and collective dimension, to which all peoples of Africa are entitled to enjoy. Being a human right, as it is enshrined in the African Charter (1981: Art 22), implies legal obligations, including state parties' duty to cooperate for development to ensure its realisation. Besides the African Charter, the AfCFTA Agreement and its ancillary Protocols are established by treaty. It implies legally binding obligations on African state governments that have ratified the treaty regarding their commitments to intra-African trade. Six years after the AfCFTA entered into force in 2019, implementation has remained unacceptably sluggish.

This chapter highlights the lethargy in implementing the AfCFTA Agreement and thus, raises questions about why member states seem to renege on their legal obligations to put in place, the enabling and supportive environment necessary for improving the livelihood circumstances of their peoples about the pan-African vision. For a comprehensible flow of the theoretical argument and analysis, this chapter first delves into a scrutiny of the core standards of pan-Africanism to illustrate the values of collectivism and solidarity that they embody and are crucial for any efforts to liberate Africa. The discussion then unfolds into the concept of the right to development, weighing in on the duty to cooperation, which incorporates cooperation through intra-African trade. The AfCFTA Agreement is then further explored, with a focus on member states' undertakings, which they are, however, disinclined to implement for no apparent reason. The chapter concludes with the argument that implementation of the AfCFTA is critical in facilitating the pursuit of socio-economic self-determination, a key aspect of the right to development, if the ultimate goal of liberation from persisting unfreedoms is to be achieved.

4.2 Core Ideals of Pan-Africanism

The core ideals of pan-Africanism discussed in this section is intended to underscore the standards of well-being suited for Africa, the thresholds for the attainment of those standards and the benchmarks for measurement that must set the pace and the processes of development across the continent. It is also intended to highlight the parameters for creating the version of Africa that embodies and upholds genuine Africanness, the worth and dignity of its peoples and the assertive viewpoints from which they desire to be perceived and understood. The literature on pan-Africanism lists several interwoven ideals (Nantulya, 2024). For this chapter, the ideals are summed up into three, namely; sovereign entitlement to the African common heritage, unity and commonality of purpose and collective socio-economic self-determination.

4.2.1 Sovereign Entitlement to The African Common Heritage

Pan-Africanism is based on its philosophical grounding in African nationalism; the feeling of belonging to Africa and the attendant obligation to safeguard ownership of the African patrimony and common heritage as an ancestral birth right. It thrives on the creed that the vast endowments of natural resources across the continent belong to and ought to be protected and bequeathed to succeeding generations of the peoples of Africa. Regrettably, the resources have frequently been plundered and often abusively exploited to the benefit of external stakeholders while Africa is left impoverished and undeveloped. Sovereign entitlement to the African common heritage assures permanent ownership and the power of control over and governance of the resources. It also guarantees the collective right of free disposal of the resources and entitlement to fair distribution of the proceeds for the livelihood sustainability benefits and well-being of the peoples of Africa. In other words, Africa's natural resource endowments are recognised as a common heritage belonging to its peoples, who are entitled to assert legitimate claims thereof.

Customary international law, which is supported by jurisprudence of the International Court of Justice (2005: Paras 243–248) and East Timor, Portugal v Australia, Jurisdiction, Judgment (1995) and the range of binding and non-binding instruments, is explicit in recognising peoples' permanent ownership and control over their natural resources (United Nations Declaration on the Rights of Peasants and Other People Working in Rural Areas, Resolution A/HRC/RES/39/12, 2018:Art 17; United Nations Declaration on the Rights of Indigenous Peoples, Resolution 61/295, 2007: Arts 25, 26 & 28; International Covenant on Economic, Social and Cultural Rights (ICESCR), 1966:Art 2(1); International Covenant on Civil and Political Rights (ICCPR), 1966:Art 1(2); United Nations General, 1962:Para. 1; United Nations, 1952).

The international law framework that protects permanent ownership over natural resource wealth does not contemplate a lesser standard for the peoples of Africa, who have long been dispossessed and have had their entitlement to the said resources contravened with impunity. Asserting permanent ownership, taking control of and utilising Africa's natural wealth and resources to create development is a human rights guaranteed. United Nations Declaration on the Right to Development Resolution A/RES/41/128 (1986:Art 1(2)) provides that the human right to development entails the full realisation of the entitlement to self-determination, which obligates asserting permanent sovereignty over their natural resource endowments. To be alienated from this right as has been the case in Africa, means that legitimate expectations on pan-Africanism and the right to development remain elusive.

African Charter (1981:Art 22(1)) endorses the right to economic, social, and cultural development, which incorporates the equitable sharing of the common heritage. This is read in context to imply the right to communal ownership and beneficiation from the shared patrimony by all the peoples of Africa. The African patrimony, otherwise referred to as the African common heritage, encompasses the extensive range of natural resource endowments that belong to the peoples of Africa and have been preserved over the centuries and bequeathed to present and future generations (Ngang, 2020, pp. 62–63; Ngang, 2021a, pp. 67–70; Ngang, 2022, pp. 20–22). The pan-African self-determination claim to permanent sovereign entitlement to the abundance of natural resources on the continent is entrenched in the African Charter (1981:Art 21 et seq), which explicitly states that:

1. All peoples shall freely dispose of their wealth and natural resources. This right shall be exercised in the exclusive interest of the people. In no case shall a people be deprived of it.
2. In case of spoliation the dispossessed people shall have the right to the lawful recovery of its property as well as to an adequate compensation.

It is accordingly prohibited to rob the peoples of Africa of their natural resource possessions. If such happens, the dispossessed peoples are entitled to full restitution or to reparations for the loss. The natural resources may however, be freely disposed of, if such disposal satisfactorily benefits the peoples to whom the natural resources lawfully belong. Noting that the natural wealth and resources on the continent are not evenly and proportionately distributed, the principles of free disposal and exclusive interest enjoin state governments (guarantors of this right), to strategically consider equitable (re)distributive measures in ensuring collective prosperity. Equitable (re)distribution of the resources is possible through the free exchange of goods and services attainable through intra-African trade under the AfCFTA. The potential of intra-African trade in fostering unity and a common purpose for the advancement of Africa can hence, not be overlooked.

4.2.2 Unity and Commonality of Purpose

At the core of the pan-African movement is the implicit acknowledgement and conviction that beyond perceived differences and separations by geographical demarcations, inclination to the spirit of solidarity and commonality of purpose among all people of African descent and indigeneity is solidly anchored on a shared identity. It obtains from an incontestable ancestry and a common destiny that underlines communal interests and aspirations. The idea of unity is buttressed by the apprehension that in the absence thereof, the fragmentations, vulnerabilities, and resultant hurdles that Africa has been subjected to over the centuries as a result of slavery, colonialism, neocolonialism, and economic globalisation will deepen, to the disadvantage and peril of the peoples of Africa. It emphasises the collective pursuit of genuine political liberation, socio-economic and cultural emancipation, empowerment, and upliftment in view of improving living standards and livelihoods for Africans (Frick et al., 2006, p. 235).

It cannot be overstated that unity implies survival, absent which, Africa faces the threat of re-colonisation or obliteration through subtle contemporary forms and models of dominances. Unity and the complete integration of the 55 sovereign states of Africa into a single political unit has so far been difficult to achieve due to a combination of complex dynamics. At the formation of the OAU as the pioneer institutional manifestation of pan-Africanism, unity was frustrated by factional ideological differences between the Casablanca, Monrovia, and Brazzaville groups of states that failed to agree on a common purpose for Unity (Okhonmina, 2024). The OAU opted for nationalism, national sovereignty, and guardianship of the colonial borders inherited at independence, which arguably produced no strategic benefit for the continent. When the AU succeeded the OAU in 2002, its trajectory has increasingly prioritised unity—the attainment of which has, however been sluggish.

Political unity is according to Okhonmina (2024), seemingly unattainable. Political unity for Africa is indeed, constrained by roadblocks mounted by the shallow egotistic and rent-seeking obsession by state governments to protect national interests. It is thus, more strategic to rather prioritise commonality of purpose in advancing the pan-African agenda for transformation. The AU upholds as one of its principal objectives enshrined in the Constitutive act of the African Union (2000:Art 3(d)), to uphold and articulate a common stance on all issues that are of continental interest and beneficial to the peoples of Africa. Conceived in this sense, commonality of purpose is apparently, more responsive to the commitment to shared prosperity achievable through intra-African trade under the auspices of the 2063 African Agenda for Development (African Union Commission, 2015:Paras 73, 74(e) & 72(h). More on intra-African trade is discussed in Sect. 4.4.

4.2.3 Collective Socio-Economic Self-Determination

Pan-Africanism hinges on the affirmation of self-sufficiency, self-reliance, and the conviction that the populations are legitimately endowed with the entitlement to determine their political future and to freely make economic, social, and cultural development choices without external meddling, control, or paternalistic influences. Drawing on the consciousness of the capacity to self-govern, the pan-African ideology significantly influenced the framing of self-determination as a principle of international law. Several UN instruments endorse self-determination as a collective entitlement, and most significantly, as an *erga omnes* norm of international law that legitimises resistance to domination and oppression (see for example, United Nations. (n.d.). The African Charter enshrines self-determination as an inalienable and unquestionable right guarantee to the peoples of Africa (African Charter, 1981: Art 20). The provision embodies the right to existence, which empowers the populations across the continent with the liberty to make autonomous political and socio-economic and cultural development choices in accordance with their policy preferences and more so, have the liberty to resort to any legitimate means to liberate themselves.

For Africa and its peoples, self-determination is underpinned by memories of the dehumanisation, injustices, and disadvantages suffered despite recognition of the broad range of basic rights and fundamental freedoms contained in the Universal Declaration of Human Rights. While decolonisation was envisaged to rectify these wrongs, many scholars agree that at independence, most, if not all, of Africa barely gained nominal political freedom, accompanied by a range of civil liberties without any guarantees of socio-economic and cultural autonomy. While decolonisation provided the opportunity for the attainment of absolute sovereignty (Ngang, 2021a,

p. 174), the absence of full autonomy meant that post-independence efforts to advance the continent have remained sterile and unproductive (Ngang, 2021a, p. 174; Adeyeri, 2018; Maathai, 2010, pp. 48–49).

In Amartya Sen's (1993) conceptualisation of development as the liberty to choose from alternatives, he posits the removal of all forms of "unfreedoms" that limit prospects for development, hinder informed decision making and constrain rational action in overcoming underlining challenges. For the livelihood circumstances in Africa to improve, economic, social, and cultural sovereignty must be conceived not as a moral aspiration but as a legal imperative that must be achieved (Ngang, 2021b, pp. 160–163). It requires a radical and perhaps revolutionary approach to the contemporary liberation struggles for emancipation. These struggles must aim to disrupt systems of exploitation such as the World Trade Organisation (WTO), whose trade liberalisation rules disadvantage Africa in major ways (Adibe & Obiefuna, 2015; Udombana, 2005).

Perceived from this viewpoint, pan-Africanism underscores the vitality of communality, cooperation, and shared responsibility in redressing the historical injustices of subjugation, exploitation, dispossession, impoverishment, and the inequalities, which Africa has been constrained to endure. It entails recourse to aspirations for the common good in fostering collective prosperity and advancement. As a measure of self-determination, Masitera (2022) suggests that to redress the hurdles of impoverishment and inequalities in Africa, it requires incorporating the value of the common good into African political economy to enhance productive capabilities and fortify human relations and interactions. The attainment of collective self-determination is contingent upon promoting common good practices through concrete initiatives, such as the commitment to a single market for the furtherance of trade relations among African countries. The AfCFTA is perceived in this regard as a mechanism by which to harness sovereignty and hence, make the right to development a reality in Africa. It is ascertained that, being of the same nature and mutually reinforcing, self-determination can be achieved by asserting the right to development (Ngang, 2021a, pp. 173–174), which as explained in the next section, obligates the duty to cooperate for development.

4.3 Right to Development and the Duty to Cooperate

The right to development guarantees the liberty to make appropriate development choices, having to select from alternatives. The discussion on pan-Africanism in the previous section indicates a choice in favour of full autonomy in the area of socio-economic and cultural development, which is embodied in the more concrete claim to development as a human right, to which the peoples of Africa are collectively entitled and accordingly enjoined to give effect to its realisation in a cooperative manner.

4.3.1 Conviction to Prioritise the Right to Development

As earlier noted, pan-Africanism inspired claims to the human right to development, which has been endorsed as one of the unique sets of peoples' rights enshrined in the African Charter. African Charter (1981: Para 8), conveys the conviction to pay keen attention to the right to development on the basis that it embodies the mutually reinforcing civil and political rights and economic, social, and cultural rights, which cannot be dissociated. The right to development is conceived in this instance as entailing fulfilment of socio-economic and cultural entitlements as a prerequisite for the exercise of civil liberties and political freedoms.

It turned out that decolonisation only granted to Africa nominal political liberation without effective economic, social, and cultural emancipation. This has meant for African state governments, ineffective functioning in guaranteeing improved quality of life and the highest attainable standards of living for the populations. The reiteration to prioritise the right to development is majorly significant for the attainment of the pan-African vision of collective self-determination and, in essence, self-sufficiency, absent which, Africa is prone to remain subservient to exploitative external influences. Pan-Africanism continues to make waves, reverberating even stronger among the present generations of Africans both on the continent and in the diaspora. This is a telling affirmation of continuous dissatisfaction with the status quo, wherein the peoples of Africa are systematically excluded from development taking place on the continent and deprived of the benefits that accrue therefrom.

As noted in Paragraph 9 of the Preamble to the African Charter (1981), the conviction to prioritise the right to development stems from the conscious commitment to eradicate all forms of colonialism and completely liberate Africans who continue to struggle for their dignity and genuine autonomy. The total liberation of Africa does not end with the dismantling of colonial structures and systems of domination, but importantly, requires taking full sovereign control of the continent from all forms of continuous external influences. It is contingent on the extent to which Africa is capable of asserting not only political sovereignty but also socio-economic emancipation, achievable through the protection of African ancestral entitlements and permanent sovereign ownership and control over their natural resources. These resources are central to creating the conditions and the enabling environment for development to take place. The peoples of Africa are capable of appropriating and exercising effective ownership of the development processes. The African Charter (1981: Art 22) makes provision to the effect that:

1. All peoples shall have the right to their economic, social, and cultural development with due regard to their freedom and identity and in the equal enjoyment of the common heritage of mankind.
2. States shall have the duty, individually or collectively, to ensure the exercise of the right to development.

The provision highlights the fact that the right to development is a collective right recognising that all Africans are entitled to equitably enjoy communal well-being by participating in and contributing to the processes of socio-economic and cultural development. African state governments are enjoined in this regard to create a conducive, enabling, and supportive environment, including through concerted, pragmatic, proactive, and protective measures in ensuring that the normative promise in pursuing development as a human right becomes a reality for the populations across the African continent. Obtaining from the contemporary understanding that development entails improvement in human well-being and better living standards, assurance of the right to development implies that its realisation should translate into continuously bettering living conditions at for the populations. It promises that if achieved, the peoples of Africa, would invariably take advantage of the equality of opportunities to participate in and contribute to development, enjoy a fair share in the proceeds that obtain from the development process through equitable redistributive justice. In this way, they can legitimately aspire for a satisfactory quality of life and living standards that meet the threshold expectations embodied in the pan-African ideals discussed in the previous section.

Vital to the content of Article 22(2) is the duty imposed on state parties to individually or collectively enable attainment of the right to development, creating opportunities for their citizens to exercise that right. The wording suggests that if African state governments fail in their individual or collective duty to enable realisation of the right to development, legitimate right to development expectations would be truncated. The pan-African vision of collective self-determination is, accordingly, an inevitable prerequisite to creating development in Africa. Without undermining individual state's obligations, to beef up the subject matter of the discussion in this chapter, attention is directed to the collective obligation mentioned in Article 22(2), which compels state parties, by virtue of haven ratified the African Charter, to adopt and indeed, demonstrate the collective precautionary and/or proactive measures and actions they have taken in ascertaining that the right to development becomes reality.

International law is a bit more elaborate in emphasising the duty to cooperate for the realisation of development objectives (Charter of the United Nations, 1945: Art 1(3), 55, 56 & Preamble; Transforming Our World, 2015: Goal 17; Constitutive act of the African Union, 2000: Goal 7). United Nations Declaration on the Right to Development Resolution A/RES/41/128 (1986: Arts 3, 4 & 6(1)) underscores in several of its provisions the duty of states to cooperate in facilitating fulfilment of the right to development and, importantly, also in eliminating obstacles to development.

4.3.2 The Duty to Cooperate for Development

Of interest is the question of why the duty to cooperate is of ultimate importance in considerations regarding the right to development in Africa. The Preamble to the African Charter states that the human and peoples' rights contained therein, are a reaffirmation of the pledge by member states under Article 2 of the OAU Charter to completely eradicate any remnants of colonialism that still exists anywhere on the continent, to coordinate and strengthen cooperation, as well as efforts geared towards bettering living conditions on the continent with respect to the human rights standards contained in the UN Charter and the Universal Declaration of Human Rights. By further emphasising the need to give priority to the right to development, coupled with the guarantee in Article 20 on the absolute and incontrovertible right to self-determination, the African human rights ontology as it is captured in Agenda 2063, underscores the importance of self-reliance, noting that "Africa has the capability to realise her full potential in development" (African Union Commission, 2015: Paras 8 & 19). Article 22(2) of the African Charter, which embodies the duty to cooperate, is supported by the obligation clause in Article 1, affirming the undertaking by state governments, parties to the Charter to adopt appropriate domestic legislative and other relevant measures to actualise the right to development.

The duty to cooperate has the potential to foster the kind of unity and concerted action envisaged for the attainment of the shared purpose of advancing the well-being and betterment of the human conditions of the peoples of Africa, which as noted earlier, lie at the core of the ideals of pan-Africanism and also central to the realisation of the right to development. Charter of the United Nations (1945: Arts 1(3), 55 & 56) highlights the importance of international cooperation not only because it is a fundamental prerequisite in redressing development challenges but of essence also, as a legal obligation under international law necessary for creating conditions for sustainable development and for promoting higher standards of living with expanded freedoms. The ultimate aim, as stipulated in the Preamble to the Charter of the United Nations (1945) is to secure the socio-economic advancement of all peoples. Consequently, for all states around the world, including especially those in Africa, it is not a discretionary moral requirement to cooperate but indeed, a legal obligation to do so. In ensuring that rights-holders and beneficiaries exercise and enjoy equality of opportunities for development, the United Nations Declaration on the Right to Development Resolution A/RES/41/128 (1986: Art 2(3)) lays down the rule that:

> States have the duty to co-operate with each other in ensuring development and eliminating obstacles to development. States should realise their rights and fulfil their duties in such a manner as to promote a new international economic order based on sovereign equality, interdependence, mutual interest and co-operation among all States, as well as to encourage the observance and realisation of human rights.

Neither the UN Charter, the UN Declaration on the Right to Development, nor the African Charter provides clarity on what the duty to cooperate entails in concrete terms nor prescribes the forms of cooperation envisaged, which leaves the matter to legal interpretation. The Draft International Covenant on the Right to Development (2023)—which, although it is yet to be adopted and given the force of law—is, however, much more authoritative in its conceptualisation of the duty to cooperate. It outlines in its Article 13, an elaborate prescription on what cooperation for development is envisaged in actual terms, including in the area of international trade, noting that:

> 4. States Parties recognise their duty to cooperate to create a social and international order conducive to the realisation of the right to development by, inter alia:
>
> (a) Promoting a universal, rules-based, open, non-discriminatory, equitable, transparent, and inclusive multilateral trading system;
> (b) Implementing the principle of special and differential treatment for developing countries, in particular least developed countries, as defined in applicable trade and investment agreements.

The elaborate formulation of the duty to cooperate in the Draft Covenant is not at variance with Article 22(2) of the African Charter, which is too cursory in its formulation of the duty to cooperate. That notwithstanding, Article 22(2) is read expansively to encompass the duty to cooperate in the area of intra-African trade as a practical measure in promoting the right to development. It is noted that the duty to cooperate contained in Article 22(2) necessitates putting in place functional mechanisms such as the AfCFTA, which is acknowledged to have the potential to accelerate development across the continent (Ngang, 2021b, p. 154). Beyond Africa's extensive involvement in international trade within the WTO framework, the coming into force of the AfCFTA reflects the kind of "multilateral trading system" contemplated in the Draft Covenant on the Right to Development (2023: Art 13(4)(a) & (b)). Article 4 of the AfCFTA Agreement, together with related provisions in the ancillary Protocols, emphasise the obligation to cooperate on various fronts to promote intra-African trade. The AfCFTA ought, therefore, to be seen as instrumental for the attainment of socio-economic sovereignty.

4.4 AfCFTA Agreement and its Ancillary Protocols

In 2012, the Addis Ababa summit of the AU Assembly of Heads of State and Government endorsed the decision to establish the common African market and related plan of action for boosting trade among member states. The commitment to speed up intra-African trade was subsequently reiterated in the Agenda 2063 blueprint for development in Africa, adopted in 2015 (African Union, n.d.). It took 6 years to bring an initial 44 AU member states to sign the AfCFTA Agreement in Kigali, Rwanda, on 21 March 2018 (African Union, 2018). Ratification of the AfCFTA Agreement was, however, exceptionally speedy, achieved in just over a year, ushering its coming into force in July 2019, and launch of the operational phase on 1 January 2021 (African Union, n.d.). In the backdrop of sluggish implementation, it is vital to give the AfCFTA a bit more scrutiny.

4.4.1 Good Faith Reading of the Commitments to Intra-African Trade

The AfCFTA is established by treaty (AfCFTA Agreement, 2018: Arts 22, 23 & 24). It is supported by several treaty status protocols such as the Protocol on Trade in Goods and Services, Protocol on Investment, Protocol on Competition Policy, Protocol on Intellectual Property, Protocol on Digital Trade, Protocol on Women and Youth in Trade, Protocol on Rules and Procedures on the Settlement of Disputes and Protocol on the Free Movement of Persons, which together, constitute the legal framework for regulating trade and investment within the African common market (TRALAC, 2025a). Vienna Convention on the Law of Treaties Adopted by the United Nations (1969: Art 36) provides that a treaty shall be read in good faith in accordance with the objective, purposive, ordinary meaning and contextual interpretation of the terms of the treaty and any ancillary agreements or instruments in connection with the treaty.

Although referred to as "Agreement", which may be confused for ordinary agreements with no binding effect, the AfCFTA Agreement and its ancillary Protocols are indeed, legally binding instruments. Their coming into force, allocate rights and obligations to state parties, which in terms of Article 36 of the Vienna Convention, obligate compliance in good faith. The "good faith" clause, which is given clarity in light of the objective, purposive, and ordinary meaning interpretation of the AfCFTA Agreement, is crucial for proper comprehension of the instrumental role of free trade among African countries in advancing the collective pursuit of socio-economic self-determination.

Even as the AfCFTA Agreement and its ancillary Protocols impose binding obligations of state parties, there is, in reality, no effective means by which to compel the state parties to comply with the obligations they have committed to. This calls to mind, the "good faith" principle, which, for the purpose of the analysis in this chapter, is read within the context of pan-Africanism and the accompanying right to development guaranteed to the peoples of Africa. Good faith literally translates to the sincerity of intention to do something. It is argued here that pan-Africanism and the idea of a right to development originated from the legitimate expectation by the dehumanised, impoverished and berated peoples of Africa to aspire for livelihood with dignity. It also assures of expanded freedoms and of a genuine intention to make living conditions increasingly better for every individual and all peoples of African descent.

When African state governments conclude treaties such as the AfCFTA Agreement (2018: Preamble) with the solemn pledge, "We, Member States of the African Union", they basically undertake in good faith to ensure with all sincerity of intention that the provisions of the Agreement will exalt the beneficiaries. The benefits of international trade, include scaling economies, promoting economic growth and development, broadening access to a diverse range of goods and services, supporting competitiveness and innovation, facilitating skills and technology transfer, sustaining job creation and strengthening relations and cooperation (Price,

2018, pp. 1–8). Good faith in this regard, and in the context of intra-African trade exhorts member states to be strategically proactive in ensuring that the African common market benefits the peoples.

Pan-Africanism and the right to development have, since their inception several decades ago, implicitly begged for translation into reality in advancing the pursuit of socio-economic self-determination and transformation of the African development landscape. It is explicitly stated that the AfCFTA is established to "create a single market for goods, services, facilitated by movement of persons in order to deepen the economic integration of the African continent and in accordance with the Pan African Vision of 'An integrated, prosperous and peaceful Africa' enshrined in Agenda 2063" (AfCFTA Agreement, 2018: Art 3(a)). The AfCFTA is, accordingly, curated to accomplish the noble cause of pan-Africanism that continues to resonate with present generations and will be for future generations of the peoples of Africa, necessitating good faith in the performance of the obligations to ensure that intra-African trade effectively becomes a reality and beneficial.

In the absence of a compelling mechanism for enforcement, as earlier noted, good faith may not be interpreted loosely as entitling state parties to approach the free trade regime in a discretionary manner regarding whether or not to comply with their obligations under the AfCFTA Agreement. While not implying that the obligations imposed by the AfCFTA Agreement are absolute and immutable, the creed and moral force that have kept pan-Africanism and the right to development alive necessitate recourse to the good faith argument in justification of the need for member states to take their commitments to intra-African trade seriously. Nuclear Tests Case (Austl. v. Fr.) (1974) affirms that the principle of good faith is fundamental in governing the creation and performance of legal obligations under international law. Quite correctly, the good faith principle ought to continually remind member states of their obligations under the AfCFTA Agreement, which they must uphold and adhere to. Good faith requires that for the same genuine reasons that motivated the establishment of the African common market for the free movement of goods and services and of peoples across borders, the objectives and undertakings ought to be pursued with sincerity of purpose and intention.

4.4.2 Potential of Intra-African Trade to Advance Socio-Economic Development

Covering 55 member states with a combined population of 1.3 billion people (and still growing) and a gross domestic product (GDP) of approximately USD3.4 trillion, the AfCFTA beats all records as the largest free market around the world (World Economic Forum, 2025). The size of the market, backed by a colossal deposit of natural wealth and resources and a burgeoning population with enormous productive capacity, suggests that if adequately explored, the AfCFTA will pilot Africa to emergence as a leading global actor as envisaged in Aspiration 7 of Agenda

2063. Mold (2022, p. 1) notes in this regard that implementation of the AfCFTA is anticipated to boost trade within Africa by as much as USD450 billion (52%) by 2035.

AfCFTA Agreement (2018: Art 3(a) & (e) et seq) highlights, as one of its broad objectives, to support the attainment of sustainable and inclusive socio-economic development as well as structural transformation among its member states. It is noted that inclusive growth is the type of growth whose benefits extends evenly and equitably across society, creates equality of opportunities for all, and contributes uniformly in improving quality of life for all (Kyereboah-Coleman et al., 2024, p. 4). It implies that the AfCFTA has the redistributive potential of equitable benefit sharing across the continent for the attainment of collective prosperity. The objectives contained in the AfCFTA Agreement and its ancillary Protocols put together articulate the overarching vision that, if achieved, the socio-economic development landscape in Africa will experience monumental transformation and consequently, contribute to the collective well-being, improved quality of life and better standards of living for the peoples of Africa.

A decisive stance in the call to action in implementing the aspirations for development in Agenda 2063 is, first and foremost, to eradicate poverty in Africa, through enhanced investment in advancing the people's productive capabilities, achievable through the expanded opportunities that intra-African trade presents. The socio-economic benefits of the AfCFTA are of the potential to upset the extreme levels of poverty and systemic inequalities that have been a bane to the populations on the African continent (Cofelice, 2018, p. 148; Ngang, 2021a, p. 148). For instance, informal cross-border trade between neighbouring countries involving a large proportion of economically disadvantaged groups is reported to generate approximately USD18 billion annually, accounting for over two-thirds of the trade flows in some African countries (Mold, 2022, p. 16). Informal cross-border trade thus, presents a huge opportunity to those without sufficient capacity to engage in formal trade, to gain leverage and hence, actively participate in and contribute to fostering trade within the continent and of course, reap the benefits of doing so.

The potential of intra-African trade to advance socio-economic development on the continent hinges on the guarantee to take permanent sovereign ownership and control over the continent's natural wealth and resources, a prerequisite for sustained industrialisation and the value-chains to support the USD3.4 trillion continental economy. Talking about intra-African trade means creating a supportive and enabling environment where the natural resource endowments on the continent can be exploited or disposed of to the benefit of the African populations as stipulated in Article 21 of the African Charter. It envisages various scenarios where the abundance of natural resources is sustainably governed and productively utilised in advancing growth prospects and in sustaining socio-economic and cultural advancement across the continent.

A sustainable approach to the right to development governance of natural resources in Africa (Ngang, 2022) necessitates for instance, looking to the uranium from the Sahel region as a feeder to nuclear plants for electricity generation on a massive scale to power industrial complexes. It entails looking to the cobalt, lithium and other rare earth minerals from the Democratic Republic of Congo to supply the African tech industry. It equally entails self-reliance on the drilling of crude oil from the massive deposits in Nigeria, Algeria, Libya, and Angola and the tapping of natural gas from Algeria, Egypt, Nigeria, and Mozambique to fuel the African economy. The extraction of gold from Ghana, Mali, Burkina Faso, South Africa, and Sudan among others can be relied on to back a single African currency and where diamonds from Botswana, Angola, and Lesotho are cut at home to galvanise the jewellery industry. The confectionery industry is expected to blossom with a steady supply of cocoa from Côte d'Ivoire and Ghana to the factories while coffee from Ethiopia and Uganda and tea from Kenya are processed locally and distributed across the continent and globally. The choices and possibilities are endless.

Continental cross-border trade in goods and services cannot be effective without entitlement, ownership and control of Africa's inexhaustible reservoir of resources with the capacity to support intra-Africa trade, but has, over the centuries, profited external stakeholders much more than it has benefitted Africans. In most instances, the abusive exploitation of the resources rather occasioned massive human rights violations with impunity. The AfCFTA provides the opportunity to change the dynamics, necessitating transformative policies in regulating natural resource extraction on the continent. Currently, the only known measure in view of regulating the extractive sector is the Working Group on Extractive Industries, Environment and Human Rights Violations in Africa—a special mechanism established in 2009 (ACHPR, 2009; African Commission on Human and Peoples' Rights, 2025). Structural transformation envisaged by the AfCFTA Agreement entails as stipulated in Paragraph 72(d) of Agenda 2063, to industrialise national economies through beneficiation and value addition of natural resources, which is strategic for accelerating intra-Africa trade and as the African Union notes, is vital for boosting Africa's trading position in the global market and in global trade negotiations (Africa Union, d.n.a). As a starting point, trade within the African common market needs to become sufficiently robust, which is yet to be attained for reasons explained below.

4.4.3 Lethargy in Implementation

Intra-Africa trade under the AfCFTA has, according to Kiiza (2025, p. 4) been off to a sluggish start. This is in spite of the commitments undertaken by member states under the various legal instruments and the demonstrated potential of intra-Africa trade to advance the pan-Africanist right to development pursuit of socio-economic self-determination, as illustrated in the previous sub-sections. Although effective implementation and functioning of the ambitious AfCFTA project is certainly bugged by structural, logistical and infrastructural hurdles and a combination of other constraining factors, the focus here is more on the vexing aspect of political lacklusterness, which is a central determinant in being able to redress the many other limitations that are holding the AfCFTA back. Put simply, the common proverbial saying that "where there is a will, there is a way" is accurately descriptive of the reason why the way for the AfCFTA remains dreary, because genuine political commitment to fostering trade relations among African countries is glaringly lacking. Being one of the major iconic projects that Africa has embarked on, with the potential to bolster integration and bring the 55 AU member states closer and stronger, there is no convincing reason why state governments seem less triggered by it.

As of 2025, of the 54 out of 55 AU member states that have signed the AfCFTA Agreement, only 48 have ratified and deposited their instruments of ratification (TRALAC, 2025b). This is not to say that ratification has capped at 48, it is expected that the seven remaining countries will eventually also ratify the Agreement. Of major concern is whether ratification necessarily translates into implementation. It is, of course, acceptable that implementation of the AfCFTA Agreement is not a once-off initiative but rather a long term process requiring discreet strategic planning (Economic Commission for Africa, 2025). The lack of steam in the political commitment to the project and the unacceptably sluggish pace of its operationalisation cannot be overlooked. Several decades back, dating to the Lagos Plan of Action of 1980 and Abuja Treaty of 1991, African state governments conceded to group into regional economic communities like the Arab Maghreb Union; Economic Community of West African States, Economic Community of Central African States, East African Community, Common Market for Eastern and Southern Africa and the Southern Africa Development Community as building blocks to the single continental market (AfCFTA Agreement, 2018: Art 5(b); Ajibo et al., 2021, p. 4; Ajibo, 2019). If these economic blocs had been sufficiently effective in consolidating intra-regional trade as expected, integration into the continental market would probably have been accomplished without much hassle. The reality, however, as a 2024 Economic Commission for Africa Report affirms, is that African countries tend to prioritise trade outside the continent rather than among themselves (Economic Commission for Africa, 2024). Africa's largest economies being South Africa, Nigeria, and Egypt, are reportedly less committed to the continental market; the percentage of their trade on the continent being as small as 19%, 7%, and 6%, respectively (Mold, 2022, p. 15).

African state governments are noted for the habit of ratifying treaties without following through with implementation and enforcement. Several groundbreaking commitments have time and again been undertaken in Africa, but eventually, never materialised. A notable example is the idea of a right to development, which originated from Africa in the period post-independence, propagated by its founding proponents as a model for development, which, if adopted, would have positioned Africa on a solid, steady path of advancement. The right to development was enshrined in the African Charter with the emphasis on giving particular attention to its realisation. The African Charter has been ratified by 54 out of the 55 AU member states to the effect that the right to development enshrined in Article 22 imposes binding obligations on the state parties.

The obligations encompass state's primary duties to protect, to respect, to fulfil, to promote and most importantly, the duty to cooperate, such as through the mechanism of intra-African trade as illustrated earlier. The African Commission and the African Court have, in addition, developed a rich and evolving jurisprudence on the enforcement of the right to development wherein respondent states have been found in transgression of their obligations under the African Charter (African Commission on Human and Peoples' Rights v Republic of Kenya, 2017: Paras 207–211; Centre for Minority Rights Development (Kenya) and Minority Rights Group International on behalf of Endorois Welfare Council v Kenya Comm 276/2003, 2009: Para 298; Democratic Republic of Congo v Burundi, Rwanda and Uganda, 2009: Para 95; Sudan Human Rights Organisation and Another v Sudan, 2009: Para 224). This notwithstanding, implementation, and enforcement of the right to development has, in 45 years since endorsement in the African Charter, remained shrouded in obscurity. This is to illustrate that without genuine commitment, ratification of the AfCFTA Agreement may not translate to effective implementation as has been with the African Charter and ancillary treaty instruments.

For intra-African trade to be effective, it necessitates first and foremost, the free movement of persons and of goods and services across the continent. This means that besides the AfCFTA Agreement (2018), the next important instrument that member states should have prioritised is the Protocol to the Treaty Establishing the African Economic Community Relating to Free Movement of Persons, Right of Residence and Right of Establishment, (2018). In terms of Article 33(1), the Protocol requires a nominal 15 ratifications to enter into force. Surprisingly, as of 2022, only four countries, namely; Rwanda, Niger, Sao Tome and Principe, and Mali, have ratified the Protocol (Economic Commission for Africa, 2023). The Protocol makes provision in Article 10, for a common African Passport for citizens of all 55 AU member states. The common passport constitutes part of the broader initiative to promote the pan-African identity, eliminate restrictive domestic laws, abolish visa requirements and ease visa-free travel across the continent to facilitate labour mobility, knowledge, technology and skills redistribution as well as boost tourism and trade (African Union, 2025). With the snail-paced ratification of the Protocol on the Free Movement of Persons, there is no indication that visa-free movement in Africa will become a reality anytime soon without a radical shift by state governments from the narrow nationalist inclinations that breed suspicion and xenophobic sentiments towards Africans from other parts of the continent.

Contrary to sound reasoning, many African countries offer extensive visa-free travel facilities to nationals from different countries around the world, but not to Africans from elsewhere on the continent. South Africa, for example, allows visa-free entry for most EU passport holders (Department of Home Affairs, 2025), but the same does not apply to nationals from many other African countries to travel freely to South Africa. Lesotho has recently announced visa-free entry for EU nationals to the country (Sekoboto, 2025), whereas, its visa requirements for nationals from other African countries remain stringent. United States passport holders can travel visa-free to Botswana, Zambia and South Africa and visa-on-arrival to Tanzania and Zimbabwe (Van Ashwegen, 2023), while citizens from other African countries do not have the same visa-free opportunities. Chinese passport holders can travel visa-free to Angola, Benin, and Malawi (Visaindex.Com, 2025) meanwhile, holders of passports from other African countries would require an entry visa. The intriguing part is that none of these countries that grant visa-free entry to nationals from outside the continent have ratified the Protocol on the Free Movement of Persons in Africa, raising suspicion about their commitment to the success of the AfCFTA.

Timelines for the roll-out of the African Passport have, time and again, been postponed for no apparent reason. The ramifications of these incongruities on intra-Africa trade are, to say the least, not only frustrating but also compromise the extent to which Africans may expect to explore the enormous opportunities for unrestricted trade that the AfCFTA offers. Africa's richest billionaire/investor, Aliko Dangote drew attention to the ordeal in May 2024 of having to obtain visas for 35 African countries to be able to travel to explore investment opportunities within the continent, much more than it is possible for a European visitor (Madowo, 2024). Stories of this nature shun the commitment to good faith that foreign nationals from outside of Africa enjoy more rights of access to and free movement in Africa than Africans are able to travel freely and have the opportunity to invest on the continent. The legal obligations undertaken by African state governments under the AfCFTA Agreement and its ancillary Protocols oblige them to translate the provisions thereof, into relevant domestic policies and regulations as well as put in place concrete measures and actions geared towards easing and facilitating trade relations among member states absent which, the project for intra-Africa trade may end up as just an elusive fantasy. Reiterating the fact that trade among African countries has remained low since the coming into force of the AfCFTA Agreement in 2019, Aliyu (2024) underscores the need for effective implementation as a means of ensuring that its full potential impact adds positively to the living standards of Africans, particularly the most vulnerable.

The United States (US) government's (Trump Administration) recent protectionist policies, including the imposition of heavy tariffs, cancellation of USAID and the African Growth Opportunity Act (AGOA) preferential trade agreements for many African countries poses a veritable challenge especially, for fragile and least developed countries that have been deeply and exclusively dependent on these arrangements for economic survival. The implications of the US policy shift on Africa is obviously enormous (Kohnert, 2025; Nantembelele, 2023; Walter, 2025). It however, equally presents unique opportunities for diversification and for strategic positioning as alternative markets and manufacturing hubs as Bekele-Thomas (2025) writes. Whether Africa will take advantage of the opportunity to consolidate the commitment to drive the AfCFTA to effective functioning as a potent mechanism for self-reliance, is yet to be seen.

4.5 Conclusion

The legal obligations which African state governments have committed to under the AfCFTA Agreement and the normative standards that obtain therefrom oblige compliance in good faith, necessitating sincerity of purpose and of intention in fostering trade relations among member states of the AfCFTA. It entails putting in place the operating systems, mechanisms, and enabling infrastructure, facilities, and logistics to facilitate and accelerate the free movement of goods, services, and people across the continent, with respect to the duty to cooperate in ensuring that people-centred development happens as a matter of human right. The pan-Africanist right to development pursuit that continues to echo vehemently across and beyond the continent, marked by fervent calls for unity and commonality of purpose, especially among the youth population, is an increasing indication that meaningful socio-economic development cannot take place without collective self-determination. In order that the pan-Africanist right to development narratives do not end up as mere rhetoric, concrete action in the form of intra-African trade is imperative and needs to happen.

While the AfCFTA has witnessed significant milestones since the launch of its operational phase in 2021, effectiveness in implementation is hampered by major constraints, which, as illustrated in this chapter, stem from the reticence by member states in adhering in good faith to their obligations under the AfCFTA Agreement, which is established to regulate free trade across the continent. The provision in Article 25, that "No reservations shall be made to this Agreement", means that the AfCFTA Agreement has an absolute binding effect, which no state party may derogate from. The non-reservation clause basically reinforces the core ideals of a unified approach and commonality of purpose in the pursuit of socio-economic self-determination and the ultimate goal of shared prosperity in safeguarding African peoples' exclusive interest. Adhering to the commitments under the AfCFTA Agreement and its ancillary instruments is not only strategic in bringing the venerable ideology of pan-Africanism to reality, but it also provides a solid framework for the realisation of the right to economic, social, and cultural development enshrined in the African Charter as a collective entitlement to all the peoples of Africa. Foot-dragging on these issues would imply business as usual, where Africa continues to trail behind as a "losing supplier" of natural resources to the benefit of all other regions around the world except its own peoples.

Effective implementation of the AfCFTA is critical if the ultimate goal of liberation from persisting unfreedoms is to be achieved. Regarding asserting permanent ownership of their natural resources, which as noted earlier, is central to advancing intra-Africa trade, the Alliance of Sahel States (Alliance des États du Sahel) including Mali, Burkina Faso and Niger appears to be taking the lead and setting the pace as a prototype in exercising the self-determination right to socio-economic sovereignty and therefore, needs to be observed with keen interest as a potential area for subsequent research relating to trade relations between the member states of the confederation.

References

ACHPR. (2009). Resolution 148 on the Establishment of a Working Group on Extractive Industries, Environment and Human Rights Violations in Africa, adopted by the 46th Ordinary Session of the African Commission on Human and Peoples' Rights on 25 November 2009.

Adeyeri, J. O. (2018). Nationalism and political independence in Africa. In S. O. Oloruntoba & T. Falola (Eds.), *The Palgrave handbook of African politics, governance and development* (pp. 203–215). Palgrave Macmillan.

Adibe, E., & Obiefuna, O. (2015). Inequitable trade rules in World Trade Organisation (WTO): Impact on developing countries. *The Nigerian Judicial Review, 13*, 57–82.
AfCFTA Agreement. (2018). Agreement establishing the African continental free trade area adopted by the African Union at the 10th extraordinary session of the assembly of heads of state and government in Kigali, Rwanda on 21 March 2018 AU Doc TI21086_E.
African Charter. (1981). African Charter on Human and Peoples' Rights, adopted in Nairobi, Kenya on 27 June 1981 OAU Doc cab/leg/67/3 Rev.5.
African Commission on Human and Peoples' Rights. (2025). *Working Group on extractive industries, environment and human rights violations in Africa*. https://achpr.au.int/index.php/en/mechanisms/working-group-extractive-industries-environment-and-human-rights-violations
African Commission on Human and Peoples' Rights v Republic of Kenya. (2017). Appl No 006/2017 (*Ogiek Community* case).
African Union. (2018, 21 march). *AU Member Countries Create History by massively signing the AfCFTA Agreement in Kigali*. https://au.int/en/pressreleases/20180321/au-member-countries-create-history-massively-signing-afcfta-agreement-kigali
African Union. (2021). *Flagship Projects of Agenda 2063*. https://au.int/en/videos/20210131/flagship-projects-agenda-2063
African Union. (2025). *Visa-free Africa*. Retrieved May 29, 2025, from https://au.int/en/programs/visa-free-africa
African Union. (n.d.). *African Continental Free Trade Area*. https://au.int/en/african-continental-free-trade-area
African Union Commission. (2015). *Agenda 2063: The Africa we want*. African Union.
Ajibo, C. (2019). *Regional economic communities as the building blocs of African continental free trade area agreement: Challenges and way forward*. Afronomics Law. https://www.afronomicslaw.org/2019/02/04/regional-economic-communities-as-the-building-blocs-of-african-continental-free-trade-area-agreement-challenges-and-way-forward
Ajibo, C., Nwanko C. M., & Ekhator, E. (2021). Regional economic communities as the building blocs of the African continental free trade area agreement. *Transitional dispute Management*. Retrieved May 28, 2025, from https://www.transnational-dispute-management.com/article.asp?key=2847
AKERC. (2025). *Pan-Africanism*. African Kin Education Resource Centre. https://akerc.org/pan-africanism/
Aliyu, S. U. R. (2024). *Intra-African trade and macroeconomic performance of Africa: Implications for the African continental free trade area*. Munich Personal RePEc Archive Paper No 21436.
Bekele-Thomas, N. (2025). *Africa's economic crossroads: Navigating protectionism and seizing opportunity*. African Business. https://african.business/2025/05/partner-content/africas-economic-crossroads-navigating-protectionism-and-seizing-opportunity-2
Centre for Minority Rights Development (Kenya) and Minority Rights Group International on behalf of Endorois Welfare Council v Kenya Comm 276/2003. (2009). AHRLR 75 (ACHPR 2009) (*Endorois* case).
Charter of the United Nations. (1945). 1 UNTS XVI, adopted in San Francisco, United States of America on 26 June 1945.
Cofelice, A. (2018). African continental free trade area: Opportunities and challenges. *De Gruyter—The federalist Debate*, *XXXI*(3), 32–35.
Constitutive act of the African Union. (2000). Adopted by the thirty-sixth ordinary session of the Assembly of Heads of State and Government in Lomé, Togo on 11 July 2000.
Democratic Republic of Congo v Burundi, Rwanda and Uganda. (2009). AHRLR 9 (ACHPR 2009) (*DRC* case).
Department of Home Affairs. (2025). Countries exempt from South Africa visa. https://www.dha.gov.za/index.php/immigration-services/exempt-countries
Draft International Covenant on the Right to Development. (2023). Report by the Chair-Rapporteur of the Working Group on the Right to Development, Zamir Akram (Pakistan) Human Rights Council A/HRC/54/50 54th Session, 6 October 2023. At the time of writing, the draft Covenant was still undergoing intergovernmental negotiations for adoption by the UN General Assembly.

East Timor, Portugal v Australia, Jurisdiction, Judgment. (1995). ICJ Rep 90, 30 June 1995.
Economic Commission for Africa. (2023). *Experts meet to review the ECA-AUC policy report on the AU Free Movement of Persons Protocol, 29–30 March 2023, Nairobi, Kenya.* https://www.uneca.org/eca-events/stories/experts-meet-review-eca-auc-policy-report-au-free-movement-persons-protocol
Economic Commission for Africa. (2024). *African countries trading more outside the continent than amongst themselves, ECA report.* https://www.uneca.org/stories/african-countries-trading-more-outside-the-continent-than-amongst-themselves%2C-eca-report
Economic Commission for Africa. (2025). *Implementation of AfCFTA needs patience and strategy.* https://uneca.org/stories/implementation-of-afcfta-needs-patience-and-strategy
Falola, T., & Kwame, E. (Eds.). (2013). *Pan-Africanism, and the politics of African citizenship and identity.* Routledge.
Frick, N., Janari, S., et al. (2006). *History: Learner's book.* New Africa Books.
International Court of Justice. (2005). Armed activities in the territory of The Congo, *Democratic Republic of Congo v Uganda*, Judgment, ICJ Reports 2005.
International Covenant on Civil and Political Rights (ICCPR). (1966). Resolution 2200A(XXI), adopted by the UN General Assembly in 1966.
International Covenant on Economic, Social and Cultural Rights (ICESCR). (1966). Resolution 2200A(XXI), adopted by the UN General Assembly in 1966.
Kiiza, A. (2025, 23 January). Assessing five years of the African continental free trade area (AfCFTA): Proposals on potential amendments. South Centre Research Paper No 215.
Kohnert, D. (2025). Impact of Trump 2.0 on Sub-Saharan Africa. MPRA aper No. 123735, Munich Personal RePEc Archive.
Kyereboah-Coleman, A.; Abor, J. Y. & Ofori-Sasu, D.. (2024). Intra-African trade and economic growth in Africa: The role of foreign direct investment. *Afreximbank policy research working paper series—APRWPS/2024/01.*
Maathai, W. (2010). *The challenge for Africa: A new vision.* Arrow Books.
Madowo, L. (2024). *Africa's richest man says he needs 35 visas to travel in Africa—Way more than a European visitor.* CNN. https://edition.cnn.com/travel/africas-richest-man-needs-35-visas
Masitera, E. (2022). Valuing common good in addressing inequalities and poverty in African economies. In O. Mtapuri (Ed.), *African perspectives on poverty, indigenous knowledge systems, and innovation* (pp. 139–155). Springer.
Mold, A. (2022). The economic significance of intra-African trade: Getting the narrative right. Brookings Global Working Paper No 44.
Nantembelele, F. A. (2023). The effects of a US-China trade war on sub-Saharan Africa: Pro-active domestic policies make the difference. *Journal of Policy Modeling, 45*(6), 1296–1310.
Nantulya, P. (2024). *Pan-Africanism reborn.* African Centre for Strategic Studies. https://africacenter.org/spotlight/pan-africanism-reborn/
Ngang, C. C. (2020). Right to development in Africa and the common heritage entitlement. *Journal for Juridical Science, 45*(1), 62–63.
Ngang, C. C. (2021a). *The right to development in Africa.* Brill Publishers.
Ngang, C. C. (2021b). Right to development governance in the advent of the African continental free trade area. *Journal for African Law, 65*(2), 160–163.
Ngang, C. C. (2022). Sustainable right to development governance of natural resources in Africa. In C. C. Ngang & S. D. Kamga (Eds.), *Natural resource sovereignty and the right to development in Africa* (pp. 19–35). Routledge.
Nuclear Tests Case (Austl. v. Fr.). (1974). I.C.J. 253, 268 (Dec. 20).
Okhonmina, S. (2024). *Pursuing unity: Pan-Africanism in practice.* The Cairo Review of Global Affairs. https://www.thecairoreview.com/essays/pursuing-unity-pan-africanism-in-practice/
Oloruntoba-Oju, O. (2012). Pan Africanism, myth and history in African and Caribbean drama. *Journal of Pan African Studies, 5*(8), 190–209.
Price, R. (2018). *International trade: The economic benefits* (pp. 1–8). UK Department for International Trade—Analysis Group.

Protocol to the Treaty Establishing the African Economic Community Relating to Free Movement of Persons, Right of Residence and Right of Establishment. (2018). Adopted by the 13th ordinary session of the AU assembly of heads of state and government held in Addis Ababa, Ethiopia on 29 January 2018.

Sekoboto, M. (2025). *Govt approves visa-free travel for EU nationals.* Sunday Express. https://sundayexpress.co.ls/govt-approves-visa-free-travel-for-eu-nationals/

Sen, A. (1993). *Development as freedom.* Oxford University Press.

Sudan Human Rights Organisation & Another v Sudan. (2009). AHRLR 153 (ACHPR 2009) (*Darfur* case).

TRALAC. (2025a). *African Continental Free Trade Area (AfCFTA) legal texts and policy documents.* https://www.tralac.org/resources/our-resources/6730-continental-free-trade-area-cfta.html

TRALAC. (2025b). *Status of ratification.* https://www.tralac.org/resources/infographic/13795-status-of-afcfta-ratification.html

Transforming Our World. (2015). The 2030 Agenda for Sustainable Development Resolution A/RES/70/1 adopted by the United Nations General Assembly on 27 September 2015, Goal 17; United Nations Millennium Declaration Resolution A/55/L.2 adopted by the United Nations General Assembly on 8 September 2000.

Udombana, N. (2005). A question of justice: The WTO, Africa, and countermeasures for breaches of international trade obligations. *The John Marshall Law Review*, 1153–1203.

United Nations Declaration on the Right to Development Resolution A/RES/41/128. (1986). Adopted by the General Assembly on 4 December 1986.

United Nations Declaration on the Rights of Indigenous Peoples, Resolution 61/295, adopted by the General Assembly on 13 September 2007.

United Nations Declaration on the Rights of Peasants and Other People Working in Rural Areas, Resolution A/HRC/RES/39/12. (2018). Adopted by the Human Rights Council on 28 September 2018.

United Nations. (1952). General Assembly Resolution 626(VII) on the Right to Exploit Freely Natural Wealth and Resources, adopted on 21 December 1952.

United Nations. (1962). General Assembly Resolution 1803(XVII) on Permanent Sovereignty over Natural Resources, adopted on 14 December 1962.

United Nations. (n.d.). *Resolution 37/43 on the Importance of the universal realization of the right of peoples to selfdetermination and of the speedy granting of independence to colonial countries and peoples for the effective guarantee and observance of human rights.* https://www.un.org/unispal/document/auto-insert-185486/

Van Ashwegen, M. (2023, 19 April). *5 visa-free and visa-on-arrival safari destinations for US passport holders.* Discover Africa. https://www.discoverafrica.com/blog/visa-free-african-travel-destinations-for-american-passport-holders/

Vienna Convention on the Law of Treaties Adopted by the United Nations. (1969). United Nations, Treaty Series, vol. 1155, p. 331.

Visaindex.Com. (2025). *China passport visa free countries 2025.* https://visaindex.com/visa-requirement/china-passport-visa-free-countries-list/

Walter, J. (2025). *The consequences of US tariff policy for Africa.* Rosa Luxemburg Stiftung. https://www.rosalux.de/en/news/id/53428/the-consequences-of-us-tariff-policy-for-africa

World Economic Forum. (2025). *Forum friends of the African continental free trade area.* https://initiatives.weforum.org/forum-friends-of-the-african-continental-free-trade-area/home

Part II
Country Case Studies

Chapter 5
Repositioning Tunisia in the AfCFTA Era: Difficulties, Reflections, and Prospects for Progress

Insaf Guedidi

Abstract This chapter analyses Tunisia's accession to the African Continental Free Trade Area (AfCFTA) and its potential to reposition the country within African and global trade networks. It examines Tunisia's trade history, its structural dependence on Eurocentric value chains, and the opportunities and constraints presented by the implementation of AfCFTA. The analysis highlights Tunisia's challenges in building regional value chains, harmonising rules of origin, and overcoming non-tariff barriers, while also pointing to comparative advantages in agro-processing, manufacturing, and services. Using lessons from previous preferential trade agreements, this chapter argues that successful AfCFTA participation requires institutional reform, private sector engagement, logistics modernisation, and digital innovation. The findings suggest that AfCFTA can serve as a catalyst for Tunisia's structural transformation, enhancing supply chain resilience, reducing vulnerability to external shocks, and enabling more inclusive and sustainable development.

Keywords Tunisia · African continental free trade area (AfCFTA) · Regional value chains (RVCs) · Trade integration · Supply chain resilience · external shocks · Intra-African trade

I. Guedidi (✉)
WTO Chairs Programme (WCP), University of Tunis, Tunis, Tunisia

Department of Economics, Universitat Jaume I, Castelló de la Plana, Spain
e-mail: guedidi@uji.es

D. N. Yuni et al. (eds.), *From Policy to Practice: Challenges and Ways Forward on the Implementation of the AfCFTA*,
https://doi.org/10.1007/978-3-032-14051-7_5

5.1 Introduction: Tunisia's AfCFTA Framework and Trade Integration History

Tunisia's involvement in the African Continental Free Trade Area (AfCFTA)[1] marks an important step in its ongoing efforts to foster deeper trade integration and achieve sustainable economic development (Dhaoui & Kasdallah, 2024). Tunisia ratified the AfCFTA Agreement in 2020. The ratification marked a strategic pivot in Tunisia's external economic policy, aiming to deepen its integration into the African continent. According to the Tunisian Institute for Competitiveness and Quantitative Studies (ITCEQ), this accession opens access to one of the largest and most dynamic markets in the world, expected to reach a population of 2.5 billion by 2050 (Dhaoui & Kasdallah, 2024; Tralac, 2024).

Following ratification, Tunisia moved to establish a national institutional framework[2] to manage and implement the agreement. In 2023, Tunisia held awareness conferences in Tunis and Ras Jdir to mark its readiness to begin commercial operations under the AfCFTA. Organised by the General Directorate of Customs with the Ministry of Trade and GIZ, these events aimed to highlight the role of customs authorities and inform staff about the agreement's provisions and trade procedures, following the completion of all legal and technical requirements (Ministère du Commerce (Tunisie), 2023). In 2025, Tunisia hosted its first major AfCFTA-related event: a regional workshop on Authorised Economic Operators (AEOs) in Tunis. Organised with the AfCFTA Secretariat, the Ministry of Trade, and international partners, the workshop aimed to strengthen trade facilitation by enhancing technical knowledge of AEO programmes among customs officials from over 12 North and West African countries (Ministère du Commerce (Tunisie), 2025b).

Tunisia's AfCFTA strategic action plan focuses primarily on enhancing investment and competitiveness, rather than on structural transformation or diversification, positioning the country to attract investment and improve its business environment within the AfCFTA framework (Rouis & Tabor, 2012). As part of its efforts to integrate Tunisian businesses into African markets, Tunisia organised a national training campaign on the AfCFTA in February 2025. This initiative

---

[1] The AfCFTA, launched in 2018, aims to create a single African market that fosters trade, industrialisation, and sustainable development while advancing the African Union (AU)'s Agenda 2063 and United Nations (UN) 2030 goals (UNECA, 2024). Once fully ratified by all 55 AU members, it will become the world's largest free trade zone, covering 1.3 billion people and a combined GDP of 3.4 trillion USD, making it the most significant trade agreement since the World Trade Organisation (WTO)'s creation in 1995 (Gathii, 2019; WB, 2020).

[2] The Economic Commission for Africa (ECA) has led efforts to help 44 countries and five Regional Economic Communities develop AfCFTA implementation strategies. As of January 2024, 35 national and two regional strategies (IGAD and ECOWAS) have been validated, with more in progress. ECA also supported capacity building in over 15 countries. GIZ and UNDP contributed to a few national strategies, including Tunisia (UNECA, 2024).

targeted private sector actors. It reached eight key regions: Tunis, Bizerte, Béja, Sousse, Sfax, Gabès, Gafsa, and Kairouan. These trainings aimed to explore trade opportunities under AfCFTA, master rules of origin and utilise digital tools from the International Trade Center (ITC) to enhance export strategies (Ministère du Commerce (Tunisie), 2025a). These capacity-building efforts reflect Tunisia's strategic commitment to benefit from the AfCFTA and to strengthen its role in intra-African trade. Although the country has faced challenges in fully implementing the agreement, such as delays in submitting its schedule of tariff concessions and the incomplete operationalisation of its National AfCFTA Implementation Committee, despite the passage of a law to establish it, these obstacles have not deterred its broader ambitions (UNECA, 2024).

Tunisia aims to deepen its integration into African value chains and to harness the trade facilitation and industrial opportunities presented by the AfCFTA. These aspirations build on Tunisia's longstanding trade history as a strategic gateway between Europe and Africa. Between 2011 and 2019, trade consistently played a vital role in Tunisia's economy. On average, the total value of trade in goods and services equaled 104% of GDP. This underscores the centrality of international exchange to the country's economic activity. Despite its strong export orientation, Tunisia has been a net importer over the past decade, with imports totaling USD 24.6 billion compared to USD 19.1 billion in exports in 2019. However, Tunisia's exports are relatively diversified, with electrical machinery and equipment making up the largest share, around 26.9% of total exports (Raga, 2022).

As one of North Africa's most industrialised economies, Tunisia has successfully attracted foreign direct investment (FDI) through its offshore regime and investment policies particularly in the textile, agri-food, electrical, and mechanical industries. In its broader push towards global economic integration, Tunisia has prioritised export promotion, enhancing its attractiveness to investors. Central to this strategy is the offshore regime, introduced by the 1972 law and reinforced by the 1993 Investment Incentive Code and the 2017 Investment Law, which collectively eased restrictions and offered substantial benefits to export-oriented businesses. By 2016, the offshore sector accounted for 78% of Tunisia's non-energy goods exports. FDI stock represents a significant share of GDP, nearly 70%, a level high compared to other emerging and OECD countries. Inflows remained resilient in the post-revolution years, with notable increases in both the industrial and service sectors following the 2017 reforms. As of 2018, Tunisia hosted over 2000 fully exporting foreign-invested companies in the industrial and service sectors, with nearly 70% being entirely foreign-owned. The offshore regime is largely driven by European firms that operate across multiple countries in the region. In 2017 alone, non-energy FDI led to 492 investment projects totaling 1318.2 million dinars and generating over 10,000 jobs. France, Italy, and Germany remain Tunisia's key investment partners, accounting for the largest shares of FDI. Tunisia experienced a surge in foreign direct investment (FDI) in 2006, mainly due to the privatisation of its telecommunications sector. However, FDI inflows have declined in subsequent years. By 2019, FDI had dropped by 18.5% to USD 845 million, largely due to a sharp fall in investment in services (Raga, 2022; Sammoud & Dhaoui, 2019).

Building on its strong export-oriented framework and longstanding reliance on foreign direct investment, particularly through its offshore regime, Tunisia now faces a pivotal opportunity to shift its trade strategy. With the launch of the AfCFTA, the country can broaden its focus beyond traditional European partners and move towards deeper integration with African markets. This chapter explores Tunisia's evolving position within global value chains (GVCs), its preparedness to implement AfCFTA, and the potential for transitioning from a primarily assembly-based economy to one that generates greater regional value.

5.2 Building Regional Value Chains through AfCFTA

5.2.1 Intermediate Goods and Tunisia Regional Integration

The African Continental Free Trade Area (AfCFTA) offers Tunisia a strategic opportunity to reposition itself within the continent's emerging economic architecture by integrating more deeply into regional value chains (RVCs). As a country with a diversified industrial base and established trade infrastructure, Tunisia stands to benefit from expanded access to African markets, reduced trade barriers, and increased investment flows. Tunisia can leverage the AfCFTA framework to strengthen its regional linkages, diversify its export portfolio, and become a key player in value-added production networks across North, West, and Sub-Saharan Africa.

Figure 5.1 compares intra-African imports and exports for four North African countries: Algeria, Egypt, Morocco, and Tunisia. Egypt clearly stands out with exports exceeding 6.6 billion USD, far above its import level, reflecting its strong integration into African markets. Morocco and Algeria also demonstrate positive trade balances, with export volumes higher than imports, indicating active participation in intra-African trade flows and a growing regional presence.

Tunisia, however, presents a distinct trade profile. In 2023, its intra-African imports were valued at approximately 2.4 billion USD, while exports lagged behind at around 1.96 billion USD. This persistent trade gap[3] signals that Tunisia has yet to fully capitalise on the market access and integration potential offered by the AfCFTA. Despite its dual membership in both the Arab Maghreb Union (AMU) and the Common Market for Eastern and Southern Africa (COMESA), the country's export performance within Africa remains modest. By leveraging its experience in manufacturing intermediate inputs and its relatively diversified export structure, Tunisia can position itself as a strategic supplier of components within regional value chains.

---

[3] Tunisia recorded a trade surplus with African countries between 2015 and 2017, but shifted to a net goods importer position in the subsequent two years (Raga, 2022). This trend persisted through 2023, as illustrated in Fig. 1.

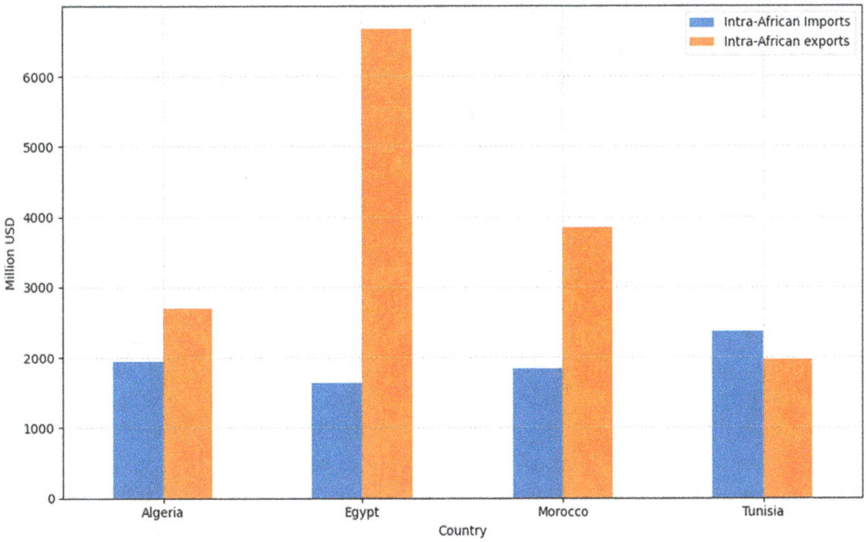

Fig. 5.1 Intra-African Imports and Exports by Country (2023). Source: Author's elaboration using Afreximbank data

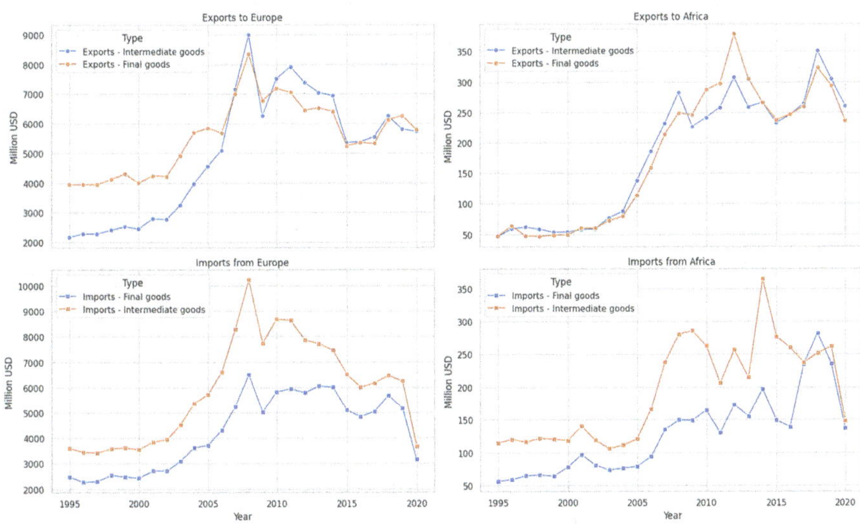

Fig. 5.2 Tunisia's trade in intermediate and final goods by region. Source: Author's elaboration using the OECD Trade in Value Added (TiVA) database

The AfCFTA presents a timely opportunity for Tunisia to reorient its trade strategy, not just to reduce its trade deficit within Africa, but also to deepen its economic integration with neighbouring markets and stimulate value-added production across the continent. The comparison (Fig. 5.2) of Tunisia's trade in final and intermediate goods with Europe and Africa from 1995 to 2020 clearly underscores the country's deep integration into European-centred GVCs. Both exports and imports with Europe, especially intermediate goods, are significantly higher and more stable over time than with Africa. Intermediate goods exports to Europe surged sharply from the early 2000s, peaking around 2008, mirroring Tunisia's role as a manufacturing and assembly hub for European industries. Imports of intermediate goods from Europe also dominate, suggesting heavy reliance on European inputs. This reflects a vertical specialisation structure where Tunisia's industrial linkages are tightly embedded in upstream and downstream European supply chains.

In contrast, Tunisia's trade with Africa, although growing, is much lower in volume and remains marginal in structure, especially in intermediate goods. The graphs show that exports and imports with African partners remain under 400 million USD throughout the period, with some growth after 2005 but lacking the scale or consistency seen with Europe. This asymmetry indicates that regional value chains within Africa are underdeveloped from Tunisia's perspective, limiting the country's potential to diversify away from Eurocentric dependence. Within the AfCFTA framework, Tunisia's challenge will be to strengthen horizontal and vertical industrial integration with African partners, particularly in intermediate goods, to rebalance trade and build resilient regional production networks.

For Tunisia, regional value chains represent a strategic avenue to diversify exports and move up the value ladder by trading more intermediate goods within Africa. The AfCFTA can play a pivotal role in enabling Tunisia to deepen its trade ties across the continent through enhanced market access and harmonised trade rules. Figure 5.3 illustrates the distribution of Domestic Value Added (DVX)[4] exported from Tunisia to African countries in 2017. The flows are heavily concentrated, with Morocco (12.0 M USD), Algeria (8.8 M USD), and South Africa (5.0 M USD) accounting for the majority of Tunisia's DVX contributions on the continent. The remaining countries receive significantly smaller amounts, mostly below 1 million USD, and many under 0.1 million USD, reflecting a fragmented and shallow level of value chain integration with the rest of Africa. This concentration suggests that while some bilateral industrial linkages are emerging, broader participation in regional value chains remains limited. AfCFTA's implementation could help rebalance this pattern by creating incentives and infrastructure for Tunisia to deepen trade in intermediate goods with a wider set of African partners.

Understanding how value is sourced across borders is key to strengthening regional production systems. Figure 5.4 illustrates the distribution of foreign value added (FVA)[5] embedded in Tunisia's imports from African countries in

[4] Domestic Value Added (DVX) captures a country's forward participation in value chains by measuring the domestic content embedded in exports that are later re-exported by partner countries to third markets. It is a key indicator of upstreamness, reflecting the extent to which a country like Tunisia contributes inputs early in the production process within regional or global value chains.

[5] Foreign Value Added (FVA) refers to the value of imported inputs that are used in a country's production and then re-exported as part of its exports. It reflects Tunisia's backward participation

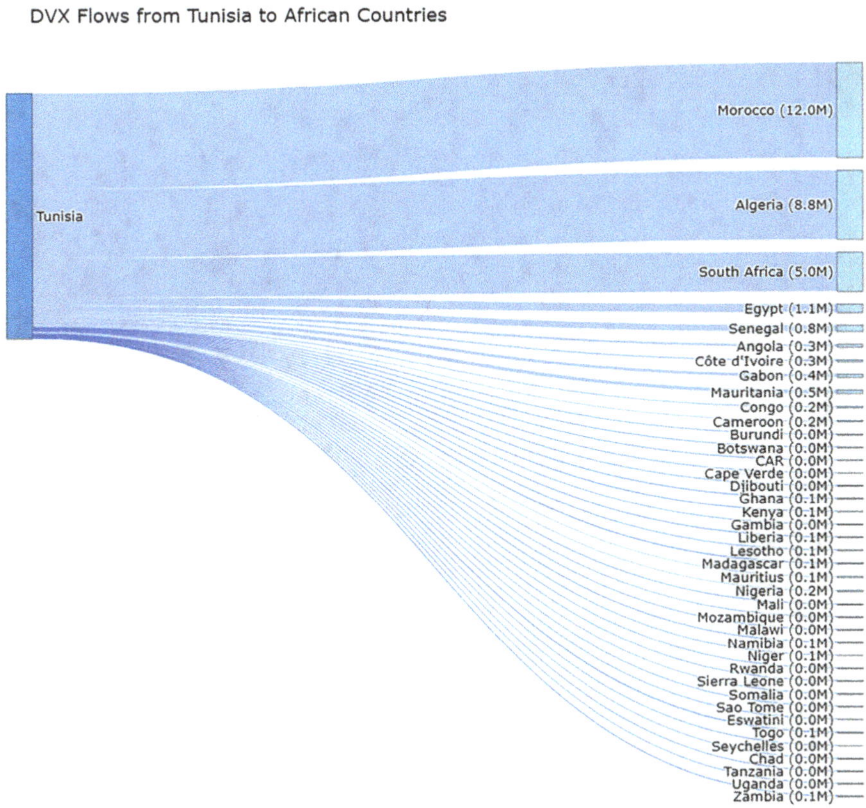

Fig. 5.3 Domestic value added (DVX) flows from Tunisia to African countries—2017. Source: Author's elaboration based on the UNCTAD-Eora Global Value Chain (GVC) Database

2017, offering insight into Tunisia's backward participation in regional value chains. The largest contributions come from Egypt (33.3 M USD), Algeria (22.6 M USD), Côte d'Ivoire (11.8 M USD), and Morocco (11.0 M USD), suggesting that Tunisia sources a significant portion of its intermediate goods from a few key partners. In contrast, most other African countries contribute marginally, typically less than 1 million USD. This highlights a limited and uneven integration of African suppliers into Tunisia's production networks. This pattern suggests that regional value chains remain underdeveloped and concentrated. It also underscores the potential of the AfCFTA to expand and diversify Tunisia's sourcing base across the continent.

The untapped potential of the AfCFTA to promote more balanced forward and backward participation in value chains across Africa is significant, but its success will depend on careful consideration of sectoral dynamics and complementarities.

---

in value chains, indicating the extent to which its exports depend on foreign intermediates sourced from other countries.

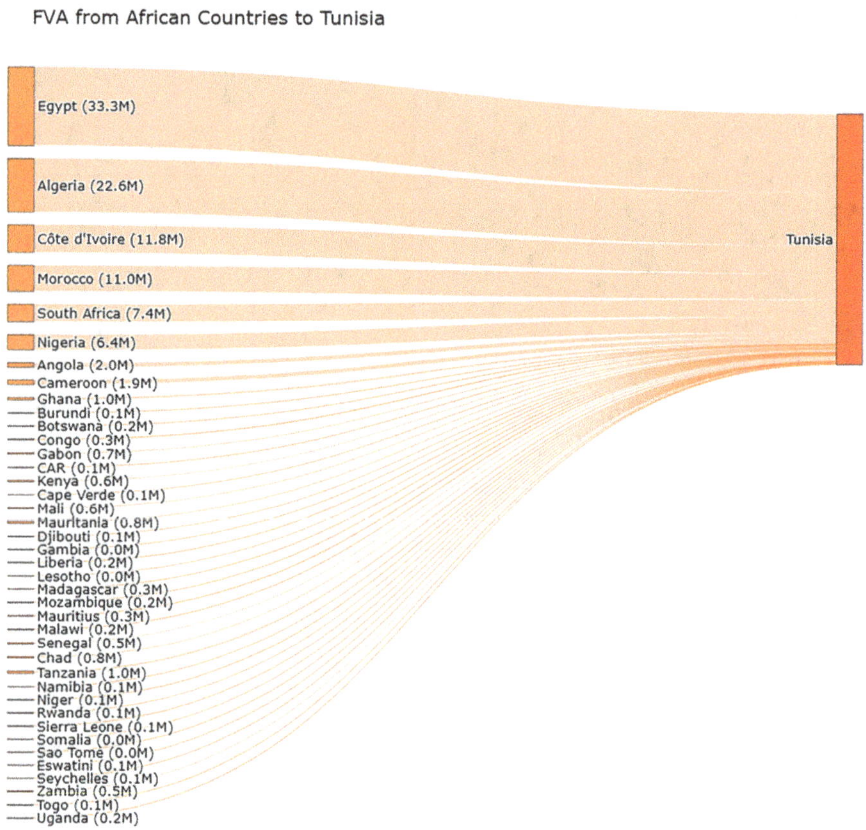

Fig. 5.4 Foreign value added (FVA) contributions from African Countries to Tunisia—2017. Source: Author's elaboration based on the UNCTAD-Eora Global Value Chain (GVC) Database

Figure 5.5 presents the sectoral distribution of Tunisia's value added in trade, where African countries are the partners. The sectoral distribution of Tunisia's Domestic Value Added (DVX) to African countries in 2017 highlights sectors where Tunisia contributes value to regional production. The largest DVX flows originate from the financial and business services sector, followed by the petroleum and chemical products, agriculture, transport, and wholesale trade sectors. This indicates that Tunisia plays a forward role in supplying both industrial and service-based intermediate inputs to select African partners. However, many other sectors, such as machinery, food, textiles, and construction, remain marginal in their DVX contributions.

The sectoral breakdown of Foreign Value Added (FVA) from African countries incorporated into Tunisia's exports is presented in Fig. 5.5. Here, the leading inputs come from textiles and wearing apparel, petroleum and chemicals, food and beverages, and machinery. This points to Tunisia's downstream reliance on key intermediate goods from its African neighbours. Interestingly, several sectors that are

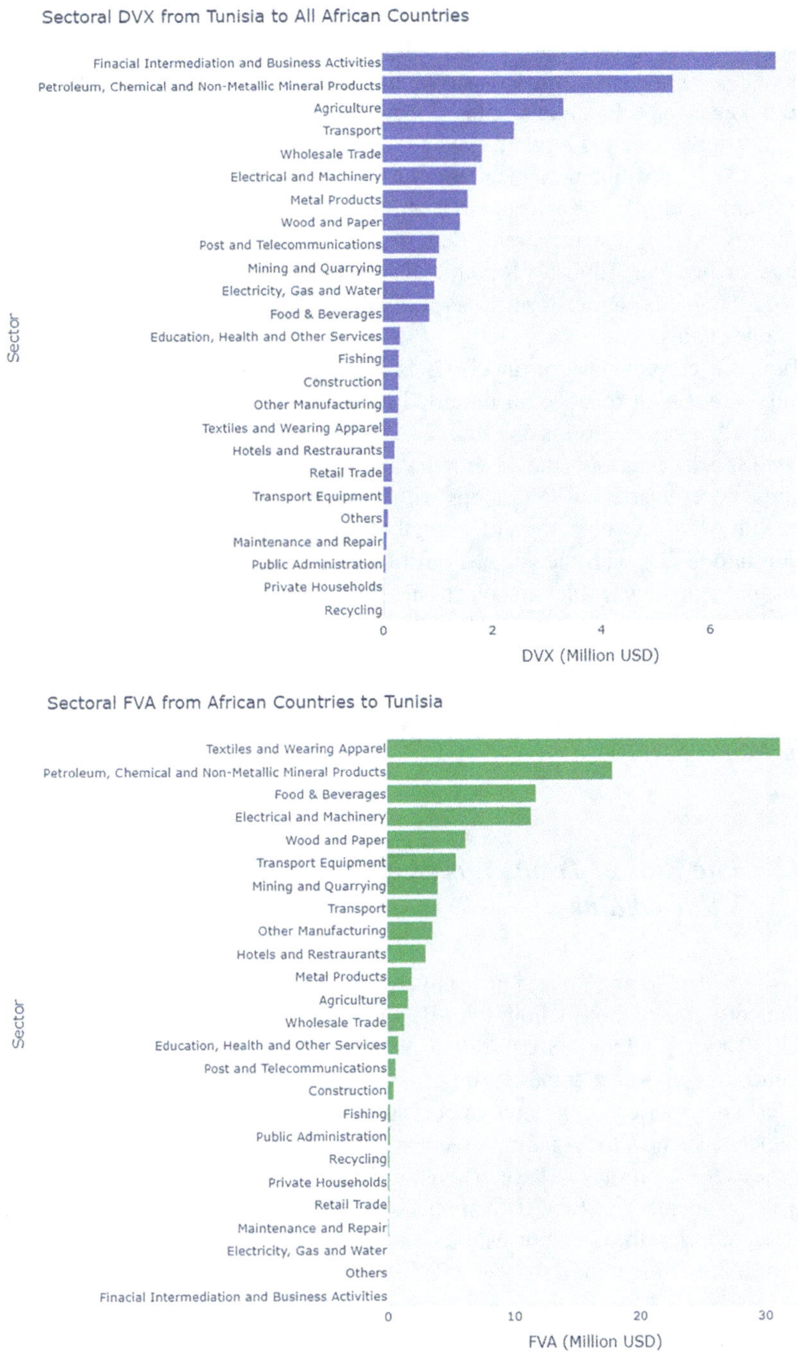

Fig. 5.5 Sectoral distribution of Tunisia's domestic value added (DVX) and foreign value added (FVA) to/from African Countries—2017. Source: Author's elaboration based on the UNCTAD-Eora Global Value Chain (GVC) Database

dominant in FVA are underrepresented in Tunisia's DVX exports, and this reveals an asymmetry in sectoral integration. In line with previous analysis, Sammoud and Dhaoui (2019) highlight Tunisia's strong integration into GVCs with notable backward linkages in sectors like textiles, chemicals, agri-food, and mechanical-electrical industries. However, forward linkages remain limited. Despite these successes, Tunisia's GVC position remains predominantly in low-value-added activities, such as assembly and basic transformation. Moreover, trade is highly concentrated with the European Union with intra-African trade remaining marginal. Moreover, the divergence between Tunisia's forward and backward sectoral linkages implies that AfCFTA could play a transformative role by promoting more reciprocal and diversified value chains.

Tunisia's current position in GVCs is heavily oriented towards the European Union, with a high reliance on imported inputs from Europe and a strong export focus on EU markets (Rouis & Tabor, 2012). This concentration exposes Tunisia to external shocks and limits the development of regional industrial ties. Transitioning towards more diversified RVC loops would not only reduce dependency but also align with AfCFTA's objectives of strengthening intra-African trade. Tunisia's integration into GVCs with the EU has positioned it as an assembly hub for low-cost inputs in sectors like textiles and electronics (Sammoud & Dhaoui, 2019). However, recent global shocks, such as the COVID-19 pandemic,[6] the war in Ukraine, and supply chain disruptions, have exposed the fragility of this model. The AfCFTA offers a strategic opportunity for Tunisia to pivot towards shorter, more resilient, and inclusive regional value chains (RVCs) by strengthening trade and industrial linkages within Africa.

5.2.2 The Role of Trade Agreements in Enabling Regional Value Chains

Over the past 15 years, Tunisia has actively engaged in numerous preferential trade agreements (PTAs), both within the MENA region and with external partners like the EU, Turkey, and the USA. While these agreements have reduced trade barriers and encouraged some domestic reforms, their overall impact has been mixed. Tunisia has experienced greater import growth than export expansion. Regional agreements, such as the Agadir Agreement, have shown more promise in boosting exports, albeit from a low base (Rouis & Tabor, 2012). Excluding the AfCFTA, Tunisia is a member of two African regional trade agreements composed solely of African countries: the Common Market for Eastern and Southern Africa (COMESA) and the Arab Maghreb Union (AMU). Figure 5.6 highlights stark differences

[6] The COVID-19 pandemic caused a parallel contraction in both imports and exports, each declining by around 15% (Raga, 2022).

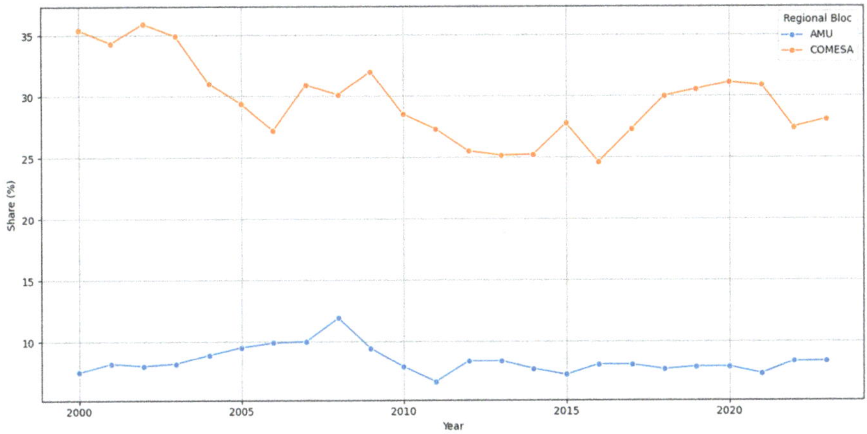

Fig. 5.6 Share of Intra-African exports (2000–2023). Source: Author's elaboration using Afreximbank data

between the AMU[7] and COMESA.[8] While COMESA consistently accounts for a significant share, ranging from 25% to 36%, AMU's contribution remains much lower, peaking at around 11.9% in 2008 but generally fluctuating between 7 and 9%.

In the case of Tunisia, these trade agreements have provided partial benefits but have not effectively fostered deep regional value chains (RVCs) within Africa (Figs. 5.3 and 5.4). These agreements often suffer from limited implementation, overlapping rules of origin, and fragmented industrial coordination. For instance, Tunisia, as one of the more trade-open members of the AMU, remains constrained by the Union's lack of implementation and low intra-regional trade. This reflects broader structural and institutional disparities among member states (Rouis & Tabor, 2012). These shortcomings are not only historical but also carry important lessons for the AfCFTA: without strong mechanisms for enforcement, harmonised rules of origin, and better institutional coordination, the continent-wide agreement risks reproducing the same weaknesses on a larger scale. In this sense, Tunisia's previous experiences underline the necessity of addressing such bottlenecks from the outset. The AfCFTA, by contrast, offers the prospect of a more coherent framework that can help overcome these gaps. For Tunisia to reap meaningful benefits, its participation must be anchored in simplified trade rules, enhanced institutional capacity, and targeted efforts to strengthen intra-African trade and investment linkages, thus avoiding the pitfalls of earlier regional trade agreements.

Tunisia's membership in the AfCFTA will not automatically translate into benefits; meaningful gains require strategic action. Drawing lessons from its experience

[7] The AMU includes Algeria, Libya, Mauritania, Morocco, and Tunisia, aiming to promote economic and political cooperation in North Africa.

[8] The COMESA brings together 21 member states, including Egypt, Kenya, Ethiopia, Uganda, Zambia, and Tunisia, forming one of Africa's largest regional economic communities.

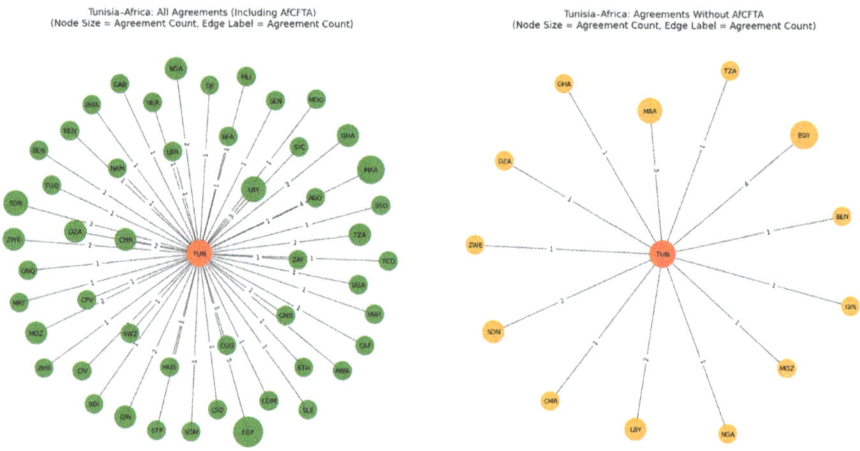

Fig. 5.7 Tunisia's trade agreements with African countries—2023. Source: Author's elaboration based on the World Bank's Deep Trade Agreements (DTA) Database

with previous trade agreements will be essential to maximise the advantages of AfCFTA and avoid the pitfalls of signing agreements that remain largely symbolic or underutilised.

Figure 5.7 reveals a significant expansion of Tunisia's trade connectivity with African countries under the AfCFTA framework. Tunisia is connected to over 45 African countries, with several countries such as Egypt, Morocco, and Côte d'Ivoire participating in three or more agreements. Without AfCFTA, Tunisia's trade ties appear limited and fragmented. Only a small cluster of countries remains connected to Tunisia, and most of them have a single agreement in place. This comparison highlights AfCFTA's role in amplifying intra-African ties. AfCFTA enables Tunisia to engage with more partners across the continent. For Tunisia, AfCFTA holds the potential to move beyond the limitations of older trade arrangements by promoting harmonised regulations and reducing non-tariff barriers.

Complex rules of origin and implementation challenges have further limited the effectiveness of these PTAs (Rouis & Tabor, 2012). In practice, Tunisian exporters have often faced complex and costly certification procedures, delays in obtaining proof of origin, and inconsistencies across agreements (Baghdadi et al., 2019; Rouis & Tabor, 2012). These barriers discouraged many firms, particularly small and medium enterprises (SMEs), from using preferential tariffs, leading to a persistent underutilisation of existing agreements. As a result, Tunisia's export diversification within Africa remained limited and its industrial linkages largely Eurocentric (Raga, 2022; Sammoud & Dhaoui, 2019).

Building on these challenges, AfCFTA introduces its own set of procedural requirements that firms must meet to access preferential treatment. To benefit from the customs advantages under the AfCFTA, goods originating from a member country must be accompanied by valid proof of origin.[9] This can take the form of either a certificate of origin or a declaration of origin included directly on the commercial invoice. These documents are mandatory to ensure that the goods qualify for preferential treatment under AfCFTA rules. The declaration of origin on an invoice under the AfCFTA can be issued by any exporter when the value of the goods does not exceed 5000 USD. For shipments above that amount, only an approved (authorised) exporter is allowed to make such a declaration, regardless of the value of the goods. To benefit from preferential treatment (i.e., reduced or zero tariffs under AfCFTA), goods must be transported directly from one AfCFTA member country to another without passing through or being altered in a third country like Europe (Belhaj, 2023). As of now, AfCFTA rules of origin cover 87.7% of tariff lines, but key sectors like textiles and garments (Chapters 51–63) and vehicles and parts (Chapter 87) have yet to reach consensus. Whether through a change in tariff heading or subheading, the value of non-originating materials, or specific processing rules, member states remain divided on which criteria to apply. This delays full agreement on these chapters (Bouzaine, 2023).

5.3 The Tariff Turnaround and Beyond: How Tunisia Can Leverage AfCFTA Preferences and Tackle Non-Tariff Barriers

Tunisia's current preferential tariff structure, as shown in Table 5.1, reveals a strategic openness towards African regional integration, particularly through its 0% Ad Valorem Equivalent (AVE) applied to COMESA Free Trade Area (FTA) members. This deep liberalisation contrasts sharply with the high tariffs still applied to non-FTA African partners like Ethiopia (19.92%). The case of Egypt (11.18%), despite being part of the AGADIR Agreement, also signals the incomplete alignment of preferential regimes across trade agreements. This highlights the need for greater coherence and harmonisation in Tunisia's regional tariff commitments.

Compared to its tariff commitments with the EU, UK, and EFTA (all around 6.85–7.74%), Tunisia's lower AVEs for certain African blocs reflect a promising regional bias. Leveraging this trend, Tunisia can use AfCFTA as a vehicle to align its tariff approach more systematically across African partners. Drawing on its COMESA experience, Tunisia is well-positioned to lead by example in AfCFTA implementation, gradually reducing tariffs for non-FTA members.

Tariff elimination forms the first cornerstone of the AfCFTA. It aims to facilitate intra-African trade by progressively reducing and ultimately removing barriers to

[9] In total, Tunisia's chambers of commerce and industry have issued 37 AfCFTA certificates of origin to date. Ref Support to Trade Agreements with Africa. In total, Tunisia's chambers of commerce and industry have issued 37 AfCFTA certificates of origin to date (GIZ, 2024).

Table 5.1 Tunisia's preferential tariff rates by trade regime (2023)

Tariff regime	Ave (%)
Preferential tariff for AGADIR countries	1.82
Preferential tariff for Algeria	7.60
Preferential tariff for EFTA countries	7.58
Preferential tariff for Egypt	11.18
Preferential tariff for European Union countries	6.85
Preferential tariff for Morocco	6.88
Preferential tariff for Turkey	7.74
Preferential tariff for the League of Arab States	1.82
Preferential tariff for the United Kingdom	6.85
Preferential tariff preference (COMESA) for Eritrea	4.43
Preferential tariff preference (COMESA) for Ethiopia	19.92
Preferential tariff for COMESA countries members of the FTA	0

Source: Author's elaboration based on ITC tariff data (https://www.macmap.org)

Note: The AVE (%) shown in the table represents the average ad valorem equivalent tariff that Tunisia applies to imports from trade partners within each specific preferential agreement. In this context, Tunisia is the reporting country, and the AVE reflects the mean tariff rate calculated across all products imported from partners under each trade regime

the movement of goods across member states. Table 5.2 provides a detailed comparison between the general AfCFTA liberalisation modalities and Tunisia's specific tariff offer under the Protocol on Trade in Goods. In line with AfCFTA requirements, Tunisia commits to liberalising 90% of its tariff lines (Category A), covering 10,506 product lines. Additionally, 7% of its lines are designated as sensitive products (Category B), totalling 817 lines, which will be liberalised over a longer timeframe. Tunisia also lists 3% of tariff lines (349 lines) under the exclusion list (Category C), consistent with AfCFTA rules, and subject to review after 5 years. Notably, these excluded products account for 9.74% of Tunisia's total imports, equivalent to 298.98 million TND. This indicates a strategic attempt to protect key domestic sectors while remaining within AfCFTA's flexibility limits. To support the effective implementation of these commitments, Tunisia has also taken concrete steps to strengthen its institutional and customs capacity. In 2023, Tunisia trained customs officials on tariff classification to prepare for implementing advance rulings, aiming to enhance transparency and predictability under AfCFTA (GIZ, 2024).

Table 5.2 AfCFTA Liberalisation Modalities (Protocol on Trade in Goods)

	Overall AfCFTA offer		Tunisia's tariff offer			
Category	Non-LDCs	LDCs	% of lines covered under AfCFTA	Number of lines covered under AfCFTA	Number of products to add or remove	Import volume (TND) and percentage of total imports
A: Level of ambition	90%	90%	90%	10,506	0	–
B: Sensitive products	7% – Subject to notification and negotiation – Negotiation method: request and offer	7% – Subject to negotiation – Negotiation method: request and offer	7%	817	0	–
C: Exclusion list	3% – Review after 5 years; subject to negotiation – Subject to anti-concentration clause (>10% of import value)	3% – Review after 5 years; subject to negotiation – Subject to anti-concentration clause (>10% of import value)	3%	349	0	298.98 million TND 9.74%
Total	100%	100%	100%	11,672	–	3070.59 million TND
Timeframe	Non-LDCs: 5 years Sensitive products: 10 years	LDCs: 10 years Sensitive products: 13 years				

Source: Author's elaboration based on data from the AfCFTA Secretariat and Bouzaine (2023)
Notes: (1) Transition Period: Tariffs will be reduced gradually in equal steps (linear approach), and liberalisation of sensitive products will begin in year 6. (2) Supplementary Modality: Member states can complement the linear approach with a request-offer negotiation method. (3) Geometric Variable: Countries willing to offer greater concessions in a shorter timeframe may do so, based on reciprocity

The AfCFTA not only calls for the gradual elimination of tariffs over a 10-year period,[10] but also emphasises the reduction of non-tariff measures (NTMs) to further facilitate intra-African trade. Non-tariff barriers on goods and services are reduced

[10] Under AfCFTA rules, tariffs on 90% of intra-African trade will be gradually eliminated, over 5 years for non-LDCs and 10 years for LDCs, beginning in 2020 (Table 5.2).

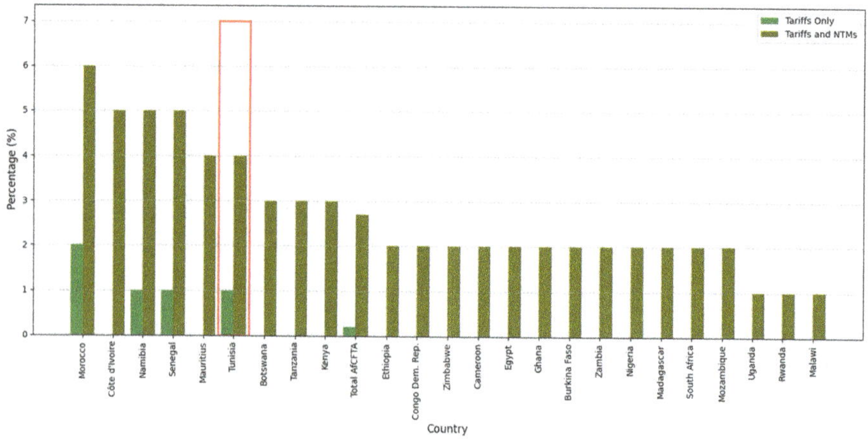

Fig. 5.8 Income Gains Due to AfCFTA in 2035. Source: Author's elaboration based on World Bank estimates (WB, 2020). Notes: (1) NTMs stand for Non-Tariff Measures. (2) The graph shows percentage changes with respect to the baseline scenario in 2035. The baseline scenario does not include policy interventions such as tariff reductions or NTM reforms

equally for all trading partners, following the most-favoured-nation (MFN) principle (WB, 2020). The impact of NTMs on firms and trade has been widely studied, including in the case of Tunisia (Baghdadi et al., 2019; Beckman et al., 2024; Garcés & Vogt, 2024; Ghali et al., 2013; Ghodsi & Stehrer, 2022). For instance, Baghdadi et al. (2019) use firm-level data to examine the effects of NTMs on Tunisian firms' imports. They show that NTMs, especially those with informational content, can enhance trade particularly for medium and large firms.

A subset of studies specifically examines scenarios under AfCFTA implementation, assessing the combined effects of NTM reduction and tariff cuts on intra-African trade flows. (Beckman et al., 2024; ElGanainy et al., 2023; Fusacchia et al., 2022; Guedidi, 2025; WB, 2020). Figure 5.8 highlights the significant role of NTMs in driving income gains under the AfCFTA. While Tunisia's income gain from tariff reduction alone is relatively modest (about 1%), the gain rises substantially to 4% when NTM reductions are included. Thus, removing regulatory and procedural barriers offers much greater potential for unlocking trade and growth.

Moreover, Tunisia's income gain from combined tariff and NTM reductions places it above the AfCFTA average of 2.7%. Tunisia's position in the mid-range of income gains across African countries suggests that its ability to benefit from the AfCFTA hinges less on tariff elimination and more on simplifying trade-related regulations, improving transparency, and harmonising standards. This reinforces the policy priority of streamlining NTMs, such as customs delays, product standards, and import licensing procedures, which often disproportionately affect small and medium-sized enterprises (Baghdadi et al., 2019).

According to ElGanainy et al. (2023) estimates, cutting intra-African tariffs by 90% and halving NTMs under the AfCFTA could raise median intra-African trade flows by 15% and real per capita GDP by 1.25%. As for agricultural trade, Hoekman et al. (2004) indicate that a 50% global cut in agricultural tariffs would generate significantly greater benefits for developing countries' exports and overall welfare than an equivalent 50% reduction in agricultural subsidies. Guedidi (2025) finds that removing both tariffs and NTMs yields the strongest gains in exports, imports, and welfare across Africa. In Tunisia, export gains are well above the African average if tariff rates dropped by 99% and NTMs reduced by 50%, reaching 180.34% (vs. 43.38% on African average). However, Tunisia's welfare gain remains modest at 0.27%, compared to the continental average of 1.91%. This suggests trade responsiveness does not fully translate into welfare benefits. Another study of Fusacchia et al. (2022) applies a global computable general equilibrium model that incorporates value-added trade structures to assess how regional trade liberalisation affects production fragmentation. Under the AfCFTA scenario, Tunisia's gross agricultural exports increase by 4.7%. Tunisia experiences a 38.8% increase in regional sourcing of foreign value-added (FVA) in its agricultural and food exports.

Services are also a key component of the AfCFTA, with liberalisation efforts extending beyond goods to include priority service sectors. In the first phase of negotiations, the AfCFTA focuses on six main service sectors: business services, communications, financial services, tourism, and transport (Bouzaine, 2023). So far, research on the economic effects of Africa's regional integration has primarily concentrated on tariff and non-tariff barriers (NTBs) related to goods. WB (2020) analysis goes further by including NTBs in services.

5.4 Opportunities Under AfCFTA

One clear advantage of the AfCFTA for Tunisia is its geographic proximity to regional African markets. However, the agreement also presents deeper opportunities for structural transformation, industrial upgrading, and broader value chain integration. The agreement could offer Tunisian firms greater access to African markets and stimulate intra-African trade, especially in manufactured goods and services where Tunisia holds comparative advantages. Furthermore, the implementation of trade facilitation measures, such as the Authorised Economic Operators (AEO) programme, positions Tunisia to benefit from more efficient cross-border procedures and enhanced competitiveness within the continent (UGTT, 2021).

The evolution of Tunisia's share in intra-African trade between 2000 and 2023 (Fig. 5.9) reveals both missed opportunities and areas for renewed engagement under the AfCFTA. While Morocco and Egypt have significantly increased their share of intra-African exports, Tunisia's export share has declined from 2.69% in 2000 to just 1.82% in 2023. This downward trend suggests that Tunisia has not yet positioned itself as a key continental supplier, despite its geographic proximity to major African markets. In contrast, peers like Egypt and Morocco have leveraged regional linkages to expand their export footprint.

On the import side, Tunisia's share of total intra-African imports decreased slightly from 3.54% to 2.79%. It still positions the country among the top regional

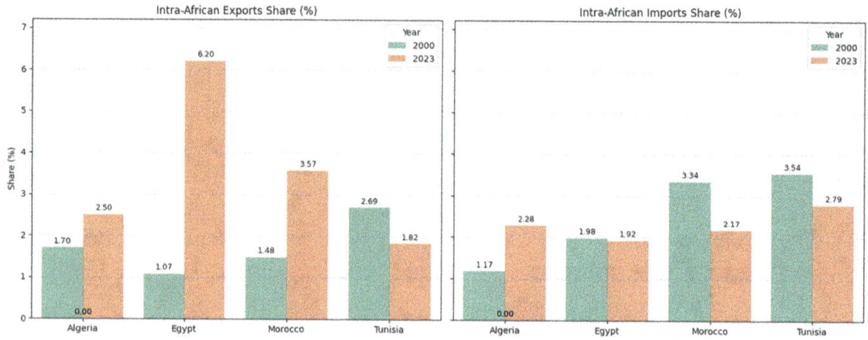

Fig. 5.9 Country share of Intra-African Trade (% of total Intra-African trade). Source: Author's elaboration using Afreximbank data

importers. This indicates the presence of established commercial ties and a relatively strong demand for African goods. The challenge, therefore, lies in converting this demand into reciprocal trade flows by boosting export capacity and improving competitiveness in sectors with growth potential.

To assess the structure of Tunisia's international trade, two key indicators are commonly used: the concentration index and the diversification index. The concentration index[11] measures the extent to which a country's exports or imports are dominated by a small number of products or partners. The diversification index,[12] on the other hand, reflects how closely a country's export structure resembles the global export structure. Together, these indices provide a comprehensive view of trade structure and are particularly useful for evaluating Tunisia's readiness to seize the opportunities offered by the AfCFTA.

In Fig. 5.10, the trade concentration highlights a key opportunity for Tunisia under the AfCFTA. Since 1995, Tunisia's export concentration index has steadily declined, indicating a gradual reduction in dependency on a narrow set of export products or markets. This trend suggests that Tunisia's export structure is becoming more diversified and resilient. It could be an important strategic asset as the country seeks to integrate into a broader African free trade area. Meanwhile, the import concentration index remains low and relatively stable, signalling that Tunisia already maintains a diverse set of import sources. This stability could be leveraged to further develop intra-African trade partnerships or to gradually replace extra-continental imports with more competitive regional suppliers under AfCFTA frameworks.

On the diversification front, the export diversification index shows a long-term downward trend, though it still remains higher than that of imports. This decline may reflect structural or competitiveness limitations in Tunisia's export sectors.

[11] The concentration index is derived from the Herfindahl-Hirschman Index (HHI). A value close to 1 indicates high concentration (i.e., trade is dominated by few products), while a value closer to 0 indicates a more balanced and diverse trade structure.

[12] The diversification index ranges from 0 to 1: a lower value indicates that the country's exports are more diversified and similar to global patterns, while a higher value reflects a more concentrated or specialised export basket.

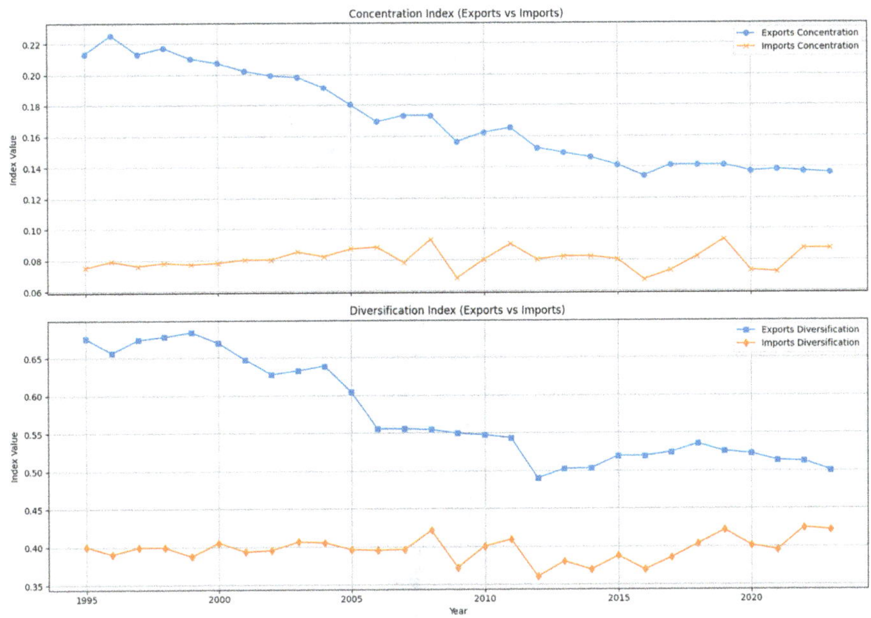

Fig. 5.10 Trade structure evolution of Tunisia (1995–2023): concentration and diversification trends. Source: Author's elaboration based on data from the UNCTADstat database

However, AfCFTA presents a strong opportunity to reverse this trajectory. Access to a wider range of African markets could stimulate export diversification, particularly in higher value-added manufacturing or service sectors. The relatively stable import diversification index further suggests room for policy action. Overall, Tunisia is partially prepared for AfCFTA integration: it has made progress in reducing export concentration but still has room to deepen diversification.

Tunisia's Revealed Comparative Advantage (RCA)[13] compares the share of a product in Tunisia's total exports to the share of that same product in world exports. Figure 5.11 illustrates Tunisia's top 15 products with the highest RCA in 2023. Several of these products demonstrate a very strong specialisation, particularly in sectors such as agro-processing (e.g., fixed vegetable oils, margarine), electrical equipment (e.g., metres and distribution devices), textiles and apparel, and non-metallic mineral products (e.g., cork and cement). The remarkably high RCA values (many exceeding 10, and some even above 15) suggest that Tunisia holds a clear and robust advantage in exporting these goods compared to the global average. These products, therefore, represent Tunisia's most export-competitive segments. They could be scaled and promoted under the AfCFTA to access broader African markets with reduced tariffs and harmonised regulations.

Figure 5.12 highlights Tunisia's top 15 export products with high potential towards African markets as projected for 2029. Each box's size represents the total

[13] An RCA value greater than 1 indicates that Tunisia is relatively more specialised or competitive in exporting that product compared to the world average.

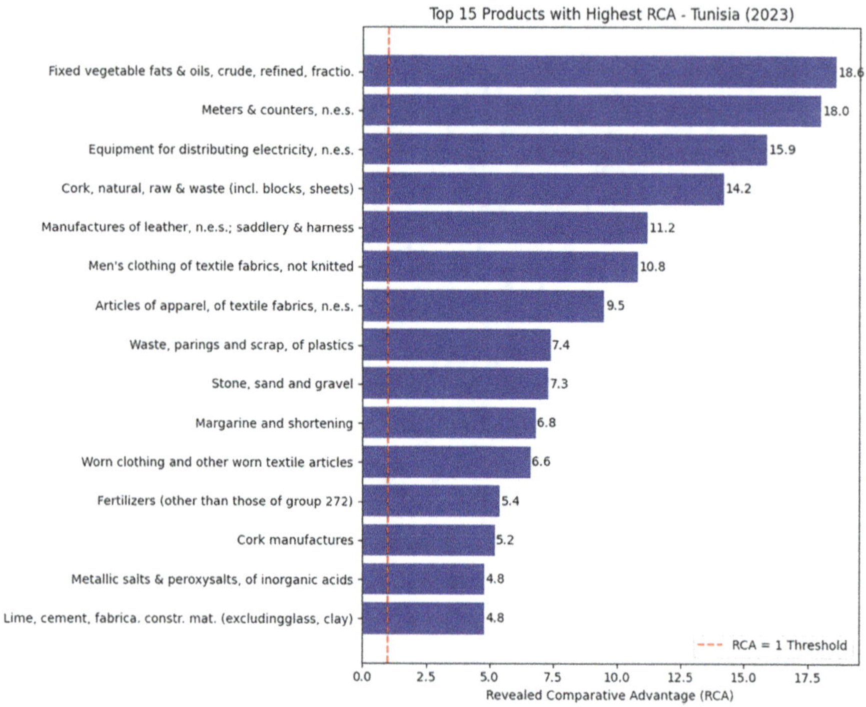

Fig. 5.11 Tunisia's top 15 products by revealed comparative advantage (2023). Source: Author's elaboration based on data from the UNCTADstat database

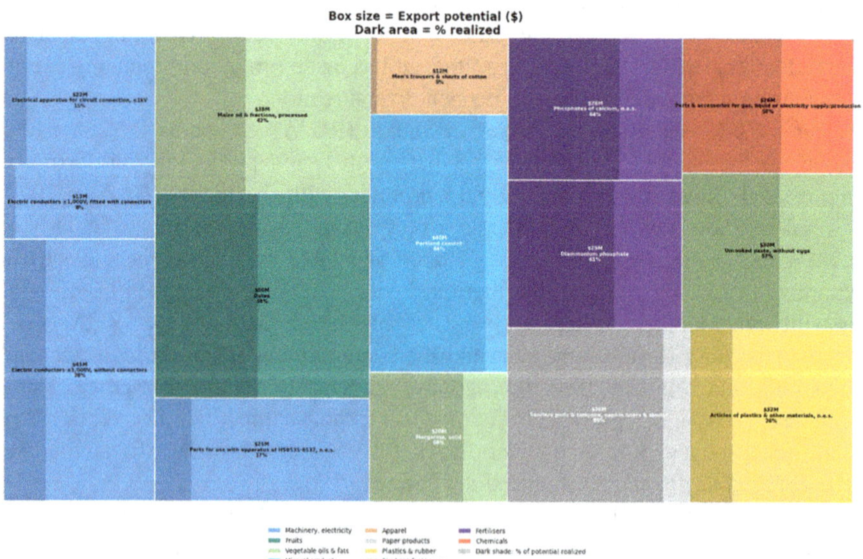

Fig. 5.12 Tunisia's top 15 products with highest export potential to Africa (projected for 2029). Source: Author's elaboration using data from the Trade Map (International Trade Centre, ITC)

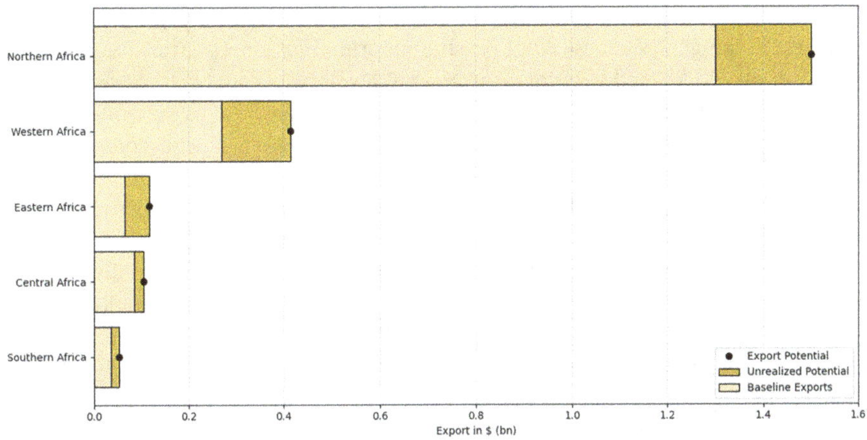

Fig. 5.13 Markets with potential for Tunisia's exports (estimate for 2029). Source: Author's elaboration using data from the Trade Map (International Trade Centre, ITC)

export potential in USD (e.g., USD 50 M for dates), while the dark-shaded portion shows how much of that potential has already been realised. Products such as Portland cement (84% realised), sanitary pads and related paper products (85%), and phosphates (64%) exhibit strong current performance, indicating Tunisia's competitiveness in these sectors. In contrast, several industrial goods like electric conductors and circuit components show low realisation rates (e.g., 28% or less), signalling substantial untapped opportunities. In the context of AfCFTA, this visualisation reveals Tunisia's sectoral diversity and export expansion prospects across the continent: from agro-industrial products (dates, margarine, maize oil) to industrial and chemical goods (plastic items, fertilisers, electrical components).

Figure 5.13 illustrates Tunisia's export potential across African sub-regions. It highlights both current export levels (baseline exports) and unrealised potential. Northern Africa stands out as the largest market, with an export potential of USD 1.5 billion, of which USD 1.3 billion is already realised, leaving USD 794 million in untapped opportunities. Western Africa follows, with a potential of USD 415 million, of which only USD 268 million has been achieved. Other regions, Eastern, Central, and Southern Africa, have smaller absolute values but still represent considerable gaps relative to their size, especially Eastern Africa, where almost 90% of the potential remains untapped. The unrealised potential across regions, particularly in West, East, and Central Africa, can be strategically pursued through trade facilitation, reduction of non-tariff barriers, and targeted support to exporters in high-potential sectors (e.g., agri-food, textiles, electrical components).

There are several potential AfCFTA opportunities for Tunisia beyond increasing trade, such as regional value chain integration, investment attraction, industrial diversification, and SME expansion, which were discussed in the previous sections of this chapter. However, it is also essential to highlight additional benefits, including job creation and enhanced supply chain resilience. As regional integration stimulates industrial activity, particularly in manufacturing, agro-processing, and logistics, it can generate new employment opportunities across various skill levels. Arouri et al. (2020) find that small firms in a developing country, such as Tunisia, play a key role in the creation of new jobs. This supports inclusive economic growth, reduces unemployment, especially among youth and women, and contributes to further poverty reduction. In North Africa, poverty rates are significantly lower than in other African regions, with less than 3% of the population living in extreme poverty (compared to 41.1% in Sub-Saharan Africa). While the AfCFTA's direct poverty reduction impact may be less dramatic in North Africa due to already low poverty levels, its indirect effects through trade, investment, and job creation remain important for enhancing inclusive growth. Regarding employment, AfCFTA is expected to generate substantial gains across the continent by 2035, with a 10.3% increase in wages for unskilled workers and 10.5% for women, especially in agriculture and female labour-intensive sectors (WB, 2020). Tunisia has shown engagement with labour provisions in the AfCFTA, although broader evidence suggests that the impact of such trade agreements on improving labour conditions has been limited to date (DTDA, 2024).

Moreover, the AfCFTA offers Tunisia a chance to enhance supply chain resilience by diversifying sourcing partners within the continent (ElGanainy et al., 2023). The COVID-19 crisis illustrated the vulnerability of Tunisia's Eurocentric trade model: GDP growth, already modest at 0.9% in 2019, collapsed by 8.8% in 2020 as lockdowns abroad disrupted inputs, tourism revenues, and offshore production chains (Marouani et al., 2022). Imports of intermediate and final goods fell sharply, particularly in the offshore regime, highlighting Tunisia's dependence on a narrow set of external suppliers (Medini & Baghdadi, 2024). By fostering shorter and more diversified regional supply chains, AfCFTA could help Tunisia cushion similar shocks in the future. For example, if African sourcing networks had been more developed during COVID-19, Tunisia could have substituted some disrupted European inputs with African ones. In this way, AfCFTA is not just a trade agreement but also a strategic insurance mechanism against external crises, providing both immediate trade cost reductions and, in the longer term, a framework for deeper integration, structural reforms, and greater resilience (WB, 2020).

5.5 AfCFTA Implementation: Strategic Challenges and Pathways

5.5.1 *Readiness and Institutional Landscape*

Including trade facilitation measures alongside tariff and NTM reductions significantly boosts Tunisia's projected income gains under the AfCFTA, from 4% (tariffs + NTMs) to 6% when trade facilitation is added. This falls slightly below the overall AfCFTA average of 7.2% (WB, 2020). To reinforce these insights, ElGanainy et al.

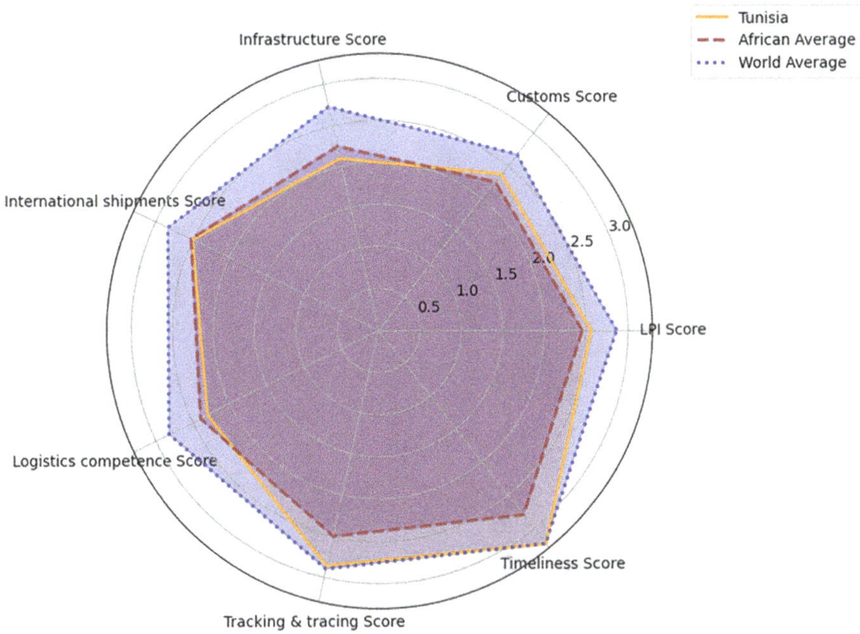

Fig. 5.14 Tunisia vs African and world averages—LPI dimensions (2018). Source: Author's elaboration based on data from the World Bank's Logistics Performance Index (LPI) database

(2023) find that the gains from tariff cuts and NTM reductions under the AfCFTA become significantly greater when combined with improvements in the trade environment. It boosts intra-African trade by 53% (compared to 15% without such improvements). This highlights the critical role of a supportive trade environment in maximising the agreement's impact.

Figure 5.14 provides a comparative overview of Tunisia's logistics performance across key dimensions. Tunisia scores above the African average in nearly every dimension, particularly in Customs, Tracking & Tracing, and Timeliness, key indicators of a well-functioning logistics system. This is critical for implementing AfCFTA commitments, such as reducing non-tariff barriers and ensuring trade facilitation. However, Tunisia still lags behind the world average, particularly in Infrastructure and Logistics Competence. These gaps suggest institutional and operational challenges that could hinder the country's ability to fully leverage AfCFTA opportunities, particularly in managing more complex, time-sensitive trade networks.

It is also important to consider broader regulatory and administrative factors captured by the Ease of Doing Business indicators. While LPI focuses on the efficiency of logistics and cross-border trade, the Ease of Doing Business framework provides a complementary perspective by assessing the overall business environment, including starting a business, obtaining permits, and enforcing contracts. The comparison of Ease of Doing Business rankings between 2000 and 2019 (Fig. 5.15) highlights

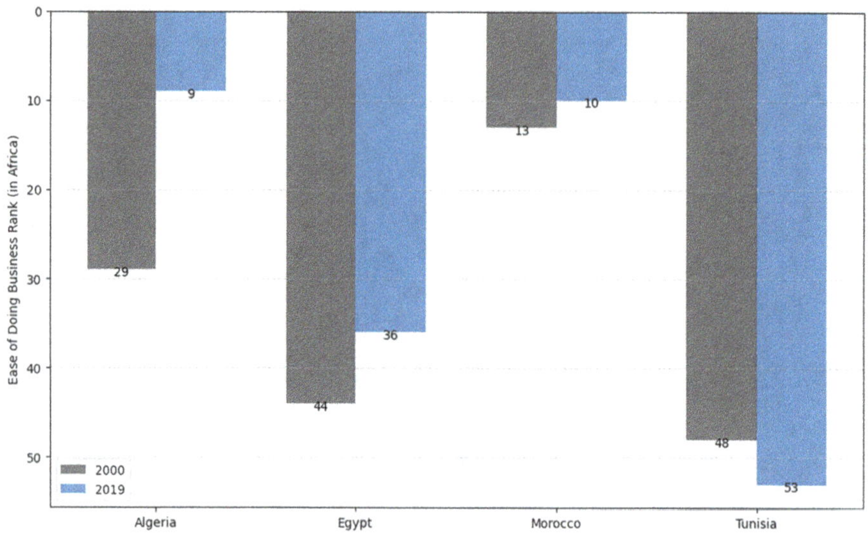

Fig. 5.15 Ease of doing business African ranking comparison (2000 vs 2019). Source: Author's elaboration using Afreximbank data

diverging institutional trajectories among North African countries. Morocco and Algeria demonstrate significant progress, improving their rankings by 3 and 20 places respectively. Egypt also shows moderate advancement, gaining eight positions. In contrast, Tunisia stands out for its declining performance, falling from 48th to 53rd place in the African ranking. A substantial administrative burden made worse by outdated or poorly designed legislative and institutional frameworks (Raga, 2022; UGTT, 2021). This erosion of business environment quality over nearly two decades suggests growing structural or administrative constraints, which may hinder Tunisia's ability to fully leverage the benefits of the AfCFTA. Tunisia's relative deterioration in doing business conditions signals an urgent need for regulatory and institutional reforms, as these are key elements that influence investment and private sector growth.

In addition to the regulatory environment captured by the Ease of Doing Business indicators, the quality of governance offers deeper insights into institutional effectiveness, the rule of law, and control of corruption, all of which critically shape the business and investment climate. In Fig. 5.16, the comparative governance indicators presented for Tunisia, the African average, and the world average in 2023 offer key insights into the country's institutional readiness for implementing the AfCFTA. Tunisia exhibits relatively stronger performance in Voice and Accountability and Regulatory Quality compared to the African average, though both remain negative, indicating structural fragility. Conversely, indicators such as Control of Corruption, Government Effectiveness, Rule of Law, and Political Stability are significantly below the world average and closely aligned, or even worse, than the African average. This suggests persistent institutional bottlenecks

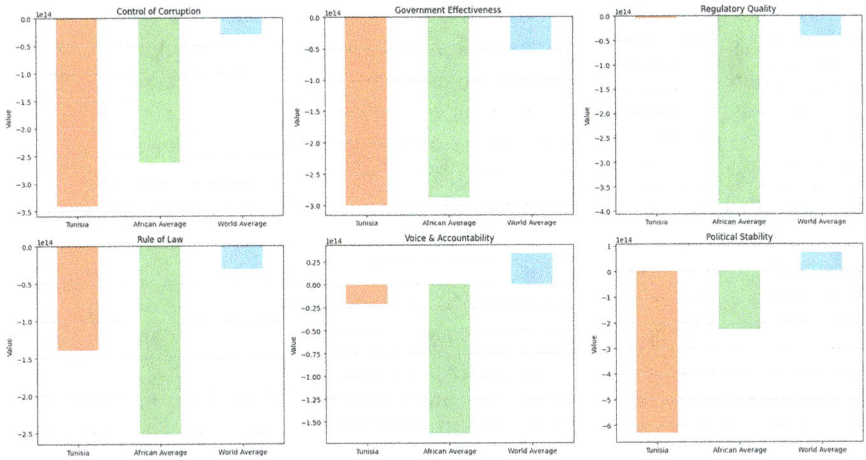

Fig. 5.16 Tunisia governance indicators (2023). Source: Author's elaboration based on data from the Worldwide Governance Indicators (WGI) database, developed by the World Bank

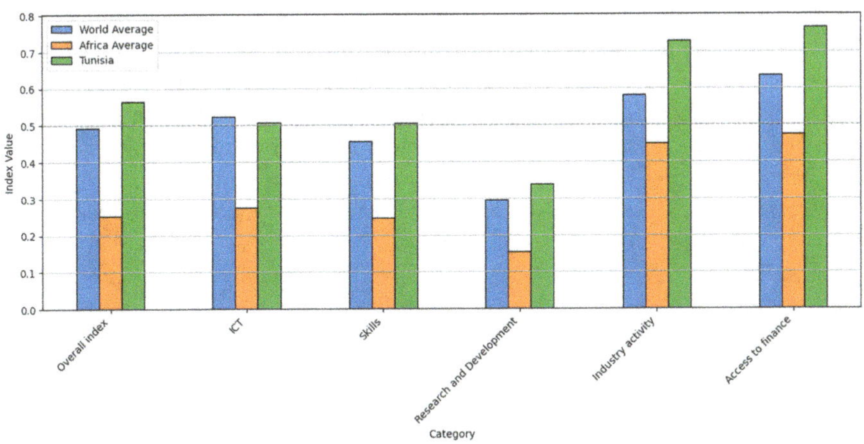

Fig. 5.17 Tunisia innovation index by category (2021). Source: Author's elaboration using data from the Global Innovation Index 2021 (WIPO, INSEAD, and Cornell University)

that may hinder transparent trade facilitation, investor confidence, and regulatory coherence within the AfCFTA framework.

Beyond governance quality, a country's capacity for innovation provides further insight into its potential for long-term competitiveness, technological advancement, and value-added production. Figure 5.17 illustrates Tunisia's performance across six key innovation-related institutional dimensions in 2021, compared to both the African and global averages. Tunisia outperforms the African average in every category, with particularly strong results in Access to Finance and Industry Activity, where its scores even exceed the global average. This indicates a relatively robust enabling environment for entrepreneurship, investment, and industrial growth. In areas such as skills and ICT, Tunisia closely aligns with global benchmarks. Tunisia is positioning itself as a digitally capable and moderately skilled economy (Dhaoui & Kasdallah, 2024; Raga, 2022).

However, Fig. 5.17 reveals relative institutional weaknesses in Research and Development (R&D), where Tunisia lags behind the global average and only slightly surpasses the African mean. This suggests that while the country is structurally ready to benefit from AfCFTA in terms of infrastructure, access to finance, and industrial base, further investment in innovation systems and scientific research is needed to fully harness long-term competitiveness. Strengthening its R&D ecosystem would help Tunisia move beyond low- and mid-tech production towards high-value activities. This will make it not just a participant but a leader in the AfCFTA landscape.

In support of the effective implementation of the AfCFTA, several key instruments have been developed to benefit Tunisia, fostering a unified and operational African market. These include the African Trade Observatory (ATO), which provides data and monitoring tools for intra-African trade flows; the AfCFTA electronic tariff book, which offers transparent and accessible tariff information for all member states; the mechanism for monitoring, notification, and elimination of non-tariff barriers (NTBs) to facilitate smoother trade; and the Pan-African Payment and Settlement System (PAPSS), which enables efficient cross-border transactions in local currencies. Together, these instruments enhance transparency, reduce trade costs, and strengthen institutional coordination across the continent. The ATO, launched by the African Union in 2019, aims to improve trade information and intelligence in Africa by ensuring that data from customs, ministries, and government agencies is automatically made public and accessible to all, especially the private sector (Bouzaine, 2023).

5.5.2 Constraints

The AfCFTA has been subject to criticism, particularly concerning its overall framework and the specific consequences it may hold for Tunisia (Africa, 2025; UGTT, 2021). Tunisia's AfCFTA implementation strategy notably lacks alignment with broader national development policies, a weakness acknowledged in its own SWOT analysis. The strategy prioritises the coordination of national and sectoral plans, yet the overall development process took approximately 2 years. This is significantly longer than countries like Cameroon and The Gambia, which completed theirs in under a year (UNECA, 2024).

Despite the strategic opportunities presented by the AfCFTA, Tunisia faces a series of constraints that are structural, institutional, logistical, and informational in nature. These are summarised below, each substantiated by evidence from earlier sections of this chapter:

Institutional and Regulatory Bottlenecks: Tunisia's declining Ease of Doing Business ranking (falling from 48th to 53rd in Africa between 2000 and 2019, Fig. 5.15) reflects persistent bureaucratic and administrative inefficiencies. Combined with weak governance indicators such as low scores on control of corruption and government effectiveness (Fig. 5.16), these weaknesses undermine investor confidence and reduce the transparency required for effective AfCFTA implementation.

Fragmented Trade Facilitation Infrastructure: Although Tunisia performs above the African average in the Logistics Performance Index (LPI), it remains below world standards, particularly in infrastructure and logistics competence (Fig. 5.14). These gaps constrain Tunisia's ability to handle time-sensitive intra-African trade and integrate into regional value chains, especially in transport corridors linking landlocked or underserved areas.

Private Sector Disengagement and Financial Constraints: National training campaigns have been implemented to raise awareness among the private sector (Ministère du Commerce (Tunisie), 2025a). However, many SMEs remain unable to penetrate African markets due to limited access to trade finance and technical assistance. This is consistent with findings that FDI inflows have declined by 18.5% by 2019, reflecting an uneven distribution of financial resources (Raga, 2022). Without targeted support, smaller exporters remain excluded from AfCFTA opportunities.

Informational and Data Gaps: Despite the availability of tools such as the African Trade Observatory (ATO) and the AfCFTA NTB reporting mechanism, their use by Tunisian firms lacks awareness of rules of origin and customs processes, as shown by persistent delays in certification and underutilisation of preferential trade agreements (Rouis & Tabor, 2012). Low digital capacity further prevents SMEs from leveraging real-time market intelligence, which inhibits their ability to navigate continental trade procedures.

Tariff Schedule and Rules of Origin Delays: Tunisia passed legislation to establish a National AfCFTA Implementation Committee, yet delays in submitting its tariff concession schedule persist (UNECA, 2024). At the continental level, unresolved negotiations on key rules of origin, particularly in textiles and automotive parts (Bouzaine, 2023), create uncertainty for Tunisian firms seeking to plan production and exports under AfCFTA rules.

Limited Industrial and Regional Linkages: As Figs. 5.3, 5.4, and 5.5 demonstrate, Tunisia's integration into African regional value chains remains shallow, with domestic value added (DVX) exports concentrated in only a few countries (Morocco, Algeria, South Africa) and many sectors marginal. Strong backward linkages (imports of African intermediate goods) contrast with weak forward linkages (exports of Tunisian inputs), highlighting Tunisia's constrained role in regional production networks.

Overdependence on EU Trade: Tunisia's trade structure remains dominated by Eurocentric value chains. Figures 5.2 and 5.5 clearly show that intermediate goods trade with Europe is several times larger than with Africa, with African flows rarely exceeding USD 400 million. This reflects Tunisia's historical role as a hub for European industries, particularly in textiles and electronics. Such dependence may create "path inertia", discouraging reallocation of trade capacity towards African partners under AfCFTA.

5.5.3 Pathways for Tunisia in the AfCFTA Context

On May 25, marking Africa Day, Tunisia took part in the first successful shipment under the AfCFTA's "Guided Trade" initiative, signalling a new phase of South-South cooperation and African economic integration. This milestone sparked the interest of several Tunisian firms, with 10 companies initially engaging in exports under AfCFTA rules. By October 2023, a total of 19 export operations had been conducted to Ghana, Cameroon, and Tanzania across sectors like construction, agri-food, and chemicals, benefiting from reduced customs duties (GIZ, 2024).

To fully leverage the opportunities of the AfCFTA and overcome the constraints outlined above, Tunisia must pursue a multidimensional strategy that combines institutional strengthening, private sector support, and regional value chain development. These pathways aim not only to increase trade volumes but also to foster structural transformation, industrial upgrading, and inclusive growth.

Strengthening institutional and regulatory capacities: Tunisia should focus on activating its AfCFTA Implementation Committee, aligning national laws with AfCFTA protocols, and advancing key trade reforms to improve transparency, reduce barriers, and strengthen its position as a regional trade hub.

Developing RVCs in strategic sectors: Tunisia should identify and invest in high-potential sectors with comparative advantages and latent export capacity, such as agro-processing, electrical equipment, construction materials, and light manufacturing. Deepening forward and backward linkages with African partners in these sectors would allow Tunisia to move up the value chain and reduce dependency on European markets.

Expanding trade facilitation and logistics infrastructure: Addressing infrastructure gaps, particularly in logistics competence and intermodal transport, is crucial for reducing trade costs and improving timeliness. Tunisia should prioritise investments in port modernisation, inland logistics zones, and digital customs systems. Participation in regional transport corridors and cross-border infrastructure projects can position Tunisia as a transit gateway between North, West, and Sub-Saharan Africa.

Mobilising the private sector and supporting SMEs: To ensure that AfCFTA benefits are widely shared, Tunisia must expand technical assistance, access to finance, and market intelligence tools for SMEs and emerging exporters. This includes scaling up training campaigns, encouraging the use of platforms like the African Trade Observatory, and promoting e-commerce channels for regional trade.

Business councils and export promotion agencies should also play a proactive role in matchmaking with African buyers.

Reducing labour market vulnerabilities and supporting inclusion: Given the dual nature of Tunisia's labour market, any trade strategy must integrate active labour policies, skills development, and formalisation incentives. Vocational training aligned with AfCFTA-target sectors (e.g., agro-processing, transport, services) and inclusive labour market institutions will be key to ensuring employment gains reach vulnerable populations, especially youth, women, and informal workers.

Leveraging digital trade and innovation systems: Tunisia's relatively strong performance in digital infrastructure, ICT skills, and access to finance positions it to lead in AfCFTA digital integration. Promoting cross-border e-commerce, digital customs clearance, and electronic certification of origin can streamline trade flows. Tunisia can also act as a regional hub for innovation in fintech and logistics tech by investing further in research, business incubators, and public-private digital partnerships.

Promoting strategic diplomacy and regional alliances: Tunisia must elevate its diplomatic engagement with African regional economic communities (RECs) and AfCFTA institutions. Active participation in AfCFTA rule-making, dispute resolution, and trade capacity-building programmes will enable Tunisia to shape outcomes that align with its industrial priorities and regional ambitions. Building strategic alliances with countries such as Egypt, Côte d'Ivoire, and Morocco, identified as key value chain partners, can also enhance trade complementarities and bargaining power.

5.6 Conclusion: Towards a New Trade Vision for Tunisia

Tunisia's accession to the AfCFTA marks a pivotal shift in the country's external economic policy, a strategic opportunity to rebalance its trade orientation beyond traditional Euro-Mediterranean ties. Despite its historical dependence on European markets, Tunisia's growing engagement with African integration frameworks presents a platform for long-term transformation. Through AfCFTA, Tunisia can reposition itself as a competitive, resilient, and regionally embedded economy by expanding market access, promoting intra-African trade, and strengthening regional value chains.

However, realising this potential requires overcoming a complex set of structural and institutional challenges. These include limited infrastructure capacity, regulatory inefficiencies, an underperforming logistics ecosystem, fragmented trade facilitation mechanisms, and a labour market weighed down by informality and youth unemployment. Moreover, Tunisia's delayed implementation of AfCFTA provisions, such as its tariff offer and rules of origin, signals the need for more coordinated and timely policy responses. Without resolving these constraints, the country risks marginalisation within Africa's emerging trade architecture.

The analysis in this chapter shows that Tunisia already possesses several competitive advantages. Its diversified manufacturing base, favourable geographic location, and moderate performance in digital and financial infrastructure provide a foundation for scaling up exports to African markets. Sectoral analysis highlights promising opportunities in agro-processing, light manufacturing, and intermediate goods, particularly in areas where Tunisia already enjoys a revealed comparative advantage. With focused investment, capacity building, and institutional coordination, these advantages can be leveraged to integrate Tunisia more deeply into African production networks.

Tunisia's new trade vision must also be inclusive. AfCFTA's benefits will only be meaningful if they extend beyond large exporters and reach small and medium enterprises, workers in the informal economy, and marginalised regions. This requires coupling trade reforms with active labour policies, support for SME formalisation, and targeted training for the youth and women who form the backbone of Tunisia's workforce. A truly transformative trade strategy must be anchored in both competitiveness and equity.

Ultimately, Tunisia's engagement with the AfCFTA offers a window to redefine its place in the global economy, from a peripheral assembly hub serving European markets to a central actor in Africa's industrial future. The pathway forward lies in strategic diversification, regional cooperation, and institutional modernisation. If approached holistically, the AfCFTA can be more than a trade agreement for Tunisia, it can serve as a catalyst for a new era of sustainable and inclusive development.

References

Africa, K. (2025). Assessing five years of the African continental free trade area (AfCFTA): Proposals on potential amendments (No. 215).

Arouri, H., Youssef, A. B., & Quatraro, F. (2020). The dynamics of high-growth firms: Evidence from Tunisia. *Eurasian Business Review, 6*(3), 323–337. https://doi.org/10.1007/S40821-016-0064-2

Baghdadi, L., Ben Kheder, S., & Arouri, H. (2019). Impact of nontariff measures on firms in Tunisia. *Review of Development Economics, 23*(4), 1562–1579. https://doi.org/10.1111/RODE.12600; REQUESTEDJOURNAL:JOURNAL:14679361;WGROUP:STRING:PUBLICATION

Beckman, J., Johnson, M. E., & Ivanic, M. (2024). Agriculture and AfCFTA: NTM reductions increase intra-Africa trade. *Agricultural Economics*. https://doi.org/10.1111/AGEC.12815

Belhaj, M. R. (2023). Spécificités des règles d'origine ZLECAf.

Bouzaine, F. (2023). Accélération de la mise-en-oeuvre de l'Accord ZLECAf: Quel est le rôle des douanes?

Dhaoui, S., & Kasdallah, E. (2024). *Analyse de performance et essai d'évaluation de l'adhésion de la Tunisie à la ZLECAf: Application d'un modèle de gravité augmenté*.

DTDA. (2024). *Labour market profile Tunisia-2023/2024*. Danish Trade Union Development Agency. http://www.ulandssekretariatet

ElGanainy, A. A., Hakobyan, S., Liu, F., Weisfeld, H., Abbas, A., Allard, C., Balima, H. W., Bteish, C., Giri, R., Meleshchuk, S., Ramirez, G., Zymek, R., Arora, V. B., Lall, S., Kett, B. R., & Pohl, M. M. (2023). Trade integration in Africa.

Fusacchia, I., Balié, J., & Salvatici, L. (2022). The AfCFTA impact on agricultural and food trade: A value added perspective. *European Review of Agricultural Economics, 49*(1), 237–284. https://doi.org/10.1093/ERAE/JBAB046

Garcés, I., & Vogt, A. (2024). Global value chain integration and non-tariff measures. *Economics Letters, 235*, 111518. https://doi.org/10.1016/J.ECONLET.2024.111518

Gathii, J. T. (2019). Agreement establishing the African continental free trade area. *International Legal Materials, 58*(5), 1028–1083. https://doi.org/10.1017/ILM.2019.41

Ghali, S., Zitouna, H., Karray, Z., & Driss, S. (2013). *Effects of NTMS on the extensive and intensive margins to trade: The CASE of Tunisia and Egypt*. http://ssrn.com/abstract=2374780

Ghodsi, M., & Stehrer, R. (2022). Non-tariff measures and the quality of imported products. *World Trade Review, 21*(1), 71–92. https://doi.org/10.1017/S1474745621000392

GIZ. (2024). *Support for Trade Agreements with Africa*.

Guedidi, I. (2025). The impact of the AfCFTA on agricultural trade and welfare in Africa: General and partial equilibrium effects. In the United Nations. Economic Commission for Africa. Subregional office East Africa (SRO-EA); United Nations. https://repository.uneca.org/handle/10855/50376

Hoekman, B., Ng, F., & Olarreaga, M. (2004). Agricultural tariffs or subsidies: Which are more important for developing economies? *The World Bank Economic Review, 18*(2), 175–204. https://doi.org/10.1093/WBER/LHH037

Marouani, M. A., Krafft, C., Assaad, R., Kennedy, S., Cheung, R., Latifi, A. D., & Wojcieszynski, E. (2022). *Tunisia COVID-19 country case study*. Working Papers. https://ideas.repec.org/p/erg/wpaper/sprr20223.html

Medini, A., & Baghdadi, L. (2024). COVID-19 shock on supply chains: Evidence from a developing country. *Journal of Industrial and Business Economics, 52*(1), 59–80. https://doi.org/10.1007/S40812-024-00307-2/FIGURES/3

Ministère du Commerce (Tunisie). (2023). *Conférence de sensibilisation de la Direction générale des douanes sur l'Accord instituant la Zone de libre échange continentale africaine (ZLECAf) à Tunis le 06.05.2023 et Ras Jdir 05.07.2023 - Accords commerciaux avec l'Afrique*. Ministère Du Commerce Tunisien. https://africatradeagreements.tn/fr/actualites/conference-de-sensibilisation-de-la-direction-generale-des-douanes-sur-laccord-instituant-la-zone-de-libre-echange-continentale-africaine-zlecaf-a-tunis-le-06-05-2023-et-ras-jdir-05-07-2023/

Ministère du Commerce (Tunisie). (2025a). Formation sur l'accord et les outils de la ZLECAf: Accompagner les entreprises tunisiennes vers les opportunités africaines - Accords commerciaux avec l'Afrique. Ministère Du Commerce Tunisien. https://africatradeagreements.tn/fr/actualites/formation-sur-laccord-et-les-outils-de-la-zlecaf-accompagner-les-entreprises-tunisiennes-vers-les-opportunites-africaines/

Ministère du Commerce (Tunisie). (2025b). *La ZLECAf renforce les capacités douanières des pays d'Afrique du Nord et de l'Ouest à travers un atelier régional sur les Opérateurs Économiques Agréés (OEA) - Accords commerciaux avec l'Afrique*. Ministère Du Commerce Tunisien. https://africatradeagreements.tn/fr/actualites/la-zlecaf-renforce-les-capacites-douanieres-des-pays-dafrique-du-nord-et-de-louest-a-travers-un-atelier-regional-sur-les-operateurs-economiques-agrees-oea/

Raga, S. (2022). Tunisia: Macroeconomic and trade profile opportunities and challenges towards implementation of AfCFTA.

Rouis, M., & Tabor, S. (2012). *Regional economic integration in the Middle East and North Africa: Beyond trade reform*. https://books.google.com/books?hl=fr&lr=&id=2Uu5Y1bgRksC&oi=fnd&pg=PP2&dq=Regional+Economic+Integration+in+the+Middle+East+and+North+Africa+mustapha&ots=xGi8n_amCa&sig=mujFjmrtvdbQFtqtQGlPxGYEurE

Sammoud, I., & Dhaoui, S. (2019). The Tunisian integration into global value chains the role of offshore regime & FDI. EMNES Working Paper, No. 21. https://south.euneighbours.eu/wp-content/uploads/2022/07/EMNES-Working-Paper-21-1.pdf

TRALAC. (2024). *Status of AfCFTA ratification*. Tralac Trade Law Centre. https://www.tralac.org/resources/infographic/13795-status-of-afcfta-ratification.html?utm_source.com

UGTT. (2021). Trade unions in AfCFTA: The issues of the AfCFTA agreement in Tunisia and its impact on the Tunisian general labour union (UGTT).

UNECA. (2024). AfCFTA implementation strategies.

WB. (2020). *The African continental free trade area: Economic and distributional effects*.

Chapter 6
Exploring the Implementation of the AfCFTA in Morocco: Challenges, Lessons, and Way Forward

Nabil Boubrahimi and Azzedine Ghoufrane

Abstract This chapter examines the opportunities, constraints, and strategic orientations associated with the implementation of the African Continental Free Trade Area (AfCFTA) in Morocco. It highlights Morocco's positioning within the dynamics of African integration, assessing both the country's strengths and the challenges it faces in contributing to the objectives of Agenda 2063 and in successfully incorporating AfCFTA provisions into its trade policy. The analysis emphasises Morocco's key assets—such as its geostrategic location, investment capacity, renewable energy potential, and proactive South–South cooperation—while also underscoring structural constraints, including insufficient integration into African regional value chains, limited productive capacities, regulatory fragmentation, and regional security risks. Drawing on flagship initiatives such as the Atlantic Initiative, the Morocco–Nigeria Gas Pipeline, and OCP's agricultural partnerships, the chapter explores how Morocco can serve as a catalyst for the development of continental value chains in critical sectors, including food security, energy transition, digitalization, and industrial value chain integration. It further identifies the institutional and legal prerequisites for effective implementation, with particular emphasis on governance, private sector involvement, and harmonisation with AfCFTA protocols. Ultimately, this chapter argues that Morocco's active engagement in the AfCFTA is essential for deepening regional integration, fostering inclusive growth, and redefining Africa's partnerships in line with sustainable development priorities.

Keywords AfCFTA · WTO · Morocco · Regional integration · Agenda 2063 · Food Security · Energy transition · South–South cooperation · Africa's development strategy

---

N. Boubrahimi (✉)
Ibn Tofail University, Kenitra, Morocco
e-mail: nabil.boubrahimi@uit.ac.ma

A. Ghoufrane
Mohammed V University, Rabat, Morocco
e-mail: a.ghoufrane@um5r.ac.ma

D. N. Yuni et al. (eds.), *From Policy to Practice: Challenges and Ways Forward on the Implementation of the AfCFTA*,
https://doi.org/10.1007/978-3-032-14051-7_6

6.1 Introduction

Regional economic integration is one of the main levers for accelerating growth and development. This process stands as a top priority in Africa's development strategy, where free trade between African countries represents one of the cornerstones of the African Union's Agenda 2063 (UNECA, 2021, 2023).

Indeed, integration offers promising prospects in terms of strengthening political and economic cooperation, promoting intra-regional trade, boosting job creation, improving the attractiveness of foreign capital, fostering the internationalisation of industrialisation drivers, and balancing external trade accounts. Geographic regions that are the most integrated possess the strongest assets to accelerate wealth creation and to enhance the resilience of their productive systems in the face of external shocks and the recessionary effects of global economic slowdowns.

From this perspective, developing a national strategy specific to the implementation of the African Continental Free Trade Area (AfCFTA) Agreement is essential to unlocking the keys to success. This has been endorsed and encouraged by numerous African governance bodies, including the 51st Conference of African Ministers of Finance, Planning and Economic Development held in May 2018.

In this context, the implementation of the AfCFTA for Morocco is necessary, based on a comprehensive and in-depth analysis of the evolution of the multidimensional relations between the Kingdom of Morocco and other African countries, as well as the country's positioning within this partnership framework. This notably involves identifying the obstacles to deepening continental integration, exploring ways to harness the potential for progress, and thoroughly restructuring Morocco's cooperative ties with key regional actors.

6.2 Situational Analysis of the AfCFTA and Development for Morocco in Terms of Opportunities and Risks

In the wake of Agenda 2063, the effective implementation of the African Continental Free Trade Area (AfCFTA) represents a crucial phase in the process of achieving genuine African economic integration. This structuring project has set itself several key objectives: the establishment of a single market for goods and services, the facilitation of capital and people flows, and the laying of the foundations for a continental customs union. The Kingdom of Morocco, which has made Africa's socio-economic development a top strategic priority, was among the first countries to sign the AfCFTA agreement.

Some African states have successfully taken major steps forward in their development processes, launching promising dynamics of democratic consolidation and socio-economic progress. These countries have adopted a proactive approach to structural reforms aimed at promoting social inclusion, harnessing growth potential, and laying the groundwork for long-term prosperity (Marcel Felicity Nagar, 2021).

Africa's human capital, the quality of its natural resources, its rich cultural heritage, and agricultural capacity are all assets that should make the continent one of the world's leading regional growth poles.

However, Africa still faces numerous challenges, including social inequalities, territorial disparities, high unemployment and poverty rates, migration flows, insecurity and armed conflicts, and the effects of climate change. Building a prosperous Africa based on inclusive growth and sustainable development requires the endogenisation of development models, the acceleration of regional integration, the revitalisation of economic diversification, and the activation of synergies and productive complementarities (Justin et al., 2020).

Morocco's African anchoring will enable it to capitalise on current global economic reconfigurations, contribute to the catch-up dynamics of African countries, accelerate the regional integration process, and support the development of a new model of continental cooperation. This new partnership framework should make it possible to better harness development potential and improve the positioning of African countries in a rapidly evolving international system.

6.3 Highlighting Morocco's Assets and Opportunities within the AfCFTA Framework

The situational analysis of the African Continental Free Trade Area (AfCFTA), applied to the context of Morocco-Africa relations, highlights the key elements emerging from a comprehensive and multidimensional assessment. Several dimensions of the AfCFTA member countries partnership are taken into account, including socio-economic, political, security, migration-related aspects, as well as those related to human development, regional integration, and the digital and environmental transitions.

These factual aspects either serve as levers for a new framework of commercial and regulatory cooperation between Morocco and Africa within the AfCFTA or represent blocking factors (weaknesses likely to exacerbate the risks and threats arising from the implementation of the AfCFTA).

In this regard, it is evident that Morocco's relationships with its African partners who have signed the AfCFTA are characterised by undeniable strengths, particularly regarding the evolution of cooperation, which is moving from a narrow, trade-centric approach to a broader, more integrated model. This model encompasses new areas of cooperation within a comprehensive agreement framework, including sustainable development, intellectual property, the inclusion of women and youth in the labour market, large-scale investment projects, climate change, and renewable energy.

One of Morocco's major assets in implementing the AfCFTA is the sustainable reinforcement of a win–win partnership with African countries, centred on constant efforts to enhance the quality of trade and investment relations.

Morocco's Atlantic Initiative reflects a visionary ambition aimed at fostering sustainable, inclusive, and shared prosperity for both the Kingdom and the West African Atlantic countries. This vision is operationalised through strategic and innovative projects that address economic, energy, political, and climate-related challenges, while reinforcing Morocco's role as a key driver of Africa's development.

- Nigeria-Morocco gas pipeline: Launched in 2016, this flagship project spans over 5700 km along the West African coast, connecting Nigeria's gas resources to Morocco and Europe through Spain. With an estimated investment of USD 25 billion, it will supply up to 40 billion m^3 annually and benefit 14 African countries, including landlocked states such as Mali and Niger.
- Dakhla atlantic port: With an initial investment of MAD 12.5 billion, the port includes facilities for trade, fisheries, and shipbuilding. Strategically located, it will boost Morocco's southern provinces, improve trade flows across West Africa, support AfCFTA implementation, and facilitate access for African partners to the Atlantic Ocean as a gateway to global value chains.
- Renewable energy and industrial projects: Complementary initiatives in Laâyoune, Dakhla, and Guelmim—including green ammonia complexes, desalination plants, large-scale solar and wind farms, and industrial free zones—are designed to reinforce Morocco's position as a strategic hub for Africa's energy transition and industrial integration.

Morocco strengthens its role within the AfCFTA through a sustainable partnership with African countries, supported by strategic projects partly financed by the African Development Bank. Notable examples include the Noor Solar Complex in Ouarzazate, the hybrid power plant in Aïn Beni Mathar, the development of the Nador West Med port and industrial zone, as well as the Guercif–Nador highway. These initiatives demonstrate how Morocco leverages regional cooperation and multilateral financing to advance its energy and infrastructure development, thereby consolidating its comparative advantages within the continental market.

In terms of trade history, Morocco maintains a privileged commercial partnership with West Africa, both in terms of trade shares and investment flows, particularly in sectors such as banking and insurance, engineering, construction, fertiliser, and agri-food exports (e.g., meat and fish preparations), as well as machinery and electrical equipment. The recent shift towards engaging with Anglophone African countries further consolidates this partnership.

These elements are expected to serve as starting points for building a more solid and mutually beneficial partnership between Morocco and AfCFTA member countries, opening up new avenues for cooperation and development. Amplifying these strengths requires a high level of political will from Moroccan and African negotiators to sustain the integration process and foster mutual trust during the implementation of the AfCFTA provisions, ensuring the commitment of the involved countries.

The strengths of the current partnership between Morocco and its African partners should be further reinforced by capitalising on the opportunities presented through the AfCFTA. Changes in the economic, social, and institutional environment present significant opportunities that Morocco and its African partners must exploit to improve their partnership and harness the untapped potential that could deepen cooperation between Morocco and AfCFTA member countries.

Furthermore, broadening the scope of the AfCFTA agreement to include deeper areas of cooperation and integration is crucial for creating a, above all, a favourable investment climate for Moroccan ventures in Africa. This would support job creation, wealth generation, and, above all, the development of a new codevelopment model based on strategic projects. This broader cooperation approach is necessitated by geopolitical and geo-economic changes affecting global trade and the successive crises experienced worldwide.

Transitioning from a purely trade-based logic focused solely on trade exchanges and nonreciprocal preferences to new, reciprocal, and more inclusive frameworks—anchored in initiatives such as the Royal Atlantic Initiative, the Morocco-Nigeria Gas Pipeline, and major OCP investments in African food security—can stimulate long-term investment, socio-economic recovery, human development, youth and women inclusion in the labour market, good governance, the rule of law, shared prosperity, and digital transformation.

On the ground, there is undeniable, untapped aggregate potential in the complementarity between Morocco and its African partners. This potential should align with the new global economic configuration (involving China, India, Russia, the USA, etc.) and can be enhanced through shared values, historical affinities, and geographic proximity. Global shifts— such as advances in ICT, health sovereignty, food security, and the energy transition—can serve the Morocco-Africa cooperation framework under the AfCFTA.

In this sense, the objectives of Morocco and its African partners under the AfCFTA should aim to establish a new foundation for cooperation that effectively addresses the priorities of African countries during implementation of the agreement. Morocco's cooperation and integration strategy must stimulate socio-economic relations from a long-term, inclusive, and strategic perspective—through investment, trade, diplomacy, and collaboration—in priority areas such as human development, governance, the rule of law, prosperity, social inclusion, food security, and the digital and green transitions.

Finally, maximising the value of Africa's natural resources through regional value chains—where Morocco holds recognised expertise (e.g., agri-food, automotive, textiles and apparel)—could facilitate the development of fairer and more mutually beneficial trade flows between Morocco and its African partners, while also reducing development asymmetries. These are the orientations that could support the establishment of a win–win partnership framework.

Despite these strengths, Morocco–Africa partnerships face several constraints. Limited productive capacities, low economic diversification, and restricted tradable goods can hinder the development of African value chains. Weak engagement of civil society and intermediary institutions, along with regional insecurity and instability, further constrain trade and investment expansion.

6.4 Constraints to Overcome and Measures Required to Address Them

The partnership relations between Morocco and Africa face several vulnerabilities that negatively impact their economic, political, and institutional performance. These challenges necessitate a joint, in-depth, and coordinated reassessment of the mechanisms required to implement actions effectively within the framework of the AfCFTA.

Firstly, Morocco faces limitations in establishing African continental value chains, which constrain intra-African productive capacities in certain sectors and increase the dependence of both Morocco and its African partners on foreign markets, resulting from a lack of economic diversification (OCDE, 2022). This situation reduces the potential for trade in goods between Morocco and its African partners. The development of African value chains, in which Morocco could play a leading role, therefore depends on improving these capacities.

Second, the limited involvement of civil society and intermediary institutions (political parties, media, trade unions, NGOs) in Morocco-Africa strategies restricts the effectiveness of implemented policies. Morocco needs to strengthen the participation of these actors to ensure local and regional ownership of projects.

Third, persistent insecurity and instability in some African regions hinder the growth of trade and investment. Morocco must consider these risks and promote targeted, secure, and sustainable cooperation initiatives.

Fourth, it is essential to harmonise legal and institutional frameworks, as well as economic and political initiatives, within a "country-to-country" negotiation framework to ensure coherence and convergence of adopted measures (Boubrahimi, & Raissi, 2020). Such harmonisation is crucial for the success of Morocco's projects in Africa and the effective implementation of the AfCFTA. Legal, institutional, and policy frameworks across countries require harmonisation to ensure coherent implementation of AfCFTA measures. The proliferation of overlapping agreements and multiple regional memberships complicates cooperation, while African countries' exposure to external shocks and geopolitical shifts risks undermining engagement.

Finally, the Morocco-Africa partnership model must take into account the room for manoeuvre that African countries have in diversifying their international relations (e.g., with China, the United States, and Turkey). The model should remain evolutionary, flexible, and non-exclusive, in order to avoid a situation where ongoing bilateral negotiations sideline or diminish the value of African countries' trade relations with Morocco.

To address these challenges, Morocco and its partners must adopt a flexible, inclusive, and adaptive model, reinforcing high-level political commitment, trust, and mutual alignment of strategies. Enhancing capacity-building, improving governance, and leveraging Morocco's expertise in agro-industry, automotive, and textiles can strengthen equitable value chains, deepen trade, and promote sustainable socio-economic development across Africa.

6.5 State of Continental Integration and Progress in the Implementation of the AfCFTA for Morocco

As part of Morocco's ongoing efforts to contribute to the implementation of the AfCFTA agreement, this structuring project requires the fulfilment of a range of legal, financial, and administrative prerequisites.

For the Kingdom, it carries strategic stakes in several priority areas, such as food and energy security, women's inclusion, youth employment, sustainable development, and digital transition. The establishment of a national AfCFTA strategy, along with the formulation of an appropriate governance model, necessitates the implementation of a roadmap that encompasses high-impact measures and actions related to these themes.

Governance plays a crucial role in the successful implementation of the AfCFTA. In this regard, the governance model will be based on existing institutional measures designed to support the AfCFTA's rollout. The National AfCFTA Implementation Committee, attached to the Directorate General of Trade under the Ministry of Industry and Trade, is the body tasked with overseeing and monitoring the AfCFTA after its implementation.

Given its composition, the committee should broaden its membership to include all relevant private sector actors, such as the Moroccan Exporters' Confederation (CME, formerly ASMEX), the General Confederation of Moroccan Enterprises (CGEM), and various professional and sectoral federations. Their representation should be institutionalised and made permanent.

Among the missions that the committee should prioritise is its role as an interface between the Kingdom of Morocco, the Regional Economic Communities, and the AfCFTA Secretariat. This will ensure a coherent and coordinated representation of Morocco's voice vis-à-vis continental partners, particularly those involved in the project. The committee should also promote Morocco's Royal initiatives to the AfCFTA governance bodies, regional economic communities, and partner African countries. Finally, the committee should oversee and monitor the effective implementation of AfCFTA-related measures. Its level of representativeness grants it a strategic dimension and would facilitate decision-making as well as the coordination of measures implemented by the relevant stakeholders.

This will enable a comprehensive understanding of the challenges and allow Morocco to fully leverage the opportunities arising from AfCFTA membership. Achieving this requires extensive awareness-raising and educational initiatives to address stakeholders' needs. The outcomes of such campaigns will provide better-informed decision-making throughout the AfCFTA implementation process.

Accordingly, it is essential to assert that the success of any national strategy for AfCFTA implementation depends on a clear and effective communication plan to disseminate information about all actions, opportunities, and strategic stakes of the agreement. Currently, several actors remain insufficiently informed about the implications of the entry into force of trade agreements, particularly the AfCFTA.

Moreover, strategic objectives must be communicated to all stakeholders as well as to the media, which can play a key role in raising awareness.

6.6 Institutional and Legal Framework for the Implementation of the AfCFTA

The successful and effective operationalisation of Morocco's vision for the implementation of the AfCFTA agreement requires the coordination and mobilisation of all stakeholders to jointly establish the necessary provisions for better ownership of the agreement by the relevant actors.

It should also be emphasised that the continued improvement of the business climate (World Bank 2020) and the attractiveness of foreign direct investment (FDI) in Morocco call for deeper institutional collaboration, legal convergence, and the simplification of trade and investment procedures. Moreover, encouraging private sector participation is essential for the establishment of a clear legal framework and the removal of regulatory barriers.

6.6.1 National Governance Framework for the AfCFTA

At the institutional level, three main objectives should guide the national body of measures and decisions required for the gradual deployment of the agreement in line with national plans and the goals of various public policies related to the agreement:

- The engagement of all stakeholders in the continental integration process. This requires enhanced and regular coordination and awareness-raising efforts to ensure effective implementation. The emergence of the desired synergies will only be possible if the stakeholders are convinced of the agreement's potential and its forecasted positive impacts in terms of business opportunities, market supply, and growth stimulation.
- The facilitation and simplification of procedures. Morocco's commitment to this African integration dynamic must not result in complex processes for operators' domestic businesses, or investors. In this regard, it is important to note that Morocco is undoubtedly a continental benchmark, particularly due to the various advances made by the State in terms of trade facilitation and compliance with international standards and regulations.
- Ongoing coordination and regular communication with the entire national economic and financial ecosystem regarding the proposed measures and strategic choices made by the government to implement the AfCFTA agreement. Decisions must be based on impact assessments and opportunity analyses, conducted in

consultation with all relevant stakeholders. This participatory approach increases the likelihood of successful implementation. The private sector is part of the AfCFTA implementation committee to support the government's policy aimed at developing Morocco's trade relations with its African partners. For example, the Moroccan Exporters' Confederation and the General Confederation of Moroccan Enterprises are the main private actors involved throughout the AfCFTA implementation process. Their members attend and participate in various consultation meetings organised to frame negotiations and prioritise actions and key areas for the implementation of the AfCFTA.

In this regard, Morocco's adoption of governance actions related to the AfCFTA agreement is essential to ensure the effectiveness and success of the national implementation action.

The measures outlined in the action plan below aim to establish a collegial decision-making framework at the national level for implementing the AfCFTA. The various committee forums would serve as both think tanks and monitoring mechanisms to foster greater appropriation by the relevant stakeholders.

6.6.2 Legislative and Regulatory Prerequisites for the Implementation of the AfCFTA in Morocco

For Morocco, normative integration is a crucial component of economic integration with African countries within the framework of the AfCFTA. It is essential for the country to have appropriate legal mechanisms in place to support its commitments and facilitate the effective participation of Moroccan companies in the continental market.

In this context, Morocco relies on several key levers:

- Harmonisation of business law and commercial regulation: Morocco can build on the standards and practices established by regional bodies such as OHADA to ensure legal and judicial security for Moroccan companies operating in Africa, while ensuring consistency between its national legislation and AfCFTA requirements. This includes business law, competition law, tax law, and intellectual property protection.
- Alignment with international WTO standards: As a member of the World Trade Organisation, Morocco must ensure that its laws and regulations comply with international standards to facilitate African economic integration and attract foreign investment.
- Establishment of a national legal framework specific to the AfCFTA: Morocco needs to develop and strengthen internal legislative and regulatory frameworks to coordinate and guide trade policies, protect investors, and ensure that companies comply with the rules of the continental market.

In summary, the success of Morocco's participation in the AfCFTA depends on its ability to harmonise national legislation with African and international standards while ensuring the legal and economic security of its companies across the continent.

6.7 Opportunities and Challenges of the AfCFTA and Morocco for the Development of African Value Chains

Aware of the challenges related to Africa's socio-economic development, Morocco has made continental integration one of its top priorities. In this regard, the Kingdom was among the first countries to sign the agreement establishing the African Continental Free Trade Area (AfCFTA).

6.7.1 Priority Areas: Food Security, Energy

6.7.1.1 Food Security

African countries share common concerns and face, as natural partners, multidimensional challenges that require a profound revision of their strategic partnership framework. In this context, it is crucial to emphasise that Morocco's implementation of the AfCFTA agreement must now be driven by themes of critical importance to the country, particularly those related to food, security, climate, and migration.

Food security and the issue of dependence on food imports are among the major challenges Morocco must address in the context of renewing the continental partnership. Food security requires that "all people, at all times, have physical, social, and economic access to sufficient, safe, and nutritious food that meets their dietary needs and food preferences for an active and healthy life" (FAO, 2011).

Food security encompasses four key dimensions: stability, availability, accessibility, and quality/safety. These dimensions cover a wide range of contributing factors, including adequate quantities and types of food, income compatibility, and the ability to access or produce sufficient food. According to the UNDP, a country ensures food security when "its population has access to good food and nutrition and can obtain food in sufficient quantity, variety, and quality to sustain their existence" (UNDP, 2012, p. 9).

It should be noted that the food security situation in Africa has deteriorated in recent years due to successive crises (financial crisis, the COVID-19 pandemic, etc.), making it one of the continents and Morocco's key development issues. Morocco can strengthen its food security within the framework of the AfCFTA by leveraging the potential for diversification in its agricultural sector, which offers significant export opportunities to African markets. Furthermore, by developing African regional value chains and securing the supply of essential products, food security can be reinforced. Intra-African cooperation facilitates the transfer of agricultural technologies, agro-industrial development, and job creation. In this context, the Moroccan Phosphate Office (OCP) is highly engaged in African countries through projects related to food security. Notably, these include the project aimed at improving agricultural productivity and soil health in West Africa—particularly in Benin, Guinea, Mali, and Togo—signed with the World Bank in 2023, as well as the agreement with the French Development Agency (AFD) to provide African farmers with sustainably produced green fertilisers specifically adapted to the needs of their crops, climates, and soils.

6.7.1.2 Energy

Regarding the reform of the energy model in Africa, it represents one of the main levers for the continent's economic development. Morocco's industrial momentum and the structural transformation of its economy inevitably depend on its ability to build a new vision for energy production and consumption. This transition is primarily driven by the expansion of renewable energy sources and by the strategic importance of ecological sustainability, infrastructure investment, and the greening of the economy.

The transition from a fossil-fuel-based energy strategy to a more sustainable alternative model requires a shift in perspective, leveraging Morocco's significant potential in renewable energy. Green sources such as solar energy, wind energy, and green hydrogen could replace traditional African exports like oil, coal, and, to a lesser extent, natural gas.

This paradigm shift is particularly crucial as it will help sustainably meet Morocco's and Africa's energy needs, reduce the volatility of fossil fuel prices, lessen dependence on energy imports, and mitigate the collateral effects of greenhouse gas emissions. Additionally, renewable energy sources are becoming increasingly competitive and are well-suited to support the growth process. The International Renewable Energy Agency (IRENA) reported that the cost of solar photovoltaic modules has dropped by 80% since 2009.

From this perspective, successive Moroccan governments have implemented energy reforms to achieve the objectives outlined in the national energy strategy, including diversification of energy supply, development of renewable energy sources, promotion of energy efficiency, and integration into regional and international markets. Moreover, Morocco has reaffirmed its commitment to the global fight against climate change and to promoting green energy by ratifying the Paris Agreement, adopting a new national climate policy, and hosting the UN Climate Change Conference "COP22" in 2016. In addition to securing its energy supply, the Kingdom is making notable progress in achieving the United Nations Sustainable Development Goals (SDG 7).

Morocco has launched important institutional reforms to transform its national energy value chain. These include the creation of the National Electricity Regulatory Authority (ANRE), the Moroccan Agency for Sustainable Energy (MASEN), the

Research Institute for Solar Energy and New Energies (IRESEN), and the Moroccan Agency for Energy Efficiency (AMEE).

In summary, Morocco's experience could benefit the revitalisation of the Afro-African energy partnership, particularly in areas such as renewable energy, energy transition, climate change mitigation, and facilitating trade.

6.7.2 Cross-Cutting Issues: Women's Inclusion, Youth Employment, Sustainable

6.7.2.1 Development, and Digital Transition

Agenda 2063 seeks to realise seven main aspirations that can effectively guide the renewal of the continental partnership, especially concerning gender issues:

1. A prosperous Africa based on inclusive growth and sustainable development;
2. An integrated continent, politically united and based on the ideals of Pan-Africanism and the vision of Africa's renaissance;
3. An Africa of good governance, democracy, respect for human rights, justice, and the rule of law;
4. A peaceful and secure Africa;
5. An Africa with a strong cultural identity, common heritage, shared values, and ethics;
6. An Africa whose development is people-driven, relying on the potential of African people, especially women and youth, and caring for children's well-being;
7. An Africa that is a strong, united, and influential global player and partner.

In this regard, the promotion of gender equality and the strengthening of promoting gender equality and strengthening gender mainstreaming in public policies across Africa, as well as combating all forms of gender-based discrimination, are crucial. To ensure good governance, the national bodies in charge of monitoring the implementation of the AfCFTA agreement should ensure the enforcement of African human rights treaties such as the "African Charter on Human and Peoples' Rights," the "African Charter on the Rights and Welfare of the Child," the "Protocol to the African Charter on Human and Peoples' Rights on the Rights of Women in Africa" (Maputo Protocol), the "African Youth Charter," and the "African Union Convention for the Protection and Assistance of Internally Displaced Persons in Africa."

This new rights-based approach aims to adopt a holistic vision that sees all categories of rights (civil and political rights, economic and social rights, individual and collective rights, etc.) as complementary and mutually reinforcing.

As an expression of solidarity-based economy, Morocco implements a proactive policy to support women and promote gender mainstreaming, particularly through state institutions such as the National Initiative for Human Development (INDH), under the Ministry of Interior and chaired by the Head of Government. Created in 2005, this initiative aims to promote democracy, good governance, and sustainable development—economically, socially, culturally, and environmentally. It has placed women's economic empowerment at the heart of its human development strategy, becoming a key driver of progress in recent years.

Within Morocco's New Development Model (NDM), the third axis, entitled "Opportunities for Inclusion and a Strengthened Social Bond," is built around four strategic choices. The first of these focuses on empowering women, promoting gender equality, and enhancing their participation. The NDM's general report recommends "promoting female entrepreneurship by improving access to financing, public aid for women-led businesses, and better social protection for female self-employed workers."

Moreover, Morocco's strategy for implementing the AfCFTA should incorporate dimensions related to the prevention of trade and investment-related disputes, as well as the regulation of issues such as competition, digital trade, and intellectual property rights. In light of both national and international experiences, strengthening dispute settlement procedures appears essential given the costs associated with economic conflicts.

To that end, Morocco's legal framework could be enriched by the AfCFTA protocols on these issues, particularly those related to competition, trade in goods and services, e-commerce, investment, and intellectual property. While the AfCFTA protocol on dispute settlement is inspired by the WTO's Dispute Settlement Understanding, it must still take into account the specific circumstances of African countries.

Competition regulation is also a fundamental aspect of African continental integration. Preventing and combating anti-competitive practices, abuse of dominant positions, and promoting fair competition should be priorities for Moroccan public authorities within the national AfCFTA strategy.

Additionally, the protection of intellectual property rights and related rights is essential for improving the business climate. Securing these rights encourages creativity and enhances Morocco's attractiveness for investment and innovation-driven companies.

Similarly, the promotion of e-commerce aligns with a global trend and responds to the imperative of digital transition, which is increasingly emerging as a crucial driver for economic development, public service modernisation, and societal progress. The AfCFTA protocol on digital trade offers legal tools that could significantly advance African countries' efforts to develop e-commerce in an integrated manner.

Having made significant strides in this area, Morocco has adopted a national strategy entitled "Digital Morocco 2030," which outlines the country's vision for digital transformation. It defines ambitions, objectives, and key initiatives aimed at positioning Morocco as a regional leader in digital innovation. By drawing on the recommendations of this protocol, Morocco can further strengthen its legal and institutional frameworks.

6.7.3 Implementation Framework of the AfCFTA

For many years, Morocco has pursued a proactive strategy aimed at continuously strengthening its South-South partnerships, particularly with countries across the African continent (CESE, 2020). In line with the Kingdom's strategic objectives to reinforce its continental anchorage, the Government is working to mobilise the necessary budgetary resources to operationalise Morocco's African vision.

Several large-scale projects have been realised with state support, notably in terms of investments in priority sectors of the African economy (telecommunications, banking, basic infrastructure, education, etc.), as well as through the sharing of expertise in various key areas such as agriculture, vocational training, and energy. The relevant ministerial departments support these efforts.

In the African arena, Morocco has multiplied its efforts to promote South-South cooperation. Enshrined in the 2011 Constitution and reaffirmed upon Morocco's return to the African Union in early 2017, this cooperation constitutes a cornerstone of its foreign policy. As an example, Morocco and the Food and Agriculture Organisation of the United Nations (FAO) signed a general agreement in 2014 in support of South-South cooperation, affirming Morocco's commitment to assist its African partners in developing sustainable rural and agricultural policies and in eradicating hunger.

This commitment materialised through the "Country Programming Framework," (CPF) signed in 2017 by the Moroccan Minister of Agriculture, Maritime Fisheries, Rural Development, Water and Forests, in which South-South and triangular cooperation play a central role. In this context, Morocco established a trust fund of approximately USD 1.2 million for the period 2014–2020, through the FAO, to support agricultural development and capacity-building in Africa. The Country Programming Framework has now been completed. An evaluation in 2021 assessed its implementation and provided lessons to guide the development of the new FAO and UN Sustainable Development System programming cycle for 2023–2027. Although the program laid the foundation for the new Country Programming Framework, which continues to strengthen Morocco–FAO cooperation, particularly in food security, sustainable natural resource management, and South–South and triangular cooperation.

Furthermore, it is important to highlight that the prospects for the operationalisation of the AfCFTA are fully aligned with the Kingdom's strategic choices, both in terms of selected priority sectors (food security, energy security, sustainability, etc.) and its objectives for expanding cooperation based on a win-win logic.

In this regard, the private sector is expected to play a key role in supporting state action as part of Morocco's African strategy. Several financial instruments have been introduced to better support Moroccan companies expanding into the continent. These include investment incentives under the new Investment Charter, which supports companies aiming to establish themselves in Africa, assistance from the Mohammed VI Investment Fund for Investment, and improved access to bank financing.

Diversifying funding sources for Morocco's AfCFTA implementation strategy is crucial for several reasons. It promotes financial sustainability, ensures greater engagement from contributors in the implementation process, and enables the establishment of governance mechanisms for tracking contributions (such as subsidies, grants, and loans) to ensure compliance with associated conditions. Morocco's potential funding sources are structured around four key pillars:

- State support through the national budget: The national budget is the primary source for financing public policies and sectoral strategies. Given the strategic importance of deepening South–South partnerships and implementing the AfCFTA, adequate and multi-year budgetary allocations should be made across the relevant ministerial departments. In this context, establishing a dedicated fund to finance actions under the national AfCFTA strategy (forums, regional trade fairs, business support, communication campaigns, etc.), possibly as a special treasury account, would be appropriate.
- Bank credit for businesses: The state is expected to develop a preferential financing offer to encourage businesses to actively participate in the AfCFTA project. Establishing subsidiaries in Africa, exporting flagship Moroccan products to continental markets, and forming partnerships (notably joint ventures) all require financial support. Financial authorities should therefore engage with the Moroccan Bankers' Association (GPBM) to set up a specific financing mechanism aligned with the AfCFTA strategy.
- Development aid: Resorting to international donors can serve as an alternative and complementary lever to traditional financing sources (national budget). African integration and the upgrading of African economies are themes eligible for development aid. The Moroccan Government is encouraged to explore opportunities in this area to bolster the financing of its strategy.
- Private sector contributions: Given the maturity of Moroccan sectors with a strong African presence (banking, telecommunications, engineering, construction companies, OCP, RAM, etc.), national champions could contribute directly or indirectly to funding the national AfCFTA implementation strategy. This could include mobilising equity or raising debt on the banking market to finance expansion into new African markets (Southern, Eastern, and Central Africa) or to support Moroccan SMEs aiming to establish operations in Africa or export products there. Such contributions would support the development of a national Africa-oriented ecosystem and enhance local integration rates.

6.8 Conclusion

In the wake of Agenda 2063, the effective implementation of the AfCFTA represents a critical phase in the process of completing genuine African economic integration. This structural project primarily aims to establish a single market for goods and services, facilitate the movement of capital and people, and lay the groundwork for the creation of a continental customs union. The Kingdom of Morocco, having prioritised Africa's socio-economic development, was among the first countries to sign the AfCFTA agreement.

Situated at the crossroads of African and European spaces, Morocco possesses the potential and assets necessary to actively contribute to the promotion of African integration and the construction of a new, mutually beneficial partnership between African countries and other regional groupings, particularly the European Union. African countries share a common history, notably linked to the challenges of post-colonial reconstruction, pan-African aspirations, external debt issues, and structural adjustment programmes. Morocco has faced the same challenges and shares the same aspirations as its African partners, including those related to continental integration, economic emergence, sustainable development, and social cohesion.

Some African states have made significant strides in their development processes and have initiated promising dynamics in democratic governance and socio-economic progress. These countries have long-term prosperity. Africa's human capital, the quality of its natural resources, its rich cultural heritage, and its agricultural capacities are all assets that should position the continent as one of the world's major regional growth hubs.

However, Africa still faces numerous challenges, including social inequalities, territorial disparities, high unemployment and poverty rates, migratory flows, insecurity and armed conflicts, and the effects of climate change. Building a prosperous Africa based on inclusive growth and sustainable development requires endogenous development models, accelerated regional integration, increased economic diversification, and the activation of synergies and productive complementarities.

Reforming Morocco's partnership model with its African partners within the framework of the AfCFTA necessarily involves a redefinition of priorities and a shift in cooperation towards a codevelopment approach. In this regard, the AfCFTA partnership framework should encompass all areas of collaboration and provide a new dimension to intra-African relations. To achieve this, it would be appropriate to rely on the implementation of the African Continental Free Trade Area and the human and sustainable development objectives of Agenda 2063 to ensure a coordinated and concerted implementation of the continental agreement, based on priorities sovereignly defined by African countries.

In this perspective, Morocco's role appears pivotal to the success of the continental integration process. Morocco continues to attract increasing numbers of investors thanks to its potential and its trajectory of development and openness. The Kingdom is now considered one of the most attractive countries on the African continent and boasting high potential.

The emergence of a new global partnership for Africa necessitates a fundamental overhaul of relationships, particularly to address imbalances and asymmetric relationships (AfDB, 2023). The AfCFTA agreement should be structured in a way that enables the continent to meet its major challenges, including sustainable growth, structural transformation, economic diversification, energy transition, political stability, peace, and security (AfDB, 2023).

Morocco's African anchoring will allow it to benefit from the current reconfigurations of the global economy, contribute to the catch-up momentum of African countries, accelerate the regional integration process, and help build a new model of continental cooperation. This new partnership framework should better harness development potential and improve the positioning of African countries in a rapidly changing international system.

References

AfDB. (2023). *African economic outlook.*

Boubrahimi, N., & Raissi, M. (2020). *AfCFTA space: Convergence clubs or asymmetry traps?* Conference proceedings, Harmattan.

CESE. (2020). *Morocco's regional integration in Africa: A strategy for sustainable development with Africa.*

FAO. (2011). *An introduction to the basic concepts of food security.*

Justin, Lin, Y. F., & Xing, H. (2020). *Endogenous structural transformation in economic development.*

Marcel Felicity Nagar. (2021). *The road to democratic development statehood in Africa: The cases of Ethiopia, Mauritius, and Rwanda.*

OECD. (2022). *Developing regional value chains to support a sustainable recovery.*

UNDP. (2012). *Africain human development report, towards a food secure future.*

UNECA. (2021). *Guidelines for developing national AfCFTA implementation strategies.*

UNECA. (2023). *Guided trade initiative: Documenting and assessing early trade experiences under the AfCFTA.*

World Bank. (2020). *The African continental free trade area: Economic and distributional effects.*

Chapter 7
An Analysis of the AfCFTA in Nigeria: Obstacles, Key Takeaways, and Pathways to Progress

Ngozi Eunice Egbuna

Abstract The AfCFTA is a transformative initiative aimed at enhancing trade relations and boosting the economic potential of countries in the African region. Nigeria effectively joined the AfCFTA by signing and ratifying its instruments on the fifth of December 2020. This study analyses the AfCFTA's implementation in Nigeria to identify the major obstacles that hinder its full implementation in Nigeria, as well as discussing effective pathways to its progress. The study shows that, despite the implementation of the AfCFTA in Nigeria, the country has continued to heavily rely on other regions and relatively less on African countries for its export and import trades. It further demonstrated that the lack of full domestication of the AfCFTA, inadequate trade-related infrastructure, among other factors, are the major obstacles hindering the full implementation of the AfCFTA in Nigeria. In light of the above, the study discussed effective pathways to the full implementation of AfCFTA in Nigeria and proposed several policy recommendations.

Keywords AfCFTA · Regional integration · Infrastructure · Diversity · International trade · Nigeria

7.1 Introduction

The African Continental Free Trade Area (AfCFTA) Agreement is considered a giant step towards economic integration and growth on the continent of Africa. The AfCFTA came with high hopes of holding great potential, capable of boosting intra-African trade and galvanising the structural transformation of countries in the

N. E. Egbuna (✉)
Prof. Ngozi E. Egbuna International Centre for Regional Integration and Trade Research, Nnamdi Azikiwe University, Awka, Nigeria

D. N. Yuni et al. (eds.), *From Policy to Practice: Challenges and Ways Forward on the Implementation of the AfCFTA*,
https://doi.org/10.1007/978-3-032-14051-7_7

African region. The AfCFTA negotiations cover areas such as trade in goods, trade in services, investment, intellectual property rights, and competition policy. It also places major emphasis on the elimination of taxes on approximately 90% of goods under the harmonised system (HS) tariff lines within 5 years, and 7% within 10 years, while the remaining 3% (not more than 10% of the import from other African countries) are to be excluded from liberalisation (Muftau, 2023; Omoju et al., 2024).

As a member of the African Union (AU), Nigeria is one of the countries that have signed and ratified the AfCFTA Agreement. However, after its initial commitments towards the establishment of the AfCFTA agreement, the country delayed signing the agreement, arising from the need to critically evaluate the agreement against the country's national and economic interests, as well as the need for proper consultations with all relevant stakeholders. However, after adequate consultations with stakeholders, Nigeria eventually signed the agreement on July 7, 2019, and ratified its instruments on December 5, 2020, making the country the 34th to formally ratify the treaty (Olajide, 2021). In readiness to fully reap the potential benefits of the AfCFTA, the Government of Nigeria incorporated the AfCFTA into its National Development Plan 2021–2025 as a transformative tool that will mainly enable Nigerian exporters to overcome obstacles associated with destination markets (Agarwal, 2023).

The AfCFTA also aims to address the growing concern about poor intra-African trade compared to trade with other regions in post-independence Africa. According to the United Nations Conference on Trade and Development's (UNCTAD's) Economic Development in Africa Report of 2019, exports from Africa to other African countries rank significantly lower than exports from Africa to other continents. The report highlighted that in 2017, intra-African exports accounted for only 16.6% of all exports, as against 68.1%, 59.4%, and 55.0% for Europe, Asia, and America, respectively (Olney, 2022). The report is even more worrisome in the case of Nigeria. In the same year, the country's imports from African countries stood at 4.0% while its exports to African countries were 12.0%, indicating that Nigeria's trade is dominated by trade with other regions. And so, the AfCFTA was projected to have the potential to reverse the trend, benefiting the African region. The AfCFTA was therefore expected to significantly increase the volume of intra-African trade, along with other potential benefits, upon successful implementation.

As the largest market in the African region, with a population of over 200 million people, Nigeria is strategically positioned to be a major player in the AfCFTA arrangement. Earlier studies (Ali, 2019; Pasara, 2020) had envisaged that Nigeria's accession to the AfCFTA treaty is considered a critical boost to the AfCFTA's viability, which will, in turn, engender improvement in the country's macroeconomic conditions, including economic growth, job creation, investment, and poverty reduction. Given the potential benefits of the AfCFTA, this study therefore seeks to analyse the major obstacles and key takeaways from the implementation of the AfCFTA in Nigeria, to provide policy recommendations for timely intervention.

7.2 An Overview of Nigeria's AfCFTA Implementation Strategy

The implementation of the AfCFTA in Nigeria is primarily under the auspices of the Presidential National Action Committee on AfCFTA (NAC-AfCFTA). The committee, which was inaugurated on November 19, 2019, was tasked with developing robust plans for the full implementation of AfCFTA in Nigeria (Muftau, 2023). The committee is made up of relevant stakeholders covering representatives from Government Ministries, Departments, and Agencies (MDAs), including the Federal Ministry of Industry Trade and Investment, Ministry of Finance, Budget and National Planning, Nigeria Export Promotion Council, Nigeria Investment Promotion Commission, Standard Organization of Nigeria, Corporate Affairs Commission, Central Bank of Nigeria (CBN), the organised private sector, academics, as well as the Civil Society Organizations (CSOs).

The NAC-AfCFTA established work streams to facilitate the implementation of the AfCFTA in Nigeria. The work streams include the Export Development Work Stream, the Non-Tariff Barrier Elimination Work Stream, the Manufacturing Work Stream, the Financial Services and Investment Mobilisation Work Stream, the Banking Sector Work Stream, the Payment System Work Stream, and the Capital Market Work Stream. Each of these work streams was created and assigned different responsibilities that broadly aimed to ensure the effective implementation of the AfCFTA Agreement in Nigeria. The implementation strategy was validated on December 7, 2022, by the Government of Nigeria, with the support of the United Nations Economic Commission for Africa (UNECA), after careful consideration of the document by relevant stakeholders in the country (Muftau, 2023).

The AfCFTA implementation strategy focused on three strategic areas or pillars:

1. Trade capacity development: This strategic pillar covers areas such as product prioritisation, Micro, Small, and Medium Enterprises (MSMEs) capacity development, special economic zones, business linkages, priority service sector selection, and service liberalisation models. Acknowledging that Nigeria's trade capacity is low, largely owing to factors such as low industrial capacity, insecurity, inadequate storage facility, low-value addition to agricultural products, the sub-optimal performance of Free Trade Zones (FTZs), as well as inadequate skills and funding among MSMEs, the implementation strategy, therefore, proposed enhancing the country's trade capacity by improving or reviving the above listed key areas.
2. Trade environment and regional integration: This strategic pillar covers areas such as capacity assessment of key trade agencies, and ECOWAS integration. This involves assessing the capacity of key trade agencies for the effective implementation of the AfCFTA. The key agencies include the Federal Ministry of Industry, Trade, and Investment, the Nigerian Association of Chambers of

Commerce, Industry, Mines, and Agriculture (NACCIMA), and the Small and Medium Enterprises Development Agency of Nigeria (SMEDAN). The pillar also highlighted ways through which existing structures of ECOWAS can be stimulated and leveraged to effectively implement AfCFTA.

3. Other pervasive issues (omnibus): This omnibus strategic pillar covers areas such as rule of origin, technical barriers, quality and conformity standards, trade dispute settlement, and MSMEs informality. The strategic document associated the country's low implementation of the Rule of Origin with its weak trade defence infrastructure. It is equally noted that MSMEs in Nigeria are predominantly informal businesses owing to the high costs and cumbersome processes required to register new businesses. The document also established that pre-shipment inspection is the most rampant non-tariff measure in the country, and as such, made recommendations. The document gave dispute settlement legal status only to state parties to establish action; however, this could also give problems to individual businesses, especially when they need to enforce their rights legally in a cross-border trade dispute. In terms of trade facilitation, the strategic document proposed facilitating measures such as the development and passage of the National Trade Policy and the implementation of the Single Window System (SWS) via Public–Private Partnership (PPP). It equally categorised the country's prioritisation into three broad groups. Exclusive products are those that should be excluded from liberalisation, including rubber, refined petroleum oil, palm oil, and fertiliser. Sensitive products cover ginger, refined oil, rice, butane, sesame, cocoa beans, cocoa butter, palm oil, soya beans, propane, sugar, cashews, spices, fertiliser, leather, cement clinkers, and gold. Non-sensitive products include all other commodities that are not listed in either the exclusive products or the sensitive products that Nigeria should liberalise completely.

7.3 Trend Analysis of Nigeria's Trade with Africa and Other Regions

AfCFTA pivots on trade agreements, and the potential the agreement holds for the countries in the region of Africa when fully implemented is huge. Particularly, it was projected in several quarters that the implementation of the AfCFTA would significantly boost the volume of trade within Africa, as well as improve the Gross Domestic Product (GDP) of the countries in the region through enhanced intra-African trade. It was equally expected that through the implementation of AfCFTA, African countries would significantly increase their trade within Africa. Therefore, this section analyses Nigeria's trading activities within Africa and other regions spanning the period from 2011 to 2024. Figure 7.1 presents the trend of Nigeria's exports to the region of Africa and other regions.

The trend of Nigeria's exports, as shown in Fig. 7.1, indicates that the country's exports to non-African region has remained significantly higher than its intra-African exports over the years. However, the country's exports trade to both regions

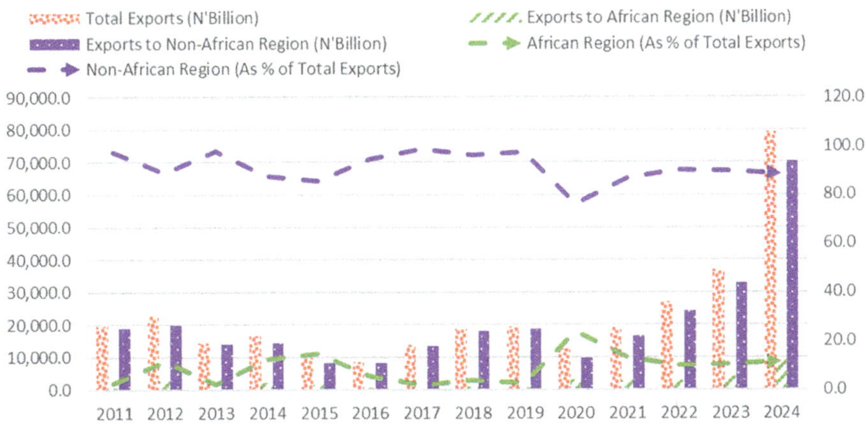

Fig. 7.1 Nigeria's exports to Africa and other regions. Source: Author Using Data from National Bureau of Statistics

present interesting trends. Specifically, Nigeria's exports to both non-African and African regions nosedived from a total exports values of N19,916.3 billion and N2530.0 billion in 2012 to exports values of N8063.9 billion and N463.5 billion in 2016 respectively, following a fall in the country's total exports fell significantly from N22,446.3 to N8527.4 in the same periods. It is important to highlight that 2016 was the year the Nigerian economy slipped into recession, as such the decline in the country's exports trade values can be largely contributed to the effects of the recession during the periods. In terms of the country's share of exports (as % of total exports) within the periods, while share of exports to non-African region recorded an increase, rising from 88.73% to 94.6%, the country's share of exports to Africa rather recorded a decline, falling from 11.3% to 5.4% within the same periods.

The trends as shown in Fig. 7.1 further reveal that Nigeria's intra-Africa exports value increased for both region between 2021 and 2024, rising from exports value of N16,431.8 billion and N2476.0 billion to N69,966.2 billion and N9120.9 billion respectively. Again, while this represents a rise in the country's share of exports to non-Africa from 86.90% to 88.47%, it represents a decline in the country's share of exports to Africa from 13.1% to 11.5% in the same periods, implying that the country's share of exports to the region of Africa rather reduced during the periods. Though these periods (2021–2024) coincided with the AfCFTA implementation periods in the country, however the periods appears rather too short to attribute the country's exports performance to its AfCFTA implementation activities.

A careful study of Nigeria's imports trade from Africa and non-African region equally presents interesting findings, as shown in Fig. 7.2.

Like in the case of exports trade, Nigeria's imports trade value declined significantly between 2011 and 2016. Specifically, while the country's total imports fell from N9892.6 billion to N8817.5 billion within the periods, its imports from Africa rather nosedived from N820.0 billion to as low as N82.7 billion. Within the same periods, the country's imports from non-Africa fell from N9072.6 billion to N8734.8

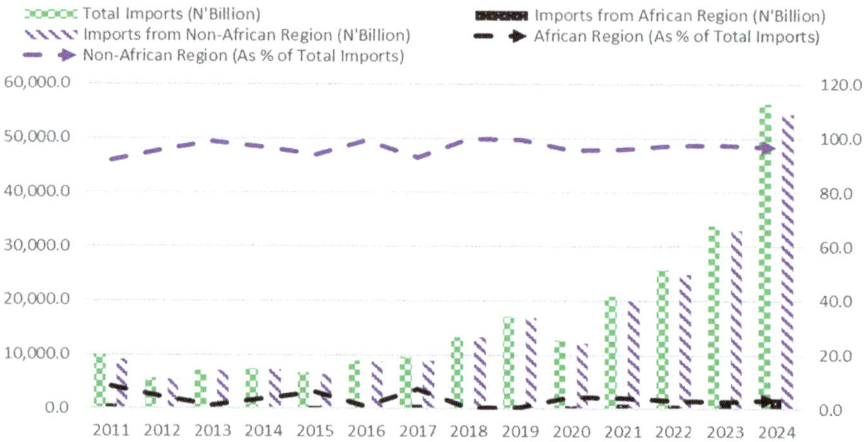

Fig. 7.2 Nigeria's imports from Africa and non-African region before and during the AfCFTA implementation. Source: Author Using Data from National Bureau of Statistics

billion. Again, as highlighted earlier, Nigeria experienced economic recession in 2016, and this may have contributed to the massive reduction in the country's imports trade values recorded in 2016. In terms of the country's share of imports, while Nigeria's share of imports from Africa reduced massively from 8.3% to as low as 0.9%, its share of imports from non-Africa rather recorded rather increase, rising from 91.7% to 99.1% in the same periods.

For the periods coinciding with AfCFTA implementation in the country, Nigeria's total imports values rose significantly between 2020 and 2024, rising from N12,700.9 billion to N56,381.3 billion. Similarly, the country's imports from Africa from N551.1 billion in 2020 to N1984.8 billion in 2024, while its imports from non-Africa increased from N12,149.8 billion to as high as N54.396.5 billion respectively in the same periods. In terms of share of imports, while Nigeria's share of imports from Africa reduced from 4.3% in 2020 to 3.5% in 2024, its share of imports from non-Africa rather rose from 95.7% to 96.5% in same periods. Clearly, AfCFTA implementation periods appears too short to attribute to any trade performance in the country so far, however it is important to mention that the country's share of imports from Africa declined within the periods. This implies that the rate at which Nigeria imported from Africa reduced, and the reduction coincided with the periods of AfCFTA implementation.

Moreover, Nigeria's top trading partners within the African region include the Ivory Coast, South Africa, Togo, Senegal, Egypt, Morocco, Swaziland, and Cameroon (see Fig. 7.3).

As shown in Fig. 7.3, Nigeria's major exports destination in Africa include South Africa, Ivory Coast, Senegal, Togo, and Namibia. Between 2020 and 2021, the country's topmost exports destination was South Africa with total exports values of N952.24 billion and N623.86 billion, respectively. This is followed by Ivory Coast with exports values of N322.44 billion and N530.76 billion. The country's exports

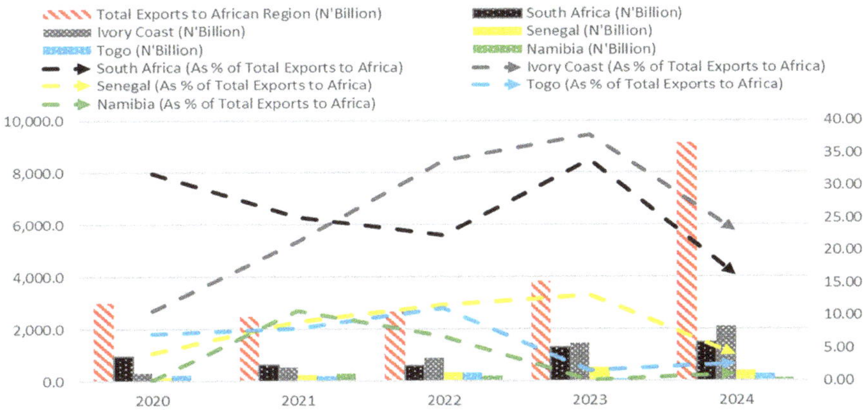

Fig. 7.3 Nigeria's top exports trading partners in Africa. Source: Author Using Data from National Bureau of Statistics

to Senegal, Togo and Namibia fluctuated within the periods (2020 and 2021). Togo took the third position on Nigeria's topmost exports destination in 2020 with exports value of N214.28 billion, Senegal took the next position with exports value of N126.61 billion, followed by Namibia with exports value of N3.10 in the same period. However, in 2021, Namibia took third position with exports value of N266.15 billion, followed by Senegal with exports value of N225.56 billion, and then Togo with exports value of N198.65 billion. In terms of share of exports (as % of total exports to Africa), except for Ivory Coast that recorded an increase in Nigeria's share of exports from 10.77% to 22.97% between 2020 and 2024, every other country experienced a fall in the country's share of exports within the same periods.

Further study of Nigeria's imports trading partners in Africa reveals the country's most imports destination as presented in Fig. 7.4.

The trends of Nigeria's imports destination in Africa from 2020 to 2024 show that the country's volume of imports from South Africa remained significantly higher than that of every other African country, and equally maintained upward trend in virtually all the periods except in 2024. Specifically, Nigeria's volume of imports from South Africa rose from N132.46 billion in 2020 to N237.24 billion in 2022, and further to N291.0 billion in 2023 before declining to N252.94 billion in 2024. The next Nigeria's topmost imports trading partner is Egypt with the country's volume of imports from Egypt rising from N39.15 billion in 2020 to as high as N107.77 before falling to N95.91 billion in 2024. Furthermore, while Morocco assumed the third position from 2020 to 2022, Togo occupied the same position from 2023 to 2024. The results of Nigeria's share of imports from Africa equally show that Nigeria imported more from South Africa than every other African country within the periods under study. The country's share of imports from Egypt Nigeria consistently increased its imports from Egypt in virtually all the periods except in 2024 when it declined from 11.95% in 2023 to as low as 4.83%. The

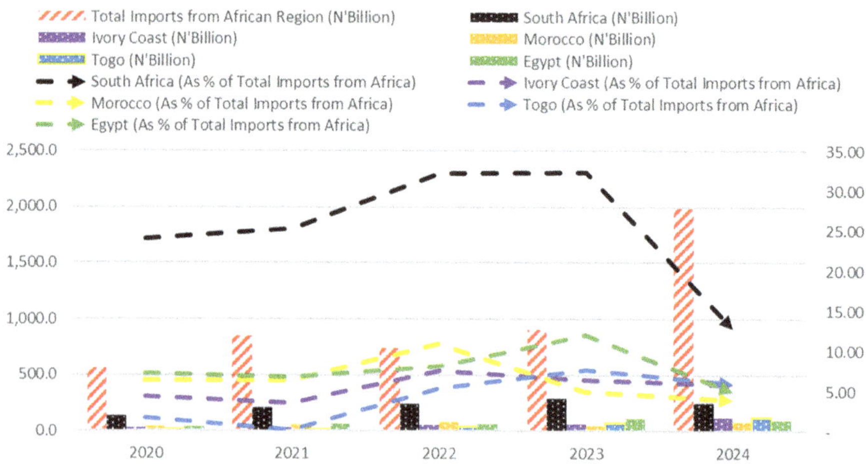

Fig. 7.4 Nigeria's top imports trading partners in Africa. Source: Author Using Data from National Bureau of Statistics

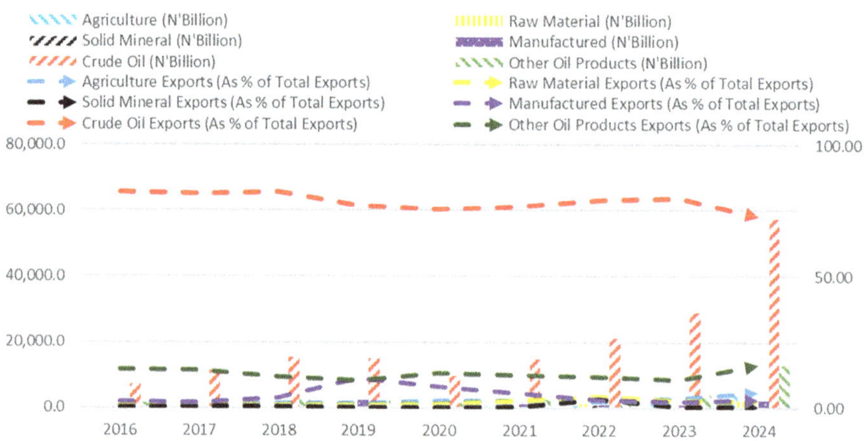

Fig. 7.5 Nigeria's top exports trading products. Source: Author Using Data from National Bureau of Statistics

country's share of imports from other African countries fluctuated within the periods but remained relatively low.

Further inquiry into the Nigeria's top trading products reveals interesting results. Figure 7.5 depicts the country's most exports trading products from 2016 to 2024.

The trends of Nigeria's exporting product reveal that crude oil is the country's topmost exports product for the entire periods. The country's crude oil exports rose from N6996.6 billion in 2016 to as high as N57,235.56 billion in 2024. While the crude oil dominated Nigeria's exports products for all the periods, however, in terms of share of exports (as % of total exports), the product a fall from 82.05% in 2016

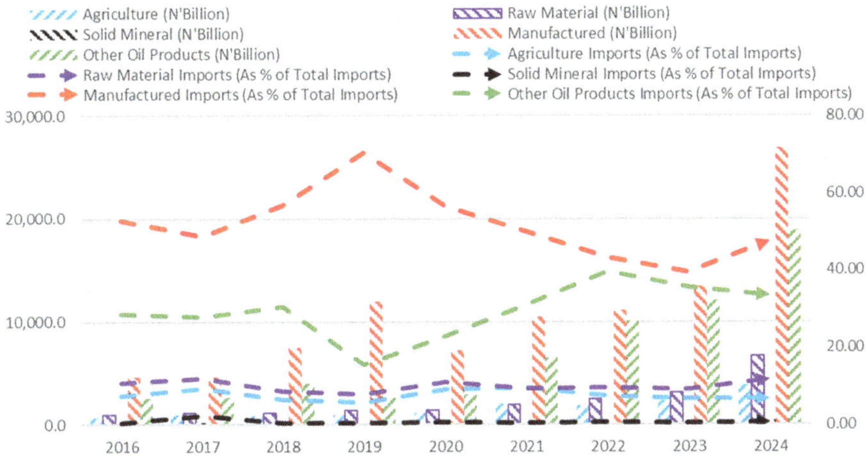

Fig. 7.6 Nigeria's top imports trading products. Source: Author Using Data from National Bureau of Statistics

to 72.37% in 2024. This is followed by other oil products that increased from N1230.8 billion to N12,783.97 billion from 2016 to 2024, representing share of exports of 14.43% and 16.16% respectively within the periods. The sixth is Solid Mineral that rose from N11.2 billion in 2016 to N260.31 billion in 2024, representing a marginal increase in the share of exports from 0.13% to 0.33% within the same periods. In all, crude oil products, agricultural products, raw materials, manufactured goods, solid mineral, as well as other crude oil products are Nigeria's top exports products. However, crude oil significantly dominants the country's exports products.

In terms of Nigeria's imports products, Fig. 7.6 presents the country's top imports products for the periods 2016 to 2024.

The results indicate that manufactured products accounts for the largest chunk of Nigeria's imports values in the entire periods. Specifically, manufactured goods accounted for imports value of N4645.2 billion in 2016, and rose to as high as N26,769.83 billion in 2024. This, however, represents a decline in the imports share of manufactured products from 52.68% in 2016 to 47.48%. The next top imports products of the country is other oil products, accounting for imports value of N2520.5 billion in 2016 and N18,813.6 billion in 2024 which represents share of imports of 28.58% and 33.37% in the same periods. Solid mineral assumed the fifth position, accounting for imports value of N49.8 billion in 2016 and N373.20 billion in 2024, and as well represents share of imports of 0.56% and 0.66% in 2016 and 2024 respectively. Overall, the results show that Nigeria's top imports products include agricultural products, raw material, manufactured products, solid mineral, and other oil products. However, the country's topmost imports product is manufactured products, followed by other oil products, while the country's least imports product of the five top imports products is solid mineral, accounting for the lowest imports values for the periods.

7.4 Major Obstacles to AfCFTA Implementation in Nigeria

Nigeria officially indicated its readiness to implement the AfCFTA Agreement after ratifying the treaty in 2020. AfCFTA is projected to have great potentials, particularly for intra-Africa trade, if fully implemented. In view of the above, Nigeria has taken some strategic steps towards ensuring the implementation of the trade agreement. Some of these steps include setting up a Presidential National Action Committee on AfCFTA, as well as incorporating the AfCFTA into its National Development Plan 2021–2025. However, the country is yet to fully implement AfCFTA. This section, therefore, critically examines the major obstacles that have hindered full AfCFTA implementation in Nigeria since it acceded to the AfCFTA.

7.4.1 Lack of AfCFTA Domestication

One of the obstacles to the effective implementation of the AfCFTA in Nigeria could be traced to the country's inability to fully domesticate the agreement. Over 4 years after Nigeria successfully subscribed to the AfCFTA Agreement, the federal government's plans to domesticate the African Continental Free Trade Area Agreement and incorporate it into its domestic legal framework are still underway. Pursuant to the legal provisions in Nigeria, international agreements must be implemented through domestic legislation before they can have any significant impact on the country's legal system.

Although Nigeria ratified the AfCFTA agreement on November 11, 2020, when the Federal Executive Council (FEC) approved the ratification, the inability of the Nigerian National Assembly to fully domesticate the AfCFTA Agreement significantly contributes in jeopardising the country's full implementation of the Agreement since it still lacks the required legal backing. The inability of the country's National Assembly to fully domesticate AfCFTA Agreement can be attributed to some factors. Among these factors is the bureaucratic procedures associated with enacting treaties into law in Nigeria, particularly treaties that relate to issues outside the Exclusive Legislative List. In a bid to give state governments a sense of belonging in the implementation of treaties such as AfCFTA Agreement that will affect them, section 12(3) of the country's 1999 Constitution provides that a bill for an Act of the National Assembly aims at implementing a treaty with regards to issues outside the Exclusive Legislative List shall not be enacted into law except it is ratified by a majority of all the States Houses of Assembly in the Federation. While this provision was made in good conscience of giving the state governments a say on such treaties, however it contributes largely to the ineffectiveness of the country's National Assembly to domesticate AfCFTA Agreement. This is largely because it is quite difficult, if not impossible to secure ratification of a majority of all the 36 States Houses of Assembly in addition to a majority of the two Houses of the country's National Assembly needed to domesticate such trade agreement (Okeke & Anushiem, 2018).

Another factor that could be constituting a cog in the wheel of the country's National Assembly in its task of domesticating AfCFTA Agreement is inadequate consultations of the country's legislature. Ideally, the easier way to get the National Assembly understand and appreciate the urgency of AfCFTA domestication would have been to allow the National Assembly to participate in the AfCFTA negotiation processes. However, this was not the case because it may amount to a double legislative task since the body would also play the constitutional role of enacting the AfCFTA Agreement into domestic laws. As such, the next desirable option to getting the legislative arm facilitate domestication of AfCFTA would have been engaging in strategic and effective advocacy to at least the relevant Committees of the National Assembly by the Presidential National Action Committee on AfCFTA on the need to domestic AfCFTA Agreement as a matter of urgency. However, there is no evidence that this has undertaken effectively.

There is also the challenge of a lacuna created in the Constitution on how a treaty bill such as AfCFTA bill should be brought before the chambers of the National Assembly for domestication. The Constitution is silent on this, that is, whether the bill should be introduced by the relevant Committees of the National Assembly or by the relevant Ministries, Departments and Agencies (MDAs). The lacuna discourages sense of responsibility, and has created room for blame games between the National Assembly and the Executive arm of the government.

7.4.2 Poor Trade-Related Infrastructure

Another major barrier to the effective implementation of AfCFTA in Nigeria is the country's poor trade-related infrastructure, especially in areas such as maritime logistics, road transportation, power/energy, etc. For instance, the country's influence on regional trade projects it as having the potential of being a maritime centre for African region, with Lagos ports like Apapa and Tin Can Island serving as huge transit points for Nigeria and its neighbouring landlocked countries. However, the current condition of the ports in Nigeria do not reflect maritime infrastructure efficient enough to handle the anticipated increase cargo flows associated with the full implementation of AfCFTA.

Currently, the ports are largely characterise by persistent congestion, poor facilities, as well as operational delays that hugely restricts trade efficiency. This corroborates a report by the Nigerian Ports Authority, which posits that significant proportion of containers, particularly in the Lagos Port Complex and Tin Can Island Port, face serious delays, largely due to logistics inefficiency (Okunsanya & Azmat, 2025). Ports such as Onne, Calabar, Warri, and Port Harcourt meant to support Lagos ports in managing the country's trade movement are equally faced with obstacles militating against their effectiveness. According to Okunsanya and Azmat (2025), Ships in Nigeria often face delays as long as 25 days before port docking, while cargo dwell times still averages 13 days as against the global standard of 4 days. The bureaucratic bottlenecks drawn from as many as more than 14 regulatory agencies worsen the delay and resulting to accumulation of demurrage and storage charges with huge financial on importers and consignees.

There is also the challenge of poor transportation links between roads and rail networks such that ports such as Calabar finds it quite difficult to service larger ships because of lack of deep-water facilities. Poor roads condition have continued to pose serious challenge for good to reach inland markets without unnecessary delays. Intra-African trade requires efficient cross-border transportation routes, effective ports and logistics facilities, and a reliable energy/power supply, among other essentials. However, the current condition of these trade infrastructure raises concern regarding their ability to handle the increased volume of trade expected under the AfCFTA full implementation. Moreover, Nigeria is yet to meet the infrastructure requirements outlined in the AfCFTA implementation. This may not be unconnected to these bottlenecks associate with the country' poor trade infrastructure.

One of the implications of the country's relatively poor trade infrastructure is that it threaten the seamless flow of goods from Nigeria to other African countries. It also has the implication of increasing the costs of production and reducing the competitiveness of made-in-Nigeria goods within the intra-African and non-African markets. A combination of these deficiencies, as well as the Nigerian government's inability to fully meet the infrastructure requirements outlined in the AfCFTA implementation, contributes to the challenge facing the country in implementing the AfCFTA.

7.4.3 Over-reliance on Crude Oil

Nigeria is mainly reliant on crude oil revenues, which account for more than 80% of its exports and foreign earnings. The National Bureau of Statistics (NBS) indicates that non-African region has remained the country's crude oil exports destination over the years. For instance, according to the NBS 2024 last quarter report, no African countries ranked among Nigeria's major trading partners. Specifically, non-African countries such Netherlands, USA, China, Belgium France, Spain, India, and Indonesia ranked as Nigeria's top exports trading partners. Although countries such as Ivory Coast, South Africa, and Ghana import crude oil from Nigeria, the volume of their imports is still significantly lower than that from non-African countries.

The Nigeria's huge dependence on non-African region for its crude oil exports can be largely attributed to the country's long trade relationship and partnership between the countries. Also, some of these countries imports more crude oil from Nigeria because of the quality of country's crude oil which suit their local demand. Nigeria's crude oil is light and sweet crude, and mainly sought after by these advanced non-African countries for its quality and suitability of being processed into different petroleum products and by-products.

However, it appears as though Nigeria has not been able to leverage its long experience of exporting to these non-Africa countries to significantly improve its intra-Africa crude oil exports. Clearly, the country can take advantage of this experience by fostering strategic trade agreement or trade partnership with countries in Africa that import crude oil. In other words, Nigeria can target African countries like Libya that largely depends on the USA for its huge crude oil imports. Nigeria can also strategically strengthen its trade relationship with the African countries (Ivory Coast, South Africa, and Ghana) that currently patronise it crude oil with the aim of increasing their patronage.

Moreover, the idea of fostering trade relationship and partnership showcases the potential the emergence of the AfCFTA Agreement represents in boosting the country's exports trade, if fully implemented by the country. However, for the country to effectively reap the AfCFTA potential benefits, it will imply channelling deliberate efforts towards addressing issues such as non-domestication of AfCFTA, poor trade infrastructure, inefficient digital infrastructure, poor cross-border security, among others, capable of jeopardising the AfCFTA potential benefits to the country, in this case, the huge market the AfCFTA Agreement presents to Nigeria for its crude oil exports.

7.4.4 Deplorable State of Cross-Border Security

Nigeria is still faced with the challenge of insecurity both inside and around its borders. There has been an increasing incidence of banditry, transnational organised crime, and high-handedness of state security operatives, as well as the activities of non-state actors, among others, threatening cross-border security. For instance, the menace of Boko Haram affecting the Lake Chad Basin, which cuts across some parts of Nigeria, Cameroon, Chad, and Niger has defiled interventions of state security apparatus, which includes military, immigration, and customs around border areas. As such, in October 2019, Nigeria and several other African countries, including Kenya, Rwanda, Ethiopia, and South Africa, had to close their borders to curtail cross-border smuggling and the rising incidence of insecurity at the time (Ogbonna et al., 2023).

Poor cross-border security has serious negative implication on both trade flows and road transportation costs. In fact, following a recent case study by the West African Association for Cross-Border Trade in Agro-Forestry-Pastoral and Fisheries Products (WACTAF), exporters along the west coast of the continent opine that it costs as high as N10.84 million to transport a truckload of goods worth N100 million by road from Lagos, Nigeria to Accra, Ghana with insecurity related levies and charges contributing significantly (Bassey, 2025). Owing to cross-border insecurity, some transporters have resulted to longer routes, which also increase both transportation costs and delivering periods. It equally mounts upward pressure on insurance costs since insurance costs tend to rise with rising incidence of insecurity. While the issue of cross-border insecurity may no longer be as threatening as it was in 2019 when some borders were closed, it still presents serious hurdles for cross-border trading, particularly in the country's implementation of the AfCFTA.

7.4.5 *Inefficient Digital Infrastructure/Limited ICT Equipment*

Though, Nigeria's digital economy has experienced improvement in the recent past, arising mainly from reforms in telecommunications and finance. According to the the Africa International Trade and Commerce Research (2024), the country has recorded improvement in facilitating digital trade resulting to enhanced access to online platforms and services, digital entrepreneurship ecosystem, as well as digital finance, especially in areas such as Fintech and digital payments, e-commerce, and digital services. However, with the increasing wave of digitalization and technology across the globe, which is now at the heart of almost every aspects of trade, the country's digital infrastructure still remains relative inefficient to significantly support AfCFTA full implementation.

ODI Global (2024) establishes that Nigeria still grapples with challenges of internet connectivity gaps, digital operational instability, inefficient ICT equipment, cybersecurity threats, and digital literacy gaps. According to the report, Nigeria's current fixed broadband penetration rate still remains less than 1% and centres more around the major cities, mainly Lagos State of Nigeria. More so, the country's plan of implementing an electronic single window system is still farfetched, with serious implications on the costs of compliance by the entrepreneurs. Addressing these digital infrastructure challenges, which will in turn strengthen the country's digital infrastructure is vital in ensuring that Nigeria fully implement AfCFTA. In fact, efficient digital infrastructure equally aligns with the broad goal of the AfCFTA Digital Protocol and therefore should addressed imperatively.

7.4.6 *Low Level of Awareness Among Micro, Small and Medium Enterprises (MSMEs)*

Micro, Small and Medium Enterprises (SMEs) contribute significantly to Nigeria's gross domestic product, and accounts to as high as over 96% of Nigeria businesses. AfCFTA provide great opportunities that MSMEs in Nigeria could leverage to boost their trading across the African region. However, most MSMEs in Nigeria lack basic knowledge about AfCFTA implementation and its provisions for them. The June, 2025 report by the Department Agenda for Western Nigeria (DAWN), suggests that more than 67% of MSMEs in Nigeria have no knowledge of AfCFTA implementation. According to the report, only about 18% of the MSMEs are aware of AfCFTA implementation. The low level of AfCFTA awareness among MSMEs poses significant challenge to their effective participation, as well as the AfCFTA full implementation. This also raises concern about the claim of wide consultation by the Nigerian government during the AfCFTA negotiation stage, and as well highlights the need for effective sensitisation on AfCFTA across the country.

7.4.7 Export Barriers/Trade Impediments

AfCFTA full implementation in Nigeria is not only affected by the Nigerian factors alone. There are also other challenges faced by the Nigerian businesses as they gain access to other African markets which are capable of affecting the AfCFTA full implementation. Some of the challenges such as poor trade-related infrastructure, cross-border insecurity, etc. earlier discussed are not peculiar to Nigeria but cuts across many African countries, and as such constitute major constraints to Nigerian businesses trading in other African countries. Many African countries grapples with poor road, rail and port infrastructure. There are still cases of insecurity and conflict in several trade routes in Africa, including the Sahel and Lake Chad Basin which has continued to increase the risk both for traders and their commodities. The condition of most roads in the region is poor and hinder trade facilitation across the region. For instance, the region of Africa is still faced with serious infrastructure challenge and therefore will need to upgrade over 60,000 km of its regional roads, as well as complete the missing links in the Trans-African Highways in order to meet the volume of trade AfCFTA will attract (Economic Commission for Africa, 2024). These hurdles create massive challenges to movement of goods, as well as increase their intra-African cost of trade and pose serious problem to Nigerian businesses trading in other African countries.

Another major challenge that many African countries face which affect Nigerian business communities and hinder effective intra-African trade is the problem of corruption which appears to be endemic across many African countries. According to Transparency International (2024), the region of Sub-Saharan Africa (SSA) is still characterised with massive corruption. Specifically, the Corruption Perception Index (CPI) by the Transparency International (TI), the SSA region recorded as low as 33 out of 100 in 2024, with 90% of countries in the region scoring below 50. The 33 recorded by SSA countries is significantly lower than the global average of 43 score for the year and indicates that the region still grapples with the problem of persistent corruption. Corruption which encompasses bribery, smuggling, as well as other illicit practices has remained a major challenge for businesses in Africa, and as such constitute problems to Nigerian businesses exporting to other African countries. Specifically, the illicit payments increase the costs of doing business and therefore makes it difficult for the businesses to compete favourably.

Among other major challenges also facing Nigerian businesses exporting to other African countries is the problem poor access to reliable market information. In many African countries, trade-related critical information such as trade regulation, market regulation, and potential buyers are not readily available or accessible in the public domain, and where they are available, most of them are usually unreliable. Most African countries still lack the culture of producing reliable data and making them publicly available. As such, some of these Nigerian businesses, especially SMEs grapple with this challenge of having access to reliable data (trade regulations, tariffs, potential buyers or partners) needed to boost their intra-Africa trade. This creates the problem of business uncertainty and makes it difficult for these Nigerian businesses to identify and access reliable new exports opportunities within the African region.

7.5 Key Takeaways from the Analysis and Policy Implications

The analysis of AfCFTA implementation in Nigeria has revealed some interesting findings and key lessons that warrant emphasis. The key takeaways and lessons are therefore discussed concisely below:

1. In preparation for joining AfCFTA, the Government of Nigeria took some strategic steps to guarantee its full implementation in the country. These plans and strategic steps included holding wide stakeholders' consultations on AfCFTA implementation in Nigeria, conducting a critical evaluation of the AfCFTA agreement against the country's national and economic interests, setting up the National Action Committee on AfCFTA (NAC-AfCFTA) to produce robust plans and strategies for AfCFTA full implementation in Nigeria, among others. The combination of these strategic actions led to Nigeria's signing and ratification of the AfCFTA instruments on 5 December 2020. However, a lot still needs to be done, especially from policy perspective to ensuring that the country fully implement the AfCFTA. To this effect, there is need for the current administration to demonstrate political will and commitment toward the full implementation of the AfCFTA in Nigeria. The President Muhammadu Buhari led administration initiated the AfCFTA process in Nigeria by signing and ratifying its instruments before handing over power to the current administration led by President Bola Ahmed Tinubu on May 29, 2023. Therefore, the onus lies on the current administration to prioritising and demonstrating its commitment to full implement AfCFTA. To achieve this, there is need for allocating and releasing the adequate resources needed for AfCFTA, as well as signalling relevant MDAs, stakeholders, and committees responsible for AfCFTA implementation to rise to their responsibilities as a matter of urgency.
2. Though Nigeria has started AfCFTA implementation, the country is yet to fully domesticate the AfCFTA agreement and incorporate it into its domestic legal framework. This is crucial for the AfCFTA's full implementation in the country, as Section 12 of the Nigerian 1999 Constitution stipulates that domestic legislation must domesticate international agreements before they can take full effect

within the country's legal system. This lack of full legal domestic backing therefore, contributes to hindering the country's full implementation of AfCFTA.

This is quite crucial because giving the AfCFTA agreement a legal backing by enacting it into law makes the Ministries, Departments, Agencies (MDAs), organisations, stakeholders, etc., responsible for the full implementation of AfCFTA in Nigeria, to rise to their responsibilities owing to stipulated legal implications of any negligence in that regard. The full domestication will encourage organisations and other concerned citizens to intensify advocacy to relevant authorities, also enabling them to advocate for the need for full AfCFTA implementation in the country. Therefore full domestication of the AfCFTA agreement can be achieved by ensuring that the country's National Assembly sees the importance of giving the agreement the force of law. This can be championed by the National Action Committee on AfCFTA (NAC-AfCFTA), and the committees can be reconstituted for effectiveness if they are no longer effective. The committee should also engage the relevant Committees of the National Assembly on strategic advocacies geared towards AfCFTA domestication. The NAC-AfCFTA should equally set time frames for full domestication of the AfCFTA agreement and work towards actualising it.

There is also the need to address the lacuna created by the 1999 Constitution about how treaty bills will be introduced at the chamber of the National Assembly. The constitution should therefore be clear on whose responsibility it is to introduce the bill, relevant committees of the National Assembly or relevant MDAs. This will give sense of responsibility to the committees or MDAs necessary to enable them do the needful and on time.

3. Nigeria's trade-related infrastructure, especially in maritime logistics, road infrastructure, and power/energy is still relatively inefficient in handling the increased volume of trade expected from AfCFTA full implementation. The AfCFTA requires efficient cross-border transportation routes, effective ports and logistics facilities, and a reliable energy supply to fully implement it. Nigeria's trade-related infrastructure is not yet efficient enough to fully implement the AfCFTA. Nigeria is also yet to meet the infrastructure requirements outlined in the AfCFTA implementation, largely due to the relatively poor nature and inadequacy of its trade-related infrastructure.

   There is need for Nigeria to prioritise meeting the infrastructure requirements as outlined in the AfCFTA implementation strategy to facilitate intra-African trade. The country should therefore tackle head-on the challenges associated with its maritime logistics, poor road network, massive port congestion, and delays, among others to ensure seamless inflow and outflow of goods.The Government of Nigeria can explore the option of public–private partnerships to address some of the trade-related infrastructural deficiencies. There is also a need for Nigeria to expedite action on its section of the ECOWAS road corridor (the Abidjan-Lagos corridor). The project, which is still at the design stage, can be expedited owing to its importance in facilitating intra-Africa trade, as well as AfCFTA. The project connects Abidjan, Côte d'Ivoire, to Lagos, part of Nigeria, traversing through Ghana, Togo, and Benin. Therefore, it is crucial for AfCFTA implementation in Nigeria. The Nigerian Government should also prioritise strengthening its power sector to ensure a stable and affordable power supply. An unstable power supply compels most manufacturing and export industries to rely on generators. This drives up the cost of production and makes it difficult for most manufacturers to produce at competitive prices.

4. The trend analysis of Nigeria's exports trade indicate that over the years, Nigeria has been depending on non-African regions for its exports trade. The results show that the country's share of exports to non-African region has been hovering around as high as 97.38% and 88.47% from 2011 to 2024 compared to its share of exports to Africa that hovered around 2.6% and 11.5% in the same period. This highlights Nigeria's relatively low exports trade within the region of Africa, and therefore suggest that the country has not been able to leverage its long experience of massive exports trade to non-African region to boost its intra-Africa exports. In terms of the country's imports trade, the trend analysis equally reveal that Nigeria largely depends on non-African region for its trade imports. The country's share of imports from non-African region hovered around as high as 91.7% and 96.5% compared to its share of imports from Africa that hovered around 8.3% and 3.5% in the same period. It is therefore believed that given the Nigeria's long experience of huge exports and imports trade with non-African region, the country can tremendously boost its exports and imports trade in Africa while leveraging the long trade experience.
5. The study also found that within the African region, Nigeria depends mostly on countries like South Africa, Ivory Coast, Senegal, and Togo for its intra-African export trade, and South Africa, Egypt, Ivory Coast, and Swaziland for its intra-African imports trade. Of these countries, only Ivory Coast and Togo are close enough. This indicates that Nigeria is not optimising its closest neighbour trade, and this is partly due to the poor or non-existent road and rail infrastructure.
6. Trend analysis of Nigeria's top trading products revealed that the country still depends largely on crude oil export trade and relatively less on its manufactured goods. This therefore highlights the need for greater emphasis on industrialisation if the country is to benefit significantly from the full implementation of the AfCFTA.

The need for Nigeria to diversify is imperative. Most African countries may not have the needed refining capacity to warrant patronising Nigeria's crude oil. This makes it paramount for Nigeria to fully diversify its economy away from crude oil and be deliberate about exploring other exportable products, especially those in which the country has a comparative and competitive advantage over many other African countries. This can be achieved through research and development (R&D) and by fostering partnerships between research institutes (those with a significant focus on manufacturing goods) and relevant industries in the country. The Nigerian Government can incentivise the partnership while relevant MDAs such as the Federal Ministry of Industry Trade and Investment, Ministry of Finance, Budget and National Planning, Nigeria Export Promotion Council, Nigeria Investment Promotion Commission, Standard Organization of Nigeria, Corporate Affairs Commission, Central Bank of Nigeria (CBN) provide relevant supports (oversight function, funding, etc.) for effectiveness. There still exist exportable products (cocoa butter, rubber, palm kernel oil, textiles, and garments, among others) in different parts of Nigeria that the country has yet to fully explore for exports. Nigeria should therefore leverage its commodities, even for manufacturing (value-added) export trade, by integrating into key regional value chains.

7. The Nigerian Government should also leverage the increasing wave of digitalisation across Africa to promote digital trade and AfCFTA implementation in the country. This can be achieved by investing massively in robust digital infrastructure to expand broadband access and efficient internet connectivity. This will also warrant the Nigerian Government to develop a comprehensive digital trade framework, create a supportive environment for digital trade, and strengthen cybersecurity and data protection measures necessary for effective digital trade. Given the technical nature of digital trade, Nigerian Government can also support MSMEs through digital literacy, digital tools, and e-commerce aggregator platforms. This will facilitate the implementation of AfCFTA and strategically position MSMEs to benefit from it in the country.
8. Nigeria's Government should promote capacity building and awareness creation, especially for Micro, Small, and Medium Enterprises (MSMEs) on AfCFTA opportunities and implementation. Despite over 4 years of AfCFTA ratification and implementation in Nigeria, awareness of the opportunities AfCFTA implementation holds for MSMEs and how they can leverage these opportunities remains poor. The Nigerian government can popularise the AfCFTA opportunities for MSMEs, as well as build their capacity to leverage the opportunities the trade agreement holds for MSMEs in Nigeria. This will enhance MSMEs' chances of gaining access to a larger market, improve competitiveness, and boost their sales and profitability.
9. The study also reveals that Nigerian businesses exporting to other countries in African face some hurdles capable of affecting AfCFTA full implementation in Nigeria, and therefore should be addressed. Many African countries still grapple with inadequate road, rail and port infrastructure. The region of Africa is equally characterised with high level of corruption militating against trade facilitation across the region as demonstrated by the 2024 Corruption Perceptions Index by the Transparency International. Most countries in the region also lack accessible and reliable trade-related information/data. The findings therefore makes it imperative for countries in the region to prioritise existing infrastructure corridors and foster new ones capable of facilitating trade in the region. As such, road corridors such as the ECOWAS road corridor, the Lobito corridor that connects Angola, Zambia and the Democratic Republic of Congo, and also the Lamu Port, South Sudan-Ethiopia Transport (LAPSSET) corridor that links Kenya, Ethiopia and South Sudan should be prioritised as a matter of urgency. Also, like the case Southern African Development Community (SADC) and the East African Community (EAC), other regions in Africa need to develop regional infrastructure master plans that align to their regional development goals. Effective regional development plans enhance connectivity and integration

within the region. In terms of corruption, there is need for countries in Africa to effectively strengthen their anti-corruption agencies. This can be achieved through effective anti-corruption reforms. There is also the need for countries in Africa to always make available and on time reliable trade-related information/data. This will entail strengthening national statistical offices of countries in Africa to develop and maintain robust trade-related websites where information/data on trade regulations, tariffs, potential buyers and partners, among others can be reliably sourced. This will go a long way in boosting the trade of Nigerian businesses trading in other African countries, as well as contribute in Nigeria's full implementation of AfCFTA.

7.6 Conclusion

This study focused on the analysis of AfCFTA implementation in Nigeria with particular interest in the major obstacles hindering its effective implementation in the country. The study is motivated by the potential benefits full AfCFTA implementation holds for Nigeria, and the significant role the country, as the giant of Africa, plays. The study analysed secondary data sourced mainly from the National Bureau of Statistics (NBS), including the NBS data on Nigeria's Foreign Trade Statistics Reports from the periods preceding the implementation of AfCFTA in Nigeria, using qualitative techniques and descriptive tools.

The study's findings suggest that, despite the implementation of the AfCFTA in Nigeria, the country records more trade with countries outside Africa than with those within. The study also revealed that obstacles such as the lack of full AfCFTA domestication, inadequate trade-related infrastructure, over-dependence on crude oil, and cross-border insecurity, among others are the major hurdles frustrating the effective implementation of AfCFTA in Nigeria. The study there discussed effective policy implications that should advance the full implementation of the AfCFTA in Nigeria, which includes enacting the AfCFTA agreement into law in line with the provisions of the country's 1999 constitution, diversification of the country's economy, embarking on intensive trade-related infrastructural development, leveraging the globally increasing digitalization to promote digital trade in the country, among others. In conclusion, a serious political commitment and innovative leadership are required to implement AfCFTA in Nigeria and address the major obstacles discussed in this study. If these obstacles militating against AfCFTA full implementation are addressed, the country will most likely reap the potential benefits of AfCFTA.

References

Africa International Trade and Commerce Research. (2024). *Advancing implementation of the AfCFTA protocol on digital trade in Nigeria*. https://africainternationaltrade.com/2024/07/24/advancing-implementation-of-the-afcfta-protocol-on-digital-trade-in-nigeria/

Agarwal, P. (2023). *Seizing the opportunity: Nigeria's path to market access in services under*.

Ali, N. A. (2019). Building a smart deal for Nigeria in the AfCFTA negotiations: Issues, processes and policy directions. In *Trade facilitation capacity needs: Policy directions for national and regional development in West Africa* (pp. 47–65). Springer.

Bassey, E. (2025). *Rising cross-border charges threatens AfCFTA goals*. The Nation. https://thenationonlineng.net/rising-cross-border-charges-threatens-afcfta-goals/

Economic Commission for Africa. (2024). *Prospectives: The long winding road defining Africa's infrastructure development*. https://www.uneca.org/stories/perspectives-the-long-winding-road-defining-africa%E2%80%99s-infrastructure-development

Muftau, I. (2023). *Overview of the African continental free trade area (AfCFTA) and challenges of implementation: Nigeria and South Africa's implementation as case studies* (Doctoral dissertation, University of British Columbia).

ODI Global. (2024). *Implementing the AfCFTA digital trade protocol in Nigeria: Three crucial considerations*. https://odi.org/en/publications/advancing-implementation-of-the-afcfta-protocol-on-digital-trade-in-nigeria/

Ogbonna, C. N., Lenshie, N. E., & Nwangwu, C. (2023). Border governance, migration securitization, and security challenges in Nigeria. *Society, 60*(3), 297–309.

Okeke, C. E., & Anushiem, M. I. (2018). Implementation of treaties in Nigeria: Issues, challenges and the way forward. *Nnamdi Azikiwe University Journal of International Law and Jurisprudence, 9*(2), 216–229.

Okunsanya, L., & Azmat, M. (2025). Unlocking Nigeria's potential: Experts' opinion-based insights on the economic impact of logistics challenges. In *Supply Chain Forum: An International Journal*. https://doi.org/10.1080/16258312.2025.2497310

Olajide, D. A. (2021). The African continental free trade area (AfCFTA) and its applicability in the west African clime: Nigeria in focus. Available at SSRN 3770896.

Olney, W. W. (2022). Intra-african trade. *Review of World Economics, 158*(1), 25–51.

Omoju, O., Ikhide, E., Osigwe, A., Nghargbu, R., Nechifor, V., El, M. A., & Ferrari, E. (2024). *The impacts of the African continental free trade area on the Nigerian economy*. JRC.

Pasara, M. T. (2020). An overview of the obstacles to the African economic integration process in view of the African continental free trade area. *Africa Review, 12*(1), 1–17.

Transparency International. (2024). *Corruption perceptions index*. https://www.transparency.org/en/cpi/2024

Chapter 8
An Analysis of the AfCFTA in Ghana: Implementation, Obstacles, Key Takeaways, and Pathways to Progress

Festus Ebo Turkson and Agyapomaa Gyeke-Dako

Abstract The African Continental Free Trade Area (AfCFTA) represents a bold step towards economic integration across Africa. Its secretariat, headquartered in Accra, Ghana, plays a unique and strategic role in implementing this agreement. This chapter examines the background of the AfCFTA and its envisioned role in shaping Ghana's economic trajectory. The chapter analyses key takeaways from Ghana's participation in the AfCFTA, focusing on the potential benefits, including enhanced intra-African trade, job creation, and industrial development. It also highlights emerging opportunities for Ghanaian businesses while confronting critical obstacles, including infrastructure deficits, regulatory disparities, and transitional costs. Drawing on empirical data and authoritative sources, this chapter provides a detailed analysis of the AfCFTA's key pathways in Ghana, offering insight into how the country can position itself as a significant beneficiary of continental integration.

Keywords Ghana · AfCFTA · Trade policy · Regional integration · Economic development · Trade facilitation · Barriers to trade

8.1 Introduction

Ghana has been at the forefront of implementing the AfCFTA. It was among the first countries to ratify the agreement and notably hosts the AfCFTA Secretariat in its capital, Accra. This positioning enhances Ghana's diplomatic influence and trade leadership in Africa (Ghana Investment Promotion Centre, 2021). Furthermore, the government of Ghana has introduced several initiatives, including the National AfCFTA Policy Framework and Action Plan, aimed at preparing businesses,

---

F. E. Turkson · A. Gyeke-Dako (✉)
University of Ghana, Accra, Ghana
e-mail: FTurkson2@ug.edu.gh; agyeke-dako@ug.edu.gh

D. N. Yuni et al. (eds.), *From Policy to Practice: Challenges and Ways Forward on the Implementation of the AfCFTA*,
https://doi.org/10.1007/978-3-032-14051-7_8

particularly small and medium-sized enterprises (SMEs), to fully leverage the trade agreement (Ministry of Trade and Industry, 2022).

The significance of AfCFTA for Ghana is broad. According to the World Bank (2020), successful implementation could boost Ghana's real income by 9% by 2035 and lift more than 300,000 Ghanaians out of extreme poverty. Intra-African exports are projected to rise by over 20%, especially in manufacturing sectors such as agro-processing, textiles, and pharmaceuticals. These prospects emerge at a time when Ghana is seeking to diversify its economy beyond cocoa and raw mineral exports, reduce youth unemployment, and enhance industrial productivity (Chivunga et al., 2024; UNCTAD, 2019).

Ghana's trade history reveals a persistent dependence on primary commodity exports, including cocoa, gold, and crude oil, alongside a growing need to industrialise and diversify exports. Ghana's trade with African partners, especially within ECOWAS, remains modest. Intra-African trade represents only 17% of Ghana's total trade, mirroring the broader continental average of 15% (UNCTAD, 2019). AfCFTA presents an opportunity to alter this pattern by offering duty-free access to a wider range of African markets, especially in manufactured goods, agribusiness, and services.

Yet, Ghana's road to fully benefiting from AfCFTA is not without challenges. Structural constraints, including poor transport infrastructure, limited digital readiness, overlapping trade regulations, and revenue losses resulting from tariff reductions, pose significant obstacles (Abrego et al., 2020; Tralac, 2022). The role of political will, policy coordination, and investment in trade facilitation infrastructure will therefore be critical.

This chapter critically analyses Ghana's engagement with AfCFTA. It provides a contextual background, explores expected benefits and sectoral opportunities, and highlights policy and implementation challenges. Drawing on a multidisciplinary range of literature and empirical data, this chapter aims to provide a comprehensive understanding of how Ghana can position itself as a continental trade hub under the AfCFTA.

The organisation of this chapter is as follows: Sect. 8.2 provides an analysis of Ghana's trade relationships within the African continent. Section 8.3 delineates Ghana's role in the African Continental Free Trade Area (AfCFTA), while Sect. 8.4 assesses the current status of AfCFTA implementation in Ghana. The potential benefits of AfCFTA for Ghana are discussed in Sect. 8.5. Section 8.6 identifies the opportunities available to Ghanaian businesses under the AfCFTA. Sections 8.7 and 8.8 examine the key challenges associated with implementing the AfCFTA and offer strategic policy recommendations, respectively, to conclude the chapter.

8.2 Ghana's Intra-African Trade Relations

Ghana is ranked among the 10 largest economies in Africa, with an estimated GDP of $88.3 billion in 2025 (IMF 2025). With an annual average growth rate of 4.5% between 2015 and 2024, Ghana is one of the fastest-growing economies in Africa. Indeed, the IMF estimates that Ghana will be among the five SSA countries that are likely to be among the fastest-growing economies in the world by 2025, with growth rates averaging above 5%. With a population of 35.1 million, Ghana has an estimated per capita GDP of $2519. This figure is approximately 32% higher than the projected average per capita GDP of $1914 for Sub-Saharan Africa in 2025. The services sector is the largest contributor to Ghana's GDP, accounting for 47% of the total in 2024. Although the industrial sector experienced the highest growth rate at 7.1%, the services sector followed with a growth rate of 5.9%, and the agricultural sector had a growth rate of 2.8%. In terms of contribution to GDP, the industrial sector ranks second at 30.8%, while the agricultural sector comes in third at 22.2%.

8.2.1 Contribution to Global Trade (Including Africa)

Ghana's external trade performance has shown significant improvement over the period 2020 to 2024 (Table 8.1). Exports (f.o.b. basis) increased steadily from US$14,472 million in 2020 to US$20,222 million in 2024. Imports also rose, albeit at a slower pace, from US$12,429 million in 2020 to US$15,241 million in 2024. Not surprisingly, total trade volume expanded from US$26.9 billion in 2020 to US$35.4 billion in 2024. The trade balance remained positive, with a notable increase from US$2043 million in 2020 to US$4981 million in 2024, reflecting Ghana's strengthened export performance relative to imports. This trend shows the country's improving trade dynamics and its growing capacity to generate foreign exchange.

Table 8.1 Ghana's global trade (2020–2024)

	2020	2021	2022	2023	2024
Indicator	(Amounts in millions of US$)				
Exports, *f.o.b.*	14,472	14,728	17,276	16,703	20,222
Imports, *f.o.b.*	12,429	13,629	14,621	14,009	15,241
Total trade	26,901	28,357	31,897	30,712	35,463
Trade balance	2043	1099	2655	2694	4981
Trade shares	(% of total trade)				
Exports, *f.o.b.*	53.8	51.9	54.2	54.4	57.0
Imports, *f.o.b.*	46.2	48.1	45.8	45.6	43.0
Total trade	100.0	100.0	100.0	100.0	100.0

Source: Bank of Ghana (2025)

Table 8.1 also presents Ghana's export and import shares as a percentage of total global trade from 2020 to 2024. Exports (f.o.b.) consistently constituted a greater share of Ghana's total trade compared to imports. Notably, the export share has increased steadily since 2022, rising to 54.2% in 2022, 54.4% in 2023, and reaching 57.0% in 2024. Correspondingly, the import share decreases over the same period, falling from 45.8% in 2022 to 43.0% in 2024. This shows a gradual strengthening of Ghana's export sector relative to its imports, suggesting an improving trade balance. Overall, Ghana's export performance appears to be on a positive trajectory within its global trading activities.

Figure 8.1 presents a breakdown of Ghana's trade distribution across various regions. Significant shifts can be observed in Ghana's trade, particularly with its notable trade partnerships. The Far East consistently held the largest share, reaching a peak of 31.6% in 2021.

The European Union (EU) was the second-largest partner, with a trade share of 21.8% in 2020, gradually decreasing to 15.6% by 2024. Trade with "Other EU" countries fluctuated, notably rising to 24.1% in 2023 before settling at 19.7% in 2024. Africa's share remained relatively stable, hovering between 14.7% and 16.8%, indicating a steady intracontinental trade relationship. ECOWAS maintained a modest share, peaking at 7.0% in 2021 and 2023 but dropping to 5.1% in 2024. North America's share was comparatively low, declining from 8.1% in 2020 to 5.0% in 2024. This suggests a diversification of Ghana's trade partners, with less reliance on traditional blocs and a notable expansion into new markets by 2024.

Ghana's export destination profile from 2020 to 2024 demonstrates notable shifts in the country's trade relationships, as reflected in the shares of exports directed to various regions and trading blocs (Fig. 8.2). Africa consistently remained a significant destination for Ghana's exports, with its share fluctuating between 20.2% and 24.2%. ECOWAS saw a steady increase from 6.8% in 2020 to a peak of 10.1% in 2023 before declining sharply to 6.5% in 2024. The EU initially accounted for 20% of Ghana's exports in 2020, rising to 25.2% in 2021, but then experienced a marked

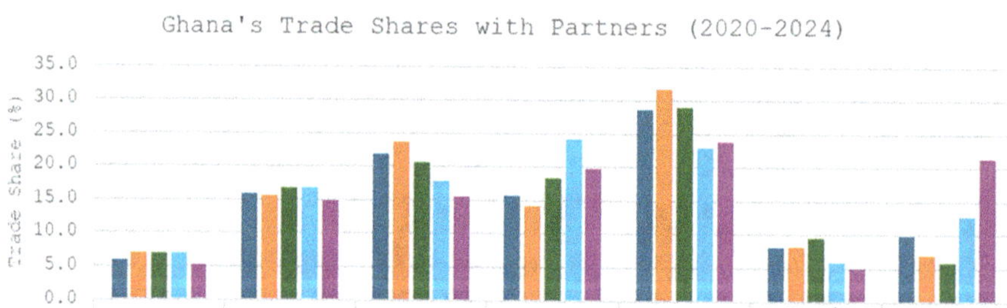

	ECOWAS	Africa	EU	Other EU	Far East	North America	Others
2020	5.8	15.8	21.8	15.8	28.6	8.1	9.9
2021	7.0	15.6	23.6	14.2	31.6	8.2	6.9
2022	6.9	16.7	20.6	18.3	29.0	9.6	5.8
2023	7.0	16.8	17.8	24.1	22.8	5.8	12.7
2024	5.1	14.7	15.6	19.7	23.7	5.0	21.3

Fig. 8.1 Ghana's trade shares with partners (2020–2024). Source: Bank of Ghana (2025)

	ECOWAS	Africa	EU	Other EU	Far East	North America	Others
2020	6.8	20.9	20	22.6	20.2	4.7	11.6
2021	9.1	21.3	25.2	21.7	23.3	4.2	4.3
2022	9.4	22.8	19.5	26	21.6	7.2	2.9
2023	10.1	24.2	13.4	31.2	13.9	3.6	13.7
2024	6.5	20.2	10.4	26.4	13.3	2.9	26.8

Fig. 8.2 Ghana's export destinations. Source: Bank of Ghana (2025)

decline, falling to just 10.4% in 2024. In contrast, the "Other EU" category, which includes non-EU European countries, experienced a significant surge, particularly in 2023, when it reached 31.2%, and remained relatively high at 26.4% in 2024.

The Far East region's share of Ghana's exports remained relatively stable from 2020 to 2022, hovering around 20–23%, but declined sharply to 13.3% by 2024. North America consistently represented a minor share, fluctuating between 2.9% and 7.2%, with a peak in 2022, followed by a decline. Overall, it can be observed that Ghana has a dynamic export landscape, characterised by a declining reliance on the EU and Far East, a fluctuating yet resilient African market, and a recent expansion into less conventional markets. These trends suggest Ghana's export strategy is adapting to global economic shifts, seeking broader market access and reducing dependence on a few major trading partners.

Ghana's export composition from 2020 to 2024, as shown in Fig. 8.4, highlights the dominance of gold, which consistently makes up the largest share of exports. This emphasises gold's critical role in Ghana's economy. Crude oil exports fluctuated between 19.1% and 31.4%, averaging 24.1% and peaking in 2022 before declining due to global price volatility. Cocoa contributed an average of 14%. Non-traditional exports (NTEs), such as processed goods and agricultural products, averaged 13.6%. Figure 8.3 shows that Ghana's exports are significantly reliant on gold, crude oil, and cocoa, which together comprise over three-quarters of total export earnings in 2024. However, the stable NTE performance indicates gradual diversification. This evolving structure reflects Ghana's resources and strategic policy shifts aimed at enhancing value addition and entering new markets.

Figure 8.4 shows Ghana's import shares by origin from 2020 to 2024. The Far East was the primary source, fluctuating between 33.4% in 2023, a peak of 40.5% in 2021, and 37.6% in 2024, driven by major economies like China, which supplied various manufactured goods and machinery. The EU was the second-largest source, with its share declining from 24% in 2020 to 22.4% in 2024, indicating reduced dependence on European suppliers. The "Other EU" category showed volatility,

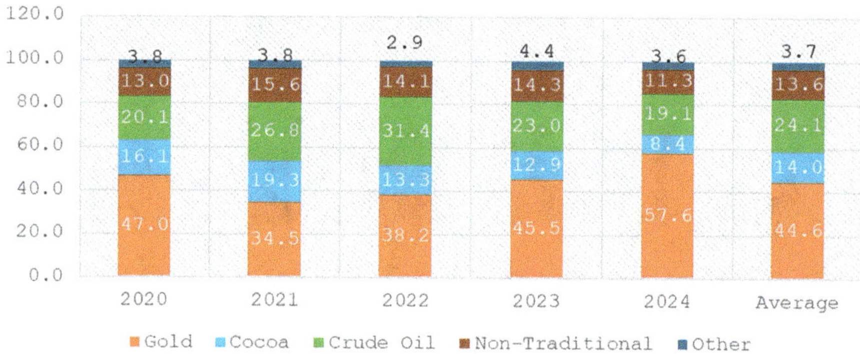

Fig. 8.3 Ghana's export products (2020–2024). Source: Bank of Ghana (2025)

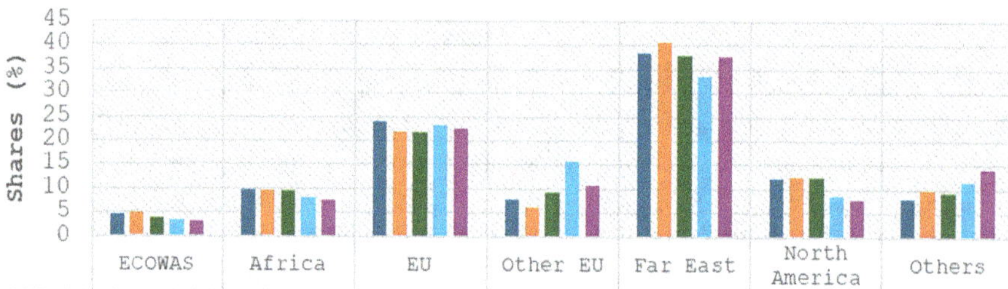

	ECOWAS	Africa	EU	Other EU	Far East	North America	Others
2020	4.6	9.8	24	7.8	38.3	12.1	8
2021	4.7	9.4	21.8	6	40.5	12.5	9.8
2022	3.9	9.5	21.8	9.2	37.8	12.4	9.3
2023	3.3	7.9	23.1	15.6	33.4	8.5	11.5
2024	3.2	7.5	22.4	10.7	37.6	7.7	14.1

Fig. 8.4 Ghana's import shares by origin (2020–2024). Source: Bank of Ghana (2025)

starting at 7.8% in 2020, dipping to 6% in 2021, rising to 15.6% in 2023, before moderating to 10.7% in 2024. African imports, including those from ECOWAS, declined from 9.8% in 2020 to 7.5% in 2024, with ECOWAS' share decreasing from 4.6% to 3.2%, indicating weaker intra-African trade links. North America peaked at 12.5% in 2021 but dropped to 7.7% by 2024, reflecting fluctuating demand for goods from the USA and Canada. These trends underscore Ghana's evolving trade landscape, characterised by a strong focus on Asian markets, declining European engagement, and global sourcing strategies.

Figure 8.5 illustrates Ghana's import composition, which features a dynamic structure with intermediate goods accounting for the largest share, averaging 36.4%, peaking at 39.6% in 2020. Oil and gas imports, the second-largest category, averaged 25.6%, rising from 15.2% in 2020 to 32% in 2023, then slightly declining to 29.4% in 2024 due to fluctuating global energy prices and domestic demand. Consumption goods averaged 15.3%, decreasing from 17.6% in 2020 to 13.2% in 2022, then rebounding. Capital goods averaged 15.7%, peaking at 18.7% in 2021 and dropping to 12.4% in 2023. The "others" category contributed the smallest

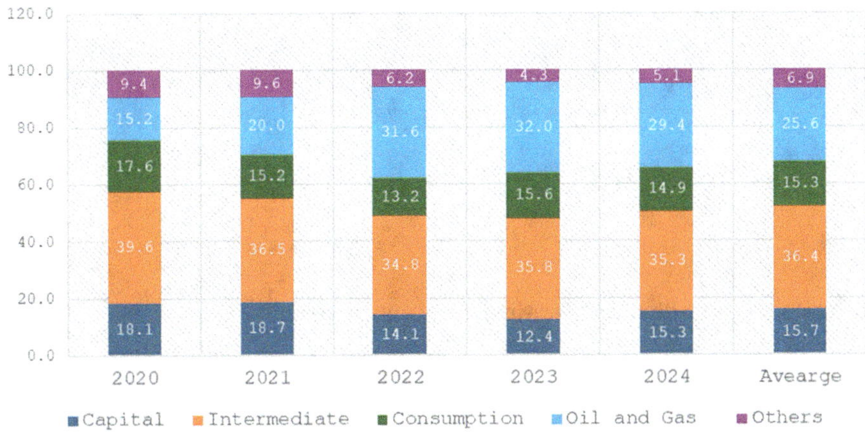

Fig. 8.5 Ghana's import products (2020–2024). Source: Bank of Ghana (2025)

share, averaging 6.9%, declining from 9.4% in 2020 to 4.3% in 2023, before experiencing a slight increase in 2024. Overall, Ghana's imports reflect a focus on industrial activity and adaptation to domestic consumption and investment cycles, with intermediate and oil and gas imports emphasising the country's integration into global supply chains and reliance on foreign inputs for economic growth.

8.2.2 *Ghana's Intra-African Trade*

8.2.2.1 Total Intra-African Trade

Regarding intra-African trade, Ghana's trade within Africa, which encompasses both exports and imports, increased from $4243 million in 2020 to $5228 million in 2024. The peak was observed in 2022 at $5328 million, after which there was a slight contraction in 2023, followed by a modest recovery in 2024 (see Table 8.2). As a percentage of its total Global trade, Ghana's intra-African trade generally increased from 15.8% in 2020 and peaked at 16.8% in 2023 before dropping to 14.7% in 2024. The overall growth in trade volume shows Ghana's increasing integration into the African market, despite intermittent fluctuations. This suggests a cautious approach to intra-African trade, possibly influenced by domestic economic adjustments, currency fluctuations, or shifts in consumer and industrial demand. However, as shown in Table 8.2, Ghana consistently maintained a positive trade balance within intra-regional trade throughout the period, with surpluses ranging from $1.807 billion in 2020 to $2.942 billion in 2024. The trade balance reached its highest point in 2024.

Table 8.2 Ghana's trade with Africa

	2020	2021	2022	2023	2024	2020	2021	2022	2023	2024
Indicator	Amounts in millions of US$					Per cent (%) shares of global				
Exports, f.o.b.	3025	3137	3939	4042	4085	20.9	21.3	22.8	24.2	20.2
Imports, f.o.b.	1218	1281	1389	1107	1143	9.8	9.4	9.5	7.9	7.5
Total trade	4243	4418	5328	5149	5228	15.8	15.6	16.7	16.8	14.7
Trade balance	1807	1856	2550	2935	2942	n.a.	n.a.	n.a.	n.a.	n.a.

Source: Bank of Ghana (2025)

8.2.2.2 Composition and Destination of Intra-African Exports

Ghana's exports (f.o.b.) to destinations within the African subregion steadily increased, from $3025 million in 2020 to $4085 million in 2024. The most significant increase occurred between 2021 and 2022, when exports surged by $802 million. Ghana's exports within the African market accounted for between 20.2% and 24.2% of its total exports, peaking in 2023 before declining in 2024. This generally shows Ghana's sustained export-led trade surplus within the African market and a marginally reduced share in imports.

In 2023, Ghana's exports to Africa (refer to Fig. 8.6) primarily consist of mineral commodities and manufactured goods. Gold accounts for 32% of the total trade value, establishing Ghana as a vital supplier of precious metals to African markets.

The export categories reveal a diverse manufacturing base, with petroleum oils making up 5% and iron and steel products at 4%. Exports of electrical energy (4%) underscore Ghana's role as a key regional energy provider, particularly relevant to West Africa's efforts to integrate its energy sector. Ghana also exports various manufactured items, including unglazed ceramics (3%), toilet paper (2%), and packing lids (2%). Additionally, specialised inputs such as nitrogenous fertilisers (2%) and cleaning products (2%) demonstrate Ghana's capacity to support regional agricultural and industrial needs. As shown in Fig. A81, the composition of exports has remained fairly consistent since 2020. Leading the exports are crude petroleum oil at 33%, followed by electrical energy at 12%, trade data discrepancies at 7%, and palm oil at 7%. Other notable exports include unglazed ceramic flags, refined petroleum oil, and wheat or meslin flour, each accounting for smaller portions.

South Africa emerges as Ghana's dominant African trading partner, accounting for 32% of total intra-African exports in 2023 (32% in 2020). As illustrated in Fig. 8.7 and Appendix Fig. A8.2, there is also a significant degree of regional integration within West Africa (though the shares have marginally declined since 2020), with Burkina Faso at 18%, Côte d'Ivoire at 10%, Togo at 8% and Mali at 7%, all representing notable export destinations in 2023. Beyond these primary destinations, Ghana maintains modest yet consistent trade relationships across the continent, with Uganda and Nigeria serving as important markets in East and West Africa, respectively. There is a limited presence in North African markets, including Tunisia, Algeria, and Morocco.

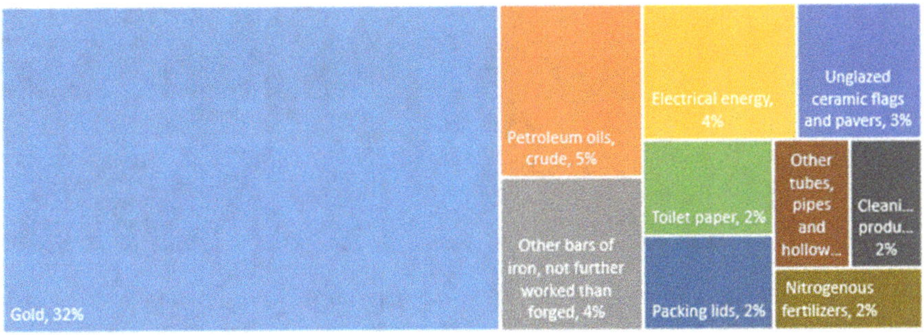

Fig. 8.6 Ghana's intra-african exports in 2023-top 20 products. Source: Data from https://atlas.hks.harvard.edu/

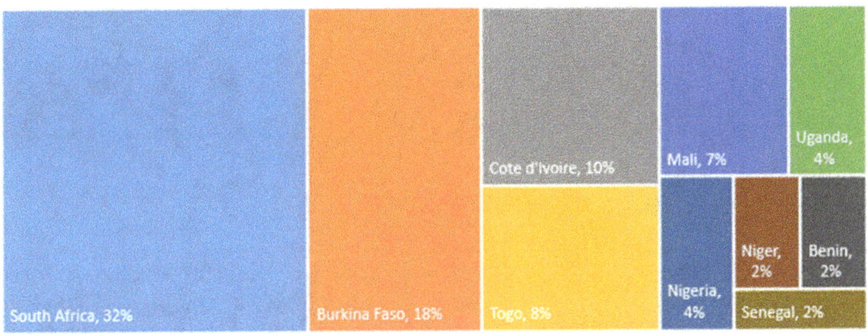

Fig. 8.7 Ghana's top export destinations in Africa in 2023 (top 20 destinations). Source: Data from https://atlas.hks.harvard.edu/

8.2.2.3 Composition and Origin of Intra-African Imports

Intra-African imports (f.o.b.) also increased, albeit at a slower and more fluctuating pace, at $1218 million in 2020, peaking at $1389 million in 2022, and then slightly declining to $1143 million by 2024 (see Table 8.2). As given in Table 8.2, imports from African origin (as a share of global trade) declined steadily from 9.8% in 2020 to 7.5% in 2024. Between 2020 and 2023, Ghana's imports from Africa underwent notable changes. In 2020, the imports comprised aircraft and spacecraft (10%), crude petroleum oil (9%), and makeup preparations (4%), alongside motor vehicles and special-purpose vessels, each accounting for 4%. By 2023 (refer to Fig. 8.8), imports became more concentrated, with cement emerging as the top import at 10%, followed closely by trade data discrepancies and refined petroleum oils, each at 8%. Other significant imports included frozen fish (5%), hot-rolled iron bars (4%), and makeup preparations (3%). The top 10 products represented a broad spectrum of industrial, agricultural, and consumer goods.

In 2023, South Africa is Ghana's largest import partner from Africa, contributing 22% of total imports, followed by Côte d'Ivoire at 16%, Egypt at 13%, and Burkina

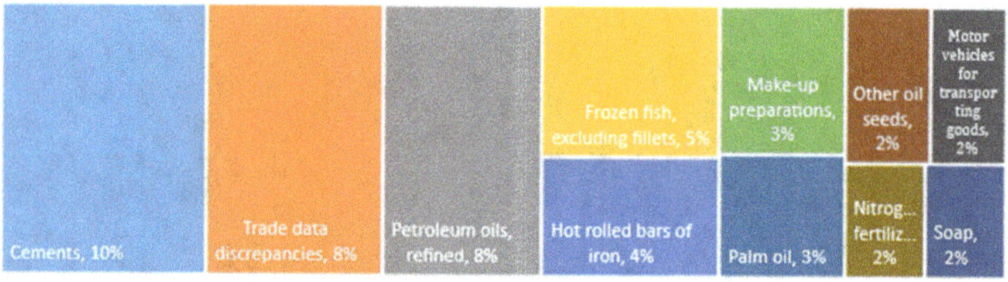

Fig. 8.8 Ghana's intra-African imports in 2023—top 10 products. Source: Data from https://atlas.hks.harvard.edu/

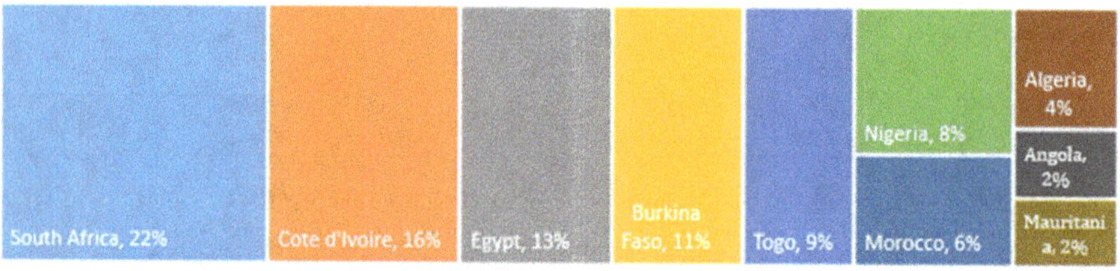

Fig. 8.9 Origin of Ghana's imports from Africa in 2023 (top 10 destinations). Source: Data from https://atlas.hks.harvard.edu/

Faso at 11%. Other countries, each represented less than 10%, included Togo, Nigeria, and Morocco. In 2020 (refer to Appendix Fig. A8.4, Nigeria was Ghana's largest import partner, accounting for 25%, closely followed by South Africa at 23%, which together made up nearly half of all imports from Africa. Next were Côte d'Ivoire (16%), Morocco (8%), and Egypt (6%). This structure reveals Ghana's dependence on a few African countries and limited product range, highlighting vulnerabilities to supply disruptions and opportunities for diversification (Fig. 8.9).

8.3 Ghana's Role in the AfCFTA

Ghana was among the first countries to ratify the AfCFTA Agreement in 2018 and has since positioned itself as a leading continental implementer of its provisions. In July 2019, Accra was selected to host the AfCFTA Secretariat, a decision that symbolically highlights Ghana's strategic commitment to Pan-Africanism and trade integration. The Secretariat, operational since 2020, oversees the administration, implementation, and monitoring of the agreement, playing a critical role in dispute resolution and technical coordination (African Union, 2018).

Ghana's engagement in the African Continental Free Trade Area (AfCFTA) is driven by the pursuit of several strategic objectives. These objectives encompass the following:

1. Facilitating market access for Ghanaian goods and services across the continent.
2. Fostering innovative Ghanaian products with significant export potential.
3. Encouraging demand for "Made in Ghana" goods across Africa.
4. Providing timely, accurate market trend information for Ghanaian businesses.
5. Promoting innovative financial instruments for trade in Africa.
6. Enhancing the value addition of Ghanaian goods for export to other African nations, thereby advancing the economy along the value chain.

To further operationalise its role, the Government of Ghana, through the Ministry of Trade and Industry, has launched the National AfCFTA Policy Framework and Action Plan. This strategy aims to enhance Ghana's productive capacity by aligning domestic trade laws with AfCFTA protocols, supporting SMEs in engaging in cross-border trade, and investing in trade-related infrastructure (Ministry of Trade and Industry, 2022). The National AfCFTA Coordination Office (NCO), established under this framework, serves as the link between Ghanaian stakeholders and the Secretariat, facilitating private sector participation, public awareness campaigns, and capacity-building efforts.

8.4 National AfCFTA Policy Framework and Action Plan

This policy framework has been developed to enhance Ghana's participation in intra-African trade while ensuring a consistent and stable policy environment that fosters private sector development. It provides clear and transparent guidelines for implementing the government's vision of maximising the benefits of the African Continental Free Trade Area (AfCFTA).

The National AfCFTA Policy Framework consists of seven key components.

8.4.1 Component One: Development of Ghana's AfCFTA Trade Policy

Ghana's AfCFTA Trade Policy component aims to accelerate trade development by adopting and implementing Ghana's trade initiatives that are consistent with and focused on increasing trade within Africa. The policy aims to enhance Ghana's exports to other AfCFTA markets and ensure that AfCFTA rules and regulations are effectively integrated into Ghana's legal framework. This will help Ghana fulfil its obligations under the AfCFTA. Ghana's trade policy, in alignment with the African Continental Free Trade Area (AfCFTA), is designed to establish and implement a framework for engagement among the government, the private sector, and civil society.

This framework aims to enhance their contributions to the formulation and execution of the AfCFTA. The policy also includes the implementation of import defence measures, competition policy, and intellectual property rights to mitigate losses arising from unfair trade practices while maximising the trade opportunities presented under the AfCFTA. Furthermore, an initiative to establish dispute settlement procedures has been prioritised to ensure the effective and timely resolution of issues that impede access for Ghanaian exporters to other markets within the AfCFTA.

8.4.2 Component Two: Trade Facilitation

The Trade Facilitation component aims to expedite the movement of goods across both existing and new trade corridors. Its main objective is to reduce the cost and time it takes for goods to travel from Ghana to various destinations in Africa. To achieve this, the initiative focuses on ensuring swift and efficient cargo clearance processes at ports and border posts, all within a safe and secure environment. Additionally, the policy framework seeks to prevent non-tariff barriers and technical standards from obstructing Ghana's trade with Africa. Furthermore, the Integrated Customs Management System (ICUMS) constitutes a vital platform for facilitating streamlined trade operations, which will greatly facilitate the movement of goods across the borders, significantly reducing the trade costs of doing business within the continent. For instance, as noted by Codjoe (2023), the Noepe-Akanu one-stop border post, where Ghanaian and Togolese customs officials work hand-in-hand, is a good example of how integrated border management can be used to simplify the process for traders.

8.4.3 Component Three: Enhancing Productive Capacity

This component focuses on improving local production capabilities for Ghanaian products intended for the African market, while also integrating Ghana into regional value chains.

Ghana has significant industrial potential to establish itself as a hub for industrial and manufacturing activities in Africa. Although Ghana's productivity (in terms of value-added per worker) rose from US$2645 to US$4844 between 2000 and 2020, its manufacturing sector has lagged behind in Sub-Saharan Africa (SSA), with an annual manufacturing value-added (MVA) share of GDP averaging 9.1% compared to 11.3% for SSA. Notably, between 2021 and 2023, Ghana's MVA increased remarkably to 11.2%, approaching the SSA average MVA of 11.6% over the same period (ILO, 2024; World Bank, 2025). This situation primarily stems from insufficient domestic capacities, including shortages of raw materials, a lack of skilled human resources, outdated supply chain channels, and inefficient infrastructure. For the Government of Ghana, the goal of enhancing productive capacity is to facilitate the nation's transition from an agrarian to an industrialised economy. In relation to

AfCFTA, there is a focus on increasing the proportion of manufactured goods exported to Africa and integrating the Ghanaian economy into regional and global value chains through improved access to competitive production factors, enhanced productivity, and growth in the manufacturing sector.

The Ghanaian government has outlined its strategic objectives aimed at enhancing productive capacity. These include improving access to high-quality raw materials and necessary inputs in sufficient quantities for key sectors, all while ensuring competitive pricing. Furthermore, the government plans to prioritise the adoption and integration of modern machinery and technology in these strategic sectors to boost productivity. It will also focus on enhancing the availability and quality of managerial and entrepreneurial skills in these areas, with an emphasis on improving access to warehousing, storage, and distribution facilities across the value chain of key sectors. Among other policies, it is anticipated that Ghana will encourage its businesses to adopt innovative technologies and equipment in production processes. Additionally, it will develop a policy and incentive framework to attract investments into selected strategic manufacturing sectors, particularly in agro-industries, for value addition and value chain processing.

8.4.4 Component Four: Trade-related Infrastructure

The component on trade-related infrastructure emphasises developing and financing infrastructure projects, particularly in multimodal transportation, including ports, roads, highways, railways, and aviation, as well as communication and energy.

The development of efficient multimodal infrastructure, supported by robust telecommunications and ICT systems, as well as strong transport, energy, and water systems, is crucial for reducing trade costs and enhancing competitiveness. The continent's inadequate infrastructure hampers trade flow and raises distribution costs. Estimates suggest that poor infrastructure adds 30–40% to the cost of goods traded in Africa. Trade costs in Africa are significantly higher than in other regions, mainly due to non-policy-induced non-tariff barriers (Mbabazi et al., 2006; Turkson, 2012, 2015; Turkson et al., 2020). Trade-related infrastructure is essential for promoting trade in Africa. However, Ghana faces similar infrastructural challenges that hinder local enterprises, reducing their competitiveness and ability to capitalise on AfCFTA opportunities. Rising input costs and unreliable power sources increase production expenses, leading to delivery delays and substantial sales losses. Poor road networks and neglected access roads to production sites and markets escalate transaction costs and prolonged delivery times. The inadequately developed intra-African transport network (rail, road, air) limits market access and raises trade expenses, further compounded by a lack of warehousing and distribution facilities at destination markets.

Turkson et al. (2020) emphasised that inadequate infrastructure and trade facilitation measures primarily drive high trade costs in Sub-Saharan Africa. Similarly, Wilson et al. (2008) noted that, compared to Asia and Latin America, Africa's higher trade costs result from significant logistics, regulatory, and infrastructural barriers, which complicate the movement of goods and lead to low intra-regional trade. Additionally, transport costs in Africa are about 2.5 times higher than in developed nations (see Portugal-Perez & Wilson, 2008).

Trade infrastructure initiatives, such as rehabilitating railways, expanding port facilities, developing the inland port at Tema (not Boankra, which is inland), and enhancing aviation infrastructure, are set to improve the efficient movement of goods and services between Ghana and its neighbours. With some projects nearing completion, Ghanaian businesses will benefit from the African Continental Free Trade Area (AfCFTA).

Additionally, this component aims to provide reliable, accessible, and competitively priced energy for trade businesses under the AfCFTA and establish a world-class intermodal logistical hub for in-country and subregional connectivity with markets across Africa by December 2026.

8.4.5 Component Five: Trade Finance and Development

The Trade and Development Finance component seeks to improve access to trade and development financing for Ghana's private sector, thereby promoting the production and marketing of Ghanaian goods in the African market.

In the realm of international trade, trade finance includes a broad range of financial products designed to facilitate business transactions between importers and exporters globally. The success of trading activities across the continent under the AfCFTA will depend on the establishment and availability of dependable, sufficient, affordable, and accessible national financial products. These are essential for both long-term capital investments in producing tradable goods and services, as well as for short-term settlements of trade debts and related payments.

Africa traditionally relied on the global financial system for transactions. With the launch of the AfCFTA, African nations must pursue innovative and cost-effective financing for intracontinental trade. The African financial landscape is complex, featuring non-convertible currencies, protective regulations, and inadequate structures that fail to support intra-African trade. Current international trade frameworks heavily depend on international financing, which is often inaccessible to many Ghanaian exporters, like letters of credit and trade credits. Additionally, financing cross-border investments among African nations is even more challenging and could hinder regional growth if unaddressed.

The Pan-African Payment System, designed to streamline cross-border payments, relies heavily on the active participation of local financial sector stakeholders. Their involvement is crucial for creating tailored trade finance solutions, ensuring exporters receive timely financial support.

The Ghanaian government advocates for a Special-Purpose Vehicle (SPV) to enhance production and marketing under the AfCFTA. It also aims to strengthen Export Finance Institutions to provide specialised support for AfCFTA exports.

Furthermore, the government plans to create a national African Customer Due Diligence (ACDD) Repository Platform for registering exporters and supporting Export Trade Houses, improving marketing services for AfCFTA products.

8.4.6 Component Six: Trade Information

The component on Trade Information seeks to provide greater access to information on opportunities for intra-African Trade and Investment.

Adequate and accessible trade information is vital for effectively implementing the African Continental Free Trade Agreement. Information regarding regulations, procedures, requirements, agreements, market opportunities, and risks is often difficult to find and access. Typically, there is significant information asymmetry concerning intra-African trade. A clear framework for gathering and sharing information on continental trade with Ghanaian businesses and entrepreneurs is lacking. The processes for collecting, processing, and disseminating information among businesses, policymakers, and relevant stakeholders in Ghana are not well-defined. Furthermore, the lack of reliable information on trade opportunities, customs formalities, and procedures greatly increases the cost of doing business in the region.

Many businesses in Ghana struggle to access the African market compared to those in other regions. Current trade information platforms in Ghana are disjointed and lack coordination. There is no robust framework for establishing regional networks to share data on businesses, exports, and market opportunities across Africa. To improve access to vital information for Ghanaian businesses, the government is creating a Ghana Trade Information Repository, which will supply market access data on African markets for enterprises engaging in trade under the AfCFTA and enhance the capabilities of institutions offering trade information on the AfCFTA in Ghana.

8.4.7 Component Seven: Factor Market Integration

The component on Factor Market Integration advocates for the implementation of relevant protocols regarding the free movement of people, investment, and factors of production.

Strengthening African integration is crucial for the success of the AfCFTA in boosting intra-African trade. To achieve this, it is necessary to enhance the mobility of production factors (labour, enterprise, and capital) within and between regions. Although the AU and ECOWAS have developed instruments to promote the free movement of people, residence rights, and the establishment of businesses, many African nations have not fully adopted them. This is due to insufficient ratification, restrictive national laws, and an inability to establish complementary agreements for mutual recognition of certification qualifications.

To capitalise on AfCFTA opportunities, Ghana must implement policies for the free movement of goods, services, and labour migration, and align cross-border establishment rules. It also needs to negotiate agreements on certification and recognition. To support Ghanaian businesses in Africa, the government plans to implement the Protocol of the Treaty Establishing the African Economic Community concerning the Free Movement of Persons, Right of Residence, and Right of Establishment. It will align national laws with the AU Protocol and conclude agreements for mutual recognition of qualifications. The government aims to develop Mutual Recognition Agreements with countries offering current and prospective labour market opportunities across Africa.

8.5 Status of AfCFTA Implementation in Ghana

In anticipation of the commencement of trading under the African Continental Free Trade Area (AfCFTA) protocols, Ghana has revised and realigned specific existing government initiatives to enhance the country's preparedness for the AfCFTA. Among the most significant of these initiatives is the One District, One Factory (1D1F) programme, which was initiated in 2017. Furthermore, the government has introduced the Strategic Anchor Industries programme, developed regional industrial parks, and established the National Export Development Strategy, which was initiated in October 2020. Beyond these, various implementation arrangements have been made, including those related to the Institutional and Policy Framework, Trade Facilitation, Capacity-Building, and Payment Systems. Trading activities have also commenced under AfCFTA.

8.5.1 Institutional and Policy Framework

8.5.1.1 National AfCFTA Policy Framework and Action Plan (NPFAP)

As part of Ghana's AfCFTA Strategy, the Government of Ghana launched the National AfCFTA Policy Framework and Action Plan (NPFAP) in 2022 to boost trade with Africa, focusing on aligning national trade policies with AfCFTA obligations, enhancing private sector readiness, and industrialisation and job creation. NPFAP issues guidelines for Ministries, Departments, and Agencies (MDAs) to create a supportive business environment that integrates its local economy into regional or continental markets and boosts trade performance.

Indeed, effective participation in the AfCFTA in Ghana is anchored in the decentralisation of the implementation of the National Action Plan. In line with the government's directive, MDAs and MMDAs have incorporated the projects into their annual budgets. This approach has ensured that financing the activities outlined in the National Action Plan is included in the national budgets of the respective MDAs and MMDAs. It is estimated that implementing all these activities will require approximately USD 9 billion between 2022 and 2027.

8.5.1.2 The Inter-Ministerial Facilitation Committee (IMFC)

The government has established the Inter-Ministerial Facilitation Committee, which serves as the policy oversight body responsible for ensuring the development, guidance, and compliance of government policies with the AfCFTA. Chaired by the Minister of Trade and Industry, the committee includes the Ministers responsible for Foreign Affairs and Regional Integration, Justice and Attorney-General, Finance and National Security, as well as a representative from the Office of the President.

The primary function of the IMFC is to ensure that participation in the AfCFTA aligns with the Government's development strategy and policy objectives. They are also responsible for ensuring that the Government's commitments in respect of the AfCFTA are fulfilled. The IMC reports to the President through the Chair of the IMFC.

To provide strategic guidance and direction for implementation, as well as advisory inputs for policy alignment, the National AfCFTA Steering Committee (NSC), comprising the Chairs of the Technical Working Groups, has been established. The NSC reports to the IMFC.

8.5.1.3 National AfCFTA Coordination Office

Ghana established the National AfCFTA Coordination Office (NCO) in March 2020 under the Ministry of Trade and Industry as a central body to coordinate the country's strategic and tactical responses to the AfCFTA Agreement. The NCO serves as a liaison between the Ghanaian government, the AfCFTA Secretariat, and various stakeholders, ensuring that Ghana maximises its benefits from the agreement. The establishment of the NCO aligns with Ghana's ambition to become a trade hub in Africa and to leverage the AfCFTA for economic transformation, private sector growth, and increased intra-African trade. The office ensures that Ghana's private sector, particularly non-resource-based sectors, can fully capitalise on the new continental market opportunities.

In line with its coordination role, the National Coordination Office is committed to establishing an efficient operational network among all key institutions involved in implementing the AfCFTA in Ghana. These include the GRA-Customs Division, the Ghana National Chamber of Commerce and Industry, the Ghana Food and Drugs Authority, the Ghana Standards Authority and the Ghana Export Promotion Authority, amongst others. The NCO has also actively engaged non-state actors, including financial institutions, entrepreneurs, and private sector associations.

8.5.2 Trade Facilitation, Capacity-Building and Payment Systems

Geographically, Ghana is strategically positioned along the Gulf of Guinea, serving as a potential logistics hub for West Africa. The government has invested in major infrastructure projects, including the expansion of Tema and Takoradi ports, aviation upgrades, and rail linkages, all of which align with the goals of the AfCFTA.

Regarding trade facilitation and capacity-building, the government of Ghana has introduced new customs procedure codes since 2022 to streamline AfCFTA-related trade. These codes facilitate the management of reliefs and privileges under the AfCFTA within the Ghana Revenue Authority's (GRA) automated customs system, enabling the efficient processing of imports, exports, and transit goods under the agreement. About 30 Ghanaian companies have received Certificates of Origin, allowing them to export under AfCFTA rules. Ghana has introduced measures such as new customs codes, capacity-building programmes, and enterprise-level support to help companies navigate AfCFTA requirements and expand into African markets. The Ghana Export Promotion Authority (GEPA) and related agencies provide support for SMEs, including logistical assistance and market access facilitation.

Ghana officially launched the Pan-African Payment and Settlement System (PAPSS) in Accra on January 13, 2022, making the system available for public use in the country. PAPSS is meant to facilitate trade in local currencies across African countries, reducing the over-reliance on the U.S. dollar and lowering transaction costs. Ghana's first actual cross-border transaction using PAPSS occurred on March 8, 2023, when a Ghanaian company made a supplier payment from GCB Bank in Ghanaian cedis to a recipient in Nigeria, who received the payment instantly in Naira. This marked a significant milestone in Ghana's active use of PAPSS for real-time cross-border payments.

8.5.3 Trading Activities

Ghana's trading activities have been conducted under the Guided Trade Initiative (GTI) so far. The GTI plays a crucial role in operationalising the AfCFTA, promoting trade, and fostering economic integration among countries within Africa. It enables State parties to pilot-test the AfCFTA rules and procedures, while also identifying areas that require improvement. It is intended to help build confidence and trust among State Parties (i.e. member states), traders, and investors.

Ghana launched the GTIs in October 2022 as one of only eight countries (out of 29) that as at the time, had fully met the requirements for participation. As noted by Codjoe (2023), trading under the GTIs commenced with approximately 96 products on the transaction list, which included batteries, coffee, sugar, pasta, tea, dried fruits, ceramic tiles, and processed meat products. These products aligned with the AfCFTA's objective of value chain development.

Although Ghana has reportedly assisted 30 companies to obtain Certificates of Origin to export goods under the initiative, 14 Ghanaian companies have been actively engaged in 40 trades across the continent, exporting products such as beverages, cosmetics, palm oil, and ceramics to South Africa, Guinea, Kenya, and Cameroon. According to Codjoe (2023), the majority of these transactions are imports with comparatively fewer exports from Ghana heading to other GTI countries. Goods imported into Ghana under the GTI so far include shipments of tea and batteries arriving from Kenya, coffee beans from Rwanda, meat products and cement from Egypt, as well as tea and dried fruits from Cameroon. During the first quarter of 2023, the National AfCFTA Coordination Office (NCO) reported that two Ghanaian companies had been exporting palm oil products to Kenya and ceramics to Cameroon under the pilot trading programme. Table 8.3 summarises the companies, their products and the first recorded GTI destinations.

While Kasapreko and Ghandour carried Ghana's first-ever AfCFTA shipment in January 2021, establishing proof of concept for the agreement, KEDA's 20 million m^2/year tile plant signifies that Ghana is now exporting heavy-manufactured goods duty-free within Africa, rather than only raw commodities. The trading activities of G-mith and Mazia under AfCFTA indicate that micro- and women-led enterprises are exploiting GTI preferences once certificates of origin and logistics support are obtained. In 2024, the GTI was expanded to cover 24 additional African countries, broadening potential trading partners and product range. The government of Ghana aims to support approximately 180 companies in exporting to AfCFTA markets, with a focus on job creation and value addition.

While trade between Ghana and other GTI countries may still be modest, evidence suggests that the initiative has effectively enhanced economic engagement among Sub-Saharan African nations, particularly in terms of trade between Ghana and Kenya. Local enterprises, including Kasapreko Company Limited, a well-known producer of alcoholic and non-alcoholic beverages, have leveraged the African Continental Free Trade Area (AfCFTA) and the trade facilitation measures

Table 8.3 Selected AfCFTA participants from Ghana

Company	Main product (s) shipped under AfCFTA	First-reported GTI destination (s) and year
Kasapreko company ltd	Ready-to-drink alcoholic and soft beverages (e.g., Alomo bitters)	20-ft container of beverages to South Africa (Jan 2021)
Ghandour cosmetics ltd.	Hair- and skin-care products (creams, lotions, hair relaxers)	20-ft container to Guinea (Jan 2021)
Benso oil palm plantation (BOPP)	Palm-kernel oil products	Bulk drums to Kenya, Oct 2022
KEDA Ghana ceramics co. ltd. (Ywyford)	Floor and wall ceramic tiles	Container to Cameroon, Oct 2022
G-mith Enterprise	Natural lime-based deodorants	Small-batch shipments to Kenya & Rwanda, 2023
Mazia co Enterprise	Honey, flavoured teas, dried-fruit snacks	Cameroon, Kenya & Rwanda (2023)

by both the Ghanaian government and similar authorities to export their products to other African nations, anticipating the complete implementation of the AfCFTA.

8.6 Obstacles Facing Ghana Under AfCFTA

While the African Continental Free Trade Area (AfCFTA) presents Ghana with unprecedented economic prospects, its successful implementation is not without formidable challenges. These obstacles span structural, institutional, financial, political, and socio-economic dimensions. Addressing them is essential if Ghana is to maximise the benefits of continental trade integration and avoid worsening existing disparities.

One of the most critical challenges is Ghana's infrastructure deficit, which continues to hinder trade competitiveness. Despite efforts to expand ports and improve road networks, the quality and coverage of transport infrastructure, particularly rail, road linkages, and border facilities, remain inadequate to support the seamless movement of goods and services. Efficient trade depends on regional connectivity, yet many trade corridors are characterised by delays, high transport costs, and logistical inefficiencies. According to Onwuka and Udegbunam (2019), even existing regional trade blocs, such as ECOWAS, COMESA, and EAC, have struggled to fully implement their free trade arrangements due to persistent infrastructure bottlenecks. For AfCFTA to thrive, Ghana must prioritise sustained investments in trade facilitation infrastructure, including digital customs systems, warehousing, and efficient port clearance processes.

Another major concern is the fiscal impact of tariff liberalisation. As a lower-middle-income country with a narrow tax base, Ghana relies significantly on trade taxes for government revenue. The removal of tariffs on 90% of traded goods under AfCFTA could lead to considerable short-term revenue losses. While efficiency gains and wider economic growth may compensate for this overtime, the transitional period could strain public finances and affect government spending on social services and infrastructure. According to Ajibo (2019), governments must consider alternative revenue mobilisation strategies such as value-added tax (VAT) efficiency, improved domestic tax collection, and economic formalisation. Without adequate compensation mechanisms, this revenue gap may undermine fiscal stability and public support for AfCFTA.

Ghana must also contend with the challenge of limited productive capacity among its domestic industries. Many Ghanaian firms, especially small and medium-sized enterprises (SMEs), lack the scale, technology, and capital to compete effectively in an open continental market. The danger is that without strategic support, Ghana could become a net importer within AfCFTA, with more industrialised countries flooding its markets with manufactured goods. This asymmetry could widen the trade deficit and weaken local industries unless accompanied by deliberate industrial policy, access to affordable credit, and capacity-building programmes.

UNECA (2020a) warns that liberalisation without corresponding investments in productive capacity may worsen inequality and deepen structural weaknesses.

Another serious challenge is the persistence of non-tariff barriers (NTBs), which may undermine the benefits of tariff reductions. NTBs such as import quotas, licencing requirements, product standards misalignment, and bureaucratic red tape continue to restrict market access across Africa. Even with AfCFTA protocols in place, countries may exploit these instruments to protect domestic industries under the guise of safety or quality control. Ghana, like other member states, needs robust institutional frameworks to detect and address NTBs while simultaneously harmonising its trade regulations with AfCFTA protocols. Abrego et al. (2020) note that even at the global level under the World Trade Organisation (WTO), NTBs have proven difficult to fully eliminate, making this a significant obstacle for AfCFTA's smooth functioning.

Furthermore, political will and policy consistency remain crucial variables in the implementation of the AfCFTA. While Ghana has demonstrated leadership in ratification and policy formulation, regional trade agreements often falter due to shifting political priorities, changes in government, or protectionist tendencies. The risk is that competing national interests could override regional commitments, especially during economic downturns or election cycles. Ensuring continuity in trade policy, strengthening institutional independence, and building a national consensus around AfCFTA goals will be essential to sustain momentum. As Obeng-Odoom (2020) argues, trade integration in Africa cannot succeed without a stable political environment and genuine commitment to long-term regionalism.

Technical capacity constraints also pose a serious threat to implementation, particularly in areas such as trade negotiation, standards compliance, digital trade systems, and monitoring mechanisms. Many state institutions and private sector actors in Ghana lack the expertise, equipment, or data systems required to comply with AfCFTA protocols. This is compounded by limited funding for training, infrastructure, and coordination. For least developed countries (LDCs) on the continent, including many of Ghana's trading partners, the lack of readiness may lead to uneven implementation and disparities in trade gains. Ajibo (2019) warns that unless accompanied by significant technical and financial support from regional and international partners, many countries may struggle to meet the operational demands of AfCFTA.

Finally, Ghana's trade strategy must navigate complex relationships with non-African trade blocs and partners. While AfCFTA aims to boost intra-African trade, it should not come at the cost of isolating the continent from global trade networks. If AfCFTA is implemented in a way that overly shields domestic markets from global competition, it risks undermining external trade relations, foreign investment, and technology transfers. As Abrego et al. (2020) suggest, a gradual reduction in Most-Favoured Nation (MFN) tariffs complemented by AfCFTA liberalisation can ensure that Africa remains integrated in the global economy while benefiting from regional consolidation.

While these challenges are significant, they are not insurmountable. With the right reforms and sustained commitment, Ghana can emerge as a central player in Africa's integration agenda and reap long-term gains from the AfCFTA.

8.7 Benefits of AfCFTA to Ghana

The African Continental Free Trade Area (AfCFTA) presents Ghana with transformative benefits, including expanded trade volumes, economic diversification, industrial development, and poverty reduction. By eliminating tariffs on 90% of goods and reducing non-tariff barriers, AfCFTA enhances market access across Africa and promotes economies of scale for Ghanaian producers and exporters. The benefits can be categorised into trade, income, welfare, production, employment, and industrial competitiveness.

8.7.1 Enhanced Trade and Market Access

AfCFTA provides Ghanaian businesses with access to a single African market of over 1.4 billion people, allowing Ghana to overcome the constraints of its relatively small domestic market. The removal of trade barriers is expected to increase Ghana's exports, especially to markets outside the ECOWAS region, such as those in North, Central, and Southern Africa.

According to the UNECA (2020b), the AfCFTA is expected to boost intra-African trade by over 52% by 2025. Ghanaian exports, particularly in processed cocoa, textiles, pharmaceuticals, aluminium products, and agro-processed goods, are expected to benefit significantly. Intra-African exports tend to be more diversified and have higher value-added content compared to exports to non-African markets, providing Ghana with the opportunity to deepen its industrial base.

> Tariff elimination under the AfCFTA could increase Africa's exports by $560 billion, with a large share expected from manufactured goods (World Bank, 2020).

8.7.2 Income Growth and Poverty Reduction

One of the most significant macroeconomic benefits of AfCFTA is its potential to raise incomes and reduce poverty. World Bank simulations project that AfCFTA will raise Africa's income by $450 billion by 2035, with Ghana among the top gainers due to its early ratification, location, and relatively diversified economy.

For Ghana specifically, income could grow by approximately 9%, while over 300,000 Ghanaians could be lifted out of extreme poverty (World Bank, 2020). The wage gains are expected to be fairly distributed across skilled and unskilled labour, which is critical for inclusive development. Wage levels are projected to increase by 10.3% for unskilled workers and 9.8% for skilled workers (Abrego et al., 2020).

8.7.3 Industrial Development and Value Chain Integration

AfCFTA supports Ghana's industrial transformation agenda under initiatives such as "One District, One Factory (1D1F)" and the National Export Development Strategy. By connecting Ghanaian producers to regional value chains, AfCFTA incentivises the production of semi-processed and finished goods for African markets. This is crucial for reducing the country's reliance on raw commodity exports and mitigating price volatility.

> AfCFTA is expected to lead to a 29% increase in intra-African industrial goods trade by 2040 (UNCTAD, 2021).

Moreover, manufacturers in Ghana stand to benefit from cheaper intermediate goods and raw materials from other African suppliers, reduced input costs from harmonised customs procedures, lower logistics costs and access to new investment and partnership opportunities through regional supply chains.

8.7.4 Business Expansion and Job Creation

The liberalisation of trade in both goods and services under AfCFTA can stimulate business growth, particularly among Ghana's small and medium-sized enterprises (SMEs). SMEs comprise over 85% of Ghana's businesses, and the AfCFTA offers them an unprecedented opportunity to expand beyond the national market (Asamoah, 2024).

As businesses grow and expand operations, job creation is expected in agroprocessing, light manufacturing, transport, logistics, financial services, fintech, and tourism.

This aligns with the government's Ghana CARES "Obaatan Pa" programme, which identifies the AfCFTA as a key driver of post-COVID-19 recovery and job creation.

8.7.5 *Consumer Welfare and Innovation*

Consumers in Ghana are expected to benefit from a greater variety of goods and services at competitive prices due to increased competition from continental suppliers, lower transaction and import costs and improved service quality (Aziegbe-Esho & Verhoef, 2022).

Moreover, trade liberalisation encourages technological upgrading and innovation, as firms seek to remain competitive in a larger market. The expected rise in knowledge and technology transfers, along with increased investor confidence, could position Ghana as a hub for knowledge and services in the region.

8.8 Opportunities for Ghana under AfCFTA

Ghana's early commitment to the African Continental Free Trade Area (AfCFTA), coupled with its hosting of the AfCFTA Secretariat, positions it strategically to capitalise on the emerging trade architecture. The opportunities span multiple sectors, ranging from manufacturing and services to logistics and digital trade, and align with Ghana's broader development goals of economic diversification, industrialisation, and job creation.

One of the most significant opportunities lies in the expansion of Ghana's manufacturing and agroprocessing sectors. The removal of intra-African tariffs and the streamlining of non-tariff barriers open access to a single continental market of over 1.4 billion people. Ghanaian producers in sectors such as cocoa processing, aluminium, textiles, pharmaceuticals, and beverages now have greater prospects for exporting to new African markets beyond the Economic Community of West African States (ECOWAS). These sectors, which have long been hindered by limited domestic demand and fragmented markets, can now scale production and benefit from economies of scale. The One District, One Factory (1D1F) initiative, which supports decentralised industrial development across Ghana, can leverage AfCFTA to integrate its outputs into continental value chains and drive rural industrialisation. UNCTAD (2021) notes that intra-African exports of industrial products are expected to increase by 29% by 2040, providing a solid basis for Ghana's industrial sector to flourish under the AfCFTA.

In addition to goods, the liberalisation of trade in services under AfCFTA provides Ghana with a competitive edge in sectors where it already has significant capabilities. Ghana's growing Information and Communication Technology (ICT) ecosystem, vibrant financial services industry, and expanding creative and educational services can now reach broader African markets. The country's success in fintech, particularly mobile money and digital banking, positions it as a leader in digital services export. According to the Overseas Development Institute (2023), Ghana is among the African countries best poised to lead the implementation of AfCFTA's digital trade provisions. This opens up opportunities for cross-border service provision in telecommunications, business outsourcing, education, consultancy, and digital financial services, enhancing Ghana's profile as a regional service hub.

Ghana's strategic location along the Gulf of Guinea, combined with its growing investments in transport and logistics infrastructure, presents another opportunity under AfCFTA. The expansion of the Tema and Takoradi ports, improvements to the Accra-Tema motorway, and ongoing development of the Boankra Inland Port and rail networks are positioning Ghana as a trade and transit hub for West Africa. These infrastructure projects are designed to facilitate cross-border trade and logistics for both coastal and landlocked neighbours, including Burkina Faso, Mali, and Niger. The adoption of the Pan-African Payment and Settlement System (PAPSS), which facilitates transactions in local currencies, further enhances Ghana's capacity to serve as a gateway for AfCFTA trade. According to the Ghana Shippers Authority (2022), these developments significantly enhance Ghana's potential to become a corridor economy that facilitates the flow of goods and services across the subregion.

The AfCFTA also presents vital opportunities for private sector growth, particularly among small and medium-sized enterprises (SMEs). In Ghana, SMEs account for over 85% of businesses and play a central role in employment and economic dynamism. The agreement facilitates their entry into regional markets through simplified customs procedures, harmonised product standards, and targeted government support. The National AfCFTA Coordination Office (NCO) has played a crucial role in equipping SMEs with the necessary training, trade documentation, and financial tools to export competitively. These initiatives are helping Ghanaian businesses transition from informal and domestic markets into more formalised, regional value chains, boosting both their resilience and growth potential.

In addition to supporting domestic businesses, AfCFTA significantly enhances Ghana's attractiveness to foreign and regional investors. By providing access to a continent-wide market under a unified trade regime, Ghana becomes a preferred base for investors seeking to serve the African market. Its relative political stability, improving ease of doing business, and trade-ready infrastructure make it an ideal destination for investments in manufacturing, agribusiness, renewable energy, and ICT. World Bank (2020) projects that AfCFTA could catalyse over $130 billion in investment opportunities in Africa's manufacturing sector alone by 2030. Ghana is poised to attract a significant share of this investment, particularly in sectors aligned with its national industrial development strategies.

Finally, AfCFTA offers a vehicle for promoting inclusive development, particularly in empowering women and youth. The agreement's commitment to gender equality and youth employment aligns with Ghana's demographic profile and entrepreneurial landscape. Initiatives such as She Trades Ghana and the Youth in Export programme can leverage AfCFTA frameworks to connect women-led and youth-owned businesses to new markets, enhance their capacity, and access targeted funding. These developments not only promote social equity but also harness the economic potential of underrepresented groups, thereby expanding the overall gains of trade liberalisation.

8.9 Pathways to Progress

The African Continental Free Trade Area (AfCFTA) presents a transformative opportunity for Ghana to reposition its economy within a more integrated and dynamic African market. As the host of the AfCFTA Secretariat and an early ratifier of the agreement, Ghana has demonstrated strong political will and strategic foresight in aligning itself with the continent's trade liberalisation agenda. The potential benefits for Ghana are considerable, encompassing expanded market access, industrial growth, enhanced employment opportunities, poverty reduction, and the development of the private sector. Sectors such as agroprocessing, manufacturing, digital services, and logistics are particularly well-positioned to benefit from the removal of trade barriers and the development of larger continental value chains.

However, these benefits are not automatic. Ghana must overcome several structural and institutional challenges to fully leverage the AfCFTA. Issues such as infrastructure deficits, fiscal risks, limited productive capacity, non-tariff barriers, potential loss of international trade tax revenue from joining the AfCFTA, political unpredictability, and technical readiness could delay or diminish the agreement's impact. If left unaddressed, these challenges could result in uneven gains, regional trade imbalances, and missed economic opportunities.

To maximise its strategic advantage under AfCFTA and ensure broad-based national development, Ghana must take proactive and coordinated steps. The following policy recommendations are the pathways to making progress under the AfCFTA:

First, the government should prioritise investment in trade-related infrastructure. The Minister of Roads has spent the first 6 months of 2025 touring the country to examine the state of roads in Ghana. However, Also, some allocations in the 2025 budget have been committed to the "Big Push Programme", which will be used to support road infrastructure, including roads, railways, ports, and digital trade systems. However, the government needs to pay attention to railways, ports, and the digital trade system to facilitate the movement of goods and services, thereby reducing delays and costs. Public-private partnerships and concessional funding from multilateral institutions should be leveraged to close infrastructure gaps that currently inhibit regional connectivity and increase trade costs.

Second, Ghana must implement fiscal adjustment strategies to address potential revenue losses from tariff reductions. The government should commit to its promise of strengthening revenue mobilisation by expanding tax collection systems, improving VAT collection efficiency, and broadening the tax base to enhance revenue without placing a significant burden on citizens. This may involve expanding the domestic tax base, improving VAT collection efficiency, and formalising the informal sector. Currently, the Ghana Revenue Authority, in collaboration with the Ministry of Finance, is conducting a nationwide consultation process to educate key players in the trade and business sectors about the VAT reforms and solicit their feedback. Additionally, the government should negotiate for compensation mechanisms under AfCFTA to support transitional financing.

Third, productive capacity enhancement must be central to Ghana's industrial policy. Support for SMEs through access to affordable credit, export financing, technology transfer, and skills development is essential to ensure competitiveness in a liberalised market. Local firms need targeted incentives to upgrade and scale up export-oriented production.

Fourth, Ghana should strengthen its institutional capacity to implement, monitor, and enforce AfCFTA protocols. This includes upgrading the capabilities of border agencies, trade ministries, and standards authorities, as well as enhancing coordination between the public and private sectors. The role of the National AfCFTA Coordination Office should be expanded to ensure broader stakeholder engagement.

Fifth, there is a need to address non-tariff barriers and regulatory misalignments through regional cooperation and harmonisation of standards. Ghana should work closely with the AfCFTA Secretariat and neighbouring countries to monitor and resolve NTBs through the dispute settlement mechanisms and technical committees established under the agreement.

Sixth, inclusive trade policies should be adopted to ensure that women, youth, and informal traders benefit from AfCFTA. Programmes that support female-led businesses, youth entrepreneurship, and access to regional markets must be scaled up to promote equitable participation in continental trade.

Ultimately, Ghana should strike a balance between its regional ambitions and a forward-looking global trade strategy. This means utilising AfCFTA as a platform to enhance competitiveness while maintaining strategic partnerships with global partners. A dual-track approach, one that deepens regional integration while expanding global market access, will enhance Ghana's long-term resilience and global positioning.

Appendix (Figs. 8.10, 8.11, 8.12, and 8.13)

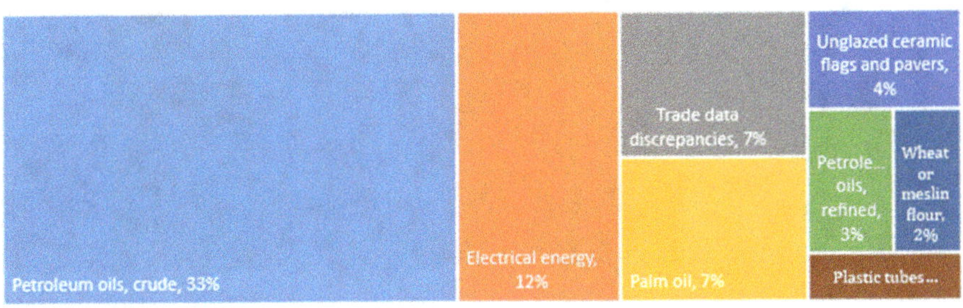

Fig. 8.10 Ghana's intra-African exports in 2020 (top 10 products). Source: Data from https://atlas.hks.harvard.edu/

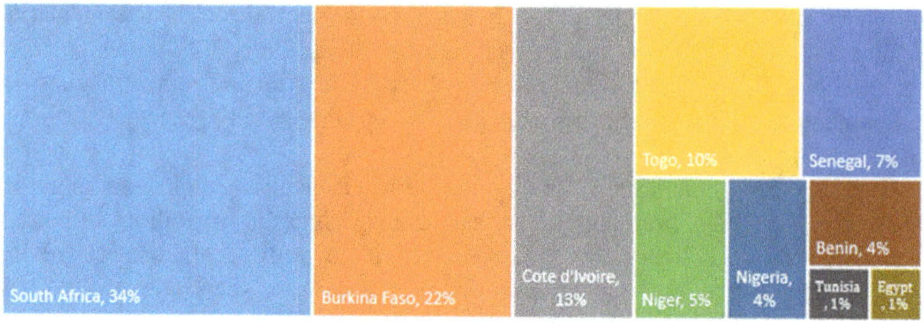

Fig. 8.11 Ghana's export destinations in Africa in 2020 (top 10 destinations). Source: Data from https://atlas.hks.harvard.edu/

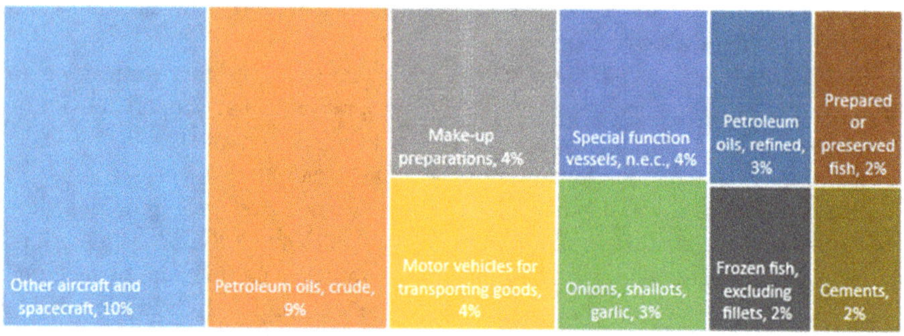

Fig. 8.12 Ghana's intra-African imports in 2020- top 10 products. Source: Data from https://atlas.hks.harvard.edu/

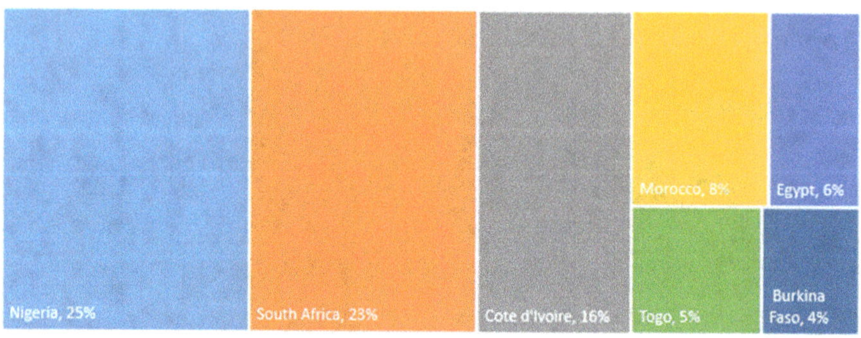

Fig. 8.13 Origin of Ghana's imports from Africa in 2020 (top 10 originating partners). Source: Data from https://atlas.hks.harvard.edu/

References

Abrego, L., de Zamaroczy, M., Gursoy, T., Issoufou, S., Nicholls, G. P., Perez-Saiz, H., & Rosas, J. N. (2020). The African continental free trade area: Potential economic impact and challenges. *IMF staff discussion notes SDN/20/04*, International Monetary Fund, may 2020.

African Union. (2018). *Agreement establishing the African continental free trade area (AfCFTA).*

Ajibo, C. C. (2019). African continental free trade area agreement: The euphoria, pitfalls and prospects. *Journal of World Trade, 53*(5), 871–894.

Asamoah, G. N. (2024). *The impact of the African continental free trade area (AfCFTA) on Ghana: A computable general equilibrium approach.* University of Rome La Sapienza.

Aziegbe-Esho, E., & Verhoef, G. (2022). Reaping the benefits of the African continental free trade agreement (AfCFTA): The role of human capital development. *Africa Review, 15*(1), 1–23.

Chivunga, M., Abudu, D., & Lemma, A. (2024). *Advancing AfCFTA digital trade implementation in Ghana. ODI Global Research Report (Oct. 2024).* ODI.

Codjoe, D. (2023). *How ready is Ghana for the AfCFTA? Perspectives on African Trade and Integration, Tralac Blog.* https://www.tralac.org/blog/article/16243-how-ready-is-ghana-for-the-afcfta.html

Ghana Investment Promotion Centre. (2021). *AfCFTA prospects & challenges.* Retrieved April 24 2025, from https://gipc.gov.gh

Ghana Shippers Authority. (2022). *Maximising AfCFTA gains: Ghana takes the lead.* Retrieved April 24 2025, from https://shippers.org.gh

ILO. (2024). *The African continental free trade area: An opportunity to promote social and labour issues across the continent? [Policy Brief].* International Labour Organisation.

International Monetary Fund (IMF). (2025). World Economic Outlook Database. Washington, D.C.: IMF. Available at: https://www.imf.org/en/Publications/WEO/weodatabase/2025/October

Mbabazi, J., Milner, C., & Morrissey, O. (2006). Trade openness, trade costs and growth: Why sub-Saharan Africa performs poorly, CREDIT Research Paper No. 06/08.

Ministry of Trade and Industry. (2022). *National AfCFTA policy framework and action plan.* Ministry of Trade and Industry-Ghana.

Obeng-Odoom, F. (2020). The African continental free trade area. *American Journal of Economics and Sociology, 79*(1), 167–197.

Onwuka, O. N., & Udegbunam, K. C. (2019). The African continental free trade area: Prospects and challenges. *Conflict Trends, 2019*(3), 3–10.

Portugal-Perez, A., & Wilson, J. S. (2008). *Trade costs in Africa: Barriers and opportunities for reform.* World Bank policy research working paper 4619. The World Bank.

Tralac. (2022). *How ready is Ghana for the AfCFTA?* Trade Law Centre. Retrieved May 2 2025, from https://tralac.org

Turkson, F. E. (2012). *Using observable trade data to measure bilateral trade costs in developing countries: Evidence from sub-Saharan Africa. CREDIT research paper 12/06.* The University of Nottingham, Centre for Research in Economic Development and International Trade (CREDIT).

Turkson, F. E. (2015). Integration and regional trade in Sub-Saharan Africa. In O. Morrissey, R. Lopez, & K. Sharma (Eds.), *Handbook of trade and development* (pp. 210–231). Edward Elgar Publishing.

Turkson, F. E., Mensah, R. A., & Barimah, A. (2020). Does trade facilitation promote bilateral trade in sub-Saharan Africa? Policy and issues. In G. O. A. Odularu, M. Hassan, & M. Babatunde (Eds.), *Fostering trade in Africa - Trade relations, business opportunities and policy instruments, advances in African economics, social and political development.* Springer.

UNCTAD. (2019). *Trade and development report.* United Nations Conference on Trade and Development.

UNCTAD. (2021). *Economic development in Africa report: Reaping the potential benefits of the AfCFTA for inclusive growth.* United Nations Conference on Trade and Development.

UNECA. (2020a). *Boosting intra-African trade through AfCFTA*. United Nations Economic Commission for Africa.

UNECA. (2020b). *AfCFTA: Boosting intra-African trade through trade facilitation and infrastructure*. United Nations Economic Commission for Africa.

Wilson, J. S., Njinkeu, D., & Fosso, B. P. (2008). *Expanding trade within Africa: The impact of trade facilitation*. Policy Research Paper 4790. The World Bank Development Research Group.

World Bank. (2020). *The African continental free trade area: Economic and distributional effects*. Retrieved May 20 2025, from https://www.worldbank.org/en/topic/trade/publication/the-african-continental-free-trade-area

World Bank. (2025). *World development indicators database.*

Chapter 9
Navigating the Implementation of the African Continental Free Trade Area (AfCFTA) in Kenya: Issues, Lessons Learnt, and Strategies

Tabitha Kiriti-Nganga

Abstract This chapter examines Kenya's experience with the implementation of the African Continental Free Trade Area focusing particularly on the Guided Trade Initiative (GTI). It outlines the strategic policy frameworks, institutional mechanisms, and export achievements underpinning Kenya's participation in trade in the African region. The analysis identifies key challenges, including non-tariff barriers, complex rules of origin, poor infrastructure, limited internet access, political instability, and difficulties in accessing finance for small and medium enterprises (SMEs). Drawing from the lessons learnt during the initial phase of the GTI, this chapter proposes targeted strategies such as trade facilitation, investment in transport and digital infrastructure, harmonization of standards, stakeholder engagement, and improved regulatory alignment. This chapter concludes that Kenya can enhance its competitiveness and deepen its integration into AfCFTA by addressing structural gaps and fostering inclusive, SME-driven growth.

Keywords AfCFTA · Guided trade initiative · Kenya · Intra-African trade · SMEs · Trade facilitation · Rules of origin · Non-tariff barriers · Infrastructure · Digital trade · Economic integration

9.1 Introduction

The African Continental Free Trade Area (AfCFTA) was established in 2018 as part of the African Union Agenda 2063 to create a single continental market of 55 Member States. The agreement entered into force on May 30, 2019, and Africa officially began trading under it on January 1, 2021. Kenya and Ghana were the first

T. Kiriti-Nganga (✉)
Department of Economics and Development Studies, University of Nairobi, Nairobi, Kenya
e-mail: tkiriti@uonbi.ac.ke

D. N. Yuni et al. (eds.), *From Policy to Practice: Challenges and Ways Forward on the Implementation of the AfCFTA*,
https://doi.org/10.1007/978-3-032-14051-7_9

two countries that deposited the instruments of ratification of AfCFTA in 2018 (African Union, 2021).

Kenya is a proactive participant in Africa's economic integration efforts, exemplified by its early ratification and deposit of instruments for the AfCFTA in 2018. In June 2022, Kenya was selected as one of seven countries to pilot the initial phase of the AfCFTA implementation. Two months later, in August, the country launched its AfCFTA implementation strategy for the period 2022–2027. This strategy focuses on enhancing, diversifying, and growing Kenya's exports to African markets, while aiming to achieve a 5% annual increase in real value-added within the manufacturing sector. Key goods targeted for export include fisheries, pharmaceuticals, fertilizers, paper products, industrial chemicals, livestock, fruits and vegetables, spices, artisanal goods, minerals, and petroleum. The strategy also emphasizes priority service sectors such as professional services, tourism, education, healthcare, finance, ICT, cultural and sports services, and transport and logistics (International Trade Administration, 2022).

The Strategy focuses on priority sectors under the AfCFTA for goods, services, and regional value chains, drawing from Kenya's Integrated National Export Development and Promotion Strategy (INEDPS) and aligning with the objectives of the Big Four Agenda.

Under INEDPS, the government aimed to increase manufacturing's contribution to GDP from 8.3% in 2017 to 15% by 2022. The Strategy outlines key drivers and enablers aimed at achieving its objectives, including the promotion of domestic exports following tariff liberalization in non-LDC African countries for products such as fresh vegetables, flowers, coffee, tea, soaps, detergents, textiles, and clothing. Kenya aims to enhance its economic growth through this strategic initiative (International Trade Administration, 2022).

Kenya's AfCFTA National Implementation Strategy is designed to achieve several core objectives. These include strengthening the country's production capacity, boosting the export of goods and services both within Africa and internationally, and creating more employment and income-generating opportunities for its citizens. The strategy also seeks to support broad-based economic growth that aligns with Kenya's broader economic transformation agenda (International Trade Administration, 2022).

To meet these goals, the strategy focuses on several key priorities. These involve enabling smooth trade in goods and services, improving the competitiveness and productivity of local manufacturers and exporters, and promoting inclusive participation in AfCFTA-related trade—particularly for women, youth, and persons with disabilities (International Trade Administration, 2022).

Kenya's AfCFTA Implementation Strategy includes a comprehensive framework for coordination, communication, monitoring, and evaluation to ensure effective execution of the agreement. Central to this framework is the establishment of the National Implementation Committee (NIC), which brings together representatives from government institutions, private sector bodies, academic and research organizations, and civil society groups. The NIC is tasked with overseeing the implementation of the AfCFTA Strategy and Agreement, identifying and managing potential risks, and mobilizing the financial resources required for successful implementation (Government of Kenya, 2022; UNECA, 2022).

NIC's roles include implementing the AfCFTA Agreement and Strategy, managing risks, and securing financing for implementation. The communication strategy involves national sensitisation on the scope of the AfCFTA Agreement, its implications for Kenya, and related econometric modelling results. Sensitisation campaigns will also target the private sector, highlighting the benefits to African businesses, trade opportunities, and market access requirements in priority countries for specific commodities and services (International Trade Administration, 2022).

Civil society organizations and other stakeholders are being engaged through focused awareness campaigns addressing key AfCFTA issues such as free movement of people, environmental protection, and food security. Moreover, tailored initiatives for women and youth highlight business opportunities and trade facilitation tools. The National Implementation Committee (NIC) extends its outreach to external stakeholders—including Kenya's diplomatic missions abroad, foreign governments and missions in Nairobi, international NGOs, trade and economic operators, and regional and global organizations—to enhance Kenya's representation and influence within AfCFTA processes (International Trade Administration, 2022; Vellum Kenya, 2022).

The Monitoring and Evaluation (M&E) framework established by the National Implementation Committee (NIC) involves preparing quarterly progress reports that measure performance against predetermined indicators. Additionally, comprehensive annual reports will be developed to capture key challenges encountered, insights gained, and practical recommendations for improvement. The strategy also outlines a 5-year evaluation schedule aimed at reviewing the relevance, efficiency, effectiveness, long-term impact, and sustainability of the implemented activities (International Trade Administration, 2022).

If effectively executed, the strategy envisions shifting Kenya's economy towards export-led growth, fostering a vibrant local market, and reinforcing the country's role as a regional trade hub and centre for ICT innovation (International Trade Administration, 2022).

9.2 Kenya's Participation in Intra-African Trade Pre-Guided Trade Initiative (GTI)

In 2022, Kenya's trade in goods within the African continent reached US$5.3 billion, accounting for 19% of its total goods trade. There was a 10% growth in this trade compared to 2021. Key trading partners—Uganda, Tanzania, Egypt, and South Africa—contributed 62% of Kenya's intra-African trade (International Trade Centre, 2023).

In the same year, Kenya's exports to other African countries reached approximately US$3 billion, accounting for 41% of the country's total exports. These exports grew by 8% compared to 2021. Key export products included tea (9%), palm oil (6%), flat-rolled iron or non-alloy steel products (5%), medicaments (5%), and cement. The primary destination markets were Uganda, Tanzania, and Rwanda, which collectively accounted for 54% of exports to other African countries. Most of Kenya's key markets are members of the East African Community (EAC) and the Common Market for Eastern and Southern African (COMESA), excluding South Africa. Uganda was the primary destination, receiving 28% of Kenya's total exports while exporting 39% to the rest of Africa (International Trade Centre, 2023) as shown in Fig. 9.1.

In 2022, Kenya's imports to other African countries were valued at US$2.3 billion, representing 11% of its total imports. These imports increased by 11% compared to 2021. Key imports included maize (9%), coal (6%), sugar cane or beet (6%), fertilizers (3%), and semi-processed iron or non-alloyed steel goods (4%). Most of these imports (74%) came from South Africa, Tanzania, Egypt, and Uganda. South Africa was the leading source of these imports, accounting for 23%, followed by Tanzania at 20% and importing 26% to the rest of Africa (International Trade Centre, 2023; Tralac (Trade Law Centre), 2022a; COTU, 2024) as shown in Fig. 9.2.

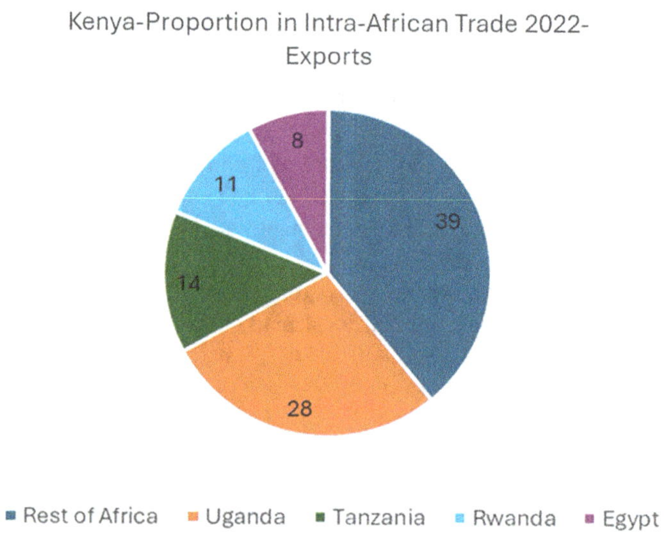

Fig. 9.1 Kenya-proportion in intra-African trade 2022–exports. Source: https://www.tradeunionsinafcfta.org/wp-content/uploads/2024/11/Kenya-Trade-Fact-Sheet-1.pdf

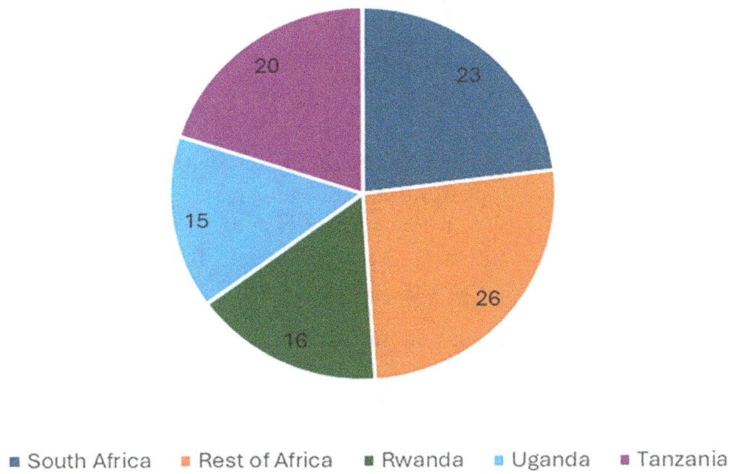

Fig. 9.2 Kenya-proportion in intra-African trade 2022-imports. Source: https://www.tradeunionsinafcfta.org/wp-content/uploads/2024/11/Kenya-Trade-Fact-Sheet-1.pdf

9.3 Kenya's Participation in Intra-African Trade Under the Guided Trade Initiative (GTI)

The Guided Trade Initiative was launched in Accra, Ghana, on 7 October 2022. It was designed to enable meaningful commercial transactions and evaluate the functional, institutional, legal, and trade policy environment under the African Continental Free Trade Area (AfCFTA Secretariat, 2023a). The AfCFTA GTI was designed to foster trade within the African continent by facilitating exports and imports between participating State Parties, with guidance from their national AfCFTA committees.

The initiative seeks to enable meaningful and commercially impactful trade within the AfCFTA framework; assess the agreement's operational, institutional, legal, and policy structures to ensure their effectiveness as well as to build trust and confidence among economic stakeholders across the African continent (AfCFTA Secretariat, 2023b). This initiative was a significant move towards boosting intra-African trade and strengthening economic cooperation across the continent.

The AfCFTA GTI aims to promote ongoing trade under the AfCFTA framework. It seeks to create a ripple effect by expanding opportunities for small and medium enterprises (SMEs), youth, and women in trade, ultimately fostering Equitable and lasting economic expansion (UNECA, 2023a).

The initiative aims to enhance value chain development by trading a diverse range of products, such as ceramic tiles, batteries, tea, coffee, processed meat products, corn starch, sugar, pasta, glucose syrup, dried fruits, and sisal fibre. Countries outside the GTI may join if they meet specific criteria and in line with the African Union (AU) 2023 Theme of "Accelerating the Implementation of the AfCFTA." The GTI scope widened to include more participants and products. By September 2023,

31 countries were part of the GTI (AfCFTA Secretariat, 2023c). These countries include:

- East Africa: Kenya, Tanzania, Uganda, Rwanda.
- Central Africa: Burundi, Cameroon, Central African Republic, Democratic Republic of Congo (DRC), Congo (Brazzaville), Equatorial Guinea, Gabon.
- North Africa: Algeria, Egypt, Tunisia, Morocco.
- Southern Africa: Angola, Botswana, Malawi, Namibia, South Africa, Zimbabwe.
- West Africa: Côte d'Ivoire, Ghana, Nigeria, Senegal, Togo.
- Island States: Cabo Verde, Comoros, Madagascar, Mauritius, Seychelles.

Key traded items include agricultural goods (e.g., mushrooms, flowers, moringa), foodstuffs (e.g., powdered milk, honey, fortified corn porridge), and processed goods (e.g., beverages, meat products, nut butters, fabrics), among others (UNECA, 2023b). This effort supports greater intra-African trade under the AfCFTA framework.

Kenya has successfully exported 21 diverse products, such as tea, soaps, machinery, and energy-saving jikos, under the AfCFTA Guided Trade Initiative (AfCFTA Secretariat, 2023a). Other products exported include bushes, soda ash, hides, and honey, demonstrating the country's strong manufacturing capabilities and strategic use of the opportunities provided by AfCFTA.

Kenya has exported goods to several African countries under the GTI, with Ghana, Nigeria, and South Africa among the recipients. Significantly, Ghana became the primary market for Kenya's exports during the first phase of the Guided Trade Initiative (AfCFTA Secretariat, 2023b).

Kenya dispatched its inaugural shipment under the AfCFTA agreement to Ghana on October 5, 2022. This significant achievement was made possible through the AfCFTA Secretariat's Guided Trade Initiative, after the East African Community (EAC) officially published the Provisional Schedules of Tariff Concessions for Category A products in September 2022.

Under the GTI framework, Kenya's total value of consignments is approximately USD five million. Kenya has successfully exported goods to Ghana, South Africa, Nigeria, Senegal, and Togo, with over 78 Certificates of Origin (CoOs) issued by the Kenya Revenue Authority (KRA) under AfCFTA (AfCFTA Secretariat, 2023c). The exported products include tea, plastic products, hides and skins, energy-saving stoves, batteries, and machinery.

Despite some challenges, the worth of Kenya's outbound trade to African region increased marginally from USD 3 billion in 2022 to USD 3.1 billion in 2023. Imports also grew from USD 2.3 billion in 2022 to USD 2.69 billion in 2023 (UNECA, 2023b).

However, three consignments did not receive preferential treatment and were therefore subjected to full import duties. The second shipment of stoves to Ghana was fully taxed, as preferential access was not granted. Similarly, a shipment of hides and skins destined for Ghana faced full duties due to the absence of preferential terms. In the case of alcoholic beverages exported from Kenya, the lack of preferential treatment also resulted in the application of full duties (AfCFTA Secretariat, 2023c).

On 21 December 2023, Kenya, Ghana, and Egypt held a virtual meeting to sort out the problems related to GTI implementation. The goal was to enhance trade operations and foster cooperation among the involved parties. Key recommendations included:

(a) GTI Subcommittee on Customs—reactivate to promptly resolve trade concerns.
(b) AfCFTA Tools Utilization—promote the use of AfCFTA reporting and monitoring tools to address non-tariff barriers (NTBs).
(c) Improved Communication—strengthen communication channels through bilateral and face-to-face engagements, with updated contact information.
(d) Certificates of Origin—ensure timely notification to the AfCFTA Secretariat upon issuance to streamline trade processes and improve data integration (AfCFTA Secretariat, 2023b).

9.4 Key Agencies Responsible for AfCFTA Implementation in Kenya

Kenya has actively prepared for what seemed like seamless trade under Intra-African trade enabled by AfCFTA Guided Trade Initiative (GTI). It set up an Ad Hoc Committee uniting trade facilitation institutions and regulators to identify companies, products, and connect them to financing and product improvement opportunities, aligning with the AfCFTA's market standards (AfCFTA Secretariat, 2023a). Key regulatory measures include notifying the competent authority, securing official stamps and signatures, and consistently updating requirements (UNECA, 2023a). Kenya has developed essential trading documents, such as gazetted tariff offers, a national implementation strategy, and certificates of origin, ensuring readiness for the AfCFTA Guided Trade Initiative (AfCFTA Secretariat, 2023c).

9.4.1 Main Implementing Agencies

The Ministry of Industry, Trade, and Investment (MITI), working jointly with various government bodies, oversees the execution of the African Continental Free Trade Area (AfCFTA) in Kenya. The primary institution tasked with this role is the Kenya Revenue Authority (KRA), specifically through its Customs & Border Control Department (C&BC). KRA handles the issuance of preferential proofs of origin, such as AfCFTA certificates of origin (RoO).

Exporters previously operating outside the AfCFTA framework are now being facilitated to export under the agreement. The Kenya Revenue Authority (KRA) is also training customs officers posted at key border locations—Malaba, Busia,

Isebania, Namanga, Loitoktok, Taveta, Lungalunga, and Moyale—on their responsibilities in signing and issuing AfCFTA certificates of origin. Furthermore, four Rules of Origin (ROO) desks have been set up in Loitoktok, Taveta, Lungalunga, and Moyale to offer stakeholders guidance on AfCFTA regulations and address related issues (Kenya Revenue Authority, 2023a). Additionally, four Rules of Origin desks have been established in Loitoktok, Taveta, Lungalunga, and Moyale to provide stakeholders with information on AfCFTA provisions and related concerns (AfCFTA Secretariat, 2023a).

9.5 Procedures for Registration as an AfCFTA Exporter

Kenyan businesses intending to export goods under the AfCFTA arrangement must register with the Customs & Border Control Department at one of the designated Rules of Origin offices located in Nairobi, Mombasa, Nakuru, Eldoret, or Kisumu. During registration, they are required to submit a copy of their business registration certificate, KRA Personal Identification Number (PIN) certificate, and, where applicable, a specific business licence—such as a horticultural permit or a mining licence for mineral exports. The eligibility of goods is assessed based on the criteria outlined in Annex 2 of the Protocol on Trade in Goods (AfCFTA Secretariat, 2023b). Once approved, exporters are issued a reference number and may then purchase AfCFTA certificates of origin at a cost of USD 3 each. To proceed with exportation, they must complete and submit the AfCFTA certificate of origin together with the export invoice, customs declaration, and other supporting documents, all in triplicate (Kenya Revenue Authority, 2023b).

To facilitate the implementation of AfCFTA, the Kenya Revenue Authority (KRA) has submitted a list of designated contact persons and authorized signatories for AfCFTA Certificates of Origin to the AfCFTA Secretariat. It has also initiated awareness campaigns targeting both the business community and KRA personnel. Additionally, KRA has set up Rules of Origin desks at various One Stop Border Posts (OSBPs) to enhance awareness and address origin-related issues. The Business Transformation Office (BTO) within the Customs & Border Control Department has been assigned the responsibility of updating customs systems and procedures to ensure compliance with AfCFTA requirement (AfCFTA Secretariat, 2023c; Kenya Revenue Authority, 2023a).

9.6 Issues Facing Implementation of the AfCFTA in Kenya

The African Continental Free Trade Area offers significant potential benefits but faces challenges that could impact its effectiveness.

9.6.1 *Non-tariff Barriers*

Non-tariff barriers (NTBs) are a key issue affecting the development of value chains across African borders. These NTBs include quantitative restrictions, various licences, special fees for foreign exchange, total bans and regulations, among others. Non-tariff barriers obstruct the smooth execution and enforcement of the AfCFTA agreement (UNECA, 2023b). Key challenges include non-recognition of quality certificates due to the lack of harmonized sanitary, phyto-sanitary, and technical standards at the continental level; rejection of approvals issued by national chambers of commerce or other authorized entities of Member States that Kenyan companies could be trading with; complex licencing procedures; prohibition of certain imports, even when these goods are included on the approved list and originate from the continental economy and road harassment and malpractices, further complicating trade logistics (AfCFTA Secretariat, 2023a). In December 2021, Kenya introduced a ban on poultry imports from Uganda, prompting a retaliatory move from Uganda, which restricted agricultural exports from Kenya. These non-tariff measures significantly disrupted trade between the two nations. Nevertheless, in 2023, Kenyan President William Ruto revoked the ban on Ugandan agricultural goods, contributing to the normalization of trade ties between the two countries (UNECA, 2023b).

9.6.2 *Rules of Origin*

Rules of origin are crucial in determining which products qualify as African goods under the AfCFTA. These rules ensure that customs officials apply the correct tariffs (AfCFTA Secretariat, 2023a). The implementation of the African Continental Free Trade Area agreement in Kenya faces significant hurdles, one of the most prominent being the complexity of the Rules of Origin. These rules are essential in determining whether goods qualify for preferential treatment under AfCFTA, but they present a series of challenges that hinder effective execution.

Firstly, the RoO under AfCFTA are often complex and product-specific, making them difficult for businesses—particularly small- and medium-sized enterprises (SMEs)—to interpret and comply with. Many Kenyan exporters struggle with understanding the technical details required to prove that their products meet origin requirements, which creates a barrier to accessing AfCFTA markets (AfCFTA Secretariat, 2023b).

Moreover, awareness and capacity among both the private sector and government officials remain limited. Numerous businesses are not adequately informed about the RoO procedures or their significance in accessing tariff preferences. Simultaneously, there is a need for continuous training of customs and border officials to ensure they apply RoO consistently and correctly across various border points (Kenya Revenue Authority, 2023a).

Administrative and logistical issues further complicate the process. Exporters must gather and submit a range of documentation—including certificates of origin, business registration, and licencing documents—which can be time-consuming and expensive. This bureaucracy discourages participation in intra-African trade, particularly among smaller businesses that lack the resources to navigate the process (UNCTAD, 2022).

Infrastructure gaps also present a challenge. While Kenya has established Rules of Origin desks at select One Stop Border Posts (OSBPs), such as in Loitoktok, Taveta, Lungalunga, and Moyale, these facilities are not widely accessible to businesses operating in other regions. This limits the reach and effectiveness of RoO services and restricts broader national implementation (Kenya Revenue Authority, 2023b).

Additionally, verification and enforcement mechanisms are not yet fully developed. There are risks of fraudulent claims regarding product origin, which can erode trust in the system and spark trade disputes between countries. To mitigate this, Kenya must invest in robust verification systems and consider digital solutions to streamline and secure RoO processes (AfCFTA Secretariat, 2023c).

Finally, inconsistencies in how RoO are applied across AfCFTA member states further complicate trade. Kenya may encounter challenges when its RoO interpretations or enforcement practices differ from those of neighbouring countries, leading to delays and increased transaction costs at borders (UNECA, 2021a).

9.6.3 Access to the Internet

Access to the internet reduces poverty and boosts economic growth through cost savings in various sectors. Africa has uneven internet penetration rates. For example, Southern Africa has a penetration rate of 66%, Eastern Africa 26%, and Central Africa 24% (Kamer, 2022). Kenya has an internet penetration of 40.8%. Low internet access hinders business opportunities and the dissemination of AfCFTA benefits in local languages. It also reduces or hampers digital trade (UNECA, 2023a).

9.6.4 Poor Infrastructure

Africa requires USD 130-USD 170 billion annually to address its infrastructure needs (UNECA, 2021b). Kenya's first tea consignment to Ghana under the GTI took 6 months to reach its destination, which is longer than expected. Due to the absence of functional local shipping lines, goods intended for African destinations often take lengthy detours to regions like the European Union (EU), the Middle East, or even as far as Australia before finally reaching their target African markets. This inefficiency underscores the need for improved regional shipping infrastructure (UNECA, 2023a). Northern and Southern Africa have better infrastructure compared to Western, Eastern, and Central Africa. Just 43% of the population is served by roads that are accessible throughout the year, resulting in high transportation costs (UNECA, 2023b).

In addition, power outages, for example, in Kenya, force many companies to invest in diesel generators, which increases their production costs. Hence, this makes them uncompetitive. In Africa, only 6% of agricultural lands are irrigated, underutilising water resources (African Development Bank, 2023). On the other hand, Kenya has significant untapped irrigation potential, estimated at 1.342 million hectares. However, only about 180,503 hectares (13.5% of this potential) have been developed. Irrigated land makes up just 1.7% of the total agricultural land but contributes around 3% to the country's GDP. Poor infrastructure hinders the effective implementation of AfCFTA (UNECA, 2023a).

In addition, the AfCFTA agreement faces a significant challenge as a result of insufficient infrastructure to prevent smuggling and unlawful activities. Many African countries struggle with monitoring and controlling activities around their land borders, which is crucial for enforcing AfCFTA rules and regional economic communities. As trade increases under AfCFTA, this problem is likely to grow if not promptly addressed (AfCFTA Secretariat, 2023c).

9.6.5 Unsustainable Supply Chains

Intra-African supply chains are struggling due to poor infrastructure, high costs of production and insecurity. The colonial past has led to similar trade patterns in many African countries, a lack of value addition and importing, characterized by the export of raw materials and the import of finished goods. Transportation costs within Africa, as cited by the African Development Bank (2023), can increase the price of traded goods by up to 75%, posing a significant non-tariff barrier that could impact the African Continental Free Trade Area.

9.6.6 Insecurity and Corruption

Intra-African supply chains are hampered by more than just poor infrastructure and high costs. Insecurity is a major issue, as heavy reliance on land routes for cross-border trade exposes these supply chains to violent conflict and extremist activities such as Al-Shabaab in East Africa, Boko Haram in West Africa and M23 in Eastern DRC. Military personnel intended to secure these routes, but their actions often complicate matters with extortion. This forces traders to choose between longer, inefficient routes or risking their safety, with extortion costs often passed on to consumers (UNECA, 2023a).

In Africa, the transportation of goods to and from ports is usually by road along transport corridors that are often teeming with corrupt law enforcement officers who extort, intimidate, and harass truck drivers in search of bribes. Corrupt customs, health, and immigration officers working at the different borders in the transport corridors also contribute negatively to the implementation and enforcement of the AfCFTA agreement by allowing illegal goods to enter or leave the country, or failing to enforce the rules of origin for goods entering the country (AfCFTA Secretariat, 2023c).

These issues reduce the market appeal and global competitiveness of African products, contributing to a decline in cross-border trade and posing a threat to the African Continental Free Trade Area. For AfCFTA to succeed in increasing regional trade across Africa and achieving trade-driven industrialisation, enhancing the competitiveness of African imports is crucial (UNECA, 2023a).

9.6.7 Political Instability

Political instability in regions such as the Democratic Republic of the Congo (DRC), Sudan, and South Sudan creates tensions that hinder trade openness in Africa. These tensions lead to countries withdrawing from regional initiatives and closing borders, which delays goods transportation, disrupts supply chains, and limits trade between African countries. As a result, these factors impede the successful implementation of the African Continental Free Trade Area agreement (UNECA, 2023b).

Political instability also presents a major barrier to the effective implementation of the African Continental Free Trade Area (AfCFTA) agreement in Kenya. Although the AfCFTA aims to boost trade among African nations by lowering tariffs and non-tariff barriers, its success depends on a stable political environment that ensures policy consistency, institutional coordination, and investor confidence.

One of the key impacts of political instability is the disruption of policy continuity. In Kenya, recurring political tensions—especially during election cycles—often result in leadership changes and shifts in policy direction. These disruptions delay the enactment of trade-related reforms and hinder the rollout of essential AfCFTA mechanisms, such as customs harmonization and trade facilitation systems (UNECA, 2021c). A sustained political commitment is vital for long-term planning and for ensuring the consistent implementation of regional trade agreements.

Moreover, political instability undermines investor confidence. Uncertainty stemming from unrest or governance challenges discourages both domestic and international investors from engaging in trade sectors that could benefit from expanded market access under AfCFTA. In the absence of a reliable and secure business environment, many Kenyan enterprises may avoid venturing into regional markets, limiting their participation in continental trade (African Development Bank (AfDB), 2022).

In addition, political unrest can disrupt trade facilitation. Protests, ethnic conflicts, and related disturbances can affect the operation of critical infrastructure, including ports, highways, and border posts. Such disruptions impede the free flow of goods and increase transaction costs, counteracting AfCFTA's objective of streamlining trade across African borders (World Bank, 2021).

Institutional coordination also suffers during politically unstable periods. Effective AfCFTA implementation requires close collaboration between government bodies such as the Ministry of Trade, the Kenya Revenue Authority (KRA), and national standards agencies. However, political instability often leads to administrative delays, fragmented decision-making, and reduced inter-agency cooperation, all of which impede the country's ability to meet its obligations under the agreement (Tralac (Trade Law Centre) 2023).

Finally, political crises tend to divert attention and resources away from long-term economic development priorities. Investments in key areas like trade infrastructure, capacity-building, and digital systems—critical for AfCFTA implementation—may be postponed or deprioritized in favour of addressing short-term political or security concerns (UNCTAD, 2022).

9.6.8 Lack of Strong Regulatory Environments

For the AfCFTA to succeed, it is essential that regulations related to labour market flexibility, entrepreneurship, and business operations are conducive to business growth. However, according to the World Bank (2024a) *Business Ready* report, many African countries still face significant gaps in establishing robust regulatory frameworks that support a thriving business environment.

A robust regulatory environment is a critical enabler of the African Continental Free Trade Area (AfCFTA), as it provides the legal and institutional foundation necessary for efficient cross-border trade. However, the lack of strong and coherent regulations in Kenya presents a significant obstacle to the agreement's effective implementation. Despite the promise of market expansion and reduced trade barriers under AfCFTA, Kenya's regulatory shortcomings continue to hinder its ability to fully capitalize on these benefits.

One of the primary issues is regulatory inconsistency and inefficiency. Kenyan businesses, particularly small- and medium-sized enterprises (SMEs), often encounter complex, overlapping, and sometimes contradictory trade and business regulations. These inefficiencies increase compliance costs and prolong administrative processes, creating barriers to entry and discouraging formal participation in intra-African trade (World Bank, 2024b). Without streamlined procedures and efficient service delivery, firms are less likely to engage in cross-border commerce, thereby limiting the country's integration into the AfCFTA framework.

Moreover, weak enforcement of trade-related laws undermines legal certainty and fair competition. In Kenya, delays in contract enforcement, lack of clarity in dispute resolution mechanisms, and insufficient protection of intellectual property rights contribute to a business environment that is perceived as unpredictable. These shortcomings discourage both local entrepreneurs and foreign investors from pursuing opportunities that AfCFTA is intended to create (UNCTAD, 2022).

Additionally, the regulatory framework in Kenya lacks the necessary business-friendly provisions related to labour flexibility, taxation, and entrepreneurship. For instance, rigid labour laws and burdensome tax regimes can deter new investments and stifle innovation—both of which are essential for expanding trade capacity and value addition under AfCFTA (African Development Bank (AfDB), 2022).

Furthermore, limited harmonization between Kenya's domestic regulations and regional trade standards impedes seamless trade with other AfCFTA member states. Inconsistencies in product standards, customs documentation, and certification procedures lead to trade bottlenecks at border points, increasing the cost and time of doing business across African borders (UNECA, 2021c). These technical and procedural mismatches undermine the broader objectives of AfCFTA, which include the creation of a unified continental market and the facilitation of smooth, rules-based trade.

In summary, Kenya's weak regulatory environment poses a significant challenge to AfCFTA implementation by creating systemic inefficiencies, reducing investor confidence, and restricting the competitiveness of Kenyan businesses in the continental market. Addressing these issues will require comprehensive regulatory reforms, improved institutional capacity, and stronger alignment with regional and continental trade norms.

9.6.9 Unharmonized Regulatory Frameworks

A key challenge faced by Kenyan traders is the absence of clear trade regulations and the inadequate collaboration between stakeholders, including government agencies and the private sector. In addition, regulatory differences among African nations pose significant challenges for businesses. Each country enforces unique standards and regulations for product standards in terms of quality, safety, and labelling, causing confusion and higher compliance costs for exporters. These inconsistencies deter cross-border trade. Additionally, diverse customs procedures and documentation requirements contribute to the complexity, leading to delays and increased costs (UNECA, 2023a).

9.6.10 Limited Awareness of the AfCFTA Framework

Additional challenges involve a lack of adequate knowledge about trade processes and regulatory obligations in the target market. Many Kenyan traders and officials are unaware of the AfCFTA rules, which need to be simplified and translated into local languages for better understanding. Some traders submit incomplete documentation, leading to border delays. Semi-illiterate farmers and traders struggle with knowledge about moving agricultural goods and livestock across member states. This lack of understanding affects both the private and public sectors, including officials who may not fully grasp the rules or procedures of the AfCFTA. This level of lack of awareness or ignorance was witnessed during the first phase of the GTI. For example, within the GTI, certain companies assumed that trade liberalization under the AfCFTA meant goods would enter the importing country free of tariffs and exempt from local taxes. UNECA (2023b) highlighted that many exporters and importers lacked awareness and understanding of the AfCFTA's tariff liberalization regime. This misconception led some to believe that trading under the regime would mean zero tariffs and no domestic taxes, discouragement, which would deter them. The report emphasized the importance of improving information exchange and collaboration between border control agencies and businesses to enhance the business community's grasp of the implementation and structure of AfCFTA's tariff schedule.

9.6.11 Lack of Economic Freedom

The Economic Freedom Index Report (2024) indicates that most African countries are economically unfree, which hinders societal well-being. Despite efforts in trade liberalization, without broader economic reforms, structural economic transformation is unlikely (Gwartney et al., 2024). Mauritius, South Africa, Botswana, Uganda, Kenya, The Gambia, Seychelles, and Cabo Verde are among the few African nations that are positioned in the upper half of global economic freedom rankings, while the majority fall well below. To harness the benefits of the AfCFTA, extensive reforms are essential to enhance economic freedom across all facets of life (Gwartney et al., 2024).

9.6.12 Protectionism

Countries might back out of their AfCFTA commitments in favour of protectionist policies, which will significantly reduce the benefits of the agreement. Protectionism has supporters across the region, especially among the politically connected elite who resist competition from other African producers. This has already happened in the past, such as Nigeria's 2019 border closure that led to higher food prices in dependent neighbouring countries (Golub et al., 2019).

9.6.13 Small and Medium Enterprises (SMEs) Access to Finance

Small and medium enterprises play a crucial role in African economies, making up nearly 90% of private sector businesses, generating roughly 85% of jobs, and accounting for about 35% of the continent's GDP. Despite their significance, many African governments lack SME-friendly policies, hindering their growth and regional integration. One of the challenges Kenyan exporters face is limited access to financing for export activities, which restricts market expansion. The African AfCFTA presents an opportunity for SMEs to expand their markets and enhance their role in the supply chain. However, access to finance is a significant challenge for businesses in Africa, including Kenya, with 24.7% of firms citing it as their primary obstacle. Small and medium enterprises are particularly affected, often failing to grow and sometimes collapsing within three years. Major contributing factors include the demand for substantial collateral, elevated interest rates, strict credit assessment procedures by banks, and the absence of proper documentation or audited financial statements. These barriers significantly impede SMEs' ability to secure necessary financial resources, according to the UNECA's 2020 Economic Report and the World Bank Enterprise Survey (UNECA, 2020a; World Bank, 2021).

9.6.14 Inefficiency in Borders

Border inefficiencies, such as lengthy customs wait times and ineffective procedures, are a major non-tariff barrier (NTB) that disrupts trade, leading to congestion and higher business costs. The African Union highlights that enhancing border management and customs efficiency could lower trade costs significantly and boost the success of the AfCFTA (African Union, 2021).

The successful implementation of the African Continental Free Trade Area in Kenya is significantly impeded by inefficiencies at the country's border posts. Although the AfCFTA aims to promote seamless trade across Africa by reducing tariffs and eliminating non-tariff barriers, its success depends heavily on the effectiveness of border operations. In Kenya, several longstanding issues at border crossings continue to undermine the agreement's potential.

One of the primary challenges is the delay in goods clearance at border points. Kenyan traders often face extended wait times due to congestion, manual customs processing, and limited operating hours. These delays increase transaction costs, disrupt supply chains, and reduce the competitiveness of Kenyan exports. Small and medium-sized enterprises (SMEs), in particular, are disproportionately affected, as they typically lack the resources to absorb such inefficiencies (UNECA, 2021c).

In addition to time delays, border inefficiencies raise the overall cost of trade. Duplicative inspections, poor infrastructure, and limited coordination among government agencies contribute to increased logistical expenses. These hidden costs dilute the advantages of tariff reductions offered under AfCFTA, making regional trade less appealing despite its potential benefits (World Bank, 2021). While Kenya has introduced One Stop Border Posts (OSBPs) with neighbouring countries to streamline processes, their impact remains limited due to weak inter-agency collaboration, incompatible systems, and low levels of awareness among traders (Tralac (Trade Law Centre) 2023).

Customs-related challenges further exacerbate the situation. Many customs systems remain outdated or only partially digitized, and inconsistencies in documentation and procedural requirements often lead to confusion and delays. Additionally, a lack of training among customs officials on AfCFTA protocols—such as rules of origin and preferential tariff treatment—results in uneven implementation and greater risk of non-compliance (UNCTAD, 2022).

Corruption at border posts also contributes to inefficiency. Demands for informal payments and other forms of rent-seeking behaviour introduce unpredictability and increase trade costs. These practices discourage formal trade and weaken the transparency that AfCFTA seeks to promote across the continent (African Development Bank (AfDB), 2022).

Effectively border inefficiencies in Kenya—including operational delays, elevated trade costs, inadequate customs systems, and corruption—pose serious challenges to the implementation of AfCFTA. Addressing these issues requires coordinated investments in infrastructure, full digitization of customs procedures, stronger inter-agency cooperation, and capacity-building for border and customs officials. Without such reforms, Kenya risks falling short of the transformative opportunities offered by continental trade integration.

9.7 Key Lessons Learnt

Expanded prospects for developing the African market have been taken advantage of, with certain firms showing determination to swiftly benefit from the trade advantages offered under the AfCFTA's preferential framework (UNECA, 2021c). The success of trade under the African Continental Free Trade Area relies heavily on the establishment and effective functioning of national institutional mechanisms, like implementation committees, to coordinate stakeholder participation (Tralac (Trade Law Centre), 2022a). The active participation of the private sector, encouraged through ongoing business to business (B2B) engagement among AfCFTA member states is essential for fully harnessing the trade advantages offered by the agreement (AfCFTA Secretariat, 2021).

Collaboration among regulatory bodies, including standards organizations, customs authorities, and trade facilitation agencies, is essential to reduce cross-border delays (ITC (International Trade Centre), 2021a). Challenges such as logistical barriers, particularly for small consignments, need to be addressed. This requires intensified awareness campaigns, capacity-building programmes, and innovative,

African-specific solutions for trade finance and transportation (AU (African Union), 2021).

Other key areas to focus on include value addition and product diversification. Margia, an experienced Kenyan tea farmer, is hopeful about the African Continental Free Trade Area opening new markets for Kenyan tea, emphasizing the need for farmers to diversify their markets and add value to their tea products to secure better returns, thereby addressing frustrations over low prices in traditional markets (Daily Nation, 2022).

Efficient transport and logistics systems are vital for enhancing trade flow. Therefore, strengthening and expanding distribution and logistics networks across various markets is crucial to facilitate and speed up the movement of goods within the AfCFTA framework (UNECA, 2020b). African countries must prioritize infrastructure development and investment to ensure the successful implementation of the AfCFTA. Lindah Oluoch, CEO of the Kenya Tea Growers Association, echoed these sentiments while highlighting logistical challenges. She noted that Kenya's first tariff-free tea consignment to Ghana under the Guided Trade Initiative took an unexpectedly long six months to arrive. Oluoch called for improvements in infrastructure, such as efficient road and rail networks, to unlock the full potential of the AfCFTA. She also advocated for regional collaboration in East Africa to establish trade corridors and rail systems, which could reduce transport times, boost competitiveness, and enhance market access across the continent (Business Daily Africa, 2023).

SMEs, particularly those led by youth, women, and persons with disabilities—that deal in low-volume exports often encounter high transportation and logistics expenses, limiting their ability to compete in external markets. Providing targeted support to these businesses is essential. Consolidating their shipments could help them achieve economies of scale and strengthen their case for accessing discounted or preferential freight rates (ITC (International Trade Centre), 2021b).

An interview with a highly placed official in Kenya's State Department for Trade makes the following as lessons learnt in the first phase of the GTI that can make the second phase of the GTI more effective in supporting the implementation of the AfCFTA. That there is need to build capacity by sensitizing and strengthening the capacity of trade facilitation agencies and regulators; creating forums for consultation and idea-sharing between organizations and businesses to facilitate matchmaking and other collaborative efforts; developing a database of GTI-identified products and companies for matchmaking and networking; simplifying certification processes and procedures; partner with freight and supply chain providers to assist the GTI initiative; Create a financing facility for exporters, including SMEs, and explore concessions from airlines/cargo services and finally, promote the Inclusion of women, young people, and marginalized populations through awareness, affordable business financing, and inclusion in national strategies (Kenya Ministry of Trade, 2024).

This can be done by encouraging digital trade. Digital trade significantly boosts the growth of SMEs by streamlining customs procedures through the adoption of ICT, as outlined in the AfCFTA's Trade Facilitation Agreement. This will improve data sharing, paperwork filing, and cargo examination procedures (AfCFTA Secretariat, 2021). By leveraging digital platforms, businesses can overcome inadequate infrastructure, enhance supply chain management with real-time tracking, and efficiently manage inventory. This streamlining reduces logistics costs and facilitates the movement of cross-border goods, promoting intra-African trade and economic growth (Tralac (Trade Law Centre), 2022b). Kenyan SMEs can utilize the AfCFTA hub, a digital platform that provides essential market opportunities and regulatory information, enabling SMEs to navigate intra-African trade seamlessly (AfCFTA Hub, 2023).

There is also a need to establish regional value chains and sign mutual recognition agreements (MRAs) for standards. These measures can enhance trade efficiency, inclusivity, and sustainability under the AfCFTA framework (UNECA, 2021a).

9.8 Strategies to Enhance Trade Under the AfCFTA

9.8.1 Trade Facilitation for Kenyan Traders, Especially SMEs

Trade facilitation initiatives, such as streamlined customs processes, digitized border procedures, and simplified clearance documentation, are essential to expedite the movement of goods, especially for small- and medium-sized enterprises (SMEs). In Kenya, these measures can reduce time and costs associated with cross-border trade, making local exporters more competitive within AfCFTA markets. Fast-tracking trade logistics through tools like the African Trade Observatory and the AfCFTA e-Tariff Book will enhance access to market data, customs requirements, and tariff information (AfCFTA Secretariat, 2021; UNECA, 2021b).

9.8.2 Enhanced Business Matchmaking Among AfCFTA Member States

Kenya should prioritize the creation of structured platforms and databases to facilitate matchmaking between businesses across AfCFTA member states. Such networks can help Kenyan producers identify reliable buyers, distributors, and collaborators across Africa. Regional expos, B2B networking forums, and online hubs like the AfCFTA Hub can be useful tools in identifying synergies and catalysing cross-border value chains (Tralac (Trade Law Centre), 2022a; AfCFTA Hub, 2023).

9.8.3 Simplification of Trade Regulations and Enhanced Information Sharing

Transparency can be improved by simplifying trade regulations and ensuring consistent information dissemination by relevant agencies. Kenyan authorities should automate and publicly share procedures, timelines, and costs for trade-related processes. This would help to reduce regulatory uncertainty and build trust between traders and institutions, which is especially important for new and informal sector traders entering AfCFTA markets (ITC (International Trade Centre), 2021a; Tralac (Trade Law Centre), 2022b).

9.8.4 Harmonization and Alignment of Standards and Certification Procedures

Kenya, alongside other member states, should align national standards with AfCFTA recognized benchmarks and mutual recognition agreements (MRAs). This would prevent duplication of compliance procedures, reduce trade barriers, and accelerate the approval of goods across borders. Harmonization would also improve product quality and competitiveness in regional markets (AU (African Union), 2021; UNECA, 2020b).

9.8.5 SME Financing, Especially for Women- and Youth-Led Businesses

Financing is a critical bottleneck for SMEs, particularly those owned by women and youth. There should be targeted funding programmes, concessional credit lines, and partnerships with financial institutions to enable access to affordable capital. This funding would help exporters address freight costs, invest in quality packaging, and scale production capacity. It would also help women-led enterprises navigate male-dominated value chains (ITC (International Trade Centre), 2021b; AfCFTA Secretariat, 2021).

9.8.6 Capacity-Building and Stakeholder Engagement

Continuous capacity-building through training sessions, workshops, and stakeholder dialogues is essential for improving awareness of AfCFTA provisions, especially the Guided Trade Initiative. Kenyan SMEs, regulators, and trade support institutions must understand rules of origin, documentation, dispute resolution, and digital tools. Engagement would also foster public-private partnerships for better policy alignment (Kenya Ministry of Trade, 2024; Tralac (Trade Law Centre), 2022b).

9.8.7 *Increased Investment in Physical Infrastructure*

Poor infrastructure continues to hamper intra-African trade. Kenya must scale up investments in rail, road, maritime, and air transport networks to improve last-mile connectivity. Upgrades to key corridors such as the Northern Corridor will ease congestion and reduce shipment times. These investments are crucial for the timely delivery of consignments under AfCFTA and for positioning Kenya as a trade logistics hub (Business Daily Africa, 2023; UNECA, 2020b).

9.8.8 *Investment in Digital Infrastructure and Promotion of Digital Trade*

Digital infrastructure enables e-commerce, online payments, real-time logistics tracking, and efficient customs procedures. Kenya should promote internet access in underserved regions and invest in ICT infrastructure to support cross-border digital trade. Platforms like the AfCFTA Hub should help SMEs access trade intelligence and regulatory guidance, while digital payments and customs automation can reduce transaction costs (AfCFTA Hub, 2023; AU (African Union), 2021).

9.9 Conclusion

Kenya's participation in the AfCFTA under the Guided Trade Initiative underscores both the promise and complexity of regional trade integration. Despite early successes and a clear strategic vision, multiple structural and policy-related barriers—such as border inefficiencies, fragmented regulations, political instability, and insufficient infrastructure—continue to impede progress. Nevertheless, Kenya's experience offers valuable lessons for future implementation phases. The country's ability to leverage digital tools, improve trade logistics, engage the private sector, and support women- and youth-led SMEs will be crucial for sustained success. Strengthening institutional coordination, simplifying trade procedures, and investing in infrastructure and capacity-building remain priority areas. If these challenges are effectively addressed, Kenya is well-positioned to become a regional trade hub and a leader in advancing the goals of the AfCFTA across the continent.

References

AfCFTA Hub. (2023). *Empowering SMEs through digital platforms*. https://www.afcfta.app

AfCFTA Secretariat. (2021). *Trade facilitation and private sector engagement under the AfCFTA*. African Union Commission. https://afcfta.au.int

AfCFTA Secretariat. (2023a). *Annex 2 to the protocol on Trade in goods: Rules of origin*. African Union.

AfCFTA Secretariat. (2023b). *Guided trade initiative: Progress report and member participation update*. https://afcfta.au.int

AfCFTA Secretariat. (2023c). *Report on the implementation of the AfCFTA agreement: Challenges and progress*. https://afcfta.au.int

African Development Bank. (2023). *African economic outlook 2023: Mobilizing private sector financing for climate and green growth in Africa*. https://www.afdb.org/en/documents/african-economic-outlook-2023.

African Development Bank (AfDB). (2022). *African economic outlook 2022: Supporting climate resilience and a just energy transition in Africa*. https://www.afdb.org/en/documents/african-economic-outlook-2022

African Union. (2021). *Enhancing border management and customs cooperation for AfCFTA*. https://au.int

AU (African Union). (2021). *Boosting intra-African trade: Addressing trade finance and logistics challenges*. African Union Commission. https://au.int/en/documents

Business Daily Africa. (2023, April 15). *AfCFTA tea consignment delay exposes logistics gaps*. https://www.businessdailyafrica.com

Daily Nation. (2022, September 7). *Kenyan tea farmers look to AfCFTA for new markets*. https://www.nation.africa

Golub, S. S., Mbaye, A. A., & Golubski, C. (2019). *Structural transformation and employment creation in Nigeria: The role of the informal sector*. Brookings Institution. https://www.brookings.edu

Government of Kenya. (2022). *National AfCFTA implementation strategy (2022–2027)*. https://www.yunbaogao.cn/index/partFile/5/uneca/2022-08/5_31570.pdf

Gwartney, J., Lawson, R., & Murphy, R. (2024). *Economic freedom of the world: 2024 annual report*. Fraser Institute. https://www.fraserinstitute.org

International Trade Administration. (2022). Export.gov overview. U.S. Department of Commerce. https://www.trade.gov

International Trade Centre. (2023). *Kenya: Intra-African trade performance report 2022*. https://www.intracen.org/

ITC (International Trade Centre). (2021a). *Making AfCFTA work for SMEs: Addressing freight and logistics barriers*. ITC Publications.

ITC (International Trade Centre). (2021b). *Making the AfCFTA work for African businesses: Key challenges and opportunities for SMEs*. ITC Publications. https://intracen.org

Kamer, L. (2022). *Internet penetration rate in Africa 2022, by region*. Stat https://www.statista.com/statistics/1171911/internet-penetration-rate-in-africa-by-region/

Kenya Ministry of Trade. (2024). *Insights from the guided Trade initiative: Lessons from phase one*. State Department for Trade.

Kenya Revenue Authority. (2023a). *AfCFTA implementation framework and guidelines*. https://www.kra.go.ke

Kenya Revenue Authority. (2023b). *AfCFTA implementation guidelines and exporter registration procedures*. https://www.kra.go.ke

Tralac (Trade Law Centre). (2022a). *AfCFTA implementation: The role of national institutions and digital solutions*. https://www.tralac.org

Tralac (Trade Law Centre). (2022b). *AfCFTA implementation: The role of national institutions and digital solutions*. Tralac. https://www.tralac.org/resources/publications.html

Trade Law Centre (Tralac) (2023), Tralac Annual Conference Report 2023, 18–19 May 2023 in Kigali, Rwanda, file.html Central Organization of Trade Union (2024), https://www.tradeunionsinafcfta.org/wp-content/uploads/2024/11/Kenya-Trade-Fact-Sheet-1.pdf

UNCTAD. (2022). *Economic development in Africa report 2022: Rethinking the foundations of export diversification in Africa.* https://unctad.org/publication/economic-development-africa-report-2022

UNECA. (2020a). *Economic report on Africa 2020: Innovative finance for private sector development in Africa.* United Nations Economic Commission for Africa. https://repository.uneca.org

UNECA. (2020b). *Infrastructure development for the AfCFTA: Unlocking trade potential.* UNECA. https://www.uneca.org

UNECA. (2021a). *AfCFTA and African market expansion: Policy priorities and opportunities.* UNECA. https://www.uneca.org

UNECA. (2021b). *Facilitating cross-border trade through a coordinated African response to COVID-19.* https://repository.uneca.org/handle/10855/43784

UNECA. (2021c). *Infrastructure development in Africa: Needs and funding.* https://www.uneca.org

UNECA. (2022). *Kenya launches its national AfCFTA implementation strategy.* United Nations Economic Commission for Africa. https://www.uneca.org/stories/kenya-launches-its-national-afcfta-implementation-strategy

UNECA. (2023a). *AfCFTA yearbook 2023: Unlocking Africa's trade potential.* https://www.uneca.org

UNECA. (2023b). *Status of implementation of the African continental free Trade area: Advancing regional integration for Africa's development.* United Nations Economic Commission for Africa. https://www.uneca.org

Vellum Kenya. (2022, August 12). *Unpacking Kenya AfCFTA national implementation strategy 2022–2027.* Vellum Kenya.

World Bank. (2021). *Kenya enterprise survey 2021.* https://www.enterprisesurveys.org

World Bank. (2024a). *Business ready 2024: Advancing business-environment reforms.* https://www.worldbank.org/en/publication/business-ready.

World Bank. (2024b). *Business ready 2024: Building enabling business environments.* https://bready.worldbank.org

Chapter 10
Navigating the Implementation of the AfCFTA in Rwanda: Issues, Lessons Learned, and Strategies

Aristide Maniriho, Jonas Barayandema, and François Niragire

Abstract Rwanda's ongoing implementation of the African Continental Free Trade Agreement (AfCFTA) provides a critical case study for understanding the complexities of continental economic integration. Despite a robust political commitment, significant impediments persist. These include pervasive non-tariff barriers, inadequate regional infrastructure, and limited productive capacity. Further challenges arise from complex rules of origin, restricted access to trade finance and market intelligence, as well as institutional and human capital limitations. Drawing from Rwanda's proactive engagement and historical regional integration efforts, several key lessons emerge. These highlight the imperative of proactive policy harmonisation, the demonstrable efficacy of trade facilitation reforms, and the transformative potential of digitalisation. Additionally, the necessity of robust private sector engagement and the fundamental importance of regional value chain development are evident. Based on these insights, strategies to optimise Rwanda's AfCFTA engagement include intensified efforts to dismantle non-tariff barriers, strategic infrastructure investments, and enhanced productive capacity with export diversification. Improved access to trade finance and market information, coupled with strengthened institutional frameworks, are also crucial for enhancing trade. These measures, underpinned by sustained regional cooperation and digitalisation, are essential for Rwanda to fully realise the AfCFTA's transformative economic potential.

A. Maniriho (✉)
Department of Economics, University of Rwanda, Kigali, Rwanda
e-mail: a.maniriho1@ur.ac.rw

J. Barayandema
Department of Finance, University of Rwanda, Huye, Rwanda
e-mail: j.barayandema@ur.ac.rw

F. Niragire
Department of Applied Statistics, University of Rwanda, Huye, Rwanda
e-mail: fniragire@ur.ac.rw

D. N. Yuni et al. (eds.), *From Policy to Practice: Challenges and Ways Forward on the Implementation of the AfCFTA*,
https://doi.org/10.1007/978-3-032-14051-7_10

Keywords AfCFTA · Rwanda · Trade barriers · Regional integration · Economic development

JEL Codes F13 · F15 · L86 · O24 · R38

10.1 Introduction

The African Continental Free Trade Area (AfCFTA) stands as a monumental and transformative initiative, poised to reshape the continent's economic landscape. Officially launched in March 2018 in Kigali, Rwanda, and commencing operational trade in January 2021, the AfCFTA aims to establish the world's largest free trade area, encompassing all 55 member states of the African Union (Maniriho et al., 2025; Vhumbunu, 2020). Its overarching objective is to foster deep regional economic integration by progressively eliminating tariffs and non-tariff barriers, thereby facilitating the free movement of goods, services, capital, and persons, and ultimately creating a single continental market (Ogbole & Ogochukwu, 2022). This ambitious undertaking is driven by the imperative to accelerate intra-African trade, enhance industrialisation, stimulate sustainable economic growth, and uplift the living standards of African citizens (Selelo, 2024). For Rwanda, a landlocked nation strategically positioned in East Africa and renowned for its proactive stance on regional integration and a consistently improving business environment, the AfCFTA represents a pivotal opportunity to further diversify its economy, attract investment, and solidify its role as a regional trade and logistics hub.

Rwanda's engagement with the AfCFTA is not merely symbolic; it is deeply rooted in the country's long-term vision for socio-economic development encapsulated in its Vision 2050 (MINECOFIN, 2020). This vision emphasises a shift from an agrarian-based economy to a knowledge-based, service-oriented, and industrialised one. The AfCFTA, with its promise of a unified market of over 1.3 billion people and a combined Gross Domestic Product (GDP) exceeding $3.4 trillion (Ogbologu, 2024), offers a crucial pathway to achieving these ambitious goals. By providing preferential access to a vast continental market, the agreement is expected to stimulate domestic production, encourage economies of scale, attract foreign direct investment, and foster the development of regional value chains, thereby bolstering Rwanda's manufacturing and service sectors (Ghafoori, 2024; World Bank, 2022). Furthermore, given Rwanda's landlocked geography, the AfCFTA's focus on trade facilitation and the reduction of transit costs is particularly pertinent, as it has the potential to significantly enhance the competitiveness of Rwandan exports and reduce the cost of imports.

The Government of Rwanda's commitment to the AfCFTA has been demonstrably strong and unwavering. This was prominently showcased by Kigali hosting the extraordinary summit that formally launched the agreement in 2018. Furthermore, Rwanda distinguished itself as one of the earliest signatories and ratifiers of the AfCFTA Agreement, signalling its profound belief in the transformative power of continental integration. Even more remarkably, Rwanda was the first African nation to ratify the Protocol on Free Movement of Persons and the African Passport, underscoring its forward-thinking approach to facilitating cross-border movement, which is intrinsically linked to trade and investment (Agwu, 2021; Soutar, 2021). This proactive and pioneering stance reflects a deep-seated understanding within Rwandan policymaking circles of the strategic imperative to leverage regional platforms for national development. This early engagement and rapid ratification not only set a positive example for other African Union member states but also provided Rwanda with a head start in terms of preparing its domestic regulatory frameworks and engaging its private sector for the opportunities and challenges that lie ahead.

However, the journey of implementing an agreement of such unprecedented scale and complexity is not without its formidable challenges. While the vision and political will are strong, the practicalities of translating the AfCFTA's provisions into tangible economic benefits for Rwanda necessitate a nuanced understanding of the existing impediments and a strategic approach to overcoming them. For a landlocked country like Rwanda, issues about efficient transit routes, reliable and affordable logistics, and the seamless movement of goods across multiple borders become even more pronounced. The elimination of tariffs, while significant, is merely one component of a successful free trade area. The persistence of non-tariff barriers (NTBs) (Kinzius et al., 2019), including cumbersome customs procedures, divergent regulatory standards, lengthy administrative processes, and inadequate infrastructure, can negate the benefits of tariff liberalisation and continue to inflate the cost of doing business across African borders (Walumweya & Kawimbe, 2024).

Moreover, for Rwanda to fully capitalise on the expanded market access offered by the AfCFTA, there is an imperative to enhance its domestic productive capacity and diversify its export base. While Rwanda has made commendable strides in improving its business environment and attracting investment, its manufacturing sector, though growing, still requires significant enhancement to compete effectively within a much larger continental market. Many Rwandan businesses, particularly Micro, Small, and Medium-sized Enterprises (MSMEs), face inherent limitations in terms of technology adoption, access to affordable finance, economies of scale, and adherence to international quality standards (Rubunda, 2023). These structural constraints, if not adequately addressed, could limit the ability of Rwandan firms to tap into the new export opportunities created by the AfCFTA.

Furthermore, the operationalisation of the AfCFTA involves intricate technical details, particularly concerning rules of origin (RoO) and sanitary and phytosanitary (SPS) measures, which can be complex for businesses to navigate. Understanding and complying with these technical aspects is critical for Rwandan exporters to ensure their products qualify for preferential treatment under the agreement. The absence of comprehensive and easily accessible information on market opportunities, regulatory requirements across different member states, and potential business partners also poses a significant challenge for Rwandan enterprises seeking to expand their reach across the continent.

Ultimately, the success of AfCFTA implementation depends on the establishment of robust institutional frameworks and the availability of adequately skilled human capital within both government agencies and the private sector. Building the capacity of trade policymakers, customs officials, and private sector actors to effectively understand, interpret, and leverage the AfCFTA's provisions is a continuous process that demands sustained investment. Without these foundational elements, the transformative potential of the AfCFTA for Rwanda risks being underrealised.

This chapter aims to provide a comprehensive and rigorous analysis of Rwanda's ongoing experience in implementing the AfCFTA. It systematically examines the key issues and challenges encountered by Rwanda in its efforts to operationalise the agreement, drawing on current data and observations. Building on these insights, this chapter then distils critical lessons learned from Rwanda's initial phases of engagement with the AfCFTA, as well as from its broader experiences in regional economic integration. Finally, drawing on these lessons and a forward-looking perspective, the chapter proposes a set of concrete, actionable strategies designed to optimise Rwanda's engagement with the AfCFTA, enabling the nation to fully capitalise on the opportunities presented by this historic continental undertaking and mitigate the inherent challenges. By offering a detailed academic examination of Rwanda's journey, this chapter seeks to contribute to the broader discourse on AfCFTA implementation across Africa, providing valuable insights for policymakers, businesses, and development partners committed to fostering a more integrated and prosperous continent.

10.2 AfCFTA Implementation Issues in Rwanda

Despite Rwanda's commendable political will and proactive engagement with the African Continental Free Trade Area (AfCFTA), the practical implementation of this ambitious agreement faces numerous systemic and specific challenges within the Rwandan context. These issues, which are not unique to Rwanda but are often amplified by its landlocked geography and developing economic structure, span across critical domains including non-tariff barriers, infrastructure, productive capacity, regulatory complexities, access to finance, and institutional capabilities. Addressing these impediments is paramount for Rwanda to fully harness the transformative potential of the AfCFTA.

10.2.1 Persistent Non-Tariff Barriers (NTBs) and Trade Facilitation Gaps

While the AfCFTA fundamentally aims to liberalise trade through tariff elimination, the continued prevalence of non-tariff barriers (NTBs) represents a significant impediment to seamless intra-African trade for Rwandan businesses (Ogbologu, 2024; Samunderu, 2024a). These insidious barriers manifest in various forms, significantly increasing the cost and time of cross-border trade, thereby eroding the benefits derived from reduced tariffs. For Rwanda, as a landlocked nation, the impact of NTBs is particularly acute, as its goods must transit through multiple jurisdictions before reaching destination markets or international ports.

Key NTBs affecting Rwandan trade include cumbersome and non-harmonised customs procedures, excessive and often redundant documentation requirements, arbitrary levies and charges imposed at borders, and frequent delays at border crossings. These inefficiencies translate directly into higher logistics costs, which are already among the highest globally for African trade. Studies indicate that non-tariff measures can increase the cost of African trade, far outweighing the impact of average applied tariffs (Stender & Vogel, 2023). The lack of uniformity in regulatory standards across different member states, coupled with inconsistent application of existing trade regulations, creates unpredictability and adds layers of complexity for Rwandan exporters (Twum, 2022). For instance, differing sanitary and phytosanitary (SPS) measures and technical trade barriers (TBTs) can act as de facto barriers, particularly for agricultural products and processed foods, which are key components of Rwanda's export diversification strategy.

Moreover, the insufficient implementation of the Protocol on Free Movement of Persons by a majority of African Union member states directly impacts trade interactions. While Rwanda was a pioneering signatory and first to ratify this protocol (Wassie et al., 2022), the limited number of other countries that have followed suit means that Rwandan traders and business professionals still face visa restrictions and bureaucratic hurdles when seeking to explore market opportunities or establish business relationships across the continent. The immobility of human capital and business acumen directly constrains the expansion of trade networks and the development of regional value chains, which are crucial for the success of the AfCFTA (Ajibo, 2023).

10.2.2 Inadequate Infrastructure and Logistics Deficiencies

The ambitious objectives of the AfCFTA are intrinsically linked to the availability of robust, efficient, and integrated infrastructure networks across the continent. Despite Rwanda's commendable investments in domestic infrastructure, particularly in its road network and digital connectivity, significant deficiencies persist in regional infrastructure and logistics, posing substantial challenges to its implementation of the AfCFTA (Ajewumi et al., 2024). High transportation costs, a pervasive issue across Africa, continue to undermine the competitiveness of Rwandan products in continental markets (Habimana, 2023; Twum, 2022).

The primary reliance on road transport for intra-African trade, exacerbated by the absence of well-developed regional railway networks and efficient multi-modal transport systems, contributes to significant delays, higher freight costs, and limited cargo capacity (Samunderu, 2024b). For a landlocked country like Rwanda, the efficiency of transit corridors such as the Northern and Central Corridors is paramount (Lakmeeharan et al., 2020; Sanawar, 2025). However, these corridors often suffer from bottlenecks at border points, inadequate port infrastructure in coastal states, and fragmented logistics services, leading to unpredictable transit times and inflated costs (Balbaa, 2022). While efforts are underway to address these issues, the scale of investment required to bridge Africa's infrastructure gap remains immense (Mafusire et al., 2017). Furthermore, the quality of logistics services, including warehousing, freight forwarding, and cold chain facilities, still needs significant improvement to support increased trade volumes and the movement of perishable goods (Rodrigue & Notteboom, 2014). These infrastructural deficits contribute to higher trade costs, making Rwandan exports less attractive and imports more expensive, thereby limiting the realisation of AfCFTA's trade-boosting potential.

10.2.3 Limited Productive Capacity and Diversification Constraints

While the AfCFTA promises expanded market access, Rwanda's current productive capacity, particularly in its manufacturing sector, requires substantial enhancement to fully capitalise on these opportunities (Twagirimana & Twagirimana, 2019). The industrial sector's contribution to Rwanda's GDP, at 22% in 2023, reflects ongoing efforts towards industrialisation, yet many Rwandan businesses, especially Micro, Small, and Medium-sized Enterprises (MSMEs), struggle with scaling up production, meeting quality standards, and competing with more established and diversified regional players (Assamah & Yuan, 2023).

Rwanda's export base, although diversifying, remains heavily reliant on primary commodities. To effectively leverage the AfCFTA, there is a critical need to move up the value chain, fostering more sophisticated manufacturing, processing, and service capabilities (World Bank, 2022). This structural transformation requires significant investment in modern technology, a substantial upgrade of industrial skills, and improved access to affordable finance for retooling and expansion (Li, 2024). Without adequate productive capacity, Rwanda risks becoming primarily an import market within the AfCFTA, rather than a significant exporter of value-added goods and services, which could lead to trade imbalances and limited job creation (Kamutando et al., 2025). The lack of specialised knowledge and experience in international marketing, as well as limited business contacts across the continent, further constrain the ability of Rwandan firms to identify and penetrate new AfCFTA markets (Twum, 2022).

10.2.4 Complexity of Rules of Origin (RoO) and Non-Tariff Measures (NTMs)

The intricate nature of rules of origin (RoO) within the AfCFTA framework presents a significant operational hurdle for Rwandan businesses seeking to benefit from preferential tariffs (Okoroma, 2024; Samunderu, 2024a). Determining the "originating status" of products, which dictates their eligibility for tariff reductions, often involves complex calculations and stringent documentation requirements that can be particularly burdensome for smaller enterprises lacking specialised expertise or administrative capacity (Kim et al., 2023). The varying and often inconsistent RoO across Africa's multiple Regional Economic Communities (RECs) further complicates compliance, adding layers of complexity to cross-border transactions (Nyirongo, 2023). For Rwandan manufacturers relying on inputs sourced from various countries, adhering to these product-specific rules can be challenging and costly, potentially disincentivising their participation in regional value chains (Tsowou & Davis, 2021).

Beyond RoO, the effective and harmonised application of other non-tariff measures (NTMs) such as sanitary and phytosanitary (SPS) measures and technical trade barriers (TBTs) remains a challenge. While these measures are crucial for consumer protection and fair trade, their inconsistent application, lack of transparency, or use as disguised protectionist tools can act as significant trade barriers (Uddin & Uddin, 2024). Rwanda, like many African countries, needs to strengthen its national infrastructure for quality assurance, standardisation, and conformity assessment to meet and enforce these standards effectively, thereby ensuring its products are readily accepted across the AfCFTA market (Nyamangirazi, 2024).

10.2.5 Limited Access to Trade Finance and Inadequate Market Information

Access to affordable and appropriate trade finance is a critical constraint for Rwandan businesses, particularly MSMEs, aspiring to engage in intra-African trade. Commercial banks often perceive intra-African trade as high-risk due to factors such as perceived political instability, currency convertibility issues, and limited credit information, leading to restrictive lending practices, high collateral requirements, and elevated interest rates (Okoroma, 2024). This financial bottleneck limits the ability of Rwandan exporters to secure working capital, invest in necessary production upgrades, manage currency fluctuations, and offer competitive payment terms to regional buyers (Rubunda, 2023; Twum, 2022). Despite the advent of initiatives like the Pan-African Payment and Settlement System (PAPSS), the underlying challenges in financial inclusion for smaller businesses persist (Okoroma, 2024).

Furthermore, a pervasive lack of readily available, reliable, and up-to-date information on market opportunities, regulatory requirements, and potential trade partners across the vast AfCFTA market constitutes a significant impediment (Sabela et al., 2024). Many Rwandan enterprises, particularly those new to exporting, lack detailed knowledge about specific demand trends in various African markets, the unique regulatory landscapes of potential destination countries, or how to identify credible business partners for sourcing raw materials or distributing products (Arnold, 2022). This information asymmetry can lead to missed opportunities, suboptimal market entry strategies, and increased risks for businesses venturing into new continental markets (Harrison, 2022). The absence of comprehensive national and regional trade portals, or the underutilisation of existing ones, exacerbates this challenge, leaving many businesses without the necessary intelligence to make informed decisions (Abdulganiyu et al., 2023).

10.2.6 Institutional and Human Capacity Limitations

The effective implementation of an agreement as comprehensive as the AfCFTA demands robust institutional frameworks and a well-trained, knowledgeable workforce within both government agencies and the private sector (Alexander, 2023). Within government, there is a continuous requirement to enhance the technical expertise of officials involved in trade policy formulation, negotiation, customs administration, standards enforcement, and dispute resolution mechanisms under the AfCFTA (Nagu, 2023). A lack of deep understanding of the agreement's legal and technical nuances can lead to delays in domestication of protocols, inconsistent application of rules, and an inability to fully advocate for Rwanda's interests in ongoing negotiations.

For the private sector, particularly MSMEs, there is a clear deficit in awareness and understanding of the AfCFTA's provisions, opportunities, and operational requirements (Ajibo, 2023). Many Rwandan export enterprises lack the necessary export capacity, including specific information on market access opportunities, experience in dealing with international standards and quality requirements, international marketing skills, and the necessary business contacts (Lwesya, 2021). This gap in human capital and institutional readiness impedes the effective utilisation of the agreement, preventing businesses from strategically positioning themselves to harness the benefits of a liberalised continental market (Husain, 2024). Without targeted training and widespread dissemination of practical information, the AfCFTA risks remaining an abstract policy concept rather than a tangible tool for economic growth at the enterprise level.

10.3 AfCFTA Implementation in Rwanda: Lessons Learned

Rwanda's engagement with the African Continental Free Trade Area (AfCFTA), alongside its broader and sustained commitment to regional economic integration within bodies such as the East African Community (EAC) and the Common Market for Eastern and Southern Africa (COMESA, of which it is a member through its EAC membership), offers a rich tapestry of experiences from which crucial lessons can be drawn. These lessons are vital for optimising its future implementation strategies and can provide valuable insights for other African nations embarking on similar integration journeys. The operational phases of the AfCFTA, though nascent, combined with Rwanda's historical policy trajectory, underscore several critical factors contributing to or impeding successful trade liberalisation and economic integration.

10.3.1 Proactive Policy and Regulatory Alignment Are Crucial

One of the most salient lessons from Rwanda's approach to the AfCFTA is the profound importance of proactive policy and regulatory alignment. Rwanda's swift ratification of the AfCFTA Agreement in 2018, making it one of the earliest signatories, and its subsequent deposit of the ratification instruments (Agwu, 2021; Soutar, 2021), demonstrated a strong and immediate national commitment. This early engagement was not merely symbolic; it provided a significant head start in terms of initiating domestic legal and regulatory reforms necessary to align with the AfCFTA framework. Such foresight allows for a more phased and less disruptive integration of the continental agreement into national economic policies.

Furthermore, Rwanda's pioneering role in ratifying the Protocol on Free Movement of Persons and the African Passport in 2018 (Matlosa, 2023) stands out as a testament to its forward-thinking approach. This action signifies a profound understanding that the free movement of people is not merely a social or political objective, but an economic imperative intrinsically linked to the efficient flow of goods, services, and capital within a free trade area (Mlambo et al., 2022). The early adoption of these protocols allows for the preliminary assessment of their domestic implications and the commencement of necessary adjustments, setting a positive example for other African Union member states that have been slower to ratify. This proactive stance minimises potential delays and uncertainties once the broader continental implementation gains momentum.

10.3.2 Prioritising Trade Facilitation Reforms Yields Tangible Benefits

Rwanda's sustained and incremental efforts in improving its overall "ease of doing business" environment, particularly within the domain of trade facilitation, offer compelling evidence of its positive impact on economic efficiency. The country's impressive ranking (38th globally among 190 economies in 2020) in the World Bank's Ease of Doing Business report underscores a consistent policy focus on streamlining bureaucratic processes and reducing administrative burdens (World Bank, 2020). This commitment predates the full operationalisation of the AfCFTA but has significantly prepared Rwanda for the agreement's trade-liberalising objectives.

A key aspect of this success has been the widespread implementation of the World Trade Organisation's (WTO) Trade Facilitation Agreement (TFA) (Hassan, 2020), which Rwanda has largely adopted. Specific reforms, such as the operationalisation of electronic single-window systems, which allow for the submission of standardised information and documents at a single entry point (Yigezu, 2021), have dramatically reduced processing times and enhanced transparency in customs procedures. Similarly, the simplification of documentation requirements and the adoption of risk-based inspections have not only expedited border clearances but also contributed to a significant reduction in trade transaction costs (Ogoti, 2018). This experience unequivocally demonstrates that addressing behind-the-border and at-the-border trade facilitation bottlenecks is a fundamental prerequisite for unlocking the full potential of tariff liberalisation under the AfCFTA. Without these efficiencies, the benefits of reduced tariffs can be easily negated by the lingering costs of delays and administrative complexities.

10.3.3 Digitalisation and Technology Adoption Are Enablers for Overcoming Geographic Barriers

For a landlocked country like Rwanda, geographical constraints inherently present significant challenges to trade. However, a crucial lesson emerging from Rwanda's experience, particularly in the nascent stages of AfCFTA implementation, is the transformative power of digitalisation and technology adoption in circumventing these barriers. Rwanda's strategic national focus on ICT development, evident in the robust growth of its ICT sector (Ghafoori, 2024), provides a fertile ground for such digital trade initiatives. The lesson here is clear: proactive investment in digital infrastructure, fostering digital literacy, and promoting e-commerce platforms can empower businesses, particularly Micro, Small, and Medium-sized Enterprises (MSMEs), to tap into the wider continental market irrespective of physical proximity to ports or major trade routes. The integration of digital solutions, such as electronic payment systems (Okoroma, 2024) and online trade information portals, can further streamline transactions, reduce costs, and enhance transparency across the AfCFTA.

10.3.4 The Imperative of Robust Private Sector Engagement and Capacity Building

The success of the AfCFTA ultimately rests on the private sector's ability to seize the opportunities it presents. Rwanda's experience has underscored the critical importance of early, sustained, and targeted engagement with businesses (Bernatzki et al., 2022). Initiatives such as the AfCFTA Private Sector Engagement Strategy, which aims to drive value addition and regional value chain integration (Ajewumi et al., 2024; Ajibo, 2023), are vital. Rwanda's participation in the AfCFTA Guided Trade Initiative (GTI), a pilot project involving eight member states for identified commodities (Agarwal & Tayo, 2024), has provided Rwandan businesses with invaluable practical experience in navigating the new trading regime. The GTI has enabled firms to test the market, identify challenges, and adjust their strategies to the new market dynamics.

However, the initial challenges reported by Rwandan trading companies participating in such initiatives, including persistent issues with visa restrictions (as noted earlier), customs procedures, and distribution networks in partner countries (Behuria, 2017), underscore a crucial lesson: private sector engagement must be accompanied by comprehensive capacity building. Many Rwandan export enterprises lack the necessary skills and information, including knowledge of potential market access opportunities, experience in dealing with international standards and quality requirements, international marketing skills, and relevant business contacts (Akimana, 2017). Therefore, ongoing efforts to provide tailored training, market intelligence, and business development services are indispensable to ensure that businesses, particularly MSMEs, can effectively participate in and benefit from the AfCFTA. This also necessitates strengthening public–private dialogue mechanisms to ensure that the private sector's concerns and practical challenges are regularly communicated to policymakers and integrated into implementation strategies.

10.3.5 Regional Value Chain Development Is Fundamental to Industrialisation, and Diversification

Rwanda's long-term economic strategy is firmly anchored in industrialisation and export diversification, aiming to transition from a reliance on primary commodities to higher-value-added goods and services (MINECOFIN, 2020). A key lesson learned is that the AfCFTA's true transformative potential lies not merely in facilitating trade in existing goods but in fostering the development of robust regional value chains (RVCs). RVCs enable countries to specialise in specific stages of production where they have a comparative advantage, resulting in increased efficiency, competitiveness, and resilience to global shocks (Okoroma, 2024).

Rwanda's strategic establishment of special economic zones (SEZs) and industrial parks, which host a growing number of manufacturing plants (Nduwimana, 2018; Newman & Page, 2017), reflects a commitment to creating an enabling environment for industrial growth and RVC integration. The lesson is that such targeted industrial policies, coupled with efforts to attract investment in manufacturing and processing, are essential. By focusing on developing specific sectors with strong backwards and forward linkages to other African economies, Rwanda can position itself as a key node within continental production networks. This approach ensures that the benefits of expanded market access translate into domestic industrial growth, job creation, and technological upgrading, rather than simply increasing imports. Successful RVC development requires harmonised standards, efficient logistics, and cross-border investment facilitation to enable seamless production and trade flows across national boundaries (Okoroma, 2024).

In short, Rwanda's journey with AfCFTA implementation, while marked by commendable strides, highlights a series of critical lessons. These include the strategic advantage of proactive policy alignment, the demonstrable benefits of persistent trade facilitation reforms, the transformative potential of digitalisation, the absolute necessity of robust private sector engagement coupled with targeted capacity building, and the fundamental importance of fostering regional value chains for sustainable industrialisation. These lessons provide a solid foundation for refining future strategies and ensuring that Rwanda fully leverages the opportunities presented by the continental free trade area.

10.4 Strategies for the Successful Implementation of AfCFTA in Rwanda

To fully harness the transformative potential of the African Continental Free Trade Area (AfCFTA), Rwanda must adopt a comprehensive and multi-pronged strategic approach that systematically addresses identified challenges and leverages lessons learned from its initial implementation phases. These strategies encompass a blend of policy reforms, targeted infrastructure development, robust private sector support, and significant human capital development, all underpinned by a commitment to regional cooperation and digitalisation. The ultimate aim is to position Rwanda as a competitive and well-integrated player within the burgeoning continental market.

10.4.1 Intensifying Efforts to Eliminate Non-Tariff Barriers (NTBs)

The continued prevalence of NTBs remains a significant impediment to intra-African trade for Rwanda, diminishing the benefits of tariff liberalisation (Muhirwa et al., 2024). Therefore, a primary strategic imperative is to intensify efforts in their elimination:

Proactive advocacy for harmonised and transparent trade facilitation measures: Rwanda must continue to play a leading role in advocating within the AfCFTA Secretariat and relevant Regional Economic Communities (RECs), such as the East African Community (EAC) and COMESA, for the accelerated elimination of NTBs. This includes consistently pushing for the full operationalisation and strengthening of the AfCFTA Non-Tariff Barriers Mechanism, ensuring that reported barriers are swiftly investigated and resolved (Achancho, 2023). Furthermore, Rwanda should champion the harmonisation of customs procedures, documentation requirements, and trade regulations across the continent, advocating for common standards and best practices that reduce complexity and costs for traders.

Deepening digitalisation of customs and border procedures: Building on its strong ICT foundation (Ghafoori, 2024), Rwanda should further invest in and integrate advanced digital platforms for customs administration, port management (for transit goods), and border control. Expanding the functionalities of existing electronic single-window systems to cover all trade-related processes, implementing pre-arrival processing of goods, and leveraging risk-based inspections will significantly reduce processing times and opportunities for rent-seeking behaviour (Clark & Bernard, 2022). The interoperability of these digital systems with those of key transit and destination countries within the AfCFTA would create seamless cross-border data flows, thereby further enhancing efficiency.

Strengthening cross-border cooperation and coordinated border management: Bilateral and multilateral agreements with neighbouring countries are essential to optimise transit routes. This involves pursuing joint customs controls, establishing integrated border posts where agencies from both sides operate side by side, and fostering greater information sharing among border agencies to enhance efficiency and combat illicit trade (Shaker, 2025). Dialogue forums with customs and trade facilitation agencies of transit countries (e.g., Kenya, Tanzania) should be institutionalised to address persistent bottlenecks and ensure consistent application of trade rules.

Sustained advocacy for full implementation of the protocol on free movement of persons: As a strong proponent and early ratifier (Matlosa, 2023), Rwanda should continue to champion the full ratification and implementation of the Protocol on Free Movement of Persons by other AfCFTA member states. Easier movement of traders, skilled labour, and business professionals across borders will significantly facilitate trade, investment, and the establishment of regional business networks, addressing issues currently faced by Rwandan traders (Dushimimana, 2021). This includes promoting the issuance of visas on arrival and, ultimately, the universal adoption of the African Passport.

10.4.2 Strategic Infrastructure Development and Logistics Optimisation

Addressing Rwanda's landlocked status and the high cost of logistics is the success of the AfCFTA. Strategic investments in infrastructure and logistics are crucial:

Prioritising investment in key regional transport corridors: *Rwanda must continue to advocate for and contribute to the development of key regional transport corridors* (Otele & Guguyu, 2023), *including road and rail networks that connect it efficiently to major ports (Mombasa, Dar es Salaam) and production centres in neighbouring* countries. This necessitates close collaboration with EAC and COMESA partners, as well as leveraging financing mechanisms such as the AfCFTA Adjustment Fund's General Fund, which specifically supports trade-enabling infrastructure (Okoroma, 2024). Strategic public-private partnerships (PPPs) should be explored to attract necessary investment in large-scale infrastructure projects.

Enhancing logistics and warehousing capabilities: Developing modern logistics hubs, strategically located dry ports (e.g., Kigali Logistics Platform), and state-of-the-art warehousing facilities is essential to improve efficiency in cargo handling, storage, and distribution (Sadiq et al., 2021). Investing in cold chain logistics is also critical for diversifying exports to include perishable agricultural products. This involves attracting private sector investment in logistics services, promoting the adoption of logistics technologies, and developing a skilled logistics workforce.

Promoting multi-modal transport solutions: Diversifying transport options beyond predominant road transport will enhance resilience and reduce costs. This includes greater utilisation of air cargo for high-value and time-sensitive goods, expanding airfreight capacity, and exploring viable inland waterway transport options where feasible. The integration of various transport modes will create a more robust and cost-effective supply chain for Rwandan businesses within the AfCFTA.

10.4.3 Boosting Productive Capacity and Export Diversification

To fully capitalise on market access, Rwanda must enhance its ability to produce competitive goods and services:

Targeted sectoral development and value addition: Rwanda should intensify its efforts to identify and strategically develop sectors with high potential for export growth under the AfCFTA, with a strong focus on value-added products. This includes agro-processing, light manufacturing (e.g., textiles, garments, construction materials), pharmaceuticals, and a range of services (e.g., ICT, tourism, financial services) (World Bank, 2022). The new Industrial Policy should be effectively implemented to enhance the competitiveness and sophistication of locally produced goods, moving beyond the export of raw materials.

Strengthening support for Micro, Small, and Medium-sized Enterprises (MSMEs): MSMEs are the backbone of Rwanda's economy, but often face significant constraints in engaging in international trade (Poole, 2021). Tailored support programmes are crucial, including facilitating access to affordable trade finance (e.g., through credit guarantees, concessional loans from development banks), providing technical assistance for product development and quality upgrades, and offering business development services such as market research and export coaching. Leveraging digital platforms to connect MSMEs with regional markets and financing opportunities is vital.

Promoting Regional Value Chain (RVC) integration: Rwanda should actively encourage its businesses to integrate into regional value chains by fostering backwards and forward linkages with firms in other AfCFTA member states. This can be achieved through targeted investment promotion (e.g., joint ventures, special economic zones designed for RVCs), business-to-business (B2B) matchmaking platforms, and incentives for regional sourcing of raw materials and intermediate goods (Poeschel et al., 2025). This strategy aligns with Rwanda's objective of building export-driven industries (MINECOFIN, 2020).

Fostering innovation and technology adoption in production: Encouraging the adoption of modern production techniques, automation, and digital technologies (e.g., Industry 4.0 applications) will enhance the efficiency, quality, and competitiveness of Rwandan products (Peter et al., 2023). This requires sustained investment in research and development, promoting a culture of innovation, and facilitating technology transfer from more advanced economies (Amini Sedeh et al., 2022).

10.4.4 Simplifying Rules of Origin (RoO) and Accelerating Standards Harmonisation

The technical complexities inherent in the African Continental Free Trade Area (AfCFTA) necessitate focused strategic consideration. Addressing these intricate technicalities is crucial for the effective implementation of the agreement. Consequently, dedicated strategic attention is indispensable to navigate these challenges. *Active and informed participation in RoO negotiations:* Rwanda must continue to actively participate in ongoing AfCFTA negotiations on Rules of Origin to advocate for simplified, transparent, and trader-friendly rules that accommodate nascent industries and diverse supply chains. Advocating for flexible rules that allow for greater regional content will encourage the development of RVCs.

Comprehensive capacity building on RoO compliance: Provide extensive training and technical assistance to Rwandan businesses, particularly MSMEs, on understanding and complying with AfCFTA rules of origin. This includes developing user-friendly guides, digital tools (e.g., online RoO calculators), and dedicated advisory services to demystify the compliance process (Ismail et al., 2023; Lowdermilk, 2013).

Accelerating harmonisation of standards and technical regulations: Advocate for and actively participate in regional initiatives aimed at harmonising product standards, technical regulations, and conformity assessment procedures across the AfCFTA. Establishing mutual recognition agreements for testing and certification, as well as strengthening regional accreditation bodies, will reduce the burden of multiple inspections and certifications, thereby facilitating trade (Katsieris, 2024). Rwanda's national standards body should be adequately resourced to align with continental standards.

10.4.5 Enhancing Access to Trade Finance and Market Information

Addressing financial and informational asymmetries is crucial for businesses:

Developing innovative and accessible trade finance mechanisms: Collaborate with the Central Bank (National Bank of Rwanda), commercial banks, and regional financial institutions, such as Afreximbank, to develop innovative and affordable trade finance products tailored for intra-African trade. This includes expanding the use of credit guarantees, factoring, forfaiting, and supply chain finance. Leveraging the Pan-African Payment and Settlement System (PAPSS) for efficient and low-cost cross-border payments will be crucial in reducing transaction costs and improving liquidity (Okoroma, 2024).

Promoting financial inclusion for MSMEs: Expand financial literacy programmes and improve MSMEs' access to formal financial services and digital payment solutions. This includes leveraging mobile money platforms and fintech innovations to reach underserved segments of the business community, enabling them to participate more effectively in regional trade.

Establishing a centralised and user-friendly AfCFTA information hub: Develop a comprehensive national online platform that serves as a one-stop shop for reliable and up-to-date information on AfCFTA provisions, market opportunities, rules of origin, customs procedures, and contact details for relevant government agencies and business support organisations (Belay, 2024). This platform should be multilingual and easy to navigate for businesses of all sizes.

Facilitating Business-to-Business (B2B) linkages and market intelligence: Organise regular physical and virtual trade fairs, business forums, and B2B matchmaking events to connect Rwandan businesses with potential partners and buyers across the AfCFTA market (Njiru et al., 2021). Investing in market intelligence tools and providing advisory services on market entry strategies, consumer preferences, and competitive landscapes in specific African markets will empower Rwandan exporters to make informed decisions.

10.4.6 Strengthening Institutional and Human Capital Capacity

The effective implementation of the AfCFTA requires continuous investment in human capital and robust institutional frameworks:

Targeted capacity building for Government Agencies: Invest in specialised and continuous training programmes for government officials involved in trade policy formulation, negotiation, customs administration, standards enforcement, and dispute resolution mechanisms under the AfCFTA framework. This ensures a deep and evolving understanding of the agreement's legal, technical, and commercial aspects.

Widespread private sector awareness and training programmes: Implement comprehensive and practical awareness campaigns and training programmes for the private sector, particularly MSMEs, on the opportunities and operational requirements of the AfCFTA. These programmes should cover practical aspects such as export procedures, market entry strategies, quality standards, and navigating cross-border trade challenges (Oyebamiji, 2024). Collaboration with business associations (e.g., Private Sector Federation) is crucial for effective outreach.

Fostering robust Public-Private Dialogue (PPD): Institutionalise regular and meaningful dialogue mechanisms between the government and the private sector (Charles, 2024). The National Implementation Committees (NICs) serve as a key platform for this engagement, ensuring that private sector concerns, challenges, and recommendations are systematically identified and integrated into AfCFTA implementation strategies (Chitanda & Semedo, 2023). This collaborative approach fosters ownership and ensures policy relevance.

Strategic investment in skills development: Align national educational and vocational training programmes with the emerging demands of the AfCFTA, focusing on skills relevant to industrialisation, digital trade, logistics, and services sectors. This includes vocational training in quality control, export marketing, foreign languages (relevant to other African markets), and digital proficiency to build a workforce capable of capitalising on continental opportunities (Belinga & Nayihouba, 2024).

By meticulously implementing these multifaceted strategies, Rwanda can effectively navigate the complexities of AfCFTA implementation, overcome existing challenges, and leverage its strategic position and proactive policy environment to become a significant beneficiary of the continental free trade area, contributing meaningfully to Africa's integrated and prosperous future.

10.5 Conclusion

Rwanda's journey in implementing the African Continental Free Trade Area (AfCFTA) presents a compelling case study of a proactive nation navigating the complexities of regional economic integration. As meticulously detailed in this chapter, despite commendable political will and early engagement, Rwanda faces a multifaceted array of systemic and specific challenges. These impediments, encompassing persistent non-tariff barriers, inadequate regional infrastructure, limited productive capacity, complex rules of origin, constrained access to trade finance, and institutional limitations, underscore the formidable task ahead for a landlocked, developing economy.

However, Rwanda's experience thus far is not solely defined by these hurdles. Crucially, its sustained commitment to regional integration within frameworks like the EAC and COMESA has yielded invaluable lessons. The emphasis on proactive policy and regulatory alignment, demonstrated by swift AfCFTA ratification and pioneering efforts in free movement protocols, has provided a strategic head start. The discernible benefits of prioritising trade facilitation reforms, including the adoption of electronic single-window systems and risk-based inspections, offer a clear blueprint for enhancing trade efficiency. Furthermore, the transformative power of digitalisation and technology adoption has emerged as a critical enabler for overcoming inherent geographic disadvantages. The imperative of robust private sector engagement and capacity building, alongside the fundamental importance of fostering regional value chain development, are recognised as indispensable for translating market access into tangible economic growth and diversification.

Drawing upon these insights, the proposed strategies offer a concrete roadmap for Rwanda to deepening the digitalisation of customs procedures, and strengthening its AfCFTA engagement. Intensifying efforts to eliminate non-tariff barriers through proactive advocacy, deepening the digitalisation of customs procedures, and strengthening cross-border cooperation is paramount. Strategic investments in regional transport corridors, coupled with enhanced logistics and warehousing capabilities and the promotion of multi-modal transport solutions, will address critical infrastructural deficits. Simultaneously, boosting productive capacity and export diversification through targeted sectoral development, robust support for MSMEs, and active promotion of regional value chain integration will ensure Rwanda can competitively supply the continental market.

Ultimately, Rwanda's success in the AfCFTA will hinge on a sustained, coordinated, and adaptive approach. By systematically addressing the identified challenges and diligently applying the lessons learned, Rwanda stands to not only mitigate inherent risks but also to fully capitalise on the transformative opportunities presented by this historic undertaking. This chapter serves as a valuable contribution to the broader discourse on AfCFTA implementation across Africa, offering practical insights for policymakers, businesses, and development partners committed to fostering a more integrated, prosperous, and resilient continent. The trajectory of Rwanda's integration offers a microcosm of the continent's aspirations, highlighting that with strategic foresight and persistent effort, the promise of the AfCFTA can indeed be realised.

References

Abdulganiyu, J., Musa, M. N., Matayo, V. A., Saidu, A. A., & Ahmed, A. A. (2023). Integrating business intelligence and small and medium enterprises for shifting Africa from consumption to a production and industrialised economy. *Spectrum International Journal of Multidisciplinary Research, 1*(2), 1–9.

Achancho, E. E. (2023). Exploring the possibilities of legal harmonisation of non-tariff barriers of RECs for the achievement of the AfCFTA. *Comparative and International Law Journal of Southern Africa, 56*(2-3), 1–31.

Agarwal, P., & Tayo, T. (2024). *Promoting women entrepreneurship under the guided trade initiative*.

Agwu, F. A. (2021). Globalization, populism, nationalism and the African continental free trade area. In *Foreign policy in the age of globalization, populism and nationalism: A new geopolitical landscape* (pp. 261–339). Springer.

Ajewumi, O. E., Afolabi, J. A., & Joe-Akunne, I. (2024). *Regional trade agreements and economic integration in Africa: Assessing the impact of the African continental free trade area (AFCFTA)*.

Ajibo, C. C. (2023). AfCFTA and regional value chain development: Confronting the barriers and changing the orthodoxy. *Journal of World Trade, 57*(4), 7.

Akimana, V. (2017). Internal and external factors affecting exporting SMEs in Rwanda. In *Management challenges in different types of african firms: Processes, practices and performance* (pp. 37–58). Springer.

Alexander, K. (2023). *A view from the south: Making sense of the organisational reality of social enterprises in sub-Saharan Africa*.

Amini Sedeh, A., Pezeshkan, A., & Caiazza, R. (2022). Innovative entrepreneurship in emerging and developing economies: The effects of entrepreneurial competencies and institutional voids. *The Journal of Technology Transfer, 47*(4), 1198–1223.

Arnold, S. (2022). Drivers and barriers of digital market integration in East Africa: A case study of Rwanda and Tanzania. *Politics and Governance, 10*(2), 106–115.

Assamah, D., & Yuan, S. (2023). Can smaller powers have grand strategies? The case of Rwanda. *Insight on Africa, 15*(1), 108–127.

Balbaa, M. E. (2022). *International transport corridors*. Tashkent State University of Economics.

Behuria, P. (2017). *The political economy of import substitution in the 21st century: The challenge of recapturing the domestic market in Rwanda*.

Belay, R. (2024). AfCFTA and African air cargo: Evaluating effects and proposing seamless logistics solutions, with a case study of Ethiopian airlines. *SSRN Journal*. https://doi.org/10.2139/ssrn.4794032

Belinga, V., & Nayihouba, K. A. (2024). Upgrading skills for Africa's economic transformation 1. In *Making the African continental free trade agreement a success* (pp. 198–233). Routledge.

Bernatzki, T., Busse, M., & Hoekstra, R. (2022). Promoting Rwanda's business environment: Impact of reforms and drivers of change. *Development Policy Review, 40*(2), e12578.

Charles, G. (2024). Regional and national public-private dialogue structures in Tanzania: Design, agenda and challenges. *Tanzania Journal of Development Studies, 22*(1), 57–80.

Chitanda, Y., & Semedo, J. L. T. (2023). *AfCFTA national implementation committees: Scoping options and support mechanisms*. AfCFTA National Implementation Committees.

Clark, J., & Bernard, D. (2022). Customs in a world of enhanced trade facilitation. In *Customs matters: Strengthening customs administration in a changing world*. International Monetary Fund.

Dushimimana, G. (2021). *Exploring cross-border cooperatives and small-scale traders in eastern Africa with a focus on Rwanda: What matters and why* (doctoral dissertation, master's thesis presented at the international institute of social studies. The Hague, The Netherlands).

Ghafoori, M. (2024). *Revolutionizing economic growth through ICT: Rwanda's path to digital empowerment*.

Habimana, V. (2023). *Rationalization of international trade and investment agreements: Case of east African community* (Doctoral dissertation, Anglia Ruskin Research Online (ARRO)).

Harrison, R. T. (2022). "Pennies from heaven"? Market failure, circuits of capital and policy support for business angels: The case of cross-border angel investment. *Journal of Business Venturing Insights, 17*, e00311.

Hassan, M. (2020). Africa and the WTO trade facilitation agreement: State of play, implementation challenges, and policy recommendations in the digital era. In *Fostering trade in Africa: Trade relations, business opportunities and policy instruments* (pp. 5–38). Springer.

Husain, D. I. (2024). *Enhancing economic competitiveness*.

Ismail, N. S., Khalid, H., Yaakob, H., Md Husin, M., Yap, C. C., Roslan, I. N. S., & Ruslan, M. A. (2023). Using design thinking methodology to transition from paper to digital system. *Journal of Design Thinking, 4*(2), 289–304.

Kamutando, G., Edwards, L., Tuyishimire, C., & Twum, A. (2025). *Shifting the dial: Using the AfCFTA to boost export growth and diversification in Rwanda*. International Growth Centre.

Katsieris, D. (2024). Accreditation, certification and inspection: Impact on global trade. In *Handbook of quality system, accreditation and conformity assessment* (pp. 1–18). Springer.

Kim, S., Chung, D., Kim, K., Park, S., Cha, W., & Lee, S. (2023). *A study of enhancing utilization of rules of origin in Korea's FTAs: A focus on the agri-food exporters (English summary report 2023.10)*. Korea Rural Economic Institute.

Kinzius, L., Sandkamp, A., & Yalcin, E. (2019). Trade protection and the role of non-tariff barriers. *Review of World Economics, 155*(4), 603–643.

Lakmeeharan, K., Manji, Q., Nyairo, R., & Poeltner, H. (2020). Solving Africa's infrastructure paradox. *McKinsey & Company, 6*, 17–25.

Li, L. (2024). Reskilling and upskilling the future-ready workforce for industry 4.0 and beyond. *Information Systems Frontiers, 26*(5), 1697–1712.

Lowdermilk, T. (2013). *User-centered design: A developer's guide to building user-friendly applications*. O'Reilly Media.

Lwesya, F. (2021). SMEs' competitiveness and international trade in the era of global value chains (GVCs) in Tanzania: An assessment and future challenges. *Small Business International Review, 5*(1), e325.

Mafusire, A., Brixiova, Z., Anyanwu, J., & Meng, Q. (2017). Infrastructure deficit and opportunities in Africa. In *Infrastructure in Africa* (pp. 545–568). Policy Press.

Maniriho, A., Barayandema, J., & Kayisire, P. (2025). Effects of African continental free trade area on enhancing exports and welfare in selected east African community countries. *The International Trade Journal, 39*(2), 2511040. https://doi.org/10.1080/08853908.2025.2511040

Matlosa, K. (2023). The free movement of persons and African integration. In *The quest for unity* (pp. 265–289). Routledge.

MINECOFIN. (2020). *Rwanda vision 2050*. Ministry of Economic Planning and Finance (MINECOFIN).

Mlambo, V. H., Thusi, X., Zubane, S., & Mlambo, D. N. (2022). The African continental free trade area: Challenges and possible successes. *Latin American Journal of Trade Policy, 5*(12), 75–106.

Muhirwa, Y. D., Iradukunda, N., & Waweru, M. (2024). Effects of non-tariff barriers on promotion of east African community integration: A case of Magasins Généraux du Rwanda. *African Journal of Empirical Research, 5*(3), 1116–1130.

Nagu, Y. (2023). *Implementing the African continental free trade agreement (AfCFTA): Policies, regulations, laws and institutions required for development* (Doctoral dissertation, University of Cape Town).

Nduwimana, E. (2018). *The role of special economic zone on job creation in Rwanda a case study of Kigali special economic zone (2014–2017)* (Doctoral dissertation, University of Rwanda).

Newman, C., & Page, J. M. (2017). *Industrial clusters: The case for special economic zones in Africa (No. 2017/15)*. WIDER Working Paper.

Njiru, N., Wanyoike, F. N., & Baltenweck, I. (2021). *Enhancing market access through business-to-business platforms: Key lessons and insights from northern Kenya*. CGIAR.

Nyamangirazi, N. (2024). Whether the African continental free trade area (AFCFTA) agreement satisfies the requirements for 'legality' under the applicable WTO law governing regional trade agreements (RTAS).

Nyirongo, R. (2023). *Navigating compliance challenges in African regional integration, Faculty of Law, Department of Commercial Law*. http://hdl.handle.net/11427/39190

Ogbole, O. K., & Ogochukwu, I. J. (2022). African continental free trade area and economic integration in Africa. *Africa's International Relations in a Globalising World: Perspectives on Nigerian Foreign Policy at Sixty and Beyond, 211*(2), 4.

Ogbologu, O. B. (2024). Charting the path to African prosperity: Unravelling the economic dynamics of the African continental free trade agreement. *Nnamdi Azikiwe University Journal of International Law and Jurisprudence, 15*(1), 92–102.

Ogoti, T. N. (2018). *Effect of customs risk based management systems on trade facilitation in Kenya revenue authority* (doctoral dissertation, KESRA/JKUAT-unpublished research project).

Okoroma, B. I. (2024). *Facilitating trade through rules of origin: A consideration of the African continental free trade area*. Univesity of Calgary.

Otele, O., & Guguyu, O. (2023). Region-centric infrastructure policies and the regional politics surrounding Chinese railway projects: Insights from the East Africa region. *Politics & Policy, 51*(5), 919–935.

Oyebamiji, O. (2024). Overcoming barriers to intra-African trade: The role of AfCFTA in dismantling colonial crop legitimacy, shipping constraints, and transportation challenges. *Journal of Economics and Political Sciences, 4*(1), 1–19.

Peter, O., Pradhan, A., & Mbohwa, C. (2023). Industry 4.0 concepts within the sub–Saharan African SME manufacturing sector. *Procedia Computer Science, 217*, 846–855.

Poeschel, F. G., Boland, C., de Lange, T., Ruhs, M., & Saka-Helmhout, A. (2025). *Engaging the private sector in global skills partnerships: Exploring the potential of international business-to-business approaches*.

Poole, D. L. (2021). *Entrepreneurs and SMEs in Rwanda*.

Rodrigue, J. P., & Notteboom, T. (2014). The cold chain and its logistics. *The Geography of Transport Systems, 1*, 288–310.

Rubunda, E. (2023). *Finance structure and the growth of small and medium size manufacturing Enterprises in Rwanda* (Doctoral dissertation, JKUAT-COHRED).

Sabela, P. T., Masuku, M. M., & Mlambo, V. H. (2024). Unleashing the development potential of Africa's women through African continental free trade agreement (AfCFTA). *Journal of Contemporary African Studies, 42*(1), 1–17.

Sadiq, M., Ali, S. W., Terriche, Y., Mutarraf, M. U., Hassan, M. A., Hamid, K., & Guerrero, J. M. (2021). Future greener seaports: A review of new infrastructure, challenges, and energy efficiency measures. *IEEE Access, 9*, 75568–75587.

Samunderu, E. (2024a). Contextual setting of the African air transport market. In *The economic effects of air transport market liberalisation. Advances in African economic, social and political development*. Springer. https://doi.org/10.1007/978-3-031-61864-2_2

Samunderu, E. (2024b). Liberalisation of trade regime under AfCFTA: A perspective analysis on Africa's single market. In *The economic effects of air transport market liberalisation: A perspective analysis of the single African air transport market (SAATM)* (pp. 641–730). Springer.

Sanawar, S. (2025). *Role of spatial planning in improving freight efficiency* (Doctoral dissertation, SPA Bhopal).

Selelo, S. (2024). Promoting intra-African trade through agenda 2063 to accelerate continental economic growth for sustainable development. *OIDA International Journal of Sustainable Development, 17*(12), 185–194.

Shaker, S. A. (2025). The impact of trade facilitation inequality on bilateral trade: the case of India–Middle East–Europe economic corridor (IMEC). *Journal of Shipping and Trade, 10*(1), 7.

Soutar, N. (2021). *The political economy of the African continental free trade area (AfCFTA): A policy analysis of the prospects and challenges.*

Stender, F., & Vogel, T. (2023). Murky trade waters: Regional tariff commitments and non-tariff measures in Africa. *The Journal of International Trade & Economic Development, 32*(7), 1058–1082.

Tsowou, K., & Davis, J. (2021). Reaping the AfCFTA potential through well-functioning rules of origin. *Journal of African Trade, 8*(Suppl 2), 88–102.

Twagirimana, E., & Twagirimana, R. G. (2019). Rwanda in Africa continental free trade area: Challenges-opportunities analysis. *Rwanda Research Paper Series, 2*, 62–79.

Twum, A. (2022). Using trade to propel high growth: Lessons from Rwanda's export performance in the past decade. Final Report.

Uddin, M., & Uddin, M. S. (2024). Non-tariff barriers on technical, sanitary and phytosanitary measures: An overview under WTO Laws. *International Journal of Global Community, 7*(2), 105–122.

Vhumbunu, C. H. (2020). The African continental free trade area. *Africa Insight, 50*(1), 122–143.

Walumweya, M., & Kawimbe, S. (2024). Enhancing economic integration through cross-border trade optimization in eastern and southern Africa: Insights for policy and practice. *GSJ, 12*(8), 52.

Wassie, M. A., Kornher, L., & von Braun, J. (2022). *African continental free trade agreement: A review of analyses of likely impacts and challenges of implementation.*

World Bank. (2020). *Doing business 2020: Comparing business regulations in 190 economies.* World Bank group.

World Bank. (2022). *World development report 2022: Education and human capital development.* World Bank.

Yigezu, H. (2021). Assessment on the effect of electronic single window implementation (Doctoral dissertation, St. Mary's University).

Chapter 11
Lesotho and the AfCFTA: An Examination of Progress and Opportunities for the Future

Denis Nfor Yuni

Abstract The AfCFTA, with its vast market of over 1.3 billion people across the continent, presents a significant opportunity for Lesotho's businesses to expand their customer base beyond its small population and achieve economies of scale that are unattainable within its borders. Consequently, Lesotho's registration with the AfCFTA is not merely a matter of convenience; it is a matter of survival. This chapter indicates that Lesotho signed the AfCFTA agreement in 2018 and ratified it in 2020 and is currently engaged in ongoing negotiations concerning tariff concessions for trade in goods. However, implementation has been slow for Lesotho, as well as other African countries. This chapter recommends that, for Lesotho to optimise the potential benefits of the AfCFTA, it must conclude tariff concession negotiations and implement the agreed tariff reductions stipulated by the AfCFTA, adopt and enforce the agreed Rules of Origin, finalise its commitments for the liberalisation of trade in the five priority services, actively participate in Phase II negotiations and ratify protocols, enhance the capabilities of government agencies to implement and monitor AfCFTA obligations, conduct awareness campaigns, and provide capacity-building support to businesses (particularly SMEs), as well as strategically diversify products and trade destinations based on its comparative advantage.

Keywords AfCFTA implementation · International trade · Economic integration · Intra-African trade · Lesotho

D. N. Yuni (✉)
Department of Economics, University of Namibia, Windhoek, Namibia

D. N. Yuni et al. (eds.), *From Policy to Practice: Challenges and Ways Forward on the Implementation of the AfCFTA*,
https://doi.org/10.1007/978-3-032-14051-7_11

11.1 Introduction: Setting the Stage for Lesotho and the AfCFTA

11.1.1 Overview of Lesotho's Socio-Economic Context and Development Aspirations

Lesotho is a landlocked country located in the southern region of Africa, which is completely surrounded by South Africa. Lesotho is a mountainous country with high altitudes, crisscrossed by a network of rivers and mountain ranges, including the 3482 m-high peak of Thabana Ntlenyana (McKenna, 2025). The landlocked condition within South Africa implies that all land ports have access only to South Africa, and it has only one airport where planes must fly through the O.R. Tambo International Airport in Johannesburg, South Africa's airspace, before gaining access to any other country (Yuni & Tsietsi, 2025). In terms of population, statistics show that Lesotho has an estimated population of about 2.3 million people in 2024 (World Bank, 2025a), placing it in the lower quartile (25%) of the World's countries in terms of population. Lesotho's geographic location, topography, and small population directly affect access to international borders beyond South Africa, access to sea ports, and the provision of a locally attractive market.

These odds as well as other factors have placed Lesotho in a dire situation of underdevelopment and classification as a Least Developed country according to the United Nations (United Nations, 2024). The economic statistics show that Lesotho recorded a real GDP of 2.25 billion USD in 2023 (higher than the Sub-Saharan African [SSA] average of 1.99 billion), real GDP per capita of 974.4 USD in 2023 (lower than the SSA average of 1581.1 USD), and an annual GDP growth rate of 1.8% (lower than the SSA average of 2.8) in the same year (World Bank, 2025b). World Bank (2025b) further posits that Lesotho's poverty head count ratio at the national poverty line and Gini inequality index stood at 49.7%, and 44.9%, respectively, in 2017. And in terms of human capital indicators, the 2021 estimate for life expectancy at birth is 53 years for Lesotho, which is lower than her peers, such as Eswatini with 57 years, 61 years for Botswana, and the sub-Saharan average of 60 years (Yuni & Tsietsi, 2025).

This explains why the government of Lesotho have consciously put in place short-, medium-, and long-term strategic plans/goals to promote development in the country. The national long-term policy documents for Lesotho include the Vision 2020, the National Strategic Development Plan (NSDP) I that covers 2012/13–2016/17, the National Strategic Development Plan (NSDP) II that covers 2018/19–2022/23, alongside other legislations and programmes. The government of Lesotho is currently implementing the NSDP II which was "extended to 2027 following the implementation failure in the past three years" (Lesotho News Agency, 2023). The NSDP II seeks to create a private sector-led and export-driven economy, with a strong emphasis on improving productivity and competitiveness in key priority sectors, while addressing infrastructure gaps, strengthening human capital, and promoting good governance. This clearly highlights the development aspirations of

Lesotho, and the African Continental Free Trade Agreement (AfCFTA) provides a pathway to achieving this development aspirations.

11.1.2 Introduction to the AfCFTA and Rationale for Lesotho's Engagement with the AfCFTA

The overarching goal of the AfCFTA is to establish a unified African market that facilitates the free movement of goods, services, capital, and people, thereby boosting intra-African trade, driving economic integration, and promoting sustainable and inclusive development across the continent (African Union, 2018). The AfCFTA seeks to eliminate trade barriers across Africa, promote industrialisation and value chains, enhance investment and competition policies, provide support for small- and medium-sized enterprises (SMEs) in regional and global trade, and support improvements in transport, logistics, and digital infrastructure to reduce the cost and time of trade, etc. These goals resonate with the development aspirations of Lesotho in the last 3 decades and will probably be retained in future strategic development plans. Specifically, the NSDP II, as extended, aligns with at least four key objectives of the AfCFTA as given in Table 11.1.

It is therefore evident that a key rationale for Lesotho's engagement with the AfCFTA, is embedded in the alignment of the goals of the AfCFTA with its prevailing developmental aspirations. Beyond the strategic alignment of both policy documents as explained above, Lesotho's engagement with the AfCFTA is a strategic move to overcome its inherent economic limitations, diversify its economy, enhance its competitiveness, attract investment, create jobs, and ultimately achieve its long-term development aspirations by leveraging the power of continental integration. The AfCFTA, with its vast market of over 1.3 billion people in the continent (World Bank, 2020), offers a significant opportunity for Lesotho's businesses to expand their customer base beyond its small population and achieve economies of scale that are impossible within its own borders. In addition, the AfCFTA provides a platform to diversify its export base into other sectors like agriculture (high-value crops and livestock products), light manufacturing, and services, reducing over-reliance on a few sectors, particularly textiles and apparel, and remittances from migrant workers, thereby plummeting vulnerability to sector-specific shocks and external factors.

The AfCFTA's objective of reducing tariffs and non-tariff barriers will make Lesotho's exports more competitive in the African market, thereby encouraging local industries to enhance their productive capacity and competitiveness. Furthermore, access to a larger market can incentivise value addition to raw materials, moving Lesotho up the value chain and could catalyse Lesotho's industrialisation agenda. Another critical advantage of the AfCFTA is that it offers Lesotho opportunities beyond its landlocked condition, without which it will be perpetually heavily rely on its neighbour, South Africa, for trade and transit. The AfCFTA deepens regional integration across the continent, fostering broader economic ties with

Table 11.1 Strategic alignment between the AfCFTA objectives and the key priority areas of the NSDP II

No	Theme	AfCFTA—objectives	NSDP II—key priority areas (KPAs)
1.	Boosting intra-African trade and economic growth	Article 3, a: To create a single market for goods, services, facilitated by the movement of persons, capital and natural resources, in order to deepen the economic integration of the African continent and establish a continental free trade area (CFTA)	KPA 1: Inclusive and sustainable economic growth and job creation • Objective 1.1: Enhance productive capacity and competitiveness of key sectors (this directly relates to being able to trade effectively within the AfCFTA) • Objective 1.2: Promote export diversification and market access. The AfCFTA provides a significant new market to access • Objective 1.3: Improve the business environment and attract investment. A larger, integrated market under the AfCFTA can be a strong investment pull
2.	Fostering regional integration and cooperation	Article 3, g: To foster and promote regional value chains; and Article 3, h: To enhance cooperation on all trade-related areas, including trade facilitation, rules of origin, investment, intellectual property rights and competition policy	KPA I - objective 1.3: Operational industrial clusters and integrated supply chains KPA 4: Enhanced human capital development, which aims to develop a skilled workforce capable of participating in and benefiting from regional value chains and the opportunities presented by the AfCFTA
3.	Private sector-led growth and industrialisation	Article 3, g: Aims to promote industrial development through diversification and regional value chain development, facilitating the movement of goods and services across member states	KPA I: Focuses on enhancing inclusive and sustainable economic growth through private sector-led job creation. Key outcomes include: • Objective 1.2: Diversified products and effective business linkages • Objective 1.3: Operational industrial clusters and integrated supply chains • Objective 1.7: Functioning incubation centres and industrial parks

Table 11.1 (continued)

No	Theme	AfCFTA—objectives	NSDP II—key priority areas (KPAs)
4.	Infrastructure development	Article 3, a: Also seeks to improve trade-related infrastructure to reduce transaction costs and enhance connectivity among African countries	KPA III: Emphasises building enabling infrastructure to support economic activities. Key outcomes include: • Objective 3.1: Sustainable quality transport network • Objective 3.2: Sustainable energy production and use • Objective 3.4: Economic-friendly ICT infrastructure

Source: Author's analysis of the Agreement establishing the African Continental Free Trade Area (African Union, 2018) and the NSDP II Strategic Focus (Government of Lesotho, 2023)

other African nations. Hence, Lesotho's industries can access a broader range of intermediate goods and raw materials from different African countries, potentially at more competitive prices.

Lesotho's registration with the AfCFTA is therefore not just a choice of convenience, it is one of survival. It is fundamental to Lesotho's food security, industrialisation, and ultimately economic growth and development. Lesotho's economic, and political power dynamics and growth imperatives within the South African region and beyond is largely dependent on its ability to minimise dependence in whatever guise and create wealth and prosperity for her people. The AfCFTA offers such an opportunity which is unmatched with any other opportunity that could potentially offer similar benefits currently.

11.2 Understanding Lesotho's Economic Profile in the Context of Regional Trade

11.2.1 Macroeconomic Environment and Sectorial Contribution to Lesotho's GDP

To understand the macroeconomic environment of Lesotho, there is a need to examine its fiscal and monetary instruments. In terms of the fiscal instruments, World Bank (2025b) posits that the proportion of Lesotho's GDP dedicated to general government final consumption expenditure has seen significant growth, from 8.1% in 1970 to 43.5% in 2009. Even though it decreased to 35.6% in 2023, this figure is still considerably higher than the world average (16.5%), the Sub-Saharan African average (15.6%), and that of its peers, Burkina Faso (20%) and Botswana (28.9%).

This greatly contrasts the domestic credit to private sector as a percentage of GDP where Lesotho records 24.9% in 2023, which is considerably lower when compared to the world average of 142%, the SSA average of 33.4%, Burkina Faso (31.6%), and Botswana (30.1%). This infers that the economy of Lesotho is largely driven by the government with relatively lower private sector participation. It is worth noting that, Lesotho's heavy reliance on Southern African Customs Union (SACU) receipts, which accounted for around 40% of its revenue in 2023, raises important questions about the nation's fiscal sustainability (Yuni, 2025).

Lesotho has a fixed exchange rate with the South African Rand based on the Common Monetary Area (CMA) agreement. The CMA comprises of Lesotho, South Africa, Namibia, and Eswatini; and seeks to facilitate trade and investment flows among member countries, by removing exchange rate restrictions and promoting the free flow of funds for economic growth and development in the region. Lesotho's monetary policy is therefore largely influenced by the monetary policy of South Africa's central bank. The World Bank (2025b) further posits that Lesotho's current account balance as a percentage of GDP has been negative since 2009 and was −7% in 2023. This has crucial implications for how Lesotho must design its policies to participate in the implementation of the AfCFTA.

In terms of sectorial contribution, the service sector contributes the most to GDP in Lesotho. In 2023, the service sector value added as a percentage of GDP was 50.6% followed by the manufacturing sector value added as percentage of GDP of 14% and then the agriculture, forestry, and fishing value added of 6.6% of GDP (World Bank, 2025b). This makes sense given the socio cultural contexts discussed earlier. On one hand, the high altitude and limited arable land explains the low agricultural value added contribution to GDP. In contrast, the service sector value added indicator includes value added in wholesale and retail trade (plus hotels and restaurants), transport, and government, financial, professional, and personal services such as education, health care, and real estate services, which Lesotho apparently has a comparative advantage in. It is also worth noting that the potential for the tourism industry in Lesotho is infinite and could significantly grow the service sector value added exponentially based on its unique topography and climate. Hence, though Yuni et al. (2023) argue that the manufacturing sector has comparative advantage relative to the agricultural sector in Lesotho, the service sector trumps them both, not only based on available statistics but much more due to its potential.

11.2.2 The Role of Regional Economic Communities and Existing Trade Agreements

Lesotho's engagement with the AfCFTA cannot be dissociated from its already existing commitments and agreements with other Regional Economic Communities or blocs. The key trade agreements that Lesotho is party to, include: the SACU Agreement, Southern African Development Community Free Trade Area

(SADC-FTA), Economic Partnership Agreement (EPA) with the EU, and the African Growth and Opportunity Act (AGOA).

The SACU agreement provides for duty-free trade among member states and a common external tariff on goods imported from outside the union, which Lesotho adheres to. This does not strictly align with the AfCFTA which requires a similar trade agreement for all countries in SSA, implying no external tariff to non-SACU members within the region. Similarly, the SADC Free Trade Area seeks to eliminate tariffs and non-tariff barriers among 16 member states, including: Angola, Botswana, Comoros, Democratic Republic of the Congo, Eswatini, Lesotho, Madagascar, Malawi, Mauritius, Mozambique, Namibia, Seychelles, South Africa, Tanzania, Zambia, and Zimbabwe. However, the implementation of the SACU trade agreement has been less adequate relative to the SADC trade agreement, with some countries maintaining significant trade barriers with member states (Organisation for Economic Co-operation and Development, 2017). The EPA with the EU is part of the SADC EPA that provides for asymmetric trade liberalisation, with the EU opening its markets to SADC exports more rapidly than SADC opens its markets to EU exports (European Commission, 2025). And the United States' AGOA agreement provides eligible SSA countries, including Lesotho, with tariff-free entry into the U.S. market for a broad spectrum of products.

Lesotho's participation in these trade agreements presents opportunities and challenges for its integration into the AfCFTA. For example, these institutional frameworks and mechanisms for regional cooperation imply that Lesotho has had a similar experience in trade agreements such as the AfCFTA and could therefore be leveraged to facilitate the AfCFTA implementation. The regional initiatives to harmonise customs procedures, improve infrastructure, and reduce non-tariff barriers can complement AfCFTA efforts to boost intra-African trade with fewer countries or regional blocs to agree with. The trade agreements outside Africa, such as the AGOA and the EPA, will also significantly benefit Lesotho if it is strategically positioned to garner raw materials from the region at competitive prices for exports even beyond Africa, based on these agreements.

The Challenges of these trade agreements are, however, significant and are perceived to potentially be a limitation to the implementation of the AfCFTA. Lesotho's membership in multiple regional trade agreements with overlapping objectives and sometimes conflicting obligations could create challenges in harmonising its trade policies under the AfCFTA. Another key challenge is that Lesotho's participation in trade agreements like the EPA can limit Lesotho's policy space and flexibility in pursuing its development objectives under the AfCFTA. For instance, implementation of the EPA may restrict Lesotho's ability to impose tariffs on imports from the EU, even if such tariffs are needed to protect domestic producers or offer subsidies or other forms of support to local industries. Similarly, while AGOA is a non-reciprocal agreement, it still creates a specific trade relationship that could influence Lesotho's trade policies, as is the case with EPA. Hence, the need for the Lesotho government to consciously put in place measures that mitigate the risks from the EPA and AGOA.

Nevertheless, the future of AGOA has become increasingly uncertain, especially with the 2025 Trump tariffs and other trade policies that imply a drastic change in America's global trade policy. A discontinuation of the AGOA will be particularly challenging for Lesotho whose textile industry has been heavily reliant on this preferential access to the U.S. market. The AfCFTA may then become a viable market alternative to the textile production in Lesotho. An efficient integration into the AfCFTA will therefore require that the government builds capacity to negotiate and implement trade agreements, ensuring that its interests are effectively represented in regional and continental forums. A key takeaway from the experience with the trade agreements is the importance of diversifying Lesotho's exports - a lesson highlighted by the country's reliance on textile production, which grew under AGOA but now faces uncertain sustainability.

11.3 The AfCFTA Agenda in Lesotho: History, Current Status and Implementation Efforts

11.3.1 Lesotho's Ratification of the AfCFTA Agreement: Timeline and Implementation Efforts

On the 21 March 2018, in an Extraordinary Summit in Kigali, Rwanda, Lesotho was among the 44 African Union member states that signed the Agreement Establishing the AfCFTA (African Union, 2018). This demonstrated Lesotho's commitment to the ideals of continental free trade. Then, the AfCFTA showed a huge promise for economic development in the creation of a single continental market for goods and services. The United Nations Conference on Trade and Development (UNCTAD) had predicted that implementing the tenets of the AfCFTA such as reducing intra-African tariffs, has the potential to increase intra-African trade by as much as 33% and reduce the continent's trade deficit by 51% (UNCTAD, 2021). While the United Nations Economic Commission for Africa in 2018, projected that intra-African trade could rise by 52% by 2022 compared to trade levels in 2010 (Infomineo, 2018). In addition, on the 20 October 2020, the parliament of Lesotho ratified the AfCFTA agreement and subsequently deposited their instruments of ratification, schedules of tariff concessions, and offers in respect of Trade in Services with the Commission as of the 27 November 2020 (African Union, 2020).

Lesotho's ratification of the AfCFTA by completing the domestic legal procedures required to be a member of the free trade area makes it a state party legally bound by its provisions. Lesotho, via SACU and SADC, is currently involved in the ongoing negotiations regarding the schedule of tariff concessions for trade in goods which aims to liberalise tariffs on up to 90% of tariff lines over a period as mandated by the AfCFTA (Bowmans, 2023; United Nations Economic Commission for Africa, 2023). Lesotho has yet to pronounce itself on the ongoing negotiations on liberalising trade in services across five priority sectors, agreement on the Rules of Origin, and the Phase II negotiations covering Investment, Intellectual Property

Rights, and Competition (IIPRC) Policy. Though the operational phase of the AfCFTA was launched on 7 July 2019 during the 12th Extraordinary Session of the African Union Assembly held in Niamey. Trading under the AfCFTA officially commenced on the 1st of January 2021, but the actual flow of goods and services under the new preferential terms in Lesotho as well as other countries has been gradual due to ongoing negotiations on various protocols and implementation challenges (Africa, 2025; African Union, 2019; Kararach et al., 2023). The lack of completion of these negotiations have limited the full implementation of the AfCFTA in Lesotho and its ability to take advantage of the exponential opportunities that come with it.

There are several steps that Lesotho needs to take to fast-track the implementation of the AfCFTA.

- First, there is need to conclude negotiations on its schedule of tariff concessions and implement the agreed tariff reductions in line with the agreed timelines. This will only be feasible with the adjustment of its national customs procedures and laws to align with the AfCFTA requirements.
- Also, Lesotho needs to adopt and implement Agreed Rules of Origin for various products by incorporating them into its national trade regulations and ensure effective enforcement.
- Lesotho also needs to actively participate in and finalise its commitments for the liberalisation of trade in the priority service sectors and implement the necessary regulatory reforms.
- Lesotho also needs to actively engage in the ongoing Phase II negotiations on the IIPRC Policy and consider ratifying these protocols once finalised to deepen its integration into the continental market further.
- The need to ensure that the Ministry of Trade, Industry, Business Development and Tourism, the Ministry of Finance and Development Planning, and other relevant government agencies and institutions have the capacity and resources to effectively implement and monitor Lesotho's obligations and benefits under the AfCFTA.
- It is also imperative to conduct nationwide awareness campaigns to inform businesses, especially SMEs, about the AfCFTA opportunities and provide capacity-building support in market access, export development, and compliance with AfCFTA requirements.

In summary, the AfCFTA presents significant opportunities for growth by expanding market access and stimulating intra-African trade. However, countries not adequately prepared for increased competition and market openness may face challenges, including the risk of local industries being outcompeted. Ultimately, the AfCFTA will be beneficial to all parties based on theoretical (Absolute Cost Advantage, Comparative Cost Advantage, and Heckscher-Ohlin Theory, etc.) and empirical literature on the gains of trade. However, growth rates in such an open market will largely be driven by the ability to produce in terms of quality and quantity, level of human capital, technological advancement, institutional frameworks, political stability, business environment and the entrepreneurial spirit of residents amongst others.

11.3.2 International Trade Statistics in Lesotho and Implications for the Implementation of the AfCFTA

To understand international trade statistics that are relevant to the implementation of the AfCFTA in Lesotho, the study examines the custom duties that Lesotho levies to imports from SSA and those levied to imports from the rest of the World. As well as the value of Lesotho's exports/imports to/from SSA and non-SSA countries, in a bit to understand Lesotho's trade with SSA compared to the rest of the World.

The Lesotho Applied Harmonised System (AHS) Duty Free Tariff Lines Share in percentage for all products refers to a trade policy indicator that shows the proportion of tariff lines for which Lesotho applies zero customs duties (i.e., duty-free access) to imports from the entire world, based on the AHS tariff schedule. It therefore shows what percentage of product categories Lesotho allows to enter the country without tariffs, when imported from any country in the world or region, based on its current applied tariff schedule and not necessarily what is bound at the WTO or AfCFTA.

Table 11.2 provides that Lesotho allowed duty-free access for 100% of fuels, stone and glass, hides and skin, food products, and vegetables imported from SSA countries between 2018 and 2021. However, for wood, raw materials, plastic or rubber, footwear, and textile and clothing, Lesotho instituted import duties that ranged between 1% and 7% for SSA. This consideration is not evident for import duties from the World at large. No product records a 100% free import duty from the World and for some products such as foot wear, Lesotho allowed duty-free access

Table 11.2 Lesotho AHS duty free tariff lines share in percentage for all products from SSA and world between 2018 and 2021

	2018		2019		2020		2021	
Description	SSA	World	SSA	World	SSA	World	SSA	World
Fuels	100	90	100	90	100	90	100	90
Stone and glass	100	74.24	100	74.24	100	74.5	100	74.5
Hides and skin	100	40.29	100	40.29	100	40.29	100	40.29
Food products	100	71.12	100	71.38	100	71.38	100	71.38
Vegetables	100	79.32	100	79.35	100	79.02	100	79.08
Wood	99	75.15	99	75.15	99.03	75.22	99.08	75.38
Raw materials	98.79	84.96	98.79	84.98	98.8	84.72	98.8	84.72
Plastic or rubber	98.16	66.03	98.16	66.05	98.16	66.05	98.17	66.94
Footwear	93.75	41.88	93.14	39.95	94.35	34.89	94.35	34.89
Textile and clothing	97.61	46.55	97.62	46.38	97.62	46.33	97.62	46.33

World Integrated Trade Solutions (WITS) (2025)

for only 34.89% from the World in 2021, implying that about 65% of foot wear imports from the world had some import duty levy.

It is, however, important to note that this does not show the impact of the AfCFTA on Lesotho's import duties. First, the analysis combines all countries in SSA and the World which does not cater for peculiar bilateral/regional agreements that will reflect in the import duties for each country and subsequently in the world. Second, this analysis does not estimate causality. However, Table 11.2 clearly shows that for the period analysed—2018–2021, the Lesotho government has levied custom duties on products from outside SSA than from within SSA. Nevertheless, majority of the exports and imports come from South Africa. In 2022, for example, Lesotho imported a total value of 1,446,109.75 USD from South Africa, (constituting about 77.36% of the total imports from the World) and exported a total value of 3384.14 to South Africa (amounting to 86.02% of total exports to the World) (World Integrated Trade Solutions (WITS), 2025). Hence, it explains why the custom duties charged to SSA is negligible relative to the rest of the World.

A further analysis of the value of imports/exports from/to the SSA and non-SSA region is demonstrated on Table 11.3. Table 11.3 shows that, for all products, the volume of exports to SSA amounted to 41.6% in 2018 (and 46.6% in 2021) of total exports to the World, implying about 58.4% (and 53.4% in 2021) of Lesotho's exports is destined for non-SSA countries. Hence a growth of the export value to SSA by 12% between 2018 and 2021. However, this trend varies considerably for individual products. For example, over 80% of the export value of capital goods, intermediate goods, animal, footwear, fuels, metals, hides and skins, machine and electrical products, minerals, plastic/rubber, transportation, and wood were destined for SSA in 2021. Meanwhile, the value of exports for raw materials destined for SSA was only 24.4% in 2021 and that for stone and Glass was only 0.3% in the same year. Conversely, the value of imports from SSA as a percentage of import from the World for all products increased from 71.1% to 77% between 2018 and 2021. Besides intermediate goods and textile and clothing, the value of over 70% of all the major products was destined for SSA in 2021.

Summarily, Table 11.3 shows that Lesotho's exports to SSA are less than its imports from SSA. This could be due to the fact that most of the products it currently trades in have higher demand outside the SSA than within the SSA. Diversification of products and trade destinations is therefore imperative to optimising the gains of implementing the AfCFTA. For example, Lesotho could take advantage of the comparative advantage it has particularly based on its unique topography and climate within the region to offer specialised tourism services that will be uncommon in the region such as skiing, snow tourism, high-altitude trekking/hiking, and the Basotho pony trails and equestrian tourism that could be developed in many districts of Lesotho.

Table 11.3 International trade-related indicators for Lesotho in 2018 and 2021

Description	2018			2021			2018			2021		
	Export to SSA (US$ thousand)	Export to World (US$ thousand)	Exports to SSA as a % of export to world	Export to SSA (US$ thousand)	Export to World (US$ thousand)	Exports to SSA as a % of export to world	Import from SSA (US$ thousand)	Import from world (US$ thousand)	Import from SSA as a % of import from world	Import from SSA (US$ thousand)	Import from world (US$ thousand)	Import from SSA as a % of import from world
All products	367,156.9	882,385.3	41.6	441,894.1	948,535.2	46.6	1,154,422.3	1,624,617.3	71.1	1,284,051	1,667,948.7	77.0
Capital goods	49,126.9	56,802.8	86.5	74,071.1	74,271.3	99.7	215,505.4	285,683.1	75.4	211,849.9	247,518.0	85.6
Consumer goods	264,218.7	621,093.6	42.5	268,905.2	590,107.0	45.6	595,903.4	763,199.0	78.1	647,518.5	752,341.8	86.1
Intermediate goods	43,954.7	50,015.6	87.9	40,081.1	43,898.9	91.3	212,074.5	428,084.0	49.5	299,624.7	538,224.2	55.7
Raw materials	9730.2	154,302.8	6.3	58,609.4	239,894.8	24.4	119,975.1	136,112.4	88.1	124,286.7	128,334.3	96.8
Animal	3471.1	4042.1	85.9	5314.6	5743.0	92.5	59,746.3	65,461.0	91.3	62,731.1	63,190.8	99.3
Chemicals	1444.5	1937.2	74.6	2626.5	3032.2	86.6	74,195.6	112,482.9	66.0	88,321.7	124,955.0	70.7
Food products	74,297.1	74,921.2	99.2	67,833.0	88,190.3	76.9	127,401.6	139,798.7	91.1	152,675.1	157,130.9	97.2
Footwear	8884.0	10,606.7	83.8	7792.5	7794.0	100.0	23,014.3	25,652.6	89.7	24,758.2	25,418.0	97.4
Fuels	365.4	435.4	83.9	325.7	325.8	100.0	202,894.8	217,391.7	93.3	216,729.8	226,447.7	95.7
Hides and skins	370.5	396.2	93.5	502.4	504.3	99.6	7954.5	8987.9	88.5	13,861.8	14,027.1	98.8
Mach and Elec	61,981.2	71,444.8	86.8	69,095.7	69,272.9	99.7	164,688.5	226,775.6	72.6	160,913.6	190,806.6	84.3
Metals	1351.3	1899.7	71.1	2157.6	2219.7	97.2	66,145.7	76,306.4	86.7	79,313.7	89,499.8	88.6
Minerals	1434.6	1591.1	90.2	1499.9	1506.5	99.6	11,161.8	12,521.0	89.1	14,293.6	14,602.1	97.9

Miscellaneous	1687.4	1934.5	87.2	1989.0	2462.4	80.8	34,139.9	45,977.1	74.3	41,946.2	51,944.7	80.8
Plastic or rubber	1715.1	1912.9	89.7	2097.7	2100.0	99.9	37,332.9	49,285.9	75.7	42,089.9	50,264.1	83.7
Stone and glass	573.0	138,430.7	0.4	591.5	176,021.6	0.3	13,044.6	14,519.8	89.8	15,206.0	15,494.2	98.1
Textiles and clothing	191,329.3	549,744.1	34.8	255,938.2	560,285.1	45.7	115,458.4	330,541.9	34.9	136,300.6	360,922.5	37.8
Transportation	6225.7	7073.7	88.0	9315.1	9547.9	97.6	76,831.6	125,958.3	61.0	62,517.8	89,513.2	69.8
Vegetable	6528.6	9738.4	67.0	9910.9	14,589.7	67.9	91,487.0	106,106.0	86.2	121,311.2	126,824.2	95.7
Wood	5498.4	6276.6	87.6	4903.9	4940.0	99.3	48,924.9	66,850.4	73.2	51,080.8	66,907.7	76.3

11.3.3 Domestic Institutional Frameworks and Coordination Mechanisms for AfCFTA Implementation in Lesotho

At least six key institutions are relevant to establishing a robust domestic institutional framework for implementing the AfCFTA in Lesotho. They include the Ministry of Trade, Industry, Business Development and Tourism; the Ministry of Finance and Development Planning; the Revenue Service Lesotho (RSL); the Bureau of Statistics; the Private Sector Organisations; and the Lesotho Regulatory Departments and Quality Control.

The Ministry of Trade, Industry, Business Development and Tourism is the premier government body responsible for trade policy formulation and implementation in Lesotho. It plays a crucial role in coordinating AfCFTA-related activities, including policy alignment, stakeholder engagement, and monitoring implementation progress. They are expected to spearhead the development of Lesotho's national AfCFTA implementation strategy which should have immediate middle and long term goals and implementation strategies in the interest of Lesotho. Considering the primary role of the Ministry of Finance and Development Planning, it is expected to provide the financial resources necessary for the facilitation and implementation of the AfCFTA such as allocating budget for AfCFTA-related activities, ensuring that AfCFTA implementation is aligned with national development plans, mobilising domestic and external resources to support AfCFTA implementation and monitoring the fiscal impact of the AfCFTA.

Revenue Service Lesotho is responsible for customs administration, including the collection of tariffs and the enforcement of trade regulations (Revenue Service Lesotho, 2024). Effective implementation of the AfCFTA will require the LRA to adapt its systems and procedures to the new trade regime, especially with reference to the pending issues such as tariff liberalisation, rules of origin, and trade facilitation. Though the Bureau of Statistics is a government department under the Ministry of Finance and Development Planning, it is specifically tasked with establishing a system for national official statistics covering economic, social, demographic (including human resources), and environmental sectors, that are aligned with Lesotho's development priorities (Bureau of Statistics, 2004). It will therefore play a crucial role in collecting, analysing, and disseminating trade data, accurately and timely, to monitor the impact of the AfCFTA and inform policy adjustments. There may be a need to improve the BOS's capacity to track new trade flows and indicators arising from the AfCFTA.

Private Sector Organisations such as the Lesotho National Development Corporation (LNDC) and the Lesotho Chamber of Commerce and Industry (LCCI) represent the interests of businesses and play a crucial role in facilitating private sector participation in Lesotho in general, and will no doubt do the same for the AfCFTA. These organisations can help disseminate information to their members, provide training, and advocate for policies that support AfCFTA implementation amongst businesses in Lesotho. Standard and quality control institutions are other key institutions that should be considered for the smooth implementation of the AfCFTA. Industries in Lesotho have historically depended on the South African Bureau of Standards for voluntary standards services and quality assurance programmes. Currently, Lesotho is engaged in a regional Standardisation, Quality, Accreditation, and Metrology (SQAM) initiative under SADC, which seeks to harmonise standards across all member countries (Logistics Cluster, 2025).

Effective coordination among these institutions and stakeholders is crucial for successfully implementing the AfCFTA. Lesotho, therefore, needs to establish mechanisms that ensure policy coherence, minimise duplication of efforts, and facilitate effective communication across these institutions. Another key institution worth mentioning is the Southern African Customs Union because coordination within SACU is essential to ensure a smooth transition to the AfCFTA regime. Lesotho has established a National AfCFTA inter-ministerial Implementation Committee to oversee the practical aspects of the AfCFTA. This committee will be crucial for coordinating policies and actions carried out by all relevant institutions. Their job cannot be complete without actively promoting private sector engagement, stakeholder awareness and capacity building, and regional coordination in terms of harmonising policies and procedures within SACU. A robust monitoring and evaluation framework is needed to track Lesotho's progress in implementing the AfCFTA and to be proactive in strategies that need to be implemented.

Lesotho's strategic position, entirely surrounded by South Africa, elevates the importance of its diplomatic representation in South Africa. The diplomatic offices are expected to promote trade, protecting national interests, facilitating investment ties, and supporting Basotho nationals abroad, all through the lens of commercial diplomacy. The United States International Trade Administration (2025) states that "Lesotho's position limits its access to global markets, forcing businesses to rely exclusively on South African ports and infrastructure". Therefore, by advocating within South Africa, these offices can help reduce border inefficiencies and improve customs procedures, given Lesotho's reliance on South African ports and transport infrastructure. To strengthen AfCFTA outcomes, these offices can coordinate implementation of mutually beneficial policies, streamline firm-level compliance with standards, and facilitate participation in regional value chains.

11.4 Challenges Faced by Lesotho in the Implementation of the AfCFTA

The immediate challenges faced by Lesotho in the implementation of the AfCFTA will not be unrelated to its negotiating power in the ongoing agreements and the capacity that is required for every aspect of the implementation, which may be causing delays with full implementation. To effectively implement the AfCFTA and capitalise on its opportunities, Lesotho needs to develop specific capacity and skill sets in: negotiations, trade agreement analysis, trade policy formulation, customs modernisation, rules of origin administration, trade facilitation, logistics and supply chain management, standards development and harmonisation, quality assurance, technical regulations, productive capacity and industrial development, investment promotion, financial services: and trade/economic communication skills for massive sensitisation and reporting.

In the short, and medium term, Lesotho will face challenges such as the overlapping memberships of RECs earlier discussed, the limited productive capacity and industrial development, infrastructure deficits, lack of diversification, competition from other countries, lack of information and awareness, financial constraints and compliance with the diverse non-trade barriers in other African countries, which could limit its access to those markets. For example, inadequate transport, logistics, and energy infrastructure exacerbated by its landlocked status can significantly increase trade costs and reduce Lesotho's competitiveness. Also, Lesotho will face increased competition from other African countries, some of which have more developed industrial sectors, lower production costs, or better infrastructure. More importantly, implementing the AfCFTA requires significant investments in infrastructure, technology, and capacity building which may not constitute Lesotho's priorities given the fiscal pressures it currently experiences.

Trade-related data that was collected by the National University of Lesotho World Trade Organisation (NUL-WTO) research chair exemplifies some of these challenges. An analysis of this data set showed that about four out of five of the sampled firms (78.5%) find exportation to be either extremely difficult or fairly difficult, while about 66.9% found importation to be either fairly easy or extremely easy (Yuni & Machema, 2024). The report further highlighted that factors such as insufficient information on foreign markets, standards compliance, competitiveness, cost of export customs, border procedures, limited access to trade finance, poor Infrastructure, insecurity and inadequate transport links tend to have a moderate to significant negative impact on export activities in Lesotho. Meanwhile, customs and border procedures, cost of import, standards compliance and limited access to trade finance constitute moderate constraints on firms' ability to import. The ability to export and import is at the very core of the implementation of the AfCFTA and so these challenges must be taken seriously.

In the long run, Lesotho will need a robust monitoring and evaluation framework that tracks transactions, highlights emerging trends, and responds proactively to market-induced tendencies that have the potential to improve growth indicators or constitute challenges for the economy. Such a framework also requires adequate capacity building, legal provisions, and policies that could manage its implementation. Experiences from the current regional economic communities that Lesotho belongs to could be leveraged to design such frameworks for the implementation of the AfCFTA.

11.5 Conclusion: Charting a Course for Lesotho's Prosperous Future within the AfCFTA

In spite of Lesotho's small population, topography and landlocked condition, the full implementation of the AfCFTA offers opportunities that could significantly change its socioeconomic dynamics. The chapter highlights that, the AfCFTA offers a significant opportunity for Lesotho's businesses to expand their customer base beyond its small population and achieve economies of scale that are impossible within its own borders.

It also highlights that the objectives of the AfCFTA aligns significantly with the long term development aspirations of Lesotho. The chapter also analyses the sectorial contributions to GDP as well as the demographic and geographic attributes of Lesotho and concludes that Lesotho has comparative advantage in the service sector, relative to the manufacturing and agriculture sector. In addition, Lesotho participates in several regional trade agreements, including SACU, SADC-FTA, EPA with the EU, and AGOA with the USA which presents both opportunities and challenges for its integration into the AfCFTA that it should consider.

This chapter also clearly shows that Lesotho signed the AfCFTA agreement in 2018 and ratified it in 2020, demonstrating its commitment to continental free trade. Lesotho is involved in ongoing negotiations regarding tariff concessions for trade in goods. However, the actual implementation of the flow of goods and services under AfCFTA terms has been gradual for Lesotho and other countries due to ongoing negotiations and implementation challenges. Lesotho applies varying levels of import duties on products from the rest of the world. In contrast, imports from SSA generally have lower duties, though a significant portion of Lesotho's imports and exports is with South Africa. And the key institutions for AfCFTA implementation in Lesotho include: the Ministry of Trade, Industry, Business Development and Tourism; the Ministry of Finance and Development Planning; Revenue Service Lesotho; the Bureau of Statistics; Lesotho Regulatory Departments and Quality Control; and the Private Sector Organisations (e.g., LNDC, LCCI).

The challenges that Lesotho may face in the Implementation of the AfCFTA abound. The immediate key challenges include concluding the negotiations and building the capacity required for every implementation aspect. In the short and medium term, Lesotho will face challenges such as the overlapping memberships of RECs earlier discussed, the limited productive capacity and industrial development, infrastructure deficits, lack of diversification, competition from other countries, lack of information and awareness, financial constraints and compliance with the diverse non-trade barriers in other African countries, which could limit its access to those markets. In the long run, Lesotho may be constrained to have a robust monitoring and evaluation framework that tracks transactions, highlights emerging trends and responds proactively.

The Strategic Importance of the AfCFTA for Lesotho's Long-Term Development cannot be over-emphasised. The full implementation of the AfCFTA provides opportunities for value chain development and regional integration, boosting small and medium-sized enterprises and entrepreneurship, opening up new market opportunities for Lesotho's SMEs within the continental market, and promote employment creation, skills development, and poverty reduction. Ultimately, taking advantage of the opportunities that come with the AfCFTA may lead Lesotho on a path of economic growth and sustainable development. Nevertheless, these key recommendations need to be considered to optimise these opportunities.

- Conclude tariff concession negotiations and implement agreed tariff reductions. There is need to fast-track the process of aligning national customs procedures and laws with AfCFTA requirements so as to enable the effective commencement of trade under the AfCFTA, and unlocking the opportunities that it brings for Lesotho.

- Adopt and implement agreed Rules of Origin which is essential to determine the nationality of goods traded under the AfCFTA, ensuring that the preferential treatment is accorded to products originating from member states.
- Also, Lesotho needs to actively participate in and finalise its commitments for the liberalisation of trade in the five priority service sectors under the AfCFTA, which is crucial for diversifying Lesotho's economy and enhancing its competitiveness.
- The need to actively engage in Phase II negotiations (IIPRC Policy) and ratify protocols which is vital for deepening Lesotho's integration into the continental market.
- In addition, there is urgent need to strengthen the capacity of government agencies to implement and monitor AfCFTA obligations, in the form of training, technical assistance, and financial support to these agencies. This is supported by Brookings Institution (2024).
- The government of Lesotho should urgently conduct awareness campaigns and provide capacity-building support to businesses in general and particularly SMEs. Businesses need to be sensitised to the expectations, regulations and market dynamics that will be witnessed under the implementation of the AfCFTA.
- Diversify product and trade destinations to optimise the gains of AfCFTA, especially by taking advantage of its unique topography and climate to offer specialised tourism services, thereby reducing its reliance on traditional exports and expanding its market reach within the continent.
- Improve diplomatic engagements with South Africa in order to reduce border inefficiencies and improve customs procedures.

References

Africa K. (2025). *Assessing five years of the AfCFTA*. Retrieved from https://www.southcentre.int/wp-content/uploads/2025/01/RP215_Assessing-Five-Years-of-the-AfCFTA_EN.pdf

African Union. (2018). *Agreement establishing the African continental free trade area*. Retrieved from https://au.int/sites/default/files/treaties/36437-treaty-consolidated_text_on_cfta_-_en.pdf

African Union. (2019). *Operational phase of the African continental free trade area launched*. African Union. https://au.int/en/articles/operational-phase-african-continental-free-trade-area-launched

African Union. (2020). *Report submitted to the 13th extraordinary session of the assembly on the African Continental Free Trade Area (AfCFTA)*. https://au.int/sites/default/files/newsevents/workingdocuments/39710-wd-ext_assembly_au_2_xiii_e.pdf

Bowmans. (2023). *Harnessing Africa's free trade agenda—Trade in goods under the AfCFTA*. Retrieved May 4, 2025, from https://bowmanslaw.com/insights/harnessing-africas-free-trade-agenda-trade-in-goods-under-the-afcfta/

Brookings Institution. (2024). *How to catalyze AfCFTA implementation in 2024*. https://www.brookings.edu/wp-content/uploads/2024/01/ForesightAfrica2024-Ch4.pdf

Bureau of Statistics. (2004). *Bureau of Statistics*. http://www.bos.gov.ls/

European Commission. (2025). *EPA with SADC (Southern African Development Community). Access2Markets*. https://trade.ec.europa.eu/access-to-markets/en/content/epa-sadc-southern-african-development-community

Government of Lesotho. (2023). *National strategic development plan II 2023/24–2027/28*. Ministry of Public Works and Transport. Retrieved from http://www.publicworksandtransport.gov.ls/digicom/uploads/NSDP_II_2023_24_2027_28.pdf

Infomineo. (2018). *The Africa continental free trade area: Benefits, costs and implications*. https://infomineo.com/agriculture/africa-continental-free-trade-area/#:~:text=Despite%20the%20many%20benefits%20this,7

Kararach G., Kedir A. M., Kahsay T., & Abraha A. (2023). *Implementing the African continental free trade agreement: Evidence from southern Africa (AfDB working paper No. 379)*. African Development Bank. https://www.afdb.org/sites/default/files/documents/publications/wps_no_379_implementing_the_african_continent_free_trade_agreement_evidence_from_southern_africa.pdf

Lesotho News Agency. (2023). *NSDP II extended again*. https://www.gov.ls/development/nsdp-ii-extended-again/

Logistics Cluster. (2025). *Lesotho regulatory departments and quality control*. https://lca.logcluster.org/12-lesotho-regulatory-departments-and-quality-control

McKenna, A. (2025). *Thabana Ntlenyana mountain*. Britannica. https://www.britannica.com/place/Thabana-Ntlenyana

Organisation for Economic Co-operation and Development. (2017). *Economic surveys: South Africa (July 2017)*. https://www.tralac.org/news/article/11921-south-africa-find-new-ways-to-boost-growth-and-job-creation.html

Revenue Service Lesotho. (2024). *About us*. https://www.rsl.org.ls/about-us

UNCTAD. (2021). *AfCFTA could boost maritime trade in Africa*. United Nations Conference on Trade and Development. https://unctad.org/press-material/afcfta-could-boost-maritime-trade-africa

United Nations. (2024). *Least developed country category: Lesotho profile*. https://www.un.org/development/desa/dpad/least-developed-country-category-lesotho.html

United Nations Economic Commission for Africa. (2023). *The AfCFTA—What you need to know: Frequently asked questions & answers (issue 1)*. African Trade Policy Centre. https://www.uneca.org/african-trade-policy-centre/flipbook.

United States International Trade Administration. (2025). Lesotho — Market challenges. In: *Lesotho country commercial guide*. U.S. Department of Commerce. Retrieved August 13, 2025, from https://www.trade.gov/country-commercial-guides/lesotho-market-challenges

World Bank. (2020). *The African continental free trade area: Economic and distributional effects (report No. 151239)*. World Bank. https://www.worldbank.org/en/topic/trade/publication/the-african-continental-free-trade-area

World Bank. (2025a). *The world bank in Lesotho*. https://www.worldbank.org/en/country/lesotho/overview

World Bank. (2025b). *World bank open data*. https://data.worldbank.org/

World Integrated Trade Solutions (WITS). (2025). *Lesotho trade indicators 2022*. https://wits.worldbank.org/CountryProfile/en/Country/LSO/Year/2022

Yuni, D. N. (2025). The macroeconomic environment of international trade in Lesotho. In Yuni & Tsietsi (Eds.), *A compendium on international trade in Lesotho*. AOSIS Publishers.

Yuni, D. N., & Machema, R. (2024). *An appraisal of international trade issues in Lesotho: Being a technical report of the data collection exercise on international trade issues in Lesotho carried out by the research pillar of the National University of Lesotho, World Trade Organisation (NUL-WTO) Research Chair*. Retrieved from https://nulwtochair.org.ls/

Yuni, D. N., Makhetha, L., & Lelimo, S. (2023). Analysing the relationship between industrialization and economic growth in Lesotho. *Cogent Economics & Finance, 11*, 2. https://doi.org/10.1080/23322039.2023.2285620

Yuni, D. N., & Tsietsi, T. (2025). An overview of the context of international trade in Lesotho. In Yuni & Tsietsi (Eds.), *A compendium on international trade in Lesotho*. AOSIS Publishers.

Chapter 12
Advancing the AfCFTA Agenda in South Africa: Insights and Future Prospects

Adelia Jansen van Rensburg and Marie-Luce Kuhn

Abstract This paper assesses South Africa's strategic role in advancing the African Continental Free Trade Area (AfCFTA) and evaluates how it can optimise the agreement's benefits for continental integration. Although South Africa was instrumental in shaping the AfCFTA framework, its ability to fully leverage the agreement is constrained by persistent domestic challenges, including energy insecurity, infrastructure deficits, and limited industrial capacity. These weaknesses threaten competitiveness and risk diminishing South Africa's influence in the wider regional market. The paper reviews the status of AfCFTA negotiations and implementation and identifies key opportunities for South Africa to diversify exports and deepen regional value chains. To translate these opportunities into tangible outcomes, the study advances a trade policy strategy built around a three-tiered framework: foundational structural reforms and industrial development, measures to strengthen trade and investment capacity, and supporting diplomatic and institutional interventions to drive regional integration. The study concludes with policy recommendations to ensure South Africa's effective and sustained engagement with the AfCFTA, reinforcing both national competitiveness and Africa's broader integration agenda.

Keywords Regional integration · The AfCFTA · South African trade policy · South Africa

12.1 Introduction

Various scholars and policymakers have emphasised the AfCFTA's transformative potential for Africa's economic development. If fully implemented, it could lift 30 million people out of extreme poverty, create 7.5 million jobs (World Bank, 2020),

A. J. van Rensburg (✉) · M.-L. Kuhn
School of Economic Sciences, North-West University, Potchefstroom, South Africa
e-mail: Adelia.JansenVanRensburg@nwu.ac.za; mlm@ibis.co.za

D. N. Yuni et al. (eds.), *From Policy to Practice: Challenges and Ways Forward on the Implementation of the AfCFTA*,
https://doi.org/10.1007/978-3-032-14051-7_12

raise intra-African trade by 52.3% and potentially double trade (UNECA, 2019). Empirical research estimates that the AfCFTA could increase welfare gains by US$18 billion, GDP by 3.15%, household per capita income by 1.94% (Alagidede et al., 2024) with potentially 725 product–country combinations with sustained export potential (Mhonyera & Meyer, 2023). It should be noted, however, that these benefits remain unevenly distributed amongst different African economies due to disparities in industrialisation, resources, debt, and institutional capacity.

The AfCFTA has several distinctive features. Encompassing 54 of the 55 African Union member states, it brings together a market of 1.3 billion people with a combined GDP exceeding US$3 trillion (African Export-Import Bank, 2024) making it the largest regional trade arrangement to date in terms of membership.

A further defining characteristic is its comprehensive scope—an approach long advocated by regional integration scholars (Hartzenberg, 2011; Kayizzi-Mugerwa et al., 2024). This approach extends beyond traditional trade in goods and tariff reductions to include services, investment, competition policy, digital trade, and the removal of non-traditional trade barriers. South Africa—one of the Africa's most advanced economies, with a well-developed services sector and a rapidly expanding digital economy—has been a strong advocate for the inclusion of these newer-generation trade issues in Africa's regional integration agenda, due to the significant potential it could hold for economic and trade expansion (The DTIC, 2021).

Another distinctive feature is the AfCFTA's "development integration" emphasis, which focusses not only market integration but infrastructure development, industrialisation, and export diversification. Regional integration scholars again, have long argued for such an alternative model for Africa's integration ambitions, noting that Western, Eurocentric approaches to integration fail to account for Africa's "unique history, evolution, and structural characteristics" (see Draper, 2019; Gibb, 2009). This development focus has the potential not only to deepen integration and expand intra-African trade but also to drive long-term structural transformation (see Efogo, 2020). South Africa has consistently promoted this development approach in the AfCFTA, maintaining that Africa's economic potential will remain unrealised without necessary infrastructure improvements, increased productive capacity, and economic diversification (see Davies, 1994),

Another notable feature is the AfCFTA's emphasis on the important role existing Regional Economic Communities (RECs) in Africa can play in realising the objectives of the AfCFTA. These blocs are central to enhancing intra-African trade—which remains relatively low (see Ferreira et al., 2022; Fofack et al., 2021) despite its immense untapped potential. In fact, Turkson et al. (2023) argues, that the AfCFTA's effectiveness will depend exclusively on how successfully the RECs can facilitate trade under the agreement.

Another feature that is of importance, is that the AfCFTA makes provision for an African-framed trade dispute resolution mechanism—an alternative that is especially critical as it is designed to be more accessible and responsive to Africa's unique challenges and to address Africa's low participation in dispute resolution (Kugler, 2021). As the continental forerunner in dispute resolution, South Africa's experience and guidance has been instrumental in shaping the inclusion of this provision and to support its effective implementation going forward.

Finally, the AfCFTA includes provisions to accommodate the varied development levels of its members through special and differential treatment (Sommer & MacLeod, 2019) and variable geometry (Taye, 2019). This feature supports the continent's diverse economic landscape and it allows countries to implement their commitments at different paces (Páez, 2024). South Africa has always promoted inclusivity, advocating for a trade regime that supports both major and emerging economies in Africa.

In summary, the AfCFTA has various distinctive features and over the years, South Africa has been an important driving force in the formation, operational design and implementation of many of these features.

12.2 Status of the AfCFTA Negotiations and Way Forward

This section will provide an overview of the AfCFTA agreement, its status in terms of negotiation and implementation, the challenges it will face going forward and South Africa's strategic role in determining its successful implementation.

12.2.1 Trade in Goods

Trade in goods remains the cornerstone of the AfCFTA, driving economic growth, job creation, poverty reduction (Songwe et al., 2021; Tshedza & Lee, 2023) and diversification through regional value chains (Ajibo, 2023). It also offers the greatest potential for integration, particularly given Africa's relatively low levels of development and limited participation in newer-generation trade areas. The Protocol on Trade in Goods serves as the primary instrument to facilitate goods trade under the AfCFTA, primarily through the implementation of preferential tariffs (African Union, 2018).

South Africa, through SACU, submitted its consolidated tariff offer in 2023 (Southern African Customs Union (SACU), 2025) with preferential trade commencing in January 2024, with its first shipments directed to Ghana and Kenya under the Guided Trade Initiative (GTI) (Erasmus, 2024a). While trade continues, the finalisation of rules of origin negotiations remains essential for the agreement to achieve full operational status.

12.2.2 Rules of Origin

Rules of origin are critical because they determine whether products are produced and processed in Africa and qualifies for preferential tariff treatment. Their primary purpose under the AfCFTA is to support Africa's broader industrialisation and beneficiation objectives (Isheloke & von Blottnitz, 2020; Opoku & Yan, 2019) and to prevent trade deflection and transhipment (Kniahin & De Melo, 2022).

The slow pace of rules of origin negotiations has emerged as a key barrier to fully operationalising the AfCFTA. Delays stem from the complexity of the rule's negotiations, which must account for Africa's diverse levels of development, industrial capacities, and competing national interests (Chawarika et al., 2024). During the negotiations, South Africa, for instance, with its more advanced and complex industrial base, has advocated a product-specific rules approach and stricter criteria to protect domestic sectors (particularly high-value, high-tariff industries such as textiles, clothing, and automobiles) whereas less developed economies push for greater flexibility (see MacLeod et al., 2023; The DTIC, 2025a; Tsowou & Davis, 2021). As a result, to date, only 92.4% of rules of origin have been agreed, with the remaining 7.6% (mainly in the textile and automotive sectors), still under negotiation (The DTIC, 2025b).

In the interim (under the GTI) countries issue certificates of origin on a case-by-case basis (Erasmus, 2024a).

Without clear and widely accepted rules of origin, the AfCFTA risks remaining largely theoretical rather than functioning. Properly implemented rules are essential to transform the agreement from "on paper" integration into actual trade. As Africa's most industrialised economy, South Africa stands to benefit significantly from goods trade under the AfCFTA (see Sect. 12.4.1) and should therefore actively advocate for the swift conclusion of the outstanding rules.

12.2.3 Trade in Services

The services sector has become increasingly vital to Africa's economic growth and development, employment creation, skills development (Baccini et al., 2023; Simo, 2020). Between 1998 and 2015, Africa's services exports expanded six times faster than merchandise exports, underscoring its importance in continental trade (Signé & Van der Ven, 2019).

The Protocol on Trade in Services provides the main legal framework for liberalising and promoting services under the AfCFTA (African Union, 2018; Simo, 2020). During the services negotiations, members adopted a GATS-plus, positive-list, request-offer approach to scheduling commitments, whereby each state submits an initial offer to all others, which can then request modifications or improvements. Although these commitments are designed to be reciprocal, practical challenges may lead to bilateral rather than collective approaches (Trade Law Centre, 2023).

This may present several challenges, including the inherent complexity of services negotiations (Feketekuty, 2008), Africa's limited technical expertise and negotiating capacity (Jansen Van Rensburg et al., 2020) and complexities surrounding its implementation, including regulatory diversity, infrastructure constraints, and national systems that are unharmonised.

As Africa's leading services economy South Africa stands to gain substantially from the liberalisation of services trade (Sect. 12.4.2). However, progress is slow given that its draft schedule of commitments still awaits Cabinet approval (The DTIC, 2025b). The finalisation of this process and the resuming negotiations should therefore be a strategic priority. South Africa's extensive experience in services negotiations positions it to play a pivotal role in the implementation process, particularly by providing regulatory expertise, institutional support, and technical assistance to other member states.

12.2.4 Protocol Competition Policy

Africa's competition landscape is dynamic and evolving, characterised by emerging regulatory frameworks, regional disparities, and growing recognition of the importance of effective competition policies (Hartzenberg, 2012). The Protocol on Competition Policy serves as the central instrument for fostering a more integrated and competitive African market. While progress on its implementation continues (The DTIC, 2025b), several challenges remain. For instance, competition law is still relatively new across much of the continent, with only 25 countries having fully operational frameworks (Okadia et al., 2021) and overlapping mandates between national and regional bodies complicate coordination (Kigwiru, 2020). Additionally, limited institutional capacity, particularly in smaller economies, constrains both enforcement and participation (Gachuiri, 2019).

South Africa stands out as a continental leader in competition regulation, with one of Africa's most advanced legal frameworks and well-established enforcement institutions, including the Competition Commission and the Competition Tribunal. This institutional strength and regulatory expertise position South Africa to play a pivotal role in shaping and implementing the AfCFTA's competition policy framework.

12.2.5 Protocol on Investment

Intra-African investment holds considerable potential to enhance productive capacity, generate employment and finance sustainable development. Despite Africa attracting considerable inward investment flows, intra-African investment remains relatively low, accounting for only 5–17% of total flows (Ayele et al., 2023). The AfCFTA Investment Protocol seeks to establish a unified and predictable investment environment to attract more intra-regional investment, however, progress is constrained by several challenges. These include the need to harmonise national policies, improve transparency, manage risks associated with the termination of Bilateral Investment Treaties, and strengthen dispute resolution mechanisms (see Laryea & Fabusuy, 2019; Raga et al., 2022).

As a continental leader in investment policy, South Africa is well-positioned to support the implementation of the protocol by providing regulatory expertise, fostering policy coherence, and promoting a transparent and inclusive investment climate. In doing so, it can play a pivotal role in unlocking the transformative potential of intra-African investment.

12.2.6 Intellectual Property (IP) Rights

Intellectual property (IP) is central to fostering innovation, protecting creators, and building competitive industries, making it a critical driver of economic growth across the continent. The AfCFTA Protocol on Intellectual Property Rights, advances this objective and includes annexes on plant varieties, geographical indications, patents, copyrights, traditional knowledge, and emerging technologies, with further annex negotiations scheduled beyond 2025 (The DTIC, 2025b). However, negotiations and implementation face significant hurdles, including Africa's fragmented IP landscape, overlapping and sometimes conflicting regimes, inconsistent legal frameworks, and limited institutional capacity (Adebola, 2020; Ncube, 2022; Ogbodo, 2024).

As one of the continent's leaders in IP regulation, South Africa is well-positioned to support the protocol's development and implementation by leveraging its strong legal and institutional frameworks, providing technical guidance, and helping to build enforcement capacity across member states.

12.2.7 AfCFTA Digital Trade Protocol (DTP)

Africa's digital economy has significant potential to accelerate inclusive growth, with projections estimating that Africa's Internet economy could reach $712 billion by 2050 and that it could eventually contribute 8.5% to GDP (Jansen van Rensburg, Strydom, et al., 2021; Lemma et al., 2022; International Finance Corporation (IFC), 2024). The AfCFTA Protocol on Digital Trade is designed to help realise this potential through harmonised rules on data governance, cross-border data flows, cybersecurity, consumer protection, and emerging technologies. In terms of its negotiation status, several of the Protocol's annexes were finalised in February 2025, including the world's first rules of origin for digital goods and services under any free trade agreement (The DTIC, 2025b; Trade Law Centre, 2024). The Protocol requires 22 ratifications to enter into force, after which member states will have 5 years to align its domestic legislation with its provisions.

Implementation, however, will face significant challenges, given the persistent infrastructure gaps, uneven levels of digital maturity, regulatory divergence, and limited skills and institutional capacity (Beyleveld & Sucker, 2023; Jansen van Rensburg, Strydom, et al., 2021). As Africa's leading digital trade nation, South Africa is well-positioned to drive harmonisation efforts, provide technical assistance, and support capacity-building initiatives to unlock the continent's digital potential.

12.2.8 AfCFTA Dispute Resolution Mechanism

As mentioned in the introduction (Sect. 12.1), the AfCFTA also makes provisions for the establishment of a comprehensive, African-led dispute resolution framework (African Union, 2018; Demamu, 2024). The Framework has been operationalised through the establishment of the Dispute Settlement Body (DSB) which will enable state-to-state disputes in Africa using a Panel and Appellate Body that will oversee consultations, conciliation, mediation, and arbitration. While modelled on aspects of the WTO system, the dispute resolution mechanism under the AfCFTA, is designed to be more accessible and responsive to Africa's unique challenges, addressing the continent's historically low participation in WTO and regional dispute (Kugler, 2021). It will also enhance legal security (Ansong, 2025), reduce reliance on the WTO, and empower African nations to resolve conflicts independently (Bore, 2020). This alternative is especially critical given the WTO's prolonged Appellate Body crisis (Wolfe et al., 2020).

Ongoing work under these provisions involves completing the Investment Protocol's Annex and finalising the Rules of Origin (RoO)—both of which are critical prerequisites for initiating disputes. South Africa, with its extensive experience in WTO processes and trade-related dispute settlement, has played an instrumental role in shaping this provision and is well-positioned to support its effective implementation going forward.

In summary, while progress under the AfCFTA is tangible, a lot of work remains. Trade in goods has advanced through the GTI and tariff offers, yet unresolved rules of origin and sensitive product lists continue to constrain full liberalisation. Services, competition, investment, and intellectual property require sustained technical work and domestic reforms, while digital trade offers transformative potential but demands substantial infrastructure development and capacity-building. To this end, its priorities should include finalising rules of origin, accelerating services commitments, providing technical support in competition, investment, and IP, leading harmonisation in digital trade, and supporting the establishment of an effective dispute settlement system. South Africa, given its economic weight, institutional depth, and leadership in negotiations, is uniquely positioned to help translate AfCFTA agreements into functioning markets.

12.3 South Africa's Strategic Position in Africa and Regional Integration

South Africa plays a central role in shaping Africa's economic, trade, and regional integration agenda.

Its economic importance is evident. South Africa's GDP is estimated at over US$ 403 billion in 2024 (Statista, 2025) and it is Africa's most advanced and diversified economy in terms of industry, mining, agriculture, services, digital trade and finances (see Sect. 12.2.4). Its financial system, underpinned by robust capital markets and a well-regulated banking sector, already enjoys a strong presence in many African countries, including Botswana, Namibia, Malawi, and Zambia (World Bank, 2022).

In terms of trade South Africa remains Africa's largest partner both within and outside the continent. In 2023, South Africa exported approximately US $29.7 billion worth of goods to Africa, which represented about 27% of its total global exports. Key markets include Mozambique, Botswana, Zimbabwe, Namibia, Zambia, Eswatini, the DRC and Lesotho with major exports including light oils, coal, ferrochromium, chromium ores, vehicles, and iron ores (International Trade Centre (ITC), 2025). In 2023, South Africa imported goods worth approximately US $9.4 billion from Africa, which accounted for about 8.8% of its total global imports. Imports were mainly sourced from Nigeria, Eswatini, Namibia, Mozambique, Botswana, Angola, Lesotho, Zambia, Zimbabwe, and Algeria were dominated by petroleum oils, gold, natural gas, odoriferous substances, diamonds, and electricity (International Trade Centre (ITC), 2025). Beyond Africa, China, the United States, and Germany are South Africa's leading trade partners—accounting for around 9%, 8%, and 6% of exports, and 20%, 8%, and 8% of imports respectively—with key exports in precious metals, ores, and minerals, and key imports in fuels, machinery, and electrical equipment (International Trade Centre (ITC), 2025).

Another important trade aspects, is that South Africa also functions as a southern gateway for African trade. The Port of Durban—one of the busiest on the continent—serves as an important gateway for other Southern African countries, facilitating access for six landlocked countries (Mthembu & Naude, 2023; Scholvin & Draper, 2012). Institutionally, agencies such as the DTIC, SARS, and ITAC strengthen trade facilitation, customs enforcement, competition regulation, and investment promotion, areas where many African economies face persistent capacity constraints (Attia, 2021).

South Africa's important role in regional integration and trade in Africa also necessitates special mention. Since 1994, South Africa's participation in RECs has expanded significantly (Nganje & Ayodele, 2021). As mentioned in the introduction of this chapter, RECs are recognised as critical building blocks for the AfCFTA (Gumede, 2021; Wapmuk & Ali, 2022) each contributing unique strengths despite variations in economic size and policy priorities (Vambe, 2024). The Southern African Customs Union (SACU), the world's oldest, has long been central to South Africa's regional integration agenda (Soko, 2008) and continues to serve as a strategic platform for advancing intra-regional trade under the AfCFTA through coordinated tariff offers, harmonised standards, pilot initiatives, and capacity building.

12.4 Review of the Literature: Opportunities for SA within the AfCFTA

12.4.1 Opportunities in Regional Goods Trade

In terms of goods trade, South Africa stands to benefit substantially from the AfCFTA. Empirical evidence supporting this, is clear. Ferreira et al. (2022) for instance, identified 782 untapped export opportunities across 35 African markets, with 40% of these opportunities in new untapped products (mainly manufactured and processed goods) and markets (particularly in Northern and Western Africa).

Sector-specific studies highlight significant export potential for South Africa's agriculture sector. Seti and Daw (2022) found that full tariff liberalisation under the AfCFTA could yield an additional US$199 million in agricultural trade for South Africa, with the largest gains identified in sugar cane, maize, citrus fruit, cigarettes, and sauces. Similarly, Annandale (2022) reported that South African agricultural exports to Africa already reached substantial amounts between 2012 and 2021 (amounting to US$1.3 billion in 2021) with processed products accounting for more than 65% of total agricultural exports to Africa. The author also shows that, while most processed exports were concentrated in SACU (50%) and SADC (90%), unprocessed goods—such as maize, apples, potatoes, and frozen beef—show even greater untapped potential.

12.4.2 Opportunities in Regional Services Trade

South Africa's services sector stands to benefit significantly from expanded market access under the AfCFTA. Accounting for over two-thirds of GDP and employment (Bhorat et al., 2018), the sector has strong potential to drive structural transformation but then it *must* become more export-oriented (Jules et al., 2021). This will present a challenge because South Africa's services trade with Africa remains limited. According to Jansen Van Rensburg et al. (2020) only around 10.6% of South Africa's exports are destined for African markets (primarily Angola, Nigeria, and Eswatini) while only 5.5% of imports originate from the continent (mainly Egypt and Angola). Moreover, the country has struggled to shift from traditional services to high-technology services (Bhorat et al., 2018) and South Africa's services trade with Africa remains concentrated in only a few services sectors (primarily transport, travel, and other business services) that account for roughly 80% exports and 75%

of imports (Jansen Van Rensburg et al., 2020). Diversification of services exports is therefore critical.

South Africa already has substantial opportunities in services trade, with comparative export advantages identified in transport, tourism-related travel, personal, cultural and recreational services, government, business, and financial services, *provided* these sectors are further developed. Key African markets with strong export potential include Kenya, Namibia, Egypt, Mozambique, Zambia, Tanzania, Nigeria, Djibouti, Uganda, and Lesotho (Jansen Van Rensburg et al., 2020).

12.4.3 Opportunities in Regional Digital Trade

The AfCFTA also presents opportunities for South Africa in the realm of digital trade. Projections suggest that it could contribute 15–20% to South Africa's GDP by 2025, with annual growth of 10–15% over the next 5 years (International Trade Administration (ITA), 2025). The country's digital economy has expanded rapidly, supported by improved connectivity, the growth of e-commerce and digital services and the uptake of emerging technologies. Its digital infrastructure—specifically mobile banking and fintech—has significant potential to drive cross-border digital trade in Africa forward (Jansen van Rensburg, Viviers, et al., 2021).

The persistent challenges that remain in measuring cross-border digital trade flows (World Trade Organisation, 2023) makes it difficult to identify digital trade opportunities for South Africa, but despite this limitation, several opportunities seem to exist. Ferreira et al. (2025) for instance, developed a Digital Readiness Index for Africa, structured around three pillars: infrastructure, skills, and the business environment and their analysis identified South Africa (together with Egypt, Morocco) as one of the most digitally prepared countries in Africa, given its robust ICT infrastructure, high mobile penetration, advanced digital skills, targeted ICT investment, supportive policy frameworks, stable governance, and strong youth participation in the digital economy.

Going forward, South Africa should prioritise strengthening its digital trade capabilities to fully leverage these opportunities.

12.4.4 Opportunity to Tap into Regional Value Chains (RVCs)

South Africa also has much to gain in terms of regional value chain creation. According to Fofack and Mold (2021), the AfCFTA also has significant potential to deepen and create new and more RVCs. Recent literature has stressed that it is not so much how much a country trades that matters, but rather the degree of value-addition it can add and benefit from and the extent to which it is integrated into regional or global value chains (Mold et al., 2022).

As the African country with the highest domestic and foreign value added and the most regionally integrated, South Africa can capitalise on these opportunities. These goals might not be too difficult to pursue given that South African exports already dominate value chains in Southern Africa. For instance, it exports knitted fabric to Eswatini, which is then used to make garments for the South African market (Nyagah, 2025). Numerous other examples exist. South Africa can play a leading role in developing and anchoring RVCs in industries to boost industrialisation and job creation. Capitalising on these opportunities will not only be advantageous to South Africa—studies have shown that South Africa could become an intra-regional trade and industrial development engine on the continent, by linking its value chains to other African countries (Banga & Balchin, 2023; Black et al., 2021; Miao, 2023).

12.4.5 Opportunities for the Private Sector

The private sector, particularly small- and medium-sized enterprises (SMEs), plays a vital role in driving economic growth and job creation (UNECA, 2019). The critical role of the private sectors/SMEs in leveraging AfCFTA opportunities have been well document in literature (see Ajibo, 2024; Mugano, 2023). It shows that SMEs will expand exponentially in the AfCFTA through the uptake of preferences and expanded market access opportunities.

South Africa already holds a competitive advantage in Africa, given the size and diversity of its SMEs and their strong presence across Africa. Domestically, SMEs account for 91% of formal businesses, employ 60% of the workforce, and contribute around 34% to GDP (The Banking Association of South Africa, 2021). They operate across diverse sectors—including retail, mining, manufacturing, automotive, banking, telecommunications, services, and energy—supporting export diversity. South African SMEs also have a notable footprint on the continent; in 2016, four supermarket chains (Shoprite, Pick n Pay, Spar, and Massmart) operated 554 stores outside the country (Fofack & Mold, 2021).

12.4.6 Opportunities for Intra-African Investment

South Africa is well-positioned to expand its role as both a leading source and destination of intra-African investment, accounting for over 32% of the continent's inward FDI flows while also ranking as the largest outward investor in Africa (Agarwal et al., 2024). Outward investment has historically outpaced inward flows (Nordås, 2001), highlighting significant untapped opportunities in both directions. Key sectors for increased inward and outbound investment include mining, manufacturing, agriculture and agro-processing, retail, services, renewable energy, infrastructure, and tourism (Ameyaw & Panibratov, 2025; Chizema et al., 2021; InvestSA, 2023).

By leveraging its institutional strength and technical expertise, South Africa can foster public–private partnerships, channel investment into high-growth sectors such as renewable energy, real estate, retail, and digital infrastructure, support the development of regional value chains, and, under the AfCFTA, create a more predictable and attractive environment for African investment through coherent frameworks, enhanced investor protection, and effective dispute resolution.

In summary, South Africa has various export opportunities under the AfCFTA and these opportunities are spread across goods trade services, digital trade, regional value chains, SMEs, and investment. Table 12.1 summarises these findings.

12.5 Review of the Literature: Implementation Challenges

The AfCFTA holds vast potential for fostering economic growth, regional integration, and industrial development across Africa. However, its successful implementation in South Africa faces significant political, economic, infrastructural, trade, and private-sector challenges. This analysis will explore these challenges and discuss how they may impede the country's ability to capitalise on the opportunities the AfCFTA offers fully.

12.5.1 Political Challenges

The success of the AfCFTA depends mainly on political commitment from South Africa's government. Unfortunately, the country has faced heightened political uncertainty marked by leadership changes, inconsistent policies, factionalism, and corruption (Noor, 2024). These issues undermine good governance and could weaken the political will needed to implement the AfCFTA effectively. Without strong and consistent political support, the country risks failing to leverage the agreement's full potential.

Additionally, South Africa's legal framework is not fully aligned with the AfCFTA's provisions and objectives. This is a continental-wide challenge (see Kuhlmann & Agutu, 2020; Vambe, 2024). To comply, South Africa must undertake extensive reforms in its trade laws and regulatory systems. This task would be time-consuming and complex, further complicated by the country's existing trade commitments, capacity constraints, and lack of sufficient technical expertise within the government.

Table 12.1 Potential opportunities for South Africa under the AfCFTA

Area	Key market and sector opportunities	Supporting studies
Goods trade	782 untapped export opportunities across 35 African markets; 40% in new products and markets, specially manufactured and processed goods; high-potential markets include Northern and Western Africa	Mhonyera and Meyer (2023), Ferreira et al. (2022)
Agriculture	+US$199m potential trade value from full tariff liberalisation; high-demand products: sugar cane, maize, citrus, cigarettes, sauces; processed goods dominant (65% of exports 2012–2021); key markets include SACU and SADC countries	Seti and Daw (2022), Annandale (2022)
Services	Comparative export advantages in transport, travel & tourism, personal, cultural and recreational services, government, business, and financial services; key African markets: Kenya, Namibia, Egypt, Mozambique, Zambia, Tanzania, Nigeria, Djibouti, Uganda, Lesotho	Bhorat et al. (2018), Jansen Van Rensburg et al. (2020), Jules et al. (2021)
Digital trade	Digital economy could contribute 15–20% to GDP by 2025; high potential in fintech, e-commerce, mobile banking; SA among most digitally ready countries in Africa (with Egypt and Morocco)	International Trade Administration (ITA) (2025), Ferreira et al. (2025)
Regional value chains (RVCs)	SA already integrated in Southern Africa; potential to anchor RVCs in textiles, agro-processing, and manufacturing; opportunity to boost industrialisation and job creation across Africa	Fofack and Mold (2021), Nyagah (2025), Black et al. (2021), Miao (2023)
SMEs	SMEs can leverage AfCFTA preferences and expanded market access; sectors include retail, mining, manufacturing, automotive, banking, telecoms, services, energy; SA SMEs already operate widely across the continent (e.g., Shoprite, Pick n Pay)	Mugano (2023), Ajibo (2024), Fofack and Mold (2021)
Investment	SA = 32% of Africa's inward FDI and $5.2bn outward FDI (2019); high-growth sectors include renewable energy, real estate, retail, digital infrastructure; opportunities to foster public–private partnerships and regional value chain development	Agarwal et al. (2024), Chizema et al. (2021), InvestSA (2023), Ameyaw and Panibratov (2025)

Source: Authors own compilation, based on the literature

12.5.2 Economic Challenges

While South Africa is one of the most advanced economies in Africa, it is facing a decline in its global competitiveness. In 2024, the country ranked 60th out of 67 in the IMD World Competitiveness Rankings, reflecting ongoing challenges such as high unemployment, electricity supply problems (load-shedding), corruption, rising debt, and political instability (International Trade Administration, 2024). These factors contribute to South Africa's weakening economic growth, which averaged only 0.7% over the past decade.

South Africa also faces significant structural problems, including the world's highest unemployment rate (at 31.9% in Q4 2024) and Gini coefficient (0.63) and one of the world's highest poverty rates at 63% (World Bank, 2025). These deep inequalities hinder broad participation in cross-border trade and make it difficult for the broader population to benefit from regional economic integration.

Additionally, despite having Africa's most advanced industrial base, South Africa's industrialisation has been slow, marked by premature deindustrialisation (Andreoni & Tregenna, 2021). In addition, South Africa's industrial base remains heavily reliant on extractive industries, limiting its capacity to diversify and fully leverage the AfCFTA's objectives of industrialisation and economic diversification, a challenge increasingly highlighted in recent trade literature (Isheloke & von Blottnitz, 2020; Opoku & Yan, 2019).

The country's key economic sectors are also under significant stress. The manufacturing sector, which contributes 15% to GDP, faces substantial challenges due to low productivity, weak business conditions, and structural economic constraints. Similarly, the transport sector, contributing 11% to GDP, faces infrastructure deficiencies, security challenges, and rising operational costs, while the mining sector, which contributes almost 9% to GDP face rising costs, labour conflicts and declining ore grades have led to job losses, mine closures, and a reduction in FDI (Ntlhoiseng, 2023). Lastly, agriculture, contributing almost 3% to GDP, faces challenges such as land reform, water scarcity, and inadequate infrastructure, all of which limit its productivity (AgriSA, 2024).

Given South Africa's dependence on mining, manufacturing, agriculture and transport the country faces significant hurdles in its efforts to diversify its economy and to increase trade. Its over-reliance on resource-based exports has meant that South Africa's export performance has been underwhelming in recent decades, lagging other countries. The limited number of export markets, lack of export diversity, high business costs (and the declining competitiveness as a result) also contribute to its underperformance in terms of exports (Stern & Ramkolowan, 2021).

To fully benefit from the AfCFTA, South Africa must address these challenges by scaling up production, reducing its reliance on extractive industries, and shifting towards value-added production. The AfCFTA's regional trade opportunities allow South Africa to diversify its exports and strengthen its business sector's competitiveness.

12.5.3 Infrastructure Challenges

South Africa's infrastructure, though relatively advanced compared to other sub-Saharan countries, is rapidly deteriorating, limiting its trade capacity (Erasmus, 2024b). This decline is driven by sluggish economic growth, constrained public spending on infrastructure, and persistent load-shedding (The Conversation, 2024), which also hampers manufacturing productivity and SME growth, restricting the country's ability to meet the increased consumer demand anticipated under the AfCFTA.

Water infrastructure is facing serious challenges due to inadequate investment, recurring droughts, water scarcity, and inefficient management, with significant losses from leaks and illegal connections (The Conversation, 2024). A reliable water supply is essential for industrialisation, agriculture, and SME operations, making these issues critical for South Africa's AfCFTA readiness.

Transport and logistics infrastructure also present major constraints. Approximately 80% of South African trade relies on road transport, yet deteriorating road networks, port congestion, rising costs, theft, truck hijackings, and delays at border posts create persistent inefficiencies (Khuzwayo, 2018). Analysis using the Global Competitiveness Index, Logistics Performance Index, and Road Quality Index shows that, while South Africa continues to rank highest in Africa for logistics and road quality, its global rankings are falling, highlighting ongoing inefficiencies in roads, ports, and other logistics systems (Sefume & Jansen Van Rensburg, 2025). The collapse of the railway system and underperformance at major ports, such as Durban and Cape Town—which rank among the lowest globally for port efficiency—further exacerbate these challenges. Collectively, these infrastructure deficits undermine South Africa's regional trade competitiveness and hinder effective cross-border trade within Africa.

12.5.4 Trade Challenges

While Sect. 12.4 highlights South Africa's numerous export opportunities under the AfCFTA, the country faces several trade-related challenges that could limit its ability to fully capitalise on these opportunities. A major concern is customs and border inefficiencies, which are particularly critical given South Africa's borders span over 4800 km with six countries, encompassing 53 land ports of entry, 11 international airports, and eight seaports (Knowlton, 2023). Border processes are often slow and inefficient, with outdated technology, staff shortages, and corruption contributing to delays and higher trade costs (Mamokhere & Chauke, 2020).

Non-Tariff Barriers (NTBs) also remain a significant obstacle, despite AfCFTA efforts to reduce tariffs and streamline trade, as extensively documented in the literature (Penda, 2021; Trade Law Centre, 2019). These barriers include inconsistent customs procedures, excessive documentation, and varying product standards across member states, while informal fees, corruption, and differing Sanitary and Phytosanitary (SPS) measures further complicate trade, particularly for agricultural exports. Effectively addressing NTBs, alongside improving border efficiency, will be essential for enabling South Africa to leverage the full benefits of the AfCFTA and promote seamless cross-border trade.

12.5.5 Private-Sector Challenges

Section 12.4.5 highlights the opportunities for South African SMEs under the AfCFTA; however, these businesses face significant barriers to accessing broader African markets. Key challenges include inadequate infrastructure, limited access to finance, and difficulties in entering new markets (Mugano, 2023). SMEs also contend with the costs and complexities of formalising operations to comply with AfCFTA regulations, which restricts their participation in cross-border trade.

Furthermore, as discussed earlier, inefficient logistics systems, non-tariff barriers, and inconsistent regulatory frameworks continue to constrain SME growth. Additionally, informal businesses, which make up a substantial portion of South Africa's entrepreneurial sector, are largely excluded from AfCFTA benefits (The DTIC, 2023). Addressing these challenges will be crucial for the AfCFTA's success. Harnessing the potential of the informal sector and integrating these businesses into the AfCFTA framework is crucial as it will enable them to access new markets. This will also ensure inclusive growth and broader economic development.

12.5.6 Labour Market Challenges

As mentioned, the AfCFTA offers significant potential for job creation, particularly in sectors such as industrialisation and value-added trade. However, South Africa faces considerable labour market challenges that must be addressed to benefit fully from the AfCFTA. These include high unemployment, skills mismatches, and a lack of investment in skills development (Festus et al., 2016). To fully harness the AfCFTA's opportunities, South Africa must invest in large-scale skills development initiatives aligned with emerging growth sectors, particularly digital services, and manufacturing. By improving vocational training and fostering industry-academia partnerships, South Africa can also better prepare its workforce to compete in a more integrated African market.

In summary, the AfCFTA presents significant opportunities for South Africa but faces numerous challenges that could undermine its ability to capitalise on these benefits. This includes political instability, economic structural issues, infrastructure deficits, trade barriers, and private-sector limitations all contribute to these challenges. See Table 12.2.

12.6 Policy Recommendations for Advancing the AfCFTA

South Africa faces both immense opportunities and significant challenges in implementing the AfCFTA (Sects. 12.5 and 12.6). Going forward, its effective participation in the AfCFTA will depend on its ability to translate opportunity into tangible

Table 12.2 Potential challenges for South Africa under the AfCFTA

Category	Key challenges/issues	Implications for AfCFTA	Analytical insights/ counterpoints
Political	Leadership changes, inconsistent policies, factionalism, corruption; legal framework not fully aligned with AfCFTA	Weak political will may limit implementation and full utilisation of AfCFTA	Strong political commitment and legal reforms are critical; alignment with continental rules is complex and time-consuming (Kuhlmann & Agutu, 2020; Vambe, 2024)
Economic	Slow economic growth (0.7%), high unemployment (31.9%), inequality (Gini 0.63), over-reliance on extractive industries	Limits broad participation in regional trade and industrial diversification	Need to diversify exports, develop value-added sectors, and enhance competitiveness (Andreoni & Tregenna, 2021; Stern & Ramkolowan, 2021)
Infrastructure	Deteriorating roads and transport systems, port inefficiencies, energy crisis (load-shedding), water scarcity	Hinders trade capacity, increases costs, slows cross-border operations	Investments in energy, transport, and water infrastructure are foundational; infrastructure deficits constrain SME growth (Erasmus, 2024b; Khuzwayo, 2018; Sefume & Jansen van Rensburg, 2025)
Trade	Border inefficiencies, customs delays, non-tariff barriers (NTBs), inconsistent SPS measures	Reduces trade efficiency and competitiveness	Streamlining customs, reducing NTBs, and harmonising standards are essential for intra-African trade (Penda, 2021; Trade Law Centre, 2019)
Private sector	SMEs face financing, regulatory, and market access challenges; informal sector largely excluded	Limits SME participation in AfCFTA and inclusive growth	Policies must support SME formalisation, capacity building, and market integration (Mugano, 2023; The DTIC, 2023)
Labour market	High unemployment, skills mismatches, lack of investment in skills development	Reduces ability to benefit from industrialisation and value-added trade	Investment in vocational training, digital skills, and industry-academia partnerships is necessary (Festus et al., 2016; UNECA, 2019)

Source: Authors own compilation, based on literature

economic gains while overcoming deep-rooted structural challenges. Achieving this requires a coherent trade policy strategy anchored in a multi-tiered policy response. The proposed framework prioritises reforms and interventions across three tiers: foundational policy measures, trade and competitiveness measures, and supporting measures. Ranked from most to least urgent, these tiers address the structural, institutional, and operational constraints that currently limit South Africa's capacity to harness continental trade, investment, and industrialisation opportunities. The subsequent discussion elaborates on these tiers and outlines specific recommendations for a sequenced and coordinated policy approach.

12.6.1 *First Tier: Foundational Policy Measures*

South Africa's slow growth, industrial underperformance, and infrastructure deficits must be addressed through structural reforms, industrial strengthening, export diversification, prioritisation of high-potential sectors, and strategic investments to boost competitiveness and inclusive growth. These measures will subsequently be explained.

12.6.1.1 Structural Reforms

The South African economy continues to face deep structural challenges. To drive faster, inclusive growth and reduce inequality, structural reforms must be accelerated. Key priorities should include resolving energy insecurity to ensure reliable power for industry, upgrading logistics and transport networks to lower trade costs, and enhancing digital and water infrastructure to support economic activity. Streamlining regulatory processes will reduce barriers for businesses, while reforms that improve the investment climate can attract both domestic and foreign capital. Addressing these constraints will stimulate job creation, boost productivity, and strengthen competitiveness, ensuring that the benefits of growth are broadly shared.

12.6.1.2 Strengthening Industrial Capacity and Aligning Policy with AfCFTA Opportunities

South Africa's industrial base remains narrow, concentrated in mineral extraction, raw materials, primary products, and low value-added exports. To fully harness AfCFTA opportunities, this must be addressed by expanding manufacturing capacity, diversifying industrial structures, and realigning industrial policy with regional trade priorities. Strategic interventions should include promoting energy-intensive and high-potential sectors, scaling up agro-processing, fostering industrial clusters, and strengthening regional value chains with neighbouring countries. By shifting from raw material exports towards value-added goods and leveraging export incentives, South Africa can enhance manufacturing competitiveness, deepen regional integration, and lay the foundation for sustainable industrial growth across Africa.

12.6.1.3 Prioritising Export Diversification and High-Potential Sectors

South Africa's export performance has been deteriorating, with composition heavily concentrated in a narrow range of commodities and traditional services. To strengthen competitiveness and resilience under the AfCFTA, diversification into higher-value sectors is critical. Additionally, increasing competitiveness in sectors such as manufacturing, agriculture and agro-processing, and services (transport, travel, finance, ICT, and digital trade) should remain a top priority.

12.6.1.4 Supporting SMEs and Entrepreneurship to Enhance Regional Participation

As noted in Sect. 12.5, South African SMEs face multiple constraints that hinder their participation in regional trade. Targeted support programmes should expand access to affordable finance, technical assistance, trade readiness initiatives, and simplified rules of origin. Establishing regional trade facilitation centres and digital platforms, combined with collaboration with African development banks, will increase capital access, strengthen market linkages, and empower SMEs to participate meaningfully in AfCFTA markets, thereby promoting inclusive growth.

12.6.1.5 Addressing Investment Gaps Through Coordinated Regional Financing Solutions

Persistent trade, infrastructure, and industrial investment gaps should be addressed through coordinated mobilisation of capital and blended-finance solutions. Leveraging public funds, guarantees, and development finance institutions can de-risk strategic projects in transport, energy, and trade corridors. Regional platforms such as the Integrated Africa Infrastructure Growth Fund and Afreximbank-backed facilities can streamline implementation, align investments with AfCFTA priorities, and catalyse private-sector participation in strengthening Africa's integrated market.

12.6.2 Second Tier: Trade Competitiveness Measures

South Africa's trade performance or competitiveness can be addressed through targeted interventions focussing strengthening trade infrastructure and connectivity, digitising and harmonising customs procedures, eliminating non-tariff barriers to improve market access, modernising trade processes and logistics, and building capacity and technical readiness across institutions. These measures will subsequently be explained.

12.6.2.1 Strengthening Infrastructure and Connectivity for Cross-Border Trade

Inadequate transport, roads, ports, and ICT infrastructure limits intra-African trade. Key investments in road, rail, ports, and energy networks should be prioritised. Modernising major border posts such as Beitbridge and Lebombo, improving digital customs clearance, and aligning transport corridors with regional flows will reduce costs, facilitate smoother trade, and position South Africa as a logistics hub for Southern Africa.

12.6.2.2 Harmonising Customs Procedures Through Digital Integration

Fragmented customs procedures increase costs and delays. South Africa should implement a fully digitised National Single Window (NSW) system to integrate inspection and documentation processes across agencies. This will reduce port congestion, enhance transparency, and set a regional benchmark for efficient trade facilitation, following best practice examples such as Côte d'Ivoire.

12.6.2.3 Addressing Non-tariff Barriers to Improve Market Access

Exposure to NTBs—including quotas, delays, and technical regulations—constrains trade. South Africa should actively engage with the AfCFTA NTB Monitoring Mechanism, collaborating with private-sector stakeholders and the Secretariat to ensure rapid resolution of barriers. This will facilitate smoother flows and reinforce South Africa's role in advancing regional integration.

12.6.2.4 Enhancing Trade Facilitation Through Process Modernisation

Inefficient trade processes should be addressed by adopting best practices, introducing integrated port community platforms, opening freight rail networks to private operators, and implementing harmonised digital trade rules under the AfCFTA Digital Trade Protocol. These measures will reduce bottlenecks, cut costs, and accelerate cross-border trade.

12.6.2.5 Technical Assistance and Capacity Building for Trade Readiness

South Africa's limited institutional and technical capacity hampers AfCFTA readiness. Continuous training on rules of origin, customs compliance, and regulatory standards is essential. Building a pool of skilled negotiators, economists, and legal experts, alongside a cross-government coordination mechanism, will strengthen coherence, enable rapid responses to challenges, and improve competitiveness.

12.6.3 Third tier: Other Supporting Policy Measures

South Africa faces challenges in leadership, legal harmonisation, institutional capacity, and evidence-based policy, which can be addressed by promoting regional leadership, harmonising legal and policy frameworks, strengthening institutional and negotiation capacity, establishing monitoring and evaluation systems, and investing in research and evidence generation. These measures will subsequently be explained.

12.6.3.1 Promoting Regional and Continental Leadership Through Engagement

South Africa should continue leveraging its political influence in continental governance and regional coordination to champion collaboration, foster accountability, and ensure compliance with AfCFTA timelines. High-level engagement through AU, SADC, and SACU platforms, coupled with showcasing national success stories, will reinforce commitment and strengthen regional integration.

12.6.3.2 Legal Frameworks, Policy Implementation and Dispute Resolution

Slow domestic adoption of AfCFTA protocols and weak alignment to regional legal frameworks could hinder benefits. South Africa should incorporate commitments systematically into national legislation and harmonise regulations within SACU and SADC. It can support the alignment of legal and regulatory frameworks across the continent by sharing its expertise in services, competition, intellectual property, and investment law. Legal harmonisation will enhance trade predictability and attract investment. South Africa should also continue to actively participate in shaping and strengthening AfCFTA's dispute resolution mechanisms, enabling fair settlement of trade disagreements.

12.6.3.3 Building Institutional and Negotiation Capacity

Weak institutional capacity combined with a shortage of skilled negotiators limit effective AfCFTA implementation. Strengthening institutions such as SARS, investing in human capital and negotiators (especially negotiators with a key knowledge in the remaining priority areas such as rules of origin, services, digital, etc.) and active participation in the AfCFTA mechanisms are crucial to address these challenges. Enhanced capacity will improve regulatory harmonisation, safeguard national interests, and facilitate robust negotiation of services, investment, competition, and intellectual property protocols.

12.6.3.4 Monitoring and Evaluation for Evidence-Based Policy

The absence of systematic tracking of AfCFTA implementation is a key gap. Establishing robust monitoring and evaluation systems to track trade barriers, assess effectiveness, and identify bottlenecks is essential. Publishing progress reports and making adjustments based on evidence will promote transparency, accountability, and better outcomes.

12.6.3.5 Investing in Research and Evidence Generation

Limited AfCFTA-focused research constrains informed policymaking. Mobilising academic and policy institutions to conduct studies, impact assessments, and innovation research is critical. Empirical research on sectors showing high export performance for South Africa should be a key priority. Regional research collaboration and strategic funding will generate actionable insights to guide effective policy design and implementation going forward.

This structured and multi-tiered policy response with its three tier policy measures (foundational, trade and competitiveness measures and other supporting measures) and the recommended policy solutions are summarised in Table 12.3.

12.7 Conclusion

South Africa's participation in the AfCFTA is both a strategic necessity and a transformative opportunity. As Africa's most industrialised economy, it holds a pivotal role in shaping continental integration. The AfCFTA offers expanded market access, export diversification, and deeper value chains, but these gains depend on addressing structural challenges such as energy insecurity, logistics inefficiencies, regulatory fragmentation, and weak investment flows.

To translate these opportunities into tangible outcomes, the study proposes a trade policy strategy built around a three-tiered framework: foundational structural reforms and industrial development, measures to strengthen trade and investment capacity, and supporting diplomatic and institutional interventions to drive regional integration. Each one of these tiers include policy recommendations to ensure South Africa's effective and sustained engagement with the AfCFTA, reinforcing both national competitiveness and Africa's broader integration agenda.

Ultimately, the AfCFTA is more than a trade agreement—it is a platform for reconfiguring Africa's economic geography and enhancing its global bargaining power. For South Africa, realising these transformative opportunities depends on effectively implementing the proposed three-tiered trade policy strategy. By pursuing foundational structural reforms, strengthening trade and investment capacity, and deploying targeted diplomatic and institutional measures, South Africa can consolidate its competitiveness, expand its influence in regional value chains, and lead

Table 12.3 Summary of policy recommendations

Tier and policy measure	Recommended solution
Foundational measures	
Structural reforms	Upgrade energy, transport, digital, and water infrastructure; streamline regulations
Industrial capacity and policy	Expand manufacturing, diversify industries, develop regional value chains
Diversify exports and prioritise sectors with high export potential	Diversify exports, and prioritise and invest in goods, agriculture, services, digital trade
SME support	Provide trade finance, technical assistance, simplified rules of origin, regional support
Investment gaps	Mobilise blended finance, public-private partnerships, regional investment platforms
Trade competitiveness measures	
Infrastructure and connectivity	Modernise roads, rail, ports, border posts; align transport corridors
Customs procedures	Implement national single window, digitise processes
NTBs	Engage AfCFTA NTB mechanism, resolve barriers
Trade facilitation support	Integrated port platforms, open freight rail, harmonise digital trade rules
Technical assistance and capacity	Training, skilled negotiators, cross-government coordination
Supporting measures	
Regional and continental leadership	Champion collaborative governance, reinforce accountability
Legal frameworks and dispute resolution	Incorporate AfCFTA commitments, harmonise regulations
Institutional and negotiation capacity	Strengthen SARS, train staff, strengthen AfCFTA dispute mechanisms
Monitoring and evaluation	Establish M&E, monitor trade barriers, adjust policies
Research and evidence generation	Mobilise research bodies and coordinate studies, especially empirical studies on sectors showing high export potential

Source: Authors own analysis of policies and recommendations

in emerging sectors such as digital trade and services. Success will require coordinated action across all tiers, ensuring that domestic reforms and continental engagement reinforce one another. Failure to adopt this comprehensive approach risks not only eroding South Africa's influence but also limiting its ability to shape and benefit from Africa's emerging single market.

References

Adebola, T. (2020). *Mapping Africa's complex regimes: Towards an African centred AfCFTA, intellectual property protocol* (Vol. 1, pp. 233–290). Oxford Acedemic.

African Export-Import Bank. (2024). *African trade report 2024: Climate implications of the AfCFTA implementation*. African Export-Import Bank.

African Union. (2018). *Agreement establishing the AfCFTA (AfCFTA)*. https://au.int/sites/default/files/treaties/36437-treaty-consolidated_text_on_cfta_-_en.pdf

Agarwal, P., Ayele, Y., McGarrell, R., Murinde, V., Ng'eno, R., & te Velde, D. W. (2024). *Exploring data on foreign direct investment to support implementation of the AfCFTA protocol on investment. ODI data analysis*. ODI.

AgriSA. (2024). *Key issues for South African agriculture leadership in the seventh administration*. https://agrisa.org.za/agri-sa/challenges-facing-south-african-agriculture-seventh-administration/

Ajibo, C. C. (2023). AfCFTA and regional value chain development: confronting the barriers and changing the orthodoxy. *Journal of World Trade, 57*(4), 577–592.

Ajibo, C. C. (2024). AfCFTA, Micro, Small and Medium-Sized Enterprises and Barriers: Prospect for Optimisation of Preferences, Manchester. *Journal of International Economic Law, 21*(1), 54–70.

Alagidede, I. P., Adjasi, C. C., Graham, M., & Mensah, J. O. (2024). Welfare effects of the AfCFTA: A simulation analysis. *Journal of African Political Economy and Development, 9*(1), 1–13.

Ameyaw, A. K., & Panibratov, A. (2025). Two decades of foreign direct investment in Africa: A systematic literature review, integrative framework, and agenda for future research. *European Journal of International Management, 27*(1), 1–47.

Andreoni, A., & Tregenna, F. (2021). The middle-income trap and premature deindustrialisation in South Africa. In *Structural transformation in South Africa: The challenges of inclusive industrial development in a middle-income country* (pp. 237–260). Oxford University Press.

Annandale, D. L. (2022). *The AfCFTA (AfCFTA): Opportunity or pipedream for South Africa's agricultural exports* (Doctoral dissertation, Stellenbosch: Stellenbosch University).

Ansong, A. (2025). Domesticating AfCFTA dispute settlement through reciprocity. In *International investment law reform* (pp. 101–116). Routledge.

Attia, S. (2021). The role of trade facilitation and other policy strategies in the successful implementation of AfCFTA. *Global Trade and Customs Journal, 16*(11/12), 595–600.

Ayele, Y., Belete, M., & te Velde, D. W. (2023). *The AfCFTA Protocol on Investment: Issues and Potential Impacts*. Overseas Development Institute Policy Brief.

Baccini, L., Fiorini, M., Hoekman, B., & Sanfilippo, M. (2023). Services, Jobs, and Economic Development in Africa. *The World Bank Research Observer, 38*(1), 147–178.

Banga, K., & Balchin, N. (2023). Linking Southern Africa to South Africa's exports: New opportunities for regional value chains. *The World Economy, 46*(2), 346–362.

Beyleveld, A., & Sucker, F. (2023). Regulating cross-border data flows under the AfCFTA protocol on digital trade: The what, why, how, where and when. *Manchester Journal of International Economic Law, 20*(2), 299–326.

Bhorat, H., Steenkamp, F., Rooney, C., Kachingwe, N., & Lees, A. (2018). Understanding and characterising the services sector in South Africa. *Industries Without Smokestacks, 275*, 275–295.

Black, A., Edwards, L., Ismail, F., Makundi, B., & Morris, M. (2021). The role of regional value chains in fostering regional integration in Southern Africa. *Development Southern Africa, 38*(1), 39–56.

Bore, O. (2020). Dispute settlement mechanisms in African RECs: Lessons and new developments. *African Journal of Legal Studies, 12*(3-4), 242–265.

Chawarika, A., Tibugari, H., Moyo, D., & Mutengwa, T. T. (2024). The SADC-EPA rules of origin and their implications for regional integration. *Cogent Social Sciences, 10*(1), 2361530.

Chizema, D., Kleynhans, E. P., Bezuidenhout, H., & Mhonyera, G. (2021). Identifying the determinants of outward foreign direct investment decisions of South African retail enterprises investing into Africa. *Acta Commercii-Independent Research Journal in the Management Sciences, 21*(1), 895.

Davies, R. (1994). Approaches to regional integration in the Southern African context. *Africa Insight, 24*(1), 11–17.

Demamu, A. Y. (2024). A framework of AfCFTA dispute settlement mechanism: Legal challenges. *Journal of International Dispute Settlement, 15*(3), 440–456.

Draper, P. (2019). Breaking free from Europe: Why Africa needs another model of regional integration. In *Regionalism in a changing world* (pp. 75–90). Routledge.

Efogo, F. O. (2020). AfCFTA and structural transformation in Africa. *Africa Insight, 50*(1), 90–106.

Erasmus, G. (2024a). *South Africa's participation in the Guided Trade Initiative of the AfCFTA*. https://www.tralac.org/blog/article/16333-south-africa-s-participation-in-the-guided-trade-initiative-of-the-afcfta.html#_ftn3

Erasmus, G. (2024b). *Infrastructural development under the AfCFTA*. https://www.tralac.org/blog/article/16303-infrastructural-development-under-the-afcfta.html

Feketekuty, G. (2008). *A guide to services negotiations. A handbook of international trade in services* (p. 542). Oxford University Press.

Ferreira, L., Viviers, W., & Cameron, M. (2022). *Export development and diversification opportunities in the AfCFTA: the case of South Africa*. In: Paper presented at the WCP Virtual International Conference on International Trade and Investment (ICITI2022) on: "AfCFTA: Challenges and Opportunities", 7–8 September 2022.

Ferreira, M., Jansen Van Rensburg, S. J., & Ferreira, L. (2025). Africa's digital readiness: The construction of a digital readiness index for Africa (Doctoral dissertation). [North-West University].

Festus, L., Kasongo, A., Moses, M., & Yu, D. (2016). The South African labour market, 1995–2015. *Development Southern Africa, 33*(5), 579–599.

Fofack, H., Dzene, R., & Hussein, O. A. M. (2021). Estimating the effect of AfCFTA on intra-African trade using augmented GE-PPML. *Journal of African Trade, 8*(Suppl. 2), 62–76.

Fofack, H., & Mold, A. (2021). The AfCFTA and African trade—an introduction to the special issue. *Journal of African Trade, 8*(suppl. 2), 1–11.

Gachuiri, E. (2019). Approaching competition policy in the AfCFTA. In *Inclusive trade in Africa* (pp. 167–176). CRC Press.

Gibb, R. (2009). Regional integration and Africa's development trajectory: Meta-theories, expectations, and reality. *Third World Quarterly, 30*(4), 701–721.

Gumede, V. (2021). The African continental free trade agreement and the future of RECs. *Journal of Contemporary African Studies, 39*(3), 470–483.

Hartzenberg, T. (2011). *Regional integration in Africa (No. ERSD-2011-14)*. WTO Staff Working Paper.

Hartzenberg, T. (2012). Competition policy in Africa. In *European yearbook of international economic law* (pp. 147–200). Springer.

International Finance Corporation (IFC). (2024). *Economy Africa 2020 – Africa's $180 billion internet economy future*. https://www.ifc.org/en/insights-reports/2020/google-e-conomy

International Trade Administration. (2024). *South Africa: Market overview*.

International Trade Administration (ITA). (2025). *South Africa: Digital economy overview*.

International Trade Centre (ITC). (2025). *Trademap*. https://www.trademap.org/Index.aspx

InvestSA. (2023). *South Africa investment conference 2023: Case booklet*. https://www.investsa.gov.za/wp-content/uploads/2023/05/South-Africa-Investment-Conference-2023_Case-Booklet_online.pdf

Isheloke, B. E., & von Blottnitz, H. (2020). *Regional mineral beneficiation policy interventions in the SADC: Industry perspectives*. International Mineral Processing Congress.

Jansen van Rensburg, S. J., Viviers, W., Parry, A., Cameron, M., & Grater, S. (2020). A strategic framework to expand South Africa's services trade. *South African Journal of International Affairs, 27*(3), 339–361.

Jansen van Rensburg, S. J., Viviers, W., Parry, A., Strydom, P. D., Kühn, M. L., Orkoh, E., Grater, S., Hoffman, A., & Joubert, B. (2021). *Africa's digital future: From theory to action* (p. 420). AOSIS.

Jansen van Rensburg, S. J. J., Strydom, P. D., Viviers, W., Kühn, M. L., & Parry, A. (2021). Economic development and industrialisation in the digital era: Where does Africa stand? In *Africa's digital future: From theory to action* (pp. 39–66). AOSIS.

Jules, K., Govender, D., & Bridgman, D. (2021). *Services as a driver of economic growth and job creation in South Africa: Can the AfCFTA assist?* SAIIA Policy Insights, 115.

Kayizzi-Mugerwa, S., Anyanwu, J. C., & Conceição, P. (2024). Regional integration in Africa: an introduction. *African Development Review, 26*(S1), 1–6.

Khuzwayo, D. (2018). An investigation into road freight challenges faced by transport companies in South Africa, Master's Dissertation, University of KwaZulu-Natal.

Kigwiru, V. K. (2020). Cooperation on competition policy within the AfCFTA. *Manchester Journal of International Economic Law, 17*(1), 98–121.

Kniahin, D., & De Melo, J. (2022). A primer on rules of origin as non-tariff barriers. *Journal of Risk and Financial Management, 15*(7), 286.

Knowlton, D. (2023). *Streamlining customs procedures: Trade efficiency in South Africa.* https://info.expeditors.com/horizon/streamlining-customs-procedures-boosting-trade-efficiency-in-south-africa.

Kugler, K. (2021). The AfCFTA's success depends on effective dispute settlement mechanisms for the private sector. *Global Trade and Customs Journal, 11*, 558–563.

Kuhlmann, K., & Agutu, A. L. (2020). The AfCFTA: Toward a new legal model for trade and development. *Georgetown Journal of International Law, 51*(4), 753–798.

Laryea, E., & Fabusuy, O. (2019). African countries and international investment law: The right to regulate or appropriate regulation, or both? *Australasian Review of African Studies, 40*(2), 27–54.

Lemma, A., Parra, M. M., & Naliaka, L. (2022). *The AfCFTA: unlocking the potential of the digital economy in Africa.*

MacLeod, J., Luke, D., & Guepie, G. (2023). The AfCFTA and regional trade. In D. Luke (Ed.), *How Africa trades* (p. 23). LSE Press.

Mamokhere, J., & Chauke, K. R. (2020). The multiplicity of challenges faced by South African borders: A case study of Limpopo Province. *Journal of Public Affairs, 20*(3), e2123.

Mhonyera, G., & Meyer, D. F. (2023). Impact of AfCFTA welfare trade: Nigeria and South Africa export competencies. *Sustainability, 15*(6), 5090.

Miao, G. (2023). *South Africa's integration into global value chains: Status, risks and challenges.* Economic Research and Statistics Department, South African Reserve Bank.

Mold, A., Munyegera, K. G., & Mukwaya, R. (2022). *What trade-in-value added databases tell us about continental integration–and what it means for the AfCFTA.*

Mthembu, S. M., & Naude, M. J. (2023). The impact of disruptions on the operations and performance of the Durban Port. In: *Conference proceedings* (p. 206).

Mugano, G. (2023). SMEs and the AfCFTA. In *SMEs and economic development in Africa* (pp. 142–157). Routledge.

Ncube, C. B. (2022). Intellectual property and the AfCFTA: Lessons and recommendations for the IP protocol. *Journal of International Trade Law and Policy, 21*(2), 105–121.

Nganje, F., & Ayodele, O. (2021). South African foreign policy. In *Oxford research encyclopedia of international studies.* Oxford University Press.

Noor, S.O. (2024). *South Africa's 2024 elections: Political change and democratic uncertainty.* https://democracyinafrica.org/south-africas-2024-elections-political-change-and-democratic-uncertainty

Nordås, H. K. (2001). *South Africa: A developing country and net outward investor.*

Ntlhoiseng, T.M.P. (2023). *Challenges and opportunities for innovation in the South African mining industry* [Master's dissertation, University of the Witwatersrand, Johannesburg].

Nyagah. (2025). *Negotiating jobs in the clothing and textiles industry.* https://tradeunionsinafcfta.org/negotiating-jobs-in-the-clothing-and-textiles-industry/

Ogbodo, J. A. (2024). Beyond the 'spaghetti bowl': Assessing the role of the AfCFTA protocol on intellectual property in Africa's complex regulatory environment. *Journal of Intellectual Property Law and Practice, 20*, 308.

Okadia, F., Wa-Kyendo, E., Njeru, M., Jattani, D., & Kemboi, L. (2021). Designing an AfCFTA-driven continent-wide competition policy around the RECs. *The Antitrust Bulletin, 66*(4), 556–575.

Opoku, E. E. O., & Yan, I. K. M. (2019). Industrialisation as a driver of sustainable economic growth in Africa. *The Journal of International Trade & Economic Development, 28*(1), 30–56.

Páez, L. (2024). Africa's LDC trade: Harnessing the variable geometry of the AfCFTA and Beyond. *Journal of World Trade, 58*(3), 437.

Penda, C. N. (2021). Eliminating 'thick' borders: Analysing the legal framework on non-tariff barriers in the Africa continental free trade area agreement. *Strathmore Legal Review, 6*, 167.

Raga, S., te Velde, D. W., Kimosop, V., & Mashiwa, M. (2022). *AfCFTA investment protocol: Issues and opportunities for Kenya*. ODI.

Scholvin, S., & Draper, P. (2012). The gateway to Africa? Geography and South Africa's role as an economic hinge joint between Africa and the world. *South African Journal of International Affairs, 19*(3), 381–400.

Sefume, F., & Jansen van Rensburg, S.J. (2025). [*Analysing the sustainability of intra-SACU trade in the context of existing infrastructure challenges*]. [Unpublished master's thesis]. North-West University.

Seti, T. M., & Daw, O. D. (2022). The implications of the AfCFTA on South African agricultural trade: An application of the partial equilibrium mode. *South African Journal of Economic and Management Sciences, 25*(1), 4302.

Signé, L., & Van der Ven, C. (2019). *Keys to success for the AfCFTA negotiations*. Brookings Institution Policy Brief.

Simo, R. Y. (2020). Trade in services in the AfCFTA: Prospects, challenges, and WTO compatibility. *Journal of International Economic Law, 23*(1), 65–95.

Soko, M. (2008). Building regional integration in Southern Africa: Southern African Customs Union as a driving force? *South African Journal of International Affairs, 15*(1), 55–69.

Sommer, L., & MacLeod, J. (2019). How important is special and differential treatment for an inclusive AfCFTA (AfCFTA)? In *Inclusive Trade in Africa* (pp. 69–86). Routledge.

Songwe, V., Macleod, J. A., & Karingi, S. (2021). The AfCFTA: A historic moment for development in Africa. *Journal of African Trade, 8*(2), 12–23.

Southern African Customs Union (SACU). (2025). *Implementation AfCFTA in SACU*.

Statista. (2025). *African countries with the highest Gross Domestic Product (GDP) in 2024*. https://www.statista.com

Stern, M., & Ramkolowan, Y. (2021). *Understanding South Africa's trade policy and performance*. Economic Research and Statistics Department, South African Reserve Bank.

Taye, S. D. (2019). *Variable geometry of African integration and its implication on AfCFTA* (Master's thesis, University of Pretoria (South Africa).

The Banking Association of South Africa. (2021). *SME*. https://www.banking.org.za/what-we-do/sme/?cn-reloaded=1

The Conversation. (2024). *South Africa's municipalities aren't fixing roads, supplying clean water, or keeping the lights on: A new study explains why*. 29 September 2024.

The DTIC. (2021). *A trade policy for industrial development and employment growth*. https://www.thedtic.gov.za/wp-content/uploads/SA_Trade_Policy.pdf

The DTIC. (2023). *Guide to the African continental free trade agreement*. http://www.thedtic.gov.za/wp-content/uploads/Guide-to-the-ACFTA_2023.pdf

The DTIC. (2025a). *African regional integration*. https://www.thedtic.gov.za/sectors-and-services-2/1-4-2-trade-and-export/market-access/african-regional-integration/

The DTIC. (2025b). *Update on the AfCFTA agreements*. Email exchange, 24 February 2025.

Trade Law Centre. (2019). *The intra-African non-tariff barrier dilemma: the challenges facing the AfCFTA approach*.

Trade Law Centre. (2023). *Trade in services in the AfCFTA: Factsheet.*
Trade Law Centre. (2024). Tralac: Annual conference, AfCFTA protocol on digital trade.
Tshedza, S. T., & Lee, K. S. (2023). How will AfCFTA Impact on South Africa's Socio-economic Position? *Journal of African Foreign Affairs, 10*(3), 103–120.
Tsowou, K., & Davis, J. (2021). Reaping the AfCFTA potential through well-functioning rules of origin. *Journal of African Trade, 8*(2), 88–102.
Turkson, E., Oduro, A. D., Baffour, P. T., & Quartey, P. (2023). Regional integration and non-tariff barriers to intra-sub-Saharan Africa trade. *The World Economy, 46*(2), 396–414.
UNECA (2019). *AfCFTA: Questions & answers*. Addis Ababa. https://repository.uneca.org/handle/10855/43253
Vambe, B. (2024). Advancing the AfCFTA (AfCFTA): Lessons from the Southern African development community protocol on trade. *Comparative and International Law Journal of Southern Africa, 57*(3), 25.
Wapmuk, S., & Ali, J. M. (2022). The AfCFTA (AFCFTA) and regional economic integration: Prospects and challenges. *Zamfara Journal of Politics and Development, 3*(1), 15.
Wolfe, R., Saluste, M., Hoekman, B. M., Fiorini, M., & Mavroidis, P. C. (2020). WTO dispute settlement and the appellate body: insider perceptions and members' revealed preferences. *Journal of World Trade, 54*(5), 667.
World Bank. (2020). *The AfCFTA: Economic and distributional effects*. World Bank.
World Bank. (2022). *South Africa financial sector assessment program.* https://documents1.worldbank.org/curated/en/099130102222273926/pdf/P170707006239f0520b3340726cc02a6858.pdf
World Bank (2025). *South Africa overview.* https://www.worldbank.org/en/country/southafrica/overview
World Trade Organisation (Ed.). (2023). *Handbook on measuring digital trade* (2nd ed.). World Trade Organisation. https://www.wto.org/english/res_e/booksp_e/digital_trade_2023_e.pdf

Chapter 13
Unlocking Growth Through the AfCFTA Protocol on Investment: The Case of Cameroon

Manfred Kouty

Abstract Cameroon was among the early adopters of the AfCFTA, ratifying the AfCFTA Agreement in 2019 and actively participating in negotiations, including the development of the Protocol on Investment (PoI), which was adopted in February 2023. The PoI aims to promote and protect intra-African investment in the AfCFTA and harmonise coexisting national, bilateral, and regional investment regulations on the continent. Article 52 (2) of the PoI stipulates that "State Parties shall, within 5 years from the entry into force of this Protocol, bring their national laws, regulations and policies into alignment with this Protocol". The objective of the study is to analyse the current regulatory frameworks governing investment in Cameroon and identify convergences and divergences about the Protocol PoI. After presenting the instruments regulating investment in Cameroon, we have analysed their coherence/divergence according to the five dimensions of PoI: investment promotion and facilitation, investment protection, sustainable development, investor obligations, and dispute resolution. We find some convergences between the regulatory framework governing investment in Cameroon and PoI. However, some elements of PoI, including physical protection and security of the investor, sustainable development, and investor obligations, need to be explicitly introduced in the legislation.

Keywords AfCFTA · Investment · Regulations · Cameroon

JEL Classification L51 · O16 · O55 · P48

M. Kouty (✉)
International Relations Institute of Cameroon (IRIC), Yaoundé, Cameroon

D. N. Yuni et al. (eds.), *From Policy to Practice: Challenges and Ways Forward on the Implementation of the AfCFTA*,
https://doi.org/10.1007/978-3-032-14051-7_13

13.1 Introduction

Foreign capital inflows, particularly Foreign Direct Investment (FDI), are a significant driver of economic growth, especially in developing countries. FDI can enhance economic growth by increasing investment, boosting productivity, and fostering technological advancements (Lucas Jr, 1988; Sala-I-Martin, 1996; Solow, 1956; United Nations, 2024). However, the effectiveness of FDI in promoting growth can depend on various factors, mainly the regulatory framework. Prior research suggests that a country's capacity to attract FDI is associated with its legal and regulatory environment (Hossain & Rahman, 2017; Sokang, 2018; UNCTAD, 2024).

Africa is one of the regions in the world which receives less foreign capital inflows. Transparent and predictable legal and regulatory environments for investment are critical in the region (Wamkele Mene, 2023). To boost its structural transformation and benefit from the opportunities offered by the African Continental Free Trade Area (AfCFTA), the African Union Assembly of Heads of State and Government adopted the Protocol on Investment (PoI) at its 37th Ordinary Session on 19 February 2023. The PoI is a key component of the AfCFTA agreement and provides a framework for investment across the African continent, including investment guarantees, freedom of economic activity, and dispute settlement mechanisms. The successful implementation of the AfCFTA PoI will be crucial to realising the full potential benefits of the AfCFTA agreement for African economies. According to World Bank research, intra-Africanthe full implementation of the AfCFTA Agreement could increase intra-African FDI by 68% and external investment by 122% (Kher et al., 2024). The AfCFTA PoI will also promote structural transformation in Africa, harness the business potential of private initiatives, and translate it into long-term outcomes for host communities.

Following the adoption of the PoI, the focus is now on its implementation, which aims to translate its objectives from policy declarations into actual economic gains and enhanced investments. Article 52 (1) of the PoI provides that "Each State Party shall apply appropriate measures to bring effect to the rules and procedures set out in the provisions of this Protocol". Article 52 (2) stipulates that "State Parties shall, within five (5) years from the entry into force of this Protocol, bring their national laws, regulations and policies into alignment with this Protocol". The Protocol is therefore an opportunity to align the African investment treaty landscape with modern treaty practice.

Cameroon is one of the first signatories of the AfCFTA Agreement and has taken an active part in PoI negotiations. Thanks to Presidential Decree No. 2019/586 of 31 October 2019, Cameroon ratified the AfCFTA Agreement and became the 33rd State Party when it deposited the instrument of ratification on 1 December 2020.

The objective of the study is to analyse the current regulatory frameworks governing investment in Cameroon and identify convergences and divergences about the Protocol PoI. It is organised as follows. The following section presents the AfCFTA Investment Protocol, while Section 13.3 presents an overview of FDI inflow and economic growth in Cameroon. Section 13.4 analyses the investment policy framework in Cameroon. Section 13.5 concludes by presenting some policy implications.

13.2 The AfCFTA Protocol on Investment (PoI)

The PoI to the Agreement Establishing the AfCFTA was adopted on 19 February 2023 by the African Union Assembly of Heads of State and Government in its 37th Ordinary Session. The PoI aims to promote and protect intra-African investment in the AfCFTA and harmonise coexisting national, bilateral and regional investment regulations on the continent.

Beyond the preamble, the Protocol consists of 54 articles divided into eight (8) parts comprising: general provisions; investment promotion and facilitation; investment protection standards; sustainable development-related matters; investor obligations; institutional arrangements; management and settlement of disputes and final provisions.

- Part 1: General provisions (Definition, objectives, scope of application, admission of Investment and denial of benefits);
- Part 2: Investment promotion and facilitation (investment promotion, investment facilitation, incentives for sustainable investments, national focal points, publication of information and non-disclosure of confidential information);
- Part 3: Investment protection standards (National treatment, exceptions to national treatment, Most-favoured nation treatment, Exceptions to Most-favoured nation treatment, Interpretation of non-discrimination, Administrative and judicial treatment, Physical protection and security, Expropriation, Exceptions to expropriation, Compensation for expropriation, Transfer of funds, Exceptions to transfer of funds);
- Part 4: Sustainable development-related issues (Right to regulate, Minimum standards on the environment, labour and consumer protection, Investment and climate change, Investment, public health and pandemics, Pursuit of development goals, Human resources development, Transfer of Technology);
- Part 5: Investor obligations (Relation to State party obligations, compliance with national and international law, Business ethics, human rights and labour standards, Environmental protection, Indigenous peoples and local communities, Socio-political obligations, Anti-corruption, Corporate social responsibility, Corporate governance, Taxation and transfer pricing);
- Part 6: Institutional arrangements(Committee on investment, Establishment of the Pan-African trade and investment Agency, Technical assistance, capacity building and cooperation);
- Part 7: Management and settlement of disputes (State-State dispute settlement, dispute prevention and grievance management, Dispute resolution, Investor liability);

- Part 8: Final provisions (Entry into force, Relationship with other international investment agreements, Notification, Application, Amendments, Authentic texts).

According to the PoI, "Investment" means an enterprise or company, which is established, acquired or expanded in conformity with the laws and regulations of a Host State by an investor which maintains substantial business in the territory of that Host State. The enterprise or company may possess assets, such as:

(a) shares, stocks, or any other form of participation in the enterprise/company or another enterprise/company;
(b) movable and immovable property, including mortgages, liens, pledges, and any other similar rights as defined in conformity with the laws and regulations of the State Party in whose territory the property is situated;
(c) intellectual property rights such as copyrights, patents, trademarks, industrial designs, trade names, know-how and goodwill to the extent they are acquired, maintained and protected under the law of the Host State;
(d) rights conferred by the law of the Host State or under contract, including licences to cultivate, extract or exploit natural resources; or,
(e) rights under contracts, including turnkey, construction, production, management, concession or other contracts.

13.3 Overview of FDI Inflows and Economic Growth in Cameroon

13.3.1 FDI and the Promotion of Economic Growth in the Literature

The theoretical analysis of the effects of foreign capital inflow, particularly foreign direct investment (FDI), on economic growth is based on the exogenous growth and endogenous growth theories.

In the exogenous growth theory, also known as the neoclassical growth model, developed by Solow (1956), economic growth results from the accumulation of exogenous factors of production, such as labour and capital stocks, or from an increase in factor productivity. The neoclassical model highlights the importance of FDI in facilitating the host economy to attain effective investment more than their internal savings. From this perspective, FDI promotes economic growth by increasing the volume and/or efficiency of investment in the host country (Sala-I-Martin, 1996; Solow, 1956).

The endogenous growth framework also emphasises that FDI is a significant driver of economic growth by promoting the technological transfer, diffusion and spillover effects (Lucas Jr, 1988; Romer, 1986; Sala-I-Martin, 1996).

13.3.2 *FDI Inflow in Cameroon*

Structurally, FDI inflows to Cameroon are low compared to its economic potential. The FDI represent 889 million (USD) in 2022 (Table 13.1).

In the same year, the stock of FDI is 6446 (million UDS). The number of greenfield investment is also low.

To boost its economic growth and structural transformation, Cameroon prioritises investment attraction as part of its economic development strategy. This policy is contained in the National Development Strategy 2020–2030 (NDS30), the new reference framework of Vision 2035 of Cameroon, which seeks to transform Cameroon into an emerging economy through industrialisation (MINEPAT, 2020). The NDS30 envisions strong and sustainable growth at an average annual rate of 5.6% to accelerate the industrialisation process. However, financing resources are the main constraint faced by the NDS30. The estimated need is around 88 trillion FCFA. That is why the authorities relye heavily on FDI (Kouty & Lemma, 2025). The adoption of the PoI is consistent with the NDS30 because it will enable Cameroon to create an enabling environment for investments.

13.4 The Investment Policy Framework in Cameroon and the Implementation of PoI: Divergences or Convergences

In this section, after presenting the instruments regulating investment in Cameroon, we will analyse their coherence or divergence according to the five dimensions of PoI: investment promotion and facilitation, investment protection, sustainable development, investor obligations, and dispute resolution.

Table 13.1 Evolution of FDI in Cameroon

Foreign direct investment (FDI)	2020	2021	2022
FDI inward flow (million USD)	675	964	889
FDI stock (million USD)	8931	5558	6446
Number of greenfield investments[a]	11	8	4
Value of greenfield investments (million USD)	204	198	95

Source: UNCTAD (2024)

[a] Greenfield investments are a form of foreign direct investment where a parent company starts a new venture in a foreign country by constructing new operational facilities from the ground (LLOYDS Bank, 2025)

13.4.1 Instruments Regulating Investment in Cameroon

The legal instruments regulating investment in Cameroon consist of national regulations, as well as regional, bilateral, and multilateral agreements.

13.4.1.1 National Regulations

Without claiming to be exhaustive, the main national regulations on investment are:

- Law No. 98/013 of 14 July 1998 Relating to Competition;
- Law N°2002/004 of April 19, 2002, on the Charter of Investments in the Republic of Cameroon;
- Law No.2006/12 of 29 December 2006 to Lay Down the General Regime for Partnership Contracts;
- Law No. 2013/004 of April 2013 to lay down private investment incentives in the Republic of Cameroon;
- Decree No 2008/2304/PM of 29 July 2008 to specify the terms and conditions for the implementation of the special taxation regime of structuring projects of the General Taxation Code;
- Law No. 2008/009 of 16 July 2008 setting the fiscal, financial, and accounting regime applicable to partnership contracts;
- Ordinance No. 2008/001 of 13 May 2008 to amend some provisions of Law No. 2002/004 of 19 April 2002 to Institute the Investment Charter of the Republic of Cameroon;
- Law No. 2010-1 of 13 April 2010 to Promote Small-and Medium-sized Enterprises in Cameroon;
- Law No.2013/2011 of 10 December 2013 Governing Economic Zones in Cameroon;
- Law No. 2015/018 Of 21 December 2015 Governing Commercial Activity In Cameroon;
- Law No. 2017/015 of 12 July 2017 to amend and supplement specific provisions of Law No. 2013/004 of 18 April 2013 to Lay Down Private Investment Incentives in the Republic of Cameroon;
- Law No. 2017/10 of 12 July 2017 To Lay Down the General Rules and Regulations Governing Public Establishments;
- The finance law of the current financial year.

13.4.1.2 International Regulations

According to the UNCTAD investment policy hub,[1] Cameroon has 20 Investment Related Instruments (IRIs), 11 Treaties with Investment Provisions and 18 bilateral Treaties.

13.4.1.3 Bilateral Regulations

Cameroon has signed bilateral investment treaties with Germany (1963), Switzerland (1964), the Netherlands (1966), the Belgium-Luxembourg Economic Union (1981), Romania (1981), the United Kingdom (1985), the USA (1989), Italy (2004), and China (2014), Canada (2014), and the Republic of Korea (2013). It has also signed treaties that are not yet in force with Egypt (2000), Guinea (2001), Mali (2001), Mauritania (2001), Mauritius (2001), Morocco (2007), and Türkiye (2012).

13.4.1.4 Free Trade Area

Number of FTAs with Investment provisions: 8 (Cameroon-UK EPA; EU-Cameroon EPA; Cotonou Agreement; AU Treaty; ECCAS Treaty; OIC Investment Agreement; CEMAC Convention on Liberation; CEMAC Investment).

13.4.1.5 Multilateral Regulations (Table 13.2)

13.4.2 Analysis of Convergence/Divergence Between PoI and Cameroon's Investment Framework

13.4.2.1 Investment Promotion and Facilitation

The Investment Promotion Agency (IPA) is the of the primary institution responsible for investment promotion in Cameroon. Created in 2005 by Decree No. 2005-310 of September 1, 2005, the objectives of IPA are to promote the country's trade mark abroad, propose measures that can attract foreign investors, as well as collect information on investment opportunities the country offers.

The Charter (Law No. 2002/004 of April 19, 2002, on the Charter of Investments in the Republic of Cameroon) contains several fiscal incentive regimes that are

[1] https://investmentpolicy.unctad.org/international-investment-agreements/countries/34/cameroon?type=tips.

Table 13.2 Cameroon's investment related instrument (IRIs)

Agreements	Type of agreement	Investment policy/dimension covered
WTO GATS agreement	Multilateral	Entry and establishment
WTO TRIMS[a] agreeement	Multilateral	Entry, establishment and incentives
WTO TRIPS[b] agreement	Multilateral	Protection
WTO SCM[c] agreement	Multilateral	Incentives
WTO agreement on technical barriers to trade (TBT)	Multilateral	Facilitation
WTO agreement on trade facilitation	Multilateral	Facilitation
WTO agreement on investment facilitation	Multilateral	Protection and facilitation
World Bank's multilateral investment guarantee agency (MIGA)	Plurilateral	Protection
IMF	Plurilateral	
OHADA[d]	Plurilateral	Protection and treatment
OAPI[e]	Plurilatéral	Protection
Oran[f]	Plurilateral	Investment garanties and trade facilitation
ISO[g]	Plurilateral	Investment garanties and trade facilitation
ICSID convention	Multilatéral	Protection
Charter of economic rights and duties of states	Multilateral	Guidelines, principles, resolutions, and similar
ILO tripartite declaration on multinational enterprises	Multilateral	Guidelines, principles, resolutions, and similar
Islamic corporation for the insurance of investment credit	Plurilateral	

Source: author, based on literature
[a] Trade-related investment measures
[b] Trade-related intellectual property rights
[c] Subsidies and countervailing measures
[d] The treaty on the harmonization of business law in Africa (OHADA)
[e] African intellectual property organization was founded in Bangui in 1977
[f] Organisation Régionale Africaine de Normalisation created in 1977
[g] International organisation for standardization

likely to serve as a taxation base for the execution of significant projects. These regimes are classified into two major groups as follows:

- The group of investment incentive regimes governed by the General Taxation Code and aligned to the IPA of Cameroon. These regimes are closely linked to the financial law of the financial year and include: exemption from VAT for certain purchases; free registration of deeds for the formation, extension, and increase of capital; exemption from registration duties during the installation phase, and several other benefits in the operational phase.
- The Partnership Contracts special regime. This regime is well known to be stable and specific and includes reimbursement by the contractor's budget of the VAT

related to local imports and purchase of materials; free registration conventions and acts.

Additionally, common incentives are granted to investors during the establishment and operation phases. In particular, any investor may benefit from a tax credit provided it meets one of the following criteria: (1) hires at least five graduates each year, (2) combats pollution, or (3) develops public interest activities in rural areas.

The Law N° 2013/11 of December 16, 2013, provides for the creation of "Economic Zones," defined as an area made up of one or more geographical areas that are serviced, developed, and equipped with infrastructure, with a view to enabling the entities located there to produce goods and services in optimal conditions. This law is Decree No. 2019/195 of April 17, 2019, which establishes the modalities for the creation and management of Economic Zones in Cameroon.

13.4.2.2 Investment Protection

National treatment: In Cameroon, the State guarantees equal treatment in carrying out an activity by the principles and provisions of competition law (Article 10 of the Charter).

Most-favoured nation treatment: Apart from the national defence and security areas, there are no sector-specific restrictions, limitations, or requirements applied to foreign ownership and control. In Cameroon, a foreign investor may invest in any sector on the same basis as a domestic investor. Foreign investors can also enter joint ventures and public-private partnerships with the government.

Restrictions on inflow and outflow of funds: Law N°2002/004 of April 19, 2002, on the Charter of Investments guarantees to any individual or corporate entity with established economic activity or wishing to establish an economic activity in Cameroon the freedom to repatriate foreign capital invested and profits made by that exploitation as well as repatriation of salary savings made by expatriate staff. However, the same law requires that foreign exchange and capital transfers be made by the rules of the Central African Economic and Monetary Union (CEMAC), which imposes restrictions on the repatriation of foreign capital.

Expropriation and compensation: In Cameroon, the law contains express protection against expropriation, which applies equally to domestic and foreign investors. The Decree N°0.85–9 of July 4, 1985, and the subsequent implementation of Decree N°87-1872 of December 16, 1987, outline the procedures governing expropriation for public purposes and conditions for compensation. According to articles 2 and 3 of Decree N°87-1872 of December 16, 1987, the State may expropriate privately-owned land with compensation.

13.4.2.3 Sustainable Development

As stated in the investment charter, business law is critical for sustainable development in Cameroon. For instance, Section 8 of Law N°2013/004 of 18 April 2013, which establishes private investment incentives in the Republic of Cameroon, states that any investor may benefit from a tax credit provided that they combat pollution. In addition, Section 14 states that specific incentives may be provided to enterprises which carry out investments that contribute to the attainment of the following priority objectives:

- the fight against pollution and environmental protection;
- Promotion and transfer of innovative technologies and research and development.

13.4.2.4 Investor Obligations

Regarding investor obligations, Cameroon has subscribed to the African Charter on Human and Peoples' Rights (Article 24 provides for the right to a clean, healthy, and sustainable environment). However, certain aspects, particularly those related to Business Ethics and Corporate Social Responsibility, are still absent in investment laws.

13.4.2.5 Dispute Settlement

In Cameroon, foreign investors have the arbitration, and international arbitration. For example, section 26 of the Law N° 2013/004 of 18 April 2013 to lay down private investment incentives in the Republic of Cameroon states that:

- Investors granted the incentives hereunder must first seek the Control Committee in case of dispute to seek an amicable settlement;
- They may, where amicable settlement has not been obtained, refer the dispute to an arbitration body recognised by the State of Cameroon.

At the international level, Cameroon has adopted a uniform act on arbitration (the Uniform Act) of OHADA. The Uniform Act and outlines basic rules applicable to any arbitration where the seat of arbitration is in an OHADA member state. Cameroon has also ratified the "International Centre for Settlement of Investment Disputes" (ICSID) Convention on January 3, 1967, and the New York Convention on February 19, 1988.

13.5 Conclusion

At its 37th Ordinary Session on 19 February 2023, the African Union Assembly of Heads of State and Government adopted the Protocol on Investment (PoI). The PoI is a key component of the AfCFTA agreement and provides a framework for investment across the African continent, including investment guarantees, freedom of economic activity, and dispute settlement mechanisms. To implement the PoI, important domestic measures and reforms within the State Parties are required. Article 52 (2) of the PoI stipulates that « State Parties shall, within five (5) years from the entry into force of this Protocol, bring their national laws, regulations and policies into alignment with this Protocol ».

The objective of the study was to analyse the current regulatory frameworks governing investment in Cameroon and identify convergences and divergences in relation to the Protocol PoI. After presenting the instruments regulating investment in Cameroon, we have analysed their coherence/divergence according to the five dimensions of PoI: the investment promotion and facilitation, the investment protection, sustainable development, the investor obligation, and dispute resolution. Our analysis shows some convergence between the regulatory framework governing investment in Cameroon and PoI. However, some aspects of PoI need to be explicitly introduced in the legislation. It is about:

- Provisions relating to the physical protection and security of the investor;
- the issue of sustainable development;
- Investor obligations (must be clarified and extended to environmental concerns, human rights and the protection of the rights of indigenous peoples and local communities; ethics and corruption).

In short, Cameroon need to update it investment charter in accordance with the PoI.

References

Hossain, S., & Rahman, Z. (2017). Does governance facilitate foreign direct investment in developing countries? *International Journal of Economics and Financial Issues, 7*(1), 164–177.

Kher, P., Forneris, X., Obadia, E., & Wager M. G. (2024). *African continental free trade area is an opportunity to recharge investment, growth and jobs; World Banc blogs*. https://blogs.worldbank.org/en/psd/african-continental-free-trade-area-is-an-opportunity-to-recharg

Kouty, M., & Lemma, A. (2025). *Unlocking growth through the AfCFTA digital trade protocol: A focus on e-commerce in Cameroon. ODI global briefing paper*. ODI Global. https://www.odi.org/en/publications/unlocking-growth-through-the-afcftadigital-trade-protocol-a-focus-on-e-commerce-in-cameroon

LLOYDS Bank. (2025). *Cameroon: Investing in Cameroon*. https://www.lloydsbanktrade.com/en/market-potential/cameroon/investment

Lucas, R., Jr. (1988). On the mechanics of economic development. *Journal of Monetary Economics, 22*(3), 3–42.

Ministry of Economy, Planning and Regional Development (MINEPAT). (2020). Cameroon Vision 2035: The reference framework for development action (Version). Scribd. https://www.scribd.com/document/509849554/CAMEROON-VISION-2035

Romer, P. (1986). Increasing returns and long-run growth. *Journal of Political Economy, 94*, 1002–1037.

Sala-I-Martin, X. X. (1996). Regional cohesion: Evidence and theories of regional growth and convergence. *European Economic Review, 40*(6), 1325–1352. https://doi.org/10.1016/0014-2921(95)00029-1

Sokang, K. (2018). The impact of foreign direct investment on the economic growth in Cambodia: Empirical evidence. *International Journal of Innovation and Economic Development, 4*(5), 31–38. https://doi.org/10.18775/ijied.1849-7551-7020.2015.45.2003

Solow, R. M. (1956). A contribution to the theory of economic growth. *The Quarterly Journal of Economics, 70*(1), 65. http://piketty.pse.ens.fr/files/Solow1956.pdf

UNCTAD. (2024). *Outward FDI policies: Promotion and facilitation—Regulation andscreening. Investment Policy Monitor No. 27.*

United Nations. (2024). *World investment report 2024: Investment facilitation and digital government*. United States of America.

Chapter 14
Positioning Chad for Success in the African Continental Free Trade Area: Strategic Pathways for a Landlocked Economy

Douzounet Mallaye

Abstract The African continental free trade area (AfCFTA) represents a transformative opportunity for African economies to enhance intra-continental trade and accelerate economic diversification. This study examines Chad's strategic position within emerging continental market, analysing the country's comparative advantages, structural challenges, and potential pathways for maximising benefits from trade liberalisation. Using a mixed-method approach combining document analysis, trade data evaluation, and policy review, we identify key sectors where Chad possesses competitive advantages, including petroleum products, livestock, gum arabic, sesame, and cotton. The research reveals that while Chad faces significant challenges from infrastructure deficits, institutional weaknesses, and limited productive capacity, the AfCFTA presents substantial opportunities for developing regional value chains and expanding service exports. We propose a strategic framework for Chad's successful integration into the continental market, emphasising targeted investments in export-ready sectors, infrastructure development, trade facilitation, and institutional capacity building. The findings contribute to the literature on trade policy in landlocked developing countries evidence-based recommendations for policymakers navigating regional integration processes.

Keywords African continental free trade area (AfCFTA) · Chad · Regional integration · Trade liberalisation · Export diversification · Landlocked economies · Comparative advantage

---

D. Mallaye (✉)
LAEREAG, University of NDjamena, NDjamena, Chad

D. N. Yuni et al. (eds.), *From Policy to Practice: Challenges and Ways Forward on the Implementation of the AfCFTA*,
https://doi.org/10.1007/978-3-032-14051-7_14

14.1 Introduction

The African Continental Free Trade Area (AfCFTA), established in 2018 and operationalised in January 2021, represents one of the most ambitious economic integration initiatives in African history. With 54 signatories and 44 ratifying countries, the AfCFTA aims to create a single market of 1.3 billion people with a combined GDP of approximately US$3.4 trillion. The agreement seeks to eliminate tariffs on 90% of goods, progressively liberalise trade in services, and address non-tariff barriers that have historically constrained intra-African trade (Signé, 2018; UNECA, 2020).

Chad, as a landlocked country in Central Africa with significant economic challenges, presents an intriguing case study for examining how vulnerable economies can position themselves to benefit from continental trade liberalisation. Despite having ratified the AfCFTA agreement in June 2018 as one of the first countries to do so, Chad faces substantial structural impediments to fully leveraging the opportunities presented by the agreement. With an economy heavily dependent on petroleum exports (approximately 85% of export revenues), limited industrial capacity, and significant infrastructure deficits, Chad must develop strategic approaches to diversify its export base and enhance its competitiveness within the emerging continental market (World Bank, 2020a).

This research addresses a critical gap in the literature regarding the specific challenges and opportunities that landlocked, resource-dependent economies face in continental free trade initiatives. While existing studies have examined the general macroeconomic implications of the AfCFTA (Abrego et al., 2020; Songwe et al., 2019), few have provided granular, country-specific analyses of strategic positioning for vulnerable economies, such as Chad. This paper contributes to the literature by analysing Chad's comparative advantages, identifying key sectors with export potential, and developing a strategic framework for maximising benefits from the AfCFTA.

The following research questions guide the study:

1. What sectors and product categories present the most significant potential for Chad to develop competitive advantages within the AfCFTA framework?
2. What structural and institutional constraints might limit Chad's ability to benefit from trade liberalisation under the AfCFTA?
3. What strategic policy interventions could enhance Chad's capacity to successfully integrate into regional value chains and expand trade under the AfCFTA?

The remainder of this paper is structured as follows: Sect. 14.2 provides a review of relevant literature on regional integration, trade liberalisation in developing economies, and the specific context of the AfCFTA. Section 14.3 outlines the methodological approach employed in the study. Section 14.4 presents an analysis of Chad's economic structure and trade patterns. Section 14.5 identifies sectors with comparative advantages and potential. Section 14.6 examines the key challenges and constraints facing Chad in the context of the AfCFTA. Section 14.7 develops a strategic framework for Chad's successful integration into the continental market. Finally, Sect. 14.8 offers concluding remarks and policy recommendations.

14.2 Literature Review

14.2.1 Regional Integration and Economic Development

Regional economic integration has long been recognised as a potentially powerful driver of economic growth and development in emerging economies. The theoretical foundations for regional integration are rooted in classical and neoclassical trade theories, which posit that trade liberalisation leads to welfare gains through specialisation. Liberalisation leads to welfare gains through specialisation according to comparative advantage, economies of scale, and enhanced competition (Balassa, 1961; Krugman, 1991; Viner, 1950). For developing countries, regional integration offers particular advantages, including expanded market access, opportunities for industrial development through regional value chains, and enhanced bargaining power in multilateral negotiations (Draper, 2013; UNCTAD, 2013).

However, the empirical literature on regional integration in developing countries reveals mixed outcomes. Studies by Venables (2003) and Foroutan and Pritchett (1993) suggest that regional integration agreements among developing countries often generate limited trade creation and can sometimes lead to trade diversion, particularly when integration occurs among countries with similar factor endowments and production structures. More recent research by Mevel and Karingi (2012) and Saygili et al. (2018) suggests that the benefits of regional integration are significantly dependent on complementary policies addressing non-tariff barriers, infrastructure development, and productive capacity.

14.2.2 The African Continental Free Trade Area: Opportunities and Challenges

The AfCFTA represents a new paradigm in African regional integration, moving beyond the existing patchwork of Regional Economic Communities (RECs) to create a continental market. Studies by the United Nations Economic Commission for Africa (UNECA, 2018) and the World Bank (2020b) project significant potential gains from the AfCFTA, including increases in intra-African trade of 15–25%, reduction in trade costs, and welfare gains of US$16.1 billion. Notably, the AfCFTA is expected to generate structural transformation by promoting industrialisation and the development of regional value chains (IMF, 2019; Songwe et al., 2019).

However, the literature also identifies significant challenges that may constrain the realisation of these benefits. Abrego et al. (2020) highlight the uneven distribution of gains across countries, with resource-rich and more industrialised economies potentially capturing a larger share of benefits. Research by Fabricius (2020), supported by Luke and MacLeod (2019) emphasises the importance of addressing non-tariff barriers, enhancing productive capacity, and improving trade-related infrastructure to capitalise on the opportunities presented by the AfCFTA fully.

14.2.3 Landlocked Developing Countries in Trade Agreements

Landlocked developing countries (LLDCs) face unique challenges in international trade due to their geographical disadvantages. Research by Faye et al. (2004) and Limão and Venables (2001) demonstrates that landlocked countries face significantly higher trade costs, with transportation costs estimated to be 50% higher to those of coastal countries. These elevated costs erode competitiveness and limit the ability of LLDCs to participate effectively in international trade.

Studies by Arvis et al. (2011) and Borchert et al. (2012) suggest that the successful integration of LLDCs into regional and global markets necessitates targeted interventions to reduce trade costs, including infrastructure development, trade facilitation measures, and enhanced cooperation with transit countries. The research of Christ and Ferrantino (2011) and Shepherd and Wilson (2006) suggests that reductions in time delays at borders and improvements in logistics can generate substantial gains for landlocked countries, potentially offsetting geographical disadvantages.

14.2.4 Chad's Economy and Trade in Regional Context: Historical Constraints on Intra-African Trade

Research on Chad's economic structure and trade patterns remains limited, particularly in the context of regional integration initiatives. Studies by the World Bank (2015, 2018a) and the IMF (2019) have analysed Chad's macroeconomic challenges, highlighting the country's heavy dependence on petroleum exports and vulnerability to commodity price shocks. These studies emphasise the need for economic diversification and structural transformation to enhance resilience and promote sustainable growth.

14.2.4.1 Historical Analysis of Chad's Limited Intra-African Trade Participation

Chad's minimal participation in intra-African trade represents a critical constraint that requires historical analysis. According to Koerner and Cook (2017), Chad's intra-African trade performance has consistently lagged behind continental averages since independence, with several structural factors contributing to this limitation:

Colonial trade orientation legacy: Chad's trade patterns were established during the colonial period with strong orientation towards France and European markets. The CFA franc monetary system and preferential trade arrangements with former colonial powers created institutional barriers to South-South trade development (Cogneau & Mesplé-Somps, 2007).

Geographic and infrastructure constraints: As emphasised by Raballand and Kunaka (2011), Chad's landlocked position and limited transport infrastructure have historically directed trade flows through Cameroon to European markets rather than fostering intra-African connections. The lack of direct transport links to major African markets has perpetuated this pattern.

Limited regional economic community engagement: Despite membership in the Central African Economic and Monetary Union (CEMAC) since 1994 and the Economic Community of Central African States (ECCAS), Chad has not effectively leveraged these platforms for trade expansion. Research by Avom and Gbetnkom (2018) demonstrates that CEMAC members, including Chad, have achieved limited trade integration due to similar production structures, inadequate infrastructure, and weak implementation of community policies.

Petroleum economy distortions: The commencement of oil production in 2003 further oriented Chad's economy towards global energy markets, reducing incentives for regional agricultural and livestock trade development (Magrin, 2013). This resource-driven export model marginalised traditional sectors that could have formed the basis for intra-African trade.The existing literature on Chad's trade potential has focused primarily on specific sectors, notably petroleum, agriculture, and livestock. Research by Behnke (2012) and Koussou et al. (2012) examines the potential of Chad's livestock sector, highlighting its contribution to export revenues and identifying constraints to sector development. Studies by Mustapha (2017) and Giraud (2013) analyse the potential of agricultural exports such as gum arabic, sesame, and cotton, noting their historical importance and future prospects.

However, there remains a significant gap in the literature regarding Chad's strategic positioning within the AfCFTA framework. This paper aims to address this gap by providing a comprehensive analysis of Chad's comparative advantages, constraints, and strategic options for maximising benefits from continental trade liberalisation.

14.3 Methodology

This study employs a mixed-methods approach, combining quantitative analysis of trade data with qualitative assessment of policy documents and institutional frameworks. The research design was guided by the need to triangulate findings from multiple sources and methods, thereby enhancing validity and reliability.

14.3.1 Data Sources

The study draws on multiple data sources:

1. Trade data: Export and import statistics were collected from the International Trade Centre's Trade Map database, covering the period 2001–2018, with supplementary data from UNCTADstat and the Observatory of Economic Complexity (OEC).
2. Policy documents: Key national strategy documents were analysed, including Chad's National Development Plan (2017–2021), National Trade Strategy (2016), Industrial and Economic Diversification Master Plan, and available AfCFTA implementation documents.
3. Economic indicators: Macroeconomic data were sourced from the World Bank's World Development Indicators, the International Monetary Fund's World Economic Outlook database, and Chad's National Institute of Statistics.
4. Sectoral studies: Sector-specific analyses from organisations such as Food and Agriculture Organization (FAO), United Nations Industrial Development Organization(UNIDO), and the African Development Bank were reviewed to gain insights into potential growth sectors.

14.3.2 Analytical Framework

The analytical framework for this study integrates three complementary approaches:

1. Revealed comparative advantage (RCA) analysis: Following Balassa (1965), we calculated RCA indices for Chad's export products to identify sectors, where the country possesses comparative advantages in international markets. The RCA index is calculated as: $RCAij = \frac{\frac{Xij}{Xi}}{\frac{Xwj}{Xw}}$ where Xij represents country i's exports of product j, Xi represents country i's total exports, Xwj represents world exports of product j, and Xw represents total world exports.

2. Trade complementarity index (TCI): To assess the potential for expanded trade between Chad and other African regions, we calculated the TCI, which measures the extent to which the export profile of one country matches the import profile of another. The TCI is calculated as: $TCI_{ij} = 100 - \Sigma\left(\frac{m_{ik} - x_{jk}}{2}\right)$ where m_{ik} is the share of product k in country i's total imports and x_{jk} is the share of product k in country j's total exports.
3. SWOT analysis: A structured evaluation of strengths, weaknesses, opportunities, and threats was conducted to provide a comprehensive assessment of Chad's position within the AfCFTA context.

14.3.3 Limitations

The study acknowledges several limitations. First, trade data for Chad, particularly for informal cross-border trade, may be incomplete or imprecise. Second, the COVID-19 pandemic has introduced significant uncertainty into economic projections and trade patterns, potentially affecting the medium-term validity of some findings. Third, the implementation of the AfCFTA is still in progress, with many operational details yet to be finalised, creating uncertainty about the precise impact of the agreement on specific sectors and products.

14.4 Chad's Economic Structure and Trade Patterns

14.4.1 Macroeconomic Overview

Chad's economy has experienced significant volatility over the past two decades, largely driven by fluctuations in oil production and prices. Following the commencement of oil production in 2003, the economy experienced rapid growth, with the GDP growth rate reaching 31% in 2004. However, this growth has not been sustained, with the economy contracting by 3% in 2016 and achieving only modest growth of 0.7% in 2017 (World Bank, 2020b).

The sectoral composition of Chad's economy reveals the continued importance of agriculture, despite the emergence of the petroleum sector. Agriculture, including livestock, accounts for approximately 50% of GDP and employs about 80% of the workforce. The industrial sector, dominated by petroleum activities, contributes approximately 15% of GDP, while services account for the remaining 35% (INSEED, 2018).

Several structural factors, including limited infrastructure, weak institutional capacity, and vulnerability to climate change and security challenges have constrained Chad's economic development. The country's Human Development Index

(HDI) ranking of 187 out of 189 countries in 2019 underscores the significant development challenges it faces (UNDP, 2020).

14.4.2 Export Structure and Dynamics

Chad's export structure has undergone a significant transformation since the commencement of oil production in 2003. Before oil exploitation, agricultural products dominated exports, with cotton accounting for approximately 50% of export revenues and agricultural products collectively representing over 90% of exports. By 2018, petroleum products accounted for approximately 88% of export revenues, with agricultural and livestock products contributing just 10% (International Trade Centre (ITC), 2020).

Despite this transformation, several non-oil export sectors continue to demonstrate resilience and potential. Livestock exports, particularly to Nigeria and Cameroon, remain significant, with an estimated value of 140 billion FCFA annually. Gum arabic exports have grown steadily, with Chad establishing itself as the world's second-largest producer after Sudan. Other promising export products include sesame, which has experienced an annual growth rate of approximately 83% between 2012 and 2016, and cotton, which retains historical importance despite challenges (Ministry of Commerce, 2018).

The geographical orientation of Chad's exports has also evolved. Before oil production, the European Union was the primary destination for Chad's exports (77% in 2001), followed by China (8%) and the USA (7%). By 2018, the USA had become the largest market (42%), followed by the European Union (35%) and Asian countries (20%). Notably, intra-African exports remain limited, accounting for just 1% of Chad's total exports in 2018 (International Trade Centre (ITC), 2020) (Fig. 14.1).

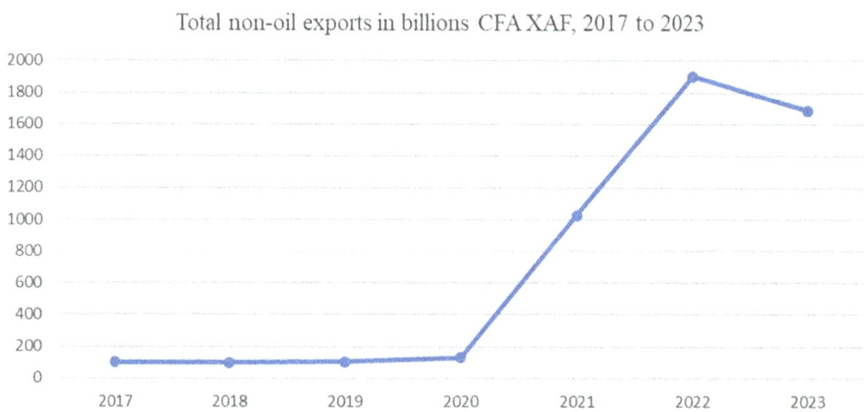

Fig. 14.1 Total exports in billions in local currency (CFA XAF), 2017–2023. Source: Author's calculations using INSEED dataset

For 2017–2020, the exports remain relatively stable, fluctuating slightly around 100–130 billion CFA XAF. However, there is a dramatic jump in 2021, reaching over 1025 billion CFA XAF, and an even higher level in 2022 near 1900 billion CFA XAF. In 2023, the value declined to approximately 1683.66 billion CFA XAF, yet the values remain an order of magnitude higher than the pre-2021 levels.

This dramatic change is worth a closer look. Factors to consider might include: shifts in export composition or emerging new export sectors and external economic factors influencing trade.

14.4.3 *Historical Analysis of Chad's Intra-African Trade Performance*

14.4.3.1 Geographic Orientation Evolution

The geographical orientation of Chad's exports has evolved significantly but remains oriented towards non-African markets. Before oil production, the European Union was the primary destination for Chad's exports (77% in 2001), followed by China (8%) and the United States (7%). By 2018, the United States had become the largest market (42%), followed by the European Union (35%) and Asian countries (20%). Notably, intra-African exports remained limited, accounting for just 1% of Chad's total exports in 2018 (International Trade Centre (ITC), 2020).

14.4.3.2 Structural Factors Limiting Intra-African Trade

1. CEMAC integration challenges: Despite being a founding member of CEMAC, Chad has not effectively leveraged this regional platform. The monetary union has facilitated some trade flows, but structural similarities among member countries have limited trade creation. Chad's trade with CEMAC partners represents less than 3% of total trade, with Cameroon being the dominant partner primarily serving as a transit corridor rather than an end market.
2. ECCAS underutilisation: Chad's participation in ECCAS has yielded minimal trade benefits. The organisation's focus on political integration rather than trade facilitation, combined with ongoing conflicts in several member states, has limited its effectiveness as a trade promotion mechanism.
3. Bilateral agreement limitations: Chad has signed bilateral trade agreements with several African countries, including Nigeria, Sudan, and Libya. However, implementation has been constrained by infrastructure limitations, bureaucratic obstacles, and security concerns, particularly along the Nigeria-Chad and Sudan-Chad borders.

14.4.3.3 Informal Cross-Border Trade Dynamics

Despite limited formal intra-African trade, Chad engages in substantial informal cross-border trade, particularly in livestock, agricultural products, and consumer goods. Estimates suggest that informal trade may represent 30–40% of total cross-border flows, particularly with Cameroon, Nigeria, and Sudan (CILSS, 2016). This informal trade reflects underlying comparative advantages that could be formalised and expanded under the AfCFTA framework.

14.4.4 Import Structure and Regional Dependencies

Chad's imports are dominated by industrial products, machinery, vehicles, and processed foods. Between 2001 and 2018, industrial products consistently represented over 70% of total imports. The geographical sources of imports have diversified over time, with Asian countries (particularly China) gaining market share at the expense of European and American suppliers. By 2018, Asian countries accounted for 34% of Chad's imports, followed by the European Union (28%) and the United States (23%) (International Trade Centre (ITC), 2020).

Regional trade patterns reveal Chad's dependence on neighbouring countries for certain imports. Cameroon supplies refined sugar (33% of imports from Cameroon), diesel (16%), cement (8%), and soap (6%). Nigeria provides petroleum products (over 50% of imports from Nigeria), along with various manufactured goods. These patterns highlight the potential for enhanced regional integration through the AfCFTA (Ministry of Commerce, 2018).

14.4.5 Services Trade

Although data on Chad's services trade remains limited, available information indicates significant import dependency in key service sectors, including transportation, business services, and telecommunications. The country's service exports are minimal, with some activity in tourism and business services. The underdevelopment of Chad's services sector represents both a challenge and an opportunity in the context of the AfCFTA, which includes provisions for liberalising trade in services (UNCTAD, 2019).

14.5 Identifying Sectors with Comparative Advantage and Export Potential

14.5.1 Results of Revealed Comparative Advantage Analysis

Our analysis of revealed comparative advantage (RCA) indices for Chad's exports identifies 11 product categories where the country demonstrates comparative advantage (RCA > 1). These products include:

1. Gum arabic (RCA = 167.4).
2. Sesame seeds (RCA = 42.3).
3. Raw cotton (RCA = 38.7).
4. Crude petroleum oils (RCA = 12.5).
5. Live animals (RCA = 8.9).
6. Cotton fabrics and fibres (RCA = 7.2).
7. Cereals, particularly maize (RCA = 6.8).
8. Preserved fruits and fruit juices (RCA = 3.6).
9. Sugar products (RCA = 2.4).
10. Vegetable oils (RCA = 1.7).
11. Leather and hides (RCA = 1.5).

These findings align with previous studies by the World Bank and other institutions that have identified similar patterns of comparative advantage in Chad's export structure. The high RCA values for agricultural products such as gum arabic and sesame seeds indicate significant potential for export expansion in these sectors.

14.5.2 Priority Sectors for AfCFTA Engagement

Based on our analysis of comparative advantages, market potential, and alignment with national development priorities, we identify five priority sectors for Chad's engagement in the AfCFTA:

1. Livestock and meat products: Chad possesses one of Africa's largest livestock populations, with over 93.8 million heads of cattle, sheep, goats, and camels. The livestock sector neighbouring countries, particularly Nigeria and Cameroon. The AfCFTA presents opportunities to formalise and expand these trade flows, develop value-added processing (such as meat processing and leather goods), and access new markets in West and North Africa.
2. Gum arabic and natural gums: As the world's second-largest producer of gum arabic, Chad has substantial potential to increase production and add value through processing. The global market for natural gums is expanding due to growing demand in the food, pharmaceutical, and cosmetic industries. The AfCFTA could facilitate improved access to processing technologies, regional

value chain integration, and direct market access to African pharmaceutical and food processing industries.

3. Oilseeds and vegetable oils: Chad's production of sesame, groundnuts, and shea nuts has grown significantly in recent years, driven by favourable growing conditions and increasing international demand. These products offer opportunities for value addition through processing into oils and other derivatives. Regional markets in North and West Africa, accessed through the AfCFTA, could provide important outlets for these products.
4. Cotton and textiles: Despite challenges, cotton remains an important export crop for Chad. The AfCFTA could support the revitalisation of the textile industry through improved access to regional markets, integration into regional value chains, and potential collaboration with more advanced textile producers in North and East Africa.
5. Petroleum products and petrochemicals: While crude petroleum dominates Chad's exports, opportunities exist to develop downstream industries producing refined petroleum products and basic petrochemicals. The AfCFTA could facilitate regional market access for these products, particularly in neighbouring countries that currently import refined products from outside Africa.

14.5.3 Chad's Export Powerhouses: Strategic Analysis of Comparative Advantage Sectors (2017–2023)

The data reveal compelling evidence of Chad's evolving export dynamics across three strategic agricultural commodities, where the country holds a significant comparative advantage. Sesame and cotton have emerged as transformative export pillars, both experiencing substantial growth and demonstrating resilience in the face of global market volatility. Meanwhile, Arabic gum exports have followed a concerning downward trajectory. This analysis examines the performance, competitive dynamics, and strategic implications for these critical exports.

Sesame exports have undergone remarkable expansion, growing 219% from 8.36 billion in 2017 to 26.68 billion in 2023. This performance demonstrates: (1) Exceptional growth momentum—The value tripled between 2017 and 2021, reaching a peak of 34.41 billion in 2021; (2) Post-pandemic resilience—despite the 35% decline in 2022, exports rebounded by 20% in 2023, and (3) Market positioning strength—The consistent double-digit performance since 2019 confirms Chad's growing influence in global sesame markets. The data that Chad has successfully captured the expanding global demand for sesame, driven by increased consumption in food industries, health-conscious markets, and Asian economies. This growth trajectory positions sesame as Chad's premier agricultural export with significant potential for further value-addition opportunities.

Cotton exports demonstrate the most dramatic transformation among Chad's key commodities, with a remarkable 243% increase from 7.38 billion in 2017 to 25.35

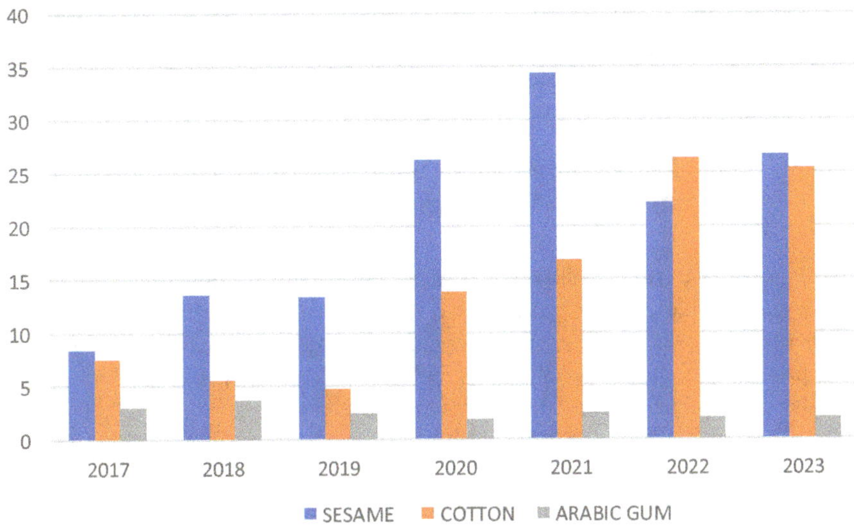

Fig. 14.2 Export performance (in billions) of goods for which Chad exhibits a comparative advantage, 2017–2023. Source: Author's calculations using the INSEED dataset

billion in 2023. The performance reveals: (1) Exceptional recovery resilience—after initial decline (2017–2019), cotton exports nearly tripled in 2020; (2) Strategic market positioning—continued strong growth through 2021, with a remarkable 57% jump in 2022; and (3) Stability establishment—the minor 4% decline in 2023 suggests stabilisation at this new, much higher plateau. Cotton's exceptional performance likely reflects Chad's success in addressing production constraints, quality improvements, strategic market diversification, and possibly favourable price dynamics in international markets. This transformation makes cotton a cornerstone of Chad's future agricultural exports.

In stark contrast to sesame and cotton, Arabic gum exports have shown a troubling 34% decline, from $ 2.94 billion in 2017 to $ 1.94 billion in 2023. The data indicates: (1) Structural decline pattern—after a brief rise in 2018, exports show a consistent downward trend; (2) Limited pandemic recovery—unlike other commodities, gum exports failed to rebound meaningfully post-pandemic and (3) competitive position erosion—stable but low values in 2022–2023 suggest Chad is losing market share.

This trajectory raises critical concerns about Chad's competitive position in the Arabic gum market, particularly increasing. The decline likely reflects a combination of production challenges, quality issues, market access limitations, and competition from other countries that produce similar products.

In conclusion, Chad's export performance in its comparative advantage sectors shows both impressive success stories and concerning challenges. Sesame and cotton have transformed into powerful export engines with continued growth potential, while Arabic gum requires urgent intervention to reverse its decline (Fig. 14.2).

Now, it is essential to examine with whom Chad trades in Africa for products where it has a comparative advantage.

14.5.4 Strategic Analysis: Chad's Intra-African Trade Patterns in Comparative Advantage Products (2017–2023)

The data reveals critical patterns in Chad's intra-African trade for its three key export commodities: cotton, sesame, and Arabic gum. These patterns demonstrate distinct trading relationships, market concentrations, and vulnerability points that have profound implications for Chad's regional trade strategy. This analysis examines these trade dynamics and their strategic significance.

14.5.4.1 Arabic Gum: Regional Trade Collapse in a Declining Sector

The Arabic gum data reveals the most concerning pattern of all three commodities:

- Market evaporation: Virtually all regional trading relationships have deteriorated to minimal levels.
- Nigeria's fluctuation: The only relatively active trading partner, Nigeria, shows extreme volatility with no stable pattern.
- Negligible volumes: By 2023, only Nigeria remains as a measurable destination at just 0.0675 billion, representing only 3.5% of Chad's total Arabic gum exports.
- Structural decline: The collapse in regional trade mirrors the overall sector decline (from 2.94 billion in 2017 to 1.94 billion in 2023).

This pattern suggests a fundamental loss of competitiveness in regional markets, likely due to quality issues, pricing challenges, or supply constraints. The data indicates Chad's Arabic gum sector faces existential challenges in maintaining its regional market position (Table 14.1).

Table 14.1 Evolution of regional trade in Chad's arabic gum (2017–2023)

Country/Year	2017	2018	2019	2020	2021	2022	2023
Cameroon	0.094	0.04	0.018		0.006	0.033	
Niger						0.0048	
Nigeria	0.062	0.21		0.009		0.0012	0.0675
Sudan	0.007				0.001	0.0085	

Source: Author's calculations using the INSEED dataset

14.5.4.2 Sesame: Shifting Regional Dynamics with Diversification Challenges

Chad's sesame exports reveal a complex regional trading pattern with significant transitions:

- Nigeria's diminishing role: Nigeria has shifted from dominant partner (2.79 billion in 2017, representing 33% of total exports) to relatively minor player (0.34 billion in 2023, just 1.3% of total).
- Egypt's emerging importance: Egypt has developed into a significant market with fluctuating but substantial volumes, peaking at 1.03 billion in 2020.
- Sudan's volatility: Sudan emerged as a major destination by 2021 (1.01 billion) but virtually disappeared from the export map by 2023.
- Limited penetration in North Africa: Despite some presence in Egypt, Algeria, and Libya, these markets remain underdeveloped relative to their potential.

This pattern suggests a concerning trend of declining intra-African trade for Chad's sesame, with regional exports representing a diminishing share of total exports. The substantial growth in overall sesame exports (from 8.36 billion to 26.68 billion) indicates that Chad is increasingly oriented towards global rather than regional markets for this commodity (Table 14.2).

14.5.4.3 Cotton: Concentrated Dependency on Cameroon

Chad's cotton exports in the Africa region demonstrate an extreme concentration pattern with remarkable implications:

- Cameroon dominance: Cameroon has emerged as the overwhelmingly dominant destination, absorbing 21.7 billion in cotton exports in 2023, representing over 85% of Chad's total cotton exports.
- Explosive growth trajectory: Cameroon-bound exports have surged by an extraordinary 2200% from 0.94 billion in 2017 to 21.7 billion in 2023.

Table 14.2 Evolution of regional trade in Chad's sesame (2017–2023)

Country/year	2017	2018	2019	2020	2021	2022	2023
Cameroon	0.05	0.55	0.10	0.08	0.24	0.35	0.13
Central Africa, Republic			0.09				
Algeria			0.0095	0.036		0.011	
Egypt		0.50	0.057	1.03	0.34	0.32	0.79
Libya	0.01	0.02	0.20	0.09	0.07	0.105	0.05
Niger	0.014						
Nigeria	2.79	3.81	1.51	0.53	0.90	1.42	0.34
Seychelles		0.025					
Sudan		0.41	0.28	0.11	1.01	0.018	

Source: Author's calculations using the INSEED dataset

Table 14.3 Evolution of regional trade in Chad's cotton (2017–2023)

Country/year	2017	2018	2019	2020	2021	2022	2023
Cameroon	0.94	3.53		7.43	8.75	10.95	21.7
Niger							0.006
Nigeria	1.33	0.031			0.13	0.001	0.077

Source: Author's calculations using INSEED dataset

- Negligible diversification: Other African markets remain marginal, with Nigeria's share declining dramatically and Niger representing a minimal destination (0.006 billion in 2023).

This extreme concentration creates a precarious dependency on a single market channel, making Chad's cotton sector highly vulnerable to Cameroon's economic conditions, policy changes, or bilateral relations. The data suggest that Cameroon likely serves as a transit hub rather than an end-consumer, indicating that Chad's cotton ultimately reaches global markets through this corridor (Table 14.3).

Chad's comparative advantage in these sectors can only translate to sustainable economic benefits if supported by strategic market diversification, reduced transit dependency, and stronger regional trade partnerships. Without addressing these fundamental challenges, the country risks continued vulnerability despite its production strengths in these key commodities.

14.5.5 Services Sectors with Development Potential

The AfCFTA's inclusion of services liberalisation presents opportunities for Chad to develop capacity in specific service sectors:

1. Transport and logistics services: Chad's strategic location at the crossroads of North, Central, and West Africa positions it to develop transit and logistics services. Investment in transportation infrastructure, combined with simplified border procedures under the AfCFTA, could enhance this potential.
2. Tourism services: Chad possesses unique natural and cultural attractions, including the Lakes of Ounianga (UNESCO World Heritage site), the Ennedi Plateau, and diverse wildlife in national parks like Zakouma. The AfCFTA's provisions on the movement of persons could facilitate regional tourism development.
3. Business services: With appropriate skills development and digital connectivity, Chad could develop capacity in specific business services, including accounting, consulting, and data processing.
4. Telecommunications services: The ongoing expansion of digital infrastructure, including fibre optic connectivity, creates potential for growth in telecommunications and digital services.

14.6 Challenges and Constraints for Chad in the AfCFTA Context

14.6.1 *Infrastructure Deficits*

Chad's infrastructure deficits represent a significant constraint to effective participation in the AfCFTA. The country's road network is severely limited, with only 2400 km of paved roads out of a total network of 40,000 km. This inadequate transportation infrastructure results in high logistics costs and significant delays in moving goods within the country and to international markets (African Development Bank, 2019).

Energy infrastructure is similarly underdeveloped, with an installed capacity of approximately 200 MW and an electrification rate of just 6.4% (0.6% in rural areas). This limited and unreliable electricity supply constrains industrial development and increases production costs (Ministry of Energy, 2018).

Digital infrastructure also remains inadequate, with internet penetration rates of approximately 12.5% and limited 3G/4G coverage, primarily in urban areas. The high cost of telecommunications services further constrains the development of digital trade and services (International Trade Centre (ITC), 2020).

14.6.2 *Limited Productive Capacity*

Chad's limited productive capacity capitalising for a significant challenge for capitalising on AfCFTA opportunities. The country's industrial sector is underdeveloped, accounting for less than 15% of GDP, with manufacturing contributing just 2.4%. This limited industrial base constrains the country's ability to produce competitive goods for regional markets and participate in regional value chains (UNIDO, 2020).

The agricultural sector, while important in terms of employment and contribution to GDP, is characterised by low productivity, limited use of modern inputs, and vulnerability to climate variability. These factors consistent surpluses for export markets (FAO, 2019).

Human capital limitations further exacerbate constraints on productive capacity. Educational attainment remains low, with an average of 6 years of schooling, and significant gaps in technical and vocational skills relevant to industrial development and services provision (World Bank, 2018b).

14.6.3 Trade Facilitation and Logistics Challenges

Chad faces substantial challenges in trade facilitation and logistics. The country ranked 151st out of 160 countries in the World Bank (2018a) Logistics Performance Index, with particularly low scores for infrastructure, international shipments, and logistics competence. Border procedures remain cumbersome, with numerous formal and informal checkpoints adding to costs and delays.

As a landlocked country, Chad relies on transit corridors through Cameroon (specifically, the Douala Port) and, to a lesser extent, through Libya, Nigeria, and Sudan. These transit arrangements involve complex procedures and high costs, with transportation from Douala to N'Djamena estimated to account for 30–40% of the value of imported goods (World Bank, 2018b).

14.6.4 Historical Regional Trade Agreement Underutilisation

Chad's limited success in leveraging existing regional trade agreements represents a critical constraint:

1. CEMAC limitations: Despite monetary integration through the CFA franc, trade creation within CEMAC has been minimal. Chad's trade with CEMAC partners remains below potential due to similar production structures, limited industrial development, and inadequate intra-regional infrastructure.
2. ECCAS ineffectiveness: The Economic Community of Central African States has failed to deliver meaningful trade benefits for Chad due to political instability in member countries, weak institutional capacity, and limited implementation of trade facilitation measures.
3. Bilateral agreement implementation gaps: Various bilateral trade agreements with Nigeria, Sudan, and other neighbours have yielded limited results due to poor implementation, bureaucratic obstacles, and security concerns along border areas.

14.6.5 Institutional and Regulatory Constraints

Institutional and regulatory constraints further complicate Chad's participation in the AfCFTA. The business environment presents significant challenges, with Chad ranking 182nd out of 190 countries in the World Bank's Doing Business 2020 report. Key issues include:

- Complex business registration procedures.
- Difficulties in contract enforcement.
- Limited access to finance.

- Corruption and governance challenges.
- Weak property rights protection.

Regulatory frameworks for key sectors, including agriculture, industry, and services, often lack coherence and effective implementation. Standards and certification systems remain underdeveloped, potentially limiting the ability of Chadian products to access regional markets under the AfCFTA (Ministry of Commerce, 2018).

14.6.6 *Fiscal Implications*

The implementation of the AfCFTA will have significant fiscal implications for Chad, which relies heavily on trade taxes for government revenue. Customs duties represented approximately 11.8% of total tax revenue in 2017, and the progressive elimination of tariffs on intra-African trade could result in substantial revenue losses. While the AfCFTA includes flexibility mechanisms for least developed countries (LDCs), such as Chad, including more extended implementation periods and sensitive product exemptions, the fiscal impact remains a significant concern (Olufowobi, 2023).

14.7 Strategic Framework for Chad's AfCFTA Implementation

Based on our analysis of Chad's comparative advantages, constraints, and the broader AfCFTA context, we propose a strategic framework for maximising the country's benefits from continental trade liberalisation. This framework comprises five interconnected pillars, each addressing specific aspects of Chad's AfCFTA preparation and implementation.

14.7.1 *Strategic Pillar 1: Addressing Historical Regional Trade Integration Failures*

To overcome historical constraints that have limited Chad's intra-African trade participation, specific interventions are required:

1. Revitalise CEMAC engagement: Develop a comprehensive strategy to leverage monetary union benefits through enhanced trade facilitation, harmonised standards, and coordinated infrastructure development within the CEMAC framework.

2. Strengthen bilateral trade mechanisms: Establish effective implementation and monitoring mechanisms for existing bilateral trade agreements, with particular focus on Nigeria-Chad and Sudan-Chad trade corridors.
3. Formalise informal trade flows: Develop simplified trading regimes to capture and formalise the substantial informal cross-border trade, particularly in livestock and agricultural products.
4. Build regional trade capacity: Establish specialised units within relevant ministries to focus exclusively on regional trade development and AfCFTA implementation.

14.7.2 Strategic Pillar 2: Enhancing Production Capacity in Priority Sectors

To capitalise on market access opportunities under the AfCFTA, Chad must enhance productive capacity in sectors with demonstrated comparative advantage. Key strategic interventions include:

1. Develop sector-specific investment promotion strategies for livestock, gum arabic, oilseeds, cotton, and petroleum derivatives, targeting both domestic and international investors with tailored incentives and support mechanisms.
2. Establish specialised agricultural development zones with appropriate infrastructure and extension services to boost productivity and quality in export-oriented agricultural value chains.
3. Create a dedicated industrial development fund to support modernisation and capacity expansion in priority manufacturing sectors, with a focus on value addition for agricultural and livestock products.
4. Implement targeted skills development programmes aligned with the needs of priority sectors, focusing on technical and vocational training, quality management, and export marketing.
5. Develop a national quality infrastructure system to ensure Chadian products meet regional and international standards, including testing laboratories, certification bodies, and standards information services.

14.7.3 Strategic Pillar 3: Addressing Infrastructure and Logistics Constraints

Overcoming infrastructure deficits is essential for enhancing Chad's competitiveness within the AfCFTA framework. Priority interventions include:

1. Develop strategic trade corridors linking production zones to domestic markets and international gateway points, with prioritisation based on economic impact and export potential.
2. Establish specialised logistics platforms at key border crossings and in major production zones to facilitate storage, consolidation, and efficient movement of export goods.
3. Accelerate energy infrastructure development in industrial zones and agricultural processing areas, with a focus on renewable energy solutions where feasible.
4. Strengthen digital infrastructure to support e-commerce and digital trade, including expanded broadband access and digital payment systems.
5. Enhance regional infrastructure coordination through active participation in regional initiatives like the Programme for Infrastructure Development in Africa (PIDA) and the Central African Economic and Monetary Community (CEMAC) infrastructure programmes.

14.7.4 Strategic Pillar 4: Trade Facilitation and Border Management

Simplifying and modernising trade procedures is critical for reducing trade costs and enhancing Chad's participation in regional markets. Key initiatives include:

1. Implement a comprehensive National Trade Facilitation Programme aligned with the WTO Trade Facilitation Agreement and AfCFTA Protocol on Trade Facilitation.
2. Establish a modern Single Window system for trade operations, integrating customs, standards, and other border agencies to streamline procedures.
3. Develop simplified regimes for small-scale traders, particularly women involved in cross-border trade, to formalise and facilitate their participation in regional markets.
4. Strengthen cooperation with transit countries through bilateral agreements and regional frameworks to reduce transit costs and delays.

14.7.5 Strategic Pillar 5: Regional Value Chain Integration

Promoting Chad's integration into regional value chains represents a critical pathway for capturing value-added opportunities under the AfCFTA. Key strategic interventions include:

1. Identify and target specific regional value chains with high potential for Chad's participation, including livestock/leather, cotton/textiles, and oilseeds/vegetable oils.
2. Develop targeted supplier development programmes to enhance the capacity of Chadian SMEs to meet the requirements of regional value chain lead firms.
3. Establish strategic partnerships with key regional firms in priority value chains through business matchmaking, joint ventures, and investment promotion.
4. Enhance trade finance and supply chain finance mechanisms to facilitate participation in regional value chains.

14.8 Conclusion and Policy Recommendations

14.8.1 Conclusion

This study has examined Chad's strategic positioning within the emerging African Continental Free Trade Area, analysing the country's comparative advantages, constraints, and potential pathways for maximising benefits from continental trade liberalisation. Our analysis identifies significant opportunities for Chad to leverage its natural resource endowments, agricultural potential, and strategic location to enhance trade performance and economic diversification through the AfCFTA.

The research highlights several sectors with demonstrated comparative advantage and export potential, including livestock and meat products, gum arabic, oilseeds, cotton, and petroleum derivatives. These sectors align with national development priorities and offer opportunities for value addition and integration into regional value chains. Additionally, the study identifies emerging opportunities in the services sector, including transport, tourism, and business services.

However, the analysis also reveals substantial challenges that may constrain Chad's ability to capitalise on AfCFTA opportunities. These include significant infrastructure deficits, limited productive capacity, trade facilitation and logistics challenges, institutional and regulatory constraints, and fiscal concerns related to tariff liberalisation. Addressing these challenges requires a comprehensive and coordinated approach, as outlined in the strategic framework proposed in this study.

The findings contribute to the broader literature on trade policy in landlocked developing countries and provide evidence-based insights for policymakers navigating regional integration processes. The study underscores the importance of complementary policies and investments to ensure that trade liberalisation generates inclusive and sustainable benefits.

14.8.2 Policy Recommendations

Based on our findings, we propose the following policy recommendations:

For the government of Chad:

1. Develop and adopt a comprehensive AfCFTA Implementation Strategy that explicitly addresses historical constraints on intra-African trade participation and articulates clear mechanisms for regional market integration.
2. Establish dedicated institutional mechanisms for AfCFTA coordination, including a high-level implementation committee with specific mandates for regional trade development.
3. Prioritise infrastructure investments that directly support export development and regional connectivity, with particular focus on transport corridors linking to multiple African markets.
4. Implement targeted industrial policies to support the development of priority sectors with export potential, moving beyond the current petroleum-centric model.
5. Accelerate trade facilitation reforms to reduce the time and cost of cross-border trade, particularly through simplified procedures for small-scale traders engaged in informal regional trade.

For regional economic communities and the AfCFTA secretariat:

1. Develop specific support mechanisms for countries with historically limited intra-African trade participation, including technical assistance and targeted infrastructure investments.
2. Strengthen monitoring and evaluation frameworks to track the distribution of benefits from the AfCFTA and identify countries requiring additional support.
3. Enhance coordination between the AfCFTA and existing regional integration arrangements to ensure coherence and address implementation gaps that have limited regional trade development.

For development partners:

1. Align development assistance with AfCFTA implementation priorities, focusing on productive capacity, infrastructure, and trade facilitation investments that address historical regional trade constraints.
2. Support the development of regional value chains that include previously marginalised producers through technical assistance and market linkage programmes.
3. Provide targeted support for trade-related capacity building, particularly in areas of standards compliance and regional market development.

The successful implementation of the AfCFTA presents a significant opportunity for Chad to overcome historical constraints on regional trade participation and diversify its economy. Realising this potential will require strategic vision, coordinated policy interventions, and sustained commitment from all stakeholders to address the structural factors that have limited Chad's integration into African markets.

The successful implementation of the AfCFTA presents a significant opportunity for Chad to diversify its economy, enhance trade performance, and accelerate sustainable development. Realising this potential will require strategic vision, coordinated policy interventions, and sustained commitment from all stakeholders. The framework and recommendations presented in this study aim to contribute to this important endeavour.

References

Abrego, L., Amoz, M., Patillo, C., Presbitero, A., Stucka, T., & Toscani, F. (2020). *The African continental free trade area: Potential economic impact and challenges*. IMF Staff Discussion Note, SDN/20/04.

African Development Bank. (2019). *Chad economic outlook: Macroeconomic performance and prospects*. Abidjan, Côte d'Ivoire.

Arvis, J. F., Raballand, G., & Marteau, J. F. (2011). *The cost of being landlocked: Logistics costs and supply chain reliability*. World Bank Publications.

Avom, D., & Gbetnkom, D. (2018). CEMAC trade integration: What are the obstacles? *Journal of Economic Integration, 33*(2), 1465–1489.

Balassa, B. (1961). *The theory of economic integration*. Richard D. Irwin.

Balassa, B. (1965). Trade liberalisation and "Revealed" comparative advantage. *The Manchester School, 33*(2), 99–123.

Behnke, R. (2012). *The economics of pastoral livestock production in Sudan*. Feinstein International Center, Tufts University.

Borchert, I., Gootiiz, B., Grover, A., & Mattoo, A. (2012). Landlocked or policy locked? How services trade protection deepens economic isolation. World Bank Policy Research Working Paper, 5942.

Christ, N., & Ferrantino, M. J. (2011). Land transport for export: The effects of cost, time, and uncertainty in Sub-Saharan Africa. *World Development, 39*(10), 1749–1759.

CILSS. (2016). *Cross-border trade in the Sahel Region*. Permanent Interstate Committee for Drought Control in the Sahel.

Cogneau, D., & Mesplé-Somps, S. (2007). Inequality of opportunity for income in five countries of Africa. *Research on Economic Inequality, 15*, 99–128.

Draper, P. (2013). *The shifting geography of global value chains: Implications for developing countries and trade policy*. World Economic Forum.

Fabricius, P. (2020). *What's holding up Africa's free trade area?* Institute for Security Studies.

FAO. (2019). *Agricultural transformation in Chad: Challenges and opportunities*. Food and Agriculture Organization of the United Nations.

Faye, M. L., McArthur, J. W., Sachs, J. D., & Snow, T. (2004). The challenges facing landlocked developing countries. *Journal of Human Development, 5*(1), 31–68.

Foroutan, F., & Pritchett, L. (1993). Intra-Sub-Saharan African trade: Is it too little? *Journal of African Economies, 2*(1), 74–105.

Giraud, P. N. (2013). *The gum Arabic economy in Chad: Constraints and challenges*. Paris School of International Affairs.

IMF. (2019). *Regional economic outlook: Sub-Saharan Africa*. International Monetary Fund.

INSEED. (2018). *Annual statistical report*. National Institute of Statistics, Economic and Demographic Studies, N'Djamena, Chad.

International Trade Centre (ITC). (2020). *Trade map - Trade statistics for international business development*. www.trademap.org

Koerner, R., & Cook, S. (2017). Trade patterns in francophone Africa: The role of historical links. *Journal of African Economies, 26*(3), 294–318.

Koussou, M. O., Duteurtre, G., & Djamen, P. (2012). The development of dairy value chains in Chad. *Livestock Research for Rural Development, 24*, 9.

Krugman, P. (1991). Increasing returns and economic geography. *Journal of Political Economy, 99*(3), 483–499.

Limão, N., & Venables, A. J. (2001). Infrastructure, geographical disadvantage, transport costs, and trade. *The World Bank Economic Review, 15*(3), 451–479.

Luke, D., & MacLeod, J. (2019). *Inclusive trade in Africa: The African continental free trade area in comparative perspective*. Routledge.

Magrin, G. (2013). The Chad oil experience: An economic success story? *Review of African Political Economy, 40*(137), 503–516.

Mevel, S., & Karingi, S. (2012). *Deepening regional integration in Africa: A computable general equilibrium assessment of the establishment of a continental free trade area followed by a continental customs union. Selected paper for the 7th African Economic Conference.*

Ministry of Commerce. (2018). *National trade strategy of Chad*. Ministry of Commerce and Industry, Republic of Chad.

Ministry of Energy. (2018). *Energy sector development strategy*. Ministry of Petroleum and Energy, Republic of Chad.

Mustapha, M. B. (2017). Sesame value chain development in Chad: Challenges and prospects. *Journal of Agricultural Extension, 21*(3), 128–139.

Olufowobi, O. (2023). THE AFRICAN CONTINENTAL FREE TRADE AGREEMENT (Af C FTA)-TAX MATTERS ARISING. Available at SSRN 5267860.

Raballand, G., & Kunaka, C. (2011). *The impact of regional liberalisation and harmonisation in road transport: The case of the Central African economic and monetary union*. World Bank Policy Research Working Paper, 5614.

Saygili, M., Peters, R., & Knebel, C. (2018). *African continental free trade area: Challenges and opportunities of tariff reductions*. UNCTAD Research Paper No. 15.

Shepherd, B., & Wilson, J. S. (2006). Road infrastructure in Europe and Central Asia: Does network quality affect trade? World Bank Policy Research Working Paper, 4104.

Signé, L. (2018). *African continental free trade area: Challenges and opportunities of tariff reductions*. Brookings Africa Growth Initiative.

Songwe, V., Moyo, B., & Muriuki, M. (2019). *The African continental free trade area: An opportunity for informal cross-border trade*. Brookings Institution.

UNCTAD. (2013). Economic development in Africa report 2013: Intra-African trade - Unlocking private sector dynamism. In *United Nations Conference on Trade and Development.*

UNCTAD. (2019). Services trade in Africa. In *United Nations Conference on Trade and Development.*

UNDP. (2020). *Human development report 2020*. United Nations Development Programme.

UNECA. (2018). *An empirical assessment of the African continental free trade area modalities on goods*. United Nations Economic Commission for Africa.

UNECA. (2020). *Creating a unified regional market: Towards the implementation of the African continental free trade area in Central Africa*. United Nations Economic Commission for Africa.

UNIDO. (2020). *Competitive industrial performance report 2020*. United Nations Industrial Development Organization.

Venables, A. J. (2003). Winners and losers from regional integration agreements. *Economic Journal, 113*(490), 747–761.

Viner, J. (1950). *The customs union issue*. Carnegie Endowment for International Peace.

World Bank. (2015). *Republic of Chad: Diagnostic trade integration study (DTIS) update*. World Bank.

World Bank. (2018a). *Logistics performance index: Connecting to compete*. World Bank.

World Bank. (2018b). *Republic of Chad systematic country diagnostic: Priorities for ending extreme poverty and promoting shared prosperity*. World Bank.

World Bank. (2020a). *Doing business 2020*. World Bank.

World Bank. (2020b). *The African continental free trade area: Economic and distributional effects*. World Bank.

Chapter 15
Bridging Isolation Through Continental Integration: Africa's SIDS in the AfCFTA

Sawkut Rojid and Tasneem Wafiiqah Rojid

Abstract This paper critically assesses the prospects and limitations of Africa's Small Island Developing States (SIDS)—Cape Verde, Comoros, Madagascar, Mauritius, São Tomé and Príncipe, and Seychelles—within the framework of the African Continental Free Trade Area (AfCFTA). Despite the AfCFTA's potential to enhance intra-African trade, reduce barriers, and foster economic integration, African SIDS face structural challenges that inhibit their full participation. These include geographic remoteness, limited economies of scale, narrow export bases, underdeveloped infrastructure, and heightened climate vulnerability. Through a comparative analysis, the study reveals significant disparities in institutional capacity, regional connectivity, and integration readiness across the island states. The paper argues for the implementation of targeted interventions such as flexible rules of origin, accelerated liberalisation of services, strategic infrastructure investment, and a dedicated AfCFTA support mechanism for SIDS. Moreover, it identifies strategic niches—digital trade, blue economy, regional tourism, and service exports—through which African SIDS can strengthen their contribution to continental value chains. The findings highlight the urgency of a differentiated integration strategy that recognises the specific developmental needs of island economies. Ensuring their meaningful inclusion is not only essential for their resilience and growth but also for the overall equity and credibility of the AfCFTA.

Keywords African continental free trade area (AfCFTA) · Small island developing states (SIDS) · Regional integration · Trade policy · Regional value chains · Climate vulnerability · Africa

---

S. Rojid (✉)
Ministry of Tertiary Education, Science and Research, Ebene, Mauritius

T. W. Rojid
United Nation Industrial Development Organization (UNIDO), Vienna, Austria

D. N. Yuni et al. (eds.), *From Policy to Practice: Challenges and Ways Forward on the Implementation of the AfCFTA*,
https://doi.org/10.1007/978-3-032-14051-7_15

15.1 Introduction

The AfCFTA presents a transformative mix of opportunities and challenges for African nations, though their impact will vary widely across the continent. Africa's six island states [or small island developing states (SIDS) as they are often referred to)]—Cape Verde, Comoros, Madagascar, Mauritius, São Tomé and Príncipe, and Seychelles contend with more limited prospects and disproportionately severe challenges relative to other nations on the continent.

The AfCFTA aims to remove trade barriers and harmonise the rules of trade across the African continent. Its key pillars—such as the liberalisation of goods and services, rules of origin, investment protocols, and dispute settlement mechanisms—are designed to facilitate deeper economic integration.

Like in the case of other African countries, AfCFTA offers enormous opportunities for Africa's SIDS. Particularly, it offers a potential mechanism for "bridging" SIDS isolation. However, to benefit from the AfCFTA, Africa's SIDS must overcome structural and institutional constraints that hinder effective participation. Africa's SIDS occupy a unique and often underrepresented space in continental development discourse. These Africa SIDS face several constraints hindering their ability to take full advantage of the expanded market access under the AfCFTA. These include

- Limitations in realising economies of scale due to their small market size and resource constraints,
- Geographical isolation leading to higher transportation costs to mainland Africa, and.
- Relatively narrow production bases, although these bases differ considerably among the countries. These combined.

These countries face a distinctive set of vulnerabilities. They struggle to fully integrate into the regional value chains offered by AfCFTA. Their unique set of challenges that in fact threaten their sustainability include:

- Their vulnerability to climate change, particularly rising sea levels and increased frequency of extreme weather events like hurricanes, which can devastate infrastructure and livelihoods.
- Their limited terrestrial natural resources, with limited arable land, minerals, and forests or large marine resources which have not yet been fully tapped into the sustainable use, due to a lack of technology, investment, infrastructure, or capacity. However, marine resources face environmental degradation, including coastal erosion, coral reef damage, and pollution, which together weaken the ecosystems that provide food, protect against storms, and support tourism.
- Their frequent natural disasters, like cyclones, droughts, and floods, destroy infrastructure, disrupt economies, and exacerbate environmental damage.
- Their underdeveloped infrastructure in terms of transportation, energy, water supply, and communication systems limit economic growth and the ability to exploit resources efficiently. The only exception is Mauritius.

While the AfCFTA holds the promise of reconfiguring Africa's economic geography, the extent to which Africa's SIDS can benefit from this integration initiative remains uncertain without deliberate policy attention and tailored support.

This chapter critically assesses the structural constraints facing these island economies, evaluates the opportunities presented by the AfCFTA, and identifies the conditions under which these countries can participate meaningfully in continental value chains and markets. By focusing on Africa's SIDS, this analysis addresses a critical gap in the AfCFTA policy narrative. It argues that the successful integration of these states into the continental framework will not only enhance their economic resilience but also serve as a test case for the inclusivity and adaptability of the AfCFTA itself.

15.2 Comparative Economic and Social Profile of African SIDS

African SIDS exhibit diverse economic structures, development levels, and demographic dynamics. These island economies are defined by their small populations, limited natural resources, and geographic isolation, which collectively result in constrained domestic markets and a strong dependence on external economic linkages. Their economies are among the most open in the world, relying heavily on imports for consumption and capital goods, as well as exports or remittances to earn foreign exchange.

On the social front, human capital development is uneven across African SIDS. Mauritius and Seychelles boast high literacy rates, good health indicators, and access to tertiary education, allowing them to pursue service-based economic models. Mauritius and Seychelles have high Human Development Index (HDI) scores of 0.802 and 0.796, respectively. On the other hand, Comoros and São Tomé and Príncipe face challenges related to limited access to quality education, high youth unemployment, and brain drain. These constraints limit local innovation and reduce the ability to scale high-productivity sectors that require technical skills or digital capacity. Life expectancy is highest in Mauritius (75.6 years) and lowest in Comoros (64.7 years). Fertility rates remain high in the Comoros, Madagascar, and São Tomé (around 4 births per woman), which drives faster population growth and poses an additional strain on social services.

Economic performance varies widely. Seychelles and Mauritius lead the region in terms of GDP per capita, at approximately USD 22,000 and USD 10,900, respectively (Table 15.1), driven by robust services sectors including tourism, finance, and ICT. In contrast, Madagascar has the lowest GDP per capita (USD 575), reflecting a large population and an economy still reliant on agriculture and extractives. Chart 1 presents the growth rates for these countries for the period 2005–2024, with comparisons to global and African averages. Cabo Verde and Seychelles had higher-than-global peaks and more severe downturns, while Comoros, Madagascar, and

Table 15.1 Key economic and social indicators

Indicator	Cape Verde	Comoros	Madagascar	Mauritius	São Tomé & Príncipe	Seychelles
Population (million)	0.6	0.9	30.3	1.3	0.2	0.1
Population Growth Rate (%/year)	1.10%	2.20%	2.60%	0.30%	1.90%	0.50%
Life Expectancy (years)	74.5	64.7	66.2	75.6	70	74.2
Fertility Rate (births/woman)	2.2	4	3.9	1.4	3.9	2.4
GDP (US$ billion)	2.5	1.4	17.5	14.2	0.6	2.3
GDP per capita (US$)	4,100	1,550	575	10,900	2,700	22,000
GDP growth (2024 est.)	4.70%	3.20%	4.00%	3.50%	2.90%	5.10%
Inflation (2024 est.)	3.50%	5.80%	8.90%	5.10%	7.20%	2.90%
Unemployment rate	11.50%	~12%	~13%	7.50%	~10%	~3%
Main Industries	Tourism, services	Agriculture, remittances	Agriculture, mining	Services, finance, ICT	Agriculture, tourism	Tourism, fisheries
Main Export Sector	Fish, clothing	Vanilla, cloves	Nickel, textiles	Textiles, sugar, ICT	Cocoa, palm oil	Fish, tourism services
Remittances (% of GDP)	~10–12%	~15–20%	~3%	~1%	~7–8%	<1%
Exchange Rate System	Pegged to Euro	Pegged to Euro (KMF)	Managed floating	Floating (MUR)	Pegged to Euro	Floating
Public Debt (% of GDP)	~120%	~38%	~54%	~78%	~97%	~65%
Debt Vulnerability	High	Moderate	Moderate	Low	High	Moderate
Current Account Balance (% GDP)	-8.50%	-6.00%	-3.50%	-11.20%	-10.00%	-5.10%
Human Development Index (HDI)	0.667 (Medium)	0.546 (Low)	0.533 (Low)	0.802 (High)	0.625 (Medium)	0.796 (High)

Source: Data are estimates for 2023–2024 from World Bank, IMF WEO, and national sources; GDP per capita Figures are in nominal USD; Inflation and GDP growth are estimates for 2024

Mauritius often followed or slightly outperformed the global average. São Tomé and Príncipe mostly trailed the global trend in the later years. GDP growth in 2025 is expected to range from 2.7% in São Tomé and Príncipe to over 5.3% in Cabo Verde, indicating continued growth momentum in the islands. Growth would be principally driven by the primary sector in (Comoros, Madagascar and Sao Tome and Principe) and tourism in Seychelles, Mauritius and Cabo Verde.[1]

A defining feature of African SIDS is their narrow economic base, typically concentrated in one or two sectors such as tourism, agriculture, or offshore services (Table 15.1). This over-reliance on a few sectors makes these economies highly vulnerable to external shocks, such as pandemics, fluctuations in commodity prices, or disruptions to international travel. For example, Mauritius and Seychelles have built globally competitive tourism industries, with Mauritius also developing robust textile manufacturing, financial services, and ICT sectors. In contrast, Comoros and São Tomé and Príncipe remain heavily reliant on agriculture and donor-funded public services, with limited diversification.

These island nations also face heavy dependence on external financing. Countries like Cabo Verde and Comoros rely extensively on remittances from their diasporas, which form a significant part of GDP (between 10–20 per cent as shown in Table 15.1), providing essential income and foreign exchange and supporting

[1] For a detailed analysis on growth projections visit the African Economic Outlook 2025.

household consumption and investment. These flows are much lower in Mauritius and Seychelles. Additionally, foreign aid and concessional loans are vital for funding infrastructure, education, and health services, especially in São Tomé and the Comoros, where domestic revenue mobilisation is weak. However, this external dependence raises concerns about debt sustainability, with two of the six African SIDS classified as at high risk of debt distress due to rising borrowing and limited fiscal space (Cabo Verde and São Tomé and Principe—Table 15.1). These two countries show high debt vulnerability, with public debt exceeding 97–120% of GDP. Mauritius and Seychelles maintain more moderate debt levels, while Comoros shows the lowest debt-to-GDP ratio at around 38%.

Compounding these vulnerabilities is the high exposure of African SIDS to climate change and natural disasters. These islands are particularly susceptible to sea-level rise, tropical cyclones, coastal erosion, and flooding, all of which threaten livelihoods, tourism infrastructure, and agricultural productivity. For instance, the Seychelles and Comoros frequently suffer from cyclones and storm surges, which damage homes, roads, and ports. Climate-related shocks also increase the costs of doing business and public infrastructure maintenance, while reducing investor confidence in long-term projects (Table 15.2).

In addition to environmental risks, these economies face deep-rooted structural and institutional challenges. High transportation and logistics costs due to remoteness, combined with small labour pools and skills mismatches, hinder private sector development and investment. While Mauritius and Seychelles have developed relatively strong institutions and good governance frameworks, other African SIDS continue to struggle with bureaucratic inefficiencies, limited public service delivery, and weak regulatory systems. These factors constrain efforts to build competitive industries and attract foreign direct investment beyond traditional sectors.

Despite these challenges, African SIDS are actively pursuing economic diversification strategies to enhance resilience and reduce external dependence. Mauritius has made significant progress by transitioning from a mono-crop sugar economy to a multi-sector model that includes tourism, finance, ICT, and education. Cabo Verde is positioning itself as a transport and renewable energy hub in West Africa, leveraging its strategic location. Meanwhile, Seychelles is pioneering blue economy initiatives, linking marine conservation with sustainable tourism and fisheries. However, the pace of transformation in countries like Comoros and São Tomé and Príncipe

Table 15.2 Key tourism statistics

Country	Tourism Share of GDP (%)	Average Tourism Revenue share of GDP (1995-2020) (%)
Cabo Verde	9.3 (2020)	17.7
Mauritius	13.6 (2023)	15.5
Madagascar	6.3 (2018)	4.3
Seychelles	65 (2018)	33.7

Source: Globaleconomy.com

Fig. 15.1 GDP growth rates by country in comparison with global and African averages. Source: World Development Indicators (WDI)

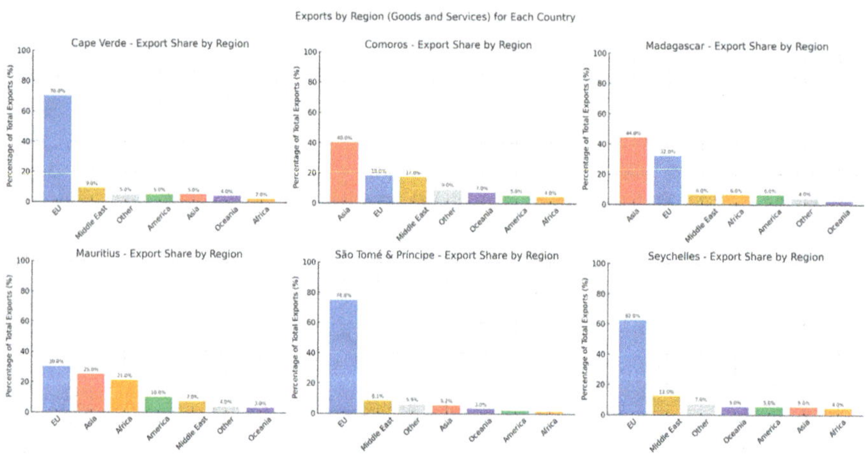

Fig. 15.2 African SIDS exports by region (%). Source: World Development Indicators (WDI)

remains slow, often hindered by political instability, limited investment, and weak human capital (Figs. 15.1, 15.2, and 15.3).

While African SIDS share many structural vulnerabilities due to their small size and isolation, their economic performances and development trajectories vary widely. Building economic resilience will require sustained investments in climate adaptation, economic diversification, institutional strengthening, and human capital development. Enhanced regional cooperation, better integration into global value

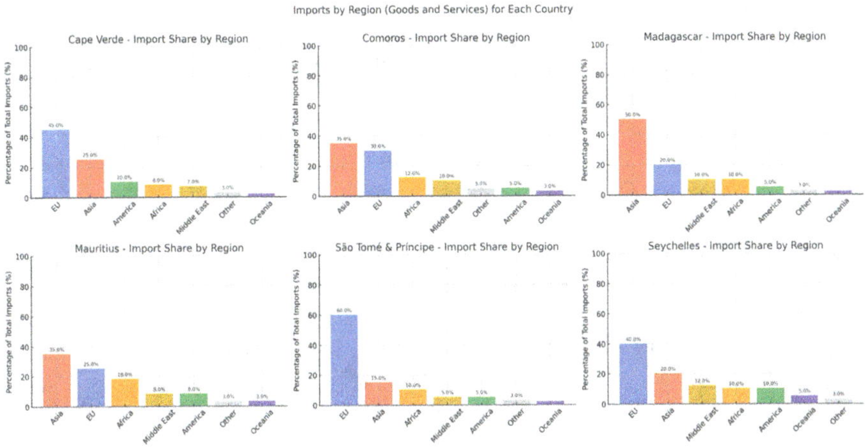

Fig. 15.3 African SIDS imports by region (%). Source: World Development Indicators (WDI)

chains, and strategic use of diaspora networks can further support their long-term development goals.

15.3 Trade Structure of Africa's SIDS

Economic diversification remains limited in most of these islands, thereby increasing their exposure to external shocks, including global price fluctuations, supply chain disruptions, and climate-related risks. Geographic remoteness, high logistics costs, and limited productive capacities further constrain their participation in global value chains (data used in this section is from World Bank 2023, 2024).

Africa's SIDS' main export sectors reflect their natural endowments and economic strategies. Tourism, fish and seafood dominate in Seychelles and Cape Verde; tourism, textiles and sugar are key in Mauritius; and agricultural products such as cocoa, vanilla, and cloves are major exports for São Tomé and Príncipe, Comoros, and Madagascar.

Across the region, current account deficits persist due to a high dependence on imports for fuel, machinery, food, and capital goods. In 2023, Mauritius recorded a current account deficit of −11.2% of GDP, Cape Verde −8.5%, and São Tomé nearly −10%. These imbalances are financed through remittances, tourism receipts, and external aid. Trade facilitation remains a priority, especially in Comoros and Madagascar, where port delays and customs inefficiencies increase transaction costs. Efforts to boost trade resilience include investing in infrastructure (ports, transport, ICT), expanding regional trade corridors, and supporting small-scale producers with standards compliance and market access. Greater emphasis on value addition—for example, local processing of fish, spices, or cocoa—can help raise export revenues and reduce vulnerability.

The following provides some trade statistics by country:

- Cape Verde's total goods and services exports were approximately US$1.158 billion in 2024. As a share of GDP, exports stood at 38.36% in 2023, down slightly from 38.68% in 2022. The long-term average is around 28%. The top exported product category was prepared and preserved foods, which accounted for approximately 73.7% of total goods exports, followed by clothing (9.5%) and footwear (5.7%). Total service exports in 2023 were approximately US$ 716 million, with travel and tourism being the main category, accounting for 75.8 per cent of total service export revenues ($543 million). Tourism (i.e., travel + passenger transport) accounted for around 48% of total exports (goods + services) in 2023, making Cape Verde one of Africa's countries with the highest tourism export dependency. Despite a relatively high level of trade openness, Cape Verde has a chronic trade deficit, with imports more than five times larger than exports. Cape Verde's exports—both goods and services—go to Europe, particularly Portugal and Spain, with virtually no notable trade with African partners.
- Comoros' total exports of goods and services in 2023 are estimated at US$140.1 million. Goods exports are modest: approximately US$31 million in 2023, while service exports stand at about US$86.65 million. Goods exports depend heavily on agricultural exports—particularly vanilla, cloves, and ylang-ylang, which constitute more than 80% of total goods exports. Cloves (whole fruit, cloves and stems) represent the dominant goods export, accounting for around 71% of goods exports. Singapore, France and other EU countries are key destinations. Travel (tourism): 76.55% of commercial service exports. As of 2020, international tourism receipts accounted for 26.84% of total exports. Comoros has a current account deficit of approximately −6% of GDP. Export earnings remain vulnerable to fluctuations. African destinations are not prominent, and while the Comoros shares close geographic proximity with Madagascar, intra-African exports remain minimal and unquantified in most official data—likely less than 5%.
- Madagascar is relatively more export-diverse. Total exports of goods and services reached approximately US$ 5.22 billion in 2023, which represents around 32.5% of GDP. Goods exports are around US$ 4.0 billion, while service exports stood at approximately US$ 1.2 billion. Nickel and cobalt account for 25–30% of exports, followed by vanilla (20%), textiles, and seafood. Madagascar has benefited from trade preferences under AGOA (US) and the EU's Everything But Arms (EBA) arrangement. Madagascar exports approximately 5.6%–6% of its exports to Sub-Saharan Africa. The bulk of this African trade is with South Africa, which alone imported over USD 200 million worth of Malagasy products in 2023. However, the country's main export markets remain outside the continent, notably France, the USA, and Japan. Travel and tourism account for 32.1% of total service exports and represent around 7.8% of total exports in 2020. Trade-to-GDP ratio remains moderate (around 30%), and logistics and infrastructure bottlenecks continue to hinder competitiveness.

- Mauritius is the most trade-diversified country in the region, with exports of goods and services equivalent to close to 60% of GDP. In 2023, it exported approximately USD 2.6 billion worth of goods and USD 2.3 billion in services. The main export categories are Prepared or preserved fish (approximately 14.2%), sugar (raw & refined) (approximately 12.5%) and garments (approximately 5.4%). Key export markets include France, South Africa, the UK, and India. Mauritius benefits from trade agreements with COMESA, SADC, the EU, and China, and continues to enhance its trade facilitation ranking and export sophistication. Among the African SIDS, Mauritius is the most regionally integrated in terms of exports, with about 21% of total exports destined for African countries. The two largest African partners were South Africa, which accounted for 12.7% of exports (approximately USD 251 million), and Madagascar, with 8.1%. Mauritius is a net exporter of services, particularly in tourism, finance, and information and communication technology (ICT), though these services are mostly consumed by clients outside the continent. Travel and tourism accounts for 59.4% of services exports and 16.8% of total exports.
- São Tomé and Príncipe is the least integrated in global trade. Its total exports are estimated to be around US$85 million in 2023, of which around US$65 million are exports of services. Cocoa beans make up over 80% of merchandise exports, followed by fish and vegetable oils. Travel services (tourism) accounted for approximately 72% of service export revenues. The country runs a very large trade deficit (imports exceed exports by more than 15 times), with a current account deficit near −10% of GDP. Export growth is constrained by limited diversification, scale, and access to finance and markets. It trades mostly with European countries, such as the Netherlands, Portugal, Poland, and France, and has negligible exports to its African neighbours.
- Seychelles, although smaller, is extremely trade-reliant, with exports of goods and services representing more than 80% of GDP. Total exports of goods, services and primary income were around US$2.38US$2.38 billion in 2023, of which approximately US$1.7 billion were for exports of services. Exports of goods are dominated by Prepared or preserved fish (especially tuna, skipjack, and bonito), which represent roughly 90% of the goods export value. The Seychelles economy is heavily service-oriented (83.7% of GDP), with tourism as the backbone. Tourism is the most important non-government sector, directly employing ~15% of the formal workforce, with substantial indirect employment in transport, banking and construction. The Seychelles' tourism and seafood exports are primarily oriented towards the United Arab Emirates, France, and the UK. Less than 3% of Seychelles' exports go to African countries, highlighting its economic orientation towards international, rather than regional, markets. The Seychelles is highly exposed to fluctuations in European market demand, changes in fishing quotas, and external tourism shocks.

Their trade dynamics highlight a persistent trend of economic orientation towards global markets, with only limited engagement in intra-African trade. Despite their geographic position within the African continent, these countries primarily export most of their goods and services to destinations outside Africa, mainly to Europe, Asia, and the Middle East. Cape Verde, Comoros, São Tomé and Príncipe, and Seychelles have extremely low export engagement with Africa, typically exporting less than 5% of their goods to the rest of the continent, with most trade flowing towards Europe and Asia. For example, Cape Verde's exports are heavily concentrated in Europe, particularly Spain and Portugal, and rely on tourism, fish products, and light manufacturing. The Comoros, an exporter of cloves, vanilla, and ylang-ylang (used in perfumes), sends the bulk of its goods to non-African countries, such as India and France, with limited trade links to nearby African nations, including Madagascar.

Mauritius and Madagascar exhibit relatively stronger trade ties within Africa. Mauritius exports approximately 9% of its goods to African countries, with South Africa and Madagascar among its top destinations. Its export basket includes textiles, sugar, processed food, and seafood, while the services sector—particularly finance and tourism—plays a critical role in its overall economy. Mauritius has also taken a strategic approach to engaging African markets, leveraging trade agreements within COMESA and SADC to deepen regional integration. Similarly, Madagascar, with a more commodity-driven economy, sends about 6–7% of its goods exports—such as vanilla, cloves, nickel, and textiles—to African partners.

The trade landscape of African SIDS remains uneven. While Mauritius and Seychelles exhibit more mature and integrated trade systems, others, such as Comoros and São Tomé, are still heavily reliant on primary commodities, with minimal diversification. Strengthening export capacity, regional linkages, and institutional trade support will be crucial to enhancing resilience and harnessing the potential of the blue and green economy in the region. Despite their African identity and proximity to the continent, these islands remain only marginally integrated into African trade networks.

The lack of regional integration can be attributed to several structural and logistical challenges. These island nations often face high transportation costs, limited maritime connectivity with mainland Africa, and a historical dependence on former colonial powers and traditional trade corridors that lie outside the continent of Africa. Furthermore, their export baskets—dominated by tourism, fisheries, agricultural commodities, and light manufacturing—are more aligned with demand in wealthier, developed markets. Efforts to improve this could involve enhanced transport connectivity, targeted trade policies, and deeper regional cooperation to reduce dependency on distant markets. Strengthening trade ties within Africa would not only help balance their economic relationships but also increase resilience against global market volatility.

15.4 Structural Challenges across Diverse Island Economies

African SIDS exhibit both shared characteristics and notable distinctions that influence their participation and shape their engagement with the AfCFTA. Although they are geographically isolated, they are strategically positioned along key maritime routes. They all share a common interest, aligned with those continental African countries, in leveraging AfCFTA to overcome trade barriers and expand regional integration.

They all face common structural challenges such as geographic isolation, limited natural resources, small domestic markets, dependence on imports and vulnerability to external economic shocks and climate change. Their economies are largely service-oriented, with tourism, fisheries, and maritime trade playing key roles, offering potential areas of collaboration and intra-African trade expansion under AfCFTA. Their levels of infrastructure development, institutional readiness, and trade diversification vary significantly.

Despite these shared challenges, there are significant differences in economic structure, institutional capacity, infrastructure, and level of integration into regional and global value chains that impact their readiness to fully capitalise on AfCFTA opportunities. Mauritius, for example, stands out as a regional leader with a well-diversified economy that includes financial services, textiles, ICT, and tourism. Its strong legal frameworks, high levels of foreign direct investment, and experience in negotiating trade agreements have enabled it to become one of the most active African economies in global trade. These characteristics position Mauritius as a frontrunner among island states in utilising AfCFTA to broaden its export markets. Seychelles also boasts relatively advanced economic and governance systems, particularly in maritime and fisheries management. In contrast, Comoros and São Tomé and Príncipe remain among the least developed, grappling with fragile institutions, underdeveloped infrastructure, and high dependence on donor support. Madagascar, while larger and richer in natural resources, faces political instability and logistical hurdles that impede its integration into regional value chains. Cape Verde's geographic remoteness from mainland Africa and reliance on remittances and services also complicate its path towards deeper trade integration under AfCFTA.

In terms of trade composition and connectivity, most of these countries primarily trade with partners outside Africa—particularly Europe and Asia—due to colonial legacies, established supply chains, and limited direct maritime links to mainland African markets. AfCFTA offers a framework to change this by creating a single continental market with reduced tariffs, harmonised trade rules, and greater cooperation in areas such as transport, customs, and standards. However, for island nations to fully benefit, complementary investments in port infrastructure, shipping services, digital connectivity, and trade facilitation measures will be essential. Furthermore, their limited industrial bases mean they will need targeted support to move beyond primary goods and tourism into more value-added sectors that can compete in a larger African market.

These island economies face significant barriers to fully capturing AfCFTA benefits. Islands' economies face significant barriers to fully capturing AfCFTA benefits, ranging from transport and logistical hurdlesand concentrated export sectors not aligned with continental demand. Madagascar shows the most potential, with statistical data illustrating both current deficits and modest projected gains under AfCFTA. However, even here, systemic constraints limit its transformative impact.

Cape Verde is similarly constrained by its insular geography and limited trade base. The country's economy relies heavily on services—particularly tourism and remittances—which are not the primary focus of AfCFTA's trade in goods protocols. Cape Verde's maritime connectivity is limited, and shipping costs are among the highest in Africa, which hampers its integration with continental markets. Its industrial base is small, and it lacks significant agricultural exports that could benefit from tariff liberalisation. While the country has made strides in infrastructure development, key bottlenecks remain, especially in port operations and customs administration. Customs systems, although improving, still fall short of the efficiency needed for full compliance with the AfCFTA's rules. These limitations mean that Cape Verde is currently not well-equipped to take advantage of preferential access to African markets, unless special consideration or assistance is provided. Moreover, Cape Verde's dependence on services such as tourism and remittances means its tradable goods sector is underdeveloped, making it harder to capitalise on tariff reductions under AfCFTA.

Comoros suffers from acute capacity and institutional challenges. With a fragile political environment, the country struggles to maintain investor confidence or build consistent trade policy frameworks. Comoros depends heavily on a few export commodities—mainly vanilla and cloves—which are vulnerable to global price swings and climate shocks. Intra-African trade is minimal, and its geographic isolation leads to prohibitively high transportation costs. Port infrastructure is underdeveloped, and bureaucratic red tape creates bottlenecks in customs procedures. Even if AfCFTA opens markets, Comoros lacks the productive capacity and logistical infrastructure to exploit these opportunities in the short to medium term.

Madagascar has made modest strides in regional trade but continues to face serious structural barriers under AfCFTA. Intra-African trade accounts for only around 10% of its total exports, which means it remains largely disconnected from the continental market. The country's export profile is narrowly concentrated, with unwrought nickel accounting for 25% of exports in 2023, followed by vanilla (~8%), cloves (7.6%), and titanium ores (5.2%). Deficiency in infrastructure, including inadequate road and port systems, customs inefficiencies, and non-tariff barriers such as challenges with meeting sanitary and phytosanitary standards, significantly limit Madagascar's ability to capitalise on AfCFTA's market opportunities. Additionally, complex rules of origin under AfCFTA may pose compliance challenges for many Malagasy exporters.

Mauritius, despite being one of the most advanced economies in the region, confronts its AfCFTA-specific constraints. The country's economy is heavily reliant on services. Although Mauritius maintains a services trade surplus, the AfCFTA's current emphasis on goods over services means these strengths remain underleveraged.

Moreover, Mauritius's export model relies on re-exporting processed goods, such as textiles, sugar, and tuna, which are sensitive to strict rules of origin. AfCFTA mandates that 90% of tariff lines be liberalised, and Mauritius, through SACU and SADC, has committed to such reductions, but regional value content (RVC) thresholds and cumulative origin rules complicate compliance. Although the country has implemented electronic certification systems to support trade, many SMEs cannot navigate the administrative demands of AfCFTA.

São Tomé and Príncipe, one of Africa's smallest economies by GDP and population, faces even more extreme constraints. It is the most vulnerable and least diversified economy in Africa. Its tiny industrial and agricultural base means it produces very few tradable goods. Like Comoros and Cape Verde, it has limited maritime and air connectivity to mainland Africa, which restricts its potential for scaling trade. The country relies heavily on imports and foreign aid, and its capacity to implement complex trade rules or participate in negotiations is severely limited due to a shortage of skilled personnel. Institutional capacity is also very low, with limited human and technical resources to implement the legal and administrative aspects of the AfCFTA agreement. Given its dependence on food and fuel imports, the country is highly exposed to external price shocks and global supply chain disruptions. These factors make São Tomé and Príncipe particularly vulnerable to being left behind under AfCFTA unless it receives targeted technical assistance and capacity-building.

The Seychelles faces a unique mix of challenges and limitations. It is one of Africa's wealthiest nations in nominal terms, yet it has a very small and undiversified export base. The vast majority of its merchandise exports are processed fish. Its trade trends create a large and persistent trade imbalance. Seychelles' manufacturing sector relies almost entirely on imported inputs, making it difficult to meet AfCFTA's rules of origin. Moreover, its policy focus on sustainability and environmental protection makes large-scale industrial development—often central to AfCFTA gains—less feasible. Seychelles' strong focus on eco-tourism and sustainability may limit its engagement with certain sectors that benefit from AfCFTA, such as manufacturing or agriculture. As such, Seychelles' ability to participate in AfCFTA is constrained not only by economic structure but also by deliberate policy choices and physical limitations.

Economically, these SIDS face constraints related to their narrow production and export bases, with many heavily depending on a few vulnerable sectors, such as tourism, agriculture, and fisheries. These sectors are not only seasonal but also highly susceptible to external shocks, including climate change, global commodity price fluctuations, and geopolitical disruptions. For example, climate-induced events such as cyclones and rising sea levels pose existential threats to both infrastructure and livelihoods, adding another layer of risk to their trade and development aspirations.

Institutionally, many of these countries have limited technical and administrative capacity to implement the often-complex trade-related reforms required by the AfCFTA, such as tariff reductions, rules of origin compliance, and harmonisation of standards. Customs modernisation, trade facilitation, and regulatory alignment remain underdeveloped in several of these states, thereby undermining their ability to engage efficiently in cross-border trade. Digital readiness is also uneven, with gaps in e-commerce platforms, digital payment systems, and information and communications technology (ICT) infrastructure, which are increasingly essential for participating in modern trade ecosystems.

Furthermore, the small size of their populations and economies restricts their bargaining power in trade negotiations and makes it difficult to attract large-scale investment or achieve economies of scale. Many of these countries also struggle to access trade finance and lack the industrial base needed to transition from raw material exporters to value-added producers—a key objective of the AfCFTA. Without significant technical assistance, investment in infrastructure, and deliberate policy inclusion, these island nations risk being left behind in the continental integration process.

To ensure that the AfCFTA is truly inclusive and beneficial for all African states, the specific constraints of island countries must be acknowledged and addressed through targeted interventions, such as support for infrastructure development, digital transformation, capacity-building, and the creation of dedicated mechanisms to enhance their participation in regional value chains. Only then can these small island economies fully leverage the potential of the AfCFTA and make meaningful contributions to Africa's broader development agenda.

15.5 Strategic Fit of African SIDS within the AfCFTA Framework

The heterogeneity of these island states calls for coordinated regional policies, such as the AfCFTA, to strengthen resilience, advance inclusive development, and ensure sustainable growth across this strategically important region. While Mauritius and Seychelles have successfully transitioned towards high-value services and sustained development, others face persistent structural challenges, including high debt burdens, reliance on remittances, and demographic pressures. All these countries possess strategic advantages and specialised capacities that, if harnessed effectively, can play a pivotal role in advancing both their national development goals and the broader objectives of the AfCFTA.

While African SIDS face significant challenges, they also possess distinct strategic assets that can be harnessed under the AfCFTA. From acting as maritime and digital gateways to exporting services, leading in climate-friendly trade, and integrating into regional value chains, these island states can make significant contributions to Africa's economic integration. To realise this potential, however, they require targeted support, policy flexibility, and active participation in AfCFTA's ongoing development. If these elements are in place, African SIDS can emerge not as peripheral players but as vital engines of innovation, sustainability, and inclusive growth within the AfCFTA. African SIDS potential includes the following:

Connectivity and gateway potential: Due to their maritime geography, African SIDS are naturally poised to serve as connectivity and logistics hubs between mainland Africa and global markets. Many are strategically located along important shipping routes in the Atlantic and Indian Oceans. For instance, Mauritius and Seychelles have advanced port facilities and are situated in key positions to facilitate transhipment, logistics services, and maritime trade. With targeted investment in port infrastructure, air-sea corridors, and maritime services as part of the AfCFTA's broader integration efforts, these island nations could serve as gateways for intra-African and African trade to the global market. Their role as bridges between mainland Africa and the world is further enhanced by the relative political stability, trade-friendly policies, and strong business environments that many of these nations offer. In this regard, African SIDS can help reduce trade transaction costs and contribute to the seamless movement of goods and services across borders.

Service-oriented economies: African SIDS are disproportionately strong in the services sector, which aligns well with AfCFTA's Protocol on Trade in Services. Countries like Mauritius have globally recognised capabilities in financial services, ICT, legal arbitration, education, and health tourism. These services are in growing demand across the continent, especially as African economies diversify and digitise. By leveraging the AfCFTA framework, African SIDS can position themselves as regional service exporters. They can lead in setting service standards, creating regional centres of excellence, and promoting cross-border service delivery through digital platforms and sectoral liberalisation. This would also encourage foreign direct investment (FDI) in services, supporting inclusive growth and knowledge transfer.

Integration into regional value chains (RVCs): Given their export-oriented nature and experience in niche markets, African SIDS can play a critical role in regional value chains, particularly in sectors like fisheries, agriculture, food processing, and marine products. For example, Seychelles and Comoros are key players in the blue economy, with developed fishing industries and marine tourism offerings. Meanwhile, São Tomé and Príncipe producehigh-quality cocoa that could be integrated into West Africa's cocoa-to-chocolate value chain. Participation in regional value chains helps SIDS overcome the limitations of their small domestic markets and lack of raw materials by linking them into broader African production networks. This encourages trade-led industrialisation, value addition, and deeper economic integration with mainland partners.

Tourism and sustainable trade: Tourism remains a cornerstone of SIDS economies, contributing significantly to GDP, employment, and foreign exchange earnings. However, it is also a sector highly vulnerable to global shocks. AfCFTA presents an opportunity for SIDS to diversify and regionalise their tourism industries. Through coordinated branding, marketing, and service liberalisation, African SIDS can offer multi-destination tourism packages with mainland African countries, boosting tourist inflows and resilience. Moreover, by prioritising eco-tourism and sustainable tourism models, African SIDS can align their trade offerings with Africa's green growth agenda. They can serve as models for sustainable tourism, showcasing how environmental conservation and economic development can go hand in hand.

Digital trade and innovation: With their limited landmass and high transport costs, African SIDS are natural candidates to benefit from digital trade. E-commerce, fintech, remote education, and telemedicine are sectors with strong potential, especially in more technologically advanced SIDS like Mauritius. Through AfCFTA's emerging Protocol on E-Commerce and digital economy strategies, SIDS can overcome geographic disadvantages and become regional leaders in digital service delivery. Investing in digital infrastructure, cross-border payment systems, and digital trade platforms will further integrate SIDS into Africa's digital transformation. This will also enhance their ability to trade remotely, build knowledge economies, and attract tech-driven investment.

Green trade and climate leadership: African SIDS are among the most vulnerable countries in the world to climate change and environmental degradation. However, this challenge also presents an opportunity for them to lead on climate-smart trade policies under AfCFTA. These countries can become exporters of sustainably harvested marine products, renewable energy solutions, and environmental consulting services. They can also advocate for the inclusion of green clauses in AfCFTA protocols, ensuring that trade liberalisation supports climate adaptation and low-carbon development. SIDS' experiences and commitments under global climate agreements (e.g., the Paris Agreement) position them as natural leaders in championing sustainable trade practices in Africa.

Special and differential treatment (SDT) advocacy: Due to their small economies, limited production capacity, and geographic isolation, African SIDS require special policy considerations to fully benefit from AfCFTA. These include longer implementation timelines, simplified customs procedures, technical assistance, and capacity-building support. By coordinating as a bloc, African SIDS can advocate for Special and Differential Treatment (SDT) within AfCFTA. This would ensure that trade rules are adapted to their unique circumstances and do not disproportionately disadvantage them. Forming a SIDS caucus within AfCFTA governance structures—like SIDS representation in UN forums—could help amplify their voice in continental negotiations.

Gateway to global markets: Several African SIDS have well-established trade and investment agreements with major global economies, including the European Union, India, China, and regional blocs like ASEAN. For example, Mauritius has signed trade agreements with China and India, in addition to being part of the Eastern and Southern Africa EPA with the EU. This enables SIDS to act as bridges between Africa and the global market. Foreign investors seeking entry into the African continent may find it easier to use African SIDS as entry points, given their political stability, investor-friendly environments, and legal frameworks. This positions SIDS as key players in helping to globalise the AfCFTA and attract foreign capital into African value chains.

15.6 Policy Recommendations

15.6.1 *Tailored Rules of Origin for Island States*

To ensure that Africa's SIDS fully participate and benefit from the AfCFTA, a differentiated and flexible policy approach is needed. This requires simplifying requirements for regional content and allowing greater cumulation for African SIDS to qualify for AfCFTA preferences. One critical recommendation is the adaptation of AfCFTA's Rules of Origin to the realities of SIDS. These countries often rely heavily on imported intermediate goods due to their limited industrial base. The current origin criteria—such as minimum regional value content or product-specific transformation rules—can exclude their exports from preferential access. Simplifying these rules by lowering thresholds or introducing flexible cumulation provisions would allow island exporters to qualify more easily for AfCFTA preferences, boosting trade flows and participation. UNCTAD (2019) notes that rules of origin should be made simple and business friendly for the gains expected from the African Continental Free Trade Area to be realised.

15.6.2 *Service Sector Prioritisation*

Another priority area is the acceleration of services liberalisation under the AfCFTA. Island economies like Mauritius, Seychelles, and Cape Verde have strong service sectors—especially in tourism, financial services, and ICT—that offer clear comparative advantages. However, the current AfCFTA implementation focuses more on goods than services. Policymakers should push for fast-tracking the Protocol on Trade in Services, particularly in sectors that align with the island's capabilities. This would enable SIDS to leverage their strengths more effectively and integrate through non-goods trade channels. The AfCFTA aims to create a single liberalised market for trade in services through the Protocol on Trade in Services which was signed in 2019

15.6.3 *Infrastructure and Connectivity Investment*

Investment in maritime and digital connectivity is also essential. Geographic isolation is a fundamental barrier for these states, resulting in high logistics costs and unreliable transport links. Regional shipping initiatives—such as subsidised sea freight routes, shared port infrastructure, or coordinated air cargo logistics—could significantly reduce these barriers. At the same time, expanding digital infrastructure, including electronic customs clearance systems, online trade portals, and interoperable certification systems, would facilitate smoother cross-border trade and reduce administrative burdens. The SAMOA Pathway for SIDS emphasised the importance of transport and connectivity together with trade facilitation, and the use of advanced technologies to enable SIDS to easily integrate into large markets (UN-OHRLLS (2020)).

15.6.4 Customs and Trade Facilitation Support

It is essential to provide technical assistance to modernise customs systems and streamline documentation processes for small traders and SMEs. Institutional capacity-building and technical assistance should be a central component of AfCFTA support for SIDS. Many of these countries face acute shortages of trade experts, customs officers, and technical specialists who can effectively implement or monitor trade policies. Through the AfCFTA Adjustment Facility, African Union bodies, and development partners, targeted training programmes, funding for trade facilitation equipment, and policy advisory services should be prioritised. These efforts should particularly benefit smaller economies, such as the Comoros and São Tomé and Príncipe, which face the greatest implementation challenges.

15.6.5 Dedicated AfCFTA Support Window for SIDS

To institutionalise long-term support, the AfCFTA Secretariat and the African Union should establish a dedicated SIDS Support Mechanism. This could take the form of an Adjustment Fund or similar initiatives to address the unique needs of SIDS. This facility could provide tailored financial support, facilitate peer learning among island states, and offer policy exemptions or phase-in periods where appropriate. Such a mechanism would recognise the unique development context of SIDS and ensure their needs are systematically addressed throughout AfCFTA implementation.

The UNCTAD is developing a dedicated SIDS strategy and Trust Fund to support Small Island Developing States (UNCTAD (2021)). While this is not formally framed as an “AfCFTA Support Window,” it aligns with AfCFTA-related aims—such as enhancing productive capacities, improving connectivity, facilitating digital transformation and customs modernisation, and strengthening FDI and trade facilitation reforms tailored for SIDS vulnerabilities.

15.6.6 Regional Cooperation among Island States

Greater regional cooperation among the island states themselves can amplify the voices of African SIDS and maximise resource efficiency. By collaborating on issues such as joint shipping lines, regional branding of export products, or shared trade facilitation systems, these countries can overcome common constraints. A coordinated platform for island states within the AfCFTA framework—modelled on other regional economic groups—could help them negotiate collectively and pool technical expertise.

15.7 Conclusion

Africa's SIDS stand at a strategic crossroads in the unfolding AfCFTA integration process. While the promise of expanded continental trade offers significant opportunities for these nations, it also exposes deep structural asymmetries that, if unaddressed, may exacerbate their economic isolation. Their geographic remoteness, small domestic markets, limited export diversification, and dependence on services and imported inputs place them at a relative disadvantage in traditional goods-based trade frameworks.

Yet, these same constraints underscore the importance of inclusive and differentiated integration strategies. Leveraging their comparative advantages in tourism, financial services, and the blue economy sectors, improving connectivity and customs systems, and ensuring flexible rules of origin can help transform these vulnerabilities into pathways for deeper integration. The AfCFTA must therefore be more than a uniform market—it must be a responsive platform that recognises and supports the specific development needs of all member states.

By tailoring trade protocols, investing in capacity-building, and institutionalising special support mechanisms for African SIDS, the AfCFTA can become a truly transformative tool, not just for market access, but for economic resilience and regional solidarity. Bridging the isolation of Africa's Island economies will not only empower these nations but will also enrich the continental value chains and economic dynamism envisioned in Africa's Agenda 2063.

In summary, addressing the specific constraints of Africa's SIDS within the AfCFTA framework requires more than general trade facilitation—it demands targeted, context-sensitive solutions. Flexible rules of origin accelerated services liberalisation, investments in connectivity, and strengthened institutional capacity are not optional but essential to ensuring these island economies can meaningfully participate in and benefit from continental integration. The establishment of a dedicated SIDS support mechanism and deeper regional cooperation among the islands themselves would further enable them to overcome their shared vulnerabilities. By implementing these recommendations, the AfCFTA can become a more inclusive and equitable trade architecture—one that leaves no member state behind, regardless of its size, location, or level of development.

References

African Development Bank (AfDB). (2022). *African economic outlook 2022: Supporting climate resilience and a just energy transition in Africa*. AfDB. https://www.afdb.org/en/documents/african-economic-outlook-2022

African Union (2020) *Agreement establishing the African Continental Free Trade Area (AfCFTA)*. https://au.int/en/treaties/agreement-establishing-african-continental-free-trade-area

Globaleconomy.Com. (2024). *Tourism statistics by country*. https://www.theglobaleconomy.com

IMF. (2023). *World economic outlook: A rocky recovery*. International Monetary Fund. https://www.imf.org/en/Publications/WEO

International Trade Centre (ITC). (2021). *Expanding trade in Africa: How AfCFTA can make a difference*. ITC. https://intracen.org/resources/publications/Expanding-Trade-in-Africa

OECD. (2020). *Economic outlook for southeast Asian Island States*. Organisation for Economic Co-operation and Development.

UNCTAD. (2019). *Rules of origin key to success of African continental free trade area*. United Nations Conference on Trade and Development. https://unctad.org/news/rules-origin-key-success-african-continental-free-trade-area

UNCTAD. (2021). *Vulnerability profile of Small Island developing States (SIDS)*. United Nations Conference on Trade and Development. https://unctad.org/webflyer/vulnerability-profile-sids

United Nations Economic Commission for Africa (UNECA). (2021). *Assessing regional integration in Africa IX (ARIA IX): Next steps for the AfCFTA*. UNECA. https://www.uneca.org/publications/assessing-regional-integration-africa-ix

United Nations Office of the High Representative for the Least Developed Countries, Landlocked Developing Countries and Small Island Developing States (UN-OHRLLS). (2020). *Small island developing States in Africa: Challenges and opportunities*. UN-OHRLLS. https://www.un.org/ohrlls/content/african-small-island-developing-states

World Bank. (2023). *World development indicators (WDI)*. https://databank.worldbank.org/source/world-development-indicators

World Bank. (2024). *Africa's pulse: Economic growth amid high debt and climate risk*. World Bank. https://www.worldbank.org/en/region/afr/publication/africas-pulse

Part III
Conclusion

Chapter 16
Trends and Projections on the Implementation of the AfCFTA

Puruweti Siyakiya and Rorisang Lesaoana

Abstract This paper synthesises key trends and projections shaping the ongoing implementation of the AfCFTA, highlighting both progress and persistent challenges and offering policy recommendations. Current trends indicate a gradual but determined movement towards operationalisation, marked by the ongoing finalisation of crucial protocols such as those on Rules of Origin (ROO), Investment, and Digital Trade. While initial trade under the AfCFTA has commenced, widespread benefits are contingent on the full implementation of these foundational elements and the effective resolution of non-tariff barriers (NTBs). The AfCFTA is expected to drive industrialisation, foster the development of regional value chains, and diversify African economies away from commodity dependence. Furthermore, digital transformation is projected to play a pivotal role, streamlining trade processes, enhancing financial inclusion and unlocking new opportunities for small and medium enterprises and informal traders. However, realising these projections necessitates accelerated investment in critical infrastructure (transport, energy, and digital platforms), strengthened regulatory and institutional frameworks, and sustained political commitment from member states. Addressing the digital divide, building human capacity, and ensuring inclusive participation of all stakeholders, particularly women and youth, remain crucial for the AfCFTA to achieve its full potential and reshape Africa's economic trajectory on the global stage.

Keywords Africa · African continental free trade area · Economic growth · Intra-African trade · Industrialisation · Market integration

JEL Classification F02 · F13 · F15

P. Siyakiya (✉) · R. Lesaoana
Department of Economics, National University of Lesotho, Maseru, Lesotho

D. N. Yuni et al. (eds.), *From Policy to Practice: Challenges and Ways Forward on the Implementation of the AfCFTA*,
https://doi.org/10.1007/978-3-032-14051-7_16

16.1 Introduction

The AfCFTA offers significant economic opportunities for African countries as it boosts intra-African trade, accelerates and promotes the African continent's industrial growth and transformation through industrialisation, stimulates the development of regional value chains (RVCs), and enhances the continent's economic integration in the global economy (Fofack & Mold, 2021). Additionally, the agreement can raise the continent's low productivity and promote higher investment, thereby helping to increase income levels and reduce poverty (Abrego et al., 2019). Additionally, FTAs typically provide member countries with comparable market access to their trading partners. Additionally, Aniche (2023) emphasises that the AfCFTA offers a platform for African countries to renegotiate trading conditions through market access provisions, following agreements with the United States, the Republic of China, and the European Union (EU).

Most African countries face persistent trade barriers, including NTBs, weak institutions, and inadequate infrastructure, which contribute to disparities in economic development and industrial capacity. According to Ezugwu and Duruji (2023), the AfCFTA is one way to address the economic challenges, transform economies and foster deep integration on the continent. The AfCFTA agreement could also double intra-African trade, increase the national income of member states by sevenfold, and lift about 30 million Africans out of extreme poverty (Maliszewska et al., 2020). Intra-African trade agreements have facilitated, to a considerable extent, a gradual lowering of tariffs on goods, with effectively applied tariffs decreasing from over 20% in 1997 to 11.8% in 2016 and a significant increase in welfare gains (Abrego et al., 2019). Literature posits that trade reduces poverty and increases growth (Dollar & Kraay, 2003, 2004; Le Goff & Singh, 2014; Matthew & Adegboye, 2014; McCulloch et al., 2001; Winters et al., 2004). The agreement is projected to attract more foreign direct investment (FDI), increase trade and diversification and stimulate economic growth.

Secondly, through diversification, RVCs development and value addition and beneficiation, AfCFTA will promote the continent's industrialisation. These are expected to reduce over-reliance on commodity exports and, at the same time, increase the production of manufactured commodities in the African continent. Industrialisation and increased production of manufacturing products will make African economies more resilient to global economic shocks (Siyakiya et al., 2023). In addition, through infrastructure improvements, reduced trade costs and technological innovation, AfCFTA is envisaged to enhance the continent's competitiveness.

Last but not least, the AfCFTA is poised to promote inclusive and sustainable development. The creation of job opportunities, the reduction of poverty and improvements in living standards within the continent will make this achievable. Also, through increased economic activity, poverty can be reduced and living standards improved in Africa. Increased economic activity and job creation will reduce poverty and improve living standards. The diversification of production will lead to an expansion of industries and services, thereby creating employment opportunities for young people and women. Accordingly, it is essential to note that successfully implementing the AfCFTA necessitates addressing numerous challenges, including infrastructure gaps, trade barriers, and policy coordination.

16.2 Key Data Trends in AfCFTA Implementation

Data-driven analysis ensures that the full potential of the AfCFTA and its tangible benefits to African economies are achieved. First and foremost, it is crucial to effectively assess the implementation, progress, and economic impacts of AfCFTA. It is essential to rely on data-driven evidence when assessing the implementation and impact of AfCFTA. This is because data enables the quantification of the AfCFTA's economic growth, trade flow, and job creation effects. The data also enables policymakers to track the progress of key indicators, such as the volume of intra-African trade flows, investment flows, and tariff reductions, helps to guide policy decisions, which are critical for optimising the benefits of the AfCFTA, provides insights into the impact of various policies, enabling the development of tailored responses and can also be utilised to detect bottlenecks and issues that may arise during the implementation of the AfCFTA. The information obtained helps pinpoint the areas where intervention, if needed, can be used to improve the effectiveness of the AfCFTA.

Data is also essential for monitoring and evaluating the progress of implementing the AfCFTA. This is important for making adjustments, if needed, to ensure the achievement of AfCFTA objectives. Furthermore, using data-driven analysis can enhance accountability and transparency by providing information consistent with the AfCFTA's objectives. This builds trust and confidence among stakeholders and member states. Data can also facilitate targeted intervention and enable effective review of progress. Good data is essential for accurately and effectively reviewing the agreement's progress and targeting specific areas for intervention. The key data areas that are important for checking the implementation progress of the AfCFTA include trade statistics (exports, imports, and trade flows), tariff data and NTB information, investment data (FDI and domestic investment), economic indicators (GDP growth, employment rate, inflation rate), infrastructure data (transportation, logistics), and other data related to SMEs. According to Besada (2025), AfCFTA's full implementation could provide a launchpad for driving value addition and beneficiation, supporting industrial development and diversification, and providing stability by buffering against global economic shocks. The section uses data from various literature and sources to project the future of AfCFTA and its impact on different sectors and industries of the economies of African countries. The analyses are based on key indices on trade, industrial growth, economic growth, employment, and investment, to mention a few. An analysis of these indices on how they affect the full implementation of the AfCFTA and the possible challenges that its potential effects pose is conducted. Finally, policy and strategic recommendations are proposed for African countries to effectively implement the AfCFTA.

16.2.1 Trade and Market Integration

It is essential to analyse trade trends to effectively monitor the progress of AfCFTA implementation. Analysing data trends in the volumes and values of intra-African trade, in relation to the AfCFTA launch, requires considering several key factors. The analysis involves pre-AfCFTA and post-AfCFTA implementation. According to McCulloch et al. (2001), successive rounds of multilateral trade negotiations resulting in a dramatic increase in world trade. As a result, the African and Asian regions were the only regions to realise an increasing trend in intra-regional trade since 2008. Before the AfCFTA went into effect, intra-African trade was relatively small. In comparison with other regions, such as Asia and Europe, intra-trade in Africa has historically been significantly lower. Also, according to the Organisation for Economic Co-operation and Development,, and World Trade Organisation (2019), over 60% of merchandise exports by Africa are primarily comprised of raw materials, including mineral ores, agricultural products and oil. The contributing factors to Africa's low intra-trade and limited value addition and beneficiation are overlapping trade agreements, infrastructure deficits, NTBs and limited economic diversification. Additionally, the United Nations Conference on Trade and Development (2019) noted that ROO could drastically bring positive changes if they properly determine the nationality of products for business-friendly, flexible, simple, transparent and predictable trade. Having efficient and clear ROO is essential for ensuring the realisation of increased benefits from trade through reduced tariffs and NTBs. Notwithstanding the aforementioned challenges, intra-African trade, over the years, has gradually increased, mainly driven by regional economic communities and efforts to promote integration.

Statistics from the UNCTAD website[1] reveal that, between 2015 and 2017, prior to AfCFTA enforcement, Africa's exports to the world, compared to those from Europe (US$4109 billion), America (US$5140 billion), and Asia (US$6801 billion), averaged US$ only 760 billion. Between 2000 and 2017, the African continent's exports to the world ranged between 80% and 90%. While Europe, Asia and America's intra-exports as a proportion of total exports were 68.1%, 59.4% and 55% in 2017, respectively, that of Africa was a mere 16.6%. Furthermore, intra-African trade between 2015 and 2017 accounted for 15.2%, whereas for Europe, Asia, and America, it was 67%, 61%, and 47%, respectively. With regard to intra-regional economic community trade within the continent, the Southern Africa Development Community (SADC), Common Market for Eastern and Southern Africa (COMESA), Community of Sahel-Saharan States, Economic Community of West African States (ECOWAS) and Arab Maghreb Union had 84.9%, 59.5%, 58.4%, 56.7%, and 51.8% in 2016, respectively. Eswatini, Namibia, Zimbabwe, Uganda and Togo were among the leading African countries in intra-African exports between 2015 and 2017, with shares of 70.6%, 52.9%, 51.6%, 51.4%, and 51.1%,

[1] https://unctad.org/press-material/facts-Figures-0#:~:text=Intra%2DAfrican%20exports%20were%2016.6,America%20and%207.0%25%20in%20Oceania.

respectively. On the contrary, Chad, Guinea, Eritrea, Equatorial Guinea, Cabo Verde, Angola, Libya, and Guinea-Bissau were among the African countries that contributed the least to intra-African exports. These countries made a contribution of less than 5% to intra-African exports.

Before the AfCFTA implementation, total formal trade, excluding informal trade by small-scale cross-border traders, totalled between 12% and 18%.[2] According to the African Export-Import Bank (2018b), AfCFTA implementation would potentially increase intra-African trade by over US$84 billion, but if realised, would further increase to US$231 billion, with the biggest beneficiary being Southern Africa, followed by North Africa, West Africa, East Africa and Central Africa. Furthermore, the United Nations (2019) projected that trade liberalisation under the AfCFTA agreement would also increase intra-African trade by 15–25%. Some data suggest that the elimination of import duties and the reduction of NTBs could potentially increase intra-African trade by 52.3% under AfCFTA.[3]

The AfCFTA's primary objective is to significantly increase economic growth by enhancing intra-African trade, and since the agreement's enactment, this has been noticeable. The increase in economic activity resulting from AfCFTA's enactment presents a unique opportunity to drive sustainable development and economic prosperity for African countries by leveraging the potential of regional markets. Despite early data on intra-African trade showing a positive trend, the full realisation of the AfCFTA potential will take time after implementation. The continent focuses on shifting trade from raw materials to manufactured and value-added products. Additionally, the digital economy is crucial in driving growth. Additionally, the digital economy is crucial role in fostering trade among member states.

Nevertheless, AfCFTA implementation has been slow, with trading under AfCFTA starting on January 1, 2021, despite the agreement coming into force in May 2019. According to Abrego et al. (2020), AfCFTA could increase African exports by around US$60 billion. They further revealed that at least 2.1% of long-term income gains would be realised from increased knowledge diffusion, innovation, and regional investment. Also Moyer et al. (2021) reported that by 2063, AfCFTA implementation would potentially increase intra-African trade to 40% of African total trade.

Post-AfCFTA implementation trends indicate that the value of intra-African trade in 2022 grew by 18.6%, reaching approximately US$193.17 billion (African Export-Import Bank, 2024). Furthermore, intra-African trade increased by 3.2% between 2022 and 2023. While there has been a general trend showing an increase in intra-African trade, the continent still trades less within the region than it does with the world. The continent's intra-trade growth is hampered by infrastructure deficit, low levels of trade facilitation and persistent NTBs. The ever-changing

[2] https://www.brookings.edu/articles/intra-african-trade-and-its-potential-to-accelerate-progress-toward-the-sdgs/.

[3] https://researchfdi.com/breaking-down-the-afcfta-what-you-need-to-know-about-africas-latest-trade-initiative/#:~:text=According%20to%20the%20World%20Bank,as%20well%20as%20attract%20investment%2C.

global challenges posed by geopolitical tensions and other economic shocks also influence intra-AfCFTA trade's growth. However, improving intra-AfCFTA trade requires considering various factors, including making the data readily available, formalising or capturing informal trade, and having a clearly defined implementation timeline. There is a lack of up-to-date and comprehensive data to accurately and correctly capture the trends in intra-AfCFTA trade. Additionally, significant trade among African countries involves informal cross-border transactions facilitated by local traders. Significantly to economic growth. Additionally, the realisation of the full benefits from the AfCFTA will take time, as some member states are implementing the AfCFTA agreement's provisions at a slow pace. Since the inception of the AfCFTA, there have been positive increases in intra-African trade. However, the agreement is a long-term project whose success depends on constantly reviewing its progress and dedication to implementing its objectives.

Another important aspect that increases trade volumes among African countries is tariff reduction. Tariff reduction is AfCFTA's cornerstone since this is expected to increase intra-African trade volumes substantially. The elimination of tariffs makes it cheaper for member countries in the AfCFTA to trade among themselves. The reduction in tariffs is likely to increase trade volume among African countries. Additionally, tariff reduction will increase the competitiveness of products produced by African countries, thus stimulating demand for these products and increasing trade volumes. Reducing tariffs can also increase trade diversification by encouraging countries to shift from a heavy dependence on raw materials to value-added manufactured goods. The critical thing about trade diversification is that it can promote the development of RVCs and create new trade opportunities. According to Maliszewska et al. (2020), liberalising tariffs is key because it would stimulate Africa's income by 0.2%.

Lower tariffs can facilitate the creation of RVCs within the continent, as components and intermediate goods can be traded affordably across borders and through specialisation and collaboration. Another important aspect is that lower tariffs can stimulate industrialisation because domestic industries can have an increased consumer base, thus encouraging investment, innovation and economies of scale. SMEs dominate the economies of most African countries; thus, lowering tariffs can stimulate the growth of these SMEs by reducing entry trade barriers and facilitating their integration into regional markets.

However, the pace and scope at which tariffs are liberalised, the lack of addressing NTBs, the lack of clear and transparent ROO, slow implementation of trade facilitation measures, and the lack of economic diversification and structural transformation could slow down the impact of tariff liberalisation on trade creation within the AfCFTA. Tariff liberalisation can vary significantly, from one African country to another and from sector to sector, depending on the capacity of each industry and the trade structure in each country. For example, Ngepah and Udeagha (2018) state that, compared to other regions, the Western and Southern African regions have continuously maintained relatively low most-favoured nation rates. A study by Zongo and Oyelami (2021) reveals that the reduction and elimination of NTBs increase bilateral exports in the medium and long term for the ECOWAS and

SADC blocs by 60.86% and 72.19%, and by 134.17% and 149.02%, respectively. African countries should have mechanisms in place to monitor and evaluate intra-African trade due to the impact of tariff reductions and make policy adjustments where possible. The AfCFTA is a crucial avenue or platform for enhancing development through increased South-South cooperation. This, and technological collaborations among African countries, thereby enhancing investment, trade, and technological collaborations among African countries, and reducing exposure to Western-led economic disruptions.

16.2.2 Industrialisation and Value Addition

Global shocks, such as escalating geopolitical tensions reflected in the Russian-Ukrainian war and the recent Israel-Gaza war, have severely affected African economies, resulting in a 6.3% decrease in merchandise trade in 2023. The slow growth of China also fuelled Africa's slow growth, as China has been the continent's leading trading partner in recent decades. The majority of African countries' exports comprise primary commodities, mainly crude oil, which constitutes over 36% of total exports by the continent. However, these commodities' prices have plummeted, resulting in a decline in exported fuels. This came against an impressive 15.93% expansion in merchandise trade from US$1.2 trillion in 2021 to US$1.4 trillion in 2022 (African Export-Import Bank, 2024). However, the decline in merchandise trade in 2023 could potentially hinder the continent's ongoing efforts and prospects for driving industrialisation and promoting value addition.

Most African countries depend on a limited range of exports, making them highly exposed to price fluctuations and demand instability. For these reasons, strategic investments in the manufacturing, agro-processing, medical and pharmaceutical, and technology-enabled services sectors could contribute to economic diversification and a more inclusive growth (Besada, 2025). Additionally, African countries' degree of economic diversification and value addition significantly determines the pace at which intra-trade occurs.

Pre-AfCFTA trade trends indicate that raw materials dominated intra-African trade, with over 60%. Only a few African countries, predominantly Egypt, Morocco, and South Africa have significant share of manufactured goods. The three countries contribute close to half of Africa's exports of manufactured goods. African countries' merchandise exports value of primary and manufactured commodities averaged 90% and 9.4%, respectively, between 1963 and 2018, compared to 27% and 72% for Asia (Organisation for Economic Co-operation and Development, and World Trade Organisation, 2019). Between 2004 and 2023, Africa's intra-exports and intra-imports averaged between 10% and 20% (Chipanda & Cilliers, 2025).

According to Chipanda and Cilliers (2025), AfCFTA's implementation is expected to significantly increase exports and imports by approximately US$2.4 trillion and US$2.2 trillion, respectively, by 2043. The shift towards intra-trade of more manufactured goods would be a great potential to boost industrialisation and value addition in the African continent. A report by the African Export-Import Bank (2024) highlighted that manufactured goods would boost intra-African trade, reduce the continent's overdependence on commodity exports and be among key drivers of economic growth. It is anticipated that intra-African trade trend will shift towards manufactured goods. This will explicitly foster Africa's industrialisation, boost intra-African trade, and also reduce the trade deficit, as the majority of African countries export more raw materials and fewer manufactured goods, and import more manufactured goods. Furthermore, the AfCFTA is expected to increase the demand for value-added products and facilitate the development of RVCs. Nevertheless, these positive benefits can be realised if challenges related to the pace of AfCFTA implementation, infrastructure and trade facilitation deficits and lack of economic diversification are addressed.

The commodity dependence by export group reveals that the bulk of exports consists mainly of raw materials, primarily mineral ores and oil. The limited exports of manufactured goods and overdependence on raw materials by African countries largely contribute to global value chains (GVCs) by supplying primary products. This makes the continent susceptible to external economic shocks with huge effects on efforts to reduce poverty and promote economic development (Chipanda & Cilliers, 2025). Growth with little industrialisation and structural change failed to translate to higher economic development, address poverty, inequality and generate meaningful employment (Siyakiya et al., 2023).

RVCs are also an important avenue for industrialisation and development. RVCs' development and GVCs' participation are key for the African continent's industrialisation and economic development desires (Mitaritonna et al., 2024). According to Black et al. (2021), there are strong linkages between RVCs and regional integration. Nevertheless, special economic zones could be one way to enhance the development of RVCs. The AfCFTA era can boost trade among African countries through commodity-based industrialisation, which can be Africa's modus operandi to foster vertical integration. Findings by Chipanda and Cilliers (2025) show that Africa's exports would be concentrated in manufactured goods in 2043.

FDI availability is also key for AfCFTA's successful implementation. Understanding the amount of FDI the continent receives is crucial for capacity-building and developing policies and regulations that align with the AfCFTA Protocol on Investment, which was adopted in 2024, aimed to boost intra-African trade. There has been a steady increase in FDI inflows into Africa during the last 30 years, rising to US$79.6 billion in 2021 from US$2.8 billion in 1990, representing a 19-fold increase. Also, between 1990 and 2022, the stock of FDI inflow rose to more than US$1 trillion from US$60 billion (Agarwal, Ayele, et al., 2024). Africa's primary sources of FDI are China, India, EU (France, Italy, and the Netherlands), Singapore, the United Kingdom, and the USA, with Egypt, Nigeria, and South Africa as the largest recipients of FDI. Nevertheless, the share of global FDI by Africa still stands low, at around 5.4% in 2021.

FDI is important for the creation of jobs, the exchange of knowledge and technology transfer. Between 2003 and 2022, major jobs were created from FDI inflows in Egypt, Ethiopia, Morocco, Nigeria, and South Africa. Intra-African FDI has been generally lower than FDI inflow into Africa from the rest of the world. World Bank data reveal that inward intra-Africa FDI stock rose to around US$23.3 billion and US$128 billion by 2017 and 2021, respectively, from about US$800 million in 2001. Most African countries received the largest share of intra-African FDI inflow from within their respective regions. A case in point, intra-African FDI inflows in Southern Africa and East Africa were more than 54% and 69%, respectively, from the same regions (Agarwal, Ayele, et al., 2024).

The sectors that received the most considerable amount of inward FDI stock in 2019 were mining and quarrying, financial and insurance, and manufacturing, with US$31 billion, US$22 billion and US$14 billion, respectively. According to Agarwal, Ayele, et al. (2024), intra-African FDI is primarily located in the services sector, particularly in business, financial, communications and tourism services, while extra-African FDI is concentrated in the natural resources sector. Between 2016 and 2021, the primary sources of intra-Africa FDI inflows were Kenya, South Africa, Mauritius, Morocco, Nigeria, and Togo, while the FDI was invested in Nigeria, Mozambique, Mauritius, Ghana, and the Democratic Republic of Congo (Agarwal, Ayele, et al., 2024; Morgan et al., 2022). The full implementation of the AfCFTA's Protocol on Investment would be a linchpin for attracting more FDI inflows, which would further drive industrialisation and RVCs development across Africa, thus expanding market access and reducing regulatory barriers. According to the World Bank,[4] the increase in FDI inflows would boost African countries' exports by up to 32% by 2035.

Industrialisation in Africa has been very slow during the past 40 years. This is the case that even though diversification and export concentration indices marginally improved. Nevertheless, Africa's performance on these indices is far lower than that of other continents, as it primarily focuses on exporting raw materials. Due to a lack of industrialisation, developing countries, including those in Africa, contributed an insignificant amount of global manufactured exports, which stood at 0.02% and 3.07% in 1988 and 2015, respectively (Organisation for Economic Co-operation and Development,, and World Trade Organisation, 2019). Industrialisation is crucial for the promotion of inclusive development through sustainable employment creation and improvements in livelihoods, as well as economic resilience to globalisation and climate change shocks (Siyakiya et al., 2023). Industrialisation is key to Africa, as well as the success of the AfCFTA.

The manufacturing sector is a crucial driver of economic growth, industrialisation and economic transformation. Its share of GDP for many African countries has been declining since 1985, although they have shown a slight increase in recent years. Africa's percentage of manufacturing value added in GDP has been the lowest. While 2025 data by the United Nations Industrial Development Organisation (UNIDO) classifies other African countries as middle-income industrialising and low-income countries, only Mauritius, Eswatini and South Africa are classified as

[4] https://www.worldbank.org/en/news/press-release/2022/06/30/free-trade-pact-could-help-lift-up-to-50-million-africans-from-extreme-poverty.

middle-income industrial economies. Many African countries' composition of exports is traditionally primary products, which makes them susceptible to global price fluctuations. Through a vibrant and robust manufacturing sector, jobs can be generated, unemployment can be reduced, value addition can be enhanced, export earnings can be increased, local supply chains can be strengthened, dependency on imports can be reduced, and technology transfer and skill development can be fostered.

South Africa, one of the Africa's most diversified and industrialised countries, is expected to play an important role in driving intra-African trade. In 2022, South Africa and SADC represented 20.5% and 47.7% of total intra-African trade, respectively (African Export-Import Bank, 2023). Also, according to African Development Bank (2022), South Africa, Morocco, Egypt, Tunisia, Eswatini, and Mauritius are the top performers in terms of the industrialisation index. The same countries also rank high on the UNIDO's competitive industrial performance index. Between 2010 and 2021, the regional industrialisation index performance was North Africa (0.66), Southern Africa (0.57), Central Africa (0.50), West Africa (0.48), and East Africa (0.47). Nevertheless, a lot has to be done to turn around the industrial prospects and fortunes of the continent. The continent's efforts to industrialise are slowed down by inadequate infrastructure, a lack of an educated and skilled workforce, limited access to finance, and a poor business environment.

AfCFTA's full implementation would help African countries to shift from the production and exportation of commodities and low-value-added products to more industrial products. Additionally, the AfCFTA would offer a valuable opportunity for African countries to diversify and industrialise. However, a lot needs to be done to industrialise the continent. As a result, policymakers should prioritise state-led industrial policy targeting sectors with high backwards and forward linkages and high-technology usage (Siyakiya et al., 2023). These could be achieved through improved regional infrastructure, ramping up the establishment of special economic zones, concessions on debts, and increased efforts on value addition and beneficiation (Acheampong & Vitenu-Sackey, 2024). The AfCFTA can contribute to industrialisation by increasing economies of scale and expanding market access, encouraging RVCs and attracting investment in industrialisation. By expanding market access, AfCFTA allows African countries to tap into a larger customer base. Instead of competing with global manufacturing giants, African countries can collaborate in RVCs in the pharmaceutical industry to reduce over-reliance on imported medicines, and in the textile and apparel industry for countries like Ethiopia, Kenya and Lesotho, to benefit from cotton producers from West African countries. Additionally, countries that are newcomers to the automobile industry can greatly benefit from South Africa's expertise in the sector.

16.2.3 Trade Facilitation and Infrastructure Development

In comparison to all other regions, sub-Saharan Africa (SSA) has the highest cost of exporting. Based on border and documentary compliances, SSA has the second-highest cost of importing, after Latin America and the Caribbean (LAC), and South Asia, respectively. Regarding ROO and related documentation, between 2010 and 2013, 13 African countries were among the 23 developing and least developed countries with 35% of the most difficult non-tariff measures applied by partner countries. Maliszewska et al. (2020) state that reducing tariffs and improving trade facilitation would ease African countries' integration into the global supply chains, thereby boosting income gains in African economies by US$292 billion. Nevertheless, these gains would require each country to reduce the burden on businesses and cross-border traders.

The Guided Trade Initiative (GTI) plays a key role in helping countries increase their trade. The GTI was launched as a pilot project in October 2022 in Accra, Ghana, to facilitate the trading of 96 commodities by eight countries. The countries were drawn from the five African regions, and they include Ghana, Tunisia, Mauritius, Egypt, Rwanda, Cameroon, Kenya, and Tanzania (Rao, 2022). GTI aims to facilitate commercially meaningful trade and assess the legal, institutional, operational, and trade policy environments. AfCFTA Secretariat provides support to these eight countries that are part of the GTI in customs clearing and shipment. Through GTI, AfCFTA Secretariat can monitor trade documents and procedures' impact on the 96 selected goods traded under the AfCFTA agreement, and assess whether reducing tariffs in line with AfCFTA procedures yields the anticipated benefits. Early results of the GTI reveal a decrease in export documentation costs by up to 35%.

The AfCFTA is a catalyst for resilience against external market dependencies and sustainable industrial growth. It is a critical path for building resilience, reducing dependency on external markets, and driving sustainable industrialisation in Africa. However, these can be achieved if structural barriers are resolved and infrastructural deficits are addressed. In that regard, enhancing RVCs and addressing trade infrastructure deficits are important. Moreover, addressing trade barriers and improving access to finance are critical. Member states must harmonise trade regulations, eliminate NTBs and scale up innovative financing mechanisms to boost intra-African trade.

Through productivity gains, economic integration and trade generally contribute to economic growth significantly. Investments in infrastructure stimulate economic growth as they increase capital accumulation and facilitate workers' transition to higher-productivity jobs. According to the literature, economic development and infrastructure improvements are positively related. Investments in infrastructure have both short-term and long-run effects on output by boosting aggregate demand and aggregate supply in the economy. Infrastructure is a key driver of social progress and economic growth, and an enabler of sustainable economic development and productivity, as it significantly contributes to achieving the Sustainable

Development Goals, enhancing human development, and reducing poverty. According to Cilliers and Chipanda (2025), in 2043 Africa's economy would grow by 5.6% and 0.2 percentage points as a result of infrastructure improvements and lack of infrastructure improvements, respectively.

Africa's infrastructure demand increases as its population grows, thereby putting more pressure on the limited infrastructure networks. The continent also relies heavily on trade, primarily involving commodities, yet it has inadequate logistical infrastructure. According to the African Development Bank (2018), Africa's annual infrastructure financing deficit is over US$100 billion. The total amount needed to finance this infrastructure deficit amounts to between US$130 billion and US$170 billion. African Development Bank (2024) further estimates that about 600 million Africans lack access to electricity. Thus, investment in infrastructure that includes energy and power is critical. The infrastructure deficit undercuts the continent's growth, making trade more expensive and reducing its ability to compete globally. With improved logistical infrastructure, better port facilities, rail and road, and power plants, Africa can tap into the global markets and maximise the benefits of AfCFTA. Cilliers and Chipanda (2025) estimate that infrastructure improvements would increase Africa's total trade by 5.6%, representing a US$272.5 billion increase. Having adequate infrastructure, including transportation networks and logistics, is key to facilitating increased trade flows in Africa. African countries should increase investments in infrastructure, particularly regional infrastructure, to enhance cross-border trading. They can also increase funding mobilisation from both the private sector and the international community so that they can augment public sector investment and close the infrastructure investment financing gap. The AfCFTA is another way through which African countries can close the infrastructure financing gap through collaboration.

Therefore, the African continent must invest heavily in regional infrastructure so that AfCFTA's goals and objectives are realised. Also, governments of African countries must prioritise the implementation of the proper reforms necessary for closing the infrastructure financing gap and improving infrastructure development across all member states. International Monetary Fund (2019) posits that improving the quality of African trade logistics could significantly boost intra-regional trade in Africa by more than 12% and reduce cross-border trade costs. Nevertheless, the AfCFTA implementation can see the light of day if more is done beyond policy declarations. According to Besada (2025), AfCFTA's successful implementation requires the development of infrastructure, harmonisation of regulations and investments in transport and logistics.

AfCFTA's success also requires a robust digital trade infrastructure development. The development in the digital economy boosts intra-trade through facilitating cross-border e-commerce and online transactions. According to Agarwal, Mba, and Lemma (2024) and Chivunga et al. (2024), digital connectivity improvements are anticipated to increase employment, trade and GDP. The AfCFTA through the

Protocol on Digital Trade,[5] harmonises digital trade regulations among African countries by enabling seamless transactions across borders.

Another important factor that can spur intra-African trade is e-commerce. The digital world has transformed Africa, as the continent is no longer confined only to a late adopter. Digital trade and e-commerce are now mainstream across the continent, and these have opened opportunities for business, innovation, and economic growth (Sourabh, 2025). The leading African countries in digital trade with well-established e-commerce markets, which are generally driven by higher internet penetration rates, advanced logistics networks, and a greater familiarity with online shopping, are Egypt, Kenya, Morocco, South Africa and Nigeria (International Trade Administration U.S. Department of Commerce, n.d). The annual growth rate of e-commerce in Africa in 2023 was 14%, with online retail revenue estimated to amount to around US$49.02 billion. A report by McKinsey and Company (2024) highlights that e-commerce in the African continent is projected to reach US$180 billion by 2024. This represents a 25% annual growth rate in comparison to a 15% for the whole world. The number of e-commerce market users in Africa is expected to increase to 609.3 million by 2027, which will increase economic growth and access to goods and services and create jobs (Musyoka, 2024). The growth in e-commerce would be driven by various factors, among them population growth, urbanisation and infrastructure development (Logis-T Africa, 2023).

In terms of payment systems adoption, the current trends are that the African continent is the global leader when it comes to mobile money dominance, since more than 70% of adults use mobile money to do various financial transactions. Also, PAPSS simplifies and enables seamless cross-border payment systems, thus reducing the cost of intra-African trade. The PAPSS allows companies to do their transactions using African currencies without the need to use a third-party currency (Chipanda & Cilliers, 2025). There is a rapid rise in fintech companies, thus driving innovation in settling payments and offering new solutions for online and mobile transactions to cater for the unbanked population.

Despite this remarkable growth, the e-commerce market in Africa is facing various challenges such as low internet penetration, limited infrastructure and lack of regulation (Africa International Trade & Commerce Research, 2024; Anyanzwa, 2024; Logis-T Africa, 2023). Going forward, e-commerce's success in Africa hinges on a number of factors, including investment in digital infrastructure so that digital connectivity can be improved, promotion of financial inclusion and expansion of access to e-commerce payment methods, harmonisation of regulations on e-commerce, fostering innovation in payment systems and implementation of measures that build trust and confidence in using e-commerce platforms. Nevertheless, most governments in Africa are slowly recognising the centrality of digital trade and e-commerce, and as a result, they are enacting policies to support their growth. By addressing the above-mentioned challenges, the digital trade ecosystem can drive

[5] https://clgglobal.com/nigeria-africas-digital-trade-champion/.

economic growth, facilitate intra-trade under the AfCFTA, as well as promote inclusive growth.

Customs and border procedures efficiency is another important factor that influences cross-border trading time and cost within the African continent. In comparison with other regions, it costs the most on average to import a container in Africa. It costs about US$2492 in Africa, while the same costs US$1488 and US$935 in LAC, and East Asia and the Pacific, respectively (Brenton & Isik, 2012). Procedures and processes that are inefficient are significant NTBs, which hinder the potential benefits that African countries can derive from the AfCFTA. According to Anyanzwa (2024), "inefficient border procedures, complex documentation requirements and lack of harmonisation between countries create major business obstacles." The barriers not only hinder intra-African trade expansion and the continent's integration into GVCs but also diminish African products' competitiveness. According to de Melo et al. (2025), importing and exporting times in customs could be reduced by 3.7 days and 1.9 days, respectively, if the trade facilitation agreement is implemented in a realistic manner. Also, the key to unlocking trade facilitation challenges is coordinated border management. Enhanced collaboration, coordination and connectivity between border agencies and the private sector can lead to faster and cheaper clearing of goods (Konar-Leacy, 2017). By reducing and streamlining customs and border procedures, Africa can realise AfCFTA's full potential benefits.

Trade facilitation measures are important, but deeper integration, which involves harmonisation of competition, intellectual property rights, e-commerce and investment policies, could stimulate market efficiency and competitiveness, attract more FDI and reduce regulatory risks.[6] Trade costs could be lowered and capital inflows could increase, thereby boosting exports as countries engage in deeper integration. Although some African countries are making efforts to improve customs and border efficiency, considerable obstacles remain on the continent as a whole. Reducing barriers to investment and trade would increase exports of apparel. The chemical, processed food, rubber and plastic products, and textiles sectors are likely to benefit the most. The time and cost of cross-border trading can be addressed by continued efforts to harmonise, automate, develop infrastructure and tackle corruption. Addressing these challenges can unlock AfCFTA's full potential, thus driving inclusive development, economic growth and Africa's integration. Additionally, it is important to utilise data for continuous monitoring and tracking of border clearance times and costs to inform future policy interventions.

---

[6] https://www.worldbank.org/en/news/press-release/2022/06/30/free-trade-pact-could-help-lift-up-to-50-million-africans-from-extreme-poverty.

16.2.4 Employment and Economic Growth Impact

The AfCFTA is projected to bring positive results to many sectors' output. This has an effect of transforming economic growth and development. The AfCFTA is also projected to contribute to employment creation differently across sectors and countries in Africa. Yaya et al. (2025) reveal that trade and unemployment rate were negatively related in the Central African Economic and Monetary Community for the period 2001 to 2021. "An increase in trade, through the removal of tariff barriers under the AfCFTA agreement, could potentially reduce the unemployment rate in the region, Yaya et al. (2025)."

The AfCFTA is expected to increase employment opportunities and wages for unskilled workers, as well as help close the wage gap between men and women (Kutortse, 2025; Maliszewska et al., 2020). Estimates indicate that the AfCFTA will create approximately 18 million additional job opportunities across African countries. Nevertheless, in some countries, the wage gap of unskilled workers, male and female, can worsen; thus, the implementation of complementary policy reforms is key. AfCFTA's implementation is projected to increase the proportion of workers in the energy-intensive manufacturing sector. Additionally, agricultural employment for unskilled labour in the sector is expected to increase in about 60% of the countries on the continent, with wages for unskilled labour in the sector anticipated to rise faster. Nevertheless, the sector's importance on the continent is expected to decline to 29.7% in 2035 from 35.9% in 2020. The employment in the sector as a proportion of total employment by region is expected to be 10.7% (North Africa), 20.9% (Central Africa), 26.7% (West Africa), 29.8% (Southern Africa), and 47.8% (East Africa) in 2035 (Maliszewska et al., 2020). Additionally, by 2035, the wages of unskilled labour and skilled labour are expected to increase by 10.3% and 9.8% respectively (Maliszewska et al., 2020). Disaggregated by gender, wages would increase faster for women than men, and by 2035, wages for women and men would be expected to increase by 10.5% and 9.9%, respectively.

The manufacturing sector is consistently identified as the sector that will benefit the most in terms of employment creation when the AfCFTA is fully implemented. Tariff reduction and the development of RVCs are projected to be among the intra-African trade drivers in manufactured goods. The AfCFTA is projected to create employment opportunities in the agricultural sector through the value addition of agro-processing, driven by increased demand for agricultural products. The agreement is also projected to increase the intra-African trade of agricultural products significantly. The subsequent effect is to drive job creation in the agricultural sector, the largest employer and significant contributor to GDP in many African countries.

However, the increase in jobs in these sectors would depend on AfCFTA's implementation, the degree of complementarity between the policies implemented to bolster job creation, and inclusivity in efforts to ensure job creation and structural transformation. Some studies predict that the full implementation of the AfCFTA could be more beneficial to women, particularly in the labour-intensive industries which employ the majority of women. Additionally, the AfCFTA presents a it is poised to create significant job opportunities for them.

According to Chipanda and Cilliers (2025), AfCFTA's implementation is projected to increase the GDP of African countries by approximately 10% and reduce poverty by over 32 million by 2043. Alternatively, by 2050, the AfCFTA could increase the GDP of Africa to a tune of US$29 trillion.[7] Generally, the agreement would have a substantial impact on wages across the continent. The agreement would also increase economic activity and productivity, potentially leading to higher earnings. Additionally, by 2043, the services and manufacturing sectors would increase by 8.1% and 10.7%, respectively.

16.2.5 Financial and Investment Flows

The AfCFTA is projected to yield positive results for the output of many sectors, particularly agriculture, automotive, digital infrastructure and innovation, energy and power supply, financial services, and the pharmaceutical industry. This has an effect of transforming economic growth and development. The manufacturing sector is expected to enjoy a lion's share of investments due to the high demand for manufactured goods in Africa. Specifically, manufacturing sub-sectors that include the agro-processing, automotive, machinery, pharmaceuticals and textile industries are expected to attract investments. The expected increase in investments in these industries could potentially expand market access and RVCs, thus making Africa an attractive manufacturing hub. Currently, there is investment in the labour-intensive manufacturing sectors across Africa. China emerges as the major source of investment in most of the light manufacturing industries across Africa, particularly the textile and footwear industries.

The African continent is endowed with vast agricultural resources. At the same time, there is an increasing demand for agricultural products both within and outside the continent. The implementation of the AfCFTA is likely to boost investments in the agro-processing industry. According to the World Bank,[8] the full implementation of the AfCFTA could potentially stimulate greater FDI flows, which are greatly needed for diversification into new industries like manufacturing, agribusiness and services, and the reduction of the continent's vulnerability to commodity price shocks.

The industries that are expected to realise an increase in investments are the food and beverage processing, leather manufacturing and textile production from local cotton. The automotive and machinery industry is also expected to attract more investments. This is because of the rising demand for vehicles and equipment. Also,

[7] https://au-afcfta.org/purpose-the-afcfta/.

[8] https://www.worldbank.org/en/news/press-release/2022/06/30/free-trade-pact-could-help-lift-up-to-50-million-africans-from-extreme-poverty.

with the growing realisation of the need for RVCs, the industry is expected to drive investments in the vehicle component manufacturing, agricultural machinery production and vehicle assembly plants. Nevertheless, investment attraction requires an affordable, reliable and stable supply of energy. The continent has the least access to electricity and a high infrastructure deficit, thus stimulating investments in different energy sources, particularly renewable energy sources, and spurring cross-border electricity grids.

The growth of trade under the AfCFTA is expected to necessitate the need for the development of digital infrastructure, innovation, transport and logistics, and a robust financial sector. These are important because modern trade is fast-moving towards the digital economy. With the high infrastructure deficit faced by the continent, it is imperative to invest in automation and financial technologies, banking, cross-border payment systems, e-commerce platforms, and high-speed internet. Also, the development of the pharmaceutical industry is expected to increase due to the fact that the AfCFTA seeks to reduce overdependence on imported medicines. This has a potential effect of creating investment opportunities and research in the industry, thus encouraging local production and supply chains. Investments in all these areas are expected to increase as the need to facilitate trade increases.

The bigger picture is that the implementation of the AfCFTA, through harmonisation of investment and trade rules, offering market access, and the creation of an integrated market, would enhance the attraction and promotion of both domestic and foreign investments. Having predictable and transparent regulations, along with an institutional framework, is crucial for boosting investor confidence. Nevertheless, the factors that influence investment in Africa require governments to have an effective implementation of the AfCFTA, craft policies that are investor-friendly, develop infrastructure, and streamline investment processes.

Financial institutions play a crucial role in supporting trade, particularly with the advent of the AfCFTA. African financial institutions, as they facilitate and finance trade across the African region, play a crucial role in this process. Beyond this, African financial institutions also support SMEs by developing tailor-made products to facilitate trade for these small firms, financing infrastructure development to smooth the flow of trade, and promoting regional integration by supporting intra-African trade and investment. The AfDB, Afreximbank, African Finance Corporation and regional and national commercial banks are among the financial institutions that currently facilitate trade within Africa. Despite the important role played by African financial institutions in facilitating trade, some challenges remain that hinder their smooth support of trade. African financial institutions face limited access to foreign exchange for financing international trade, insufficient capital to underwrite large trade finance transactions, high perceived risk, inadequate infrastructure, high regulatory hurdles, and a lack of collateral to access trade finance. Addressing these obstacles through joint efforts among African financial institutions, governments, regional bodies, and international partners is critical to fully realising the AfCFTA's potential and driving long-term economic growth across the African continent.

Africa's financial landscape is experiencing increased cross-border banking activity. These tendencies are critical to promoting trade, investment, and overall economic growth, particularly in light of the AfCFTA. A vast majority of African financial markets are tiny and highly fragmented, with banks dominating the total financial industry. In addition, African capital markets face several other issues, including a weak regulatory framework and structures, limited activity in secondary markets, a lack of diversified products, a small number of participants, limited mobilisation of local currency savings, inadequate financial infrastructure, and a shortage of listed, tradable securities.

In an attempt to address the above, the AfDB Group approved the Capital Markets Development Trust Fund (CMDTF) in November 2019. The first Phase (2020–2022) was effectively implemented in the West African region. Furthermore, in November 2022, the Committee that has oversight of CMDTF approved the CMDTF 2023–2026 Strategy to deepen the impact of CMDTF in West Africa. The CMDTF also supports the AfDB's High 5s and operational priorities, which include the Private Sector Development Strategy (2022–2026), the Regional Integration Strategic Framework (2018–2025), the Industrialisation Strategy for Africa (2016–2025), and the Gender Strategy (2021–2025).[9] Between 2019 and 2024, 13 projects across West Africa, worth a total of US$5,595,172, were approved by the CMDTF.

The current trends of cross-border banking in Africa are shifting towards regional banks, and many pan-African banks are emerging as key players in facilitating trade and investment. Most African banks are expanding internationally to improve yields, diversify operations, and assist domestic clients' global activities. As the AfCFTA are expanding and becoming increasingly vital in financing and facilitating intra-African trade. Cross-border banking, including regional banks, has improved financial access in many African countries. Fintech advances enable faster and more inexpensive cross-border payment alternatives, such as mobile money and digital wallets. However, still some challenges that hinder the proper functionality of cross-border banking. These include regulatory fragmentation, high costs, lack of interoperability, foreign currency volatility, limited market knowledge, infrastructure limitations, and regional risks, as well as contagion.

16.2.6 SMEs and Informal Sector Participation

While formal intra-African trade currently accounts for a low percentage, ranging from 12% to 18%, it is essential to note that informal cross-border trade constitutes a significant portion and, at the same time, is not fully captured; however, it could substantially increase overall intra-trade figures if properly accounted for (Andrew,

[9] https://www.afdb.org/en/topics-and-sectors/initiatives-and-partnerships/capital-markets-development-trust-fund.

2022). SMEs and the informal sector play a crucial role in the economies of African countries. SMEs account for a lion's share of businesses and employment in developing countries, including African countries. The literature shows that it is more prevalent in Africa than in other regions (African Export-Import Bank, 2020; Food and Agriculture Organisation of the United Nations, 2020). SMEs are a crucial driver of economic growth, as they account for nearly 80% of jobs in Africa (Runde et al., 2021). At the same time, the informal sector provides livelihoods and survival for the majority of the population in many developing countries, who usually rely on the informal economy (Blades et al., 2011). It creates employment and income opportunities for a substantial portion of the population, particularly the poor and less educated individuals, including many women and youth, as well as vulnerable groups facing difficulties in finding employment in the formal economy (Organisation for Economic Co-operation and Development, 2007; Tieku & Yakohene, 2023). Nevertheless, the economic benefits of the informal economy vary from country to country, depending on the structure of the economy (Gerxhani, 2004).

The AfCFTA presents many opportunities for SMEs and the informal sector by expanding market access, enabling them to participate in RVCs, allowing them to diversify markets and products, facilitating trade through reducing border delays and simplifying customs procedures, accessing financing and enhancing e-commerce and digital trade. The AfCFTA makes strides to support SMEs and the informal sector by creating a more favourable environment for them to participate in trade, developing protocols and frameworks to address the unique challenges faced by SMEs and informal traders, promoting inclusive growth, providing visibility for products and services offered by SMEs and informal traders, and developing platforms and partnerships to provide SMEs with access to market information, networking opportunities and trade finance.

The informal sector plays a massive and significant role in intra-African trade, contributing approximately US$17.6 billion annually. It is also estimated to contribute between 7% and 16% of the formal trade flows of intra-African trade, with 42% of total formal trade contributed by West African countries and between 30% and 40% of total formal trade by the COMESA and SADC trading blocs. Formal intra-African trade as a percentage of total intra-trade increased from 13.6% in 2022 to 14.9% in 2023 (African Export-Import Bank, 2024). Women account for around 60% of informal cross-border traders across the continent. Because of the immense contribution by informal cross-border traders, it is imperative to measure their activities to monitor intra-African trade for accurate data and policy formulation. SMEs also benefit through the GTI, which reduces compliance expenses that impede trade.

The overall economic transformation of Africa and the AfCFTA. Women and the youth account for a sizable amount of the continent's population, labour force, and entrepreneurial spirit, notably in the SME and informal sectors. The Protocol on Women and Youth in Trade under the AfCFTA represents a significant step that will enhance the participation of women and youth in trade. It could help youth and women improve their competitiveness, access more markets, and participate in RVCs by addressing the unique barriers and challenges they face in cross-border trading (Agarwal, 2024). The Protocol is also anticipated to improve competitiveness, support in RVCs, and create wider markets.

16.3 Challenges in AfCFTA Implementation Based on Data Trends

The AfCFTA represents a transformative opportunity for regional integration (Soutar, 2021). However, data-driven assessments reveal several inherent challenges that hinder their full realisation. It is therefore correct to say that the implementation of AfCFTA is faced with several challenges. Among other challenges, these include non-tariff barriers, infrastructure and logistical issues, insufficient financial accessibility, and policy misalignments between member states (Wapmuk & Ali, 2022). This section discusses some of the challenges that hinder the implementation of the AfCFTA. Most importantly, the discussion puts more emphasis on those challenges that have some data backing to amplify their severity of hindrance. First, NTBs and policy inconsistencies are critically discussed. Thereafter, logistical and infrastructural components, as well as financial accessibility challenges, follow suit. Lastly, the political dimension, including the policy misalignment discussion, concludes this section.

16.3.1 Persistent Non-tariff Barriers and Policy Inconsistencies

It is no new phenomenon that countries tend to capitalise more on the commodities in which they have comparative advantages. All these efforts are often driven by the global demand, which is primarily determined by tariffs. On the same note, most countries tend to focus on tariff liberalisation to create some demand. This is amplified by Tanyi (2015), who argues that AfCFTA has a trade creation effect via the tariff liberalisation route. Despite progress in tariff liberalisation, NTBs such as import quotas, technical standards, and sanitary regulations remain widespread. The African Trade Observatory (ATO) reports uneven progress in NTB reporting and resolution (African Export-Import Bank, 2018a).

Additionally, inconsistent national policies, such as export bans and licencing requirements, often contradict the objectives of the AfCFTA, undermining predictability for traders and investors. These unintended consequences often hinder the smooth flow of goods and services within the trade sphere. Figure 16.1 depicts several key indicators that function as “de facto” non-tariff barriers.

As can be seen from Fig. 16.1, the key NTBs have been disaggregated into about seven indicators with the data from the World Trade Organisation (2023). The indicators used include the following: LPI score, Customs score, Infrastructure Score,

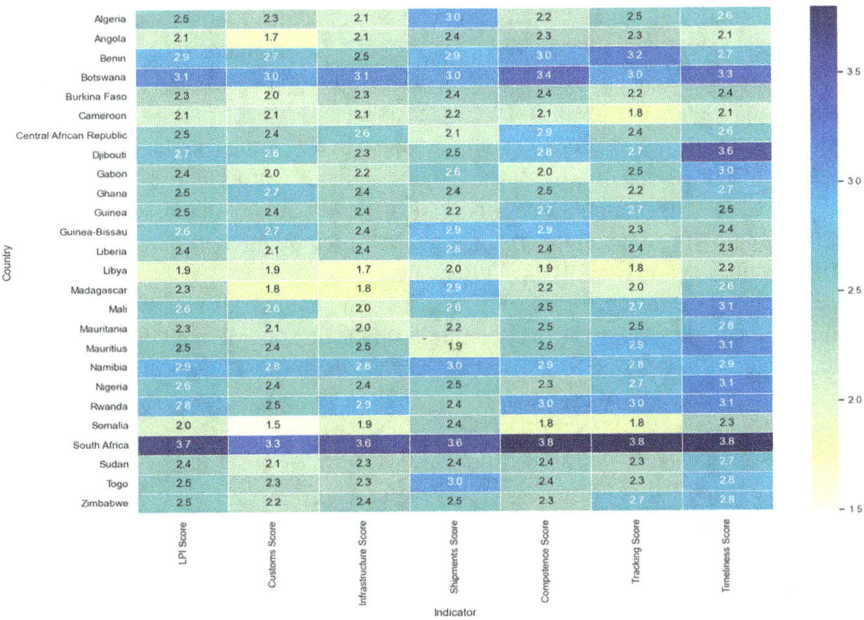

Fig. 16.1 Heatmap of NTB-related logistics scores by country (2023). Source: Authors' own with data from World Bank (2023)

Shipments Score, Competence Score, Tracking Score, and Timeliness Score. Each score ranges from 1 (poor) to 5 (excellent) and reflects the extent to which trade and transport-related bottlenecks hinder cross-border commerce, a key concern for the realisation of AfCFTA.

The Heatmap shown in Fig. 16.1 reveal some interesting facts. For starters, South Africa scores consistently above 3.6 across all categories, highlighting its role as a regional logistics hub. Its superior performance in customs efficiency (3.3), infrastructure (3.6), tracking (3.8), and competence (3.8) reflects long-standing investments in transport corridors, port infrastructure, and trade facilitation. According to Arvis et al. (2023) and the World Trade Organisation (2023), countries with such logistics capacity tend to act as regional gateways and play a disproportionate role in intra-African trade. Therefore, AfCFTA's success depends heavily on leveraging countries like South Africa as logistical anchors while lifting others towards higher performance tiers.

On the other hand, across most countries, such as Angola, the Central African Republic, Libya, and Somalia, the Customs Scores fall below 2.5, and the Infrastructure Scores are alarmingly low, often hovering around 2.0. The reflections from all these include the following issues: inefficient border control procedures, outdated trade infrastructure (e.g., ports, rail, warehousing), and limited information and communication technology (ICT) integration into customs management (Jackson, 2009; Xing, 2018). Additionally, studies such as Hoekman and Nicita (2011) and Portugal-Perez and Wilson (2012) confirm that soft infrastructure (such as customs and transparency) can have as much of a trade-boosting effect as tariff reductions, making these scores red flags for AfCFTA implementation.

Countries like Somalia, Libya, Liberia, and Cameroon are in the "cold region" in tracking and tracing (below 2.0). This suggests weak adoption of digital systems for cargo monitoring, significant gaps in data transparency across border agencies, and fragmented communication between private logistics actors and public customs authorities. As can be imagined, this erodes trust in supply chain visibility, indirectly raising the cost per shipment, and undermining regional value chain development (Shamsuzzoha et al., 2013; Widianti et al., 2021).

Generally, within the top tier (≥2.8 across indicators), there are a handful of countries, including South Africa, Namibia, Mauritius, and Rwanda. However, the Middle-Tier (2.3–2.7) is comprised of Ghana, Nigeria, Kenya, Botswana, and Benin. The last component, Low Tier (≤2.2), is comprised of Angola, Somalia, Libya, Madagascar, and the CAR. This regional disparity reveals unequal readiness levels across the continent. While Southern and Eastern Africa demonstrate moderate to strong logistics ecosystems, large parts of Central and West Africa remain structurally disconnected, posing risks to AfCFTA's core principle of continent-wide market integration.

In summary, Fig. 16.1 underscores the urgent need for harmonised customs procedures, with interconnectivity across national single-window systems and broader alignment under AfCFTA Annexes on Trade Facilitation. The current heterogeneity in policy frameworks reflects the legacy of colonial-era trade patterns and the slow implementation of WTO trade facilitation agreement provisions. Infrastructure development should not only be physical (roads, ports) but also digital, encompassing logistics tracking systems and customs automation platforms. Additionally, the projects under the Programme for Infrastructure Development in Africa (PIDA) must be tightly integrated with AfCFTA logistics corridors. This homogenisation will not only improve cross-border trade facilitation in Africa but also enhance the lives of its people, as trade can make them better off.

Several landlocked states, such as Lesotho, Chad, Mali, and Zimbabwe, rely on neighbouring countries for port access, making them uniquely vulnerable to NTBs. Regional economic communities (RECs) and AfCFTA protocols must address transit trade facilitation and harmonised documentation to mitigate these systemic disadvantages. On the other side, South Africa, Kenya, and Morocco (not pictured but relevant) can act as trade facilitation anchors. These countries could be prioritised as pilot zones for regional e-customs integration and trade digitalisation, setting precedents for scalable solutions continent-wide.

Based on the aforementioned facts, the following possible coordination mechanisms could be utilised to expedite AfCFTA implementation. First, the expansion of ATO mandate to monitor logistics and NTBs in real time. The importance of logistics monitoring and other NTB remedies cannot be overemphasised, as argued by Maniriho (2022). Furthermore, the establishment of a continent-wide NTB early warning system, building on existing mechanisms in COMESA and the Eastern African Community. There is also a need to create AfCFTA Logistics Hubs with targeted donor and public–private investment to scale capacity where it is needed most. Lastly, incentivising the adoption of smart ports and green logistics to align with both trade and environmental targets.

16.3.2 Gaps in Infrastructure and Logistics Development

The other main obstacle to the success of AfCFTA implementation is inadequate logistics infrastructure, such as roads, ports, and warehouses, which make trading within Africa difficult. Efficient trade depends heavily on physical and digital infrastructure (Nordås & Piermartini, 2004). Many countries still face serious deficits in road, rail, port, and broadband connectivity. This not only increases the cost of doing business but also prolongs lead timelines, making intra-African trade less competitive and ineffective. Figure 16.2 shows a glimpse of the distribution of LPI scores in the AfCFTA countries.

The histogram shown in Fig. 16.2 reveals that most countries score between 2.4 and 3.0, with a peak around the 2.5–2.7 range. This clustering in the lower-middle section of the distribution indicates that a majority of African and lower-income countries continue to face systemic logistics inefficiencies. The rightward taper reflects a smaller group of high-performing economies with LPI scores above 3.5. Furthermore, the uneven distribution suggests a significant logistical development gap, which could exacerbate existing inequalities within the AfCFTA. High performers (like South Africa) may disproportionately benefit, while low performers struggle with access and participation in the intra-trade sphere.

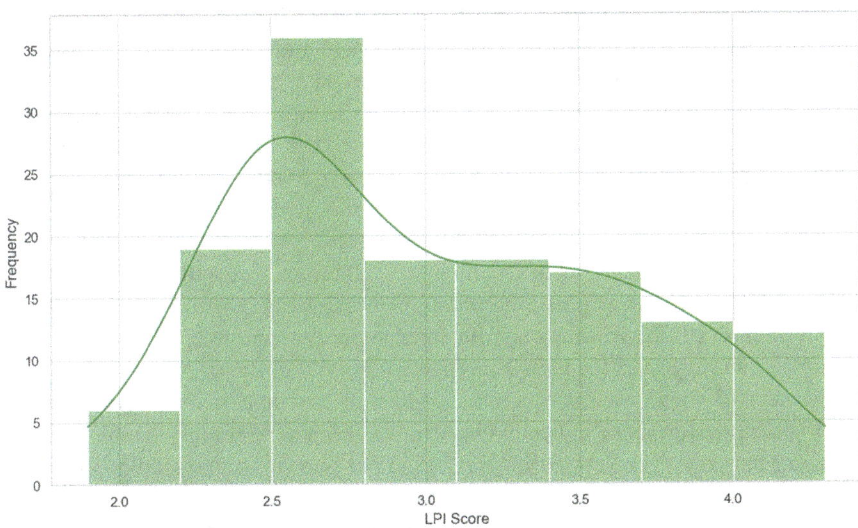

Fig. 16.2 Distribution of LPI scores in AfCFTA countries (2023). Source: Authors' own with data from World Bank (2023)

The relatively narrow tail on the right suggests that very few countries have world-class logistics systems. This finding is consistent with the African Development Bank, African Union,, and United Nations Industrial Development Organization (2022) report, which highlights the poor state of customs automation, underdeveloped ICT infrastructure, and fragmented intermodal networks in Africa. Countries below the mean LPI score (~2.7) should be prioritised in AfCFTA's Phase II and III implementation stages, focusing on critical areas such as trade facilitation reforms under the AfCFTA Protocol on Customs Cooperation and Trade Facilitation, investment in ports, roads, railways, and trade ICT infrastructure via initiatives like PIDA, among others. On the other hand, Capacity-building and technical assistance, especially in customs and tracking systems, will usher our African countries towards sustained growth in this aspect.

One may ask, what are the implications of low LPI scores? Low LPI scores translate directly into inflated trade costs and longer border delays. According to Arvis et al. (2024), a one-point increase in LPI score is associated with a logistics cost reduction of 14–18%, representing a significant potential gain for intra-African trade. Therefore, the histogram makes a compelling case for targeting logistics equalisation measures to democratise market access under AfCFTA. The fact that many scores cluster in the 2.5 range supports the urgent need for regional corridor development, such as the North-South Corridor (Northern and Southern Africa), the Central Corridor (Tanzania, Rwanda, and Burundi), and the Abidjan-Lagos Corridor (West Africa). These corridors can serve as levers of regional equalisation, lifting LPI scores via shared infrastructure and harmonised regulation.

It is imperative to note that Fig. 16.2 includes several fragile states (e.g., Chad, Central African Republic, South Sudan), which tend to reside in the lowest bins (<2.3). Their logistics disadvantages are exacerbated by conflict, limited port access, and high transport insecurity (Calì, 2014). The AfCFTA Adjustment Facility, if operationalised effectively, could channel technical and financial support towards these lagging economies. Moreover, the development of an LPI-Conscious AfCFTA Scorecard would track LPI indicators alongside tariff commitments and services liberalisation benchmarks. Likewise, mainstreaming LPI data into National AfCFTA Strategies, particularly for identifying and mitigating non-tariff barriers, would also improve the pace towards the full implementation of the AfCFTA. According to empirical evidence, the African Development Bank, African Union,, and United Nations Industrial Development Organization (2022) estimates that Africa requires over $130 billion annually in infrastructure investments. On the other hand, the World Bank's (2023) LPI shows significant disparities across RECs, with only a few countries ranking above the global average levels (World Bank, 2023).

Figure 16.3 shows the interquartile range (IQR), median, and outliers for seven key logistics performance indicators in Africa. Each box represents the middle 50% of scores across African countries, the horizontal line shows the median, and dots represent outlier countries (either over- or under-performers). Among all indicators, the Timeliness Score has the highest median (~2.7) and relatively tight IQR, suggesting that even low-performing countries manage to maintain some basic reliability in trade scheduling. This aligns with the African Export-Import Bank (2023),

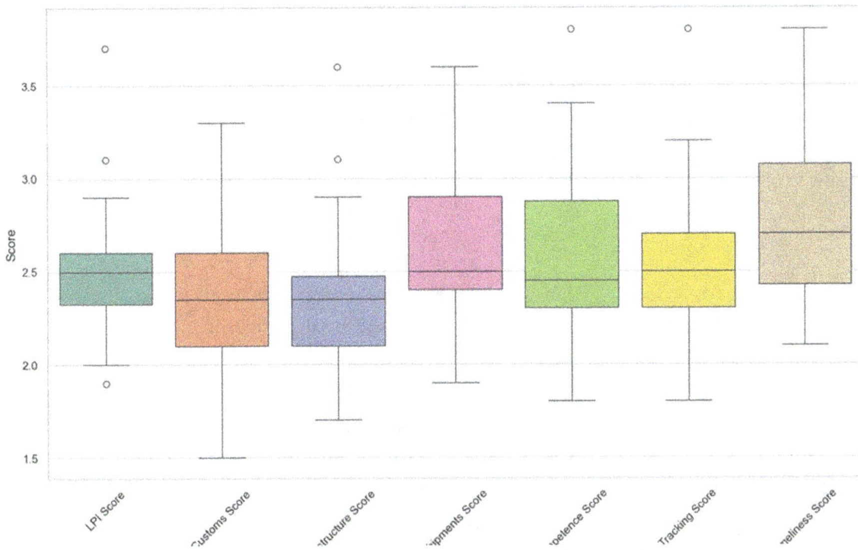

Fig. 16.3 Boxplot of logistics performance indicators across AfCFTA countries (2023). Source: Authors' own with data from the logistic performance index World Bank (2023)

indicating that investments in customs hours, clearance windows, and port automation have modestly improved delivery times in parts of West and Southern Africa. Timeliness gains may be the "low-hanging fruit" of logistics reform, offering a foundation to build broader NTB reductions.

The Customs Score and Infrastructure Score distributions have the lowest medians (~2.3) and display substantial spread. The reflections from these include inefficiencies in border management systems, low digitisation rates in customs documentation and poor road, rail, and port infrastructure (especially in landlocked or conflict-prone and fragile states). According to Portugal-Perez and Wilson (2012), weak infrastructure accounts for up to 40% of trade cost penalties in low-income countries in Africa. Unless these areas are prioritised, tariff liberalisation under AfCFTA will yield minimal gains due to persistent frictions in physical and procedural trade environments.

Both the Shipments Score and Competence Score have long whiskers and visible outliers. These indicators reflect variability in the logistics industry professionalism, operator reliability and cross-border shipment frequency and success. Outliers on the high end (e.g., South Africa, Botswana) mask a long tail of fragile performers, reaffirming earlier findings from the heatmap and histogram (Figs. 16.1 and 16.2). A regional trade pact like AfCFTA must not only promote trade volume but also equalise trade reliability through standardised procedures, digital integration, and logistics training programs. Despite technological advances globally, African countries lag in cargo tracking systems, with many scoring below 2.5 and showing tight clustering. This limits transparency, risk assessment by insurers and just-in-time trade models. As confirmed by Arvis et al. (2023) and the World Trade Organisation

Table 16.1 Synthesis: summary based on the boxplot

Indicator	Median score	Variability	NTB challenge
Timeliness	High (~2.7)	Low	Relatively manageable with modest investment
Customs	Low (~2.3)	High	Major administrative bottleneck
Infrastructure	Low (~2.3)	High	Structural constraints limiting intra-African integration
Tracking	Low (~2.4)	Moderate	Technological gap undermining supply chain transparency
Shipments	Moderate	High	Reliability is inconsistent across the continent
Competence	Moderate	High	Skill and capacity disparities in logistics service delivery

(2023) reports, digital visibility tools are essential for managing trade across fragmented customs zones and remain underdeveloped in the African context.

Table 16.1 provides a summary of the implications based on Fig. 16.3. This summary covers the critical aspects of trade facilitation indicators, including timeliness, customs, infrastructure, tracking, shipments, and competence.

Based on the earlier trends and indicators' performance, customs reforms should be front-loaded in the implementation timeline of the AfCFTA, with a focus on harmonising documentation, reducing clearance times, and expanding single-window platforms. Additionally, tracking and cargo visibility systems must be subsidised or scaled regionally, leveraging cloud-based platforms to reduce cost barriers. Public–private logistics training academies should be prioritised to improve the bottom quartile of "competence". Performance benchmarks for AfCFTA member states could be built using LPI-derived scorecards, tied to compliance incentives under the AfCFTA Adjustment Facility. Given all these, the AfCFTA full implementation will be closer to attainment, assuming all the coordination mechanism works well.

16.3.3 Limited Financial Inclusion and Access to Trade Finance

SMEs, which constitute over 80% of African businesses, face severe constraints in accessing trade finance and other financial instruments necessary for cross-border expansion (Montinari & Stracca, 2016). Financial markets remain underdeveloped and fragmented, and many traders operate without formal banking relationships. Additionally, as argued by Adegboye and Iweriebor (2018), about 80% of African inhabitants and 83% are lagging in financial accessibility. Figure 16.4 shows the severity of the credit gap, a critical indicator of trade finance as one of the most structural barriers to the effective implementation of the AfCFTA.

From Fig. 16.4, the map categorises countries by the percentage of the adult population that is unserved or underserved by formal credit markets. The data is

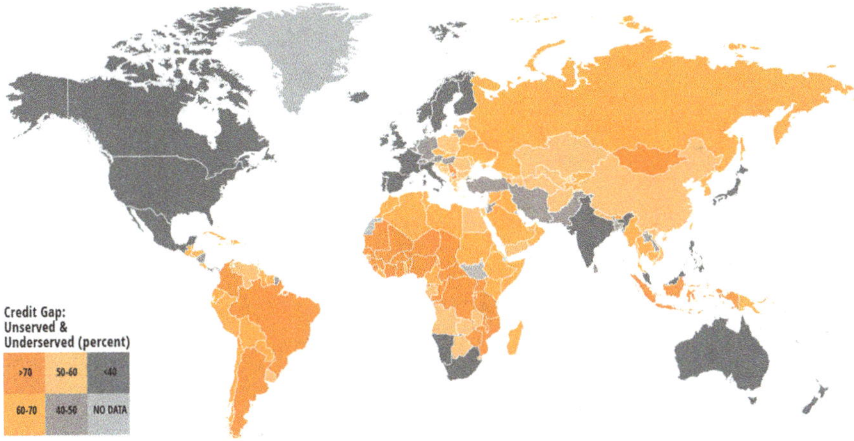

Fig. 16.4 The credit gap. Source: The International Finance Corporation (IFC)

segmented into dark orange (>70%), which signifies severely credit-constrained countries, and orange (60–70%), showing substantial financial exclusion. Light orange (50–60%) shows moderate gaps, while beige (40–50%) shows emerging markets with growing financial access. On the other hand, dark grey (<40%) shows financially inclusive countries, and light grey signifies that there is no data available.

The focus of the analysis on the AfCFTA implementation is in Africa. So, nearly all SSA countries are shaded in the orange to dark orange spectrum, indicating that over 60–70% of adults are either unserved or underserved by the formal credit system. For example, Nigeria, DRC, Ethiopia, Mozambique, and Burkina Faso fall into the highly financially excluded category. More so, Lesotho, Namibia, South Africa, and Mauritius fare slightly better but still face access constraints, particularly for informal businesses and rural populations (Mutsonziwa & Fanta, 2021). In the context of AfCFTA, this financial exclusion translates into a hidden NTB, where access to regional markets exists in theory, but firms lack the capital to exploit these opportunities. On the macroeconomic performance of these economies, are there any implications? We will see the answer to this question in the next section.

MSMEs contribute over 80% of employment and 40% of GDP in many African countries, yet they account for less than 15% of formal credit disbursements. The AfCFTA aims to integrate over 1.3 billion consumers (Döring & Engel, 2021), but without access to credit, firms cannot invest in compliance with cross-border standards. Entrepreneurs cannot scale up to meet regional demand, while women-led enterprises, which dominate the informal sector, are locked out of formal trade. Therefore, credit access becomes a de facto exclusion mechanism in a liberalised trade regime.

According to African Development Bank (2022) and Polonskaya (2022), Africa faces an $81 billion trade finance gap, limiting intra-African exports and cross-border infrastructure investments. Regional banks often lack liquidity and collateral mechanisms, especially in post-conflict or high-risk jurisdictions. Therefore, SMEs

Table 16.2 Drivers of financial exclusion

Factor	Effect on AfCFTA participation
High collateral requirements	Informal businesses are excluded from loans.
Credit bureau underdevelopment	No credit history = no risk profile
Gender bias in lending	Women-owned firms face disproportionate denials.
Rural-urban divide	Remote areas lack access to branch infrastructure.
Currency volatility	Local banks are hesitant to fund export operations.

capable of producing for export markets are often trapped in a cash-flow cycle due to short-term credit cycles and limited working capital options. Table 16.2 summarises some of the critical drivers of financial exclusion in Africa.

According to Beck (2022), structural financial sector underdevelopment in Africa stems from a combination of colonial banking legacies, macroeconomic instability, and under-regulated Fintech markets. To overcome some of the associated challenges, leveraging institutions like Afreximbank, African Guarantee Fund, and ECOWAS Bank for Investment and Development to provide risk-sharing instruments for local banks and Fintech lenders is of paramount importance. Additionally, the creation of special windows for women- and youth-led MSMEs, through programs like Affirmative Finance Action for Women in Africa and African Women Impact Fund, will aid in this regard.

In summary, it is evident that even if tariff walls fall and transport corridors improve, AfCFTA will remain a glass ceiling for millions of African entrepreneurs unless the credit gap is urgently addressed. The overwhelming dominance of orange-shaded countries in Africa (Fig. 16.4) signals a pan-continental structural barrier to trade inclusivity. Therefore, Finance must be reframed not as a peripheral service but as a core trade-enabling infrastructure, which is equivalent in importance to roads, ports, and digital platforms.

16.4 Future Projections for AfCFTA Implementation

There is no specific data that shows the growth of intra-African trade for the years 2025, 2030, and 2040. However, since the operationalisation of the AfCFTA in 2021, trade is anticipated to rise. In 2023, intra-African trade was reported to have increased to USD$192.2 billion, which is a 3.2% increase compared to 2022 (African Export-Import Bank, 2024). The World Bank[10] predicts that by 2035,

[10] https://www.worldbank.org/en/news/press-release/2022/06/30/free-trade-pact-could-help-lift-up-to-50-million-africans-from-extreme-poverty.

intra-African exports led by manufactured goods would increase by 109% under deep integration. The United Nations Economic Commission for Africa (UNECA) predicts that by 2040, the agreement could potentially increase intra-African trade by up to 25%. This represents up to US$70 billion in trade value. Other studies predict that intra-African trade would rise by a value ranging between US$50 billion and US$70 billion, equivalent to 15% and 25% of the total trade.[11] This will depend on the level of liberalisation.

According to UNECA, intra-African trade is expected to increase by 35% by 2045 (Mangeni et al., 2024). The 2025 Economic Report on Africa also anticipates that AfCFTA would potentially boost intra-African trade exports and value of cross-border trade by 45% and US$275.7 billion by 2045, respectively, while intra-African trade would increase by 60%, 48%, 34%, and 28% for agri-food, industry, services, and energy, respectively (United Nations Economic Commission for Africa, 2025). Other estimates suggest that intra-African trade would increase by 35% by 2045 if the AfCFTA is fully implemented (Mangeni et al., 2024).

Africa has historically accounted for a minor proportion of the world's population and global trade, ranging from 2% to 3%. Data by Statista[12] showed that Africa's share of global merchandise trade stood at 2.7% in 2023. Even after the establishment of the AfCFTA and its official start in January 2021, intra-African trade as a percentage of global trade declined from 14.55 to 13.7% in 2021 and 2022. During the same period, intra-African exports and intra-African imports as a percentage of total trade declined from 18.22% to 17.89% and from 12.81% to 12.09%, respectively.[13] This is shocking given that the continent has vast natural resources and a growing young population. However, limited industrialisation and low manufacturing, infrastructure deficits, overdependence on raw material exports, trade barriers, complex regulatory requirements, and vulnerability to external shocks are among the contributing factors to Africa's relatively small share of global trade.

The development of infrastructure is important for industrialisation. Having efficient transportation and logistics is key to the development of the manufacturing sector. The infrastructure, like highways and railways, ports and industrial parks, facilitates the movement of goods, supports regional and international trade and creates manufacturing hubs respectively. The other important infrastructural development is energy and power supply. The growth of the manufacturing sector requires a reliable and affordable supply of electricity. African countries can collaborate in energy infrastructure development. Of importance is also the digital infrastructure and innovation developments. The manufacturing sector of today thrives on the back of an enhanced digital infrastructure. The digital economy, through e-commerce, high-speed internet, and digital trade technologies, is an enabler of modern manufacturing. Investment in renewable energy solutions and the

[11] https://www.un.org/osaa/africa-dialogue-series/africa-dialogue-series-2023/global-concept-note.

[12] https://www.statista.com/statistics/1499938/share-of-africa-in-global-goods-trade/.

[13] https://www.uneca.org/stories/african-countries-trading-more-outside-the-continent-than-amongst-themselves%2C-eca-report.

development of the digital infrastructure are key to the development of the manufacturing sector and the successful implementation of the AfCFTA.

Digital transformation is a pillar for the successful implementation of the AfCFTA. It influences market access, trade facilitation, economic diversification, and transformation. In view of the above, the African Union, in collaboration with Africa Capacity-Building Foundation, AfDB, Africa Telecommunications Union, UNECA, World Bank and many other organisations, developed a comprehensive Digital Transformation Strategy (2020–2030)[14] that will guide a common, coordinated response to reap the benefits of the fourth industrial revolution. The future of the AfCFTA is shaped by digital transformation. Improvements in digital transformation are expected to enhance market access and e-commerce, streamline trade facilitation and logistics, revolutionise payments and financial inclusion, and foster innovation and new business models. Despite a good projection about the effect of the digital transformation on the AfCFTA, the digital infrastructure gap, the digital skills gap, regulatory harmonisation, cybersecurity, and the digital divide are still persistent in Africa. If the continent invests in infrastructure and digital technology, intra-African trade could significantly increase by 2045.

16.5 Policy and Strategic Recommendations

The AfCFTA has huge potential to reshape the economic fortunes of African countries. Boosting intra-African trade is central to unlocking Africa's economic potential. Nevertheless, unlocking its full potential requires robust policy decisions and strategic interventions. These include accelerating and deepening implementation of core Protocols, investing in enabling infrastructure and connectivity, fostering industrialisation and value addition, strengthening trade facilitation and enforcement, promoting inclusivity and awareness, and strengthening the institutional framework and coordination.

The AfCFTA has enormous potential to change the economic fortunes of African countries. However, realising its full potential requires strong policy decisions and strategic actions. These include accelerating and deepening implementation of core Protocols through completing and operationalising pending Protocols, harmonising national laws and regulations, investing in enabling infrastructure and connectivity by developing integrated transport and logistics networks, bridging the digital divide and promoting digital trade and ensuring reliable and affordable energy supplies, encouraging industrialisation and value addition, improving trade facilitation and enforcement, promoting inclusivity and awareness, and strengthening institutional frameworks and coordination. African countries can significantly accelerate the full potential of the AfCFTA if they focus on the above strategic recommendations and interconnected policies, thus resulting in sustained economic growth,

[14] https://au.int/sites/default/files/documents/38507-doc-dts-english.pdf.

employment creation, poverty reduction and a more resilient and stronger Africa with a felt presence in the global economy.

The effective and seamless implementation of the AfCFTA requires strengthening of institutional and regulatory frameworks. This is possible through a multifaceted approach that involves harmonising and simplifying regulations, building capacity and human capital development, ensuring dialogue and accountability, and strengthening institutional frameworks and governance. Additionally, it is imperative to enhance trade facilitation and customs efficiency. These have a direct effect of lowering costs for doing business, speeding delivery times and increasing competitiveness for African countries. The key strategies to enhance customs efficiency and trade facilitation for unlocking the full potential of AfCFTA implementation involve improving digitalisation and automation, enhancing transparency and predictability, leveraging technology and innovation, streamlining border procedures, and strengthening institutional capacity and cooperation.

The flourishing of the AfCFTA also depends on accelerating investments in infrastructure and digital trade platforms. The African continent has a huge infrastructure deficit amounting to US$108 billion annually. Closing this financing gap requires an enhanced public-private partnership that strengthens legal and regulatory frameworks, leveraging on mobilising domestic resources, attracting FDI through creating a favourable investment climate, strengthening project preparation facilities and prioritising strategic infrastructure by focusing on trade-enabling infrastructure. Digital trading works efficiently when there is a robust physical infrastructure. Accelerating investments in digital trade platforms involves a strong public sector investment in foundational digital public infrastructure through expanding broadband connectivity and enhancing digital identity systems, digital payment infrastructure and cloud computing infrastructure. Also important to this is incentivising private sector investment in digital platforms by regulating sandboxes and innovation hubs, offering tax incentives and grants, enabling access to venture capital and growth equity and allowing room for public-private dialogue. In addition to that, developing and promoting integrated digital ecosystems through a platform of platforms approach, offering support for micro, small, and medium-sized enterprise digitalisation, and creating data governance frameworks. Last but not least, accelerating investment in digital trade platforms requires building capacity for digital adoption and leveraging international partnerships through offering digital literacy programmes and skills development, providing technical assistance and promoting investment. Implementing and adopting these recommendations could foster deeper integration, boost intra-African trade, and drive sustainable economic development.

The successful implementation of the AfCFTA also requires building the capacity of trade-related border and customs agencies and strengthening the institutional framework. There is a need for enhancing data collection and analysis and fostering public-private dialogue for ensuring inclusive designing of policies and training of SMEs, trade negotiators and customs officials on provisions of the AfCFTA. SMEs and informal traders are the mainstay of many African countries' economies as they create employment and support economic activities. Removing barriers for them could enhance intra-AfCFTA trade, ultimately boosting inclusive growth and reducing poverty. Nevertheless, SMEs and informal traders usually face numerous obstacles, including limited access to finance, a lack of information and market intelligence, NTBs, inadequate infrastructure and logistics, and challenges related to trust and formalisation. Addressing these barriers could encourage SMEs and informal traders to make significant contributions to intra-African trade and the continent's economic development and integration.

16.6 Conclusion

The AfCFTA is poised for significant expansion in the coming years, thanks to ambitious integration initiatives and the adoption of key trends. Currently, intra-African trade accounts for a relatively low proportion of total African trade, ranging between 15% and 18%. It is the lowest compared to other regions, such as Asia (around 60%), America (55%), and Europe (around 70%). In the medium term, a positive momentum of intra-African trade is expected to continue. In the long term, it is anticipated to increase by up to 25% by 2040 and between 35% and 45% by 2045. The continent's income is expected to increase by US$450 billion by 2035, thanks to the AfCFTA. With regard to the continent's share of global trade, it remains modest, currently standing below 3%. It is projected to increase by 32% by 2035, meaning a growth in Africa's share of global trade. This increase is poised to bring in US$16 trillion in revenue generated from minerals by 2030.

Digital transformation is going to play a significant role in boosting intra-African trade by increasing market access, reducing trading costs, enhancing competitiveness and streamlining trade processes. Additionally, digital transformation could thus create significant job opportunities, thereby boosting Africa's GDP. However, there is a need for investment in key digital enablers and to accelerate the operationalisation of the AfCFTA Protocol on Digital Trade to foster and promote digital inclusion. Furthermore, the success of the AfCFTA requires offering support for SMEs and informal traders. This is because SMEs and informal traders contribute to employment creation and poverty reduction in developing countries. Share. Additionally, they represent a significant portion of businesses in Africa. The SMEs and informal traders face hurdles in trading across borders. Hence, they require financial support and customs procedures. The implementation of policies that target the empowerment of SMEs and informal traders, such as investments in physical and digital infrastructure, is crucial in boosting intra-African trade.

Nevertheless, there are many factors hampering the effective implementation of the AfCFTA. These include the presence of NTBs and policy inconsistency, gaps in infrastructure and logistics development, and limited financial inclusion and access to trade finance. Addressing these obstacles would open up significant opportunities for intra-African trade. The potential long-term effects of the AfCFTA would result in economic transformation and diversification, poverty reduction and shared prosperity, enhanced global influence and geopolitical rebalancing, as well as digital-driven leapfrogging. To summarise, the AfCFTA is anticipated to transform Africa into a more integrated, industrialised, and prosperous continent. The AfCFTA represents a strategic shift towards self-reliance and collective power, allowing Africa to leverage its demographic dividend, enormous resources, and youthful energy to become a significant player in the twenty-first-century global economy. Its success will benefit Africans while also reshaping global trade, investment, and geopolitical forces.

The key data trends in AfCFTA implementation provide a detailed picture of the evolving trade and market integration, employment and economic growth, financial and investment, industrialisation and value addition, SMEs and informal sector participation, and the infrastructure landscapes. These inform us about what is being traded, within Africa, between Africa and the world, and how the rules and infrastructure for that trade are changing. The data helps us understand both the progress of AfCFTA implementation, the challenges that arise from its implementation, and the possible solutions to overcome these challenges.

The key data insights show the growing significance of African countries in global trade, the rise of regionalism and deep trade agreements, the importance of eliminating NTBs through trade facilitation, the role of technology and e-commerce in boosting intra-African trade, and the shifting of the global supply chains. Although there has been a remarkable increase in developing countries' share of global trade, particularly, Asian countries, Africa's share is still insignificant. Also, rising NTBs such as product standards, technical regulations and sanitary measures increase significant barriers to trade, thereby increasing the costs of trading for developing countries.

These data trends suggest that the benefits from trade are substantial, but are not evenly distributed and automatic. Policymakers must address persistent challenges hindering the successful implementation of AfCFTA. These challenges include infrastructure deficit, digital divide and impact on the environment, among others. Due to unequal access to digital infrastructure and skills, some African countries and businesses in Africa are excluded from participating in the digital economy, e-commerce, thus hindering them from benefiting from AfCFTA implementation. Addressing infrastructure gaps, such as poor transportation networks and logistics, could reduce barriers to trade in many African countries.

References

Abrego, L., Amado, M. A., Gursoy, T., Nicholls, G. P., & Perez-Saiz, H. (2019). *The African continental free trade agreement: Welfare gains estimates from a general equilibrium model*. International Monetary Fund.

Abrego, L., Zamaroczy, M. D., Gursoy, T., Issoufou, S., Nicholls, G. P., Perez-Saiz, H., & Rosas, J.-N. (2020). *The African continental free trade area: Potential economic impact and challenges*. International Monetary Fund.

Acheampong, T., & Vitenu-Sackey, P. A. (2024). *Industrialisation in Africa: Leading countries and reasons for their success*. https://afripoli.org/industrialisation-in-africa-leading-countries-

and-reasons-for-their-success#:~:text=Indirect%20determinants%3A%20creating%20an%20enabling,stability%2C%20sound%20institutions%20and%20infrastructure

Adegboye, A. C., & Iweriebor, S. (2018). Does access to finance enhance SME innovation and productivity in Nigeria? Evidence from the World Bank Enterprise survey. *African Development Review, 30*(4), 449–461. https://doi.org/10.1111/1467-8268.12351

Africa International Trade & Commerce Research. (2024). *Key role of digital infrastructure in Africa's E-commerce growth.* https://africainternationaltrade.com/2024/06/11/key-role-of-digital-infrastructure-in-africas-e-commerce-growth/#

African Development Bank. (2018). *Infrastructure and its financing*. African Economic Outlook.

African Development Bank. (2022). *African Development Bank approves $40 million trade finance package to bank one limited Mauritius.* https://www.afdb.org/en/news-and-events/press-releases/african-development-bank-approves-40-million-trade-finance-package-bank-one-limited-mauritius-57633#:~:text=The%20African%20Development%20Bank%20estimates,greater%20difficulty%20accessing%20trade%20finance

African Development Bank. (2024). *Driving Africa's transformation. The reform of the global financial architecture. African Economic Outlook 2024, Issue.* https://www.afdb.org/sites/default/files/2024/06/06/aeo_2024_-_chapter_1.pdf

African Development Bank, African Union, & United Nations Industrial Development Organization. (2022). *Africa industrialization index.* https://www.afdb.org/en/documents/africa-industrialization-index-2022

African Export-Import Bank. (2018a). *The African continental free trade area, research update.* https://afreximbank.com/?smd_process_download=1&download_id=8651

African Export-Import Bank. (2018b). *Boosting intra-African trade: Implications of the African continental free trade area agreement.* African Export-Import Bank. https://media.afreximbank.com/afrexim/African-Trade-Report-2018.pdf

African Export-Import Bank. (2020). *Informal cross-border trade in Africa in the context of the AfCFTA*. African Export-Import Bank. https://afr-corp-media-prod.s3-eu-west-1.amazonaws.com/afrexim/African-Trade-Report-2020.pdf

African Export-Import Bank. (2023). *Export manufacturing and regional value chains in Africa under a new world order. (African Trade Report 2023, Issue).* https://media.afreximbank.com/afrexim/AFRICAN_TRADE_REPORT_2023.pdf

African Export-Import Bank. (2024). *Climate implications of the AfCFTA implementation*. African Export-Import Bank. https://media.afreximbank.com/afrexim/African-Trade-Report_2024.pdf

Agarwal, P. (2024). *Empowering African women in trade through AfCFTA's guided trade initiative*. https://odi.org/en/insights/empowering-african-women-in-trade-through-afcftas-guided-trade-initiative/

Agarwal, P., Ayele, Y., McGarrell, R., Murinde, V., Ngeno, R., & Te Velde, D. W. (2024). *Exploring data on foreign direct investment to support implementation of the AfCFTA protocol on investment.* O.D. Institute. https://odi.org/en/publications/exploring-data-on-foreign-direct-investment-to-support-implementation-of-the-afcfta-protocol-on-investment

Agarwal, P., Mba, S. K., & Lemma, A. (2024). *Advancing implementation of the AfCFTA protocol on digital trade in Nigeria*. O. D. Institute. https://media.odi.org/documents/ODI_Report_-_Advancing_implementation_of_the_AfCFTA_Protocol_on_Digital_Trade__mIuVg14.pdf

Andrew, M. (2022). *Reassessing the economic significance of intra-African trade*. https://coilink.org/20.500.12592/9f983r

Aniche, E. T. (2023). African continental free trade area and African union agenda 2063: The roads to Addis Ababa and Kigali. *Journal of Contemporary African Studies, 41*(4), 1–16. https://doi.org/10.1080/02589001.2020.1775184

Anyanzwa, J. (2024). *High costs, inefficient border procedures slow down intra-Africa trade.* https://www.zawya.com/en/economy/africa/high-costs-inefficient-border-procedures-slow-down-intra-africa-trade-aviwstqy

Arvis, J.-F., Saslavsky, D., Ojala, L., Shepherd, B., Busch, C., & Raj, A. (2023). *Connecting to compete 2023 (trade logistics in the global economy: The logistics performance index and its indicators, issue)*. The World Bank. https://documents1.worldbank.org/curated/en/099042123145531599/pdf/P17146804a6a570ac0a4f80895e320dda1e.pdf

Arvis, J.-F., Ulybina, D., & Wiederer, C. (2024). *From survey to big data: The new logistics performance index*. World Bank.

Beck, M. (2022). Extroverted financialization: How US finance shapes European banking. *Review of International Political Economy, 29*(5), 1723–1745. https://doi.org/10.1080/09692290.2021.1949375

Besada, H. (2025). *What US tariffs mean for Africa and the global south*. https://blogs.lse.ac.uk/businessreview/2025/04/08/what-us-tariffs-mean-for-africa-and-the-global-south/#:~:text=If%20fully%20realised%2C%20AfCFTA%20could,buffer%20against%20global%20trade%20fluctuations

Black, A., Edwards, L., Ismail, F., Makundi, B., & Morris, M. (2021). The role of regional value chains in fostering regional integration in southern Africa. *Development Southern Africa, 38*(1), 39–56. https://doi.org/10.1080/0376835X.2020.1834354

Blades, D., Ferreira, F. H. G., & Lugo, M. A. (2011). The informal economy in developing countries: An introduction. *Review of Income and Wealth, Series, 57*(Special Issue), 1–8.

Brenton, P., & Isik, G. (2012). *De-fragmenting Africa: Deepening regional trade integration in goods and services*. World Bank. https://documents1.worldbank.org/curated/en/245181468009603809/pdf/684900ESW0Whit00Box367921B00PUBLIC0.pdf

Calì, M. (2014). *Trading away from conflict: Using trade to increase resilience in fragile states*. World Bank Publications.

Chipanda, B., & Cilliers, J. (2025). *The AfCFTA*. https://futures.issafrica.org/thematic/08-afcfta/

Chivunga, M., Abudu, D., & Lemma, A. (2024). *Advancing AfCFTA digital trade implementation in Ghana*. O. D. Institute. https://www.zbw.eu/econis-archiv/bitstream/11159/701691/1/1910849324_0.pdf

Cilliers, J., & Chipanda, B. (2025). *Large infrastructure thematic futures 1-40*. https://futures.issafrica.org/thematic/11-large-infrastructure/

de Melo, J., Sorgho, Z., & Wagner, L. (2025). Reducing wait times at customs to boost trade: How implementing the trade facilitation agreement can expand trade among AfCFTA countries? *Journal of African Economies, 34*(2), 265–294. https://doi.org/10.1093/jae/ejae008

Dollar, D., & Kraay, A. (2003). Institutions, trade, and growth. *Journal of Monetary Economics, 50*(1), 133–162. https://doi.org/10.1016/S0304-3932(02)00206-4

Dollar, D., & Kraay, A. (2004). Trade, growth, and poverty. *The Economic Journal, 114*(493), F22–F49. https://doi.org/10.1111/j.0013-0133.2004.00186.x

Döring, K. P. W., & Engel, U. (2021). Regional integration and trade. In U. Engel (Ed.), *Yearbook on the African union* (Vol. 1, pp. 177–193). Koninkilijke Brill NV.

Ezugwu, O. A., & Duruji, M. M. (2023). African continental free trade area agreement (Afcfta) and the challenges of regional integration in Africa. *International Journal of Social Service and Research, 3*(11), 2719–2727. https://doi.org/10.46799/ijssr.v3i10.504

Fofack, H., & Mold, A. (2021). The AfCFTA and African trade—An introduction to the special issue. *Journal of African Trade, 8*(2), 1. https://doi.org/10.2991/jat.k.211206.001

Food and Agriculture Organisation of the United Nations. (2020). *Towards development of and action programme to address food security and nutrition challenges in landlocked countries in Africa FAO regional conference for Africa, Victoria Falls, Zimbabwe*. https://www.fao.org/3/nc555en/nc555en.pdf

Gerxhani, K. (2004). The informal sector in developed and less developed countries: A literature survey. *Public Choice, 120*(3), 267–300. https://doi.org/10.1023/B:PUCH.0000044287.88147.5e

Hoekman, B., & Nicita, A. (2011). Trade policy, trade costs, and developing country trade. *World Development, 39*(12), 2069–2079. https://doi.org/10.1016/j.worlddev.2011.05.013

International Monetary Fund. (2019). *Regional economic outlook sub-Saharan Africa navigating uncertainty*. International Monetary Fund. https://doi.org/10.5089/9781513514055.086

International Trade Administration U.S. Department of Commerce. (n.d.). *The rise of eCommerce in Africa*. https://www.trade.gov/rise-ecommerce-africa

Jackson, A. (2009). ICT and the new global investment paradigm: Challenges to cross-border trade and investment. *World Customs Journal, 3*(1), 55–61. https://doi.org/10.55596/001c.91355

Konar-Leacy, V. (2017). *Coordination, collaboration and connectivity for better border management*. https://blogs.worldbank.org/en/trade/coordination-collaboration-and-connectivity-better-border-management

Kutortse, K. D. (2025). Assessing the implication of African continental free trade area (AfCFTA) for Ghanaian women and youth entrepreneurs research. *Applied Economics, 17*(1), 1–30. https://doi.org/10.5296/rae.v17i1.22799

Le Goff, M., & Singh, R. J. (2014). Does trade reduce poverty? A view from Africa. *Journal of African Trade, 1*(1), 5–14. https://doi.org/10.1016/j.joat.2014.06.001

Logis-T Africa. (2023). *E-commerce in Africa: A rapidly growing market expected to reach $180 billion by 2024*. https://logistafrica.com/en/highlights/e-commerce-in-africa-a-rapidly-growing-market-expected-to-reach-180-billion-by-2024/#:~:text=According%20to%20the%20report%20%E2%80%9CFuture%20of%20Commerce:%20Outlook,of%2025%%20per%20year,%20compared%20to%2015%%20globally

Maliszewska, M., van der Mensbrugghe, D., Pereira, M. F. S., Osorio Rodarte, I., & Ruta, M. (2020). *African continental free trade area: Economic and distributional effects*. World Bank. https://openknowledge.worldbank.org/server/api/core/bitstreams/ef1aa41f-60de-5bd2-a63e-75f2c3ff0f43/content

Mangeni, F., Mold, A., & Signé, L. (2024). *In the promise of free trade and integration across Africa's nations*. https://www.brookings.edu/articles/the-promise-of-free-trade-and-integration-across-africas-nations/

Maniriho, E. A. (2022). *Aviation, air cargo and logistics management: A manual for air cargo handlers and shippers*. Notion Press.

Matthew, O., & Adegboye, F. B. (2014). Trade openness, institutions and economic growth in sub-Saharan Africa (SSA). *Developing Country Studies, 4*(8), 18–30. https://core.ac.uk/download/pdf/234681626.pdf

McCulloch, N., Winters, L. A., & Cirera, X. (2001). *Trade liberalization and poverty: A handbook*. Centre for Economic Policy Research.

McKinsey & Company. (2024). *Future of commerce: Outlook for 2024*.

Mitaritonna, M. C., Zheng, Y., Karingi, S., & Mevel, S. (2024). *Implementing the AfCFTA agreement and implications for Africa's regional value chains*. https://www.gtap.agecon.purdue.edu/uploads/resources/download/12342.pdf

Montinari, L., & Stracca, L. (2016). Trade, finance or policies: What drives the cross-border spillover of business cycles? *Journal of Macroeconomics, 49*, 131–148. https://doi.org/10.1016/j.jmacro.2016.06.001

Morgan, S., Farris, J., & Johnson, M. E. (2022). *Foreign direct Investment in Africa: Recent trends leading up to the African continental free trade area (AfCFTA)*. https://www.govinfo.gov/content/pkg/GOVPUB-A93-PURL-gpo223144/pdf/GOVPUB-A93-PURL-gpo223144.pdf

Moyer, J. D., Kabandula, A., Bohl, D., Hanna, T., Mayaki, I., & Bwalya, M. (2021). *Conditions for success in the implementation of the African continental free trade agreement*. https://au.int/sites/default/files/documents/38076-doc-afcftaenglishfinal20200123-2.pdf

Musyoka, M. M. (2024). *The African E-commerce boom: Trends, challenges, and future prospects*. https://africa.com/the-african-e-commerce-boom-trends-challenges-and-future-prospects/

Mutsonziwa, K., & Fanta, A. B. (2021). Small business performance: Is it access to formal or informal credit that matters? *Journal of African Business, 22*(4), 550–563. https://doi.org/10.1080/15228916.2020.1826854

Ngepah, N., & Udeagha, M. C. (2018). African regional trade agreements and intra-African trade. *Journal of Economic Integration, 33*(1), 1176–1199. https://doi.org/10.11130/jei.2018.33.1.1176

Nordås, H. K., & Piermartini, R. (2004). *Infrastructure and trade (ERSD-2004-04)*. World Trade Organisation.

Organisation for Economic Co-operation and Development. (2007). Removing barriers to formalisation. In *Promoting pro-poor growth policy guidance for donors*. OECD. https://doi.org/10.1787/9789264024786-8-en

Organisation for Economic Co-operation and Development, & World Trade Organisation. (2019). *Aid for trade at a glance 2019: Economic diversification and empowerment, aid for trade at a glance*. https://www.oecd-ilibrary.org/docserver/18ea27d8-en.pdf?expires=1640115439&id=id&accname=guest&checksum=2DCF9B437A08639AA0FEA81620B39376

Polonskaya, K. (2022). The strategies of the international chamber of commerce to eliminate double taxation. *Journal of International Economic Law, 25*(1), 74–90. https://doi.org/10.1093/jiel/jgac008

Portugal-Perez, A., & Wilson, J. S. (2012). Export performance and trade facilitation reform: Hard and soft infrastructure. *World Development, 40*(7), 1295–1307. https://doi.org/10.1016/j.worlddev.2011.12.002

Rao, P. (2022). *Afcfta's guided trade initiative takes off, set to ease and boost intra-African trade*. Africa Renewal. https://africarenewal.un.org/en/magazine/afcftas-guided-trade-initiative-takes-set-ease-and-boost-intra-african-trade

Runde, D. F., Savoy, C. M., & Staguhn, J. (2021). *Supporting small and medium Enterprises in sub-Saharan Africa through blended finance*. https://www.csis.org/analysis/supporting-small-and-medium-enterprises-sub-saharan-africa-through-blended-finance

Shamsuzzoha, A., Ehrs, M., Addo-Tenkorang, R., Nguyen, D., & Helo, P. T. (2013). Performance evaluation of tracking and tracing for logistics operations. *International Journal of Shipping and Transport Logistics, 5*(1), 31–54. https://doi.org/10.1504/IJSTL.2013.050587

Siyakiya, P., Erdoğdu, M. M., & Akay, E. Ç. (2023). Impact of industrialisation on economic development in selected African and Asian economies: The role of institutional quality and investment climate. *SN Business & Economics, 3*(12), 211–242. https://doi.org/10.1007/s43546-023-00585-3

Sourabh, P. (2025). *E-commerce in Africa, unlocking new paths for economic growth*. https://www.stattimes.com/ecommerce/e-commerce-in-africa-unlocking-new-paths-for-economic-growth-1354446

Soutar, N. (2021). *The political economy of the African continental free trade area (AfCFTA): A policy analysis of the prospects and challenges University of Cape Town]. Cape Town*. https://open.uct.ac.za/server/api/core/bitstreams/5e80cde4-73c8-4b94-85ed-e9cef3969046/content

Tanyi, K. T. (2015). Assessing Africa's two billion populated market by 2063: The facts and fallacies of a continental free trade area (CFTA). *Business and Economics Journal, 6*(154), 51–62. https://doi.org/10.4172/2151-6219.1000154

Tieku, K. T., & Yakohene, A. B. (2023). Analyzing the African continental free trade area (the AfCFTA) from an informality perspective: A beautiful house in the wrong neighborhood. *Global Studies Quarterly, 3*(3), ksad043. https://doi.org/10.1093/isagsq/ksad043

United Nations. (2019). *World economic situation and prospects 2019*. United Nations. https://desapublications.un.org/file/729/download?_ga=2.204692246.761102355.1745519798-120173571.1739182184

United Nations Conference on Trade and Development. (2019). *Made in Africa: Rules of origin for enhanced intra-African trade*. United Nations.

United Nations Economic Commission for Africa. (2025). *Advancing the implementation of the agreement establishing the African continental free trade area: Proposing transformative strategic actions*. United Nations Economic Commission for Africa. https://repository.uneca.org/handle/10855/50385

Wapmuk, S., & Ali, J. M. (2022). The African continental free trade area (AFCFTA) and regional economic integration: Prospects and challenges. *Zamfara Journal of Politics and Development, 3*(1), 15.

Widianti, K. R., Cahyadi, E. R., & Slamet, A. S. (2021). The use behavior of tracking and tracing services in e-commerce logistics. *Jurnal Manajemen dan Organisasi, 12*(1), 10–20. https://doi.org/10.29244/jmo.v12i1.35373

Winters, L. A., McCulloch, N., & McKay, A. (2004). Trade liberalization and poverty: The evidence so far. *Journal of Economic Literature, 42*(1), 72–115. https://doi.org/10.2307/3217037

World Bank. (2023). *Logistics performance indicators (LPI)*. https://lpi.worldbank.org/

World Trade Organisation. (2023). *Trade facilitation agreement facility (TFAF)*. World Trade Organisation. https://www.tfafacility.org/annual-report-2022

Xing, Z. (2018). The impacts of information and communications technology (ICT) and E-commerce on bilateral trade flows. *International Economics and Economic Policy, 15*(3), 565–586. https://doi.org/10.1007/s10368-017-0375-5

Yaya, I. M., Ndiaye, C. T., Asongu, S., & Diop, S. (2025). Analysis of the effects of the African continental free trade area (AfCFTA) on the labor market in the Central African economic and monetary community (CEMAC). *International Journal of Manpower, 46*(10), 77–102. https://doi.org/10.1108/IJM-11-2024-0741

Zongo, A. M. I., & Oyelami, L. (2021). Modeling the impact of non-tariff barriers in services on intra-african trade: Global trade analysis project model. *SSRN Journal*. https://doi.org/10.2139/ssrn.3854631

Chapter 17
Trade Facilitation, Border Management, and the Harmonisation of Policies Across AfCFTA Member States

Alouis Chilunjika

Abstract This chapter explores the ways that the African Continental Free Trade Area (AfCFTA) promotes regional integration through trade facilitation, modernisation of border administration, and policy harmonisation. Despite advancements, the full potential of intracontinental trade is still hampered by procedural and structural trade restrictions. Drawing on case studies of national reforms and empirical data from the Regional Economic Communities (RECs), this chapter emphasises how Africa's trade costs are two to three times higher than those of developed regions due to ineffective border procedures. Three important conclusions are drawn. First, customs efficiency has increased, and clearance times have decreased because of the implementation of digital border technology such as computerised single window systems. Second, policy fragmentation still exists, particularly with regard to rules of origin and tariff regimes. Third, enforcement and legal discrepancies arise from institutional misalignments between national REC commitments and AfCFTA objectives. These consist of inadequate compliance procedures and overlapping regulations. To promote a more cohesive and effective African trade environment, the chapter suggests setting up regional trade tribunals for uniform rule enforcement, accelerating Phase II AfCFTA negotiations on intellectual property, investment, and competition, and implementing digital trade protocols at the REC level to improve certification and customs interoperability.

Keywords Trade · Trade facilitation · Border management · Policy harmonisation · African continental free trade area · Member states

---

A. Chilunjika (✉)
Department of Political and Administrative Studies, National University of Lesotho, Roma, Lesotho
e-mail: a.chilunjika@nul.ls

D. N. Yuni et al. (eds.), *From Policy to Practice: Challenges and Ways Forward on the Implementation of the AfCFTA*,
https://doi.org/10.1007/978-3-032-14051-7_17

17.1 Introduction to Trade Facilitation

Trade facilitation seeks to automate, standardise, and simplify international trade processes by lowering transaction costs and minimising delays related to the movement of goods across borders (Vutula, 2025; World Trade Organization (WTO), 2023; Duval & Utoktham, 2022). Fundamentally, Zimano et al. (2019) argued that trade facilitation aims to improve the administrative, logistical, and regulatory bottlenecks that frequently impede economic competitiveness, particularly in developing and least-developed nations. This will increase the efficiency, transparency, and predictability of trade procedures. The operational scope of trade facilitation encompasses several interconnected domains. These include modernising customs to enable quicker and safer clearance of goods, such as through the use of paperless systems, electronic customs declarations, and risk-based inspections. Optimising logistics also entails enhancing multimodal transportation corridors, port infrastructure, and warehousing systems. According to De Melo et al. (2025), trade facilitation also includes regulatory coherence, including the execution of mutual recognition agreements (MRAs) for technical barriers to trade (TBT) and sanitary and phytosanitary (SPS) regulations, as well as the harmonisation of technical standards. It is impossible to overestimate the significance of trade facilitation in Africa.

Compared to nearly 60% of commerce in Europe, intra-African trade still makes up a disproportionately small 14–18% of all trade on the continent (African Development Bank (AfDB), 2023; Harris, 2022). This disparity is a result of significant non-tariff obstacles, restricted regional integration, and long-standing structural inefficiencies in border management. As a result, trade facilitation is a strategic policy requirement that can revolutionise trade in Africa rather than just being an operational issue. Moving on, effective trade facilitation is economically valuable, as demonstrated by empirical evidence. World Bank (2023) found that a 4% increase in export diversification can result from a one-day reduction in border clearance time. This is a particularly significant finding for African nations looking to advance up the value chain. According to additional estimates from the United Nations Economic Commission for Africa (UNECA) (2023), the trade facilitation provisions of the African Continental Free Trade Area (AfCFTA) could increase intra-African trade by 52% by 2030 if fully implemented. This would provide a clear path towards structural diversification and economic transformation.

Trade facilitation changes have a significant impact on broader economic integration and development, extending beyond overall trade figures. For example, more effective transit lanes, simplified customs processes, and integrated border management might save trade costs by 15–25% for landlocked nations like Lesotho, Chad, and Niger (Mateko, 2025; African Development Bank (AfDB), 2023). To improve their export competitiveness and better connect them to regional and international markets, these reductions are essential. Furthermore, Rikhotso (2025) postulated that encouraging the inclusion of small and medium-sized businesses (SMEs), especially unofficial cross-border traders, depends heavily on trade facilitation. According to research by the International Air Transport Association (IATA)

(2023), bureaucratic red tape and a lack of digital infrastructure are the primary reasons why SMEs in Africa incur compliance costs that are up to three times higher than those of major corporations. SMEs can be empowered to participate by streamlining processes, lowering documentation needs, and providing specialised support mechanisms.

Lastly, the establishment of strong regional value chains in key industries, such as pharmaceuticals, automobile manufacturing, and agro-processing, depends on improved border systems and standardised laws. Coherent trade facilitation policies are the foundation for industrial upgrading, knowledge transfer, and investment attraction-all essential components for achieving the development objectives outlined in Agenda 2063 and the AfCFTA (OECD, 2023; Nwankwo & Ajibo, 2020; Akeyewale, 2018). As such, trade facilitation is an essential component of Africa's pursuit of greater industrialisation, integration, and inclusive growth rather than a supplementary reform. As a result, it necessitates consistent policy focus, sufficient funding, and robust institutional coordination at the regional and national levels.

17.1.1 Border Management Evolution

A larger trend of institutional modernisation and digital transformation is reflected in the development of border management in Africa. In the past, manual processes, onerous bureaucracy, and widespread inefficiencies characterised border procedures on the continent, which hindered trade and compromised the integrity of customs (Dihel & Goswami, 2016; Hillberry & Zhang, 2018; Zimano et al., 2019). However, over the past 20 years, a growing understanding of how effective border management promotes national security, facilitates trade, and enhances public revenue has led to small but significant adjustments. The border systems of Africa can be categorised into three major stages of development, each representing a step closer to increased automation and effectiveness. The first stage was characterised by largely manual procedures and predominated the pre-2000s era. According to Hassan (2015), clearance delays were often 5–7 days due to the prevalence of physical paperwork, redundant inspections, and non-standardised protocol. Widespread corruption, under-invoicing, and rent-seeking behaviour flourished due to the lack of digital controls. Ineffective border controls not only increased transaction costs for legal traders but also damaged public confidence in customs officials. Corruption in customs administration was one of the top three factors preventing formal trade in sub-Saharan Africa during this time (Chiswa, 2024; Transparency International, 2023).

The second stage began to take shape after the World Trade Organisation's Trade Facilitation Agreement (WTO-TFA), which prioritised automation, simplification, and transparency in customs processes, came into effect in 2017 (Fernandes et al., 2018; Schmieg, 2019). By 2023, the TFA had been adopted by 44 African nations, leading to the implementation of the first digital reforms. Notably, nations such as Ghana, Rwanda, and Senegal led the way in this era by implementing and expanding single window systems, pre-arrival processing, and electronic customs platforms (Chiswa, 2025; Ogunleye, 2021; Tyagi & Goyal, 2023). The institutional and technical foundation for more ambitious advances was established during this decade, notwithstanding regional disparities in progress. The African Continental Free Trade Area (AfCFTA), established in 2021, marked the beginning of the third and current phase, characterised by advancements in smart borders and technological convergence. According to Vutula (2025), modern digital tools are being utilised to enhance border governance and support the trade facilitation objectives of the AfCFTA. The implementation of blockchain-enabled verification for cocoa export certificates in Ghana, for instance, has improved traceability and decreased fraud. Customs inspections and risk profiling are being supported by artificial intelligence (AI) engines in South Africa, resulting in more focused and effective enforcement. Internet of Things (IoT)-enabled cargo tracking is also being implemented along important corridors (TradeMark Africa (TMEA), 2023; Truby et al., 2022; Ogunleye, 2021), which lowers the incidence of diversion and theft.

The efficient coordination of multiple government entities, each with a distinct function in border management and compliance, is crucial to the success of digital border reforms. Figure 17.1 presents a list of important institutional players and instances of technology adoption in Rwanda, Kenya, and Nigeria, where customs, immigration, and standards agencies have adopted different technological innovations to enhance trade facilitation and digital border management:

Through these developments, border contacts are being transformed from disjointed, paper-based practices to cohesive digital ecosystems. One example that stands out is Rwanda, which has become a regional leader in trade efficiency due to improvements in border automation. The adoption of an electronic customs system reduced typical clearing times from 5 days to 6 h, increased customs revenue by 40%, and significantly decreased informal payments (Rwanda Revenue Authority (RRA), 2023). Through targeted investment, political commitment, and institutional alignment, Rwanda's experience demonstrates that even landlocked and resource-constrained nations can advance into areas with global best practices. In many nations, institutional resistance to change, inadequate infrastructure, and a lack of technical capacity obstruct the pace of digital transformation across the continent

Institution	Function	Tech Innovation Example
Customs	Revenue collection and compliance	e-Customs (Rwanda), ASYCUDA system (42 African states)
Immigration	Border security and migration control	Biometric e-gates (Kenya, South Africa)
Standards Agencies	SPS and TBT enforcement	e-Certification via Nigeria's Standards Organisation (eSON)

Fig. 17.1 Institutional players and technology adoption. Source: Author's Construction

varies significantly. In many nations, institutional resistance to change, inadequate infrastructure, and a lack of technical capacity hinder improvements. Standardised standards, system interoperability, and capacity-building programmes that support not only the technologies but also the individuals and organisations responsible for putting them into practice are necessary to guarantee that border modernisation benefits all African Union member states (Chiswa, 2025; De Melo et al., 2025; Gakwaya et al., 2020; Kieck, 2020).

17.1.2 Policy Harmonisation Imperatives

According to Vutula (2025), one crucial element of the larger regional integration strategy under the AfCFTA is the standardisation of trade-related policies among African nations. The fundamental goal of policy harmonisation is to lessen market fragmentation by coordinating international regulatory frameworks, practices, and standards to facilitate the smooth flow of commodities, services, and manufacturing inputs. Disparities in national policy, especially concerning tariffs, non-tariff measures (NTMs), customs documentation, and technical rules, lead to inefficiencies, skew trade flows, and compromise the goals of a single African market in the absence of such coherence (Chiswa, 2025; ElGanainy et al., 2023; Galal, 2024; Grinsted & Sandrey, 2015; Kayizzi-Mugerwa et al., 2014).

Similarly, strong theoretical underpinnings, most notably Jacob Viner's Customs Union Theory, which was first presented in 1950, provide support for the harmonisation argument. Viner claims that when nations match their internal trade regulations and external tariffs, trade creation is likely to occur, with more efficient imports from member nations replacing inefficient domestic output. Accordingly, Arvis et al. (2016) argued that this promotes intraregional commerce and economic specialisation in addition to improving consumer welfare. The Economic Community of West African States (ECOWAS) provides a concrete illustration of this, as the implementation of a Common External Tariff (CET) in 2015 resulted in an 18% increase in intraregional trade, despite the implementation being hindered by more than 500 product-specific exemptions (International Air Transport Association (IATA), 2023). This implies that although tariff harmonisation has observable advantages, consistent implementation and strong enforcement are necessary for its success.

The removal of non-tariff measures (NTMs), especially technical trade barriers and sanitary and phytosanitary (SPS) norms, provides a second major theoretical rationale for harmonisation. African exports are still significantly hampered by divergent NTMs, particularly in the agricultural and agro-processed industries. The fragmented and overlapping SPS and TBT measures are estimated to cost Africa more than $25 billion a year (United Nations Economic Commission for Africa (UNECA), 2023). The economic benefits of harmonising such standards are demonstrated by the East African Community's (EAC) experience. The EAC has increased milk commerce between Kenya and Uganda by 20% as a result of regional coordination that has synchronised about 74% of its dairy-related SPS criteria (East African Community (EAC), 2023). This suggests that standardisation facilitates the flow of commodities with the least amount of regulatory friction, which not only lowers compliance costs but also strengthens regional value chains.

Despite the strong case and supporting data for harmonisation, the institutional frameworks in place now paint a contradictory image. The World Trade Organisation Trade Facilitation Agreement (WTO TFA) offers a worldwide reform roadmap, and African nations are making consistent, albeit uneven, progress. Accordingly, World Trade Organization (WTO) (2023) avers that Article 7, for example, encourages the processing of customs documents before arrival and has been ratified by 31 African nations. This method enables traders to submit information before products arrive at the border, hence reducing customs waits dramatically. Article 10, which mandates the creation of computerised single window systems, has not advanced as quickly, though; as of right now, just nine African nations have completely functional systems (World Trade Organization (WTO), 2023). This technology deficiency leads to implementation asymmetries that erode regional integration and impede the achievement of cross-border policy consistency (Chang et al., 2020; Harris, 2022; Hillberry & Zhang, 2018).

17.2 Regional Perspectives and Implementation: Trade Facilitation in African Regional Economic Communities (RECs)

Regional Economic Communities (RECs) such as the Common Market for Eastern and Southern Africa (COMESA), the Economic Community of West African States (ECOWAS), the Southern African Development Community (SADC), and the East African Community (EAC) are crucial to the continent's ability to execute trade facilitation reforms successfully. The WTO Trade Facilitation Agreement (TFA) and the AfCFTA are two examples of continental and international trade frameworks that are primarily operationalised and domesticated through these RECs. For traders, customs authorities, and logistics players, their involvement is crucial in bridging the implementation gap between high-level policy pledges and practical procedural reforms. This section examines trade facilitation advancements at the REC level, enduring obstacles, and innovative opportunities under three interconnected themes: border management and control strategies, logistical performance, and policy harmonisation initiatives.

17.2.1 State of Trade Facilitation in African RECs

Trade logistics in many African nations remain severely inefficient despite several governmental commitments and small-scale changes. Sub-Saharan Africa remains the lowest-ranking region in the world, as noted by the World Bank's Logistics

Performance Index (LPI), with an average score of 2.5 out of 5 in 2023, which is lower than the global average of 3.3 (World Bank, 2023). One major issue is the high cost of logistics. Compared to 10–15% in more developed nations, logistical costs account for 40–60% of the total cost of commodities in Africa (African Development Bank (AfDB), 2023). According to United Nations Conference on Trade and Development (UNCTAD) (2023), severe infrastructure deficiencies exacerbate these expenses: just over 25% of the continent's highways are paved, and port stay durations usually vary from 7 to 21 days, which causes shipments to be delayed and transaction costs to rise.

Performance across RECs varies significantly throughout the continent. For example, with an average LPI score of 2.8, SADC has become a regional pioneer in logistics reform, and this can be attributed to efforts in modernising customs, managing corridors, and upgrading ports. On the other hand, ECOWAS trails behind with an average score of 2.2, indicating comparatively slower advancements in customs integration and infrastructural development (World Bank, 2023). The potential for integrated regional value chains is hindered by uneven implementation, which also undermines the AfCFTA's harmonisation goals.

By 2024, 44 member states of the African Union had ratified the WTO TFA; its remains patchy, particularly in the area of digital customs systems. These systems, which are crucial for decreasing manual processes, boosting transparency, and expediting cargo clearance, are only fully adopted in 15% of African nations (World Trade Organization (WTO), 2023). Similarly, due to excessive inspections, bribes, unofficial blockages, and redundant documentation requirements, non-tariff barriers (NTBs) continue to be a significant problem, contributing an estimated 15% to 30% to trade expenses (African Continental Free Trade Area (AfCFTA) Secretariat, 2023). Ghana is a good example of transformation, as the Paperless Port Initiative cut clearance times from 5 days to 4 h. However, despite this success story, rent-seeking practices and informal payments continue to exist, thereby negating the full benefits of digitisation (Ghana Revenue Authority (GRA), 2023).

The difficulties in aligning the AfCFTA with the current Regional Economic Communities (RECs) add another level of complexity. Significant discrepancies still exist in tariff schedules, rules of origin (RoO), and infrastructure standards, despite the AfCFTA's intention to expand and consolidate the benefits of the RECs. Key accomplishments and harmonisation gaps across a few chosen RECs are summarised in the table below:

Figure 17.2 highlights the achievements made by the EAC, SADC, and ECOWAS, respectively, which include the alignment of 74% of the SPS standards, the simplification of the operational trade regime, and the establishment of a common external tariff since 2015. However, despite these achievements, there are also lurking gaps or disparities. These disparities include structural, political, and technical. For instance, logistical disparities among member states, such as incompatible railway gauges, have reduced the effectiveness of regional supply chains and transportation corridors, despite the Southern African Development Community's (SADC) promotion of the use of a Simplified Trade Regime to facilitate trade for small-scale traders (Grinsted & Sandrey, 2015; Hassan, 2015; Mold, 2018; Schmieg, 2019). According to Akeyewale (2018), the extensive use of waivers also illustrates a

REC	Achievements	Harmonization Gaps
EAC	74% of SPS standards aligned	Persistent disputes over Rules of Origin (e.g., Kenya-Tanzania)
ECOWAS	Common External Tariff since 2015	Over 500 product-specific exemptions undermine CET integrity
SADC	Operational Simplified Trade Regime (STR)	Incompatible rail gauges hinder cross-border rail connectivity

Fig. 17.2 RECs' accomplishments and harmonisation gaps. Source: Author's Construction

conflict between regional economic commitments and national economic protection, despite ECOWAS having achieved tariff harmonisation on paper. The road to a fully integrated African market depends on resolving persistent inconsistencies in trade policy and border management.

17.2.2 Border Management Strategies across Africa

Modernising border posts with One-Stop Border Posts (OSBPs) has been a key component of trade facilitation, especially in the EAC. According to Zimano et al. (2019), by combining the immigration and customs departments of nearby nations into a single building, OSBPs enable speedier processing, common documentation, and cooperative inspections. By reducing typical transit times from 3 days to just 8 h, the Malaba OSBP, situated on the Kenya-Uganda border, has emerged as a showcase model (East African Community (EAC), 2023). But not every OSBP has produced the same outcomes. For instance, understaffing, inconsistent electrical supply, and coordination issues among national agencies have all contributed to the setbacks of the Beitbridge OSBP between South Africa and Zimbabwe, which have reduced the anticipated time savings (TradeMark Africa (TMEA), 2023; Zimano et al., 2019).

Customs management digital advances are also becoming more popular. Due to the Electronic Cargo Tracking System's (ECTS) real-time tracking capabilities and decreased opportunities for manipulation, Rwanda saw a 90% decrease in cargo diversion and customs fraud (Rwanda Revenue Authority (RRA), 2023). By 2025, the e-Customs initiative in Nigeria, driven by $3.2 billion public-private collaboration, is expected to modernise customs infrastructure and significantly increase revenue collection by fully automating port processes (Nigeria Customs Service (NCS), 2023). partners. Donors and development partners have significantly contributed to these reforms. By increasing clearance efficiency and reducing corruption, the European Union's partnership with Trademark Africa has facilitated the digitisation of border procedures at 15 East African locations, resulting in a projected $300 million in annual trade benefits (European Union, 2023). In a similar vein, the Africa Facility for Trade Finance (AFTRAF) of the African Development Bank has provided more than $1 billion in trade guarantees to trust, mitigate the risk of cross-border payments, and enhance private sector confidence in intra-African trade (African Development Bank (AfDB), 2023).

17.2.3 Policy Harmonisation Efforts

According to Nwankwo and Ajibo (2020), the AfCFTA's objective of a seamless continental market is still dependent on policy harmonisation. In light of this, by offering a uniform certificate of origin and streamlined customs paperwork, COMESA's Simplified Trade Regime (STR) promotes low-value cross-border trade. However, the STR's effectiveness has been limited due to uneven adoption, with only five of COMESA's 21 member nations applying it consistently (COMESA, 2023). Internal disputes over revenue-sharing formulae have halted efforts to create a customs union in the SADC area. These disputes have proven difficult to overcome and are politically sensitive (SADC, 2024). Both convergent and divergent patterns have been observed in technical standards. With 74% of its dairy standards harmonised, the EAC has achieved remarkable convergence in sanitary and phytosanitary (SPS) controls. Accordingly, East African Community (EAC) (2023) asserts that Kenya was able to expand milk exports to Uganda by 20% as a result of this policy alignment, illustrating how harmonised standards can spur trade growth. Nigeria's unilateral prohibition on the import of maize in 2021, on the other hand, violated ECOWAS' free movement regulations and increased regional economic tensions, demonstrating the negative effects of policy divergence (ECOWAS, 2022).

Since its inception in 2023, the AfCFTA's Guided Trade Initiative (GTI) has faced difficulties, providing valuable insights into the potential and challenges associated with harmonisation. Eight nations participated in this pilot programme to test standardised customs and SPS procedures. Consequently, there was a 35% rise in commerce between Ghana and Cameroon, demonstrating the beneficial effects of regulatory convergence (African Continental Free Trade Area (AfCFTA) Secretariat, 2023). The project, however, also drew attention to enduring issues. For instance, competing interpretations of the rules of origin have caused delays in commerce between Kenya and Egypt, highlighting the need for more precise and consistently enforced standards (African Continental Free Trade Area (AfCFTA) Secretariat, 2023). By and large, to fully realise the potential of the AfCFTA, a series of targeted and actionable interventions must be prioritised. The success of the AfCFTA hinges on RECs' ability to function as engines of harmonisation and catalysts for integration.

17.3 Rationale for Harmonisation of Trade Facilitation and Border Management in Africa

According to Mateko (2025), the core of Africa's aspirations for regional and continental integration is border control and trade facilitation. Harmonised trade regimes among African nations are urgently needed, as intra-African trade typically accounts for less than 15% of total trade volumes, compared to 59% in Asia and 69% in Europe (African Continental Free Trade Area (AfCFTA) Secretariat, 2023). In this vein, inconsistent technical standards, superfluous inspection processes, and disjointed customs procedures define the existing environment, which raises trade costs and lowers competitiveness (Ashurst, 2016; Chiswa, 2025; Dihel & Goswami, 2016; ElGanainy et al., 2023; Ganne, 2018; Harris, 2022). Consequently, harmonisation is not only desirable but also necessary for the AfCFTA to realise its potential as a transformational economic bloc. Under the four main axes of lowering costs and delays, boosting integration, enhancing compliance, and encouraging inclusive growth, this section explains the justification for coordinating border management and trade facilitation.

17.3.1 Reducing Trade Costs and Delays

It has long been recognised that inconsistent processes and disparate customs practices are significant contributors to high transaction costs across African borders. According to the World Bank (2023), landlocked nations such as Malawi, Uganda, and Burundi are most affected by these inefficiencies, with additional expenses ranging from 30% to 50% higher than those of coastal economies. One prominent example is the Northern Corridor, which connects Mombasa, Kenya, Kampala, Uganda, and Kigali, Rwanda. Due to human paperwork, duplication checks, and ill-coordinated inspections, goods trucks spend around 40% of their transit time at borders along this corridor (TradeMark Africa (TMEA), 2023).

The benefits of harmonisation through unified border operations and standardised paperwork have become evident. When Ghana implemented a National Single Window system, for example, the number of customs paperwork needed dropped from over 10 to just four, resulting in a 70% reduction in cargo clearing times (Ghana Revenue Authority (GRA), 2023). In the same vein, coordinated procedures were effective when combined inspections at the Rwanda-Uganda border post at Gatuna cut the average processing time from 48 hours to just 6 h (East African Community (EAC), 2023). By reducing transit times from 18 to 10 days and minimising damage to road infrastructure, the Central Corridor between Tanzania and Burundi has established unified axle-load requirements, thereby improving freight reliability (African Development Bank (AfDB), 2023). To this effect, RECs ought to invest in digital customs systems that are compatible with one another and establish OSBPs. These measures decrease transit times, improve operational coherence, and reduce opportunities for corruption.

17.3.2 Enhancing Regional and Continental Integration

Realising the goals of the AfCFTA, which aims to create a single market for goods and services among 54 nations, depends on harmonising border and trade facilitation procedures. However, progress is hindered by the inconsistent use of key tools such as trucking regulations, sanitary and phytosanitary (SPS) measures, and rules of origin (RoO) (de Melo et al., 2020; Fernandes et al., 2018; Rikhotso, 2025; Tyagi & Goyal, 2023; Vutula, 2025). For example, because SADC and ECOWAS have different interpretations of the RoO, South African auto exporters have faced non-tariff barriers when trying to access the Nigerian market (Rikhotso, 2025; United Nations Economic Commission for Africa (UNECA), 2023). The experience of the Tripartite Free Trade Area (TFTA), which includes SADC, EAC, and COMESA, and aimed to harmonise 183 trade regulations, offers even more lessons. Africa's regional trade structure, however, remains deeply fragmented politically and institutionally, with only about 40% of these regulations being implemented so far (African Union Development Agency (AUDA-NEPAD), 2023). It is estimated that inconsistencies in SPS and transport regulations cost the dairy industry in East Africa over $200 million annually (COMESA, 2023). Therefore, the AfCFTA Trade Facilitation Protocol (2024) should establish standardised ICT solutions, such as ASYCUDA World, for all RECs, ensuring data exchange and digitising border processes.

17.3.3 Improving Compliance and Transparency

Despite broad support for the WTO Trade Facilitation Agreement (TFA), there remains a significant gap between its promises and actual implementation. According to World Trade Organization (WTO) (2023), Article 10 of the TFA mandates the creation of national single window systems, but only 22 African countries have fully implemented this requirement. The results are more positive for countries that have adopted the World Customs Organisation (WCO) SAFE Framework and implemented policies like Authorised Economic Operators (AEOs). For example, adopting AEOs reduced contraband and smuggling in Botswana by 60% (World Customs Organization (WCO), 2023). Modernised customs procedures, which increase transparency, also reduce discretionary power. Nigeria has experienced a 45% drop in bribery cases due to its e-Customs system, which uses automated processing and biometric verification (Transparency International, 2023). In Rwanda, blockchain-based clearance systems, which eliminated 90% of manual processes, have greatly reduced rent-seeking and manipulation opportunities (Rwanda Revenue Authority (RRA), 2023; Tyagi & Goyal, 2023).

From the standpoint of the private sector, border uncertainty continues to be a major barrier. According to a report by the International Air Transport Association (IATA) (2023), 68% of African companies believe that inconsistent procedures and erratic delays are the biggest obstacles to commerce. Best-practice platforms like Kenya's TradeNet, which unifies more than 40 agencies into a single online system, show how centralised coordination can lower transaction costs and boost business confidence (Kenya Revenue Authority (KRA), 2023). RECs should, therefore, set up regional anti-corruption dashboards that are connected to the Non-Tariff Barrier (NTB) reporting system of the AfCFTA. Tools for transparency and real-time data analytics can assist in monitoring and quickly removing informal obstacles.

17.3.4 Facilitating Inclusive and Sustainable Economic Growth

To achieve broader development goals, especially those related to sustainability, industrialisation, and inclusiveness, coordinated trade facilitation is essential. Standardised processes significantly lower entry barriers for small-scale traders, especially in landlocked countries. Harmonising clearance at the Kazungula OSBP between Zambia and Botswana reduced transaction costs for Malawian SMEs by 25%, boosting their market access (SADC, 2023). Similarly, impact has also been shown by gender-sensitive trade facilitation efforts. The EAC's STR, which minimises costs for low-value transactions and simplifies customs procedures, increased women's participation in cross-border trade by 30% (UN Women, 2023). These results emphasise the importance of designing trading systems that address the needs of underrepresented groups.

Harmonised trade practices also speed up the flow of processed goods and intermediate goods, which promotes agro-industrialisation and value addition. Exports of processed cocoa increased by 18% in 2023 as a result of Ghana's customs procedures being in line with AfCFTA guidelines (GIPC, 2024; Galal, 2024). African Development Bank (AfDB) (2023) estimates that standardised SPS certificates might open up an extra \$90 billion in intra-African agricultural commerce each year. In the same vein, the AfCFTA Protocol on Women and Youth in Trade calls for the establishment of "green lanes" at OSBPs for SMEs and women-led businesses to facilitate quicker clearance and fair access. Over and above, it can be noted that harmonising border management and trade facilitation practices throughout Africa is more than just a technical fix; it is a strategic necessity for realising the continent's full economic potential (de Melo et al., 2025; Duval & Utoktham, 2022; Vutula, 2025). African businesses continue to incur large costs due to the fragmentation of trade documentation, disparate customs systems, and inconsistent regulatory frameworks; intraregional trade expenses are still two to three times higher than the global average (Chiswa, 2025; Galal, 2024; World Bank, 2023). More than just individual reforms are needed to remove these obstacles; a methodical harmonisation of systems throughout the continent is needed, supported by institutional cooperation, political will, and digital revolution.

17.4 Sectoral and Thematic Focus: Infrastructure, Digital Trade, and Private Sector Engagement in Africa's Trade Facilitation Agenda

According to the African Continental Free Trade Area (AfCFTA) Secretariat (2023), with intra-African trade still making up less than 15% of Africa's total trade volume, compared to regions like Europe (69%) and Asia (59%), the AfCFTA offers a once-in-a-lifetime chance to boost intra-African trade. However, the continent's capacity to fully benefit from the AfCFTA is still constrained by structural issues with digital integration, transit infrastructure, and private sector participation. To unlock Africa's trade potential and create a competitive, integrated African market, this section examines three crucial areas: digital trade facilitation, transportation and logistics infrastructure, and private sector involvement.

17.4.1 Infrastructure and Logistics Corridors: The Arteries of Intra-African Trade

Africa continues to have the world's weakest transport and logistics system. Sub-Saharan Africa came in last place in the 2023 Logistics Performance Index (LPI) with an average score of 2.5 out of 5, which is far lower than the global average of 3.3 (World Bank, 2023). All modes of transport are affected by core deficits:

- Road transport: While South Asia has 50% paved roads and OECD nations have over 90% paved roads, just 26% of Africa's roads are paved. Road freight prices are two to three times higher than the global average, averaging \$0.08 to \$0.15 per ton-kilometre throughout the continent (African Development Bank (AfDB), 2023; United Nations Conference on Trade and Development (UNCTAD), 2023).
- Rail infrastructure: With just 2.5 km per 1000 km^2, Africa has the lowest rail density in the world, significantly less than Europe's 22 km. By requiring expensive transhipment at borders, the employment of many incompatible rail gauges (Cape, metre, and standard) exacerbates inefficiencies (African Union Development Agency (AUDA-NEPAD), 2023).
- Port performance: There is a lot of traffic in African ports. Whereas ports like Singapore and Rotterdam have cargo dwell times of 2–4 days, the average cargo dwell time is 14–21 days. Additionally, according to United Nations Economic Commission for Africa (UNECA) (2023), 85% of African ports lack contemporary digital logistics and container handling facilities.

Mixed results are reflected in the performance of critical corridors. The installation of OSBPs has reduced transit times by 30% on the Northern Corridor (Mombasa-Kampala-Kigali), which accounts for approximately 40% of East Africa's trade; however, bribery and other informal barriers persist (East African Community (EAC), 2023). Since the port was granted a concession in 2003, the volume of goods moving via the Maputo Corridor has increased by 18% annually as a result, efficiency is also undermined, as only 32% of the roads meet the requirements. Consequently, efficiency is also undermined, as only 32% of the roads meet international Class I requirements (African Development Bank (AfDB), 2023). The development of dry ports in Zambia and Zimbabwe has reduced transit times for products bound for the Democratic Republic of Congo (DRC) from 21 to 9 days via the Walvis Bay Corridor. According to the Namibia Ports Authority (2023), however, because of inadequate rail connectivity, 78% of freight still travels by road.

17.4.2 Digital Trade Facilitation: Revolutionising Border Management

Improving cross-border efficiency and modernising customs depend heavily on digital technologies. A single platform for traders to input all trade-related data makes paperwork easier using Electronic Single Window Systems (e-SWS). While Rwanda digitised 92% of declarations through its e-Customs platform (Rwanda Revenue Authority (RRA), 2023), Ghana's National Single Window cut clearance times from 5 days to 4 h (Ghana Revenue Authority (GRA), 2023). With 42 agencies integrated, Nigeria's e-Trade system has reduced document processing by 60% (Nigeria Customs Service (NCS), 2023). Only 18 African nations, however, now have functional e-SWS systems. The lack of supporting legislative frameworks, system compatibility, and high initial expenditures (from $15 million to $50 million per system) are obstacles to wider adoption (World Trade Organization (WTO), 2023; United Nations Conference on Trade and Development (UNCTAD), 2023).

To improve inspection efficiency, emerging technologies are also used to reduce fraud. For example:

- The Kenya-Uganda dairy corridor implemented a blockchain-based SPS certification system that resulted in a 40% decrease in certificate fraud (TradeMark Africa (TMEA), 2023; Tyagi & Goyal, 2023).
- The TradeSecure technology in South Africa makes it possible to issue and track SPS documents in real time.
- The Zambian AI-powered risk engine has lowered the frequency of physical inspections by 35% (Vutula, 2025; ZRA, 2023).

Despite these advancements, cybersecurity threats are disproportionately high in Africa. According to African Union Development Agency (AUDA-NEPAD) (2023) and Interpol. (2023), only nine African nations have fully implemented data protection regulations, and the continent suffers 35% more cyberattacks targeting trade systems than the global average.

17.4.3 Private Sector Engagement in Trade Facilitation

The private sector plays a pivotal role in the design, execution, and long-term success of trade facilitation initiatives. Trade intermediaries, such as freight forwarders and customs brokers, play a crucial role in ensuring last-mile compliance and maintaining supply chain continuity.

- Ethiopian Airlines' investment in cold chain logistics led to a 25% increase in perishables trade, while DHL's e-commerce platform decreased delivery times by 40% across important corridors (International Air Transport Association (IATA), 2023; DHL, 2023).
- Accredited customs brokers in Senegal cut clearance times by 50% (World Customs Organization (WCO), 2023).
- In Kenya, licenced agents handle over 68% of total declarations, improving the contact between traders and customs authorities (Kenya Revenue Authority (KRA), 2023).

Public-private partnerships (PPPs) have also played an important role in infrastructure delivery. Several successful models include:

- The Lekki Deep Sea Port in Nigeria, a joint venture between China Harbour and Lagos State, has reduced port congestion by 30%.
- The Doraleh Port in Djibouti, managed by China Merchants Ports, reduced Ethiopia's import expenses by 15%.
- Tanzania's Standard Gauge Railway (SGR), built by a Turkish-Portuguese partnership, increased transport capacity to ten million tonnes annually.

However, not all public–private partnerships have been flawless. Ghana's Tema Port development was delayed by 2 years due to bureaucratic paralysis, and Kenya's SGR project incurred debt servicing costs of $3.2 billion, raising concerns about its long-term budgetary viability (African Development Bank (AfDB), 2023; United Nations Economic Commission for Africa (UNECA), 2023).

AfCFTA's full potential will be realised if the continent can holistically integrate its physical infrastructure, digital trade systems, and private sector stakeholders. The existing infrastructure gap alone requires an estimated $130 billion in yearly investments, the majority of which must be funded through blended finance and PPPs (PIDA, 2023). Simultaneously, the complete installation of electronic single windows must be prioritised by 2027 across all borders. Institutionalising private sector participation through dedicated frameworks within RECs and national trade policies will ensure that both large and small businesses play a crucial role in Africa's trade revolution. Only by concurrently addressing infrastructure, technology, and governance will enable the African continent transform its trade corridors into true engines of sustainable, inclusive, and resilient development.

17.5 Policy Coherence and Challenges in African Trade Facilitation

The AfCFTA's successful implementation is dependent on the harmonisation of trade policy and border procedures. While regional economic integration has advanced significantly during the last decade, Africa's trade environment remains plagued by inconsistencies, regulatory misalignments, and institutional fragmentation (Akeyewale, 2018; Chiswa, 2025; de Melo et al., 2025; Grinsted & Sandrey, 2015; Hillberry & Zhang, 2018; Nwankwo & Ajibo, 2020; Rikhotso, 2025; Vutula, 2025). These problems not only raise transaction costs but also undermine the continent's ability to compete in global markets. This part examines three critical areas where policy coherence is essential: tariff and non-tariff measures, border agency cooperation, and legal-institutional frameworks. It highlights the potential for strategic reform and improved implementation across the continent.

17.5.1 Harmonising Tariff and Non-Tariff Measures

17.5.1.1 Common External Tariffs (CETs) and Rules of Origin (RoO)

The inconsistent application of Common External Tariffs and Rules of Origin (RoO) across Africa's Regional Economic Communities (RECs) exemplifies the continent's fragmented trade architecture. For example, in 2015, the ECOWAS implemented a CET to streamline and standardise regional trade (Ashurst, 2016; Dihel & Goswami, 2016; Ogunleye, 2021). However, many exclusions have substantially reduced its effectiveness. According to the International Trade Centre (ITC) analysis from 2023, ECOWAS member states have awarded over 500 product-specific waivers, effectively distorting trade flows and undermining the CET's integrity. While the EAC is more stable in its use of CET, it has experienced internal conflict. Revenue-sharing disagreements between Kenya and Tanzania have periodically eroded confidence in the tariff system, underscoring the challenges of maintaining cooperative fiscal arrangements within a customs union (East African Community (EAC), 2023).

At the continental level, overlapping RoO frameworks further complicate the issues. South African vehicle exports to Nigeria (an ECOWAS member) and Egypt (a COMESA member) are subject to separate rules of origin, resulting in delays, confusion, and legal uncertainty. According to the African Continental Free Trade

Area (AfCFTA) Secretariat (2023), the proliferation of rules has exacerbated cross-border disputes, many of which remain unresolved due to a lack of clarity and enforcement procedures. According to a United Nations Economic Commission for Africa (UNECA) (2023) study, RoO misinterpretations are responsible for 35% of intra-African trade conflicts. However, more streamlined and harmonised procedures can produce excellent outcomes. The SADC has implemented an STR for small traders that includes a uniform certificate of origin, resulting in a 40% increase in compliance and official trade registration (Zimano et al., 2019).

17.5.1.2 Non-Tariff Measures (NTMs) and Standards Harmonisation

In addition to tariffs, NTMs, notably sanitary and phytosanitary (SPS) regulations and technical barriers to trade (TBTs), are some of the most significant impediments to intra-African trade. Accordingly, East African Community (EAC) (2023) noted that commendable progress has been made within the EAC, with 74% of SPS criteria for dairy products now harmonised among member states. This collaboration has seen a surge in trade, leading to a 20% increase in milk trade between Kenya and Uganda (East African Community (EAC), 2023). In contrast, ECOWAS has only harmonised roughly 30% of agro-processing requirements. This imbalance has resulted in Nigeria's unilateral restriction on maize imports in 2021, which violated regional trade commitments and sparked diplomatic tensions (ECOWAS, 2023). The expense of implementing TBTs is likewise unreasonable. South African exporters are counterparts, reportedly spending 15–25% more on testing and certification than their European Union counterparts, due to duplicative and fragmented procedures (International Air Transport Association (IATA), 2023). As a result, it is critical to implement a real-time NTM dashboard during AfCFTA's Phase II discussions to quickly detect, monitor, and resolve NTBs. In addition, stronger REC level SPS and TBT Committees with enforcement responsibilities and technical capacity are required to harmonise protocols.

17.5.2 Coordinating Border Agencies and Risk Management

17.5.2.1 Integrated Border Management (IBM) Models

Integrated Border Management (IBM) aims to streamline border operations by integrating the efforts of various border control agencies, including customs, immigration, and sanitary inspection authorities. Examples of successful IBM implementations are:

- Ghana's paperless port system cut customs processing time from 5 days to 4 h by merging multiple agencies into a single platform (Ghana Revenue Authority (GRA), 2023).

- The Malaba OSBP between Kenya and Uganda reduced travel time from 3 days to 8 h with consolidated border procedures and collaborative inspections (TradeMark Africa (TMEA), 2023).
- Rwanda's border post with the Democratic Republic of Congo (DRC) reduced smuggling by 60% after implementing shared risk profiles (Rwanda Revenue Authority (RRA), 2023).

Despite these accomplishments, difficulties remain. For example, the Beitbridge border between Zimbabwe and South Africa is home to 14 different agencies, many of which operate in silos with no coordinated data exchange or harmonised procedures (SADC, 2023; Zimano et al., 2019). Furthermore, more than half of African OSBPs lack automation and digital infrastructure, which limits their operational impact (African Development Bank (AfDB), 2023).

17.5.2.2 Risk Management and Customs Modernisation

Countries that have implemented risk-based clearance systems have seen increases in efficiency. The Automated Risk Engine in South Africa expedited the processing of low-risk commodities while reducing physical inspections by 45%, enabling authorities to concentrate on high-risk shipments (SARS, 2023). Nigeria saw a 60% decrease in corruption-related events during border processing when e-Customs platforms with digital manifests and biometric clearance were implemented (Nigeria Customs Service (NCS), 2023). Promoting cooperation between RECs and the WCO is essential to implement the SAFE Framework for integrated, risk-based customs clearance and establish an AfCFTA Border Agency Code that requires standardised data-sharing procedures, digital risk profiling, and joint inspections.

17.5.3 Legal and Political Challenges in Policy Harmonisation

17.5.3.1 Sovereignty Vs. Regional Integration

A recurring barrier to trade harmonisation in Africa is the conflict between regional commitments and national sovereignty. National policies might violate regional trade agreements, as they are often implemented to achieve domestic political or economic objectives. For instance, the EAC's rules on the free flow of goods and services have been criticised for being broken by Uganda's digital tax policy (East African Community (EAC), 2023). Nigeria's Automotive Industry Policy, which requires 35% local content in car production, has also been noted by the WTO as possibly conflicting with AfCFTA commitments and international trade standards (World Trade Organization (WTO), 2023).

17.5.3.2 Institutional Fragmentation and Weak Enforcement

In Africa's trade integration programme, enforcement continues to be a significant weakness. As a result of overlapping membership and institutional weariness, only 40% of COMESA's Tripartite Free Trade Area (TFTA) obligations have been fulfilled, despite the TFTA's goal of harmonising trade laws throughout COMESA, EAC, and SADC (African Union Development Agency (AUDA-NEPAD), 2023). Similarly, the AfCFTA Dispute Settlement Mechanism, which has been in place since 2021, has struggled to gain traction. Only five trade disputes have been formally lodged thus far, indicating that the mechanism is not being used to its full potential and that its procedures may not be well understood by the public (African Continental Free Trade Area (AfCFTA) Secretariat, 2023). To help member states align their domestic legal systems with their regional commitments, an AfCFTA Legal Harmonisation Fund must be established. In order to improve enforcement capacity, it is also crucial to extend the jurisdiction of regional trade courts, such as the ECOWAS Court of Justice and the East African Court of Justice (EACJ), to encompass AfCFTA-related disputes. Furthermore, it is worth noting that Africa's trade facilitation ambition requires more than a superficial alignment of customs paperwork or haphazard technology upgrades to achieve significant policy consistency. To do this, trade governance systems must be fundamentally reorganised in all the legal, institutional, and operational areas.

17.6 Outcomes, Impact, and Policy Recommendations

According to De Melo et al. (2025), significant and quantifiable economic benefits are emerging from the adoption of trade facilitation policies throughout Africa. The reforms include the participation of women and small businesses. The data suggests a trajectory of growth that, if maintained and expanded, may significantly aid in Africa's economic transition under the African Continental Free Trade Area (AfCFTA), despite ongoing hurdles. Similarly, it is worth noting that lower trade costs are one of the most apparent effects of trade facilitation, particularly for low-income African nations. According to the World Bank (2023), these nations have seen an average cost decrease of 14.3% as a result of implementing the WTO's TFA. This is far higher than the global average of 8.2%. Simplified customs processes, less documentation needs, and more stable regulatory frameworks are the leading causes of this cost savings.

Ghana and Rwanda are two notable instances of time efficiency. Clearance times in Rwanda have been drastically shortened from 5 days to just 6 h with the implementation of a completely digitalised electronic customs system. According to the Rwanda Revenue Authority (Rwanda Revenue Authority (RRA), 2023), this change resulted in a 40% increase in customs income and a 30% increase in trade volumes. According to Ghana Revenue Authority (GRA) (2023), Ghana's "paperless port" project also decreased the average cargo dwell time by 70%, saving traders an estimated $300 million a year in logistics, warehousing, and demurrage expenses. These results highlight the close relationship between economic efficiency and digital border control.

Countries that have implemented strong trade facilitation measures have seen increases in competitiveness, as well as time and cost savings. These nations rank about 30% higher in terms of trade infrastructure, international shipment reliability, and customs efficiency (World Bank, 2023). In addition to drawing in investment, these improvements in logistics performance also make it easier for domestic industries to join regional and international value chains. In addition to macroeconomic metrics, trade facilitation measures have had a significant effect on equity and inclusion, especially for women-led firms, small and medium-sized enterprises (SMEs), and informal traders. Through the simplification of customs documentation and the reduction of compliance burdens, the implementation of STRs under the AfCFTA and RECs like the EAC has resulted in a 40% increase in participation by small traders (East African Community (EAC), 2023). This has made it easier for SMEs to reach markets and join official trade networks.

There has also been a notable impact on women in the trade sector. Women's cross-border commerce participation has increased by 25% as a result of gender-responsive changes in the EAC, including the creation of special women's trade desks and the simplification of border processes (UN Women, 2023). Furthermore, Nigeria's implementation of an e-Trade platform, which includes online declarations and biometric verification, has dramatically improved the experience of women traders by reducing harassment and informal payments by 60% (Nigeria Customs Service (NCS), 2023). In addition to shielding them from exploitation, these measures enable women to expand the size of their trading operations. Another significant outcome of trade facilitation policies is the incorporation of informal traders into the official economy. An excellent illustration is the OSBP programme in Malawi. The OSBP reform resulted in a 50% decrease in informal payments, accompanied by a corresponding increase in tax compliance and formal registration. This was achieved by combining customs, immigration, and security processes into a single, coordinated operation and by providing targeted outreach to informal traders (TradeMark Africa (TMEA), 2023). This twofold advantage-the state's increased revenue and traders' increased livelihood security-shows the mutually beneficial possibilities of an inclusive trade policy.

In light of the above, it can be argued that there are observable and significant results from trade facilitation initiatives throughout Africa. They not only increase competitiveness and lower transaction costs, but also promote greater inclusion, particularly for underrepresented groups such as women and informal traders (Rikhotso, 2025). These successes serve as a reminder of the critical importance of implementing and expanding reforms within the framework of the AfCFTA. Future initiatives should focus on expanding the reach of successful innovations, strengthening institutional capacity, and ensuring that trade facilitation policies are technology-driven, inclusive, and consistent across the continent. By doing this, Africa can fully realise the potential of regional commerce as a catalyst for sustainable development and economic progress.

17.6.1 Monitoring and Evaluation Frameworks

Understanding the advancements, obstacles, and effects of trade facilitation reforms throughout Africa requires effective monitoring and evaluation (M&E). Under frameworks like the WTO TFA and the AfCFTA, nations are implementing trade-related policy changes. To analyse their success and guide mid-course corrections, data-driven policy assessment is crucial. Governments, RECs, and continental organisations are increasingly using digital dashboards, feedback loops, and performance indicators to track the quality and speed of changes. For monitoring trade logistics performance, the World Bank's LPI is one of the most popular tools. This measure provides a composite score that takes into account international shipments, infrastructure quality, tracking capabilities, timeliness, logistics expertise, and customs efficiency. As noted above, the average LPI score for Africa remains low, at approximately 2.5 out of 5. However, nations like Rwanda and Ghana, which have adopted digital customs reforms and upgraded their trade infrastructure, have seen their scores rise above 3.2, making them regional leaders in logistics performance (World Bank, 2023).

The Doing Business metrics, especially those on "Trading Across Borders," are a valuable addition to the LPI metrics. These metrics monitor the time and expenses involved in importing and exporting commodities. Because of the implementation of paperless processes, port modernisation, and customs automation, export times in nations like Kenya, Togo, and Côte d'Ivoire have reduced from 48 to 32 h (African Development Bank (AfDB), 2023). According to the World Trade Organization (WTO) (2023), nations that have adopted electronic single window systems, which enable the submission of trade-related papers via a single digital portal, have seen a 22% decrease in import-related expenses. In addition to demonstrating the effectiveness of digital tools, these Figures also act as standards for other countries implementing comparable reforms.

In addition to these global indices, Africa is using regional and continental M&E processes more frequently to evaluate and enhance trade facilitation. The AfCFTA NTB Reporting System is one such tool. It is a digital platform that allows traders to report trade-inhibiting behaviours, including arbitrary inspections, corruption, or regulatory anomalies. According to the African Continental Free Trade Area (AfCFTA) Secretariat (2023), the NTB mechanism has received over 1200 complaints since its inception, with many of these complaints being settled through bilateral consultations or policy initiatives. This technology provides a comprehensive database of trade-related issues that can inform more extensive policy changes, in addition to a grievance redress mechanism. Furthermore, real-time information on the performance of important trade routes can be obtained through systems such as Trademark Africa's Corridor Performance Monitoring System. Such platforms facilitate evidence-based decision-making, investment prioritisation, and cross-national intervention coordination by providing granular, current data (TradeMark Africa (TMEA), 2023).

17.7 Recommendations and Future Directions

To maintain and expand the benefits of trade facilitation, African nations and organisations must implement a comprehensive and well-planned set of policy changes that prioritise inclusive development, digital transformation, regional integration, and environmental sustainability. By implementing these forward-looking tactics, current gaps will be filled. Trade and trade facilitation will support the Sustainable Development Goals (SDGs) and the broader objectives of Agenda 2063 for social and economic transformation.

A key strategic priority is to establish laws and regulations for a continental customs union. As a result, nations need to accelerate the completion of the AfCFTA Phase II negotiations by 2025, especially in vital areas like intellectual property rights, investment, and competition policy. To ensure that enterprises operate within a unified legal and economic framework across Africa, these protocols are essential for minimising regulatory differences (African Union Development Agency (AUDA-NEPAD), 2023). Similarly, it is important to harmonise CETs and RoO. Discrepancies, such as ECOWAS's over 500 product-specific CET exclusions, currently weaken the integrity of regional trade systems and make it harder to build integrated supply chains (International Air Transport Association (IATA), 2023). A unified strategy would increase investor confidence, simplify compliance, and reduce conflicts.

The AfCFTA's dispute resolution process must be strengthened on the continent to ensure that its regulations are upheld and effectively implemented. According to the African Continental Free Trade Area (AfCFTA) Secretariat (2023), the establishment of a fully operational AfCFTA Appellate Body would encourage a rules-based economic environment, discourage protectionism, and offer legal certainty. In the absence of reliable enforcement, the advantages of liberalisation and harmonisation might not materialise. Concurrently, the digitisation of trade processes needs to be given top priority. By 2030, all major ports and border checkpoints should have electronic single windows installed. This should be a continental goal. According to the African Development Bank (AfDB) (2023), these technologies reduce delays and potential for rent-seeking behaviour by streamlining interactions between traders, customs, and other regulatory bodies. In addition to single windows, blockchain-based certification platforms for sanitary and phytosanitary (SPS) and technological barriers to trade (TBT) compliance should be adopted by Africa. In the high-value agriculture and pharmaceutical sectors, in particular, these platforms can enhance traceability, reduce document fraud, and promote mutual recognition of standards (World Customs Organization (WCO), 2023).

Another new area of development is climate-smart trade facilitation. As the world economy moves towards decarbonisation, Africa needs to ensure that its trade policies support the objectives of environmental sustainability. Making at least 15 main trade corridors electrified and decarbonised by 2035 is a top priority to reduce greenhouse gas emissions and attract green finance (African Union Development Agency (AUDA-NEPAD), 2023). The continent also needs to prepare exporters for the Carbon Border Adjustment Mechanism (CBAM), particularly those that trade with the EU. In light of this, protecting Africa's competitiveness in carbon-sensitive markets will require adherence to these requirements (United Nations Economic Commission for Africa (UNECA), 2023).

Lastly, trade facilitation needs to be purposefully created to encourage inclusive growth. Lawmakers should set aside 30% of the customs processing capacity at trade hubs exclusively for small-scale traders in order to assist SMEs. In the trading ecosystem, this would level the playing field for smaller players, speed up transactions, and lessen congestion (African Development Bank (AfDB), 2023). The need for gender-responsive trade changes is equally critical. The demands of female merchants should be mainstreamed in the next AfCFTA Phase III discussions, with an emphasis on digital literacy, physical safety at borders, and financial access (UN Women, 2023). Africa can make sure that the advantages of integration and facilitation are distributed fairly throughout genders and economic classes by including inclusion into the architecture of trade systems.

17.8 Conclusion

Africa's journey towards trade facilitation has yielded tangible and promising outcomes. From the modernisation of border systems and customs reforms to the notable inclusion of small and medium-sized enterprises (SMEs), women traders, and informal actors, the continent has made measurable progress in dismantling procedural trade barriers. Yet, these successes remain uneven, and persistent challenges continue to threaten the full realisation of trade facilitation as a cornerstone of continental integration. Key impediments include institutional fragmentation between national governments, RECs, and the AfCFTA Secretariat; underinvestment in critical trade-enabling infrastructure; and uneven implementation of digital systems such as electronic single windows and blockchain certification platforms. These structural and operational deficits undermine the predictability and reliability that are essential to a functioning rules-based trade regime. In order to fully realise the continent's economic potential, it is strategically necessary to harmonise border management and trade facilitation practices throughout Africa. This goes beyond simple technical changes. The complete implementation of the WTO Trade Facilitation Agreement (TFA) must be the top priority for states. This entails investing in digital innovation and capacity-building at the same time as implementing risk-based inspections, pre-arrival processing, and expedited documentation. With the correct reforms, strong governance, and inclusive execution, Africa can create a trading environment that is cohesive, effective, and fair. This ecosystem will increase economic resilience and intra-African commerce while also re-establishing Africa as a major player in international trade.

References

African Continental Free Trade Area (AfCFTA) Secretariat. (2023). *Annual implementation report*. AfCFTA Secretariat.

African Development Bank (AfDB). (2023). *African infrastructure development report*. African Development Bank Group.

African Union Development Agency (AUDA-NEPAD). (2023). *Continental rail infrastructure review*. AUDA-NEPAD.

Akeyewale, R., (2018). *Who Are the Winners and Losers in Africa's Continental Free Trade Area?* [Online] https://www.weforum.org/agenda/2018/10/africa-continental-free-trade-afcfta-sme-business/

Arvis, J.-F., Duval, Y., Shepherd, B., & Utoktham, C. (2016). Trade costs in the developing world: 1995-2010. *World Trade Review, 15*(3), 451–474.

Ashurst. (2016). *Road infrastructure in Africa*. [Online] https://www.ashurst.com/en/news-and-insights/insights/road-infrastructure-in-africa/

Chang, Y., Iakovou, E., & Shi, W. (2020). Blockchain in global supply chains and cross-border trade: A critical synthesis of the state-of-the-art, challenges and opportunities. *International Journal of Production Research, 58*(7), 2082–2099.

Chiswa, N. (2024). Unlocking Africa's economic potential: The role of PPPs in fuelling infrastructure development and investment–South Africa's perspective. *Jindal Global Law Review, 15*(1), 157–185.

Chiswa, N. (2025). Realising Africa's promise: The role of artificial intelligence and blockchain technology in achieving the objectives of the African continental free trade area. *Sustainability and Climate Change, 18*(2), 78–82.

de Melo, J., Solleder, J.-M., & Sorgho, Z. (2020). Market integration across Africa: Progress and challenges ahead. In *Working paper series 342*. African Development Bank Group.

De Melo, J., Sorgho, Z., & Wagner, L. (2025). Reducing wait times at customs to boost trade: How implementing the trade facilitation agreement can expand trade among AfCFTA countries? *Journal of African Economies, 34*(2), 265–294.

DHL. (2023). *Africa e-commerce logistics brief.* DHL International GmbH.

Dihel, N., & Goswami, A. (2016). *The unexplored potential of trade in services in Africa: From hair stylists and teachers to accountants and doctors*. World Bank Group.

Duval, Y., & Utoktham, C. (2022). *Has the trade facilitation agreement helped reduce trade costs? An ex-post analysis, in WP#2 ESCAP*. Economic and social Commission for Asia and the Pacific (ESCAP).

East African Community (EAC). (2023). *Northern corridor OSBP review*. East African Community Secretariat.

ElGanainy, A., Hakobyan, S., Liu, F., & Wesfeld, H. (2023). Trade integration in Africa: Unleashing the continent's potential in a changing world. *IMF, 2023*, 1. https://doi.org/10.5089/9798400232794.087

Fernandes, A. M., Maemir, H., Mattoo, A., & Rojas, A. F. (2018). *Are trade preferences a panacea? AGOA and African exports* (pp. 17–18). World Bank Group.

Gakwaya, O., Meier-Hahn, U., Mbouna, R., & Wannemacher, L. (2020). *Block chain in Africa: Opportunities and chal lenges for the next decade*. Smart Africa.

Galal, S. (2024). Internet usage in Africa-statistics & facts. *Statistica*. https://www.statista.com/topics/9813/internet-usage-in-africa/

Ganne, E. (2018). *Can blockchain revolutionize international trade?* World Trade Organization.

Ghana Revenue Authority (GRA). (2023). *National single window evaluation report*. Ghana Publishing Corporation.

Grinsted, J., & Sandrey, R. (2015). *The continental free trade area—A GTAP assessment*. Trade Law Centre. https://www.tralac.org/publications/article/7287-the-continental-free-trade-area-a-gtap-assessment.html

Harris, C. G. (2022). Towards a blockchain solution for customs duty-related fraud. In S. Sakr & A. Zomaya (Eds.), *Database systems for advanced applications: DASFAA 2022 international workshops* (pp. 120–134). Springer.

Hassan, M. (2015). *A WTO agreement on trade facilitation: Can it facilitate trade?* PhD thesis, University of St. Gallen. http://verdi.unisg.ch/www/edis.nsf/SysLkpByIdentifier/4279/$FILE/dis4279.pdf

Hillberry, R., & Zhang, X. (2018). Policy and performance in customs: Evaluating the trade facilitation agreement. *Review of International Economics, 26*(2), 438–480.

International Air Transport Association (IATA). (2023). *Cold chain logistics in Africa (Report No. 12–2023)*. IATA.

Interpol. (2023). *Cybersecurity threats to African trade systems*. INTERPOL General Secretariat.

Kayizzi-Mugerwa, S., Anyanwu, J., & Conceição, P. (2014). Regional integration in Africa: An introduction. *African Development Review, 26*(S1), 1–6.

Kenya Revenue Authority (KRA). (2023). *Customs and clearance efficiency review*. KRA Press.

Kieck, E. (2020). Trade facilitation and customs. In A. Mattoo, N. Rochsa, & M. Ruta (Eds.), *Handbook of deep trade agreements* (pp. 293–318). The World Bank.

Mateko, F. (2025). A SWOT analysis of regional trade advancement implementation in Africa. *African Journal of Rhetoric, 17*(1), 77–92.

Mold, A. (2018). *The case for an integrated African market—The costs of 'non-AfCFTA'*. https://www.theeastafrican.co.ke/oped/comment/Integrated-African-market%2D%2Dthe-costs-of%2D%2Dnon-AfCFTA/434750-4709126-3el6hjz/index.html

Namibia Ports Authority. (2023). *Walvis Bay corridor assessment report*. NamPorts.

Nigeria Customs Service (NCS). (2023). *e-Trade portal impact report*. NCS Publications.

Nwankwo, C., & Ajibo, C. (2020). Liberal izing regional trade regimes through AfCFTA: Challenges and opportunities. *Journal of African Law, 64*(3), 297–318.

Ogunleye, I. (2021). *Artificial intelligence for economic development in Nigeria. Taraaz and the Citris policy lab's 2021 technology and human rights fellowship program.*

Rikhotso, T. (2025). Implementation of the AfCFTA by small, micro-medium enterprises. *African Journal of Rhetoric, 17*(1), 77–92.

Rwanda Revenue Authority (RRA). (2023). *E-customs performance data*. RRA.

Schmieg, E. (2019). *EU and Africa: Investment, Trade, Development*. Stiftung Wissenschaft und Politik.

TradeMark Africa (TMEA). (2023). *Corridor performance monitoring report*. TMEA.

Truby, J., Dahdal, A., & Caudevilla, O. (2022). Global blockchain-based trade finance solutions: Analysis of governance models and impact on local laws in six jurisdictions. *Global Journal of Comparative Law, 11*(2), 167–196.

Tyagi, N. K., & Goyal, M. (2023). Blockchain-based smart contract for issuance of country of origin certificate for Indian customs exports clearance. *Concurrency and Computation: Practice and Experience, 35*(16), e6249.

United Nations Conference on Trade and Development (UNCTAD). (2023). *African trade logistics outlook (UNCTAD/DTL/2023/1)*. United Nations. https://doi.org/10.18356/24120345.

United Nations Economic Commission for Africa (UNECA). (2023). *Assessing regional integration in Africa IX*. UNECA. https://doi.org/10.54321/987654

Vutula, N. Z. (2025). Utilising trade facilitation as an efficient means of implementing the AfCFTA. *African Journal of Rhetoric, 17*(1), 176–207.

World Bank. (2023). *Logistics performance index report*. World Bank Group. https://doi.org/10.1596/978-1-4648-1987-4.

World Customs Organization (WCO). (2023). *Authorized economic operator impact study (WCO Research Series No. 5)*. WCO. https://doi.org/10.54321/2023-5

World Trade Organization (WTO). (2023). *Trade facilitation agreement implementation review (WTO Working Paper No. ERSD-2023-02)*. WTO. https://doi.org/10.30875/abcdef12.

Zimano, R. F., Chimanikire, D., & Chilunjika, A. (2019). Border management systems' intelligence and annotations on existing transit challenges in Zimbabwe. In S. Muqayi & C. Manyeruke (Eds.), *Dynamics of contemporary border management in Zimbabwe: Challenges, benefits and prospects* (pp. 37–60). Adonis & Abbey Publishers Ltd.

Chapter 18
The Socio-Economic Impacts of the AfCFTA

Sheereen Fauzel, Boopen Seetanah, and Verena Tandrayen-Ragoobur

Abstract The African Continental Free Trade Area (AfCFTA), a key initiative under Agenda 2063, is expected to drive the social and economic progress of countries of the African region. The AfCFTA includes 54 member states and aims to create a single market for commodities. It further facilitates the movement of people, capital, and investments across African countries. While the literature highlights numerous benefits from such trade liberalisation, the socio-economic impacts are rather diverse and country-dependent. The present paper critically analyses the social and economic effects of the AfCFTA, taking into consideration that different countries have varying implementation and institutional capabilities. To further probe into the impact of the AfCFTA on economic growth, an econometric analysis is conducted. Overall, the findings show the advantages of the AfCFTA in promoting the socio-economic performance of African countries.

Keywords AfCFTA · Socio-economic impacts · Dynamic fixed effect model

18.1 Introduction

The African Continental Free Trade Area (AfCFTA) is one of the leading projects of Agenda 2063. Signed in March 2018 and entered into force in 2019, the AfCFTA aims to enhance trade across countries within the African continent. Trade under the

S. Fauzel (✉)
Department of Finance and Accounting, University of Mauritius, Reduit, Mauritius
e-mail: s.fauzel@uom.ac.mu

B. Seetanah (✉)
University of Mauritius North West University, Reduit, South Africa
e-mail: b.seetanah@uom.ac.mu

V. Tandrayen-Ragoobur (✉)
Department of Economics and Statistics, University of Mauritius, Reduit, Mauritius
e-mail: v.tandrayen@uom.ac.mu

D. N. Yuni et al. (eds.), *From Policy to Practice: Challenges and Ways Forward on the Implementation of the AfCFTA*,
https://doi.org/10.1007/978-3-032-14051-7_18

agreement started on 1 January 2021 and it includes 54 of the 55 African Union (AU) member states, which represent a population of 1.4 billion people (UNDESA (United Nations Department of Economic and Social Affairs), 2022) and a market worth around USD 3 trillion annually (IMF (International Monetary Fund), 2022). The primary aim of the AfCFTA is to promote the socio-economic development of African countries. This is to be achieving through greater intra-African trade as well as reinforcing the position of the continent in the global market by strengthening Africa's collective voice and policy space in global trade negotiations.[1] With the AfCFTA, intra-African trade is forecasted to grow by more than 80% representing a rise of nearlyUS$60 billion in African exports (Abrego et al., 2020). Moreover, United Nations Economic Commission for Africa (UNECA) (2018) projected that this agreement can increase trade within Africa by more than 50% via the elimination of tariffs and the reduction of Non-Tariff Barriers (NTBs). Likewise, the World Bank (2020) projected that the AfCFTA will help in alleviating poverty by removing around 30 million Africans from extreme poverty and enhancing income levels across the member states.

Moreover, the AfCFTA aims to enhance economic integration across the African region through the creation of a single market not only for goods and services but also by being an enabler in facilitating the movement of people across Africa. Importantly, one of the main objectives of the AfCFTA remains the promotion of sustainable growth, inclusive socio-economic development and structural transformation of member states. The AfCFTA also seeks to enhance Africa's competitiveness on the foreign market and foster industrial development through the promotion of regional value chains, advancement of agricultural development and food security which remain a priority for many African nations.

Whilst greater trade liberalisation has proved to promote economic growth (Irwin, 2025; Kutu & Ohonba, 2024; Papadopoulos, 2022), yet the socio-economic impacts of the AfCFTA are rather complex. For instance, referring to its key principles, one can argue that such an agreement can have positive effects on the distribution of income as well as on the creation of employment. Other socio-economic impacts that may arise from the AfCFTA include a reduction in poverty, greater gender equality, and increased regional trade. However, these benefits will depend on various factors. These are mainly in terms of national implementation strategies, the effective removal of tariff and non-tariff barriers, and the streamlining of customs procedures. There is also a need to reform institutions and make structural adjustments to gain from the advantages offered by the AfCFTA.

Thus, this paper adds to the existing empirical literature to investigate the extent to which the AfCFTA agreement has impacted the economic performance of a sample of African countries. The trend in intra-African trade is analysed to investigate the extent to which the AfCFTA has influenced trade flows among member states on the continent. The analysis is further complemented by examining various socio-economic variables, including GDP per capita, the share of the population living in

[1] https://au.int/en/african-continental-free-trade-area.

absolute poverty, and the Human Development Index (HDI). These indicators offer a comprehensive perspective on how the AfCFTA can influence economic performance, enhance living standards, and reduce disparities and inequalities, while promoting sustainable development and inclusive growth across the continent.

This chapter is structured as follows: Sect. 18.2 reviews the related literature, while Sect. 18.3 presents the situational analysis. Section 18.4 discusses the economic model, and Sect. 18.5 analyses the findings. This chapter concludes in Sect. 18.6.

18.2 Review of Literature

18.2.1 Theoretical Link between AfCFTA (Trade Agreements) and Socio-Economic Effects

The Heckscher-Ohlin (H-O) theory (1933) explains that countries trade based on their factor endowments, primarily their factor resources, such as labour and capital (Angrist, 1995). The theory is built upon the earlier theory of comparative advantage by David Ricardo, which specifies that trade occurs based on the relative abundance of factors of production in different countries (Bernhofen & Brown, 2011; Bowen et al., 1987). Countries rich in certain resources will specialise in the production of goods and services that utilise those abundant resources, thus leading to a rise in output and economic growth. For instance, trade agreements reduce trade barriers and enhance market access. Thus, countries engaging in international trade may grow faster as they can produce more efficiently. This results in a more efficient allocation of resources internationally and advances overall economic growth (Singh, 2019).

Moreover, the new trade theory of Krugman, developed in the 1970s and 1980s, criticises the traditional trade theories and puts more emphasis on the role of increasing returns to scale, imperfect competition, intra-industry trade and product differentiation, which help to shape international trade patterns. This theory explains that even without significant differences in factor endowments or technology, countries can still trade through specialisation and access to larger markets (Ahmed, 2012). The new trade and endogenous growth theories emerged in the 1980s and 1990s, mainly due to the limitations of earlier models, which treat technological progress as an exogenous factor. The endogenous growth theory focusses on internal factors, such as investment in human capital, innovation, and knowledge accumulation, which are important engines of growth. From an international trade perspective, the endogenous growth model posits that trade can enhance these internal factors, resulting in higher growth (Gandolfo, 2013). Trade liberalisation can stimulate knowledge spillovers, capital accumulation, boost human capital, and attract foreign direct investment, which are important contributors to economic growth. Moreover, regional integration leads to structural changes as it facilitates

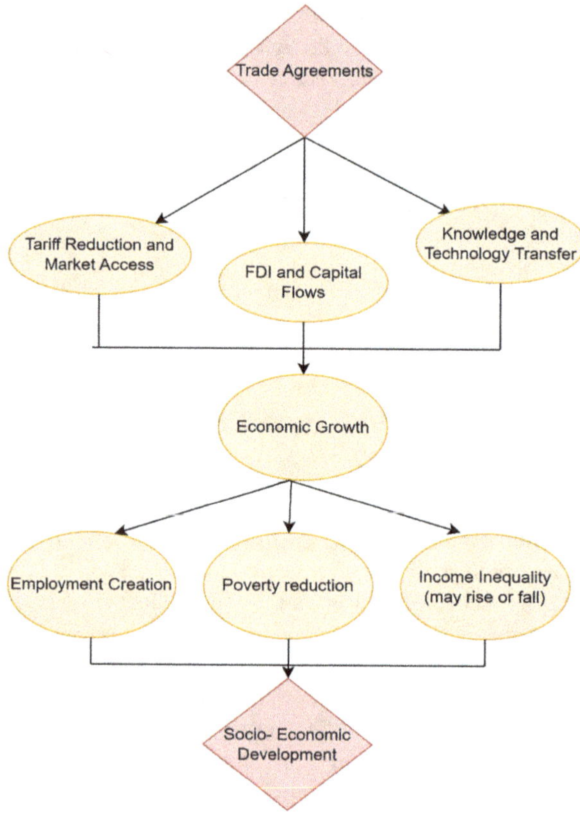

Fig. 18.1 Theoretical framework: trade agreements and socio-economic impacts. Source: Authors' compilation, 2025

specialisation through an efficient reallocation of factors of production across varied sectors of economic activity (Fei, 2022).

There is also the pro-poor trade theory, which discusses the linkage between trade, poverty and income inequality. Trade agreements can create a trade environment which helps poor households improve their economic situation. Pro-poor trade policies thus aim at narrowing the income disparity between the rich and the poor. This is mainly achieved through lower tariffs on goods mainly consumed by the low-income families. Also, the pro-poor trade theory posits that if there are barriers faced by exporters in developing countries and if these trade barriers are against the poor communities, then it will not reduce income inequality (Nicita et al., 2014). The conceptual model is shown in Fig. 18.1.

18.2.2 Empirical Review

Oloruntoba and Nshimbi (2023) argue that the AfCFTA promises socio-economic development mainly by promoting trade creation, favouring structural transformation, and reducing poverty. It also can create a large market, induce investment in manufacturing across the African continent. With the AfCFTA, there will be more trade liberalisation, and it is expected that the agreement will liberalise trade for the more technologically advanced commodities dominating African intraregional trade (UNCTAD (United Nations Conference on Trade and Development), 2021). These outcomes are crucial for the economic landscape of Africa, particularly for marginalised groups. Empirical studies have used various trade models, including ex-ante simulations using multisector, multi-country computable general equilibrium (CGE) models, and concluded that the AfCFTA has the potential to improve income and welfare of many African countries (Abrego et al., 2020). Such empirical work has analysed the removal of trade restrictions in term of both import tariff elimination, and non-trade barriers.

The AfCFTA can impact income inequality in Africa through changes in trade policies, trade patterns, and mobility of workers and capital (Pavnik, 2017). Chauvin et al. (2016) applied the CGE model to a sample of six African countries and observed that the agreement is likely to benefit rich households in some countries and benefit the poorer households in others. Moreover, rural households are observed to benefit more than urban ones in some countries under study. Hence, the impact is more heterogeneous with mixed evidence across different African countries. Similar findings were observed by a study conducted by the IMF (International Monetary Fund) (2022), which applied a model-based simulation in the African region. The results indicated that income inequality declined in poor countries exporting agricultural commodities but rose in those nations exporting manufacturing products. In contrast, Autor et al. (2014) and Dix-Carneiro and Kovak (2017) argued that if income inequality increased initially with the implementation of the AfCFTA, the same would not hold in the long run, but this long-run adjustment might take time. Dix-Carneiro and Kovak (2017) argued that if income inequality increased initially due to the AfCFTA, it wouldl not persist in the long run.

With the cut in tariffs under the AfCFTA, Jensen and Sandrey (2015b) found that there would be a general decline in government revenue due to tariff liberalisation. However, Echandi et al. (2022) argued that such losses could be neutralised, and Steenbergen (2022) suggested that an increase in economic growth could mitigate them if non-tariff barriers and trade costs were properly managed. Similarly, Abrego et al. (2020) argued that losses in tariff revenue resulting from import tariff elimination could be modest because of the low level of effectively applied intraregional import tariffs and low level of intraregional trade. It is also highlighted that the loss in tariff revenue is expected to disappear with time and be replaced with higher tax revenue as the countries experience higher consumption and income in the long run, mainly due to lower trade barriers and non-tariff barriers. However, this will depend on how effectively the countries take the necessary actions to lower the non-tariff barriers.

As per MacLeod (2021), great trade liberalisation through the AfCFTA will impact decent work and economic growth, one of the Sustainable Development Goals, in particular SDG 8. For instance, targets 8.1 and 8.2, which promote sustainable economic growth and increase economic productivity through diversification, are integral in the implementation of the AfCFTA. More so, the trade agreement is directly linked with targets 8.5–8.10 referring to achieving full and productive employment and decent work for all, with equal pay for work of equal value. These targets are also directed to the encouraging the participation of young people in employment, those young in education and training. In addition, detrimental working conditions like modern slavery, human trafficking and child labour need to be elimited so much that protecting labour rights and promoting safe and secure working environments are crucial for workers. Target 8.3, which aims to promote policies that support job creation and enterprise growth, and 8.a, which focuses on increasing aid for trade support, are seen to be indirectly linked to the AfCFTA. However, no linkage is found between AfCFTA and target 8.4 related to improving resource efficiency in consumption and production.

Chauvin et al. (2016) predicted different outcomes of the AfCFTA when they assumed scenarios like a 100% tariff cut, a 50% NTM cut, and a 30% cut in transaction costs. Their results showed that welfare for the countries studied would increase in the range of 0.1% and 2.64%. They further argued that there would be heterogeneous sectoral impacts across countries such as a rise in unskilled wages, exceeding the increase in skilled wages, in 19 out of 20 countries where there have been only tariff cuts. In addition, more skilled workers would benefit across countries where there have been improvements in NTBs and transaction costs. From the findings, it can be noted that the AfCFTA is pro-poor for some countries and pro-rich in others. Moreover, given 100% cut in tariff and a 50% NTM cut, Jensen and Sandrey (2015a) forecasted that a total African welfare gain of US$39 billion could be attained, with between -US$1.4 billion to +US$9.9 billion changes in welfare by country and −0.7% to +43% export changes by country.

They also found that there are skilled labour gains in employment relative to unskilled labour in 5 out of 9 countries, and both skilled and unskilled labour gains in employment are registered in 1 out of 9 countries. Moreover, for 3 out of 9 countries, they found that unskilled labour gains in employment relative to skilled labour, while unemployment rises in 1 out of 9 countries. Finally, there is likely to be capital gains relative to labour gains in 9 out of 10 nations.

Echandi et al. (2022) on their part considered various possibilities like a 100% tariff cut, a 50% NTB cut, and a 10% reduction in trade costs through trade facilitation and an increase in FDI inflows. They found that GDP is projected to increase from 7.1% to 9.0% with a 31.5% increase in exports. Moreover, wages are found to grow faster for skilled workers relative to unskilled workers, with a labour shift of 2.25% to 2.45% between sectors, mostly from agriculture to the manufacturing sector. The AfCFTA has great potential for employment creation, particularly in sectors such as manufacturing and services. Banga et al. (2021) noted that an enlarged market access might encourage industrialisation, and this could potentially create new jobs mainly for women and the youth. However, if weaker economies face difficulties competing, this may lead to unequal benefits, resulting in regional disparities.

Hence, while there are apparent benefits to Africa from the AfCFTA, there is still a lack of consensus across the empirical work. Therefore, there is a need for a more in-depth analysis of both the economic and social effects of this trade agreement, mainly given that different countries have different implementation capabilities. This paper builds on existing discussions and further analyses the broader socio-economic impacts of the AfCFTA.

18.3 AfCFTA and Socio-Economic Transformation in Africa

This section presents a data-driven assessment of the AfCFTA's impact since its entry into force in 2021, using various indicators, including trade, poverty, employment, and GDP growth, to evaluate key trends in socio-economic variables across African nations. As per the World Bank (2020) report, the AfCFTA represents the largest free trade area. With the AfCFTA, the continent has made significant progress in creating a integrated environment, encouraging both trade and investment flows. As a result, intra-African trade has increased (see Fig. 18.2). The data show that intra-African trade reached USD 196.5 billion in 2023 and rose to USD 213.6 billion in 2024, representing an increase of 8.7%. Intra-African trade is further forecasted to rise by 35% by 2045 after the full implementation of the AfCFTA (United Nations Economic Commission for Africa (UNECA), 2018). The Figures further

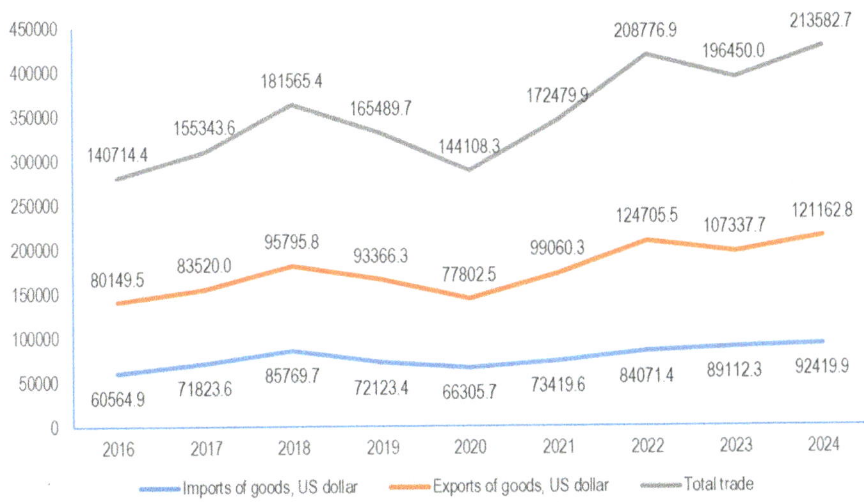

Fig. 18.2 Intra-African trade: 2016–2024. Source: Authors' Compilation, IMF Statistics, 2025

reveal significant growth in both exports and imports from 2021, although there was a decline in 2023. However, a better performance is registered in 2024. The short-term volatility in 2023 highlights the need for more comprehensive structural and institutional reforms to sustain the gains generated by the AfCFTA.

Regional trade driven by the AfCFTA offers significant opportunities to countries within the continent in their pursuit of higher sustainable development. Trade fosters sustained and inclusive economic growth through the advancement of industrial development and innovation, the creation of job opportunities and the reduction in income inequalities and poverty. Interconnected intra-African trade can help build more resilient economic structures and societies by promoting a better and efficient allocation of resources, thereby enhancing productivity and welfare for the population. The benefits of enhanced intra-African traderesulting from the implementation of the AfCFTA are likely to promote socio-economic development.

One proxy used to measure the socio-economic development of the African region is GDP per capita. Though it is not a perfect measure, it provides a broad indication of the average output per person. It serves as a general benchmark for assessing the living standards across regions within the continent. It also provides some insights into income levels and the economic well-being of the population. Despite these limitations, GDP per capita remains one of the most common indicators for tracking the socio-economic situation of societies over time. From Fig. 18.3, it can be observed that real GDP per capita peaked after 2020. The decline in 2020 was mainly due to the health pandemic, but most African economies managed to recover gradually and experienced higher per capita GDP thereafter. The highest performance was from the Middle East and North Africa.

The informal sector in Africa accounts up to 60% of intra-African trade (United Nations Economic Commission for Africa (UNECA), 2018). With the AfCFTA, whereby tariffs and non-tariffs barriers are significantly removed, cross-border

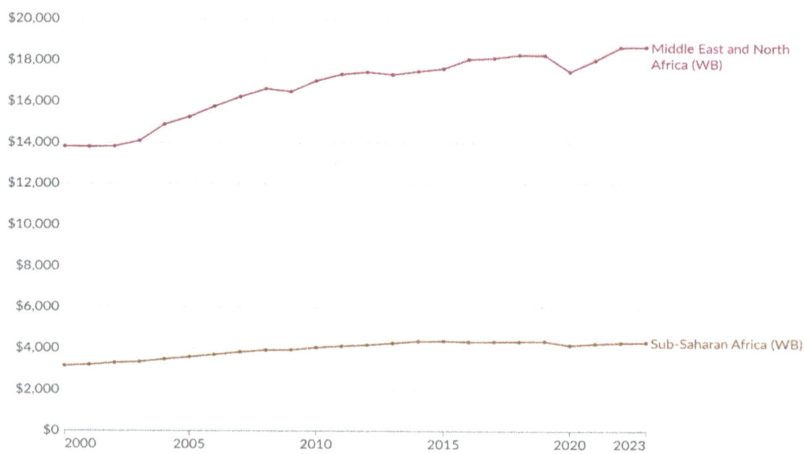

Fig. 18.3 Real GDP per capita—2000–2023. Source: Authors' Compilation, Our World in Data and World Bank, 2025

trade will increase thereby benefiting even the informal sector. Moreso, with simpler customs rules under the AfCFTA, the informal entrepreneurs will be encouraging to formalise their businesses. This will give them better access to finance, training and government support. Furthermore, as per the World Bank (2020) report, the AfCFTA is expected to lift 30 million Africans out of extreme poverty and raise the incomes of nearly 68 million others who live on less than USD 5.50 per day. This is possible if the necessary policy reforms and trade facilitation measures are implemented. The next measure used to assess socio-economic development is the share of the population living in absolute poverty (see Fig. 18.4).

Data on the percentage of people living in extreme poverty across the different regions in Africa reveals that the trend in extreme poverty starts to decline except-from 2021 for all regions across the continent, except the Middle East and Northern Africa (see Fig. 18.4). As per the predictions from the World Bank report, it is noted that Western and Central Africa experienced the largest fall in the share of people living in extreme poverty, followed by Eastern and Southern Africa, and Sub-Saharan Africa. It is expected that African nations with the uppermost initial poverty rates may benefit from major declines in poverty rates.

Another measure of socio-economic development is the Human Development Index (HDI), which is a combined measure of three important pillars in terms of health, knowledge and living standards. It is the geometric mean of normalised indicators for each of these three dimensions. The indices used for calculating the HDI are life expectancy at birth (measuring quality long and healthy life), mean years of schooling (denoting education and knowledge) and gross national income per capita (measuring decent living standard). Assuming other factors are constant, it can be noted that since the implementation of the AfCFTA in 2021, several African nations in the sample have registered incremental gains in HDI. Nations such as Uganda, Rwanda, Kenya, and Zambia experienced steady improvements between

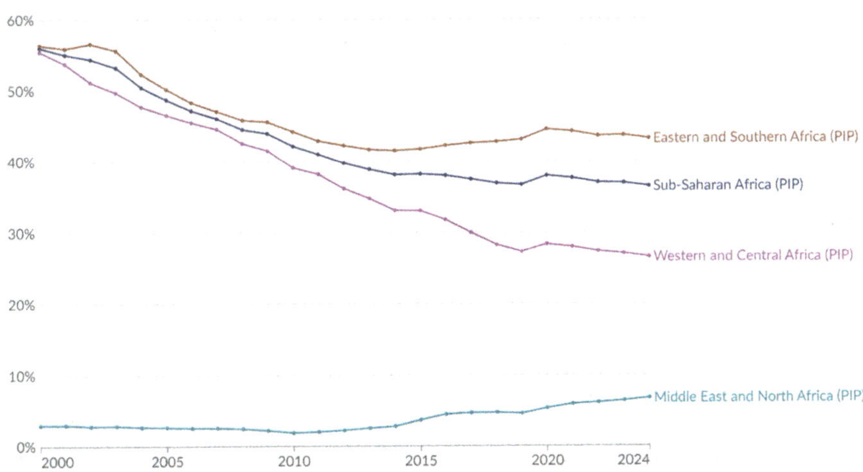

Fig. 18.4 Percentage of the population, living in extreme poverty 2000–2024. Source: Authors' Compilation from Our World in Data and World Bank Poverty and Inequality Platform, 2024

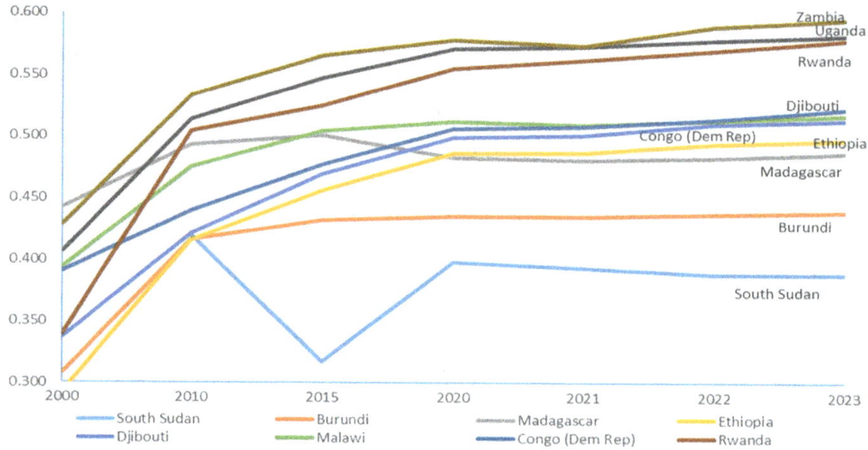

Fig. 18.5 Human development index, 2000–2023 (low HDI countries in the sample). Source: Authors' Compilation, Human Development Report, 2025

2021 and 2023, confirming the potential spillover effects of enhanced regional integration through improved trade and investment flows, as well as the positive impact on income, education, and health outcomes. In contrast, countries like South Sudan and Libya experienced a negative change in the HDI, reflecting the fragile and conflict situations in these countries. Political stability and institutional capacity remain important elements in translating trade integration into human development gains (Fig. 18.5).

High-performing economies like Egypt, Mauritius, and Seychelles have continued to perform well, with greater diversification prospects offered by the AfCFTA. This is shown in Fig. 18.6.

While the AfCFTA represents a significant milestone towards regional integration and economic transformation, HDI trends across African countries are shaped by a complex interplay of multiple factors beyond trade liberalisation. These include public investment in health and education, political stability and governance quality, external shocks like the COVID-19 pandemic, fluctuations in global commodity prices, climate-related disasters, and the inflow of foreign aid and remittances. For instance, improvements in health systems and access to primary education have contributed to gains in the HDI in countries such as Rwanda and Ethiopia.

Conversely, conflicts, political instability, and weak institutional frameworks in nations like South Sudan and Libya have hindered progress in human development, despite continental policy initiatives. Moreover, social protection programmes, infrastructure development (including digital access), and international development partnerships have all an important role in supporting income and enhancing living standards. Therefore, while AfCFTA can be a catalyst for socio-economic development, its impact is dependent on complementary domestic reforms, institutional capacity, and external macroeconomic conditions. The data highlights

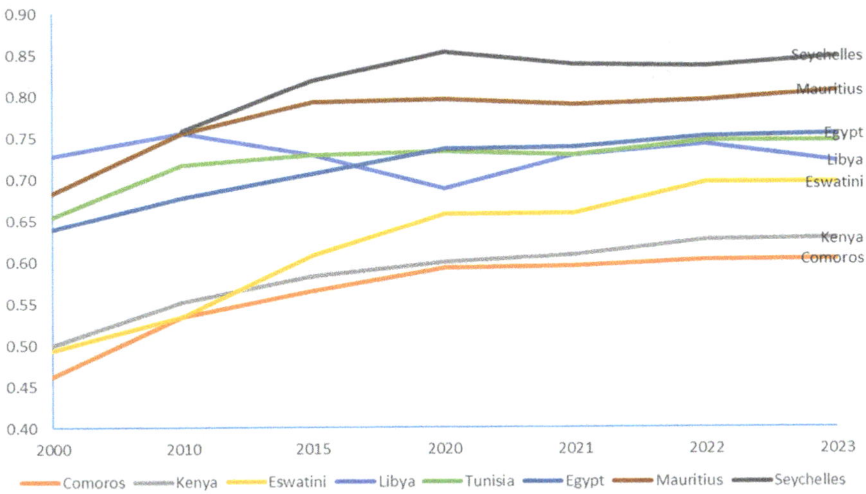

Fig. 18.6 Human development index, 2000–2023 (high HDI countries in the sample). Source: Authors' Compilation, Human Development Report, 2025

heterogeneity in socio-economic impacts, reinforcing the need for targeted strategies to enhance inclusive development across the continent.

18.4 An Econometric Analysis

The present study further examines the impact of AfCFTA on socio-economic development for a sample of member countries over the period 1994 to 2022. Several studies have analysed the impact that RTAs have on economic growth; however, few studies have investigated the extent to which the involvement of the AFCFTA can impact economic development in member countries, especially with regional integration increasing in numbers and becoming deeper and more complex. This study thus uses a panel of African countries. Due to limited data availability, selected African countries have been included in the sample. These include Burundi, Comoros, Congo, and the Democratic Republic of the Congo. Rep., Djibouti, Egypt, Eswatini, Ethiopia, Kenya, Libya, Madagascar, Malawi, Mauritius, Rwanda, Seychelles, Sudan, Tunisia, Uganda, and Zambia.

To model the effects of the AfCFTA on socio-economic development, the standard literature is followed, using a Solow Growth function augmented with the AfCFTA dummy, as specified below.

$$\text{HDI} = f\left(\text{AFCFTA dummy}, X\right) \tag{18.1}$$

HDI denotes the human development index. The AFCFTA dummy is set to one from the year in which AfCFTA was implemented, and *X* represents a set of control variables. The AFCFTA dummy is one from the year in which the AfCFTA was implemented. *X* denotes a set of variables that can affect socio-economic growth. These variables are HC (a proxy for human capital), TO (a proxy for trade openness), FDI (denotes foreign direct investment), and COVID (a dummy variable to capture the impact of the COVID-19 pandemic). The equation is written as follows:

$$\text{HDI} = f\left(\text{AfCFTA,TO,FDI,HC,COVID}\right) \tag{18.2}$$

Given the variance-stabilising effects of the log transformation, variables are expressed in logarithm form (excluding the dummy variables). This approach allows for a better interpretation of the coefficients in terms of elasticity.

With all variables in log form, Eq. (18.2) is rewritten as follows:

$$\ln \text{HDI}_{\text{it}} = \alpha_0 + \beta_1 \text{AfCFTA}_{\text{it}} + \beta_2 \text{lnTO}_{\text{it}} + \beta_3 \text{lnFDI}_{\text{it}} + \beta_4 \text{lnHC}_{\text{it}} + \beta_5 \text{COVID}_{\text{it}}\ \varepsilon_{\text{it}}$$

where β1… β5 denote the parameter estimates and ε_{it} is the random error term.

18.4.1 Variables Definition

The human development index (HDI) is used to measure the socio-economic development of the African nations under study. The same proxy was used in the study by Cruzatti (2021) to measure socio-economic development with the implementation of free trade agreements. HDI takes into consideration health, education, and economic development.

18.4.1.1 Independent Variables

The main independent variable in the study is the AfCFTA dummy taking a value of 1 when the African nations have signed the agreement and zero otherwise (See Fauzel et al., 2024).

Trade openness is proxied by the share of total trade to GDP (that is the ratio of total exports plus total imports to GDP). International trade normally boosts economic growth as it leads to more access to international markets and enhances competitiveness. A similar proxy was used by Freund and Pierola (2012) in their study on the trade-growth nexus in the presence of RTAs. Another independent variable included in the model is the foreign direct investment (FDI) which is proxied by total FDI inflows as a share of GDP.

Moreover, Oduro et al. (2014) showed that output rises with the education level in a country. Hence, the secondary enrolment rate has been included in the present study to analyse the impact of education on economic growth for the sample of countries included. Finally, a COVID dummy is included in the regression as we cannot ignore the effect of this pandemic on economic performance. The health crisis had massive effects across the globe, and African countries, which are still at the developing level, were severely affected. The COVID dummy takes a value of 1 during the COVID years and otherwise. The World Development Indicators dataset was used to extract data for the different variables used in the above econometric model.

18.4.2 *Regression Technique*

This study analyses the impact of the AfCFTA on the socio-economic development of African economies from 1994 to 2022. Following Mohsin et al. (2021), a fixed effects regression is applied, as inferred by the Hausman test.

18.5 Findings

18.5.1 *Correlation Matrix*

To assess the strength and direction of the linear association between two variables, a correlation matrix is worked out. Table 18.1 provides the correlation matrix, and no problem of serial correlation is detected. The degree of multicollinearity is relatively low across the explanatory variables in the model.

18.5.2 *Panel Unit Root Tests and Panel Cointegration Test*

Before proceeding with the estimation of the model, it is important to analyse the time series properties of the data used. As highlighted by Phillips (1986), non-stationary time series may produce biased and misleading results. Furthermore, due to the existence of cross-sectional dependence in the dataset, second-generation unit root test is used namely the Pesaran Cross-Sectional IPS test.

Table 18.1 Correlation matrix

	LHDI	LTO	LFDI	LHC
LHDI	1	0.4214	0.2362	0.5640
LTO	0.4213	1	0.4238	0.3501
LFDI	0.2362	0.4283	1	0.2057
LHC	0.5640	0.3501	0.2057	1

Source: Authors' Compilation, 2025

18.5.3 Panel Unit Root Test

As proposed by Im, Pesaran, and Shin (2003), the panel unit root test is presented. The aim of this test is to check the order in which the variables are integrated and to determine the econometric model to be used (Table 18.2). The absence of a unit root test can lead to spurious regression results. Using the Augmented Dicky Fuller technique, the panel unit root test confirms that the variables are stationary at first difference I (1).

18.5.4 Cointegration Test

After checking for stationarity of the variables, we proceeded to investigate whether cointegration exists between the variables or whether there is a long run link between the variables. To test the existence of any long-run cointegration, the Kao residual cointegration test is carried out (Table 18.3). Since the T-Statistics is greater than the p-value, the presence of a long-run relationship among the variables are confirmed.

Since the variables are stationary at first difference and cointegrated, we proceeded with estimating Eq. (18.1) by using a dynamic fixed effect as inferred by the hausman test.

Table 18.4 provides the results of the dynamic fixed effect model as selected by the Hausman test. The findings indicate that the AfCFTA dummy is positive and significant. This confirms the main purpose of the AfCFTA agreement, which is the largest African continental regional trade bloc, as indicated by Pasara and Dunga (2020). Indeed, the AfCFTA agreement is deemed to significantly increase investment, driving industrial growth and improving economic resilience among member countries. However, it can be noted that the coefficient is relatively small. It in fact shows that AfCFTA has brought along only 0.008% of socio-economic growth, and this can be explained by the fact that this agreement has been in force for a short time, probably not implemented at its desired level.

Table 18.2 Panel unit root

Description	Im, Pesaran, and Shin	Prob	Levin, Lin, and Chy	Prob
LHDI	−9.82	0.000	9.01	0.000
LTO	−7.81	0.000	−12.8	0.000
LFDI	−11.1	0.000	−14.4	0.000
LHC	−4.78	0.000	−9.23	0.000

Source: Authors' Compilation, 2025

Table 18.3 Contegration test

	t-Statistic	Prob
ADF	−6.211779	0.000

Source: Authors' Compilation, 2025

Table 18.4 Regression results; dependent variable: LHDI

Variables	Dynamic fixed effect	
	Coefficient	t-value
LHDI(−1)	0.901576***	87.91842
$AfCFTA_{dummy}$	0.007833***	2.191279
LTO	0.017511***	2.374013
LFDI	0.016681	0.517210
LHC	0.086351***	5.425129
$COVID_{dummy}$	−0.012117***	−2.844459
Constant	−0.645761***	−3.674108
Hausman test	$P < 10\%$—dynamic fixed effect selected	

Source: Authors' Compilation, 2025
Notes: *** shows significance at 1%

We expect a larger impact of this agreement on socio-economic development over time. Similarly, Alagidede et al. (2024) noted that the AfCTFTA has contributed to economic growth, welfare gain, and an increase in household per capita spending. Overall, we can argue that the AfCFTA has already started to reshape the economic landscape of Africa through the promotion of trade integration, industrialisation, and increased investment. The full impact of this agreement will, however, materialise over time. The results show early signs of the effects of the agreement on socio-economic development across African nations under study.

Among the control variables, the results show a positive and significant link between trade openness and HDI. A 1% rise in trade openness has led to a 0.018% increase in socio-economic development. Indeed, RTAs remove trade barriers, which increases trade flows between member countries. An increase in trade thereby stimulates economic growth as it allows countries to produce goods and services where they are more efficient and have a comparative advantage. This leads to greater efficiency and productivity (Okoro et al., 2020). However, there is no positive link between FDI and HDI. This is attributed to the fact that most FDI are concentrated in capital intensive sectors in Africa and this has not contributed much in creating favourable spillovers on health, education, and income. Same findings were obtained by Adams (2009) and Sghaier and Abida (2013), highlighting the fact that the effects of foreign investment depend mostly on institutional frameworks, human capital, and appropriate policies.

With the adoption of the AfCFTA agreement and the AfCFTA Protocol on Investment, new opportunities for intra-African investment are being created. Hence, over time, it is expected to see a larger positive impact of investment on socio-economic development. Human capital remains central to the development of African countries. This is in line with many previous works on the region namely Seetanah et al. (2019).

Another significant result from Table 18.2 relates to the COVID-19 variable. It is noted that the coefficient has a negative effect on HDI. Indeed, the pandemic has negatively impacted development due to its multiplier effect on trade, investment and the labour market. This is supported by Loayza and Pennings (2020) who argued that the health crisis had a long-lasting influence on emerging and developing nations. However, recovery will occur as a result of proper structural reforms. Finally, it is observed that the past level of human development strongly influences the current level. It confirms the fact that socio-economic development is further enhanced through the past achievements in components like health, education and income.

18.6 Conclusion and Policy Implications

Regional Trade Agreements (RTAs) have been increasing over the years with the aim to promote greater trade among countries in the region. As such, Africa has created the largest free trade bloc which allow African nations to use the AfCFTA as a tool to promote development. This study analyses the impact of the AfCFTA on the socio-economic development of a sample of African countries. The dynamic fixed effects model selected through the Hausman specification test is used. The results confirm that the AfCFTA has a positive and statistically significant impact on socio-economic development measured by the Human Development Index. However, the magnitude of the coefficient remains small, as the agreement was recently implemented. Its full economic impact will be felt in the longer run. Furthermore, the results indicate that trade openness and human capital are crucial pillars for African economic development. Finally, the COVID-19 dummy confirms the negative impact of the health crisis on the African continent.

18.7 Policy Recommendation

The results shows that the AfCFTA has had a positive but yet small initial effect on the socio-economic development of Africa which signals the fact that the full impact of the agreement will materialise with time mainly if there are supportive policies. Hence, it is crucial for policy makers to improve trade facilitation among the member states. The priority should be the removal of NTBs followed by complex customs procedures, burdensome standards that delay movement of goods and raise transaction costs. The harmonisation of regulations, as well as the simplification of border procedures together with improving transport and logistics infrastructure are key factors that will promote trade in the region. The use of digital platforms for trade documentation can foster greater efficiency and enhance trade. These strategies will not only ease cross-border trade but also create a conducive and business friendly environment that will attract local and foreign investors.

In addition, deeper market integration among member states requires the reinforcement of institutional frameworks that can provide stability, transparency, and effective governance. Strong institutions play a pivotal role in ensuring that trade agreements are implemented consistently. To maximise the developmental impact of foreign investment, African governments should not only attract inflows but also strategically channel them into sectors that generate broad-based social and economic benefits. Investments in education, healthcare, renewable energy, and digital infrastructure, for example, have the potential to improve human capital, enhance productivity, and foster inclusive growth. At the same time, countries must strengthen their absorptive capacity by investing in skills development, vocational training, and innovation systems, thereby ensuring that local firms and workers can benefit from technology transfers and knowledge spillovers. Such an approach would transform FDI from a source of capital inflows into a driver of long-term structural transformation and sustainable development.

References

Abrego, M. L., de Zamaroczy, M. M., Gursoy, T., Nicholls, G. P., Perez-Saiz, H., & Rosas, J. N. (2020). *The African continental free trade area: Potential economic impact and challenges*. International Monetary Fund.

Adams, S. (2009). Foreign direct investment, domestic investment, and economic growth in sub-Saharan Africa. *Journal of Policy Modeling, 31*(6), 939–949.

Ahmed, G. (2012). Krugman trade theory and developing economies. *China-USA Business Review, 11*(12), 1557.

Autor, D. H., Dorn, D., Hanson, G. H., & Song, J. (2014). Trade adjustment: Worker-level evidence. *The Quarterly Journal of Economics, 129*(4), 1799–1860.

Banga, K., MacLeod, J., & Parra, M. M. (2021). *Digital trade provision in the AfCFTA: What can we learn from south-south trade agreements?* United Nations Economic Commission for Africa.

Chauvin, N. D., Priscila Ramos, M., & Porto, G. (2016). Trade, growth, and welfare impacts of the CFTA in Africa. In *Proceedings of the CSAE conference 2016: Economic Development in Africa*. St Catherine's College.

Cruzatti, J. (2021). *Free trade agreements and development: A global analysis with local data (No. 702)*. AWI Discussion Paper Series.

Dix-Carneiro, R., & Kovak, B. K. (2017). Trade liberalization and regional dynamics. *American Economic Review, 107*(10), 2908–2946.

Echandi, R., Maliszewska, M., & Steenbergen, V. (2022). *Making the most of the African continental free trade area*. World Bank Publications-Books.

Fauzel, S. B., Tandrayen-Ragoobur, V., & Seetanah, B. (2024). Has the regional comprehensive economic partnership (RCEP) negotiations impacted on tourism flows of member countries? *Journal of Economic and Administrative Sciences, 40*(1), 4–22.

Fei, X. (2022). Trade liberalization and structural changes: Prefecture-level evidence from China. *Structural Change and Economic Dynamics, 61*, 103–126.

Gandolfo, G. (2013). Endogenous growth and trade, old and new. In *International trade theory and policy* (pp. 329–334). Springer.

IMF (International Monetary Fund). (2022). *World economic outlook (October 2022) database*.

Irwin, D. A. (2025). Does trade reform promote economic growth? A review of recent evidence. *The World Bank Research Observer, 40*(1), 147–184.

Jensen, H. G., & Sandrey, R. (2015a). *The continental free trade area: A GTAP assessment*. Trade Law Centre and United States Agency for International Development.

Jensen, H. G., & Sandrey, R. (2015b). African agricultural trade: Recent and the future. *African Journal of Agricultural and Resource Economics, 10*(2), 146–157.

Kutu, A. A., & Ohonba, A. (2024). The impact of trade liberalization on economic growth in South Africa. *International Journal of Economics and Financial Issues, 14*(6), 55–63.

Loayza, N., & Pennings, S. M. (2020). *Macroeconomic policy in the time of COVID-19: A primer for developing countries*. World Bank Research and Policy Briefs (147291).

MacLeod, J. (2021). Decent work and economic growth. In W. Leal Filho, A. M. Azul, L. Brandli, P. G. Özuyar, & T. Wall (Eds.), *Decent work and economic growth: Encyclopedia of the UN sustainable development goals* (pp. 211–220). Springer. https://doi.org/10.1007/978-3-030-38815-7_24

Mohsin, M., Ullah, H., Iqbal, N., Iqbal, W., & Taghizadeh-Hesary, F. (2021). How external debt led to economic growth in South Asia: A policy perspective analysis from quantile regression. *Economic Analysis and Policy, 72*, 423–437.

Nicita, A., Olarreaga, M., & Porto, G. (2014). Pro-poor trade policy in sub-Saharan Africa. *Journal of International Economics, 92*(2), 252–265.

Okoro, A. S., Ujunwa, A., Umar, F., & Ukemenam, A. (2020). Does regional trade promote economic growth? Evidence from economic Community of West African States (ECOWAS). *Journal of Economic Development, 22*(1), 131–147.

Oloruntoba, S. O., & Nshimbi, C. C. (2023). The AfCFTA: Promise for a globally competitive continent and Africa's development. *Journal of Contemporary African Studies, 41*(4), 351–359.

Papadopoulos, A. (2022). Trade liberalization and growth: A quantile moderator for Hoyos'(2021) replication study of Estevadeordal and Taylor (2013). *Empirical Economics, 63*(1), 549–563.

Pasara, M. T., & Dunga, S. H. (2020). Who wins and who loses under the AfCFTA? A simulation analysis across ECOWAS countries. *International Journal of Economics and Finance Studies, 12*(2), 487–504.

Sghaier, I. M., & Abida, Z. (2013). Foreign direct investment, financial development, and economic growth: Empirical evidence from north African countries. *Journal of International and Global Economic Studies, 6*(1), 1–13.

Singh, S. K. (2019). An empirical studies of the Heckscher-Ohlin model. *International Journal of Research, 6*(2), 688–693.

UNCTAD (United Nations Conference on Trade and Development). (2021). *Reaping the potential benefits of the African continental free trade area for inclusive growth.*

UNDESA (United Nations Department of Economic and Social Affairs). (2022). *2022 revision of world population prospects (database).*

United Nations Economic Commission for Africa (UNECA). (2018). *An empirical assessment of the African continental free trade area modalities on goods*. UNECA. https://www.uneca.org

World Bank. (2020). *The African continental free trade area: Economic and distributional effects*. World Bank. https://www.worldbank.org/en/topic/trade/publication/the-african-continental-free-trade-area

Chapter 19
Bridging Policy and Practice in Regional Integration: The Case Study of the AfCFTA

Tabitha Kiriti-Nganga, Denis Nfor Yuni, and Boopen Seetanah

Abstract The African Continental Free Trade Area (AfCFTA) presents a historic opportunity, but its transformative potential hinges on bridging the divide between policy and practice. This concluding chapter critically examines the implementation of the AfCFTA across Africa by analysing the challenges, strengths, lessons learned, indigenous solutions, and policy recommendations from the country case studies reviewed in the book. Valuable insights from these analyses demonstrate that most countries across Africa face similar challenges; however, some countries have adopted sterling indigenous solutions to some of the challenges experienced in other countries. Hence, this chapter posits that there is a need for significant peer learning amongst the African countries for balanced growth and sustainable development. To fully realise the AfCFTA's potential, this chapter recommends that African governments must strengthen legal and institutional frameworks, harmonise trade and customs procedures, and invest in trade-related infrastructure across member countries. Special attention should be given to supporting women, youth, and MSMEs through inclusive financing, training, and policy interventions. In addition, sustained political will, data-driven reforms, and integration of sustainable development principles are essential for aligning the AfCFTA with the Agenda 2063 goals.

Keywords AfCFTA · Regional integration · Trade policy · Implementation gaps · Intra-African trade · Agenda 2063, Africa

---

T. Kiriti-Nganga
Department of Economics and Development Studies, University of Nairobi, Nairobi, Kenya
e-mail: tkiriti@uonbi.ac.ke

D. N. Yuni (✉)
Department of Economics, University of Namibia, Windhoek, Namibia
e-mail: dyuni@unam.na

B. Seetanah
University of Mauritius, Moka, Mauritius
e-mail: b.seetanah@uom.ac.mu

D. N. Yuni et al. (eds.), *From Policy to Practice: Challenges and Ways Forward on the Implementation of the AfCFTA*,
https://doi.org/10.1007/978-3-032-14051-7_19

19.1 Introduction

The African Continental Free Trade Area represents one of the most ambitious regional integration projects in modern history. However, the journey towards regional integration in Africa has been marked by a persistent ridge between policy ambition and practical implementation. The key goals of the African Continental Free Trade Area (AfCFTA) are to create a single continental market for goods and services, with free movement of business, persons and investments; expand intra-African trade across all sectors by reducing tariffs and non-tariff barriers; and enhance the competitiveness of African industries and enterprises (African Union, 2018). It also seeks to boost industrialisation and structural transformation through coordinated trade policy, promoting sustainable and inclusive socio-economic development across Africa. While the AfCFTA articulates bold visions of unity, cooperation, and economic transformation, the practical realisation of these aspirations depends on four key enabling factors: the legal and institutional frameworks, the political will of the leadership of member states, harmonisation of customs and other trade regulations, and robust trade routes infrastructure within the region. These enablers are briefly discussed below.

The success of the AfCFTA is heavily dependent on the strength and coherence of national legal and institutional frameworks. For the agreement's provisions to be fully operational, countries must take action to enact policies and laws on customs procedures in line with the AfCFTA requirements, rules of origin, quality standards, immigration, and asset ownership, among other areas. The lack of clear institutional mandates or overlapping responsibilities can cause implementation bottlenecks and create legal uncertainty for traders and investors. Establishing the requisite policies or institutional frameworks to align with the requirements of the AfCFTA may sometimes be at odds with national development priorities and therefore require a committed political will to navigate such dilemmas. Additionally, political will is required for the allocation of resources and the promotion of sensitisation or educational programmes that will generate public support and private sector involvement. The commitment of political leaders in member states, or the lack thereof, determines whether tariff liberalisation schedules are adhered to, whether trade facilitation measures are prioritised, and whether sensitive sectors are protected or opened. At the continental level, the AU and AfCFTA Secretariat require strong backing from heads of state to promote integration, encourage dispute resolution, secure funding for trade infrastructure, and implement capacity building programmes.

Harmonisation of customs procedures and trade regulations across member states is vital for reducing trade costs and ensuring smooth intra-African commerce. Disparate rules of origin, documentation requirements, and customs clearance protocols create delays, increase transaction costs, and discourage cross-border trade. Harmonised standards, particularly in health, safety, and environmental areas, are also essential to facilitate market access and prevent technical barriers to trade. United Nations Economic Commission for Africa (2013) posits that, "harmonised rules of origin and a trade facilitation environment across the continent would greatly improve the means and cost of doing business across borders". Also, the EU Commission in 2019 posits that, the "availability of harmonised standards is a fundamental pre-requisite to disrupt remaining technical barriers to trade and allows the full interoperability of products and services in the different geographic areas" (Miglierini, 2019).

The fourth key enabling factor is the need for robust trade infrastructure, which includes roads, ports, railways, and logistics hubs. This constitutes the physical backbone of AfCFTA implementation. Poor connectivity between African countries has historically constrained intra-regional trade, as transportation has been slow, expensive, and unreliable. Most existing rail, road, and water trade routes were established in the colonial era to ferry raw materials to the then-colonial masters and provide avenues for them to sell their final products. A re-orientation of trade routes in Africa is, therefore, imperative to improve intra-African trade. It is worth noting that in the last decades, several trade corridors have been constructed, and some are currently in progress. For example, between 2004 and 2022, the African Development Bank funded the main and connecting sections of seven strategic trade corridors, totalling 7150 km of roads in Africa (African Union, 2025).

The chapters of this book provide an in-depth examination of how these four key factors, along with several others, that have influenced the implementation of the AfCFTA across Africa. The country case studies also clearly demonstrate how implementation is heterogeneous, depending on the ability to overcome general challenges and leverage comparative advantages. This chapter, therefore, analyses the 11 country case studies discussed in the book in the next section, and then highlights the general key policy recommendations identified.

19.2 A Synthesis of the Experiences from Country Case Studies

This section synthesises the key challenges, strengths, lessons learned, indigenous solutions, and policy recommendations from the preceding chapters. Table 19.1 illustrates that a substantial number of African nations encounter similar challenges in fully realising the benefits of the AfCFTA. For example, nearly all countries (Tunisia, Nigeria, Cameroon, Ghana, Kenya, Rwanda, Lesotho, Chad) suffer from inadequate and inefficient trade-related infrastructure, including poor road networks, congested ports, and unreliable energy supply. Similarly, Nigeria, Ghana, Rwanda, Lesotho, South Africa, Cameroon, and Chad face cumbersome customs procedures, differing regulatory standards, and complex administrative processes that hinder the implementation of the AfCFTA. Many countries also struggle with a narrow export base and insufficient industrial capacity to produce diverse goods that are competitive enough for continental markets. This often leads to an overreliance on primary commodities, a phenomenon observed in countries such as Nigeria, Rwanda, Lesotho, South Africa, and Chad. Other recurring challenges across the

Table 19.1 Synthesis of the experiences from country case studies

Countries	Challenges	Strengths	Lessons learned	Indigenous solutions and local initiatives	Policy recommendations
1. Tunisia	• Delays in implementing the AfCFTA tariff schedule and the National Committee • Weak logistics infrastructure • Limited customs digitalisation and inter-agency coordination • Low SME readiness and finance access • Limited awareness and usage of tools like the African Trade Observatory • Overdependence on EU Trade • Weak intra-African export diversification • Asymmetry between backward (imports) and forward (exports) value chain linkages • Unresolved rules of origin issues in key sectors (e.g., textiles, vehicles) • Corruption, low government effectiveness	• Industrial capacity with diversified manufacturing base • Strong FDI-driven offshore sector • Strong comparative advantages (cement, sanitary products, etc.) • High RCA in several goods • Strategic proximity to African and Mediterranean markets • Above-average customs, tracking, and logistics timeliness • Strong ICT access, finance, and innovation platforms • Leadership potential in fintech and logistics tech	• Experience from past trade agreements shows that partial implementation leads to missed opportunities • Overlapping rules of origin hinder impact • Experience from COVID-19 shows that overreliance on EU GVCs exposes vulnerability • Awareness and support tools are necessary for SME participation • Strength in attracting FDI can be redirected toward African integration	• Offshore Regime and Investment Law attracted over 2,000 foreign-exporting firms • Guided Trade Initiative enabled first successful exports under AfCFTA to Ghana, Cameroon, Tanzania • Customs Training and AEO Programs improved technical readiness for AfCFTA compliance • Training on ITC trade tools and rules of origin in 8 key regions improved awareness	• Activate and operationalise AfCFTA National Committee • Invest in ports, logistics zones, and digital customs • Join regional transport corridors • Expand trade finance, training, and tech tools • Match-make with African buyers through business councils • Target sectors with latent capacity (agri-food, chemicals) • Deepen both forward and backward regional value chains • Skills training for youth, women, and informal workers • Promote employment-intensive sectors under AfCFTA • Scale electronic certificates of origin, e-commerce • Strengthen digital infrastructure and PPP

2. Morocco	• Fragmented legal frameworks • Low harmonisation of political and economic initiatives • Overlapping commitments due to multiple REC memberships and trade deals • Exposure to external shocks • High reliance on external financing and energy imports • Weak engagement of NGOs, media, civil society, unions in AfCFTA processes • Insecurity in partner regions hinders investment and trade integration • Rapid population growth outpacing economic development	• Strong political will for south–south cooperation • Hub for banking, insurance, agribusiness, fertilisers, and construction • Major investments in renewable energy • Active role in OHADA and WTO commitments • Existence of gender inclusion policies • Existence of digital strategy—Digital "Morocco 2030" and AfCFTA e-commerce protocols integrated	• Legal and institutional alignment is crucial for effective agreements • COVID-19 and Energy Shocks showed that food and energy security are central to resilience strategies • Private sector needs targeted financing and legal clarity for SME expansion • National implementation must align with regional and continental bodies	• Existence of National AfCFTA Strategy and Roadmap and energy reform institutions and special AfCFTA implementation fund • South–South Cooperation Mechanism • Investment Charter and Mohammed VI Fund supports SMEs and large Moroccan firms expanding into Africa	• Align with AfCFTA, OHADA, and WTO principles on business law, IPR, and competition • Promote trade facilitation • Centre policies on gender, youth, digital rights, and human development • Offer incentives, financing, and joint venture support to firms expanding into Africa • Strengthen sector linkages in agri-food, textiles, automotive, and energy • Implement robust mechanisms for commercial dispute resolution and e-commerce regulation

(continued)

Table 19.1 (continued)

Countries	Challenges	Strengths	Lessons learned	Indigenous solutions and local initiatives	Policy recommendations
3. Nigeria	• Despite ratifying the AfCFTA agreement, Nigeria has not fully domesticated it • Poor trade-related infrastructure • Over-reliance on crude oil exports, increasing reliance on trade outside Africa • Deplorable State of Cross-Border Security • Low trade capacity due to low industrial capacity, insecurity, inadequate storage facilities, low-value addition, inadequate skills and poor funding, etc. • Informality of MSMEs • Low implementation of the Rule of Origin is associated with its weak trade defence infrastructure • Lack of optimised closest neighbour trade	• Strategic position and market size • Earlier studies suggested that Nigeria's accession to AfCFTA would critically boost the agreement's viability and improve the country's macroeconomic conditions, including economic growth, job creation, investment, and poverty reduction • Government initiatives such as stakeholder consultations, critical evaluation of the agreement, and the establishment of the Presidential National Action Committee on AfCFTA	• The lack of full domestication of the AfCFTA is a crucial hindrance to its effective implementation • Critical role of infrastructure • Need for economic diversification • Cross-border security issues directly impede cross-border trading and AfCFTA implementation • Need for awareness and capacity building for MSMEs • Sustained political commitment is key	• Establishment of the Presidential National Action Committee on AfCFTA to coordinate AfCFTA-related strategies • Workstream-based implementation approach • Captured AfCFTA in its National Development Plan 2021–2025 • Regional integration via the Lagos–Abidjan corridor to improve trade flows • Emphasis on improving digital infrastructure and building MSME e-commerce capacity	• Full domestication of AfCFTA • Address trade-related infrastructure deficiencies • Economic diversification and industrialisation: • Promote digital infrastructure and digital trade • Promote capacity building and awareness creation, especially for MSMEs, on AfCFTA opportunities and how to leverage them • Demonstrate political commitment and leadership • Promote R&D, industrial clusters, and integration into agro-processing and manufacturing value chains • Address cross-border crime and terrorism to ensure trade corridors are safe and stable

4. Ghana	• Infrastructure deficits • Regulatory disparities with other African countries hinder smooth AfCFTA implementation • Transitional costs, including changes in customs procedures, legal frameworks, and business practices, accrue to businesses and government agencies • Limited productive capacity • Increased competition could pose a challenge to nascent or less competitive Ghanaian industries • Limited access to finance for SMEs • Technical barriers to trade and sanitary and phytosanitary measures • Informal cross-border trade • Skills gaps	• Hosts the AfCFTA Secretariat, which provides a direct line to policy discussions and implementation efforts • Strong political commitment • Government initiatives like the National AfCFTA Policy Framework and Action Plan to prepare businesses • Geographic location offers strategic access to a significant regional market • Pioneering the use of the Pan-African Payment and Settlement System	• Robust and efficient infrastructure is foundational for successful trade integration • Importance of regulatory harmonisation • Need for business preparedness • Tariff elimination alone is insufficient; addressing non-tariff barriers is equally vital • Recognising the importance of SMEs and tailoring support for them is a key lesson • Industrialisation is key to competitiveness	• One District, One Factory (1D1F): A home-grown industrialisation initiative • Ghana Trade Information Repository: A national digital platform being developed to close the trade information gap • Institutions to support Ghanaian exporters with marketing and compliance services, such as Export Trade Houses	• Prioritise massive investments in critical trade-related infrastructure • Regulatory alignment and harmonisation of customs procedures to facilitate seamless cross-border trade • Enhanced productive capacity and industrialisation • Targeted support for SMEs in areas such as access to finance, market intelligence, technology adoption, and quality standards compliance • Address non-tariff barriers • Invest in education and vocational training to develop the skilled workforce required • Digitalisation of trade processes • Promote regional value chains

(continued)

Table 19.1 (continued)

Countries	Challenges	Strengths	Lessons learned	Indigenous solutions and local initiatives	Policy recommendations
5. Kenya	• Outdated border and transport infrastructure • Differing regulations across countries and RECs • Multiple and overlapping memberships	• Kenya has been a proactive participant in Africa's economic integration efforts • One of 7 pilot countries for AfCFTA Rollout in June 2022 • The AfCFTA Strategy builds on Kenya's Integrated National Export Development and Promotion Strategy (INEDPS) and the Big Four Agenda • Strong Intra-African Trade Growth	• Need for progressive liberalisation • Role of trade facilitation: Implementing trade facilitation measures is crucial • Significance of institutional frameworks	• Established 2022–2027 implementation strategy in August 2022	• Expand supply and export capacity • Prioritise facilitating effective trade in goods and services • Ensure inclusiveness of women, youth, and persons with disabilities in trade under AfCFTA • Establish the National Implementation Committee to implement the AfCFTA • Implement a Comprehensive Communication Strategy for adequate sensitisation • Implement Robust Monitoring and Evaluation Strategy

6. Rwanda	• Pervasive non-tariff barriers persist • Inadequate regional infrastructure, particularly for a landlocked country • Limited productive capacity • Inherent limitations of MSMEs • Complex Rules of Origin and SPS measures • Restricted access to trade finance and market intelligence • Institutional and human capital limitations	• Strong and unwavering political commitment to the AfCFTA • Rwanda is strategically positioned in East Africa • Proactive stance on regional integration • Rwanda's engagement with AfCFTA is deeply rooted in its Vision 2050 • The AfCFTA offers Rwanda a potential for economic diversification	• Imperative of proactive policy harmonisation • Efficacy of trade facilitation reforms • Transformative potential of digitalisation • Necessity of robust private sector engagement • Fundamental importance of regional value chain development	• Rwanda is renowned for its proactive stance on regional integration and a consistently improving business environment • First to ratify Free Movement Protocol	• Intensify efforts to dismantle non-tariff barriers • Strategic infrastructure investments to ensure efficient transit routes • Enhance productive capacity with export diversification • Improve access to trade finance and market information • Strengthen institutional frameworks to implement the AfCFTA • Continuously build capacity of trade policymakers, customs, officials, and private sector actors • Sustain regional cooperation and digitalisation

(continued)

Table 19.1 (continued)

Countries	Challenges	Strengths	Lessons learned	Indigenous solutions and local initiatives	Policy recommendations
7. Lesotho	• Slow AfCFTA implementation • Limited participation in Phase II Negotiations • Limited capabilities of government agencies to implement and monitor AfCFTA obligations • Lack of awareness and capacity building for businesses • NTBs impede intra-African trade • Limited productive capacity and export diversification • Infrastructure deficiencies • Lack of access to finance for SMEs	• Competitive advantage in services, especially tourism, education, and government services • Existing experience in trade agreements (e.g., SACU, SADC-FTA, AGOA) offers valuable lessons • Lesotho signed and ratified the AfCFTA agreement in 2018 and 2020	• Incomplete negotiations hinder implementation • Significance of capacity building and awareness • Addressing NTBs is key • Past trade agreements show that preferential access does not automatically translate into sustainable trade outcomes	• Strong alignment between AfCFTA objectives and Lesotho's NSDP II development strategy • Established a national AfCFTA inter-ministerial implementation committee to show institutional commitment	• Expedite Phase II Negotiations • Enhance government agency capabilities • Conduct awareness campaigns and capacity-building support for SMEs • Improve trade facilitation and reduce NTBs • Strengthen productive capacity and export diversification • Promote regional value chain integration • Improve trade-related infrastructure • Enhance access to finance for businesses • Improve cross-border payments systems

8. South Africa	• Corruption, weak political will, policy inconsistency, and slow legal reforms undermine AfCFTA implementation • Economic constraints such as high unemployment, inequality, poverty, and deindustrialisation • Energy insecurity and degraded logistics systems • Trade inefficiencies such as border delays, outdated customs systems, NTBs, and inadequate harmonisation of standards • Skills shortages, low vocational training alignment with trade sectors, and youth/women underrepresentation • Delays in finalising tariff offers, services liberalisation, and regulatory reforms hinder full AfCFTA participation	• Continental Leadership, as South Africa played a leading role in AfCFTA negotiations • Advanced Economy, diversified sectors, and strong regulatory institutions • Highest regional integration score (0.63/0.75) in SSA, long-standing role in SACU and SADC, and key port access (Durban) • Firms are influential across multiple sectors and already operate across Africa (e.g., retail, telecom, and banking) • Digital trade readiness with potential to be a continental digital hub	• Overreliance on mining and agriculture limits resilience; value-added products are needed for trade success • Consistent political will matters • Private sector development drives integration • South Africa's strong institutions are vital for compliance, but need continual support and coordination	• Leverage domestic institutions, such as SARS, ITAC, and DTIC, to drive regulatory harmonisation and trade facilitation • SME-led continental engagement could build on existing SME networks to deepen informal and formal regional trade ties • The use of existing RECs as catalysts to test in regional integration has been key to building AfCFTA implementation	• Accelerate structural reforms by fixing energy, logistics, and regulatory barriers • Strengthen industrial capacity • Diversify exports • Capitalise on regional value chains to develop textile, automotive, and agro-industries with partners • Modernize agriculture • Boost services trade by liberalising and modernising digital, financial, and professional services • Advance digital trade: expand infrastructure, platforms, and cross-border regulation • Invest in skill via expanding vocational training and youth inclusion

(continued)

Table 19.1 (continued)

Countries	Challenges	Strengths	Lessons learned	Indigenous solutions and local initiatives	Policy recommendations
9. Cameroon	• Cameroon's FDI remains low relative to its economic potential and industrialisation goals • Financing constraints—e.g.: the National Development Strategy 2020–2030 (NDS30) requires about 88 trillion FCFA • Though repatriation of capital is allowed, it must comply with strict CEMAC monetary regulations • Cameroon has yet to fully align its national laws with the AfCFTA Protocol on investment, especially on investor responsibilities and dispute mechanisms	• Multiple tax incentives for investors (e.g., VAT exemptions, tax credits for hiring, pollution control, and rural development) • Investment Promotion Agency (IPA) exists to promote and facilitate investments • Access to domestic and international arbitration systems (OHADA, ICSID, New York Convention)	• Effective legal infrastructure is key to attracting sustainable FDI • Existing incentives are positive but not enough to attract meaningful investment without and legal certainty • Laws lack clear articulation of responsibilities in areas such as human rights, ethics, and environmental protection	• National development strategy prioritises industrialisation, FDI mobilisation, and aligns with the goals of AfCFTA's Protocol on Investment • Tax incentive schemes • Creation of economic zones	• Fully align national investment laws with the AfCFTA • Modernise the investment charter • Enhance investment facilitation by strengthening the capacity and autonomy of the Investment Promotion Agency • Improve access to finance and capital repatriation • Promote environmentally responsible investment • Strengthen Dispute Resolution Mechanisms

10. Chad	• Infrastructure deficit • Institutional weaknesses • Limited productive capacity • Dependence on oil and primary commodities • Landlocked status • Limited access to finance for businesses, especially SMEs • Existence of Non-Tariff Barriers (NTBs) • Limited Export Diversification • Insufficient Value Addition • Skills gap in areas necessary for industrial development and competitive trade	• Strategic position in Central Africa • Comparative advantages in key sectors of production • Government commitment evident in analysing Chad's position and proposing strategies to implement AfCFTA • Emerging services sectors with potentials in transport, tourism, telecommunications, and business services	• Holistic approach to development is critical for trade integration • Diversification reduces vulnerability • Trade facilitation matters for landlocked countries • Value of capacity building is vital for effective policy implementation and trade negotiation	• Specialised agro zones • Export-Focused Industrial Fund • Prioritising trade corridors and logistics hubs that link key production zones to Douala and neighbouring markets • Gender-sensitive trade reforms • Domestic Standards Infrastructure	• Targeted investments in export-ready sectors • Prioritise investments in crucial infrastructure • Implement robust trade facilitation measures • Build institutional capacity • Economic diversification • Improve access to finance • Encourage and support value addition to primary products • Enhance skills development • Forge strategic partnerships with neighbouring countries and regional bodies

(continued)

Table 19.1 (continued)

Countries	Challenges	Strengths	Lessons learned	Indigenous solutions and local initiatives	Policy recommendations
11. SIDS	• High transport and logistics costs due to geographic isolation • Limited productive capacity and narrow export base • Heavy dependence on external (non-African) trade partners • Vulnerability to external shocks (climate and global markets) • Weak integration into continental value chains	• Strategic location for maritime trade and logistics hubs • Relatively stable policy environments in some SIDS • Openness to trade and existing global market linkages • Potential to leverage blue economy opportunities	• Market access alone is insufficient without production capacity • Regional integration benefits are uneven across country types • Trade facilitation must be tailored to small island contexts • External orientation can both support and hinder continental integration	• Promotion of blue economy sectors (fisheries and ocean-based industries) • Regional cooperation among island states • Targeted SME support in niche export sectors	• Invest in maritime connectivity and regional shipping networks • Support diversification into high-value niche sectors • Strengthen digital infrastructure to overcome geographic barriers • Design special provisions for SIDS within AfCFTA frameworks • Enhance access to finance and capacity-building for local firms

Source: Authors' analysis of country case studies

countries include access to finance and market information for MSMEs, slow domestication and implementation, cross-border security and the prevalence of informal trade.

Similarly, many African countries share common strengths that position them well for AfCFTA. Most of the countries were early signatories and ratifiers of the AfCFTA agreement, suggesting some commendable level of political commitment. Some of them have strategic geographic location and market size. For example, Nigeria is the largest market, the SIDS have Strategic maritime location along major shipping routes, Kenya is the Eastern regional hub, and South Africa is the most industrialised country in Africa. Though the strengths vary, they all have their merits and, therefore, suggest that each country can capitalise on their comparative advantage to be favourably position in the integration.

Several recurring lessons emerge from the implementation experiences. Some include the need for critical infrastructure for trade integration, the imperative of policy and regulatory harmonisation, and that private sector engagement and capacity building are essential for the countries to utilise the agreement effectively (Kenya, Rwanda, Lesotho). Additionally, overreliance on primary commodities creates vulnerabilities, as was evident during the COVID-19 pandemic and the Russia-Ukraine war. Diversification and value addition are key for sustained benefits, and addressing NTBs is as important as tariff elimination. Also, climate vulnerability must be integrated into trade policy design.

A number of indigenous solutions and national initiatives were also identified as presented in Table 19.1. These are primarily based on the establishment of AfCFTA national implementation strategies and policies, the creation of government agencies to oversee implementation, and the development of advocacy programmes. These strengths are instrumental in facilitating the implementation of the AfCFTA. It is interesting to note that what some countries highlighted as challenges, others have already addressed using indigenous solutions and national initiatives. For example, while Tunisia and Kenya have a comprehensive communication strategy to raise awareness, Nigeria and Lesotho perceived that a lack of awareness and capacity building were significant constraints. Similarly, Morocco has invested significantly in renewable energy, whereas the lack of a consistent power supply is one of Nigeria's most significant production and operational constraints. Hence, peer learning will be beneficial in addressing challenges faced and enhancing balanced growth and sustainable development.

19.3 The AfCFTA as a Buffer for External Shocks: A Case Study of the Recent Trade Disruptions of the Trump Effect

The recent pronouncements from the White House, since President Donald Trump assumed office, have disrupted global value chains, ruptured trade alliances built over decades, and, most importantly, reminded us of the power of trade disruptions.

Similar examples of policies and actions/sanctions that disrupted global trade in the twenty-first century include the United States-China Trade War of 2018 to 2020; the European Union and United States sanctions on Russia since 2014; and the China-Australia Trade Dispute of between 2020 and 2024. The recent policy announcements by President Trump is a good case study for analysing how such policies could affect socio-economic development in Africa. Such protectionist policies have been referred to as the "Trump effect", stemming from his administration's guiding mantra of "*America First*" and the broader goal of "*Making America Great Again*". This phenomenon is not unprecedented. A 2021 study found evidence of a so-called "Trump effect" on public attitudes towards trade, showing that support for Trump's protectionist stance influenced individuals across party lines (Essig et al. 2021).

On April 2, 2025, President Trump imposed a 10% baseline tariff on all U.S. imports, in what is called the *Liberation Day tariffs*, effective April 5 (Domena, 2025). In the same breath, he announced reciprocal tariffs on approximately 60 countries, with rates ranging from roughly, 11% to 50%, depending on perceived treatment of U.S. exports (U.S. President (Trump, D. J.), 2025). The April second Liberation Day, Tariffs were published in the Executive Order 14,257, titled "Regulating imports with a reciprocal tariff to rectify trade practices that contribute to large and persistent annual united states goods trade deficits". Additional tariffs such as the 25% tariff on all U.S. imports from any country importing Venezuelan oil of March 2025, 25% tariffs on steel/aluminium, and an additional 10% Tariff on BRICS-aligned Countries of July 17, 2025 all have direct and indirect implications on African countries (Trump, 2025; U.S. Department of State, 2025; Shalal & Howard, 2025).

This is coming at a time when the USA is seriously engaged in trade with several African countries, with the African Growth and Opportunity Act (AGOA) being the most visible display of international trade commitment with African countries. Evidence from the World Economic Forum suggests that apparel sales in Kenya under AGOA increased from $55 million in 2001 to $603 million in 2022, accounting for nearly 68% of the country's total exports to the US (Domena, 2025). Automotive exports to the U.S., surged by 447.3% between 2001 and 2022, with an initial increase of 1643.6% in the first year of AGOA implementation (World Economic Forum, 2023). Overall, AGOA countries shipped over US$103 billion worth of non-crude products to the U.S., with an average compound annual growth rate of 7% between 2001 and 2022 (Kerner, 2024). While these examples demonstrate the infinite potential of international trade and its positive implications for economies, they also highlight the risks associated with such trade that stem from short-term policies, which may or may not be renewed.

The prevailing fear across AGOA countries is understandable, given the enormous investments in infrastructure and other set-up costs that may not have been recouped during the 21 years of AGOA. For example, since around 2014, Ethiopia's textile and garment industrial parks have attracted US$740 million in foreign direct investment, driven mainly by AGOA benefits (World Economic Forum, 2023). These investments have set up production factories that may become redundant or constrained if the US market is suddenly closed, with no comparable alternatives. Since its enactment on May 18, 2000 (initially set to expire in 2008), AGOA has been extended twice. The decision to extend AGOA is likely to be influenced by current trade administration and geopolitical tensions, and that will be the case for subsequent extensions. Hence, the need to highlight such protectionist trade policies from global powers, which have a high tendency to leave African countries vulnerable economically and politically.

The implications of the liberation day tariffs has been to effectively nullify the benefits of AGOA, as African exporters (especially Lesotho, South Africa, Madagascar) suddenly faced tariffs of up to 50%, threatening export competitiveness, manufacturing, and job security. Similarly, the 10% tariffs on China, has a ripple effect on African exports to China and global supply chains that transit through China, potentially increasing export costs. In addition, tariffs on raw materials hamper growth in mineral-dependent economies like Zambia, DRC, and Angola. Nevertheless, these policies induce trade fragmentation that pushes African nations to pivot towards China, EU, GCC, and most importantly regional integration via the AfCFTA.

The AfCFTA serves as a buffer for external shocks such as the trump tariffs, Russia-Ukraine war, and the COVID-19, because it reduces overdependence outside the African continent. When the AfCFTA attains full maturity, it is expected to account for most intra-African trade and host dominant value chains such that external shocks are limited. This is because the AfCFTA provides a huge market that will unleash several supply options, lessening the level of vulnerability on trade for African countries, especially for exports, hence, the need to fast-track the implementation of the AfCFTA to take advantage of these strengths of regional integration in Africa.

19.4 Advancing Beyond Trade Towards Inclusive and Sustainable Development across the Continent

The AfCFTA may be the instrument or wheel that drives trade and integration within Africa, but it remains a means to an end, not the end in itself. The AfCFTA seeks to eliminate tariffs on 90% of goods, liberalise key service sectors (such as telecommunications, finance, and transport), increases cross-border investment and competition, facilitate e-commerce and digital integration, and reduces digital trade barriers (African Union, 2018;World Bank, 2022). This will deepen regional integration in Africa, reduce poverty and boost economic growth and development. A 2022 World bank report posits that, if AfCFTA's goals are fully realised, 50 million people could escape extreme poverty, real income could rise by 9%, Africa's exports to the rest of the world could increase by 32%, and intra-African exports could grow by 109% by 2035 (World bank, 2022). The United Nations Economic Commission for Africa (2023) estimates further predict a 33.5% growth in intra-African trade in

2045 as a result of the Agreement, with major trade growth projected in the agri-food sector and in industrial products. Nevertheless, these achievements will timidly translate into inclusive and sustainable development if not consciously and strategically planned for. There is a need to ensure that benefits reach all segments of the society, integrate sustainable development principles into trade policies and fashion the AfCFTA as a catalyst for broader African Agenda 2063 aspirations.

To ensure that benefits reach all segments of society, especially women, youth, informal traders and other marginalised groups, there must be policies that ensure that this is done, amidst the increased competition that will exist in a more integrated Africa. Competition generally has a way of apportioning more benefits to the strong and leaving the weak in the shadows. Already, the World Bank's (2022) report is promising, predicting that by 2035, wages will increase by 11.2% for women and 9.8% for men on average. There exist numerous ways in which these marginalised groups can be catered for. For example, women-owned SMEs could be supported with access to finance, training, and market information, as well as the implementation of preferential procurement policies that prioritise women-led enterprises. Additionally, to promote youth entrepreneurship and skills development, the government could establish AfCFTA Youth Innovation and Export Hubs to foster entrepreneurship. It could also invest in technical and vocational education aligned with AfCFTA priority sectors (e.g., manufacturing, logistics, ICT) and provide startup grants, mentorship, and incubators for youth-led businesses. Targeted financing mechanisms, social safety nets, labour protection schemes, and simplified or digitised customs procedures can significantly empower firms in the informal economy.

Other instrument of the African union, especially as regards women and youth participation, such as the AU Youth Charter, the Women and Youth Financial & Economic Inclusion 2030 Initiative, and the AU Strategy for Gender Equality & Women's Empowerment, may be critical for unlocking the full potential of the AfCFTA. For instance, the African Union (2006) provides a continental legal and policy framework for advancing the rights, development, and active participation of young people in Africa's socio-economic transformation. By encouraging entrepreneurship, innovation, and youth engagement in policymaking, the Charter aligns with the AfCFTA's goal of expanding intra-African trade through new businesses, start-ups, and digital enterprises often driven by young Africans (African Union, 2006). Similarly, the Women and Youth Financial & Economic Inclusion 2030 Initiative seeks to bridge the structural gaps in access to finance, business opportunities, and market participation for women and youth (African Union, 2023). Limited access to affordable credit, trade finance, and investment capital has been a long-standing barrier to inclusive economic growth in Africa. By addressing these constraints, the Initiative directly supports AfCFTA implementation, ensuring that small-scale cross-border traders, many of whom are women, can formalise their businesses, expand their operations, and access wider regional markets.

To effectively integrate sustainable development principles into trade policies and fashion the AfCFTA as a catalyst for broader African Agenda 2063 aspirations, it is vital to look beyond the narrow scope of trade liberalisation and consider the broader socio-economic and environmental context in which the AfCFTA operates. While the AfCFTA primarily aims to reduce tariffs, eliminate trade barriers, and enhance intra-African commerce, achieving the long-term goals of Agenda 2063, such as inclusive growth, gender equality, environmental sustainability, and structural economic transformation, requires deliberate alignment between trade policy and development priorities. This entails integrating sustainability criteria into the design and implementation of trade rules, investment protocols, industrial policy frameworks, and infrastructure development at the regional and national levels, in addition to ensuring that the benefits of trade are distributed equitably and in an environmentally responsible manner. Strategic partnerships with civil society, the private sector, and development partners across member countries can help mobilise technical and financial resources while ensuring accountability and transparency in the AfCFTA's implementation. Ultimately, attaining the broader aim and vision of Africa 2063 is not just about reforming trade rules but about reimagining trade itself as a transformative tool for achieving Africa's long-term vision of prosperity, unity, and resilience.

The outlook for the road ahead therefore necessitates a sustaining momentum and political will, especially from the leadership of the AfCFTA member countries. So far, the conceptualisation, drafting, and commencement of the AfCFTA have enjoyed significant political will from the leadership of the member states (Tayo, 2023). In the implementation process, it is clear that political will must be reinforced by continuous data-driven analysis, strategic interventions, and evidence-based reforms. This implies that African governments must move beyond passive or "auto-pilot" governance and significantly increase their funding commitments to research and development, thereby enhancing the effectiveness and efficiency of governance systems.

19.5 Conclusion and Way Forward

The AfCFTA presents a transformative opportunity, but its success hinges on bridging the gap between continental ambitions and national implementation. Countries must, therefore, own the implementation process, adapt strategies to local contexts, and commit to cooperation over competition. The analysis across multiple African nations reveals a common narrative regarding AfCFTA implementation, which is that of a continent poised for economic transformation but grappling with significant foundational challenges. Recurring obstacles include pervasive infrastructure deficits, complex non-tariff barriers, limited productive capacities, and difficulties for small- and medium-sized enterprises (SMEs) in accessing finance and market information. Many countries also face the challenge of slowly domesticating the agreement into national law. Despite these challenges, a strong political will towards regional integration, coupled with early ratification by many states, was instrumental in advancing the AfCFTA agenda. Lessons learned emphasise the critical need for domestic structural reforms, robust infrastructure, and targeted capacity building for the private sector to leverage the vast continental market effectively. The need for a more decisive political will and massive sensitisation campaigns cannot be overemphasised, especially at a time when we are witnessing increasing xenophobia from African countries like South Africa and Ghana. Xenophobia stands as one of the darkest threats of the AfCFTA integration mantra as it risks undermining the spirit of continental integration and erodes trust, mobility, and cooperation among African peoples. It is therefore incumbent upon African leaders to bring their subjects to see the positive evidence that lies in integration and provide structured plans on how to deal with the externalities of insecurity, pollution, and the extra pressure on common facilities and jobs.

Overall, on the face of it, the challenges faced during the implementation of the AfCFTA seem to outweigh its strengths. Nevertheless, the lessons learned from the process, the political will demonstrated thus far, and the regional united front on the AfCFTA agenda constitute arguably the greatest developmental force the region has witnessed since independence. These ingredients have far greater significance in overcoming prevailing challenges. With the right direction, the AfCFTA will still deliver on its mandate. In light of the challenges, lessons, and insights emerging from the case studies on AfCFTA implementation, this chapter outlines a set of practical recommendations structured across the short, medium, and long term. These recommendations are intended to guide key stakeholders, including the AfCFTA Secretariat, African Union Commission, national governments, civil society, development partners, and academic institutions, in strengthening the effective execution of the AfCFTA agenda. They are discussed below.

1. Short-term (0–2 years): Fix the "binding constraints"

- These are quick, high-impact actions that unlock trade immediately, such as:
- Simplify border and customs processes via electronic single windows and pre-clearance systems.
- Actively remove non-tariff barriers by establishing real-time NTB reporting and resolution systems.
- Reinforce political commitment through funding, public awareness campaigns (especially SMEs), and prioritisation of trade facilitation.
- Improve inter-agency coordination, especially at the level of customs, trade ministries, and standards agencies.
- Strengthen legal and institutional frameworks by aligning national laws and institutions with AfCFTA provisions on customs procedures, standards, immigration, and asset ownership.

2. Medium-term (3–5 years): Build trade capacity and systems

- Invest in trade infrastructure and logistics, such as transport corridors, dry ports (for landlocked countries like Chad), and port efficiency.
- Strengthen productive capacity and industrialisation.
- Harmonise standards and regulations.
- Reform tariff revenue dependence.

- Deepen regional value chains by promoting cross-border production networks and encourage sourcing within Africa.
- Strengthen data and monitoring systems that track trade flows.
- Establish preferential procurement policies, export hubs, vocational training programmes, and targeted financing for women, youth, and informal traders.
- Build national and regional capacity to anticipate and respond to global policy shifts, such as tariffs and sanctions by Western powers.

3. Long-term (5–15 years): Achieve structural transformation

- Build continental value chains and industrial clusters via regional manufacturing hubs that integrate upstream and downstream industries.
- Deepen services integration by liberalising finance, transport, and digital services.
- Advance digital trade and e-commerce ecosystems.
- Strengthen continental institutions such as the AfCFTA Secretariat by improving enforcement mechanisms and dispute resolution.
- Align AfCFTA with broader development agendas, such as the Agenda 2063.
- Manage political economy constraints by building compensation mechanisms for losers and social protection systems.

4. Cross-cutting strategic principles: Across all time horizons, there is need to:

- Sequence reforms pragmatically; start with facilitation, then production, and then deep integration.
- Allow flexibility for landlocked countries and small economies, cognizant of the fact that not all countries can move at the same speed.
- Shift from agreement to execution, by focusing less on negotiations, and more on implementation capacity and institutional delivery.
- Put the private sector at the centre of the AfCFTA implementation, while the government only creates the enabling environment.

References

African Union. (2006). *African youth charter*. African Union. Retrieved August 13, 2025, from https://au.int/sites/default/files/treaties/7789-treaty-0033_-_african_youth_charter_e.pdf

African Union. (2018). *Agreement establishing the African Continental Free Trade Area*. https://au.int/sites/default/files/treaties/36437-treaty-consolidated_text_on_cfta_-_en.pdf

African Union. (2023). *The women and Youth Financial & Economic Inclusion Initiative, a catalyst for inclusive development*. African Union. Retrieved August 13, 2025, from https://au.int/en/pressreleases/20230403/women-and-youth-financial-economic-inclusion-initiative-catalyst-inclusive

African Union. (2025). *2025 annual meetings: Regional corridors as drivers of continental integration*. https://www.afdb.org/en/news-and-events/2025-annual-meetings-regional-corridors-drivers-continental-integration-81924?utm

Domena A. T., (2025). *Could Trump trash the US-Africa AGOA trade pact?* https://www.dw.com/en/could-us-president-trump-trash-us-africa-agoa-trade-pact/a-72274345?utm.

Essig, J., Xu, P., Garand, J. C., & Keser, C. (2021). The "Trump" effect: Political elite and support for free trade in America. *American Politics Research, 49*(3), 328–342. https://doi.org/10.1177/1532673X21992124

Kerner, T. (2024). *AGOA forum 2024: Insights, economic benefits for Africa, and the road ahead.* Brookings. https://www.brookings.edu/articles/agoa-forum-2024-insights-economic-benefits-for-africa-and-the-road-ahead/

Miglierini, G. (2019). EU Commission: Harmonised standards to eliminate technical barriers to trade. A Communication from the EU Commission discusses actions in the field of harmonised standards needed to eliminate technical barriers to trade and achieve a true 'Single market'. https://www.ncfinternational.it/eu-commission-harmonised-standards-to-eliminate-technical-barriers-to-trade/#:~:text=The%20availability%20of%20harmonised%20standards%20is%20a,and%20services%20in%20the%20different%20geographic%20areas

Shalal, A., & Howard, N. (2025). *Trump says US nears trade deals as tariff deadline delayed.* Reuters. Retrieved from https://www.reuters.com/world/china/us-close-several-trade-deals-announcements-be-made-next-days-bessent-says-2025-07-06/

TayoT.T.(2023).*TheroadtoAfrica'ssinglemarket:Progresssofarandchallengesforthefuture*.https://afripoli.org/the-road-to-africas-single-market-progress-so-far-and-challenges-for-the-future

Trump, D. J. (2025). *Trump targets BRICS, threatens 10% tariff for "anti-American" stance.* Wall Street Journa. https://www.wsj.com/livecoverage/stock-market-today-dow-sp-500-nasdaq-07-07-2025/card/trump-targets-brics-threatens-10-tariff-for-anti-american-stance-6LQPP58OwCwc1zKbp8Uj?utm

U.S. Department of State. (2025). *On Trump Administration imposing tariffs on countries importing Venezuelan oil [Press release].* https://www.state.gov/on-trump-administration-imposing-tariffs-on-countries-importing-venezuelan-oil/

U.S. President (Trump, D. J.). (2025). *Executive order 14257—Regulating imports with a reciprocal tariff to rectify trade practices that contribute to large and persistent annual United States goods trade deficits [executive order].* American Presidency Project. https://www.presidency.ucsb.edu/documents/executive-order-14257-regulating-imports-with-reciprocal-tariff-rectify-trade-practices

United Nations Economic Commission for Africa. (2013). *Harmonizing policies to transform the trading environment: Assessing regional integration in Africa VI assessing regional integration in Africa VI.* https://archive.uneca.org/sites/default/files/PublicationFiles/aria_vi_english_full.pdf#:~:text=For%20example%2C%20harmonized%20rules%20of%20origin%20and,under%20initiatives%20led%20by%20regional%20economic%20communities

United Nations Economic Commission for Africa. (2023). *The AfCFTA, boosting regional integration through trade.* https://www.uneca.org/stories/the-afcfta%2C-boosting-regional-integration-through-trade?utm

World Bank. (2022). *Free trade deal boosts Africa's economic development.* https://www.worldbank.org/en/topic/trade/publication/free-trade-deal-boosts-africa-economic-development?utm

World Economic Forum. (2023). *How has the AGOA agreement benefited African countries?* https://www.weforum.org/agenda/2023/11/africa-us-trade-agoa-deal-expires-2025/

GPSR Compliance
The European Union's (EU) General Product Safety Regulation (GPSR) is a set of rules that requires consumer products to be safe and our obligations to ensure this.

If you have any concerns about our products, you can contact us on

ProductSafety@springernature.com

In case Publisher is established outside the EU, the EU authorized representative is:

Springer Nature Customer Service Center GmbH
Europaplatz 3
69115 Heidelberg, Germany

www.ingramcontent.com/pod-product-compliance
Lightning Source LLC
Chambersburg PA
CBHW071701150626
46733CB00003B/43
* 9 7 8 3 0 3 2 1 4 0 5 0 0 *